"*Unchanging Witness* is a timely ͚
wish to hold to the faith 'once del
anchorless confession that cannot ͞
Fortson and Grams demonstrate conclusively that not just the inspired authors of
Holy Scripture but the holy fathers of the one, holy, catholic, and apostolic Church
set forth a vision of ennobling Christian conduct that unanimously excludes homosexual practice. This text is particularly valuable for Orthodox Christians in that
it sets forth Orthodoxy's unified witness against homosexuality in modern times.
Highly recommended!"

*Bishop Basil, Diocese of Wichita and Mid-America, Antiochian
Orthodox Christian Archdiocese of North America*

"Never before have voices in the church been so confused and conflicted on sexual ethics and behavior. What does the Bible say? What does Christian tradition
say? *Unchanging Witness* is a stimulating and scholarly study to help concerned
Christians think and act more deeply in this watershed moment. The authors are
well versed in the contemporary debate and fully informed on the exegesis of the
biblical texts and the primary sources in Christian tradition and historical theology. *Unchanging Witness* is a clarion call to bold Christian action."

*Robert E. Cooley, president-emeritus and professor of biblical archaeology,
Gordon-Conwell Theological Seminary, and ordained minister, Assemblies of God*

"In this well-conceived volume, Don Fortson and Rollin Grams have convincingly
connected biblical exegesis and the teaching of the church throughout history to
enable Christ followers to respond to the pressing cultural and ethical challenges
of our day. Carefully addressing the church's entanglement with modern culture,
this significant and timely publication provides all of us with an exemplary guide
not only to understand the issues of our day but to navigate a faithful and scriptural
way forward. It is a privilege to recommend *Unchanging Witness*, which should be
essential reading for pastors, church leaders, and students alike."

David S. Dockery, president, Trinity Evangelical Divinity School

"This is a rigorous, scholarly examination of the scriptural teaching on the issue
of homosexuality and the consistent witness of the church through the ages to that
teaching. It leaves one in no doubt that the revisionist readings of Scripture currently
in vogue in the West are without foundation and are in fact a wholesale abandonment
of historic, orthodox Christianity. While the church has a pastoral obligation to all its
members, we believe this book spells out what God requires of us: to be conformed
to the character of Christ. This is a valuable resource for all pastors, priests, and theologians, especially for those of us in Africa who hold to the truth once delivered to
the saints, and hopefully a help to those who experience struggles within themselves,
to give them courage to constantly come to the cross."

*Bishop Bethlehem Nopece, Port Elizabeth Diocese,
Anglican Church of Southern Africa*

UNCHANGING WITNESS

S. DONALD FORTSON III AND ROLLIN G. GRAMS

UNCHANGING WITNESS

THE CONSISTENT CHRISTIAN TEACHING ON **HOMOSEXUALITY** IN SCRIPTURE AND TRADITION

B&H
ACADEMIC

NASHVILLE, TENNESSEE

Printed in the United States of America
1 2 3 4 5 6 7 8 9 10 • 21 20 19 18 17 16
BMS

To

*The Anglican bishops of the majority world who
have valiantly upheld historic Christian orthodoxy*

CONTENTS

FOREWORD

The body of Christ is experiencing severe fracture. Schism is taking place on a scale not seen since the sixteenth century, and the primary culprit is the claim that the church has been wrong all along in its belief that homosexual practice is a sin. The reason homosexuality has struck such a divisive chord is that essential sexual ethics are at stake when the so-called gay Christian movement gives its blessing to homosexual practice. Sexual ethics have always been part of the faith delivered once for all to the saints; unfortunately, many Christians are ignorant of that tradition. The gay Christian movement has not only challenged biblical interpretation but has also attempted to reinterpret Christian history on the issue of homosexuality. While the debated biblical texts are well known, the historical texts remain hidden to most of the Christian public. We aim to let voices from the Christian past be heard alongside the biblical witness in this critical debate.

Our book addresses the homosexual crisis in the church, primarily for a Christian audience. While much of this work may be applicable to discussions of homosexuality in society at large, our chief concern is with those who identify themselves as Christians. Many contemporary discussions of homosexuality are based on broad assertions lacking substantial grounding in the texts of the Christian tradition. Our book is intended as a resource for those who hold the historic Christian position on homosexuality. What we offer is the combined perspective of a New Testament scholar and a church historian; both are deeply concerned about the implications of this homosexual crisis for the church. Both of us fear that segments of the Christian church are approaching apostasy and believe the church will benefit from a work that applies our respective disciplines to the study of homosexuality.

As advocates of homosexuality offer a muddled message, the testimony of the Christian tradition is urgent, as is the right interpretation of Scripture in its context. Most contemporary Christian books on homosexuality put little or no emphasis on church history, and so the first part of this book uses primary source evidence to show what the church has always taught. Given recent arguments that Scripture does not view homosexual practice as sinful, the second half of the book turns to a study of the biblical texts in their ancient Near Eastern, Jewish, and Greco-Roman contexts. We argue that revisionist interpretations are not only bad exegesis but are also an abandonment of historic, orthodox Christianity.

Jesus called us to love both God and our neighbors (Matt 22:37–39); therefore, our labors stem from a love for Christ and his church. To love God is to keep his commandments (Deut 11:1; Josh 22:5; John 14:15, 21; 15:10), and the only possible unity with God and with other Christians is a unity centered on Christ and based on obedience to God. Not to warn a person who is living in sin is a terribly unloving act. Restoring those who admit their transgressions, as we humbly acknowledge our own propensity to sin, is also part of Christian love (Gal 6:1). Yet such restoration is impossible if our warnings are aimed at persons who insist their practices are not sinful. In the context of the current confusion, we intend to demonstrate that Scripture and the historic, orthodox church consistently have warned that homosexual practice is a sin. We will show that the suggestion that homosexual practice is acceptable before God is contrary to Scripture and to what all the church everywhere has always taught.

The authors wish to express their appreciation to the multitude of people who have encouraged us in this endeavor. We would like to thank our faculty colleagues who sharpened our thinking, the students who asked difficult questions, and the numerous individuals who gave us input on this project. We particularly wish to thank Susan Lindholm and Tari Williamson, who read the entire manuscript and helped us produce a clearer work. Dr. Catherine McDowell, an Old Testament professor at Gordon-Conwell Theological Seminary, offered helpful input for our chapters on the Old Testament and ancient Near Eastern context. Shawn Tayon and Elly Keuthan were most helpful in tracking down some primary sources in translation. Bradford Green assisted with research on the modern church. We further thank the editors at B&H who have worked with us to produce the final manuscript for publication. Finally, we wish to thank our families; they graciously endured years of our working on this manuscript.

Note to the reader: We would like you to be aware of two important stylistic matters. First, we have chosen to use the New Revised Standard Version of the Bible in this work because it is accepted by a broad array of denominations in the English-speaking world. We did not want our Bible translation to be a distracting issue, as we wrote this book for a broad Christian audience. Second, our work is full of quotations (some of them long) from primary texts. As this may become tedious for some readers, we have used italics to highlight those portions that are most important.

Primary sources are well marked in this book, and we hope that by citing them frequently, we provide readers with a resource to engage the discussion with understanding.

GENERAL INTRODUCTION

The church faces a critical moment over the issue of homosexuality. This crisis extends beyond *what* the church should say on the topic; it includes a crisis of authority regarding the place of Scripture and the church's witness in theology and ethics. In some communities of faith, the crisis is international and, to a great degree, a matter of church politics—but how long will a declining Western, liberal clericalism be able to dominate the growing, vibrant Christian faith of the non-Western world? In other communions the issue is a purely Western discussion of the relationship between church and culture: Will Scripture and church tradition continue to define orthodoxy, or will modern and postmodern approaches lead to the normalization of homosexuality?

We live in a time when what believers have long regarded as truth about sexuality, marriage, and biblical authority is under cross-examination. We have, as it were, returned to Eden, where the serpent posed two challenges to God's Word: (1) *Did God really say . . . ?* and (2) *Is what God said only his attempt to keep you under his commands without allowing you freedom to determine right and wrong for yourselves?* The first challenge questions *what* God actually said, whereas the second questions God's authority over liberated individuals.

The church in the West has, for several decades, been listening to a voice asking if what we have long thought about sexual ethics is really true and suggesting it is time for us to grow up, to be liberated from oppressive commands, to exercise our own authority, and to walk the last mile in a glorious march of freedom that has included such milestones as the liberation of slaves, women, and ethnic minorities. Is it not time, we are asked, to cast off the shackles of past sexual mores and embrace a new sexuality that accepts, among other things, same-sex relations—even marriage?

This book is our call back to reality. We issue that call by saying *what* God has said in his Word and by presenting *what* the church has affirmed throughout

1

its history. For some people this argument has already become *passé*, for they agree that the Scripture calls homosexuality a sin and that the church has consistently affirmed this up until the last decades. They do not care, however, for they will not subject themselves to scriptural authority or church tradition. In our view they have given up Christian dialogue altogether and are speaking *outside* the church and *against* the church in their appeals to their own experiences and reasoning, their twisting of Scripture, and their ignoring of Christian tradition. These have fallen to the second challenge suggested by Eden's serpent, that our own understanding of right and wrong should supersede God's directives.

Others, however, have succumbed to the serpent's first challenge: "Did God really say . . . ?" They doubt whether Scripture actually condemns homosexual acts. Moreover, many—particularly Protestants—have forgotten that the church's teaching should be part of any theological discussion. This book, we hope, will help those mesmerized by this challenge, those wondering whether God really said what Scripture and the church claim. Our answer to the serpent is, "Yes, God really did say that," and, "No, we will not challenge God's authority." As Paul says about those succumbing to this challenge, "Claiming to be wise, they became fools" (Rom 1:21).

Every theological discussion has several layers, what we might call tasks of theology. We suggest four:

- Interpretation of authoritative texts
- Synthesis of authoritative texts
- Formation of convictions
- Practice of convictions

In the present work our focus is largely on the first two tasks. We are interested in the interpretation of the Bible first and foremost, and this involves understanding (1) what the Bible says about homosexuality (so-called "in-the-text" interpretation); (2) how to understand what the Bible says about homosexuality in the historical and cultural contexts in which the biblical books were written ("behind-the-text" interpretation); and (3) how those texts have been interpreted by Christians ("in-front-of-the-text" interpretation). All this relates to the last two tasks of theology, the formation and practice of our convictions—particularly if we believe Scripture is the final authority for faith and practice and if we value the church's statements and practice of Christian faith in the past 2,000 years.

Part I of this work focuses on historical interpretation, working through periods of church history to see what has been stated on the issue of homosexuality. Many theological works on the subject have omitted this discussion, as though theology is a matter of reading the Bible and then discussing what it says without listening to nearly two millennia of church history. We intend to right this imbalance, even to the extent of beginning with church history.

Part II examines the biblical texts and their contexts. We suggest that after some thirty or more years of revisionist readings of relevant biblical texts, a new tendency among exegetes is to acknowledge that the traditional interpretation was correct all along. We do not intend to engage extensively with contemporary interpretation of biblical texts—there is little benefit in rehashing aging arguments or showing how many maverick interpretations of the biblical texts have surfaced. Rather, we wish to interpret the texts afresh (the first theological task). Then we will explain them within a larger, biblical ethic (the second theological task) and explain where some key contemporary interpretations have gone wrong. Frequently the issue has nothing to do with legitimate, alternative readings but with inadequate research and short-lived interpretations, which are too often used by well-known scholars.

One significant feature of our work is that we regularly quote primary sources. As we surveyed various Christian studies on the subject of homosexuality, we noted how infrequently (with some noteworthy exceptions) primary sources are presented for the reader. Too often quotations of primary sources are either lacking or are offered only as references tucked away in footnotes. We hope the present work will give readers abundant quotations from primary sources so that they are able to discuss the subject knowledgably, not having to take an interpreter's word on what a text says. Our primary objective in this book is to complete the first task of theology for the topic of homosexuality. In the first section we do this mainly by citing primary texts and, when necessary, discussing some famously misleading interpretations of the material. In the second section of the book, we engage more deeply in interpreting biblical texts since controversial interpretations—often at variance with one another—have abounded in recent times. Even as we engage alternative interpretations, we intentionally keep the focus on the texts themselves as much as possible to keep our readers engaged with Scripture on this issue.

The second task of theology is to explore the unity and diversity of biblical texts on an issue and then synthesize the material. This is sometimes a complicated and difficult task. Yet, on the subject of homosexuality, this task follows easily upon the heels of the first, for there is no diverse teaching on the subject or development of views. Both the teaching of the Bible and the teaching of Christian tradition have uniformly taught the same thing: homosexual practice is sinful. We agree with Saint Vincent of Lerins (AD 434) in his approach to determining heresy in the church. Heresy is that which is neither biblical nor universally taught. In the following quotation, "Catholic faith" means "universal faith":

I have often then inquired earnestly and attentively of very many men eminent for sanctity and learning, how and by what sure and so to speak universal rule I may be able to distinguish the truth of Catholic faith from the falsehood of heretical pravity; and I have always, and in almost every instance, received an answer to this effect: That whether I or anyone else should wish to detect the frauds and avoid the snares of heretics as they rise, and to continue sound and complete in the Catholic faith, we must, the Lord helping, fortify our own belief in two ways; first, by the authority of the Divine Law, and then, by the Tradition of the Catholic Church.

[5.] But here someone perhaps will ask, since the canon of Scripture is complete, and sufficient of itself for everything, and more than sufficient, what need is there to join with it the authority of the Church's interpretation? For this reason,—because, owing to the depth of Holy Scripture, all do not accept it in one and the same sense, but one understands its words in one way, another in another; so that it seems to be capable of as many interpretations as there are interpreters....

Therefore, it is very necessary, on account of so great intricacies of such various error, that the rule for the right understanding of the prophets and apostles should be framed in accordance with the standard of Ecclesiastical and Catholic interpretation.

[6.] Moreover, in the Catholic Church itself, all possible care must be taken, that we hold that faith which has been believed everywhere, always, by all. For that is truly and in the strictest sense "Catholic," which, as the name itself and the reason of the thing declare, comprehends all universally. This rule we shall observe if we follow universality, antiquity, consent. We shall follow universality if we confess that one faith to be true, which the whole Church throughout the world confesses; antiquity, if we in no wise depart from those interpretations which it is manifest were notoriously held by our holy ancestors and fathers; consent, in like manner, if in antiquity itself we adhere to the consentient definitions and determinations of all, or at the least of almost all priests and doctors. (*The Commonitory* 2.4-6)[1]

We believe the evidence is clear: both Scripture and the church universal ("everywhere, always, by all") have taught that homosexual practice is a sin. Those who teach otherwise are teaching heresy.

The final two tasks of theology are not taken up in detail in this work. We are not discussing how the formation of doctrine has been diversely reconceived in modern and postmodern times. Nor are we writing pastoral theology. On occasion we do address the authority of Scripture, the use of Scripture, and the importance of tradition, church discipline, biblical ethics, and the like—all relevant to the formation of convictions and pragmatic concerns. Yet it would

---

[1] "The Commonitory of St. Vincent of Lerins, for the Antiquity and Universality of the Catholic Faith Against the Profane Novelties of All Heresies," in *Sulpitius Sererus, Vincent of Lerins, John Cassian*, ed. John Schaff, trans. C. A. Heurtley, *Nicene and Post-Nicene Fathers*, vol. 11 (Edinburgh, Scotland: T&T Clark; repr., William B. Eerdmans, 1991), 132.

take a second book to explore why homosexual practice has been approved by some in the West, why biblical authority has been demoted in certain circles, why the meaning of texts has been said to lie not with the authors but with readers, why and how Western values have influenced theology and ethics, and how to counsel persons struggling with sinful sexual attractions and practices. Here, too, other books are available, although we urge readers to accept that the subjects examined in the present work are prerequisite to these other matters.[2]

Having spent the past few years identifying and interpreting relevant texts for a Christian dialogue on homosexuality and having listened to debates in society and the church on this issue for many years, we believe the textual focus we offer is essential. Too often people assume biblical texts do not speak to the issue directly, adequately, or in sufficient volume. Too often the teaching of the church throughout the centuries has been ignored by Protestants who forgot that it is, after all, relevant, or by persons who suggest that the church has been too compromised on other issues—notably, slavery and the status of women—to speak with authority. Too often in our Western context one's own experience, relationships, and reasoning dictate theological convictions and moral behavior over against Scripture and the teaching of the church. A study of texts—canonical texts and historical texts of the church—as Saint Vincent suggested, provides the necessary prescription against heresy.

Thus, our work refocuses the debate over homosexuality on the real issue. The issue is not, after all, whether the Bible addresses homosexual practice: it does. It is not whether diverse interpretations on this issue have existed in the history of the church: they have not. The issue is, rather, what is authoritative for the church in the formation of its convictions and in its practices. On the issue of homosexual practice, no person or church or group should say that biblical texts mean something other than what the church has said all along because, as we shall demonstrate, both Scripture and the church have clearly and consistently said the same thing. The issue comes down to this: the authority of Scripture and the relevance of the church's teaching. That is where we wish to leave the matter, for that is the point at which some in the church in the West are dividing from the rest of the church universal, from the teaching of the church in other centuries, and from what must indeed be considered the teaching of all Christians.

---

[2] A helpful book that addresses a number of these topics is *God, Gays and the Church: Human Sexuality and Experience in Christian Thinking*, ed. Lisa Nolland, Chris Sugden, and Sarah Finch (London: The Latimer Trust, 2008).

PART I

CHRISTIAN TRADITION AND HOMOSEXUAL PRACTICE

Introduction to Part I

CHAPTER 1

THE GAY CHRISTIAN MOVEMENT

The origins of the gay rights movement in America are usually associated with the New York Stonewall Inn riots of 1969 and the ensuing arrests of gay demonstrators. A 1965 New Year's Day Mardi Gras costume ball in San Francisco, sponsored by the Council on Religion and the Homosexual (CRH), also resulted in the arrests of homosexuals. In both instances public opinion began to shift in favor of homosexuals. The CRH, founded in 1964, was one of the first organizations to use the title "homosexual" and asserted that "one should no more deplore homosexuality than left-handedness." Thus began a concerted effort by the gay community to achieve public approval. Efforts to change the public's mind about homosexuality and "whack away at the sickness theory" led the American Psychiatric Association (APA) to remove homosexuality from the officially approved list of psychiatric illnesses in 1973.[1]

---

[1] Psychiatrist and professor Jeffrey Satinover has argued that politics corrupted the scientific process of the APA in its reclassification of homosexuality. Satinover states, "The purported scientific consensus that the press touts is a fiction." Jeffrey Satinover, *Homosexuality and the Politics of Truth* (Grand Rapids, MI: Baker, 1996), 31–40. See also Robert R. Reilly's *Making Gay Okay: How Rationalizing Homosexual Behavior Is Changing Everything* (San Francisco, CA: Ignatius, 2014), which includes a thorough overview of gay activism within psychology influencing the APA's 1975 statement that "being gay is just as healthy as being straight." Reilly asserts there is "no credible science to substantiate this assertion" (p. 127). Our own view is that sin may have psychological and physical implications, but it is not essentially a psychiatric disorder.

Gay activists have crafted an aggressive strategy for persuading straight Americans to tolerate and eventually celebrate homosexuality. Marshall Kirk and Hunter Madsen outlined this strategy in their 1989 book *After the Ball: How America Will Conquer Its Fear and Hatred of Gays in the 90s*.[2] They admitted that the campaign for gay acceptance would likely not work on intransigent religious conservatives who were "diehard homohaters"; thus, the campaign targeted ambivalent skeptics through the mainstream media by using a "keep talking" principle which over time would give the impression that homosexuality was commonplace. Homosexual behavior was to be downplayed because "gay sex habits provoke public revulsion." The primary objective with religious homohaters was to "cow and silence them as far as possible." Kirk and Madsen offered a twofold plan for dealing with the religious:

> First gays can use talk to muddy the moral waters, that is, to undercut the rationalizations that "justify" religious bigotry and to jam some of its psychic rewards. *This entails publicizing support by moderate churches and raising serious theological objections to conservative biblical teachings.* It also means exposing the inconsistency and hatred underlying antigay doctrines. Conservative churches, which pay as much lip service to Christian charity as anybody else, are rendered particularly vulnerable by their callous hypocrisy regarding AIDS sufferers.
>
> Second, gays can undermine the moral authority of homohating churches over less fervent adherents by portraying such institutions as antiquated backwaters, badly out of step with the times and with the latest findings of psychology. Against the atavistic tug of Old Time Religion one must set the mightier pull of Science and Public Opinion (the shield and sword of that accursed "secular humanism"). Such an "unholy" alliance has already worked well in America against churches, on such topics as divorce and abortion. With enough open talk about the prevalence and acceptability of homosexuality, that alliance can work for gays.[3]

The gay Christian[4] movement has followed the blueprint proposed by Kirk and Madsen in its efforts to infiltrate various denominations with the gay-rights

---

[2] The term *homophile movement* has been used to describe early gay pleas for tolerance. Today gay activists push for full acceptance and the celebration of homosexuality by society. For a thoroughly researched exposé of how gay activism has influenced Hollywood, the media, universities, public schools, and business see, Michael L. Brown, *A Queer Thing Happened to America: And What a Long, Strange Trip It's Been* (Concord, NC: EqualTime, 2011). Robert R. Reilly's *Making Gay Okay* also documents how the homosexual campaign has marched through all the institutions of American society. For the British context see Patricia Morgan, *The Marriage Files: The Purpose, Limits and Fate of Marriage* (London: Wilberforce, 2014).

[3] Marshall Kirk and Hunter Madsen, *After the Ball: How America Will Conquer Its Fear and Hatred of Gays in the 90s* (New York, NY: Doubleday, 1989), 179.

[4] The expression "gay Christian" is currently a popular term of self-identification and will be used in this chapter to identify a group of people/ideas. Though the authors believe this language

program. One of the battleground denominations for homosexuality in recent decades has been the United Methodist Church. Methodist minister Karen Booth, in her book *Forgetting How to Blush: United Methodism's Compromise with the Sexual Revolution*, chronicles destructive gay activism within her denomination. Booth evaluates the arguments of pro-gay Methodist apologists through the lens of the Wesleyan Quadrilateral—a manner of depicting the fourfold authority of Scripture, tradition, reason, and experience—pointing out that Methodist progressives regard reason and experience as more authoritative than Scripture and tradition. Traditionalists are accused of being oppressive "neo-Pharisees" on a "witch hunt" to exterminate gays and lesbians. They are guilty of "soul murder" and hate, upon which God will bring his judgment. Booth notes, "This extreme and inflammatory rhetoric could have been lifted almost verbatim from Madsen and Kirk's *After the Ball* playbook."[5]

METROPOLITAN COMMUNITY CHURCH

In the early stages of the gay Christian movement, the door was shut to gay church leadership in almost all denominations. Therefore, a few homosexuals decided to start their own "church." In 1968, former Pentecostal preacher Troy Perry, who was openly gay, gathered a small group of California homosexuals. The group eventually took the name Metropolitan Community Church (MCC), also known as the Universal Fellowship of Metropolitan Community Churches, and initiated a ministry primarily for gays, lesbians, bisexuals, and transgender persons. Now, with about two hundred congregations in the US, the MCC is comprised mostly of former Protestants and Catholics who could not find affirmation of their gay lifestyle in traditional Christian churches.

According to its website, the "MCC began as a fellowship of churches, each church linked to another through affiliation as an open and inclusive body. Collectively, MCC churches offer a picture of Christianity and religion which celebrates God's diverse creativity. At our foundation, MCC brings to bear the co-existence and complementary relationship of sexuality and spirituality; initially bringing the message of God's love to homosexual persons."[6] The MCC is committed to ending all forms of supposed discrimination against

---

is an oxymoron, it is a useful term for identifying a social group. The movement has produced its own version of Scripture and a Bible commentary—*The Queen James Bible*, which edits the KJV to "prevent homophobic interpretations." See http://queenjamesbible.com and *The Queer Bible Commentary*, ed. Deryn Guest, Robert E. Goss, Mona West, and Thomas Bohache (London, England: SCM Press, 2006).

[5] Karen Booth, *Forgetting How to Blush: United Methodism's Compromise with the Sexual Revolution* (Fort Valley, GA: Bristol House, Ltd., 2012), 181–204 provides a well-documented exposé of gay Christian tactics designed to turn a denomination away from its Christian heritage.

[6] Metropolitan Community Churches, "Our Churches," accessed September 27, 2014, http://mccchurch.org/overview/ourchurches.

persons based on sexuality, gender identity, or ethnicity. The rite of Holy Union, "the spiritual joining of two people," has been a part of MCC practice almost from the beginning.

The MCC includes churches in multiple nations, drawing together people whose common bond is often their self-identified sexual preference. The MCC has been compared to the Unitarian Universalist Church in its theology and practice, although it claims to embrace the Apostles' Creed and the Nicene Creed.[7] Most denominations do not consider the MCC a Christian body. Often the group is excluded from lists of Christian denominations in the United States. In 1983 the governing board of the National Council of Churches voted to "postpone indefinitely" the membership application of the MCC.

GAY ORGANIZATIONS

Multiple support groups for gay persons have arisen within Catholicism, Orthodoxy, and mainline Protestant denominations. These groups function as national networks that lobby within their respective denominations. The gay networks' goals are ecclesiastical affirmation of gay sexuality, the ordination of practicing homosexuals, and the blessing of same-sex unions.[8] These groups typically chastise their denominations as homophobic and heterosexist, calling on them to practice inclusion and cease unjust discrimination against gays. Gay advocates within these groups often reference an inclusive Jesus who would not discriminate. Appeals are made to new biblical scholarship that has "exploded the myths" of Christian prejudice against minority gay persons.

A typical Protestant gay organization is the GLAD Alliance, a gay advocacy group within the Christian Church (Disciples of Christ). GLAD's resources for congregations include films, books, and Bible studies directed toward transforming Christians to be "open and affirming" of homosexuality. GLAD describes its history and mission this way:

> The GLAD Alliance had its beginnings in the struggles for a more inclusive Christian Church (Disciples of Christ) in the late 1970s. Our founders sought a church that welcomes the gifts and graces of those persons who have traditionally been excluded because of their gender or sexual identities. While our mission was initially focused on working for inclusion for lesbians and gay men, GLAD's mission has since broadened to include a commitment

---

[7] MCC founder Troy Perry's autobiography, *The Lord Is My Shepherd and He Knows I'm Gay* (1972), has been a popular text within the gay Christian movement.

[8] Denomination-specific groups include Dignity USA (Roman Catholic); Orthodox and Gay (Orthodox churches); Integrity USA (Episcopal Church USA); UCC Coalition of LGBT Concerns (United Church of Christ); Lutherans Concerned, Extraordinary Lutheran Ministries (Evangelical Lutheran Church in America); Covenant Network of Presbyterians (Presbyterian Church USA), Methodists in New Directions, Reconciling Ministries Network (United Methodists), and Association of Welcoming & Affirming Baptists (Baptist).

to working for the inclusion of persons of ALL gender and sexual identities (lesbian, gay, bisexual, transgender, queer, questioning, intersex, asexual, and ally). In those early years of struggle, our mission was primarily to be a community of sanctuary, offering a safe place for lesbian and gay Disciples to gather and share their struggles. As our church and society at large has moved toward a place of greater acceptance, GLAD has been moving more and more into the realm of advocacy and activism as we seek to transform the Christian Church (Disciples of Christ) in every manifestation into a more just, welcoming, and inclusive community of faith, one that truly does welcome all to Christ's table as God has welcomed us.[9]

A host of nondenominational pro-gay organizations has made traditional Christian objections to homosexuality their prime target. While remaining off the radar screen of most evangelicals, these advocacy groups have been a potent force for assaulting historic Christianity. Typically these groups claim that they offer a new and improved version of outdated fundamentalist Christian faith. Some groups even include the word *evangelical* in their organizations' titles, claiming to embrace orthodox Christian teaching.[10] Their attacks usually focus on how Christianity has "misinterpreted" the Bible and must be corrected to align with pro-gay ideology. Any ministry to gays which suggests the possibility of healing or "conversion" to heterosexuality is a special target of vitriol. Undermining the so-called "ex-gay swindle" appears to be the prime agenda of some groups. Ex-gay testimonials subject one to vicious slander.[11]

EVANGELICAL CAPITULATION

Mainline gay arguments seeking to undermine historic Christianity have begun to bleed over into evangelicalism. An illustration of the attempt to infiltrate evangelical churches is the work of twenty-something Matthew Vines. Raised in an evangelical Presbyterian congregation, Vines has started a new organization called Reformation Project with the goal of changing the minds of conservative Christians about gay relationships. His plan is to train fifty persons from evangelical churches to argue that Scripture does not condemn same-sex sexual orientation or loving gay relationships. According to Vines, his scheme

---

[9] GLAD Alliance, "History," accessed September 27, 2014, https://sites.google.com/site/doc-gladalliance/about-us/history. One of the key GLAD leaders within the Christian Church (Disciples of Christ) is Rev. Mel White, whose writings are full of deceptive gay propaganda. See Mel White's *Stranger at the Gate: To Be Gay and Christian in America* (1994; repr., New York, NY: Plume, 1995) and *Holy Terror: Lies the Christian Right Tells Us to Deny Gay Equality* (2006; repr., Riverdale, NY: Magnus, 2012).

[10] For example, Evangelicals Concerned Inc., The Evangelical Network, and The Gay Christian Network.

[11] Pro-gay organizations claiming some Christian association include Truth Wins Out, It Gets Better, Not All Like That, Progressive Christian Alliance, Faith in America, Christians Tired of Being Misrepresented, Many Voices, and Soul Force.

is the next frontier of the gay movement, which is working to change the minds of conservative Christians about same-sex relationships.[12]

Another example of a gay evangelical is Southern-Baptist-raised Justin Lee, who started the Gay Christian Network in 2001and tells of his journey to accept his homosexual orientation in the 2012 book *Torn: Rescuing the Gospel from the Gays-vs.-Christians Debate*. It is a moving tale of his loving family and his personal grappling with same-sex attraction. He describes his disillusionment with those who tried to explain the causes of his homosexuality and his skepticism of ex-gay ministries.[13] Lee's book is likely to provoke compassion from readers, but he presents straw-man arguments as representative of traditional Christian views. This may appear convincing to those who have not studied the issue, are questioning orthodox teaching on homosexuality, or are seeking answers they want to hear.

Lee's failure to represent the robust Christian position accurately is just the beginning of his problems. When he moves to discussion of specific biblical texts, he follows the lead of pro-gay scholarship, largely discredited. Yet to those uninitiated in biblical and historical studies, the arguments may appear convincing—Lee himself seems to have found what he was looking for. In the end Lee argues that Jesus's teaching about love trumps explicit biblical prohibitions of homosexual practice. Lee asserts, "The Holy Spirit knows the purpose of God's laws and can guide us in interpreting and applying them to our situations, superseding the letter of the law when appropriate, and helping us to fulfil God's ultimate desire for us on earth: not to be slaves to a set of rules, but to live out God's unconditional agape love in every moment of our lives."[14]

Lee admits there are differences of interpretation regarding key biblical texts that reference homosexuality. The debate involves, according to Lee, "Side A," which supports same-sex marriage and relationships, and "Side B,"

---

[12] See "The Reformation Project: A Bible-Based, Gospel-Centered Approach to Inclusion," accessed September 27, 2014, http://www.reformationproject.org; Matthew Vines, *God and the Gay Christian: The Biblical Case in Support of Same-Sex Relationships* (New York, NY: Convergent, 2014).

[13] Lee argues, "We must move away from an 'Ex-Gay' Approach." Ironically, this belies his own overarching approach to Christians appreciating different perspectives. The fact is, thousands of believers have been helped by reparative therapy or experienced healing in a variety of ways, and some ex-gays joyfully experience Christian marriage. Recent powerful examples are the stories told in Rosaria Champagne Butterfield's *The Secret Thoughts of an Unlikely Convert* (Pittsburgh, PA: Crown & Covenant, 2012), Christopher Yuan's *Out of a Far Country* (Colorado Springs, CO: WaterBrook Multnomah, 2013), and David Kyle Foster's *Love Hunger* (Bloomington, MN: Chosen Books, 2014). As much as some gay Christians do not want to acknowledge this or find it foreign to their personal experiences, the gospel is powerful to transform lives, and it takes different shapes in different people's lives according to God's purposes. Absolutizing one's own experience as normative for every other person is a dead-end street.

[14] Justin Lee, *Torn: Rescuing the Gospel from the Gays-vs.-Christians Debate* (New York, NY: Jericho, 2012), 204.

which promotes celibacy for Christians with same-sex attractions. Lee's rec-ommendation for resolving the dispute is that Christians should not quarrel over such "disputable matters." From Lee's perspective, recent gay interpreta-tions of the Bible should be granted equal standing with Christian viewpoints held by the church for two millennia. Lee's discussion is devoid of any engage-ment with the history of Christianity. There are obvious reasons for this.

A few supposedly evangelical scholars have embraced a pro-gay theology. In his book *The Bible's Yes to Same-Sex Marriage: An Evangelical's Change of Heart,* mainline Presbyterian Mark Achtemeier chronicles his "growing conviction that the church's condemnation of same-gender relationships is a tragic and destructive misinterpretation of the Bible's message."[15] Achtemeier outlines the Bible's teaching on marriage between a man and woman but then argues that "same sex unions are equally as capable as their heterosexual coun-terparts of fulfilling the highest revealed purposes God has in mind for love and marriage."[16]

Achtemeier cites Christian support of slavery and the "oppression" of women as examples of what he calls "the fragment approach" to reading the Bible. He describes this approach as lifting out isolated texts of Scripture "without much consideration of their surrounding contexts or the witness of Scripture as a whole."[17] Biblical support for his attention to the "broader wit-ness of Scripture" is found in the New Testament teaching on Old Testament law. Devotion to written rules in the Bible is insufficient to align one with the will of God, Achtemeier argues. Rather, one should look to God's work in the world. Achtemeier describes how his interaction with gay individuals caused him to rethink his position:

> I allowed observations of what was actually happening in the lives of believing gay people to raise questions about the traditional condemnations of homosexuality that were based entirely on fragments of the written, bib-lical Law! Was it possible that the Holy Spirit would correct peoples' mis-understanding of the Bible surrounding this issue, in the same way as had happened with the "biblical" cases supporting slavery and the oppression of women?[18]

Achtemeier highlights the fact that neither he nor any of his children are gay; thus, his journey to embrace gay Christianity has not been motivated by family concerns. This is noteworthy since many evangelicals have changed

---

[15] Mark Achtemeier, *The Bible's Yes to Same-Sex Marriage: An Evangelical's Change of Heart* (Louisville, KY: Westminster/John Knox, 2014), xii.

[16] Ibid., 63–64.

[17] Ibid., 20.

[18] Ibid., 23. The citation of Christian views on slavery and women is misleading. See the "Excursus" at the end of Part II for a detailed explanation of this point.

their views on homosexuality only after they or family members "came out" as gay. David Gushee, a Baptist minister and professor of ethics at Mercer University, is a case in point: his sister, a single-mother, came out as a lesbian in 2008. Since that time Gushee has changed his mind about homosexuality and calls other Christians to join him in his defection from the historic faith.

One must respect Gushee for admitting that his new position is a departure from what the church has believed and taught for two millennia. According to him this is a serious matter because contemporary Christian leaders "carry profound responsibilities to the one, holy, catholic and apostolic Church. We can't simply abandon the Bible, or Church tradition, or historic Christian beliefs, just because there is a cultural movement of great power bearing down hard on us to snap our views into line with prevailing opinion. This is precisely what Church leaders (at their best) have refused to do." Despite his warning against abandoning the Bible and church tradition, Gushee proceeds to do just that and urges the church to forsake its historic position on homosexuality.[19]

Joining Gushee in this call for a changed mind is emergent church leader Brian McLaren, whose son married his same-sex partner in 2012. McLaren laments the broken relationships he experienced with fellow believers "when I 'came out' as a married heterosexual evangelical pastor who had changed my mind on LGBT equality." He challenges others to have courage and remain open to changing their minds.[20]

Former Southern Baptist pastor Danny Cortez, also with a gay son, announced to his congregation in 2014 that he had changed his mind on homosexuality. Pastor Cortez and his congregation, the New Heart Community Church of La Mirada, California, have declared themselves a "Third Way church," allowing members to disagree on the sinfulness of same-sex practice. In 2014 the Southern Baptist Convention's Executive Committee, on behalf of the Convention, declared New Heart not in cooperation with the SBC. Changing one's mind on homosexuality brings with it the consequence of division in relationships and denominations.[21]

World Vision, a leading evangelical humanitarian organization, found out the hard way that public disavowal of the historic Christian position on

---

[19] David P. Gushee, *Changing Our Mind* (Canton, MI: Read the Spirit, 2014), 16–17. New Testament scholar Robert Gagnon has described Gushee's survey of pertinent biblical texts as "embarrassingly bad exegesis." See *The Christian Post*, Robert A. J. Gagnon, October 29, 2014, "David Gushee's Gay-Switch, Biblical Scholarship, and Slanted Reporting," accessed November 15, 2014, http://www.christianpost.com/news/david-gushees-gay-switch-biblical-scholarship-and-slanted-reporting-128817. Gagnon's impressive work, *The Bible and Homosexual Practice: Texts and Hermeneutics* (Nashville, TN: Abingdon, 2002) has become a standard text.

[20] Ibid., xv.

[21] See R. Albert Mohler Jr., September 24, 2014, "Homosexuality as Dividing Line—the Inescapable Issue," accessed November 14, 2014, http://www.albertmohler.com/2014/09/24/homosexuality-as-dividing-line-the-inescapable-issue.

homosexuality has consequences. In the spring of 2014, Richard Stearns, president of World Vision United States, announced that the organization was changing its policy to allow the hiring of married gay employees. The protest from evangelicals was so widespread that in less than a week, World Vision reversed itself. A letter sent out by World Vision included this statement: "The Board acknowledged they made a mistake and chose to revert to our long-standing conduct policy requiring sexual abstinence for all single employees and faithfulness within the biblical covenant of marriage between a man and a woman." A number of high profile leaders had spoken out in opposition to World Vision's policy change and rejoiced to hear of this reversal. Other Christians, including blogger Rachel Held Evans, were outspokenly distressed at World Vision's reversal. Evans wrote, "I confess I had not realized the true extent of the disdain and stigmatization many Evangelicals have toward LGBT people."[22]

Evangelical capitulation on homosexuality will continue to produce controversy. Commitment to biblically defined sexual ethics has been a hallmark of evangelicalism, and abandonment of that commitment is viewed by the majority of evangelicals as departure from authentic Christianity.

CHALLENGING THE CATHOLIC CHURCH

One significant leader of the gay Christian movement in recent decades has been Jesuit priest, professor, and psychotherapist John J. McNeill, known for his influential book *The Church and the Homosexual*, first published in 1976. In the book, now in its fourth edition, McNeill called on the Roman Catholic Church to revise its teaching about homosexuality. He argued that new evidence in biblical studies, psychology, sociology, and history "challenged every premise on which the traditional teaching was based." According to McNeill, gay and lesbian Catholics suffer an "enormous amount of pain, psychological trauma, and potential emotional breakdown . . . caused by the interiorization of Church teaching. . . . What was bad psychology had to be bad theology and vice versa."[23]

McNeill's work was hailed as a book that "convincingly established that the Bible does not condemn homosexuality," a "major weapon for those

---

[22] *Christianity Today*, Celeste Gracey and Jeremy Weber, March 24, 2014, "World Vision: Why We're Hiring Gay Christians in Same-Sex Marriage," accessed November 15, 2014, http://www.christianitytoday.com/ct/2014/march-web-only/world-vision-why-hiring-gay-christians-same-sex-marriage.html?paging=off; *The Christian Post*, Michael Gryboski, March 27, 2014, "Evangelicals Respond to Word Vision's Reversal on Hiring Gay Married Employees," accessed November 14, 2014, http://www.christianpost.com/news/evangelicals-respond-to-world-visions-reversal-on-hiring-gay-married-employees-116901.

[23] John McNeill, *The Church and the Homosexual*, 4th ed. (Boston, MA: Beacon, 1993), xii.

fighting to change the church," and a "good book, which shatters bad myths."[24] Though the book initially received the *Imprimi Potest* of the Roman Catholic Church, a certification of official approval, the Congregation for the Doctrine of the Faith ordered the removal of the *Imprimi Potest* in 1977. McNeill was forbidden to discuss the issue of homosexuality in public and was eventually expelled from the Society of Jesus in 1987. He has continued his publishing on gay Christianity in subsequent books: *Taking a Chance on God: Liberating Theology for Gays, Lesbians and Their Lovers, Families and Friends* (1988, 1996), *Freedom, Glorious Freedom: The Spiritual Journey to the Fullness of Life for Gays, Lesbians and Everybody Else* (1995, 2009), and *Both Feet Firmly Planted in Midair* (1998), his spiritual autobiography. In 2008, his *Sex as God Intended* included a Festschrift of essays "celebrating the life and work of John J. McNeill."[25]

McNeill's influential writings are representative of an aggressive gay Christian movement demanding the church change its position on homosexuality and fully embrace gay sexuality as a legitimate expression of Christian faith. In the preface to the fourth edition of *The Church and Homosexuality*, McNeill chastised Roman Catholic bishops for their traditional sexual ethics:

> In the name of all Catholic gays, and gays and lesbians everywhere, I cry out "Enough!" Enough of your distortions of Scripture that make homosexuals the scapegoats of every disaster! Jesus himself in Luke 10:10 recognized the sin of Sodom as inhospitality to the stranger, yet you support the interpretation of that sin as homosexual activity. *Through the centuries you have supported sodomy laws that have sent thousands of gays to their deaths. You continue to claim that a loving homosexual act is condemned in Scripture, when competent scholars are nearly unanimous in admitting that nowhere in Scripture is there a clear condemnation of sexual acts between two gay men or lesbians who love each other.* Enough! Enough of your effort to reduce all homosexual acts to expressions of lust, and of your refusal to see them as expressions of deep, genuine human love! Enough of your effort to lead young gays to internalize self-hatred with the result that they are able to relate to God only as a God of fear and hate, and lose all hope in a God of love! Enough of your recent efforts to foster hatred and discrimination against us in the human community! Enough of driving us from the home of our mother, the Church, and denying us the fullness of human life and sexual love. Enough of fostering discrimination against us, even violence and gay-bashing.[26]

---

[24] Ibid., commendations on back cover of McNeil's book.

[25] John J. McNeill, *Sex as God Intended: A Reflection on Human Sexuality as Play Including Festschrift Essays Celebrating the Life and Work of John J. McNeill* (Maple Shade, NJ: Lethe, 2008). The Festschrift includes essays by Troy Perry, founder of MCC, and Mel White.

[26] Ibid., Preface, xx. McNeill's controversial comments were a caricature of historic Christianity and a misrepresentation of biblical scholarship. Scholars are not "nearly unanimous"

For the purposes of this book, we are concerned with the historical and biblical arguments presented by McNeill and other pro-gay Christian activists who seek to discredit the historic Christian church, falsely charging her with persecuting gays and supporting "sodomy laws that have sent thousands of gays to their deaths." Being a Roman Catholic, McNeill realized that in addition to his attempt at undermining traditional interpretations of Scripture, he also had to discredit the church's perspective on homosexual practice throughout church history. He argued that for two millennia Christians have been deceived by church leaders who have foisted their antigay perspectives on God's people based on erroneous ideas and misinterpretations of the Bible.

The Western Christian tradition, according to McNeill, has used three principle sources as its basis for condemning homosexual practices:

> The early Christian community, primarily drawn from among the Jews of the diaspora, were inclined to see any variation of behavior in Greek culture as a deviation from the divine law given to Israel and as the inevitable breakdown of morality due to idolatrous practices. The second major source of the condemnation of homosexual practices was an appeal to the popular Stoic philosophical concept of nature, a concept which culminated in Aquinas's version of natural law. The third source, and in some respects the most important, since it was deemed to be a divine confirmation of the first and second sources, was the prevalent version of the Sodom and Gomorrah story.[27]

McNeill places great emphasis on the church fathers' supposed misunderstanding of Sodom's sin. Due in part to McNeill's book, debunking the Sodom story has become a fundamental part of the gay Christian argument regarding Scripture and Christian history. McNeill challenges the historic interpretation, basing much of his argument on the earlier work of Derrick Sherwin Bailey in *Homosexuality and the Western Christian Tradition* (1955). In the first chapter of Bailey's book, he argued that "none of the Biblical condemnations of homosexual practices makes any mention of the Sodom story."[28] The origin of the traditional Christian idea that Sodomites were destroyed because of

---

that Scripture fails to condemn sex acts between gays "who love each other." And there is no scholarly consensus that the sin of Sodom, according to Scripture, was exclusively inhospitality.

[27] Ibid., 68. This is a misleading comment, for while the factors McNeill mentions were involved, they were not central to the early church's stance on homosexuality. The primary reason the early church maintained a negative view of homosexual practice was divine revelation in the Old and New Testaments. This will become evident to the reader in chapter 2 of the present work.

[28] D. S. Bailey, *Homosexuality and the Western Theological Tradition* (London, England: Longmans, Green and Co., 1955). Bailey explains the explicit reference to Sodom's sexual perversion in Jude 5–7 as a condemnation of men seeking sexual relations with angelic beings. Bailey comments that in Jude's view, "the sin of Sodom, though admittedly sexual ("having . . . given themselves over to fornication"), was only, as it were, incidentally homosexual; the

their homosexual acts "can be traced to its origin in a conception of the sin of Sodom which appeared first in Palestine during the second century BC." Bailey concluded that the church must judge the morality of homosexual acts as it does all other sins, for "it is no longer possible to maintain the belief that homosexual practices were once punished by a Divine judgment upon their perpetrators so terrible and conclusive as to preclude any subsequent discussion of the question."[29]

GAY SEXUALITY

There is no substantive difference between the mainstream gay movement and sexually active gays who claim Christian faith. For this reason it is imperative for the church to understand the sexual agenda of the gay community. The gay movement understands homosexual sex as a revolutionary act, which undercuts the "heteronormativity" of Western Christianized society. Achieving full social acceptance of homosexual identity must ultimately include arguing for the acceptability of homosexual practice. This entails denouncing monotheistic moral norms and substituting an atheistic pursuit of sexual pleasure as the *summum bonum* of human life. An eighteenth-century French text advocating libertine sexuality, *Philosophy in the Bedroom* written by the Marquis de Sade, has attracted renewed attention among modern gay scholars. In the book, de Sade's character Dolmance explains the superior pleasures of male homosexual sex:

> In all the world there is no mode of pleasure-taking preferable to this: I worship it in either sex; . . . 'tis with men Nature wishes men to practice this oddity, and it is especially for men she has given us an inclination. Absurd to say the mania offends Nature; can it be so, when 'tis she who puts it into our head? can she dictate what degrades her? No, Eugenie, not at all; this is as good a place to serve her as any other, and perhaps it is there she is most devoutly worshipped.[30]

---

emphasis is rather upon the sexual incompatibility of the angelic and human orders than upon any particular kind of unnatural coitus between persons of the same sex" (Bailey, 16).

[29] Ibid., 11, 26, 28. Bailey views the destruction of Sodom as a natural disaster, not the judgment of God as the biblical narrative indicates. He comments: "So sudden and complete a devastation of these prosperous cities would create an indelible impression upon the people of that time who, being ignorant of the scientific explanation, would inevitably tend to ascribe the disaster to supernatural agencies. In this way, no doubt, began the theory of a Divine visitation and judgment for sin, which developed into the familiar Sodom story of the Bible" (Bailey, *Homosexuality*, 7). Part II will deal at length with scholarly treatment of the Sodom story.

[30] The Marquis de Sade, "Philosophy in the Bedroom," trans. Richard Sever and Austryn Wainhouse. *Reclaiming Sodom*, Part II, Jonathan Goldberg, ed. (New York, NY: Rutledge, 1994), 207. Marquis de Sade (d. 1814) was an aristocrat philosopher of the French Enlightenment and was imprisoned several times for his writings. De Sade's infamous work, *120 Days of Sodom*, is a perverse tale with graphic depictions of sexual depravity and violence.

Note the idolatry incipient in this text and the language of "worship" associated with a sex act. This is the elephant in the room that many gay Christians do not want to discuss—deviant sexual acts in defiance of God's moral law that are historically known as sodomy. Preferring sex acts over obedience to God is a form of idolatry. Gay Christians want to talk about the injustices they face, committed love relationships, and such, but they minimize discussions of their sexual practice. But this is the heart of the issue: homosexual sex as an expression of one's gay identity becomes more important than submission to the revealed will of God.

Gay scholars accurately recognize that Christian influence has curbed the free and open practice of gay sex, and they intend to change this. Thus their strategy must include attacking historic Christianity (*After the Ball,* etc.) and supporting philosophy which eschews any notion of divine judgment for sexual immorality. Some are even calling for reclaiming a metaphorical Sodom in which homosexual practice is not merely tolerated but glorified. Rocky O'Donovan writes:

> But I want to (re)claim Sodom all for our very own, so I speak a new myth. I want the tiny hamlet to be Queer Space—and really, it is ours whether we want it or not. So let's take it, claim it, speak it; enough of our blood has been spilled in its name to warrant ownership of that landscape several million times over. And all because that nasty old god hates us Queer Boys—would rather kill us than look at us. So that's new? That god, rabid with his own omnipotence and made in the image of the power-hungry, jealous, White, bourgeois, straight, able-bodied male, is no friend (let alone god) of mine. . . . I like Sodom now. I feel comfortable there. Of course god destroyed it. That's what straight men like to do. And now Sodom is ours. Nobody else dares step foot/body/soul into that space. So let's take back Sodom. Let's rebuild there. They always give us wastelands and we always turn them into music and gardens, full of our passions, desires, beauties. In that space I can stand my ground. In that space I can speak about my body without fear.[31]

As radical as all this sounds to traditional Christians, some of the same themes are found among leaders of the gay Christian movement. McNeill argues for the superiority of committed, loving gay relationships, which can

---

[31] Rocky O'Donovan, "Reclaiming Sodom," in *Reclaiming Sodom*, 248. Unrestrained fulfillment of sexual desires may not stop with homoeroticism; the late well-known gay activist Franklin Kameny once wrote, "Let us have more and better enjoyment of more and better sexual perversions, by whatever definition, by more and more consenting adults. . . . If bestiality with consenting animals provides happiness to some people, let them pursue their happiness." Kameny's letter to Americans for Truth About Homosexuality (AFTAH), May 31, 2008, accessed March 26, 2015, http://americansfortruth.com/2008/05/31/gay-icon-kameny-tells-aftah-bestiality-ok-as-long-as-the-animal-doesnt-mind.

serve as role models to the divorce-ridden culture of traditional marriage. Yet McNeill incongruously suggests that casual gay sex may be a good thing:

> There are only three kinds of sexual activity between consenting adults: good, better and best sex. Apart from rape or child abuse, contrary to traditional Church teaching, it is difficult to sin seriously in a sexual gesture. . . . A danger in the present situation is that many in the gay community could lose the freshness and the joy of their celebration of God's good gift of sexuality and regress into feelings of shame, guilt, and self-loathing for any expression of their sexuality. And, of course, the conservative homophobic Churches are doing their best to produce this regression among their followers. The possibility of having caring and playful sex still exists if both partners follow the guidelines for safe sex.[32]

McNeill claims that Jesus endorsed homosexual practice, drawing on the accounts in Matthew 8 and Luke 7 of Jesus healing a Roman centurion's servant—"my beloved boy," as McNeill translates it. He comments on the story: "Here we have the most direct encounter of Jesus with someone who would today be pronounced 'gay,' and Jesus' reaction was acceptance of the person without judgment and even eagerness to be of assistance to restore the '*pais*' to health, and by implication to fully restore the loving relationship of the two, making possible the renewal of any sexual activity which they would have enjoyed together prior to the illness."[33]

In addition to his affirmation of gay sex, McNeill argues that God is providentially increasing the gay community:

> I am convinced that gay liberation is a central part of the great dialectic of human liberation that God is working out through Her/His Holy Spirit. . . . Gay people have a special need for a vision of their role in bringing about the reign of God in history to sustain them in the difficult battles ahead. . . . This presence of a visible lesbian and gay community, for the first time in my knowledge in the past three thousand years, is an integral part of this dialectic and another aspect of the rediscovery of the feminine in a new synthesis in the human personality.[34]

Little difference exists between gay Christian theology and gay secular humanist presuppositions, other than the use of "God-talk" in an attempt to sanctify gay sex.[35] The gay Christian movement is both in the world and of

---

[32] John J. McNeill, *Sex as God Intended*, 63, 65.

[33] Ibid., 89. McNeill apparently prefers a modern tolerant Jesus rather than the first-century Jewish Jesus who would have taken the book of Leviticus's condemnation of homosexual practice at face value—just like any other Jew of his day.

[34] Ibid., 113.

[35] What one finds among both secular and "Christian" gays is a relentless effort to sanitize (sanctify) their immoral behavior. Robert R. Reilly has observed, "For any individual, moral

the world. Homoerotic behavior is ultimately a profession of atheism and a declaration of war on Western society's heterosexual norms inherited from historic Christianity. Homosexual sex is indeed a revolutionary act seeking to overthrow all constraints imposed by traditional Christianity. Christianity is the opposition, from the secular humanist perspective, and this conclusion is legitimate, for homosexual practice is antithetical to everything Scripture and the Christian tradition teach about men and women, who are created by God for each other. The gay Christian movement chooses to obscure the truth and has deluded itself into embracing the fantasy that God blesses homosexual practice.[36]

THE BOSWELL THESIS

In addition to McNeill, another gay Catholic writer who has generated controversy is history professor John Boswell of Yale University. Boswell died at age forty-two of an AIDS-related illness in 1996, but his 1980 book *Christianity, Social Tolerance, and Homosexuality* left its mark on the gay Christian community. Boswell has been called the patron saint of gay Christians because of the notoriety given his book. In addition to gay Christians, some in the secular press lauded his work. But even some members of the scholarly gay community criticized the book as biased and inaccurate in its evaluation of Christian history. Boswell represents a certain point in the trajectory of historical studies on ancient Greek homosexual practices that begins, by and large, with Kenneth Dover.[37] A spate of historical studies followed Boswell's work,[38]

---

failure is hard to live with because of the rebuke of conscience. Habitual moral failure, what used to be called vice, can be tolerated only by creating a rationalization to justify it" (*Making Gay Okay*, 7).

[36] A public illustration of this phenomenon was President Obama's endorsement of homosexual marriage in 2012 and his attempt to justify this view by appealing to Jesus. Robert R. Reilly comments, "He might as well have said, Christ died to make the world safe for sodomy" (*Making Gay Okay*, 44).

[37] In 1978, Kenneth Dover produced *Greek Homosexuality*, a study of artifacts (such as vases) and literature of ancient Greece. His study largely focused on the practice of pederasty and its acceptance within Greek society. As long as free citizens did not sell themselves for sex (as did Timarchos in a case presented by the famous orator Demosthenes, which will be noted later), and as long as youths switched roles from the "beloved" (*eromenos*) to the adult "lover" of boys (*erastēs*), Greek society (particularly Athenian society) approved of pederasty. Kenneth Dover, *Greek Homosexuality* (Cambridge, MA: Harvard University Press, 1978; 2nd ed., 1989).

[38] See, for example, Michel Foucault, *The History of Sexuality*, 3 vols. (New York, NY: Random House, 1978–1986); Harold Patzer, *Die grieschische Knabenliebe* (Wiesbaden, Germany: F. Steiner, 1982); Sarah Lilja, *Homosexuality in Republican and Augustan Rome* (Helsinki, Finland: Societas Scientarium Fennica, 1983); Gundel Koch-Harnack, *Knabenliebe und Tiergeschenke: Ihre Bedeutung im pedärastischen Erziehungssystem Athens* (Berlin: Gebr. Mann, 1983); Ronald M. Springett, *Homosexuality in History and the Scripture: Some Historical and Biblical Perspectives on Homosexuality* (Washington, DC: Biblical Research Institute, 1988);

yet many nonhistorians continue to reference Boswell as though he provided a definitive work.[39] While early Christian consensus opposing all forms of homosexual practice is easily discernible from the sources, it was surprisingly challenged by Boswell in *Christianity, Social Tolerance, and Homosexuality*. Boswell's revisionist account sought to rehabilitate Christian history, making it more compatible with homosexual practice. Boswell argued:

> The early Christian church does not appear to have opposed homosexual behavior per se. The most influential Christian literature was moot on the issue; no prominent writers seem to have considered homosexual attraction "unnatural," and those who objected to physical expression of homosexual

---

Carola Reinsberg, *Ehe, Hetärentum und Knabenliebe im antiken Griechenland* (Munich, Germany: C. H. Beck, 1989); David Halperin, John Winkler, and F. Zeitlin, eds., *Before Sexuality: The Construction of Erotic Experience in the Ancient Greek World* (Princeton, NJ: Princeton University Press, 1990); David Halperin, *One Hundred Years of Homosexuality: And Other Essays on Greek Love* (New York, NY: Routledge, 1990); John J. Winkler, *The Constraints of Desire: The Anthropology of Sex and Gender in Ancient Greece* (New York, NY: Routledge, 1990); David Cohen, *Laws, Sexuality, and Society: The Enforcement of Morals in Classical Athens* (Cambridge, MA: Cambridge University Press, 1991); Wayne R. Dynes and Stephen Donaldson, eds., *Homosexuality in the Ancient World* (New York, NY: Garland, 1992); Amy Richlin, *The Garden of Priapus: Sexuality and Aggression in Roman Humor*, rev. ed. (New York, NY: Oxford University Press, 1992); Eva Cantarella, *Bisexuality in the Ancient World* (New York, NY: Yale University Press, 1992); Angeliki Laiou, ed., *Consent and Coercion to Sex and Marriage in Ancient and Medieval Societies* (Washington, DC: Dumbarton Oaks Research Library and Collection, 1993); David Konstan, *Sexual Symmetry: Love in the Ancient Novel and Related Genre* (Princeton, NJ: Princeton University Press, 1994); Bernadette Brooten, *Love Between Women: Early Christian Responses to Female Homoeroticism* (Chicago, IL: Chicago University Press, 1996); Judith Hallett and Marilyn Skinner, eds., *Roman Sexualities* (Princeton, NJ: Princeton University Press, 1997); Susan Deacy and Karen Pierce, eds., *Rape in Antiquity: Sexual Violence in the Greek and Roman Worlds* (London: Bristol Classical, 1997); Martti Nissinen, *Homoeroticism in the Biblical World* (Minneapolis, MN: Fortress, 1998); Thomas McGinn, *Prostitution, Sexuality, and the Law* (Oxford: Oxford University Press, 1998); Craig Williams, *Roman Homosexuality: Ideologies of Masculinity in Classical Antiquity* (Oxford, England: Oxford University Press, 1999; 2nd ed., 2010); Robert Gagnon, *The Bible and Homosexual Practice: Texts and Hermeneutics* (Nashville, TN: Abingdon, 2001); Thomas McGinn, *The Economy of Prostitution in the Roman World: A Study of Social History and the Brothel* (Ann Arbor, MI: University of Michigan, 2004); Marilyn Skinner, *Sexuality in Greek and Roman Culture* (Malden, MA: Blackwell: 2005; 2nd ed., Wiley-Blackwell, 2014); Rebecca Langlands, *Sexual Morality in Ancient Rome* (Cambridge, England: Cambridge University Press, 2006); Andrew Lear and Eva Cantarella, *Images of Ancient Greek Pederasty: Boys Were Their Gods* (London, England: Routledge, 2008); Mark Golden and Peter Toohey, *A Cultural History of Sexuality in the Classical World* (New York, NY: Oxford University Press, 2011); Kyle Harper, *From Shame to Sin: the Christian Transformation of Sexual Morality in Late Antiquity* (Cambridge, MA: Harvard University Press, 2013).

[39] For an exhaustive list of reviews of *Christianity, Social Tolerance, and Homosexuality*, see *The Boswell Thesis*, ed. Mathew Kuefler (Chicago, IL: University of Chicago Press, 2005), 25–26. Kuefler lists fifty-two reviews of Boswell's book.

feelings generally did so on the basis of considerations unrelated to the teaching of Jesus or his early followers. Hostility to gay people and their sexuality became noticeable in the West during the period of the dissolution of the Roman state—i.e., from the third through the sixth centuries—due to factors which cannot be satisfactorily analyzed, but which probably included the disappearance of urban subcultures, increased governmental regulation of personal morality, and public pressure of asceticism in all sexual matters. Neither Christian society nor Christian theology as a whole evinced or supported any particular hostility to homosexuality, but both reflected and in the end retained positions adopted by some governments and theologians which could be used to derogate homosexual acts.[40]

One of Boswell's arguments was that the Fathers did not understand the primary sin of Sodom to be homosexuality but inhospitality. The minimal patristic citations Boswell used to establish this point were misleading, and he ignored evidence to the contrary.[41] He also attempted to downplay the role of Old Testament prohibitions of homosexuality for the New Testament church. Boswell wrote that the Levitical Holiness Code was no longer significant for apostolic Christianity and beyond; thus, its condemnation of homosexual practice had little influence in the early church. Again Boswell ignored the patristic texts contradicting his thesis. In fact, multiple Fathers cited the book of Leviticus as the textual authority for prohibition of homosexual behavior. The notion that Old Testament condemnation of homosexual practice carried no weight in early Christianity is not substantiated in the texts.[42]

Boswell suggested that a primary reason for the early church's condemnation of homosexual activity was the ascetic impulse that emerged within Christianity. Ascetic writers used the concept of "the natural order," borrowed from Stoics, but most Christian writers did not use this idea, according to Boswell. Patristic scholar David F. Wright countered that patristic sources

---

[40] John Boswell, *Christianity, Social Tolerance, and Homosexuality: Gay People in Western Europe from the Beginning of the Christian Era to the Fourteenth Century* (Chicago, IL: University of Chicago Press, 1980), 333.

[41] Bailey, in his 1950s seminal work on the early church and homosexuality, wrote: "The Fathers of the Christian Church . . . entertained no doubt whatever that the Sodomites were peculiarly and inordinately addicted to homosexual practices, and that they were punished on this account." Bailey, 25; see chapter 10 below.

[42] See David F. Wright, "Early Christian Attitudes to Homosexuality," *Studia Patristica*, 1989: 329–33. Wright's notes list numerous patristic references that contradict Boswell's misrepresentation of the Fathers. J. Robert Wright, in his review of Boswell's book, stated, "In spite of a number of interesting references to the early church fathers, he seems not to have consulted the major patristic indexes that were available at the time of his writing, which would have lent some sense of completeness or thoroughness to his work. . . . I do not find Professor Boswell's retrospective revision of the scriptural/patristic/historical tradition convincing." J. Robert Wright, "Boswell on Homosexuality: A Case Undemonstrated," *Anglican Theological Review* 66, no. 1 (1984): 87–88. See our chapter 2 on the patristic texts.

often speak of the created nature of male and female as the basis for rejecting homosexual practice. Wright stated:

> A long list of Christian writers in East and West depict homosexual inter-course as in conflict with man's created nature. . . . Failure to accord suffi-cient weight to the natural order in the thought of Fathers like Augustine, Lactantius, and Cyprian has led Boswell to misconceive the force of this particular "ascetic attitude."[43]

Despite the absence of textual evidence to substantiate Boswell's arguments, his interpretations of the early and medieval church are uncritically exploited by gay Christian groups seeking to bolster their push for toleration of homosexual practice in the church.[44] However, as the textual evidence in the following chapters will make abundantly clear, the historic church consistently condemned every mode of homosexual behavior. The story of Sodom and Gomorrah, Old Testament law, and New Testament texts were all employed as the theological foundation for Christian views of homosexual practice. Chapters 2 and 3 will examine the historical sources from the early church and the Middle Ages, demonstrating that Boswell's thesis cannot be substantiated from the texts of Christian history.

---

[43] Ibid., 332.

[44] Typical of gay Christian response to Boswell's work is Chris Glaser's flattering comment: "Then came the milestone work of John Boswell, a medieval historian at Yale University. His tome, *Christianity, Social Tolerance, and Homosexuality*, met with academic acclaim and general surprise at its assertion, based on historical evidence, that the church has not always been intolerant of homosexuality." Chris Glaser, "The Love That Dare Not Pray Its Name: The Gay and Lesbian Movement in America's Churches" in *Homosexuality in the Church: Both Sides of the Debate*, ed. Jeffrey S. Siker (Louisville, KY: Westminster/John Knox, 1994), 152; John McNeill writes, "I will never forget my joy and sense of liberation when I first read John Boswell's critique of the traditional biblical passages used to condemn homosexuality (*Christianity, Social Tolerance, and Homosexuality*, 91–117). I agree with Boswell that it can be estab-lished with good scholarship that nowhere in Scripture, the Old and the New Testament, is there a clear condemnation of a loving relationship between two adult gay men and two lesbians." John J. McNeill, *Sex as God Intended* (Maple Shade, NJ: Lethe, 2008), 85.

CHAPTER 2

CHURCH FATHERS AND A DISTINCT CHRISTIAN LIFE

C hristianity is a tradition. It is a faith with a particular ethos, a set of beliefs and practices handed on from generation to generation. The Christian tradition may be understood as the history of what God's people have believed and how they have lived based on His Word. This tradition is not only a collection of accepted doctrines but also a set of lifestyle expectations for followers of Christ. One of the primary things handed down in the Christian church over the centuries is a consistent set of ethical instructions, including specific directives about sexual behavior. The church of every generation from the time of the apostles has condemned sexual sin as unbecoming a disciple of Jesus. At no point have any Orthodox Christian teachers ever suggested that one's sexual practices may deviate from biblical standards.

Tradition can be a good thing; the old voices often give needed perspective. Followers of Christ must listen to the voices from long ago as well as the voices of present-day Christian leaders who point us to the teaching of Scripture. The old as well as the new are necessary. G. K. Chesterton put it this way, "Tradition means giving votes to the most obscure of all classes, our ancestors. It is the democracy of the dead. Tradition refuses to submit to that arrogant oligarchy who merely happens to be walking around."[1] C. S. Lewis observed that when Christians solely rely on new books to the exclusion of old ones, they suffer from blindness because the new must be "tested against

---

[1] Gilbert K. Chesterton, *Orthodoxy* (San Francisco, CA: Ignatius, 1908), 53.

the great body of Christian thought down through the ages." The only cure for historical myopia is "to keep the clean sea breeze of the centuries blowing through our minds, and this can be done only by reading old books." Lewis likened neglecting the literature of the Christian past to the embarrassing confusion one experiences when joining at eleven o'clock a conversation that started at eight.[2]

The Protestant movement affirmed that the Bible alone is the final source of authority in matters of Christian faith and practice, but attempting to understand Scripture apart from the historic faith of the church is a precarious venture. The rich testimony of the saints provides direction and confidence for those who seek to interpret the Word of truth correctly. There is safety in numbers. The faithful testimony of the church is a bulwark against innovation in interpretation and the potential distortion of valid Christian teaching that has stood the test of time. Authentic Christian belief is discerned through the study of Holy Scripture in conversation with the historic witness of the catholic (universal) church. From conversation with the fathers and mothers of the church, believers receive godly counsel to guide contemporary pilgrims.

EARLY CHRISTIAN PERSPECTIVES

The Roman world in the centuries immediately following the ministry of Christ and his apostles included those who engaged in homosexual activity. The early church was careful to distinguish Christian behavior from pagan patterns of living, especially in the area of sexuality. Sexual purity was a hallmark of the Christian community. Though pagan writers wrongly accused Christians of participating in perverse sexual acts, the church consistently denounced fornication, adultery, and all homosexual acts as incompatible with Christian faith. A number of the Fathers wrote commentaries on Paul's epistles and consequently dealt with the apostle's perspective on homosexuality. Early Christians condemned all practices that involved members of the same gender participating in sexual acts with one another. This included pederasty, male dominance/rape, effeminacy, lesbianism, male homosexuality, transsexuality, prostitution, temple prostitution, orgies, and homosexual "marriages." It was not merely a specific type of homosexual activity that was considered unacceptable, even though specific texts mentioned specific practices (such as pederasty). The church fathers condemned the immorality underlying *all* such practices.

The early church viewed homosexuality as a sin because it involved sex with a person of the same gender. The fundamental error was not that a relationship was not mutual (as in pederasty), that it involved some sort of violence (as in homosexual acts to establish dominance), that it was not monogamous

---

[2] C. S. Lewis, "Introduction," *The Incarnation of the Word of God: Being the Treatise of St. Athanasius*, trans. by "A Religious of C.S.M.V., St. Th." (New York, NY: MacMillan, 1947).

(as in orgies), that it took place in a pagan temple (as in temple prostitution), or that it occurred outside a committed relationship. Early church literature is consistent in its teaching that none of these is the fundamental perversion addressed in ancient Christian texts on homosexuality—despite suggestions to the contrary by those wishing to argue in favor of monogamous, committed homosexual marriages.

Christians in the second and third centuries, moreover, knew of "homosexual orientation," as passages cited below on effeminacy suggest. One cannot argue, as some have in contemporary ecclesiastical disputes, that only recently have we come to the enlightened realization that some persons have an orientation toward persons of the same gender. Indeed, the Great Mother cult of Asia Minor accepted such persons as priests after they made themselves eunuchs, and the second-century author Justin makes reference to this phenomenon (*First Apology*, 27, see below).

Second-century writers approached ethics from the perspective of behavior. This is not to say they omitted references to character or outcomes, but their focus was on actions. For example, they were willing to suffer martyrdom rather than sacrifice to the local gods or the emperor or lie about being Christians when asked. Many a modern person wonders why they did not just lie for the greater good or treat the sacrifice of an animal to pagan gods as a community barbecue. The answer is that they identified acts as good or bad in themselves. This is true of sexual ethics: there was no circumstance that might make adultery acceptable, no theory of love that could allow pederasty, and no concern for orientation that could excuse homosexuality.

The following texts from the second and third centuries confirm the church's long-held views on homosexuality. They also stand as a firm challenge to Western Christians today, for they were written by individuals who suffered great loss for living against the grain of society.

ANTE-NICENE FATHERS

Teaching of the Twelve Apostles (Didache) (ca. 100)
An early Christian manual on morals and practice:

> Thou shalt not commit murder, thou shalt not commit adultery; *thou shalt not commit paederasty* (corrupt boys), thou shalt not commit fornication. ... (2.2)[3]

---

[3] *Teaching of the Twelve Apostles* 2.2 (*ANF* 7:377) 377.

Epistle of Barnabas (ca. 100)

> Thou shalt not be found a *corrupter of boys* (Gk. *paidophthoros*), nor shalt thou become like such persons. (10.6)[4]

Apology, Aristides (ca. 125)

Aristides argues against pagan conceptions of the gods. Regarding gods of the Greeks, he writes:

> Because of these stories, O king, much evil has befallen the race of men who are at this present day, since they imitate their gods, and commit adultery, and are defiled with their mothers and their sisters, and by *sleeping with males*: and some of them have dared to kill even their fathers. For if he, who is said to be the head and king of their gods, has done these things, how much more shall his worshippers imitate him! And great is the madness which the Greeks have introduced into their history concerning him: for it is not possible that a god should commit adultery or fornication or *should approach to sleep with males*, or that he should be a parricide; otherwise, he is much worse than a destructive demon. (*Apology* 9)[5]
>
> Some of their gods were found to be adulterers, and murderers, and jealous and envious, and angry and passionate, and murderers of fathers, and thieves, and plunderers. . . . some were changed into the likeness of beasts in order that they might commit adultery with the race of mortal women, and some have been reviled for *sleeping with males*: and some of them, they say, were in wedlock with their mothers and sisters and daughters; and they say of their gods that they committed adultery with the daughters of men; and from them was born a certain race which also was mortal. (*Apology* 8)[6]
>
> For if their [the Greeks'] laws are just, their gods are unjust, who have committed transgressions in killing one another and practicing sorcery, committing adultery, plundering, stealing, and *sleeping with males*, along with the rest of their other doings. (*Apology* 13)[7]
>
> The Greeks, then, O king, because they *practice foul things in sleeping with males*, and with mother and sister and daughter, turn the ridicule of their foulness upon the Christians. (*Apology* 17)[8]

---

[4] *Epistle of Barnabas* 10.6, in *The Apostolic Fathers*, trans. J. B. Lightfoot (1891; repr., Grand Rapids, MI: Baker, 1989), 278–79, 278–79. The Fathers condemn corrupting or polluting boys (pederasty) as a well-known example of homosexuality in Roman culture, but it was not the only form of homosexual practice they condemned. Any kind of sex act with a person of the same gender was forbidden to Christians.

[5] Aristides, *Apology* 9, in *Text and Studies: Contributions to Biblical and Patristic Literature*, ed. J. Armitage Robinson, vol. 1, *The Apology of Aristides, Translated from the Syriac*, 2nd ed. (1893; repr., Nendeln, Lichtenstein: Kraus Reprint Limited, 1967), 42.

[6] Ibid., 40.

[7] Ibid., 47.

[8] Ibid., 51.

Apocalypse of Peter (ca. 150)

Other men and women who cast themselves down from a high slope came to the bottom and were driven by their torturers to go up the precipice and were then thrown down again, and had no rest for this torture. These were those who *defiled their bodies, behaving like women*. And the women with them, these were those who *behaved with one another as men with a woman*. (32)[9]

Letter to the Philippians, Polycarp (ca. 155) [quoting 1 Cor. 6:10]

Knowing, therefore, that "God is not mocked," we ought to live in a manner that is worthy of his commandment and glory. . . . For it is a good thing to be cut off from the sinful desires of the world, because every "sinful desire wages war against the Spirit," and "neither fornicators nor *male prostitutes nor homosexuals* will inherit the kingdom of God," nor those who do perverse things. Wherefore we must keep away from all these things. (5)[10]

Apology, Athenagoras (ca. 177)

For those who have set up a market for fornication, and established infamous resorts for the young for every kind of vile pleasure,—*who do not abstain even from males, males with males committing shocking abominations*, outraging all the noblest and comeliest bodies in all sorts of ways, so dishonouring the fair workmanship of God (for beauty on earth is not self-made, but sent hither by the hand and will of God),—these men, I say, revile us for the very things which they are conscious of themselves, and ascribe to their own gods, boasting of them as noble deeds, and worthy of the gods. These adulterers and *paederasts* defame the eunuchs and the once-married (while they themselves live like fishes; for these gulp down whatever falls in their way, and the stronger chases the weaker: and, in fact, this is to feed upon human flesh, to do violence in contravention of the very laws which you and your ancestors, with due care of all that is fair and right, have enacted). (*Apology* 34)[11]

---

[9] *Apocalypse of Peter* 32 (*Akhmim* manuscript), in *New Testament Apocrypha*, vol. 2, *Writings Related to the Apostles; Apocalypses and Related Subjects*, rev. ed., ed. Wilhelm Schneemelcher, trans. R. McL. Wilson (Louisville, KY: Westminster/John Knox, 1992), 631. The manuscript may be a later reworking of this apocalypse and therefore not be an indisputable source from the second century. Still, it states that homosexual acts by adult men and women are sinful and will be punished. The phrase "behaving like women" is not a condemnation of men assuming the wrong (subordinate) role in sexual encounters. The text references not only men but also women involved in same-sex relations. The point is about homosexual acts, not roles.

[10] Polycarp, *Letter to the Philippians* 5, in *The Apostolic Fathers*, 2nd ed., trans. J. B. Lightfoot and J. R. Harmer, ed. Michael Holmes (1891; repr., Grand Rapids, MI: Baker, 1989), 125–26. Polycarp is alluding to and affirming 1 Cor 6:9–10.

[11] Athenagoras, *Apology* 34 (*ANF* 2:147). See also *Acts of John* 36 (ca. 200): "Likewise also thou poisoner, sorcerer, robber, defrauder, *sodomite*, thief, and as many as are of that band, ye

First Apology, Justin (ca. 155)

> But as for us, we have been taught that to expose newly-born children is the part of wicked men; and this we have been taught lest we do any one an injury, and lest we should sin against God, first, because we see that almost all so exposed (not only the girls, but also the males) are brought to prostitution. . . . And anyone who uses such persons, besides the godless and infamous and impure intercourse, may possibly be having intercourse with his own child, or relative, or brother. And there are some who prostitute even their own children and wives and *some are openly mutilated for the purpose of sodomy*; and refer these mysteries to the mother of the gods. (*First Apology* 27)[12]

Theophilus to Autolycus, Theophilus (ca. 190)

> Do you [Autolycus—an idolater and scorner of Christians], therefore, show me yourself, whether you are not an adulterer, or a fornicator, or a thief, or a robber, or a purloiner; whether you do not *corrupt boys*; whether you are not insolent, . . . All these things, then, involve you in darkness, as when a filmy defluxion on the eyes prevents one from beholding the light of the sun: thus also do iniquities, O man, involve you in darkness, so that you cannot see God. (1.2)[13]

Address to the Greeks, Tatian (ca. 160)

> Crescens, who made his nest in the great city, surpassed all men in *unnatural love* (i.e., pederasty), and was strongly addicted to the love of money. (19)

---

shall come at last, as your works do lead you, unto unquenchable fire, and utter darkness, and the pit of punishment, and eternal threatenings." *Acts of John* 36 in *The Apocryphal New Testament*, trans. M. R. James (Wortley, United Kingdom: Clarendon, 1924), 235; *Acts of John* is a Gnostic work. It maintains that Christ did not have a body (e.g., "Revelation of the Mystery of the Cross," *Acts of John* 99, p. 255), and it upholds abstinence from sex as a virtue ("Drusiana and Callimachus," *Acts of John* 63, p. 243). This quotation, however, shows that certain sexual sins can be identified apart from any thought—even in an ascetic, Gnostic text—that sex itself is wrong.

[12] Justin, *First Apology* 27 (*ANF* 1:172). This quotation would be improperly read as isolating sexual sin to prostitution. Rather, it is unpacking how and why the culture was sexually perverted. Exposure of newly born children—which was infanticide and wicked in itself—often led to a life of prostitution for both the girls and boys "rescued." Another sexual sin that resulted from this practice was incest. Moreover, the culture witnessed the prostituting of other children and wives. Finally, Justin mentioned the self-castration of priests for the purpose of homosexual acts in the Great Mother cult. Justin sought to show the multiple dimensions of the perversion. He was not trying to say that mutilation or homosexuality is only wrong when practiced as part of a cult.

[13] *Theophilus to Autolycus* 1.2 (*ANF* 2:89).

Pederasty is condemned by the Barbarians, but by the Romans, who endeavour to collect herds of boys like grazing horses, it is honoured with certain privileges. (28)[14]

The Instructor, Clement of Alexandria (ca. 200)

In this text various forms of homosexual practice are referenced. Effeminate men and masculine women, some attempting to live the role of the opposite sex and some transsexual, pederasts, male prostitutes, and those engaged in homosexual incest all receive mention.

To such an extent, then, has luxury advanced, that not only are the female sex deranged about this frivolous pursuit, but men also are infected with the disease. For not being free of the love of finery, they are not in health; but inclining to voluptuousness, *they become effeminate*, cutting their hair in an ungentlemanlike and meretricious way, clothed in fine and transparent garments, chewing mastich, smelling of perfume. What can one say on seeing them? Like one who judges people by their foreheads, he will divine them to be adulterers and effeminate, addicted to both kinds of venery, haters of hair, destitute of hair, detesting the bloom of manliness, and adorning their locks like women. . . . and *boys, taught to deny their sex, act the part of women. . . . Men play the part of women, and women that of men, contrary to nature; women are at once wives and husbands: no passage is closed against libidinousness;* and their promiscuous lechery is a public institution, and luxury is domesticated. O miserable spectacle! horrible conduct! Such are the trophies of your social licentiousness which are exhibited: the evidence of these deeds are the prostitutes. Alas for such wickedness! Besides, the wretches know not how many tragedies the uncertainty of intercourse produces. For fathers, unmindful of children of theirs that have been exposed, often without their knowledge, have intercourse with a son that has debauched himself, and daughters that are prostitutes; and license in lust shows them to be the men that have begotten them. . . . What, then, will not women with strong propensities to lust practice, when they look on men perpetrating such enormities? Rather we ought not to call such as these men, but lewd wretches (*bataloi*), and effeminate (*gynides*), whose voices are feeble, and whose clothes are womanish both in feel and dye. And such creatures are manifestly shown to be what they are from their external appearance, their clothes, shoes, form, walk, cut of their hair, look. "For from his look shall a man be known," says the Scripture, "and from meeting a man the man is known: the dress of a man, the step of his foot, the laugh of his teeth, tell tales of him." (3.1)[15]

The Sodomites, having through much luxury, fallen into uncleanness, practising adultery shamelessly, and *burning with insane love for boys*; the

---

[14] Tatian, *Address to the Greeks* 9, 28 (*ANF* 2:73).
[15] Clement of Alexandria, *The Instructor* 3.1 (*ANF* 2:276–77).

All-seeing Word, whose notice those who commit impieties cannot escape, cast His eye on them. (3.8)[16]

Apology, Tertullian (ca. 197)

But if we challenge you to comparison in the virtue of chastity, I turn to a part of the sentence passed by the Athenians against Socrates, who was pronounced a corrupter of youth. *The Christian confines himself to the female sex. . . .* (*Apology* 46)[17]

For into this dread place [Tartarus] are wont to be cast all who offend against filial piety, and such as are guilty of incest with sisters, and seducers of wives, and ravishers of virgins, and *boy-polluters*, and men of furious tempers, and murderers, and thieves, and deceivers; all, in short, who tread in the footsteps of your gods, not one of whom you can prove free from crime or vice, save by denying that they had ever a human existence. (*Apology* 28)[18]

On Idolatry, Tertullian (ca. 200)

In short, I find not dress cursed by God, except *a woman's dress on a man*; for "cursed," saith He, "is every man who clothes himself in woman's attire" [cf. Dt. 25.5]. (16)[19]

Against the Valentinians, Tertullian (ca. 200)

I should suppose the *coupling of two males to be a very shameful thing.* (11)[20]

---

[16] Ibid., 3.8, 282. See also *Acts of Thomas*: "And he led me to a place in which there were many chasms, and much ill odour and a hateful vapour was given off thence. And he made me look down into each chasm, and I saw in the (first) chasm a flaming fire, and wheels of fire were running <hither and> thither, and souls were hung upon those wheels, dashed against each other. And there was a cry there and a very great lamentation, but there was none to deliver. And that man said to me: 'These souls are kindred to thee, and in the days of reckoning they were delivered for punishment and destruction. And then (when the chastisement of each is ended) others are brought in their stead, and likewise these again to another (chasm). These are they who *perverted the intercourse of man and woman*.'" *Acts of Thomas* 6.55 in *New Testament Apocrypha,* 362. The *Acts of Thomas* is a Gnostic work. Another second-century Gnostic work, *The Gospel of Judas* 2.38 (Coptic text), condemns those men who sleep with men.

[17] Tertullian, *Apology* 46 (*ANF* 3:51). Note here—and in some other texts from this chapter—that pederasty is commented on primarily as a manifestation of homosexuality, not paedophilia. What Christians noted in particular about pederasty was that it involved same-sex relations, not that it was out of wedlock or an abuse of children, although the later was at times mentioned.

[18] Ibid., 28.

[19] Tertullian, *On Idolatry* XVI (*ANF* 3:71).

[20] Tertullian, *Against the Valentinians* XI (*ANF* 3:509). Note in the citations from Tertullian that he condemns three practices: pederasty, effeminacy, and male homosexual acts.

Commentary on the Gospel of Matthew, Origen (ca. 230)

But observe here that every great sin is a loss of the talents of the master of the house, and such sins are committed by fornicators, adulterers, *abusers of themselves with men, effeminate*, idolaters, murderers. (2.10)[21]

To Donatus, Cyprian (ca. 250)

If . . . you could gaze into secret places—if you could open the closed doors of sleeping chambers, and recall their dark recesses to the perception of sight—you would behold things done by immodest persons which no chaste eye could look upon; you would see what even to see is a crime; . . . *Men with frenzied lust rushing upon men.* (9)[22]

Symposium or Banquet of the Ten Virgins, Methodius of Olympus (ca. 300)

The inhabitants of Sodom, gathering their vintage from these vines, were provoked to an *unnatural and fruitless passion of men.* (5.5)[23]

The Refutation of All Heresies, Hippolytus (ca. 230)

The following quotation from Book 4, chapter 23, is part of Hippolytus's argument against astrology, a pseudoscience which taught that personal qualities were determined by the stars. Of interest in this text is the description of the astrologers' belief that people are born with natural characteristics about which they can do little or nothing and, in this instance, "unnatural lusts" are included for Sagittarians. The same is said of those born under Aries (chap. 25) and Capricorn (chap. 24); those under Virgo are supposedly prone to be "victims of unnatural lusts" (chap. 20). This counters the arguments of some that antiquity did not entertain the notion of homosexual orientation.

Those born in Sagittarius will be of the following description: great length, square forehead, profuse eyebrows, indicative of strength, well-arranged projection of hair, reddish (in complexion). The same by nature are gracious, as educated persons, simple, beneficent; *given to unnatural lusts*, companionable, toil-worn, lovers, beloved, jovial in their cups, clean, passionate, careless, wicked; as regards friendship, useless; scorners, with noble souls, insolent, crafty; for fellowship, useful. (4.23)[24]

---

[21] Origen, *Commentary on the Gospel of Matthew* 2.10 (*ANF* 9:500).

[22] Cyprian, *To Donatus* 9 (*ANF* 5:277–78). The sin highlighted is not frenzied lust per se but, as taught in Rom 1:27, misdirected passion of men for other men.

[23] Musconius of Olympus, *Symposium* 5.5. *St. Methodius: A Treatise on Chastity in Ancient Christian Writers*, vol. 27, trans. Herbert Musurillo (New York, NY: Paulist, 1958). Note that the sin of Sodom is considered to be homosexual practices.

[24] Hippolytus, *Refutation of All Heresies* 4.23 (*ANF* 5:34).

Apostolic Tradition, Hippolytus (ca. 230)

New converts to the faith, who are to be admitted as hearers of the word, shall first be brought to the teachers before the people assemble. And they shall be examined as to their reason for embracing the faith, and they who bring them shall testify that they are competent to hear the word. Inquiry shall then be made as to the nature of their life. . . . If a man has a wife or a woman a husband, let the man be instructed to content himself with his wife and the woman to content herself with her husband. *But if a man is unmarried, let him be instructed to abstain from impurity, either by lawfully marrying a wife or else by remaining as he is.* . . . A harlot or licentious man or one who has castrated himself, or any other who does things not to be named, must be rejected, for they are defiled. (2.16.20)[25]

On the Jewish Meats, Novatian (ca. 250)

For that in fishes the roughness of scales is regarded as constituting their cleanness; rough, and rugged, and unpolished, and substantial, and grave manners are approved in men; while those that are without scales are unclean; because trifling, and fickle, and faithless, and *effeminate* manners are disapproved. Moreover, what does the law mean when it says, "Thou shalt not eat the camel"?—except that by the example of that animal it condemns a life nerveless and crooked with crimes. Or when it forbids the swine to be taken for food? It assuredly reproves a life filthy and dirty, and delighting in the garbage of vice, placing its supreme good not in generosity of mind, but in the flesh alone. Or when it forbids the hare? *It rebukes men deformed into women.* (3)[26]

---

[25] *The Apostolic Tradition of Hippolytus*. 2.16.20, translated into English with an introduction and notes by Burton Scott Easton (New York, NY: Macmillan Company, 1934), 41–42. Of interest a few lines later is the condemnation of men who have concubines—that is, men living with women outside of marriage: "If a man has a concubine, he must desist and marry legally; if he is unwilling, he must be rejected." The only acceptable cohabitation is that involving a married man and woman.

[26] Novation, *On Jewish Meats* 3 (*ANF* 5:647). Boswell cites this text to illustrate the early Christian practice of connecting animal behavior to Mosaic law. Boswell claims, "These associations profoundly affected subsequent attitudes toward homosexual behavior." John Boswell, *Christianity, Social Tolerance, and Homosexuality*. Undoubtedly, these fanciful associations did foster opposition to homosexual behavior among the Christian population of Europe in the Middle Ages, but it was certainly not the genesis of this condemnation. Supposed pictures of human depravity in the animal kingdom merely underscored the already existing denunciation of homosexual behavior in the Old and New Testaments. Note: Novatian and his followers formed a separatist group during the persecutions, but they were orthodox Trinitarians.

NICENE AND POST-NICENE FATHERS

The church in the fourth and fifth centuries continued to regard various homosexual practices as sinful; no textual evidence from Christians disputes this.[27] Church leaders were aware of homosexual practice and denounced it in all forms as sexual sin. The sin of Sodom, clearly identified as homosexual practice, was often cited as a sin against nature and one upon which God has poured and will pour out his wrath. Documents from this period include books of church order, canons from church councils, various writings of the Fathers that include commentaries on specific biblical texts, and decrees from Christian emperors. Cumulatively these materials leave no doubt as to the church's perspective on the "vice against nature" and the church discipline required for restoring people who sinned in this manner.

Basil's Canonical Epistle (375)

> They who have *committed sodomy with men or brutes*, murderers, wizards, adulterers, and idolaters, have been thought worthy of the same punishment; therefore observe the same method with these which you do with others. We ought not to make any doubt of receiving those who have repented thirty years for the uncleanness which they committed through ignorance; for their ignorance pleads their pardon, and their willingness in confessing it; therefore command them to be forthwith received, especially if they have tears to prevail on your tenderness and have [since their lapse] led such a life as to deserve your compassion. (*Canon* 7)[28]

> He that *abuses himself with mankind*, shall do the penance of an adulterer. (*Canon* 62)[29]

De renuntiatione saeculi, Basil (ca. 360)

> If thou art young in either body or mind, shun the companionship of other young men and avoid them as thou wouldest a flame. For through them the enemy has kindled the desires of many and then handed them over to eternal

---

[27] James Brownson, in his attempt to undermine traditional Christian views on homosexuality, argues, "We find nothing of gender complementarity in the Apostles Creed, Nicene Creed, or any other ancient ecumenical creed." Homosexuality was not the subject of debate at Nicaea or any of the other ancient ecumenical councils. But silence on a question, irrelevant to debate, means nothing. As the primary sources in this chapter demonstrate, there is no question whatsoever as to where the bishops and theologians of early Christianity stood on homosexual practice. See James V. Brownson, *Bible, Gender and Sexuality* (Grand Rapids, MI: Eerdmans, 2013), 266.

[28] *The First Canonical Epistle of Our Holy Father Basil,* Canon 7 (*NPNF*[2] 14:604).

[29] Ibid., Canon 62, 608.

fire, hurling them into the *vile pit of the five cities* under the pretence of spiritual love.[30]

Homilies on Romans, Chrysostom (397)

But when God hath left one, then all things are turned upside down. And thus not only was their doctrine Satanical, but their life too was diabolical. . . . Which is an evident proof of the last degree of corruptness, *when both sexes are abandoned.* . . . For everything which transgresseth the laws by God appointed, lusteth after *monstrous things which be customary.* . . . For not the soul only, but the body also of one who hath been so treated, is disgraced, and deserves to be driven out everywhere. How many hells shall be enough for such? But if you scoff at hearing of hell and believe not that fire, remember Sodom. (1)[31]

And yet a more disgraceful thing than these is it, when *even the women seek after these intercourses*, who ought to have more sense of shame than men. (4)[32]

Confessions, Augustine (397)

Therefore those offenses which be contrary to nature are everywhere and at all times to be held in detestation and punished; such were those of the Sodomites, which should all nations commit, they should be held guilty of the same crime by the divine law, which hath not so made men that they should in that way abuse one another. For even that fellowship which should be between God and us is violated, when that same nature of which He is author is polluted by the perversity of lust. . . . But Thou avengest that which men perpetrate against themselves, seeing also that when they sin against Thee, they do wickedly against their own souls; and iniquity gives itself the lie, either by corrupting or perverting their nature, which Thou hast made and ordained, or by an immoderate use of things permitted, or in "burning" in things forbidden to that use which is against nature. (3.8)[33]

---

[30] *The Ascetic Works of Saint Basil*, trans. W. K. L. Clarke (London, England: Society for Promoting Christian Knowledge, 1925), 66. Note "the five cities" are those associated with the story of Sodom and Gomorrah. See Gen 14:8.

[31] Chrysostom, *Homilies on Romans* 4 (*NPNF*[1] 11:356, 358). Chrysostom is explaining Rom 1:26–27 as depicting homosexual acts, which he views as unnatural. The sin of homosexuality is "monstrous"; for it Sodom was judged with fire.

[32] Ibid., 356.

[33] Augustine, *Confessions* 3.8 (*NPNF*[1] 1:65). Augustine sees homosexual acts as sin against God's holy law, which is universal and not restricted to certain cultures. Homosexual acts are unnatural and an example of burning after things forbidden. Sodom's sin, according to Augustine, was homosexual activity.

City of God, **Augustine (426)**

After this promise Lot was delivered out of Sodom, and a fiery rain from heaven turned into ashes that whole region of the impious city, where custom had made *sodomy as prevalent as laws have elsewhere made other kinds of wickedness*. But this punishment of theirs was a specimen of the divine judgment to come. (16.30)[34]

He who is not scandalized at the apostle's censure of the horrible wickedness of the women who "*changed the natural use into that which is against nature*," will read all this without being shocked, especially as we are not, like Paul, citing and censuring a damnable uncleanness, but are explaining, so far as we can, human generation, which with Paul we avoid all obscenity of language.[35]

Epistle 211, **Augustine (423)**

The love which you bear to each other must be not carnal, but spiritual: for those things *which are practiced by immodest women in shameful frolic and sporting with one another* ought not even to be done by those of your sex who are married, or are intending to marry, and much more ought not be done by widows or chaste virgins dedicated to be handmaids of Christ by a holy vow. (211.14)[36]

Commentary of Ambrosiaster **(ca. 400)**

Ambrosiaster, an anonymous writer of the fourth century, commenting on Romans 1:

They were helped by the devil to carry out in practice the things which they conceive in their lusts . . . they were handed over to uncleanness that they might willingly damage each other's bodies with abuse. For even now there *are men of this type who are said to dishonour each other's bodies*. It is clear that, because they changed the truth of God into a lie, they changed the natural use (of sexuality) into that use by which they were dishonoured and condemned to the second death. . . . Paul says that the due penalty comes from contempt of God, and that it is wickedness and obscenity.[37]

CHURCH COUNCILS AND IMPERIAL LEGISLATION

The earliest church council to address the problem of homosexual practice was the Spanish Council of Elvira. The council stipulated that *stupratores*

---

[34] Augustine, *City of God* 16.30 (*NPNF*[1] 2:328). Again, note that Sodom's sin is identified as homosexual acts.

[35] Ibid., 280.

[36] Augustine, *Epistle* 211.14 (*NPNF*[1] 1:568). Here is a reference to lesbian behavior as a sin.

[37] Ambrosiaster, *Ancient Christian Texts: Commentaries on Romans and 1–2 Corinthians*, trans. Gerald L. Bray (Downers Grove, IL: IVP Academic, 2009), 12–13.

puerorum (Latin for "defilers of boys") were forbidden to take Communion even at the moment of death.

Council of Elvira (306)

> Neither give communion in the end to defilers of boys. (Canon 71)[38]

The Council of Ancyra in Asia Minor (314)

The council issued a canon that condemned those who defiled themselves with animals or men, describing the required penance for these sins.

> [Rubric] *Those who fornicate irrationally, that is, who mix with cattle or who are polluted with males.* [Text] Of those who have acted or who act irrationally; as often as they have committed such a crime before the age of twenty, after fifteen years penance they should merit the community of prayers; then, after spending five years in this community, they can have the Eucharist. However, the quality of their lives is to be discussed during the time of penance, and so they might obtain mercy. *And if they are given insatiably to these heretical crimes, they are to undertake to do penance for a longer time.* However, if this is done after age twenty by those who are married, after twenty-five years of penance they will be received into the community of prayers in which they remain for five years and then they can receive the Eucharist. If they are married and over fifty and fall into this sin, they can receive the grace of communion at the end of their lives. (Canon 16)[39]

Imperial legislation in the post-Constantinian era reflected both the influence of old Roman law as well as Christianity. All the general laws enacted since the time of Constantine I were codified under the Christian emperor Theodosius II in 450. He ordered a commission to collate the legislation of the previous century but to adapt it to new circumstances. This project was

---

[38] Our translation of the Latin text in A. W. W. Dale, *The Synod of Elvira and Christian Life in the Fourth Century: A Historical Essay* (London, England: McMillan, 1882), 336, accessed March 16, 2015, https://archive.org/details/synodofelvirachr00dale. Bailey commented on this decree from the Council of Elvira: "It is most unlikely, however, that the censure of the Church was reserved solely for those who, after baptism, continued unrepentantly their addiction to the 'love of boys;' no doubt the canon in question was framed with a particular situation in view, but subsequent legislation and Church opinion suggests that at this time no distinction was made between different kinds of homosexual offenders" (*Homosexuality and the Western Theological Tradition*, 86).

[39] *Council of Ancyra*, Canon 16, translated in Pierre J. Payer, Sex *and the Penitentials: The Development of a Sexual Code 550–1150* (Toronto, Canada: University of Toronto Press, 1984), 45. Note: Some manuscripts number this text as canon 17. See also translation in *NPNF*, Series 2, vol. 14, 70. This canon was an authority for medieval penitentials. For example, in Bartholomew of Exeter's penitential (1184), section LXIX on fornication *"contra naturam"* begins by quoting this text from the Council of Ancyra. See *Bartholomew of Exeter, Bishop and Canonist: A Study of the Twelfth Century with the Text of Bartholomew's Penitential* (Cambridge, England: Cambridge University Press, 1937), 235–36.

eventually published, with the laws taking effect in 439 in the eastern part of the empire and accepted as authoritative also in the West. Below are several pieces of legislation that became part of the compilation known as the *Theodosian Code*.

Statute of Constantius and Constans (342)
Two sons of Constantine who inherited rule of the empire after their father's death.

> When a man *"marries"* in the manner of a woman, a "woman" about to renounce men, what does he wish, when sex has lost its significance; when the crime is one which is not profitable to know; when Venus is changed into another form; when love is sought and not found? We order the statutes to arise, the laws to be armed with an avenging sword, that those infamous persons who are now, or who hereafter may be, guilty may be subjected to exquisite punishment. (*Emperors Constantius and Constans Augustuses to the People*)[40]

Statute of Valentinian, Theodosius, and Arcadius (390)

> All persons who have the *shameful custom of condemning a man's body, acting the part of a woman's*, to the sufferance of an alien sex (for they appear not to be different from women), shall expiate a crime of this kind in avenging flames in the sight of the people. (*Emperors Valentinian, Theodosius, and Arcadius Augustuses to Orientius, Vicar of the City of Rome*)[41]

BOOKS OF ORDER

Several books of church order were produced in late antiquity. These manuals for church life typically included directions for ecclesiastical practice, moral guidance, and the exercise of discipline. The following excerpts illustrate the moral imperatives associated with being a follower of Christ in post-Constantinian Christendom. While many pagan practices were outlawed by the time of Theodosius I, around 395, a strong contingent outside the church still influenced Byzantine and Roman culture toward licentiousness. The church continued to stand against pagan immorality by upholding the same standards of sexual purity it advocated during the first three centuries after Christ.

Constitutions of the Holy Apostles (c. 375)

> We believe that lawful marriage, and the begetting of children, is honourable and undefiled; *for difference of sexes was formed in Adam and Eve for*

---

[40] *The Theodosian Code and Novels and the Sirmondian Constitutions*, trans. Clyde Pharr (Princeton, NJ: Princeton University Press, 1952), 231–32.

[41] Ibid., 232.

the increase of mankind. We acknowledge with us a soul that is incorporeal and immortal, not corruptible as bodies are, but immortal, as being rational and free. *We abhor all unlawful mixtures, and that which is practiced by some against nature as wicked and impious.* (6.3)[42]

But we do not say so of that mixture that is contrary to nature, or of any unlawful practice; for such are enmity to God. *For the sin of Sodom is contrary to nature,* as is also that with brute beasts. . . . For the practisers of one sort attempt the dissolution of the world, and endeavor to make the natural course of things to change for one that is unnatural. . . . These things are forbidden by the laws; for thus say the oracles: *"Thou shalt not lie with mankind as with womankind."* "For such a one is accursed, and ye shall stone them with stones: they have wrought abomination." . . . These things the laws have forbidden, but they have honoured marriage, and have called it blessed, *since God has blessed it, who joined male and female together. And wise Solomon somewhere says: "A wife is suited to her husband by the Lord."* (6.28)[43]

"Thou shalt not corrupt boys" for this wickedness is contrary to nature, and arose from Sodom, which was therefore entirely consumed with fire sent from God. "Let such a one be accursed: and all the people shall say, So be it." (7.2)[44]

CONCLUSION

This brief survey of the early Christian centuries underscores several assertions that can be made with confidence about Christian attitudes toward homosexual practice. Given the ethnic diversity of Christians and their geographic dispersion throughout the Mediterranean world in the earliest centuries after Christ, the evident consensus on this issue is remarkable. Early Christians were committed to the teachings of the Old Testament and the emerging New Testament canon—understood as a fitting extension of the Jewish Scriptures. The sexual ethics of the Old Testament were considered the foundation of apostolic teaching in the New Testament. Thus, Christian writers freely cited both testaments as the authoritative standard for Christian faith and practice.

The church fathers were aware of homosexual practices in their culture and consistently condemned such behavior. Distinguishing themselves from

---

[42] *Constitutions of the Holy Apostles* 6.3 (*ANF* 7:454). In these fourth-century texts the phrases "unlawful mixtures" and "against nature" point to the gender complementarity of men and women, i.e., the natural sexual compatibility of the male and female by God's design in creation. Brownson in *Bible, Gender, Sexuality* has argued that the phrase "contrary to nature" (Romans 1) is "ambiguous" in the Bible. This novel idea is nowhere found in patristic literature. See more discussion of this point in part II.

[43] Ibid., 6.28, 462–63. This text cites Lev 20:13 as a binding law of God. The second reference is to Prov 12:4.

[44] Ibid., 7.2, 466.

nonbelievers was a foundational element of Christians' ethical code, consistent with the exhortations of apostolic writings to be separate and to depart from the ways of the world. *The Constitutions of the Holy Apostles* (ca. 375) rehearses this essential early Christian perspective:

> Beloved, be it known to you that those who are baptized into the death of our Lord Jesus are obliged to go on no longer in sin; for as those who are dead cannot work wickedness any longer, so those who are dead with Christ cannot practice wickedness. We do not therefore believe, brethren, that anyone who has received the washing of life continues in the practice of licentious acts of transgressors. Now he who sins after his baptism, unless he repent and forsake his sins, shall be condemned to hell-fire. (2.3)[45]

The Fathers believed homosexual practice was perverse and would lead one down the path to destruction. Same-sex sexual activity was considered a grievous sin against the Creator who designed men and women for each other. In addition to violating divine design, homosexual activity—according to early Christian writers—was an instance of humans abusing and polluting one another.

While frequent appeal was made to the Old Testament prohibitions of same-sex intercourse in the book of Leviticus, the story of Sodom also figured prominently in Christian literature addressing homosexuality. According to the Fathers, the primary sin of Sodom and Gomorrah was sexual perversion; God's judgment on these cities was considered a powerful warning to avoid all homosexual practice. The Fathers paired Paul's condemnation of deviant activity in Romans 1 with the Genesis Sodom story as evidence that God has always regarded homosexual activity as a heinous crime worthy of judgment. While there appears to be more patristic focus on male homosexuality, the Fathers were aware of female homosexual activity. Both the Old and New Testaments portrayed homoerotic behavior as sin against a holy God, the Fathers said. Believers, however, could receive forgiveness for this sin and overcome it by God's power (1 Cor 6:9–11).

The sexual ethics of Paul the apostle and the early church which followed his teaching turned the Roman world upside down. In a radical reversal of Greco-Roman values, Christian leaders instructed believers that sexual relations were only acceptable in heterosexual marriage. This exclusive view of

---

[45] Ibid., 2.3, 98. See also, *The Divine Institutes of Lactantius* (ca. 320). After listing pagan vices, including sexual sin, the author writes, "But which of these things can be laid to the charge of our people, with whom the whole of religion consists in living without guilt and without spot? Since, therefore, they see that both they and their people do those things which we have said, but that ours practice nothing else but that which is just and good, they might, if they had any understanding, have perceived from this, both that they who do what is good are pious, and they themselves who commit wicked actions are impious. . . . It is impossible that they who err in the whole of their life should not be deceived also in religion" (*ANF* 7:145).

sexuality was specifically connected to gender differences. Kyle Harper, in *From Shame to Sin: The Christian Transformation of Sexual Morality in Late Antiquity*, observes:

> In the matter of same-sex eros, the Roman world knew its own intricate tessellation of rigid limits and extreme permissiveness. Christian norms simply ate through the fabric of late classical morality like an acid, without the least consideration for the well-worn contours of the old ways. As with *porneia*, Christian hostility to venery involving members of the same sex was nurtured in Hellenistic Judaism, imported to the gentile mission, sharpened in its application and expression. Paul's letters again provided an incomplete but, really, unambiguous template for the blanket condemnation of same-sex love in early Christianity. . . . Paul's overriding sense of gender—rather than age or status—as the prime determinant in the propriety of a sexual act was nurtured by contemporary Jewish attitudes. But the analogy between male and female same-sex attraction was strikingly novel, and truly momentous. By boiling the sex act down to the most basic constituents of male and female, Paul was able to describe the sexual culture surrounding him in transformative terms.[46]

Based on careful scrutiny of the documents from this era, Harper's conclusions are most certainly correct. Boswell's attempt at writing revisionist history that suits his purposes fails any objective examination of the sources.

---

[46] Kyle Harper, *From Shame to Sin: The Christian Transformation of Sexual Morality in Late Antiquity* (Cambridge, MA: Harvard University Press, 2013), 12. Harper describes Christian usage of the term *porneia*: "The significance of *porneia*, in historical terms, was precisely that it gave a single name to an array of extramarital sexual configuration not limited to but especially including prostitution." Harper argues that the "revolution in the rules of behavior," caused by Christianization of the empire, was primarily its condemnation of all prostitution and all forms of homoeroticism.

CHAPTER 3

THE MIDDLE AGES AND CONFESSING SIN

D uring the earliest centuries of Christianity, a public rite of penance developed which functioned as the formal process of discipline for public sins such as murder, adultery, and apostasy. This was especially useful in dealing with Christians who "lapsed" during the periods of persecution but sought readmission to the church when persecution subsided. Penitents were typically welcomed back into the church by the bishop after a lengthy process demonstrating genuine repentance for sin. Eventually the practice of penance became more private, with offenders confessing their sins to a priest and the priest prescribing tasks that had to be completed in order for the offender to be forgiven. Accordingly, the need arose for manuals to guide priests in the appropriate penance for specific offenses.

As Christian monks evangelized the pagan population of Europe in the early Middle Ages, teaching new converts the sexual ethic of the Christian faith was one significant challenge. Adultery and concerns about clerical chastity arose among the Christian population, and sexual behavior became a prominent topic in medieval penitential literature.

Penitential manuals, also known as penitentials, provided general pastoral guidelines for ministering during private confession. Compilers of the manuals assembled material from various sources and allowed confessors some discretion in ministering to penitents. The penitentials provide a rather complete picture of how the medieval church understood sexual sin. Penitentials proliferated beginning in the sixth century and gained wide geographical circulation for almost 500 years. The earliest penitentials were Irish in origin, spreading to Anglo-Saxon England and then to Western Europe.[1]

---

[1] See Pierre J. Payer, *Sex and the Penitentials: The Development of a Sexual Code 550–1150* (Toronto, Canada: University of Toronto Press, 1984). Payer states, "The relative completeness of their treatment of sexual behavior, their wide geographical distribution, their temporal span

The penitentials addressed various types of homosexual behavior and could be quite graphic.[2] The penance recommended depended on the offense, the age of the offender, and the person's status in the church. The form of homosexual practice regarded as most heinous was "sodomy," which required the most severe penance, sometimes lasting ten to fifteen years.[3] The penitentials also condemned lesbian practice, but it was referenced less frequently than sex involving two males.[4] All known penitentials of the early Middle Ages have at least one canon censuring same-sex intimacy, and many penitentials have multiple canons condemning homosexual practice.[5]

Sodomy was a serious transgression and often paired with bestiality as an "irrational" sin. The penitentials were strikingly uniform in their censure of the various forms of homosexual practice. They provide historians with what Pierre Payer called an "index of medieval morality, at least an index to what was morally reprehensible."[6] Derrick Sherwin Bailey, based on his study of a dozen well-known penitentials, offered this evaluation: "Surveying the Penitentials as a whole, and comparing them with the ecclesiastical opinion and legislation . . . all homosexual practices are held to be sinful in some measure, and certain acts are regarded as transgressions of special gravity."[7]

In contrast, John Boswell argued that Christians of the early Middle Ages were tolerant of homosexual behavior and "gay sexuality was rarely singled out for special derogation."[8] Boswell's thesis stands contrary to scholarly appraisals of the historical data. Experts on penitential literature have pointed out that Boswell cited the penitentials sparingly, and he claimed that their censures of sodomy only applied to married men; he failed to observe that numerous censures were addressed to unmarried men. Either Boswell inadequately evaluated the penitentials or intentionally suppressed their content. Medievalist Allen Frantzen comments, "Boswell's portrayal seriously misrepresents the

---

of influence, and their contribution to later collections of ecclesiastical law make the penitentials key witnesses to the concerns of the early Middle Ages" (Payer, 5).

[2] Penitentials often distinguished various forms of male homosexual activity. Some penitentials distinguished the passive participant in sodomy (*molles*), sometimes translated as the "effeminate man," from the active participant. This distinction appears to be used by Paul in 1 Cor 6:10.

[3] Though the term is not used as frequently today, this book will at times use the word *sodomy* when discussing historical texts.

[4] The reduced space given to lesbianism reflects the greater freedom of men in patriarchal medieval societies and the widespread male abuse of that freedom. Never in Christendom is lesbianism affirmed.

[5] See Payer, *Sex and the Penitentials*, 135–39. Payer includes an expansive list of penitentials censuring various forms of homosexual practice. He lists thirty-one penitentials that address male homosexuality and fourteen that censure lesbian practice. See also Payer, 40–44.

[6] Ibid., 135.

[7] Bailey, *Homosexuality*, 108.

[8] John Boswell, *Homosexuality*, 180.

evidence . . . many sources show that the early medieval Church overwhelmingly disapproved of same-sex relations."[9]

EARLY PENITENTIALS

The excerpts below from various penitentials demonstrate that Boswell's thesis is incorrect. These documents address multiple homosexual behaviors, condemning them all. While the pastoral advice on appropriate penalties varies, the universal censure of homosexual practice is perspicuous.

Welch Synod, the Synod of the Grove of Victory (ca. 550)

> He who is *guilty of sodomy* in its various forms shall do penance for four, three, or two years according to the nature of the offense.[10]

A Book of David (ca. 500–525)

> Those who commit fornication with a woman who has become vowed to Christ or to a husband, or with a beast, or *with a male*, for the remainder [of their lives] dead to the world shall live unto God.[11]

Penitential of Columban (ca. 600)

> But if anyone, his sins getting the better of him, actually commits sin, if he commits homicide or the *sin of sodomy*, he shall do penance for ten years.[12]
>
> But if one *commits fornication as the Sodomites did*, he shall do penance for ten years, the first three on bread and water; but in the other seven years he

---

[9] Allen J. Frantzen, *Before the Closet: Same-Sex Love from Beowulf to Angels in America* (Chicago, IL: University of Chicago Press, 1998), 2. Frantzen argues that Boswell was dependent on Michel Foucault's *The History of Sexuality*. Of Foucault he writes, "His medievalism was remarkable only for its superficiality, lack of detail, and indifference to documents and their nuances. . . . He seems to know almost nothing about either the theology or the social practice of penance and confession." *Before the Closet*, 7–8. Frantzen's published works include an earlier book on penitential texts: Allen J. Frantzen, *The Literature of Penance in Anglo-Saxon England* (New Brunswick, NJ: Rutgers University Press, 1983). Payer also argues that the evidence does not support Boswell's thesis regarding tolerance of homosexuality in the early Middle Ages. See Payer, *Sex and the Penitentials*, 135–39.

[10] *Medieval Handbooks of Penance: A Translation of the Principle Libri Poenitentiales and Selections from Related Documents*, trans. John T. McNeill and Helena M. Gamer (New York, NY: Columbia University Press, 1990), 172. Payer describes *The Synod of the Grove of Victory* and *Excerpts from a Book of David* as not strictly speaking "penitentials" but documents containing penitential-like prescriptions which were incorporated into the early Irish manuals of Vinnian, Columbanus, and Cummean. These Irish penitentials comprised the core of the penitential tradition up to the twelfth century. See Payer, *Sex and the Penitentials*, 10.

[11] McNeill and Gamer, *Medieval Handbooks of Penance*, 173.

[12] Ibid., 250.

shall abstain from wine and meat, and [he shall] not be housed with another person forever.[13]

If any layman, indeed, commits *fornication according to the sodomic rite*, that is, commits an act of homosexuality, he shall do penance for seven years, in the first three on bread and water and salt and dry fruit of the garden; in the four remaining years he shall abstain from wine and meats; and thus his guilt shall be cancelled and the priest shall pray for him and so he shall be joined to the altar.[14]

Penitential of Cummean (ca. 650)

A *small boy misused by an older one*, if he is ten years of age, shall fast for a week; if he consented, for twenty days.[15]

So shall those who commit sodomy do penance for seven years.[16]

Penitential Ascribed by Albers to Bede (ca. 720)

In the section "Of the Capital sins," the list of sins includes "*effeminacy*" and "*sodomy*."[17]

The Burgundian Penitential (ca. 700–725)

If anyone *commits fornication as the Sodomites did*, he shall do penance for ten years, three of these on bread and water, and never sleep with another.[18]

Canons of Theodore (ca. 741)

He judged that he who often *commits fornication with a man or with a beast* should do penance for ten years. Another judgment is that he who is joined to beasts shall do penance for fifteen years. He who after his twentieth year defiles himself with a male shall do penance for fifteen years. A male who *commits fornication with a male* shall do penance for ten years. Sodomites shall do penance for seven years, and the *effeminate man* as an adulteress. Likewise he who commits this sexual offense once shall do penance for four years. If he has been in the habit of it, as Basil says, fifteen years; . . . If *a woman practices vice with a woman*, she shall do penance for three years.[19]

---

[13] Ibid., 252.

[14] Ibid., 254.

[15] Ibid., 113.

[16] Ibid., 103.

[17] Ibid., 226.

[18] Ibid., 274.

[19] Ibid., 185. This penitential is traditionally attributed to Theodore of Tarsus (690) but is of a later date. According to Bede's Penitential, a nun participating in sexual activity with another woman is assigned penance for seven years. See Bailey, 103n11.

Ecgbert's Penitential (ca. 730–60)

If *a man commits sodomy* often, or if one doing so is in orders, some hold that he must do penance for ten years; others say, for seven years; others again, for one year if he had taken the passive role (*molles*); others for one hundred days, if the offender is a boy.[20]

Penitential Regulation, **Pope Gregory III (ca. 731–41)**

If any ordained person has been defiled with the crime of sodomy, which is described as a vice so abominable in the sight of God that the cities in which its practitioners dwelt were appointed for destruction by fire and brimstone, let him do penance for ten years, according to the ancient rule. Some, however, being more humanely disposed, have fixed the term at seven years. Those also who are ignorant of the gravity of this offence are assigned three years in which to do penance. As for boys who know that they are indulging in this practice, it behoves them to hasten to amend; let them do penance for fifty days, and in addition let them be beaten with rods; for it is necessary that the crop which has brought forth bad fruit be cut down.[21]

The So-called *"Roman Penitential"* (ca. 830)

If anyone *commits fornication as [did] the Sodomites*, he shall do penance for ten years, three of these on bread and water. . . . If any layman commits fornication as the Sodomites did, he shall do penance for seven years.[22]

Collection of Regino of Prum (ca. 890)

Some consider that he who *commits fornication like a sodomist* must do penance for ten years; others seven years; others again, for one year. Some hold that if the practice is habitual, a layman must do five years penance; a *clericus*, seven years; one who is a sub-deacon or a monk, eight years; a deacon ten years; a priest, twelve years; and a bishop, thirteen years.[23]

Medieval scholar R. W. Southern summarizes the penitential perspective on homosexuality:

So far as sexual sins were concerned, the purpose of the penitential literature of the early Middle Ages had been to list all the forms of forbidden activity with suitable penances attached. Sodomy, as Boswell remarked, was only one among a large number of forbidden actions. Like adultery and every

---

[20] Translated in Bailey, *Homosexuality*, 104.

[21] Ibid., 106.

[22] *Medieval Handbooks of Penance*, 302–3.

[23] For the Latin text, see Benjamin Thorpe, *The Ancient Laws and Institutes of England*, vol. 2 (London, England: G. E. Eyre and A. Spottiswoode, 1840), 84; translation in Bailey, *Homosexuality*, 104–5.

other grave sin, it was very common, but this does not imply tolerance, as Boswell suggests, still less a growing legislative tolerance. The multiplicity of sexual sins simply reflected the extent of human depravity, and the only relevant generalization which emerges from the penitential codes down to the eleventh century is that *sodomy was treated on about the same level as copulation with animals.*[24]

KINGS AND CANONS

In addition to the penitentials, which give us the most explicit information about the church's perspective on homosexual practice in the early Middle Ages, other medieval documents also address the topic, including edicts of Christian kings and emperors, canons from church councils, and works by theologians. In the East, Christian emperors such as Justinian incorporated Christian teaching into moral codes enforced by the state. Powerful Western kings like Charlemagne issued edicts seeking to curb homosexual acts throughout their dominions. Local church councils in the early Middle Ages and ecumenical Western councils in the later Middle Ages likewise addressed sodomy, often citing previous ecclesiastical authorities.

Justinian Code (538)

Therefore, as *certain persons, instigated by the devil, devote themselves to the most reprehensible vices, and commit crimes contrary to nature,* We hereby enjoin them to fear God and the judgment to come, to avoid diabolical and illicit sensuality of this kind; in order that, through such acts, they may

---

[24] R. W. Southern, *Saint Anselm: A Portrait in a Landscape* (New York, NY: Cambridge University Press, 1995), 149–50. Pierre Payer offers this summary: "While it is too much to say with Taylor [*The History of Sex*] that the penitentials 'devoted a disproportionately large amount of their space to prescribing penalties for homosexuality,' it is certainly true that they show considerable interest in the subject. This is in sharp contrast, for instance, to the relative lack of interest shown in the heterosexual relations of unmarried lay people. Different forms of homosexual relations are carefully distinguished, and the age of the participants is important, as is ecclesiastical status, in the apportioning of penances. The numerous canons mentioning clerical homosexuality do not suggest that it was rampant, but they confirm the perfectly natural expectation that, in institutions whose populations are all of the same sex, homosexuality will probably occur and this will be reflected in works dealing with the pastoral care of such people." Payer, 43–44. Bailey's summary states, "Surveying the Penitentials as a whole, and comparing them with the ecclesiastical opinion and legislation already described, their most striking feature is undoubtedly seen to be the recognition that homosexual acts between men commonly take various forms, of which sodomy proper is only one—a distinction virtually ignored hitherto. Not all such acts are regarded as equally culpable, particularly when committed by boys or youth, and clerics and monks are expected, apparently, to conform to a higher moral standard than that required of the laity; nevertheless all homosexual practices are held to be sinful in some measure, and certain acts are regarded as transgressions of special gravity." Bailey, *Homosexuality*, 108.

not incur the just anger of God, and bring about the destruction of the cities along with their inhabitants; for We learn from the Holy Scriptures that both cities as well as men have perished because of wicked acts of this kind. . . . But if, after Our warning has been given, anyone should continue to commit these offences, he will in the first place render himself unworthy of the mercy of God, and will afterwards be subjected to the penalties imposed by the laws. We order the Most Glorious Prefect of this Royal City to arrest any persons who persist in committing the aforesaid crimes, after the publication of Our warning; in order that this city and the State may not be injured by the contempt of such persons and their impious acts, and inflict upon them the punishment of death. (Novels 77, *The Emperor Justinian to the People of Constantinople*)[25]

Justinian Code (544)

Wherefore it would not be just for us to treat with contempt His abounding kindness, His tolerance, and His infinite patience, lest, avoiding repentance, our hearts may become hardened, and We may accumulate His anger upon our heads, on the day of His vengeance. *But while we attempt to avoid committing wicked actions, and cherishing improper desires, there are persons who are guilty of abominable offences, which are deservedly detested by God. We have reference to the corruption of males, a crime which some persons have the sacrilegious audacity to perpetrate. . . . Wherefore it is proper that all those who are influenced by the fear of God should abstain from such impious and criminal acts which even are not committed by beasts, and that those who have not yet perpetrated them may hereafter be deterred from doing so.* Hence those who are given to this species of vice must hereafter not only refrain from sinning, but also show that they are penitent; prostrate themselves before God; confess their faults in the presence of the Most Blessed Patriarch, and (as has already been stated) they will reap the fruits of their repentance; so that the Almighty in his indulgence, and on account of the wealth of His compassion, may render Us worthy of His kindness; that we may all give thanks for the salvation of those who are penitent; and that the magistrates, by prosecuting the guilty, may conciliate God who is deservedly incensed against Us. *And, indeed, We consciously and wisely beseech to bring to repentance those who defile themselves with filthy practices of this kind, so that there will no longer be occasion for Us to prosecute such offences. (Novels 141, The Emperor Justinian to the People of Constantinople)*[26]

---

[25] *The Emperor Justinian to the People of Constantinople* novels 77, in *The Civil Law Including the Twelve Tables, The Institutes of Gaius, The Rules of Ulpian, The Opinions of Paulus, The Enactments of Justinian, and the Constitutions of Leo*, trans. Samuel P. Scott, vol. 16 (Cincinnati, OH: The Central Trust Company, 1932), 288–89.

[26] *The Emperor Justinian* novels 141, vol. 17, 160–61. Note the mercy inherent in this directive. While the text strongly condemned homosexual behavior, it also spoke of repentance and salvation for the sinner.

Leges Visigothorum (ca. 650)

That crime which ought always to be detested and is regarded as an *execrable moral depravity*, ought not to be left unavenged. Therefore *those who lie with males, or who consent to participate passively in such acts*, ought to be smitten by the sentence of this law—namely, that as soon as an offense has been admitted and the judge has publicly investigated it, he should forthwith take steps to have offenders of both kinds castrated. (*Lex Visigoth* 3.5.4)[27]

Sixteenth Council of Toledo (693)

If any one of those *males who commit this vile practice against nature with other males* is a bishop, a priest, or a deacon, he shall be degraded from the dignity of his order, and shall remain in perpetual exile, struck down by damnation. (Canon 3)[28]

Leges Visigothorum (693)

We are compelled by the teaching of the orthodox faith to impose the censure of the law upon indecent practices, and to restrain with the bridle of continence those who have been involved in lapses of the flesh. For we best serve the interests of the people and country with clemency and piety when we take care both to root out completely crimes of depravity, and to bring to an end evil acts of vice. Certainly we strive to abolish the detestable outrage of that lust by the *filthy uncleanness of which men do not fear to defile other men in the unlawful act of sodomy* (*stuprum*); as often, therefore, as they pollute themselves by the mutual defilement of this crime, we regard their conduct as an offence against both divine religion and chastity. Although indeed both the authority of Scripture and the decree of the secular law prohibit absolutely this kind of delinquency. (*Lex Visigoth* 3.5.7)[29]

Charles the Great (ca. 800)

A capitulary of Charles the Great indicates his shock at finding that some of the monks in his empire were practicing "sodomites." He determined to curb the evil and "dared not permit such ills any longer in any part of the realm, much less among those who should be especially chaste and devout." Charlemagne's

---

[27] *Lex Visigoth* 3.5.4, trans. and cited in Bailey, *Homosexuality*, 92. See also translation by Samuel P. Scott, *The Visigoth Code* (Boston: The Boston Book Company, 1910), 110, accessible at https://archive.org/details/cu31924072483419. This law was issued by King Kindasvinth of Gothic Spain.

[28] *Sixteenth Council of Toledo* canon 3, trans. and cited in Bailey, *Homosexuality*, 93.

[29] Ibid., 94; see also *The Visigoth Code*, translation by Scott, 111. According to Bailey, this text was a supplement to the Council of Toledo's edict added by the Gothic King Egica.

edict exhorted priests and bishops to "attempt in every way *to prohibit and eradicate this evil.*"[30]

Hincmar of Reims (845–82)

In his work on the divorce of King Lothair of Lorraine, Bishop Hincmar condemned lesbian practice:

> They do not put flesh to flesh in the sense of the genital organ of one within the body of the other, since nature precludes this but *they do transform the use of the member in question into an unnatural one*, in that they reported to use certain instruments of diabolical operation to excite desire. Thus they sin nonetheless by committing fornication against their own bodies.[31]

During the ninth and tenth centuries, a body of pastoral literature developed which scholars refer to as *Diocesan Statutes*. These documents were sets of regulations issued by bishops for the use of diocesan priests in shepherding their flocks. The statutes included censures of homosexual practices. Herald of Tours (858) issued this directive: "Those who sin irrationally [allusion to Ancyra, Canon 16], or with relatives are to be severely judged so the vices might be cut away."[32] A diocesan statue of Theodulf of Orleans (ca. 800) reads, "For just as it is more abominable to mix with a mule than with a male, so *it is a more irrational crime to mix with a male than with a female.*"[33]

In the tenth century and first half of the eleventh, an additional group of texts known as Canonical Collections emerged. These were intended to pass on the tradition of previous ecclesiastical legislation; thus, they included references to church councils, papal letters, writings of the Fathers, and penitentials. Medieval scholar Pierre Payer studied these collections and concluded:

> After a careful study of numerous collections up to 1048, both printed and in manuscript, I found that every one contains a number of texts censuring homosexual practices. Taken together with the tradition of the penitentials it is clear that prior to 1048 the church displayed a consistent and uninterrupted pastoral concern with homosexuality. . . . *Both the penitentials and*

---

[30] See Boswell, *Christianity, Tolerance and Homosexuality*, 177–78. Bailey briefly mentions antihomosexual legislation during the Carolingian period. Bailey, *Homosexuality*, 94–95. Payer presents a more expansive list of references to homosexuality during the Carolingian era in his "Introduction" to *The Book of Gomorrah: An Eleventh-Century Treatise Against Clerical Homosexual Practices*, trans. Pierre J. Payer (Ontario, Canada: Wilfrid Laurier University Press, 1982), 7–9.

[31] Boswell's translation. For Latin text, see *Christianity, Social Tolerance, and Homosexuality*, 204n132. Boswell views this as a commentary on lesbianism. It may refer to women using an artificial phallus. Bede's Penitential also makes reference to nuns "[fornicantes] per machinam." Bailey, 102.

[32] Payer, "Introduction," in *Book of Gomorrah*, 10.

[33] Ibid., 42n35, "Second Diocesan Statue."

the sections dealing with sins and confession in the collections of canon law
provide overwhelming evidence that homosexuality was included in the cata-
logues of sins worthy of frequent mention.[34]

THE BOOK OF GOMORRAH

The year 1048 was significant as it marked the election of the reforming pope
Leo IX, who was committed to revitalizing a corrupt church that had become
polluted with simony (selling church offices) and clerical immorality. Leo supported the Cluniac reform of monasteries,[35] and once elected to the papacy, he
traveled widely to press reforms throughout Christendom. During his pontificate, an acerbic exposition against clerical homosexuality was written by Peter
Damian, a monastic reformer in Italy. Damian took his message of clerical
reform to Italy, Germany, and France, earning a reputation as a fiery preacher
who publicly opposed the worldliness of fellow clergy. A central cause of his
alarm was the proliferation of sexual immorality, especially homosexual practice. He wrote the *Book of Gomorrah* (1048–54) and addressed it to Leo IX.
The treatise was a diatribe against practicing homosexuals who had infiltrated
holy orders. Damian believed homosexual practice disqualified one from
ordination, and he pressed his case with Leo IX that homosexuals should be
deposed from church office. In the preface to the *Book of Gomorrah,* Damian
wrote:

> A certain abominable and terribly shameful vice has grown up in our
> region. Unless the hand of severe punishment resists as soon as possible,
> there is certainly a danger that the sword of divine anger will be used sav-
> agely against it to the ruin of many. Alas! It is shameful to speak of, shameful
> to suggest such foul disgrace to sacred ears! But if the doctor shrinks in hor-
> ror from infected wounds, who will take the trouble to apply the cauter? If
> the one who is to heal becomes nauseated, who will lead sick hearts back to
> health? *Vice against nature creeps in like a cancer and even touches the order*
> *of consecrated men.*[36]

Damian's primary concern was the church's lack of discipline for homosexual behavior. He stated, "When someone is known to have *fallen into this*
wickedness with eight or even ten other equally sordid men, we see him still

---

[34] Ibid., 10–11.

[35] The influential French monastery of Cluny led a spiritual renewal movement, urging a
return to strict observance of the Benedictine Rule. The order reached its peak influence in the
twelfth century, when there were over a thousand Cluniac houses in Europe.

[36] Ibid., 27. Bailey doubts there was an outbreak of homosexuality in the mid-eleventh century. Damian's indignation, therefore, was a response to the conduct of "a few licentious individuals that had come to his notice" (Bailey, *Homosexuality,* 115). Payer counters that there is
an "absence of any serious caveat among respectable historians in taking Damian's claim at face
value" (*Book of Gomorrah,* 22).

remaining in his ecclesiastical position." The toleration of such behavior is "contrary to reason and against the canonical decrees of the fathers." Damian cited Pope Gregory's teaching that anyone guilty of a crime punishable by death in the Old Testament may not be promoted to ecclesiastical orders. Failure to punish those committing homosexual acts was "entirely against the norm of sacred Law and the rule of divine authority."[37]

It was an "unheard of crime" and "outrage" that some clerics committed "these great evils with their spiritual children [penitents]." Some of the priests who engaged in such behavior concealed the evil by confessing their sins to one another, Damian said. He discounted "apocryphal canons" he believed were too lax. As an example, he cited Bishop Burchard's *Decretum* (c.1008–12), a canon law collection which stated, "If anyone has *sinned as the Sodomites*, some say ten years penance; if he is in the habit, more must be added; if he has ecclesiastical rank, he is to be degraded and do penance as a lay person."[38]

For Damian, homosexual practice was the most heinous of crimes. In chapter 15 of the *Book of Gomorrah*, titled "A Deserving Condemnation of Abominable Shamefulness," he warned:

> Truly, this vice is never to be compared with any other vice because it *surpasses the enormity of all vices*. Indeed, this vice is the death of bodies, the destruction of souls. It pollutes the flesh; it extinguishes the light of the mind. It evicts the Holy Spirit from the temple of the human heart; it introduces the devil who incites to lust. It casts into error; it completely removes the truth from the mind that has been deceived. It prepares snares for those entering; it shuts up those who fall into the pit so that they cannot get out. It opens hell; it closes the door of heaven. It makes a citizen of the heavenly Jerusalem into the heir of the infernal Babylon.[39]

---

[37] Ibid., 30–34.

[38] Ibid., 41–50. Damian argued that "authentic canons" came from councils, holy Fathers, or the pope, not other individuals. Two ninth-century councils (Chalon, 813; Paris, 829) condemned the use of penitentials. The desire for uniformity in penitential practice through the use of common authorities seems the primary concern. See *Medieval Handbooks of Penance*, 401–3. Boswell argued that Hincmar and Burchard (*Decretals*) downplayed the seriousness of homosexual practice, viewing it as a variety of fornication and in some cases less serious than heterosexual sin. Boswell infamously wrote, "Indeed the evidence suggests that despite considerable local variation, attitudes toward homosexuality grew steadily more tolerant throughout the early middle ages" (Boswell, *Homosexuality, Social Tolerance and Christianity*, 206). On the contrary, there was never any ecclesiastical tolerance of homosexuality. Debate among clerics only concerned censures for homosexual practice.

[39] Ibid., 63. Damian contrasts the momentary pleasures of homosexual sex with the eternality of God's judgment: "Think how miserable it is that because of the present satisfaction of one organ's pleasure, afterwards the whole body together with the soul will be tortured forever by the most atrocious flaming fires" (*Book of Gomorrah*, 83).

Damian's pastoral concern for clerical homosexuals was evident in his address to Leo IX. He wrote:

> O, I weep for you unfortunate soul, and from the depths of my heart I sigh over the lot of your destruction. *I weep for you, I say, miserable souls who are given over to the filth of impurity.* . . . . *The iniquity of a Christian soul surpasses the sin of the Sodomites because each one now falls in a worse way insofar as he defies the very commands of evangelical grace. The knowledge of divine law vehemently accuses him, lest he find relief in a plan to excuse himself.* . . . . If suitable compunction and contrition would strike the secret recesses of your heart, I, not improperly, would rejoice in a dance of unspeakable joy. This is the reason why you in particular should be wept for because you yourself are not weeping.[40]

In the final chapter Damian defended himself against potential detractors, claiming that he was motivated by love for brethren. Those who wished to criticize Damian should also attack the Fathers, "who disputed so sharply against different sects of heretics." Damian added:

> If blasphemy is the worst, I do not know in what way sodomy is better. *Blasphemy makes a man to err: sodomy, to perish.* . . . If we are careful to search into which of these crimes weighs more heavily on the scales of divine scrutiny, sacred scripture fully instructs us in what we seek. Indeed, while the sons of Israel were led into captivity for blaspheming God and worshipping idols, the Sodomites perished in heavenly fire and sulphur, devoured in the holocaust.[41]

Leo wrote a letter of response to the *Book of Gomorrah* in which he praised Damian's "holy indignation" and zeal for virtue. He acknowledged that Damian had written fairly and rightly, yet Leo desired to distinguish between homosexual sin "that was not a long-standing practice or performed with many men" and habitual practices. Those who "restrained their desires and atoned for these shameful sins with a suitable penance," he said, should be readmitted to their previous rank. Leo concluded with a declaration of his authority in the church: "If anyone shall dare to criticize or question this decree of apostolic direction, let him know that he is himself acting in peril of his rank. *For he who does not attack vice encourages it; such a one is rightly accounted guilty [and worthy] of the [same] end as he who perishes though sin.*"[42]

---

[40] Ibid., 66–69.

[41] Ibid., 87–89.

[42] Leo IX, *Nos humanius agents*, trans. and cited in Boswell, *Homosexuality, Social Tolerance, and Christianity*, 365–66. Bailey had suggested that Leo's letter was a reproof to Peter Damian for being too harsh, but Boswell argues that the letter is full of praise. Based on the full text of the letter, Boswell appears to be correct. Leo strikes a moderate tone; however, he is

LATE MEDIEVAL VOICES

During Leo IX's pontificate, he appointed an Italian named Hildebrand as an administrator. Hildebrand (Gregory VII) was elected to the papacy in 1073 and pursued an intense program of reform and moral revival in the church. The Gregorian reform movement strengthened the bureaucracy of the church, asserted independence from secular authority, and stridently pursued a reformation of clerical morality. Though celibacy was required of all clergy, many had wives and even concubines. A widely circulated pamphlet written by Ulrich of Imola (ca. 1060) argued for allowing priestly marriage lest sinful priests commit graver offenses such as bestiality or sodomy, which had already infected much of the upper clergy.[43] The Gregorian reform also addressed widespread adultery and concubinage among the laity.

Gratian's *Concordantia discordantium canonum* (also known as *Gratian's Decretum*, ca. 1140) contained several sections on homosexual sin. The *Decretum,* based on nearly 4,000 patristic texts, conciliar decrees, and papal pronouncements, became a standard text summarizing legal precedent in the church. Gratian's work was an attempt to harmonize these sources. The *Decretum* described the "act against nature" as worse than both adultery and fornication:

> The holy Lot offered his daughters' modesty [Gen. 19:8]. That was a crime of impurity, but at least it would have been intercourse in a natural way, instead of an act against nature. He valued hospitality, something kept inviolate even among barbarians, over the shame of his own house. . . . *Crimes against nature are always and everywhere to be repudiated and punished. Such were those of the Sodomites* [Gen. 19:5]. Even if people everywhere did what they did, they would still be guilty under divine law [Lev. 18:22; Rom. 1:26; 1 Cor. 6:9], which has forbidden people to perform such acts. Indeed our very communion with God and nature, of which he is the author, is violated when *we pollute ourselves by perverted lust*. . . . The natural act is licit in marriage, and illicit in adultery. *An act against nature is always illicit and, without a doubt, disgraceful and criminal. So the Apostle [Rom. 1:26] explains that this is more damnable for both men and women, than if they sinned in a natural way by adultery or fornication.*[44]

---

forthright in his support of disciplining those practicing homosexuality. See Bailey, *Homosexuality*, 114, and Boswell, *Homosexuality, Social Tolerance, and Christianity*, 211–12.

[43] Michael Goodich, *The Unmentionable Vice: Homosexuality in the Later Medieval Period* (New York, NY: Dorset Press, 1970), 24. Ulrich wrote his pamphlet shortly after the Eastern Orthodox churches officially separated from Rome in 1054. The Orthodox churches allowed married men to be ordained but forbade those men already ordained to marry.

[44] Catholic University of America, *Marriage Canons from the Decretum of Gratian*, Case 32, question 7, ca. 12–14, trans. John T. Noonan Jr., ed. Augustine Thompson O.P., 1967, accessed September 27, 2014, http://faculty.cua.edu/Pennington/canon%20Law/marriagelaw.htm. As the *Decretum* indicates, Gratian articulated the church's view that Lot's situation in Sodom involved

In 1179 Hildegard of Bingen, a German nun and mystical writer, recorded some of her visions from God in a book known as *Scito vias Domini* ("Know the Ways of the Lord"). In the second part of *Scivias*, an abbreviated name for the same work, she wrote about a message she claimed to have received from God. It condemned all forms of homosexual practice:

> For many are found among both spiritual and secular people who not only pollute themselves in fornication with women but also assume a heavy burden of condemnation by contaminating themselves in perverted forms. How? *A man who sins with another man as if with a woman sins bitterly against God and against the union with which God united male and female.* Hence both in God's sight are polluted, black and wanton, horrible and harmful to God and humanity, and guilty of death; for they go against their Creator and His creature, which is in them. How? God united man and woman, thus joining the strong to the weak, that each might sustain the other. *But these perverted adulterers change their virile strength into perverse weakness, rejecting the proper male and female roles, and in their wickedness they shamefully follow Satan,* who in his pride sought to split and divide Him Who is indivisible. They create in themselves by their wicked deeds a strange and perverse adultery, and so appear polluted and shameful in My sight. . . . *And a woman who takes up devilish ways and plays a male role in coupling with another woman is most vile in My sight, and so is she who subjects herself to such a one in this evil deed.* For they should be ashamed of their passion, and instead they impudently usurped a right that was not theirs. And, having put themselves into alien ways, they are to Me transformed and contemptible.[45]

In 1203 Alan of Lille, a humanist theologian, wrote a poem, *De planctu natura* ("Complaint of Nature"), in which he argued that homosexual sex was unnatural, sinful, and produced unhappiness because it frustrated God's plan to link sex with the conception of children. In the poem sodomy functions as a metaphor for all forms of vice. In his *Sermones de peccatis capitalibus*, Alan argued that the two most serious crimes are homicide and sodomy. He also produced a confessor's manual, *Liber poenitentialis*, which directed penance of fifteen years for an adult practicing sodomy; a minor's penance was to last 100 days. Alan was known for combating the Cathari, a sect in France and Italy accused of practicing homosexuality.[46]

---

both the issue of hospitality and homosexual practice. It is noteworthy that Gratian tied together the story of Sodom, Levitical law, and the prohibitions of Paul, underscoring the unanimity of the biblical witness against homosexual practice. He also cited texts from Augustine and Isidore, Archbishop of Seville in 636, as ecclesiastical authorities.

[45] Hildegard of Bingen, *Scivias* 2.6, in *The Classics of Western Spirituality*, trans. Columba Hart and Jane Bishop (Mahwah, NJ: Paulist, 1990), 279.

[46] Goodich, *The Unmentionable Vice*, 33–35. Alan of Lille, *Liber poenitentialis*, ed. Jean Longere, vol. 2, Analecta Medievalia Numercensia 17 (Louvain, Belgium: Editions Nauwelaerts, 1965).

Other significant sources for understanding late medieval perspectives on homosexual practice are commentaries on Scripture. The standard medieval commentary on the Bible, known as *Glossa ordinaria (or Glossa communis)*, was compiled by Anselm of Laon and other scholars in 1117. The commentary was based primarily on extracts from the Fathers. A second standard commentary was the *Postillae super totam Bibliam*, complied by Nicholas of Lyre in 1340. The two works became the basis of most biblical study in the late Middle Ages.

The commentaries of Anselm and Nicholas, citing the Fathers, explained that the reason for Sodom's destruction with fire and brimstone was its sin against nature (sodomy).[47] Based on Leviticus 18–19 and Romans 1, sodomy was identified with idolatry. Commentary on Jude 7–8 classified sodomy with heresy: both crimes led to eternal damnation. Medievalist Michael Goodich summarized the perspective of these two medieval commentaries: "Thus, with Holy Scripture as a basic text, assisted by the standard commentaries of Anselm of Laon and later of Nicholas of Lyre, the medieval preacher or theologian was equipped with an arsenal of polemical tools and precedents in his fight against moral offenders. *Homosexual acts were classed among the gravest of sins.*"[48]

Medieval attitudes toward homosexual practice were further manifested in declarations of councils. King Baldwin II of the Crusader kingdom of Jerusalem, along with Patriarch Gormund of Jerusalem, called the *Council of Nablus* (ancient Shechem) in 1120. The council declared:

> *If any adult shall be proved to have defiled himself voluntarily by sodomitical vice whether actively or passively*, let him be burnt. . . . If any sodomist, before he is accused, shall come to his senses, and having been brought to penitence, shall renounce that abominable vice by the swearing of an oath, let him be received into the Church and dealt with according to the provisions of canons. But if he falls a second time into such practices and wishes again to do penance, he may be admitted to penance, but let him be expelled from the kingdom of Jerusalem.[49]

Two ecumenical councils addressed the "sin against nature." The popes and bishops were determined to deal with immorality, including homosexual practice, among clergy throughout Europe. Apparently, even though the church's teaching was unambiguous, enforcement of sexual standards for clergy was

---

[47] Goodich observes (*The Unmentionable Vice*, 36), "While, as Derrick S. Bailey suggests, the sin of the Sodomites may not have been homosexuality, but rather inhospitality or a desire to mix 'the heavenly and the earthly' via intercourse, there is no doubt that medieval thinkers regarded the sin of Sodom as homosexuality."

[48] Ibid., 35–39.

[49] *Neopolitanum concilium*, trans. and cited in Bailey, *HWTT*, 96.

not adequate. For this reason, ecumenical decrees ordered church law to be upheld consistently.

Third Lateran Council (1179)

Let all who are found *guilty of that unnatural vice* for which the wrath of God came down upon the sons of disobedience and destroyed the five cities with fire, if they are clerics be expelled from the clergy or confined in monasteries to do penance; if they are laymen they are to incur excommunication and be completely separated from the society of the faithful. (Canon 11)[50]

Fourth Lateran Council (1215)

In order that the morals and conduct of clerics may be reformed for the better, let all of them strive to live in a continent and chaste way, especially those in holy orders. Let them *beware of every vice involving lust, especially that on account of which the wrath of God came down from heaven upon the sons of disobedience*, so that they may be worthy to minister in the sight of almighty God with a pure heart and an unsullied body. Lest the ease of receiving pardon prove an incentive to sin, we decree that those who are caught giving way to the vice of incontinence are to be punished according to canonical sanctions, in proportion to the seriousness of their sins. We order such sanctions to be effectively and strictly observed, in order that those whom the fear of God does not hold back from evil may at least be restrained from sin by temporal punishment. (Canon 14)[51]

Pope Innocent III, who called the Fourth Lateran Council into session, wrote a widely read ascetical treatise, *De miseria humane conditionis*, before he became pope in 1198. In this work was a section titled "On Unnatural Intercourse." He wrote:

This vice causes an ignominious change, which the Apostle feared not to name: "For this cause God delivered them up to shameful lusts. For their women have changed the natural use into that use which is against nature. And in like manner the men also, leaving the natural use of the women, have burned in their lusts, one towards another: men with men, working that which is filthy." *What is more shameful than such shamefulness? What more criminal than these crimes? In the Law, intercourse of a man with a man is treated as equal to intercourse between a man and a beast.* So one reads in Leviticus: "Thou shalt not lie with mankind as with womankind because it is

---

[50] Fordam University, "Internet Medieval Sourcebook," Third Lateran Council, Canon 11. Accessed March 17, 2015, http://www.ewtn.com/library/COUNCILS/LATERAN3.HTM.

[51] Ibid., Fourth Lateran Council, Canon 14. Accessed March 17, 2015, http://www.ewtn.com/library/COUNCILS/LATERAN4.HTM. The mention of God's anger from heaven references Rom 1:18, which occurs in a chapter that goes on to discuss God's judgment on homosexual practice.

an abomination. Thou shalt not copulate with any beast, nor be defiled with it." For each of these the same penalty is prescribed: "If anyone lie with a man as with a woman, both have committed an abomination; let them be put to death; the beast also you shall kill." He who has ears to hear, let him hear; and he who has acted foolishly, let him come to his senses. . . . The penalty this crime deserved taught a lesson: "The Lord rained brimstone and fire from heaven on Sodom and Gomorrah.". . . Therefore the Lord rained out of Himself not rain and dew, but brimstone and fire: brimstone for the stench of lust, fire for the heat of passion a penalty fit for the crime.[52]

In the thirteenth century a new genre of penitential manuals emerged. These texts were more systematic than their counterparts from the early Middle Ages, concisely classifying sins along with giving the penance to be imposed for specific sins. The earliest such manuals appeared at the new University of Paris, which attracted thousands of young men and held classes not far from Parisian brothels. An influential manual written in 1224 was *Liber poenitentialis* by Robert of Flamborough, who was confessor to many of these students. His penitential book included five sections under the heading *De fornicantibus sodomitice*. Robert's manual was designed for inexperienced priests, complete with directions on how to interview a penitent carefully concerning the nature of his or her sexual sin.[53]

In 1242 a Dominican professor of law at Bologna, Paul of Hungary, wrote the *Liber de poenitentia*, which gave more than usual attention to the sin against nature. Paul's penitential included citations from Roman and canon law, the Fathers, and Scripture. He systematically dealt with sodomy, beginning with a definition, then describing its causes, heinousness, and proper punishment. Sodomy was the most severely punished sin in both Testaments and the civil law of Constantine, according to Paul. Sodomites are God's adversaries and destroyers of the human race, disobeying God's command to multiply. The basic cause of sodomy is an abundance of food, drink, leisure, and pride, Paul said. According to this text four sins in Scripture call out to God for retribution: sodomy, homicide, oppression of widows, and keeping wages from laborers.[54]

One of the most thorough theological discussions of "sins contrary to nature" in the late Middle Ages (1274) was presented by Thomas Aquinas in his *Summa Theologica*.[55] As with every topic addressed in the *Summa*,

---

[52] *On the Misery of the Human Condition* 2.24, trans. Margaret Mary Deitz (Indianapolis, IN: The Bobbs-Merrill Company, Inc., 1969), 50. Innocent connected the story of Sodom, Leviticus 18 and 20, and Romans 1 as the collective biblical indictment of homosexual practice.

[53] See sections 272–75 of Robert of Flamborough, Canon-Penitentiary of Saint-Victor at Paris, *Liber Potentientialis*, A Critical Edition with Introduction and Notes, ed. J. J. Francis Firth (Toronto, Canada: Pontifical Institute of Medieval Studies, 1971), 195–96, 229–31.

[54] Goodich, *The Unmentionable Vice*, 59–61.

[55] Thomas Aquinas, according to John Mahoney, was the first theologian to present a systematic natural law theory. See John Mahoney, *The Making of Moral Theology: A Study of the*

Thomas systematically explored a Christian view of homosexuality by using Scripture, tradition (the Fathers), and reason. Aquinas agreed with Augustine and numerous other church fathers that the crime against nature was a heinous sin violating God's natural order for procreation.[56] Any sex act that did not potentially lead to procreation was unnatural.[57] Homosexual acts were opposed to reason as well as to Scripture. The following passages from the *Summa* and Commentary on Romans demonstrate Aquinas's firm conviction that sex acts between persons of the same gender are always sinful.

> Now lust consists essentially in exceeding the order and mode of reason in the matter of venereal acts. Wherefore without any doubt lust is a sin. . . . As the Apostle says (1 Corinthians 6:20) in speaking against lust, *You are bought with a great price: glorify and bear God in your body.* Wherefore by inordinately using the body through lust a man wrongs God Who is the Supreme Lord of our body. Hence Augustine says: (De Decem. Chord. 10 [Serm. lx (xcvi de Temp.)]): *God Who thus governs His servants for their good, not for His, made this order and commandment, lest unlawful pleasures should destroy His temple which thou hast begun to be.*[58]

> The sin of lust consists in seeking venereal pleasure not in accordance with right reason. . . . First, because it is inconsistent with the end of the venereal act. On this way, as hindering the begetting of children, there is the *vice against nature* which attaches to every venereal act from which generation cannot follow.[59]

> Wherever there occurs a special kind of deformity whereby the venereal act is rendered unbecoming, there is a determinate species of lust. This may occur in two ways: First, through being contrary to right reason, and this is common to all lustful vices; secondly, because, in addition, it is contrary to the natural order of the venereal act as becoming to the human race: and this is called *the unnatural vice.* This may happen . . . by copulation with an undue

---

Roman Catholic Tradition (Oxford, NY: Clarendon, 1977), 77.

[56] The theory of natural law had its roots in the patristic era. In the second century Athenagoras said that humans were well ordered by God in creation (*Apology*, 25); Justin Martyr commented that God made humans with the rational power to choose between right and wrong (*First Apology* 28) and that "every race knows that adultery, and fornication, and homicide, and such like, are sinful" (*Dialogue with Trypho the Jew* 93); and Tertullian stated that the entire universe is ordered and guided by reason (*Apology* 11). Similarly, in the fourth century Augustine said that God's eternal law is impressed upon humanity and so everything is perfectly ordered (*De libero arbitrio* 1.5). See John Mahoney, *The Making of Moral Theology*, 77.

[57] Unnatural acts included masturbation, bestiality, *coitus interruptis* in marriage, and other forms of birth control. Typically, however, the "sin against nature" referred to homosexuality.

[58] *Summa Theologica* 2.2.153.3 in *St. Thomas Aquinas Summa Theologica*, Complete English Edition in Five Volumes, trans. Fathers of the Dominican Province, vol. 4 (repr.,Westminster, MD: Christian Classics, 1981), 1,806. The italics in all quotations from the *Summa* are those of the translators.

[59] *Summa Theologica* 2.2.154.1, vol. 4, 1,808.

sex, male with male, or female with female, as the Apostle states (Romans 1:27): and this is called the *vice of sodomy.*[60]

Now the principles of reason are those things that are according to nature, because reason presupposes things as determined by nature . . . in matters of action it is most grave and shameful to act against things as determined by nature. Therefore, since by the unnatural vices man transgresses that which has been determined by nature with regard to the use of venereal actions, it follows that in this matter this sin is the gravest of all. . . . in *sins contrary to nature, whereby the very order of nature is violated, an injury is done to God, the Author of nature.* . . . The most grievous is the sin of bestiality, because use of the due species is not observed. Hence a gloss on Genesis 37:2, "He accused his brethren of a most wicked crime," says that "they copulated with cattle." *After this comes the sin of sodomy, because use of the right sex is not observed.*[61]

They are called **shameful affections**, because their acts are not worthy of man: *it is a shame even to speak of the things that they do in secret* (Eph 5:12). For if sins of the flesh are shameful, because through them man is lowered to what is bestial in him, much more so are sins against nature, through which man sinks below the bestial: *I will change his glory into shame* (Hos 4:7). . . . In another way, something is said to be against man's nature by reason of the general class, which is animal. Now it is obvious that according to the intent of nature, sexual union in animals is ordained to the act of generation; hence, every form of union from which generation cannot follow is against the nature of an animal as animal. In line with this it is stated in the Gloss that *the natural use is that a man and a woman come together in one copulation, but it is against nature that a man pollute a man and a woman a woman.* The same is true of every act of intercourse from which generation cannot follow. . . . It should be noted that the apostle very reasonably considers vices against nature, which are the worst carnal sins, as punishments for idolatry, because they seem to have begun as idolatry, namely, at the time of Abraham, when idolatry is believed to have begun. That seems to be the reason why they are first recorded to have been punished among the people of Sodom (Gen 19). Furthermore, as idolatry became more widespread, these vices grew.[62]

In the fourteenth century a preachers' manual for moral instruction demonstrated that sexual vice, including sodomy, was a concern in the parish churches. *Fasciculus Morum* dealt with the seven deadly sins: pride, wrath, envy, avarice, sloth, gluttony, and lechery. Under its exposition of lechery, the writer commented on sodomy:

---

[60] *Summa Theologica* 2.2.154.11, vol. 4, 1,819.

[61] *Summa Theologica* 2.2.154.12, vol. 4, 1,820.

[62] Saint Thomas Aquinas, *Commentary on the Letter of Saint Paul to the Romans*, trans. Fr. Larcher, vol. 37, chapter 1, lecture 8 (Lander, WY: The Aquinas Institute for the Study of Sacred Doctrine, 2012), 52–53. Italics appear in the English translation.

The fifth and last branch of lechery is the *diabolical sin against nature called sodomy.* I pass over it in horror and leave it to others to describe it. . . . What wonder then, if Christ takes vengeance on those who scorn his commandment by getting involved, not just in simple fornication but in that *vile and abominable sin against nature* that is not to be named? To be sure, it is no wonder at all. An explicit type of this occurs in Genesis 19, in Sodom and Gomorrah, which are five cities of that region. Not only did fire and sulphur falling from above kill people and animals, but the earth opened its mouth and swallowed all the living. Thus it is certain that on account of the said sin they perished forever in hell.[63]

SAME-SEX UNIONS?

Boswell has suggested that Anselm, consecrated archbishop of Canterbury in 1093, felt homosexual attraction to some of his fellow monks and expressed it by writing of embraces and kisses in his letters to them. Boswell writes:

> Although Anselm was devoted to the monastic ideal of celibacy, he had extraordinary emotional relationships, first with Lanfranc and then with a succession of his own pupils. . . . Erotic interest appears not to have been the primary component of most of Anselm's relationships, and it was probably the strength of his character that invested such passion in relations which might have seemed casual to an outside observer. On the other hand, some of his epistolary output appears erotic by any standards.

Boswell also claimed that Anselm "prevented the promulgation of the first antigay legislation in England."[64]

R. W. Southern, an expert on Anselm, argued that Boswell did not understand medieval monastic spiritual friendship, which had nothing to do with homosexual desires. Embraces, kisses, and expressions of deep emotional attachment were acceptable between individuals living in monastic community. Southern observed, "Anselm saw the pleasure of friendship (as the pleasure of music) as a foretaste of the pleasure to be experienced at a higher degree of excellence in Heaven." The medieval kiss was a symbol of unity and in the religious context expressed intertrinitarian union of divine persons, union of the saints and union between God and man. For Anselm monastic friendships were "souls fused together in common monastic obedience . . . an indissoluble union here and in Heaven."[65]

---

[63] *Fasciculus Morum: A Fourteenth-Century Preacher's Handbook*, ed. and trans. S. Wenzel (University Park, PA: Pennsylvania State University, 1989), 687.

[64] Boswell, *Christianity, Social Tolerance, and Homosexuality*, 218–19.

[65] R. W. Southern, *Saint Anselm: A Portrait in a Landscape* (repr., Oxford, NY: Cambridge University Press, 1995), 151, 156. Consider the famous medieval tale *Sir Gawain and the Green Knight*. In it Sir Gawain is greeted daily by his host, Bertilak of Hautdesert, in a way that

Anselm was concerned about the proliferation of homosexual practice in his day and delayed in promulgating antisodomy legislation only in order to procure the bishops' full backing. In a letter explaining the need for legislation against sodomy, Anselm stated, "It must be recognized that this sin [of sodomy] has become so common that hardly anyone even blushes for it, and many, being ignorant of its enormity, have abandoned themselves to it." Long hair and effeminate clothing were forbidden to priests, and Anselm viewed them as encouraging sodomy. He noted: "As for those priests who refuse to have their hair cut, they are not to enter the church. I do not order that, if they enter the church, they shall cease to be priests, but they are to be warned that they are acting against God, and incurring damnation."[66]

Boswell argued for the existence of medieval church ceremonies that marked the commitments of same-sex couples. Ecclesiastical blessing of homosexual unions, according to him, is evident in the *adelphopoiesis* (Gk. "brother making") ceremony in the Greek and Byzantine churches. These were, in fact, ceremonies in which men pledged spiritual brotherhood to one another with a priest presiding. They had nothing to do with "same-sex marriage" or condoning homoerotic relationships. Yet Boswell cites an eleventh-century Greek text he describes as the "Office for Same-Sex Union,"

The priest<shall say>:

> Forasmuch as Thou, O Lord and Ruler, art merciful and loving, who didst establish humankind after thine image and likeness, who dist deem it meet that thy holy apostles Philip and Bartholomew be united, bound one unto the other *not by nature but by faith and the spirit.* As Thou didst find thy holy martyrs Serge and Bacchus worthy to be united together, bless also these thy servants, N. and N., joined together *not by the bond of nature but by faith and in the mode of the spirit,* granting unto them peace and love and oneness of mind. *Cleanse from their hearts every stain and impurity,* and vouchsafe unto them to love one another without hatred and *without scandal* all the days of their lives, with the aid of the Mother of God and all thy saints, forasmuch as all glory is thine.[67]

---

seems strange to most modern readers: "He clasps him tight and kisses him three times with as much emotion as a man could muster" (III.1936–37). Simon Armitage, *Sir Gawain and the Green Knight* (London, England: Faber and Faber, 2007). Quite clearly, however, the text is only describing the filial friendship between Bertilak and Gawain. The sexual indiscretion involving kisses is, in the story, rather between Bertilak's wife and Gawain. One might also consider the custom in some parts of Russia: there, even today, men greet one another with kisses on the mouth.

[66] Ibid., 149, 152.

[67] John Boswell, *Same-Sex Unions in Premodern Europe* (New York, NY: Villard, 1994), 295. This book, like his first, caught the attention of the popular press but received mixed reviews from scholars. See "The Boswell Thesis," 22. For critical book reviews of *Same-Sex Unions*, see Brent P. Shaw, "A Groom of One's Own?," *The New Republic* (July 18 1994): 33–41; Robin Darling Young, "Gay Marriage: Reimagining Church History," *First Things* (November 1994):

It is transparent in this text that the ceremony is incongruous with homosexual practice. In fact, the text classifies the union in question as in the spirit, "not by nature." And the rite calls for the brotherly union to be "without stain, impurity or scandal"—which obviously excluded sodomy in the eleventh century. It is inconceivable that a church ceremony would sanction what it otherwise condemned. Boswell's revisionist interpretation has no basis in the document itself.

The liturgy mentions not only an apostolic pair (Philip and Bartholomew) but also Serge and Bacchus (fourth century), whom Boswell considers a gay couple or "paired saints." In fact, Serge and Bacchus were Christian soldiers martyred under Emperor Maximian.[68] Because they refused to sacrifice to the gods, Bacchus was beaten to death, and Serge was beheaded a few days later. It is clear from the account of their martyrdom that the men were close Christian friends, supporting each other in the face of impending death. Boswell writes, however: "Serge and Bacchus came to represent to subsequent generations of Christians the quintessential 'paired' military saints: they were usually referred to and often pictorially depicted together (sometimes rubbing halos together and with their horses' noses touching). And they became the preeminent 'couple' invoked in the ceremony of same-sex union."[69] Contrary to Boswell's peculiar assertion, no evidence supports the two martyrs having a homoerotic relationship. Nevertheless, gay Christians continue to cite Boswell's work as historical evidence of the church blessing homosexual unions.[70]

43–48; Marian Therese Horvat, "Rewriting History to Serve the Gay Agenda," Tradition in Action, accessed September 27, 2014, http://www.traditioninaction.org/bkreviews/A_002br_SameSex.htm.

[68] For Boswell's translation of the Greek text recounting the martyrdom of saints Serge and Bacchus, see *The New Encyclopedia of Christian Martyrs*, compiler Mark Water (Grand Rapids, MI: Baker, 2001), 374–82.

[69] Boswell, *Same-Sex Unions*, 153–54. Boswell claims the famous icon of Saints Serge and Bacchus with Christ above them (at St. Catherine's monastery on Mount Sinai) mirrors a traditional Roman depiction of a deity overseeing the wedding of a husband and wife (Boswell, 194, figure 5). This icon is on the book's cover. In 1994 a gay Franciscan iconographer, Robert Lentz, created a modern icon of Sergius and Bacchus, which was first displayed in the Chicago Gay Pride Parade. Although Boswell's interpretation of the martyred pair is rejected by the Greek Orthodox and most scholars, the gay Christian community still venerates the two saints.

[70] In 2008 gay Roman Catholic John McNeill wrote: "Gay union rituals were universally found in Church documents as early as the fourth century. Boswell argues that these rituals were true marriage ceremonies. Such ritual celebrations of marriage were possible because gay couples saw each other as equal and based their relation on interpersonal love. In other words, nine centuries before heterosexual marriages were declared a sacrament [Fourth Lateran Council, 1215], the church liturgically celebrated same-sex covenants. . . . Not only did the early Christian Church see same-sex love as holy and worthy of sacramental celebration, they also saw that love as a love that would continue on for all eternity in heaven" (McNeill, *Sex as God Intended*, 128–29).

CONCLUSION

The cumulative evidence from centuries of medieval sources points to the church's unequivocal condemnation of all forms of homosexual practice. As in the patristic era, despite the geographical separation and diverse cultures of early medieval Christians, they shared a commitment to biblically defined sexual ethics. The Christian tradition's consistent message about human sexuality was handed down to medieval believers by monastic missionaries and ecclesiastical authorities.

Boswell's suggestion that Christians in the later Middle Ages were more tolerant of homosexuality than their counterparts in the early Middle Ages is inaccurate. No extant source includes an example of medieval Christians expressing toleration of homosexual behavior.

There was no medieval deviation from patristic teaching concerning the accepted code of Christian sexual morality. The medieval church was no less concerned that biblical sexual ethics be upheld as the standard of conduct for all Christians, including the clergy. Penance for homosexual practice ranged from fasting to castration to the death penalty. Boswell's argument that diversity of penance points to tolerance is confused at best and misleading at worst. In truth, all varieties of homosexual practice were condemned by the medieval church, for those activities were condemned by Scripture, the Fathers, and canon law.

In the late medieval era, when massive collections of earlier Christian writings emerged, the compilers of canon law provided a comprehensive picture of the church's views of homosexual practice. What one observes is a consistent pattern of both denunciation and pastoral care for persons guilty of homosexual sin. Pastoral implementation of penance could restore the guilty person to full fellowship with both God and the church.

The medieval penitential literature and canonical collections point to the unanimity of the church's witness through many centuries. No major shifts in either the theological principles undergirding the censure of homosexual practice or the way the church attempted to care for persons who confessed the sin are found. A fusion of judgment and mercy, to some degree, appears to have been the general pattern of the church's response to homosexual practice.

The medieval material also indicates a distinction among persons who engaged in same-sex acts. Younger boys experimenting with homosexual sex were treated far more leniently than adults, and adults who habitually engaged in homosexual acts were treated more severely than occasional offenders. The texts reveal a medieval awareness that some people felt sexual desire for persons of the same gender, but this did not legitimate acts against nature. Rather, extreme measures were taken to help persons with same-sex attraction avoid eternal damnation, from penance to strict requirements concerning their living arrangements. Homosexuality was not viewed as a psychological disorder: it was sin. While homosexuality may have been characteristic of some persons—an orientation—ethics was not reduced to a psychology of inclinations or orientations; it dealt with actions that proceeded from the wickedness of fallen humanity, a humanity that could be transformed through the work of Christ.

CHAPTER 4

RENAISSANCE AND REFORMATION CONFRONT IMMORALITY

The European Renaissance of the fourteenth to sixteenth centuries has been fertile soil for "queer history" since the 1970s. Numerous gay historians have suggested the rise of homosexual identity and urban gay subcultures during this period. Other gay scholars have critiqued the anachronism of finding distinctive homosexual identity in Renaissance texts. Part of the objection relates to Renaissance era definitions of "sodomy," which these scholars correctly argue had a broad spectrum of meaning and thus was not always connected to the concept of homosexual identity. From another angle lesbian historians point to the challenges of finding any lesbian identity in the Renaissance era because, as they argue, European culture was still patriarchal and heterosexist.[1]

Irrespective of debate about the "queer history" of the Renaissance, it is clear from ecclesiastical texts that the church's opposition to same-sex sexual relations persisted. As homosexual activity appeared to proliferate in Renaissance urban settings, the state responded with legislation to curb the spread of the "unspeakable sin." Remarkably, church and state continued to collaborate in dealing with the "sodomy" problem during this period. While there were civic statutes imposing the death penalty on persons convicted of sodomy, executions were rare and typically reserved for repeat offenders.

The Renaissance spawned what has been called the Christian humanism of northern Europe. Humanists shared with the Italian Renaissance an interest in ancient Greek and Latin texts, especially the writings of the early church fathers. Study of the New Testament's Greek text was renewed as scholars pored over manuscripts, seeking to understand more fully the roots of the

---

[1] See *Queering the Renaissance*, ed. Jonathan Goldberg (Durham, NC: Duke University Press, 1994). This is a collection of essays by gay historians skeptical of the older gay historiography.

Christian tradition. Many humanists, based on their study of Scripture in the original languages, believed church reform was necessary. This emphasis on returning to ancient Christian roots involved a renewed commitment to Christian morality, which included taking seriously biblical texts that forbade homosexual practice. In the sixteenth century the new Protestant movement joined Roman Catholics in condemning same-sex sin among clergy and the general population.

RENAISSANCE FLORENCE

In 1376 Pope Gregory IX stated that there were two abominable sins among the Florentines. One was their "usury and infidelity." The other "is so abominable that I dare not mention it"—he was referring to sodomy.[2] In the fourteenth century, Florence had harsh laws against sodomy, but courts rarely prosecuted the crime unless it involved "violent acts of assault or rape, the violation of young children, sodomy committed together with other crimes, and, less frequently and often only after years of illicit sexual activity, publicly known habitual sodomites."[3]

In the early decades of the fifteenth century, Florentine citizens, government authorities, and ecclesiastical leaders began calling for the curbing of homosexual practice. A legislative proposal in 1403 authorized the *Signoria* (executive body) to devise new statutes "for the elimination and extirpation of this vice and sodomitical crime, and for its purging and its punishment." A 1415 law expressly forbade exile, mutilation, or execution of homosexuals for a first conviction; instead, a fine of 1,000 lire and an optional flogging could be imposed by a judge. A first conviction could also result in the offender being declared ineligible to hold civic office. Only persons convicted a second time could be put to death. Michael Rocke, in his study of homosexuality in Renaissance Florence, comments on this policy:

> Apparently the regime had determined that only by making penalties less cruel and by guaranteeing—up to a point—the physical safety and civic identity of sodomites could it broaden its effective control over sodomy. The pragmatic response marked a sharp departure from the past, and heralded what would come to be the typical approach to policing sodomy in Florence throughout most of the Renaissance.[4]

---

[2] Michael Rocke, *Forbidden Friendships: Homosexuality and Male Culture in Renaissance Florence* (New York, NY: Oxford University Press, 1996), 3.

[3] Ibid., 21–25.

[4] Ibid., 26–32. Sodomy convictions in fifteenth-century Venice also increased. See Guido Ruggiero, *The Boundaries of Eros: Sex Crime and Sexuality in Renaissance Venice*, Studies in the History of Sexuality (New York: Oxford University Press, 1985).

Florence became known throughout Europe for homosexual practice among its citizens. This reputation was not without warrant as Renaissance era studies have exposed a thriving homosexual underground in Florence as well as Florentine literature and songs praising same-sex relations. But despite its proliferation, the vice *contra naturam* was consistently condemned by church and state. Rocke observes:

> If many Florentines not only named the "unmentionable vice" but also commonly practiced it, this does not mean their community as a whole approved of sodomy or accepted it without misgivings. The passion for the classical world that characterized the elite culture of the Italian Renaissance did not, as has sometimes been uncritically assumed, revive some mythic Greek ethos in which sexual relations between males enjoyed widespread and unqualified tolerance. Quite the contrary. Many people, *following the teachings of the Church*, continued to regard sodomy as a serious and potentially destructive sin, and everywhere it remained a crime punishable by severe penalties, including death by burning. Especially in the fifteenth century, the ruling class of the Republic of Florence identified this sexual practice as one of the city's most pressing moral and social problems.[5]

The Franciscan preacher Bernardino of Siena was invited by Florentine leaders to preach during Lent in 1424–25. Known throughout Italy as a powerful preacher and moral reformer, Bernardino used his Lenten sermons to boldly address the sins of the people, including sodomy. Several sermons were directed explicitly at homosexual practice and the dangers it presented. Bernardino expressed concern for the boys of the city who were being enticed into sodomy by men showering them with gifts, clothes, and money. The sermons chastised fathers who allowed their sons to be sodomized by mature men in order to further their own civic careers. Some boys even learned about the vice from their fathers. Mothers too were rebuked, specifically for dressing their sons in fine clothes (like girls), thus making them attractive to homosexual predators. According to Bernardino, some parents allowed their sons to experiment with sex, excusing their sin and not requiring them to attend confession. Young men between the ages of fourteen and twenty-five were especially susceptible to homosexual vice due to youthful lust. Some older men practiced it in their youth but abandoned it for marriage. Other mature men had become set in their attraction to boys and practiced habitual sodomy, Bernardino said.[6]

---

[5] Rocke, *Forbidden Friendships*, 4.

[6] Ibid., 36–39. Rocke comments, "But it is significant that Bernardino also attributed some sodomites' rejection of women to their erotic disposition. Sodomites were not aroused or attracted, in his view, by even the most desirable of women. In a culture and age in which sodomy was usually considered a condition of certain people but a sin that anyone could commit, and men were commonly thought capable of (and can be found) desiring both boys and women,

He also charged homosexuals with hatred of women and children, arguing misogyny was one factor driving the vile practice since some sodomites had sexual tastes only for men and despised women. Preaching on the equal worth of men and women, Bernardino said homosexuals rejected this biblical principle: "Isn't there any sodomite here who dislikes this, and says that woman isn't worth as much as man? . . . We shall speak here of the cursed sodomites, who are so blind in this wickedness of theirs that no matter how beautiful a woman may be, to him she stinks and is displeasing, nor will he ever want to yield to her beauty."[7] In one sermon Bernardino warned fathers not to marry their daughters off to men who habitually practiced sodomy. He charged those engaged in same-sex acts with hating children and rejecting God's plan for procreation, declaring, "When young men are seized by this pestilential ruin, they are hardly ever cured, and scarcely or belatedly, if at all, do they allow themselves to be united in matrimony. If by chance they take a wife, they either abuse her or they do not love her. They do not procreate children."[8] One by-product of this situation, in fact, was a decrease in Florence's population.

The sermons of Bernardino were not mere caricatures of homosexual practice in Florence. Rocke observes, "The wealth of court records in the later part of the century corroborates his [Bernardino's] descriptive remarks." The sermons likely "helped mold public sentiment and dispel indifference about controlling sodomy more vigorously."[9]

A few years after Bernardino's antisodomy sermons, the government of Florence took a significant step toward aggressively policing its city's notorious vice. In 1432 the *Ufficiali di note* (Office of the Night) was established for the purpose of searching out and prosecuting homosexuals in Florence. This unique judicial magistracy was commissioned with the sole task of reigning in the sexual culture of sodomy that saturated the city. The city's central criminal magistracy, the *Otto di guardia* (Watch of Eight), was also involved in sodomy cases during this period, but it was the Office of the Night that relentlessly pursued homosexuals. With hundreds of accusations coming forward each year and significant numbers of sodomy suspects to investigate, the Office of the Night had its hands full.

The Office of the Night functioned for seventy years in Florence, from 1432 to 1502. During these seven decades 17,000 persons in Florence, a city with a population of only 40,000, were accused of sodomy at least once: about 3,000 were convicted. In the last four decades of the fifteenth century, an average of

---

still Bernardino believed that the sexual tastes of at least some sodomites focused one-dimensionally on males and more or less precluded relations with females," 41.

[7] Ibid., 40. See Bernardino of Siena, *Prediche* (Siena, 1427), 410.

[8] Rocke, *Forbidden Friendships*, 41. See Bernardino of Siena, *Opera omnia* 2:83.

[9] Rocke, *Forbidden Friendships*, 36.

400 people were implicated each year and fifty-five to sixty were condemned for homosexual acts.[10] Rocke describes the impact of the Office of the Night:

> Through a combination of intensified surveillance, rapid summary proceedings, and the radical innovations in penalties, the Office of the Night transformed the control of sodomy in Florence. With this magistracy, the government abandoned the previous judiciary praxis of harsh but sporadic punishment directed mainly against violent same-sex rape or child abuse. Instead, it initiated a new regime of routine and fairly mild disciplining of mainly consensual homosexual relations, which were much more diffused.[11]

Dominican preacher and reformer Girolamo Savonarola moved to Florence in 1482 and preached against the immorality he observed there, calling for reform of gambling, drinking, whoring, swearing, and dancing. According to Savonarola, the city's supreme offense against God was the rampant practice of sodomy. He spoke about Florence's infamy throughout Italy for this vice and complained of citizens frequently talking and joking about it. Savonarola urged the authorities to abandon their lenient penalties for homosexual practice.[12]

The authorities heeded his exhortations. A new statute stipulated that those convicted of sodomy before age eighteen were to be punished at the discretion of the Council. Offenders over eighteen were to be pilloried for an hour at the first offense. A second offense would result in being paraded through the street and branded on the forehead. A third conviction would lead to death by burning. Since fines for first offenses were abolished, there was a sharp drop in prosecutions due to the loss of incentives for informers, who had received a share of the money collected. When authorities tried to restore the fines, Savonarola would have none of it.[13] Preaching in the cathedral in 1495, he turned to the government officials seated in a reserved section and said, "I'd like to see you build a nice fire of these sodomites in the piazza, two or three, male and female, because there are also women who practice that damnable vice. I say offer [them as] a sacrifice to God."[14]

Savonarola's severity made numerous enemies among the population of Florence and the curia in Rome. He attacked the prelates and priests of Rome for abusing women, corrupting boys, and practicing sodomy. His numerous prophecies, some of which did come true, were controversial. He was summoned to Rome by Pope Alexander VI, forbidden to preach, and eventually put

---

[10] Ibid., 4.

[11] Ibid., 7.

[12] Donald Weinstein, *Savonarola: The Rise and Fall of a Renaissance Prophet* (New Haven, NJ: Yale University Press, 2011), 154–55.

[13] Ibid., 155–56. His famous political sermon of December 14, 1494, was delivered to a packed audience in the great cathedral.

[14] *Prediche sopra i Salmi* II, 124–25 in Weinstein, 156.

in prison and tried as a heretic. On May 23, 1498, Girolama Savonarola was hanged and burned in the marketplace of Florence as a schismatic and heretic. On the day of his execution, one of the newly elected officials in Florence was said to exclaim, "Praise be to God, now we can practice sodomy."[15]

GERMANY AND SWITZERLAND

In German, *florenzen* meant "to sodomize," and a *florenzer* was one who practiced sodomy. North of the Alps was a different context from fifteenth-century Italy. Homosexual practice was not as prevalent in this part of Europe, and trials for sodomy occurred only occasionally. In court records same-sex intimacy was often described as "heresy" or "unchristian acts." Two clerics were burned by a court in Constance in 1418 for committing "heresy" with each other. In the same city in 1464, a friar and a burgher were prosecuted for "unchristian acts" they committed together. In 1471 four Regensburg men (three artisans, one merchant) who were found guilty of the "sin of unchastity which is called the mute sin against human nature" were decapitated. Compared with other capital crimes, sodomy cases in German and Swiss cities were rare. For example, during the fifteenth century in Zurich, 338 death sentences were issued by the city council. Of these, only five were for same-sex acts.[16]

One ongoing tension in European society concerned clerical immunity from secular prosecution. The church could not sentence anyone to death. Thus, sodomite clerics tried by the church were never executed but only fined or sent into exile. Civic authorities, though they generally honored church rights, were often displeased with this inequity, voicing their concern about church negligence in allowing some immoral clerics to receive little or no punishment. Cities were typically more active in prosecuting same-sex acts than the church. The church, in some instances, seemed to prefer secrecy in prosecuting sodomy among its clergy. In a 1489 judicial case in Lucerne, a threesome was found guilty of homosexual acts. Two laymen were burned to death, but a Benedictine monk was spared after the bishop of Constance applied to the city council for jurisdiction in the monk's case. The council extradited the monk to the bishop, threatening to cease cooperation with the church if the monk was not punished.[17]

---

[15] Roberto Ridolfi, *Life of Girolamo Savonarola*, trans. Cecil Grayson (New York, NY: Alfred A. Knopf, 1959), 288. Ridolfi adds this comment: "It is not difficult to imagine what deeds followed such words. Even the chronicler Parenti, a leading member of the Arrabbiati, and enemy and examiner of the Friar, feared the imminent punishment of God as he narrated the depravities and insults to religion of those times, such as the sacrilegious race run in the Duomo itself, on Christmas Eve, 1499, by [a donkey] with a thick stick suggestively thrust into its rear."

[16] Helmut Puff, *Sodomy in Reformation Germany and Switzerland 1400–1600* (Chicago, IL: University of Chicago Press, 2003), 24–26.

[17] Ibid., 35–42.

Despite church and state tension over punishing homosexual activity, the church helped shape urban legislation and the moral standards of cities. Divine law was a crucial factor in the prosecution of sodomy by city councils of the Holy Roman Empire in the fifteenth and sixteenth centuries. The Sodom and Gomorrah story of the Old Testament, with its fiery judgment from God against male homoeroticism, suggested that cities needed to be cleansed of homosexual activity lest plague and storms come upon them. Maintaining moral order in society was a high priority for magistrates in the imperial cities. Helmut Puff, in his study of sodomy during this era, observes, "Judicial activity against sodomites during the late Middle Ages coincided with the clergy's newly intensified efforts to disseminate the Word of God among laypersons."[18]

In late medieval theology *sodomia* may refer to masturbation, nonprocreative heterosexual intercourse, bestiality, and sexual contact among persons of the same gender. The term *sodomy* was so shameful that clerics were hesitant to use it in sermons or writing, though use in the confessional was a different matter. Public remarks concerning the unmentionable vice ("mute sin") were considered polluting to speaker and hearers alike. An early fifteenth-century catechism, under its treatment of the seventh commandment (forbidding adultery), discussed the different categories of lust and included the one that could not be mentioned. It stated:

> The seventh transgression concerns the command to desire naturally and where nature is naturally inclined to. These are the [sinners] *who pollute themselves with the vice that cannot be named* and of which one cannot speak properly; the [sinners] who sin against nature and [by their sins] do offend the works of nature in whatever form that occurs.[19]

With the invention of printing by the middle of the fifteenth century, devotional material for the masses became available. One devotional work, the anonymous German *Mirror for the Sinner* (c. 1476), addressed the *peccatum contra naturam* ("sin against nature") or *sodomia* as both a capital sin and one condemned by the seventh commandment. The sin was defined as "*where the natural practice of intercourse is reversed*" by people who "*commit the sin against nature with themselves, other humans, or animals.*" The author implored those guilty of these sins to confess, and he warned, "Woe to you, man or woman, that you commit these poisonous things and talk to other humans about them or teach them how to commit these acts."[20]

---

[18] Ibid., 49. Puff argues that community values—more than state repression—drove opposition to homosexual practice.

[19] Ibid., 59. Catechism (*summa*) of Ulrich von Pottenstein (ca. 1360–1417).

[20] Ibid., 62–66. Puff indicates that among northern humanists like Erasmus, censorship often was used to mask the unspeakable sin in translation and classroom instruction. See pp. 70–74.

Court records from two Reformation era Swiss cantons, Zurich (Protestant) and Lucerne (Roman Catholic), offer a glimpse of sixteenth-century male same-sex intimate relations and how authorities responded to the "heresy of sodomy." Judicial cases indicate a subculture in which sexual favors were granted between males for money, clothes, and gifts. During litigation, defendants often blamed those who first seduced them for introducing them to sodomite behavior, some claiming they had been introduced to it by Italians. The guilty typically seemed to believe their conduct was sinful.[21] Prosecution of homosexuals was often the result of community surveillance and outcries that their transgressions threatened the social fabric.[22]

During the sixteenth century in Zurich, a city with a population of about 5,000, there were only eighteen recorded investigations into charges of sodomy. The death sentence was not always decreed for those found guilty. Records indicate that out of 572 total executions in Zurich during the century, only eight people were burned at the stake for committing homosexual acts; three were beheaded. An additional 56 were executed for bestiality. Other penalties for persons convicted of sodomy included exhortation, banishment, and house arrest. In a few cases no punishment is recorded. In Lucerne, a city of about 4,000, twelve sodomy investigations are documented during the same period. Out of 181 death sentences in the city, only seven were for sodomy. Records indicate that executions for sodomy in Lucerne included drowning, decapitation, and burning at the stake.

Catholics and Protestants did not differ significantly in the way they responded to same-sex sexual acts. Often sodomy (and bestiality) was described in legal documents as "unchristian acts." In the Zurich Council's *Book of Punishments*, one gets a glimpse of how sodomy was viewed. One homosexual who coerced an apprentice into sex was executed for "*such an unchristian, shameful, vicious atrocity, malice, knavery, and heresy . . . against divine, Christian, and human law as well as against nature, all honor.*"[23] Summarizing his study of court records for sixteenth-century Zurich and Lucerne, Puff observes: "Authorities in Swiss cities did not prosecute same-sex sexual behavior consistently. When it surfaced, however, it was taken very seriously. . . . Though erotic companionship among men was, as far as one can tell, not uncommon, their sexual acts, once unearthed, were held in harsh condemnation at the local level."[24]

---

[21] Ibid., 76–89. Puff states, "Many a perpetrator seems to have had an acute sense of the danger or sinfulness of his doings," p. 85.

[22] Puff believes state powers were not the key agents in prosecutions of persons who committed homosexual acts; instead, he argues that "governments were sometimes forced to act according to community concerns," p. 87.

[23] Ibid., 94–96.

[24] Ibid., 88–89, 103–4.

PROTESTANT REFORMERS

Both northern humanists and Protestant Reformers of the sixteenth century identified sodomy with Italians. German humanists slandered the Italian humanists as pederasts and ridiculed Italian clergy for committing sodomy. Humanists north of the Alps were more distinctively Christian than their Italian counterparts. Thus, these scholars were unequivocal in their condemnation of sodomy. Humanists like Erasmus recognized the sexual depravity of the ancient Romans and were careful in handling the classical texts to the point of some censorship.[25] Northern Christian humanists detested the clerical sexual immorality that parts of the church had tolerated. In numerous ways the Christian humanists laid a foundation on which Luther built, including their condemnation of sodomy.

The sixteenth-century Protestant Reformers reiterated traditional interpretations of the Bible on homosexual practice. Aware of such activity in their societies, they discreetly condemned it in their writings and commentaries on Scripture. The abominable vice of sodomy was still largely an unmentionable sin among the Christian population, and Protestants were hesitant to depict homosexual conduct explicitly in their writings. It was common knowledge, though, that some who had taken vows of celibacy committed homosexual acts. Protestant leaders condemned this, supporting marriage between one man and one woman as God's design for laity and clergy alike.

LUTHERANS

The Protestant Reformation began with the ministry of Martin Luther in Germany, who challenged the Roman church to reform its doctrine and practice. Luther had been an Augustinian monk and was aware of the immorality among those in holy orders. During a trip to Rome as a young monk, he was shocked at the debauchery he observed among the church hierarchy.[26] The writings of Luther, Melanchthon, and the Lutheran confessions and catechism all address sexual sin.

---

[25] Ibid., 70–74. Puff observes, "While an intellectual elite north of the Alps might have reached out to a pan-European movement of learned literati, as a romanticized view of the past wants us to believe, German humanists also voiced stereotypical slurs concerning Mediterranean sexual depravity," p. 125.

[26] This was not just Luther's opinion. In 1527 Machiavelli wrote, "Nor can we have surer proof of its decay than in witnessing how those countries which are the nearest neighbours of the Roman Church, the head of our faith, have less devoutness than any others; . . . to the Church, therefore, and to the priests, we Italians owe this first debt, that through them we have become wicked and irreligious." Niccolo Machiavelli, *Discourses on the First Decade of Titus Livius*, trans. Ninian Hill Thompson (London: Kegan, Paul, Trench & Co., 1885), 56, accessed March 20, 2015, https://archive.org/details/discoursesonfir00thomgoog.

Commentary on Romans (1552)

In Martin Luther's *Commentary on Romans*, he explained what Paul meant by the notion of dishonoring one's own body (Rom 1:24):

> Very cautiously and by way of paraphrase the Apostle speaks of the per-versions of the heathen, rebuking them with such terms as "uncleanness" and "dishonour." In I Corinthians 6:9, 10 he writes (*more explicitly*): "Be not deceived: neither fornicators, nor idolators, nor adulterers, nor effeminate, nor abusers of themselves with mankind . . . shall inherit the kingdom of God." So also in Ephesians 5:3 and II Corinthians 12:21. Since to honor the body (at least in this one respect) means to be chaste and continent, or to use it properly, *so the abuse of the body, by changing its natural use, means to dishonour it. The body is disgraced and degraded most viciously not only by adultery and similar violations of chastity, but all the more by the degrading perversions (that are here named).*[27]

Commenting in "Lecture on Genesis" on the Sodom and Gomorrah story, Luther wrote:

> They departed from the natural passion and longing of the male for the female, which is implanted into nature by God, and desired what is altogether contrary to nature. Whence comes this perversity? Undoubtedly from Satan, who after people have once turned away from the fear of God, so powerfully suppresses nature that he blots out the natural desire and stirs up a desire that is contrary to nature.[28]

Luther acknowledged that sodomy was practiced in his day, though mostly in secret. He observed:

> So far the ears of the Germans are innocent of and uncontaminated by this monstrous depravity; for even though disgrace, like other sins has crept in through an ungodly soldier and a lewd merchant, still the rest of the people are unaware of what is being done in secret. *The Carthusian monks deserve to be hated because they were the first to bring this terrible pollution into Germany from the monasteries of Italy.*[29]

Luther's *Large Catechism* (1529) noted of the commandment, "You shall not commit adultery,"

> Inasmuch as this commandment is concerned specifically with the estate of marriage and gives occasion to speak of it, let us carefully note, first, how

---

[27] Martin Luther, *Commentary on Romans*, trans. J. Theodore Mueller (Grand Rapids, MI: Kregel, 1954), 47.

[28] Martin Luther, "Lecture on Genesis," *Luther's Works*, ed. Jaroslav Pelikan, vol. 3 (St. Louis, MO: Concordia, 1961), 255.

[29] Ibid., 251–52.

highly God honors and glorifies the married life, sanctioning and protecting it by his commandment. . . . Significantly he established it as the first of all institutions, and he created man and woman differently (as is evident) not for lewdness but to be true to each other, be fruitful, beget children, and support and bring them up to the glory of God. . . . The papal rabble, priests, monks and nuns resist God's order and commandment when they despise and forbid marriage, and boast and vow that they maintain perpetual chastity while they deceive the common people with lying words and wrong impressions. For no one has so little love and inclination for chastity as *those who under the guise of great sanctity avoid marriage and either indulge in open and shameless fornication or secretly in worse—things too evil to mention*, as unfortunately has been only too well proved.[30]

Augsburg Confession (1530)

The *Augsburg Confession*, prepared by Philip Melanchthon in 1530, was among the earliest Lutheran statements of faith. Presented to Charles V and the German princes, it was immediately challenged by a Roman Catholic document, to which Melanchthon replied with a commentary on the original confession, known as the *Apology of the Augsburg Confession*. In both of the Lutheran statements, Article XXIII addressed "The Marriage of Priests" and dealt with the problems caused by enforced celibacy among the clergy, one of which was homosexual practice.

> Among all people, both of high and of low degree, there has been a loud complaint throughout the world concerning the flagrant immorality and dis-solute life of priests who were not able to remain continent and *who went so far as to engage in abominable vices*. . . . The vow of celibacy has been the cause of so much frightful and unchristian offense, so much adultery, and such terrible, *shocking immorality and abominable vice* that even some honest men among the cathedral clergy and some of the courtiers in Rome have often acknowledged this and have complained that such vices among the clergy would, on account of the abomination and prevalence, arouse the wrath of God.[31]

Apology of the Augsburg Confession (1531)

> We have many reasons for rejecting the law of perpetual celibacy. But even if the law were not unjust, it is dangerous to public and private morals; this alone should keep good men from approving a burden that has destroyed so many souls. . . . It is no secret how harmful this law has been to public morals and how productive of vices and shameful lusts. . . . The destruction

---

[30] *The Book of Concord*, trans. and ed. Theodore Tappert (Philadelphia, PA: Fortress, 1959), 393–94.

[31] Ibid., 51, 54.

in the flood and the burning of Sodom and Gomorrah reveal God's wrath at human vice. Similar vices have preceded the fall of many other cities, like Sybaris and Rome.[32]

Loci Communes, Philip Melanchthon (1543)

Melanchthon said of the commandment, "You shall not commit adultery,"

> It condemns all cohabitation outside of legitimate marriage and sets forth penalties in this life and eternal torments after this life. . . . God is angry at all impurities and He either severely chastises or completely destroys those who do not respect [this commandment], as the Sodomites were destroyed. Not only were those five cities destroyed for this reason, but the evil desires of every nation gave occasion for the destruction of many others. . . . We should study these examples, apply them to ourselves as warnings from God, and resolve to be obedient to this precept and to fight against the flames of illicit desire.[33]

REFORMED TRADITION

The Reformed Tradition consistently renounced homosexual practice. When addressing the seventh commandment, Reformed writers typically listed homosexuality as one of the sexual sins condemned.

Common Places (1527), Martin Bucer, "Commentary on the Four Holy Gospels"

> Undertaking celibacy in the pursuit of physical ease is a carnal desire that advances one's own interest, not God's, and is entirely divorced from "making oneself a eunuch for the sake of the kingdom of heaven." The monks even give proof of this fact by assailing the kingdom of heaven, that is, the faith of Christ and the gospel, more fiercely than anyone else. Their life too is further proof; it is *fouler than Sodom's, so far are they from seeking even celibacy.* All their ways are nothing but hypocrisy, zeal for the belly and a fine reputation. . . . If anyone who lacks the gift attempts to live without a wife or husband, in his ungodly contempt of his true vocation he will expose himself to the danger of unchastity, and thereby he will never attain to God. . . . The man privileged not to need a wife cannot avoid embracing celibacy with the greatest joy. So let every man dedicate himself to the will of God and be ready to serve the glory of God in the calling the Father has laid upon him, and all will be well. But let no one be self-seeking or despise God's calling, however lowly it may be.[34]

---

[32] Ibid., 246.

[33] Philip Melanchthon, *Loci Communes* 154, trans. J. A. O. Preus (St. Louis, MO: Concordia, 1992), 68.

[34] "Marriage, Divorce and Celibacy" in *Common Places of Martin Bucer*, trans. and ed. D. F. Wright (Appleford, England: Sutton Courtney, 1972), 423–24. Martin Bucer was a leader of

Decades (1550), Heinrich Bullinger, "Seventh Precept of the Ten Commandments"

The *abominable sin of sodomy*, and meddling with beasts, also is plainly forbidden: against which we have most evident and express laws set down in the eighteenth and twentieth chapters of Leviticus. We have also a very severe, but yet a most just, punishment laid by God himself upon the pates of the *detestable Sodomites*: for with fire and stinking brimstone sent down from heaven he consumed those filthy men to dust and ashes; which ashes he washed away with the waves of the Dead Sea, because he would not have so much as the very cinders to remain of so wicked men. Moreover, their whole cites and fruitful fields were burnt with fire. For it was not requisite that any one jot of the substance of those most wicked men should remain undestroyed. The place where those cities sometime were situated is at this day overflown with water, and called the Dead Sea. Whereby we do consequently gather, that *the most just God will not spare the Gentiles, entangled in the very same sin, although for a time he wink at and dissemble it. Fire shall destroy both them and theirs; and they themselves shall for ever burn in hell, where nothing shall remain of them but a reproachful memory.* For in the Revelation of our Lord Jesus Christ to his apostle John we read: "And fire came down from God out of heaven, and devoured them; and the devil, which deceived them, was cast into a lake of fire and brimstone, where the beast and the false prophet shall be tormented day and night for evermore." Apoc. xx.[35]

More reserved than Luther, John Calvin seldom spoke directly about homosexual practice, but he did reference the topic when it arose in his preaching and teaching through the Scriptures. Like humanists and Luther he detested the pervasive immorality among some priests. According to Calvin homosexual practice is an indication of God's judgment; women and men are handed over by God to same-sex lust.

Institutes of the Christian Religion (1559), John Calvin

Today there is no order of men more notorious in excess, effeminacy, voluptuousness, in short, in all sorts of lusts; . . . I seem to be saying

---

the Reformed churches in southern Germany and Switzerland. He had close contact with the Lutherans in his early ministry. A young John Calvin was shaped by Bucer when they spent several years together between Calvin's two sojourns in Geneva. In the final few years of his life, Bucer moved to England, serving as regius professor of divinity at Cambridge.

[35] *The Decades of Heinrich Bullinger*, ed. Thomas Harding, vol. 1 (Grand Rapids, MI: Reformation Heritage, 2004), 418. Bullinger's *Decades* (fifty sermons) was popular in Elizabethan England, going through seventy-seven printings between 1550 and 1560. When Ulrich Zwingli was killed by Roman Catholic troops in 1531, Bullinger became the key Protestant leader in Zurich.

something unbelievable—so far has that former discipline fallen into disuse which enjoined a more exacting censure of the conduct of clergy.[36]

Commentary on the Epistle of Paul the Apostle to the Romans, John Calvin

> He brings as the first example, the dreadful crime of unnatural lust; and it hence appears that they not only abandoned themselves to beastly lusts, but became degraded beyond the beast, since they reversed the whole order of nature. . . . Paul here records those abominations which had been common in all ages, and were at that time especially prevalent everywhere; for it is marvellous how common then was that filthiness which even brute beasts abhor; and some of these vices were even popular. . . . He calls those disgraceful passions, which are shameful even in the estimation of men, and redound to the dishonouring of God.[37]

Calvin tied the Sodom story in Genesis 19 with Paul's argument in Romans 1. He commented:

> Here, in a single crime, Moses sets before our eyes a lively picture of Sodom. . . . They were not contaminated with one vice only, but were given up to all audacity in crime, so that no sense of shame was left them. And Ezekiel . . . accurately describes from what beginnings of evil they had proceeded to this extreme turpitude (Ezekiel xvi.49.) What Paul says, also refers to this same point: that God punished the impiety of men, when he cast them into such a state of blindness, that they gave themselves up to abominable lusts, and dishonoured their own bodies. (Rom.i.18.)[38]

The Heidelberg Catechism (1563)

> Can those who do not turn to God from their ungrateful, impenitent life be saved? The answer: Certainly not! Scripture says, "Surely you know that the unjust will never come into possession of the kingdom of God. Make no mistake: no fornicator or idolater, none who are guilty either of adultery or of homosexual perversion, no thieves or grabbers or drunkards or slanderers or swindlers, will possess the kingdom of God."[39]

---

[36] John Calvin, Institutes of the Christian Religion IV.5.14, ed. John T. McNeill, trans. Ford Lewis Battles, vol. 2 (Philadelphia, PA: Westminster Press, 1960), 1097.

[37] John Calvin, Calvin's Commentaries on the Epistle of Paul the Apostle to the Romans, trans. John Owen, Calvin's Commentaries, vol. 19 (repr., Grand Rapids, MI: Baker, 1979), 79.

[38] John Calvin, Commentaries on the First Book of Moses Called Genesis, trans. John King, Calvin's Commentaries, vol. 1 (repr., Grand Rapids, MI: Baker, 1979), 496–97.

[39] Question 87, in Confessions and Catechisms of the Reformation, ed. Mark A. Noll (Grand Rapids, MI: Baker, 1991), 155. Noll cites the translation published by United Church Press in 1962 as a 400th anniversary edition, which added the phrase "homosexual perversion." This translation was justified based on the citation of 1 Cor 6:9–10 as a marginal proof text. Jack Rogers makes a reasonable case for omitting the expression "homosexual perversion," but he

In a later question the *Heidelberg Catechism* dealt with the application of the seventh commandment to heterosexual married life and celibacy: "Q. 108: What does the seventh commandment teach us? Answer: "That all unchastity is condemned by God, and that we should therefore detest it from the heart, and *live chaste and disciplined lives, whether in holy wedlock or in single life*."[40]

The Second Helvetic Confession (1566)

> For marriage (which is the medicine of incontinency, and continency itself) was instituted by the Lord God himself, who blessed it most bounti- fully, and willed man and woman to cleave one to the other inseparably, and to live together in complete love and concord (Matt. 19:4ff). Whereupon we know the apostle said: "Let marriage be held in honor among all, and let the marriage bed be undefiled" (Heb. 13:4). . . . We also *detest an impure single life, the secret and open lusts and fornications of hypocrites pretending to be continent* when they are the most incontinent of all. All these God will judge.[41]

ANABAPTISTS

A number of Anabaptist groups, sometimes referred to collectively as the "Radical Reformation," emerged independently throughout Europe. Known for their commitment to holiness of life and the exercise of church discipline (the "ban"), Anabaptists taught their followers to forsake the sins of the flesh in obedience to Christ.

The New Birth (1537), Menno Simons

> Tell me, dearly beloved, where and when did you read in the Scriptures, the true witness of the Holy Ghost and criterion of our consciences, that the unbelieving, disobedient, carnal man, the adulterous, immoral, drunken, avaricious, idolatrous, and pompous man has one single promise of the kingdom of Christ and His church, yes, part or communion in His merits, death, and blood? I tell you the truth, nowhere and never do we read it in the Scriptures. But thus it is written by Paul: For if ye live after the flesh ye shall die. Adulterers, whoremongers, *perverts, effeminate*, unclean, idolaters,

---

acknowledges that 1 Cor 6:9–10 in the margin refers to "male prostitutes" and "sodomites." See Jack Rogers, *Jesus, the Bible, and Homosexuality* (Louisville, KY: Westminster/John Knox, 2009), 111–16. Rogers claims, "The Reformed confessions, properly translated, say nothing about homosexuality" (p. 60). This statement is not accurate. For example, see the *Westminster Larger Catechism*, question 139 cited in this chapter.

[40] Ibid., 160.

[41] *The Second Helvetic Confession*, chapter XXIX in The *Book of Confessions* (Louisville, KY: The Office of the General Assembly Presbyterian Church [U.S.A.], 1991), 5.246, 5.251.

drunkards, proud, avaricious, hateful persons, betrayers, and those who shed innocent blood; thieves, murderers, and those who know no mercy, those disobedient to God and Christ, will not inherit the kingdom of God unless they repent. Yes, their portion will be in the fiery lake which burns with fire and brimstone, which is the second death [1 Cor 6:9-11].[42]

ANGLICANS AND PURITANS

During the reign of Henry VIII, under the leadership of Thomas Cromwell, Parliament began to give the Church of England authority over legislation that had been the domain of the Roman Catholic Church in England. Some of that legislation dealt with sodomy.

Act in Restraint of Appeals (1533)

Forasmuch as there is not yet sufficient and condign punishment appointed and limited by the due course of the Laws of this Realm, for *the detestable and abominable Vice of Buggery [sodomy] committed with mankind or beasts*: It may therefore please the King's Highness, with the assent of his Lords spiritual and temporal, and the Common of this present Parliament assembled, that it may be enacted by authority of the same, that the same offence be from henceforth adjudge Felony, and such order and form of process therein to be used against the offenders, as in cases of Felony at the Common-law. And that offenders being hereof convict by verdict, confession, or outlawry, shall suffer such pains of death, and losses, and penalties of their goods, chattel, debts, land tenements and hereditaments, as Felons be accustomed to doe according to the order of the Common-laws of this Realm. And that *no person offending in any such offence, shall be admitted to his Clergy*, And that Justices of the Peace shall have power and authority, within the limits of their commissions and Jurisdictions, to hear and determine the said offence, as they do use to doe in cases of other Felonies. This Act to endure till the last day of the next Parliament.[43]

---

[42] *The Complete Works of Menno Simons*, trans. Leonard Verduin (Scottsdale, PA: Herald, 1986), 89–90.

[43] 25 Henry VIII c. 6 text in E. Gilson, *Codex Juris Ecclesiastici Anglici*, vol. 2 (Oxford, 1761), 1,080, translated into modern English in Bailey, *Homosexuality and the Western Theological Tradition*, 147–48. This was the first civil regulation in England on unnatural sex acts. Of the thousands of executions that took place during Henry VIII's reign, none have been proven a result of this statute. See H. Montgomery Hyde, *The Love That Dare Not Speak Its Name* (Boston, MA: Little, Brown, 1970), 40. The act was repealed twice but was reinstated by Elizabeth I (with modifications) in 1563. It remained a law in England for three centuries. The rationale for bringing back the sodomy law was "divers evil disposed persons have been the more bold to commit the said most horrible and detestable Vice of Buggery aforesaid, to the high displeasure of God." Bailey, 149–50. For an overview of homosexuality in England during this era, see Alan Bray, *Homosexuality in Renaissance England* (London, England: Gay Men's Press, 1982).

The Marrow of Theology (1629), William Ames, "Chastity"

Marriage of its own nature has a certain purity as an ordinance from God and by virtue of that ordinance becomes the means to preserve purity and chastity. 19. Marriage is the individual joining of one man and woman by lawful consent for a mutual communication of their bodies and community of life together. 20. It is *one man and one woman*, Gen. 2:22; Mal. 2:15; Matt. 19:4; 1 Cor. 7:2; Lev. 18:18. . . . 39. The joining is for bodily communication because in marriage godly offspring are first sought, Mal. 2:15. Marriage secondarily offers a remedy against the carnal desires which many without a special gift for continency have had since the fall of Adam; and these desires are so unbridled that unless help comes from this remedy men burn, so to speak, making them unfit for pious duties. They run headlong into unlawful evil unions, 1 Cor. 7:2, 9. . . . 44. Dissipation is opposed to chastity in the stricter sense, in that it is the illicit use of the things pertaining to procreation. In this sense it is called *Impurity, inordinate affection, evil concupiscence*, Col. 3:5; *lasciviousness*, Rom. 13:13; and the *Disease of concupiscence*, 1 Thess. 4:5. . . . 48. There are various kinds of dissipation: first, whoredom, or the union of an unmarried man with an unmarried woman. 1 Cor. 6:16, whether it be lewdness, the deflowering of a woman otherwise honourable, or fornication, which involves a dishonourable woman or prostitute. Second, adultery, in which at least one of the offending persons is married or betrothed. Third, incest or a union of those who are near in the flesh. Fourth, rape, when force is added to dissipation. Fifth, *any coition against nature*.[44]

The Sincere Convert (1641), Thomas Shepard

The heart is a foul sink of all atheism, *sodomy*, blasphemy, murder, whoredom, adultery, witchcraft, *buggery*; so that if thou hast any good thing in thee, it is but as a drop of rosewater in a bowl of poison; where fallen it is all corrupted.[45]

Westminster Confession of Faith (1647)

I. *Marriage is to be between one man and one woman*: neither is it lawful for any man to have more than one wife, nor for any woman to have more than one husband at the same time. II. Marriage was ordained for the mutual help of husband and wife; for the increase of mankind with a legitimate issue, and of the Church with an holy seed: and for preventing uncleanness.[46]

---

[44] William Ames, *The Marrow of Theology*, trans. and ed. John D. Eusden (Durham, NC: Labyrinth, 1983), 318–20.

[45] Thomas Shepard, *The Works of Thomas Shepard*, vol. 1 (Boston, MA: Doctrinal Tract and Book Society, 1853), 28, accessed March 19, 2015, https://archive.org/stream/worksofthomasshe01 shep#page/28/mode/2up.

[46] *Westminster Confession of Faith* in *The Creeds of Christendom*, ed. Philip Schaff, vol. 3 (repr., Grand Rapids, MI: Baker, 1993), 655. James Brownson argues the *Westminster*

Westminster Larger Catechism (1648)

In seventeenth-century England the *Westminster Larger Catechism* inter-preted the seventh commandment's prohibition of adultery to include the sin of sodomy:

> Q. 139: What particular sins does the seventh commandment forbid? The answer: In addition to failing to do what is required, the seventh command-ment forbids: adultery, fornication, rape, incest, *sodomy and all unnatural desires.*[47]

ROMAN CATHOLIC REFORM

In the sixteenth century Catholics and Protestants had intense disagreements over original sin, justification, the Mass, and a host of other issues. However, they agreed the church must deal with immorality among the clergy. It was public knowledge that some priests visited prostitutes, harbored concubines, and practiced homosexuality. Leo X (who published the infamous Papal Bull against Luther) convened the Fifth Lateran Council (1512–17), which issued a decree against clerical sexual immorality, including homosexual practice.

Fifth Lateran Council (1514)

> In order that clerics, especially, may live in continence and chastity according to canonical legislation, we rule that offenders be severely pun-ished as the canons lay down. *If anyone, lay or cleric, has been found guilty of a charge on account of which the wrath of God comes upon the sons of disobedience, let him be punished by the penalties respectively imposed by the sacred canons or by civil law.* Those involved in concubinage, whether they be lay or cleric, are to be punished by the penalties of the same canons.

Confession is here prohibiting polygamy and incest, not making an argument for marriage based on the "gender complementarity" of male and female. He conveniently skips over the fact that the textual reference is to Gen 1:27, which is clearly about gender complementarity, for God commands Adam and Eve to "be fruitful and multiply" (Gen 1:28). Also of interest in this sec-tion of the *Westminster Confession* is its acknowledgement that preventing sexual "uncleanness" is one purpose of marriage. When the Westminster divines defined sexual uncleanness, they explicitly mentioned "sodomy" in Larger Catechism Question 139. See James V. Brownson, *Bible, Gender, and Sexuality* (Grand Rapids, MI: Eerdmans, 2013), 266n2.

[47] *The Westminster Confession of Faith and Catechisms in Modern English* (Summertown, TN: Summertown Company, 2005), 116. Jack Rogers attempts to diminish the force of this language by arguing that the word *sodomy* was used to describe "sexual acts not open to procre-ation and as such applied to heterosexual as well as homosexual behavior." Rogers, *Jesus, the Bible and Homosexuality* (Louisville, KY: Westminster/John Knox, 2009), 205n47. While he is correct that historically the term *sodomy* has been used broadly, that was not how it was used in the *Westminster Larger Catechism*. The proof texts for "sodomy, and all unnatural lusts" in the *Larger Catechism* are Rom 1:26–27 and Lev 20:15–16, which explicitly describe homosexual behavior. See *The Constitution of the Presbyterian Church* (U.S.A.), Part I: *Book of Confessions* (Louisville, KY: The Office of the General Assembly, 1991), 7.249; endnote 4 for Q.139.

Concubinage is not to be allowed by the tolerance of superiors, or as an evil custom of a great number of sinners, which should rather be called a corruption, or under any other excuse; but let those involved be punished severely in accordance with the judgment of the law.[48]

The Catholic Holy Roman emperor Charles V enacted the following legislation in 1532:

If anyone commits impurity with a beast, or *man with a man, or a woman with a woman*, they have forfeited their lives and shall, after the common custom, be sentenced to death by burning. (*Constitution Criminalis Carolina*)[49]

Council of Trent (1545–63)
At the Council of Trent, the Roman Church dealt with immorality among the clergy, especially clerics who kept concubines. The bishops confirmed that habitual sexual sin could exclude one from the kingdom of God and that priests must be an example to the flock in their moral conduct.

Defending the doctrine of the divine law, which excludes from the kingdom of God not only unbelieving, but the faithful also (who are) fornicators, adulterers, *effeminate, liers with mankind*, thieves, covetous, drunkards, railers, extortioners, and all others who commit deadly sins. (Sixth Session, Chapter XV)[50]

And with what freedom shall priests be able to correct laymen, when they have to answer silently to themselves, that they have committed the very things which they reprove? Wherefore, bishops shall charge their clergy, of whatsoever rank they be, that they be a guide to the people of God committed to them, in conduct, conservation and doctrine; being mindful of that which is written, Be holy for I also am Holy. (Session 14, "Decree of Reformation")[51]

In his massive volume, *Law, Sex, and Christian Society in Medieval Europe,* James A. Brudage summarizes Catholic and Protestant perspectives on "deviant sexuality" in the age of the Reformation:

---

[48] *Fifth Lateran Council*, Session 9, May 5, 1514, accessed March 19, 2015, http://www.ewtn.com/library/COUNCILS/LATERAN5.HTM#1. This text is referencing Ephesians 5 and Romans 1 where the wrath of God comes upon the sexually immoral, explicitly those who practice homosexuality in Romans 1.

[49] *Die Peinliche Gerichsordnung Kaiser Karls V. von 1532* (Carolina), ed. Arthur Kaaufmann (Stuttgart, Germany: Reclam, 1996), 81, translated by Puff, *Sodomy in Reformation Germany and Switzerland, 1400–1600*, 29.

[50] *The Canons and Decrees of the Sacred and Oecumenical Council of Trent*, ed. and trans. J. Waterworth (London, England: Dolaman, 1848), 42.

[51] Ibid., 111.

Sixteenth- and seventeenth-century canon law and theology showed few novelties in their treatment of deviant sexual behaviour. By and large the older condemnations continued in force, and both Catholic and Protestant writers agreed that homosexual acts should be punished severely. Writers and judges seem to have been more concerned with lesbian behaviour in this period than was true earlier. Some scattered prosecutions for sexual relations between women have come to light in recent years and, while there are not many of them, they greatly outnumber those known from any earlier century in the Middle Ages. Similarly, transvestite behaviour seems to have concerned authorities during this period and to have been punished much more severely than was common previously.[52]

CONCLUSION

The Italian Renaissance, though noteworthy among gay historians for the proliferation of homosexual practice, was not an era of social toleration of homoerotic behavior. While there is evidence of increased homosexual activity in Florence, it was not condoned by Florentine citizens or the church. In fact, city government in Florence sought to curb homosexual acts, revising laws repeatedly in efforts to find effective ways to police such conduct. Reforming preachers in Italy condemned sexual sin, calling for the purging of sinners who corrupted their communities.

The Florentine situation was repeated throughout Europe as sovereigns and civil governments sought to curtail the "vice against nature." Among Renaissance-era Christian populations there was a fear of God's swift judgment against societies that did not condemn homosexual behavior. Europeans were aware that sodomy was being practiced in dark corners, and there were civil and ecclesiastical attempts to curb its proliferation and to punish perpetrators.

The Protestant Reformers were reticent to speak explicitly about homosexual activity. Sodomy was still considered an unmentionable sin too crass for public discourse. The Reformers primarily addressed the issue when it arose in the exposition of Scripture or in catechisms that dealt with the Ten Commandments. It seems homosexual practice was not a major concern of the Reformers, although they were aware of its existence and that it was a problem among the Roman clergy.

Sixteenth-century Protestant commentaries on biblical texts addressing homosexuality did not differ from the writings of ancient and medieval commentators on Scripture. Nor was there any discernible difference between Catholics and Protestants regarding the topic. Old and New Testament texts

---

[52] James A. Brundage, *Law, Sex, and Christian Society in Medieval Europe* (Chicago, IL: University of Chicago Press, 1987), 570–71. On lesbian practice he cites the case of Benedetta Carlini, described in Judith C. Brown, *Immodest Acts: The Life of a Lesbian Nun in Renaissance Italy* (New York, NY: Oxford University Press, 1986), 117–28.

were straightforward in condemning all same-sex sexual activity, as were the church fathers. Thus, the Protestant movement reaffirmed what had always been Christian teaching on this subject.

Sixteenth-century Catholic reform efforts addressed many areas of disorder within Catholicism, including the moral corruption of clergy. The canons of Trent and other papal decrees of the period dealt with the practice of sodomy among priests, calling for the swift discipline of the guilty.

In contrast to the sixteenth-century Catholic and Protestant consensus, there has been a concerted contemporary effort to distinguish between acceptable and unacceptable forms of homosexuality. Just as sexual relations between married heterosexuals are God honoring, gay scholars argue, likewise monogamous, long-term, loving homosexual relationships are legitimate expressions of human sexuality. Where supposed Christians have deserted spouses and children to pursue homosexual relationships, the adultery should be excused (some say) because the adulterous partners were homosexual all along and are now pursuing faithful relationships with same-sex partners. Present-day clergy participating in this immoral madness would be doubly condemned for adultery and homosexual practice by the Reformation-era church.

The Modern Church and the Homosexual Crisis

CHAPTER 5

ROMAN CATHOLICS AND THE ORTHODOX ON HISTORIC FAITH

B eginning with this chapter, attention will shift to contemporary Christian perspectives. The present chapter will survey the Roman Catholic and Eastern Orthodox traditions. Next will come a chapter on contemporary evangelical Protestants, followed by a concluding chapter on mainline Protestant denominations that have recently departed from traditional Christian practice. Together the three chapters will provide the big picture of where the church currently stands on the homosexual crisis of the twenty-first century.

The present chapter will look at the two traditions collectively representing the majority of global Christianity today; together they have one and a half billion members worldwide, and Roman Catholics remain the largest Christian group in the United States with about seventy-five million members. These faith traditions have in contemporary times reaffirmed the ancient church's stance on homosexual practice. In these faiths one observes a firm commitment to continuity with the historic church. The faith and practice of the church handed down through the centuries is essential to authentic Christianity for these faith traditions. On the subject of homosexuality, the Roman Catholic and Orthodox traditions have been a beacon of light reminding Protestants that the testimony of the saints is a substantive voice to be heard alongside the authoritative voice of Scripture.

ROMAN CATHOLICS

A *Code of Canon Law* issued by Pope Benedict XV in 1917 stipulated that laymen and clergy in minor orders [that is, lower than a deacon] and clerics in sacred orders [deacons, priests, and bishops] guilty of sexual sins, including sodomy, were "by that fact infamous" and subject to church censures. Laymen who committed homosexual acts likewise were censured by the church, which understood the seventh commandment (*You shall not commit adultery*) to include a prohibition of sodomy. Roman Catholics number the Ten Commandments according to an ancient pattern established by Augustine, which makes the prohibition of adultery the sixth commandment. Three canons of Benedict XV's code addressed the issue.

Code of Canon Law (1917), Pope Benedict XV

> Laity legitimately convicted of a delict against the sixth [commandment of the Decalogue] with a minor below the age of sixteen, or of debauchery, *sodomy*, incest, or pandering, are by that fact infamous, besides other penalties that the Ordinary decides should be inflicted.
>
> A cleric constituted in minor order [who is] a respondent in some delict against the sixth precept of the Decalogue shall be punished for the gravity of the fault even with dismissal from the clerical state.
>
> Clerics in sacred [orders] . . . If they engage in a delict against the sixth precept of the Decalogue with a minor below sixteen, or engage in adultery, debauchery, bestiality, *sodomy*, pandering, incest with blood-relatives or affines in first degree, they are suspended, declared infamous, and are deprived of any office, benefice, dignity, responsibility, if they have such, whatsoever, and in more serious cases, they are to be deposed.[1]

The late twentieth century was a time of vicious attack against Roman Catholicism by Western cultural elites.[2] Much of this centered on moral issues on which Catholicism was unwilling to abandon historic Christianity in order to appease its postmodern critics. Faced with such attacks, Catholics remained stalwart for Christian orthopraxis in societies advocating the legalization and acceptance of homosexuality. In 1975, the Sacred Congregation for the Doctrine of the Faith adopted the document *Persona Humana*, which spoke to the topic of human sexuality, including homosexuality. Pope Paul VI approved the declaration "on certain questions concerning sexual ethics" and ordered its publication. The text clearly affirms the historic understanding of Scripture while also encouraging pastoral care for homosexuals.

---

[1] Canons 2257–2359, in *The 1917 or Pio-Benedictine Code of Canon Law in English Translation* (San Francisco, CA: Ignatius, 2001), 748–49.

[2] See Philip Jenkins, *The New Anti-Catholicism: The Last Acceptable Prejudice* (New York, NY: Oxford University Press, 2004).

Persona Humana (1975), Sacred Congregation of the Faith

At the present time there are those who, basing themselves on observations in the psychological order, have begun to judge indulgently, and even to excuse completely, homosexual relations between certain people. This they do in opposition to the constant teaching of the Magisterium and to the moral sense of the Christian people. . . . In the pastoral field, these homosexuals must certainly be treated with understanding and sustained in the hope of overcoming their personal difficulties and their inability to fit into society. Their culpability will be judged with prudence. But no pastoral method can be employed which would give moral justification to these acts on the grounds that they would be consonant with the condition of such people. For according to the objective moral order, homosexual relations are acts which lack an essential and indispensable finality. *In Sacred Scripture they are condemned as a serious depravity and even presented as the sad consequence of rejecting God (Rom. 1:24–27; cf. also 1 Cor. 6:10, 1 Tim. 1:10). This judgment of Scripture does not of course permit us to conclude that all those who suffer from this anomaly are personally responsible for it, but it does attest to the fact that homosexual acts are intrinsically disordered and can in no case be approved.*[3]

A decade later Joseph Cardinal Ratzinger [Pope Benedict XVI], serving as prefect of the Congregation for the Doctrine of the Faith, wrote a *Letter to the Bishops of the Catholic Church on the Pastoral Care of Homosexual Persons.* The letter's purpose was to deal with a misinterpretation of the 1975 document; some Catholics had suggested that the distinction between the homosexual condition and individual actions implied that the homosexual condition was "neutral, or even good." Cardinal Ratzinger and the Congregation reiterated that the homosexual tendency or condition is "intrinsically disordered." The 1986 Letter to Bishops, approved for publication by Pope John Paul II, succinctly addressed a multitude of questions surrounding the Catholic Church and homosexuality.

Letter to the Bishops of the Catholic Church on the Pastoral Care of Homosexual Persons (1986), Congregation for the Doctrine of the Faith

An essential dimension of authentic pastoral care is the identification of causes of confusion regarding the Church's teaching. One is a new exegesis of Sacred Scripture which claims variously that Scripture has nothing to say on the subject of homosexuality, or that it somehow tacitly approves of it, or that all of its moral injunctions are so culture-bound that they are no longer applicable to contemporary life. These views are gravely erroneous. . . . The

---

[3] Roman Catholic Church, *Persona Humana: Declaration on Certain Questions Concerning Sexual Ethics,* Par. VIII, accessed September 27, 2014, http://www.vatican.va/roman_curia/congregations/cfaith/documents/rc_con_cfaith_doc_19751229_persona-humana_en.html.

Church today addresses the Gospel to a world which differs in many ways from ancient days. But the world in which the New Testament was written was already quite diverse from the situation in which the Sacred Scriptures of the Hebrew People had been written or compiled. *What should be noticed is that, in the presence of such remarkable diversity, there is nevertheless a clear consistency within the Scriptures themselves on the moral issue of homosexual behavior. The Church's doctrine regarding this issue is thus based, not on isolated phrases for facile theological argument, but on the solid foundation of a constant Biblical testimony.* The community of faith today, in unbroken continuity with the Jewish and Christian communities within which the ancient Scriptures were written, continues to be nourished by those same Scriptures and by the Spirit of Truth whose Word they are. *It is likewise essential to recognize that the Scriptures are not properly understood when they are interpreted in a way which contradicts the Church's living Tradition. To be correct, the interpretation of Scripture must be in substantial accord with that Tradition.* (par. 4–5)

In Genesis 3, we find that this truth about persons being made in the image of God has been obscured by original sin. . . . In Genesis 19:1–11, the deterioration due to sin continues in the story of the men of Sodom. There can be no doubt of the moral judgement made there against homosexual relations. In Leviticus 18:22 and 20:13, in the course of describing the conditions necessary for belonging to the Chosen People, the author excludes from the People of God those who behave in a homosexual fashion.

Against the background of this exposition of theocratic law, an eschatological perspective is developed by St. Paul when, in 1 Cor. 6:9, he proposes the same doctrine and lists those who behave in a homosexual fashion among those who shall not enter the Kingdom of God.

In Romans 1:18–32, still building on the moral traditions of his forebears, but in the new context of the confrontation between Christianity and the pagan society of his day, Paul uses homosexual behavior as an example of the blindness which has overcome humankind. . . . Finally, 1 Tim. 1, in full continuity with the Biblical position, singles out those who spread wrong doctrine and in v.10 explicitly names as sinners those who engage in homosexual acts. . . . *Thus, the Church's teaching today is in organic continuity with the Scriptural perspective and with her own constant Tradition. Though today's world is in many ways quite new, the Christian community senses the profound and lasting bonds which join us to those generations who have gone before us, "marked with the sign of faith."* (par. 6, 8)

The Church, obedient to the Lord who founded her and gave to her the sacramental life, celebrates the divine plan of the loving and life-giving union of men and women in the sacrament of marriage. *It is only in the marital relationship that the use of the sexual faculty can be morally good. A person engaging in homosexual behavior therefore acts immorally.* (par. 7)

It has been argued that the homosexual orientation in certain cases is not the result of deliberate choice; and so the homosexual person would then have no choice but to behave in a homosexual fashion. Lacking freedom, such a person, even if engaged in homosexual activity, would not be culpable. . . . What at all costs to be avoided is the unfounded and demeaning assumption that the sexual behavior of homosexual persons is always and totally compulsive and therefore inculpable. What is essential is that the fundamental liberty which characterizes the human person and gives him his dignity be recognized as belonging to the homosexual person as well. *As in every conversion from evil, the abandonment of homosexual activity will require a profound collaboration of the individual with God's liberating grace.* (par. 11)

What, then, are homosexual persons to do who seek to follow the Lord? Fundamentally, they are called to enact the will of God in their life by joining whatever sufferings and difficulties they experience in virtue of their condition to the sacrifice of the Lord's Cross. . . . The Cross is a denial of self, but in service to the will of God himself who makes life come from death and empowers those who trust in him to practice virtue in place of vice. . . . *Just as the Cross was central to the expression of God's redemptive love for us in Jesus, so the conformity of the self-denial of homosexual men and women with the sacrifice of the Lord will constitute for them a source of self-giving which will save them from a way of life which constantly threatens to destroy them. Christians who are homosexual are called, as all of us are, to a chaste life.* (par. 12)

We encourage the Bishops, then, to provide pastoral care in full accord with the teaching of the Church for homosexual persons of their dioceses. No authentic pastoral programme will include organizations in which homosexual persons associate with each other without clearly stating that homosexual activity is immoral. A truly pastoral approach will appreciate the need for homosexual persons to avoid the near occasions of sin. We would heartily encourage programmes where these dangers are avoided but we wish to make it clear that departure from the Church's teaching, or silence about it, in an effort to provide pastoral care is neither caring nor pastoral. *Only what is true can ultimately be pastoral. The neglect of the Church's position prevents homosexual men and women from receiving the care they need and deserve.* (par. 15)

The Lord Jesus promised, "You shall know the truth and the truth shall set you free" (Jn. 8:32). Scripture bids us speak the truth in love (cf. Eph. 4:15). The God who is at once truth and love calls the Church to minister to every man, woman and child with the pastoral solicitude of our compassionate Lord. It is in this spirit that we have addressed this Letter to the Bishops of the Church with the hope that it will be of some help as they care for those *whose suffering can only be intensified by error and lightened by truth.* (par. 18).[4]

In 1985, on the twentieth anniversary of Vatican II, John Paul II convoked an assembly of the Synod of Bishops. At this convocation the bishops cited the

---

[4] Roman Catholic Church, "Letter to the Bishops of the Catholic Church on the Pastoral Care of Homosexual Persons" accessed September 27, 2014, http://www.vatican.va/roman_curia/congregations/cfaith/documents/rc_con_cfaith_doc_19861001_homosexual-persons_en.html.

need for "a catechism or compendium of all catholic doctrine regarding faith and morals." The next year the pope commissioned twelve cardinals, chaired by Ratzinger, to prepare a draft of the new catechism. The commission worked for six years and produced the *Catechism of the Catholic Church* (1992), "a statement of the Church's faith and of catholic doctrine, attested to or illumined by Sacred Scripture, the Apostolic Tradition, and the Church's Magisterium." In the section on the Ten Commandments, under the sixth commandment, the catechism addressed the issue of homosexuality.

Catechism of the Catholic Church (1992)

Homosexuality refers to relations between men or between women who experience an exclusive or predominant sexual attraction toward persons of the same sex. It has taken a great variety of forms through the centuries and in different cultures. Its psychological genesis remains largely unexplained. *Basing itself on Sacred Scripture, which presents homosexual acts as acts of grave depravity, tradition has always declared that "homosexual acts are intrinsically disordered." They are contrary to the natural law. They close the sexual act to the gift of life. They do not proceed from a genuine affective and sexual complementarity. Under no circumstances can they be approved.*

The number of men and women who have deep-seated homosexual tendencies is not negligible. They do not choose their homosexual condition; for most of them it is a trial. They must be accepted with respect, compassion, and sensitivity. Every sign of unjust discrimination in their regard should be avoided. These persons are called to fulfill God's will in their lives and, if they are Christians, to unite to the sacrifice of the Lord's Cross the difficulties they may encounter from their condition.

Homosexual persons are called to chastity. By the virtues of self-mastery that teach them inner freedom, at times by the support of disinterested friendship, by prayer and sacramental grace, they can and should gradually and resolutely approach Christian perfection.[5]

In 2005 Pope Benedict XVI approved an Instruction from the Congregation for Catholic Education on the issue of homosexual ordination. The document addressed the question of "whether to admit to the seminary and to holy orders candidates who have deep-seated homosexual tendencies." The Instruction was unequivocal.

Concerning the Criteria for the Discernment of Vocations with regard to Persons with Homosexual Tendencies in view of their Admission to the Seminary and Holy Orders (2005)

From the time of the Second Vatican Council until today, various Documents of the Magisterium, and especially the *Catechism of the Catholic*

---

[5] *Catechism of the Catholic Church*, English translation (Liguori, MO: Liguori, 1994), 566.

Church, have confirmed the teaching of the Church on homosexuality. The *Catechism* distinguishes between homosexual acts and homosexual tendencies.

Regarding *acts*, it teaches that Sacred Scripture presents them as grave sins. The Tradition has constantly considered them as intrinsically immoral and contrary to the natural law. Consequently, under no circumstance can they be approved.

Deep-seated homosexual *tendencies*, which are found in a number of men and women, are also objectively disordered and, for those same people, often constitute a trial. Such persons must be accepted with respect and sensitivity. Every sign of unjust discrimination in their regard should be avoided. They are called to fulfill God's will in their lives and to unite to the sacrifice of the Lord's Cross the difficulties they may encounter.

In the light of such teaching, this Dicastery, in accord with the Congregation for Divine Worship and the Discipline of the Sacraments, believe it necessary to state clearly that *the Church, while profoundly respecting the persons in question, cannot admit to the seminary or to holy orders those who practice homosexuality, present deep-seated homosexual tendencies or support the so-called "gay culture."*

Such persons, in fact, find themselves in a situation that gravely hinders them from relating correctly to men and women. One must in no way over-look the negative consequences that can derive from the ordination of persons with deep-seated homosexual tendencies.

Different, however, would be the case in which one were dealing with homosexual tendencies that were only the expression of a transitory prob-lem—for example, that of an adolescence not yet superseded. Nevertheless, such tendencies must be clearly overcome at least three years before ordina-tion to the diaconate.[6]

In 2006 the United States Conference of Catholic Bishops issued *Ministry to Persons with a Homosexual Inclination: Guidelines for Pastoral Care,* a statement on pastoral ministry to homosexuals. The statement reiterated Catholic teaching, offering assistance to bishops in evaluating programs of ministry and providing guidance to those engaged in ministry to homosexuals. The guidelines were necessary due to the "many forces in our society that promote a view of sexuality in general, and homosexuality in particular, not in accord with God's purpose and plan for human sexuality." The bishops pro-duced the document "to offer guidance in the face of pervasive confusion." The following are excerpts from the guidelines provided by the bishops.

---

[6] Roman Catholic Church, "Concerning the Criteria for the Discernment of Vocations with regard to Persons with Homosexual Tendencies in View of Their Admission to the Seminary and Holy Orders, section 2," accessed September, 27, 2014, http://www.vatican.va/roman_curia/congregations/ccatheduc/documents/rc_con_ccatheduc_doc_20051104_istruzione_en.html.

Ministry to Persons with a Homosexual Inclination: Guidelines for Pastoral Care (2006)

They [homosexual acts] are sexual acts that cannot be open to life. Nor do they reflect the complementarity of man and woman that is an integral part of God's design for human sexuality. Consequently, the Catholic Church has consistently taught that homosexual acts "are contrary to the natural law. . . . Under no circumstances can they be approved." In support of this judgment, the Church points not only to the intrinsic order of creation, but also to what God has revealed in Sacred Scripture. *In the book of Genesis we learn that God created humanity as male and female and that according to God's plan a man and a woman come together and "the two of them become one body." Whenever homosexual acts are mentioned in the Old Testament, it is clear that they are disapproved of, as contrary to the will of God. In the New Testament, St. Paul teaches that homosexual acts are not in keeping with our being created in God's image and so degrade and undermine our authentic dignity as human beings. . . . St. Paul listed homosexual practices among those things incompatible with the Christian life.*

While the Church teaches that homosexual acts are immoral, she does distinguish between engaging in homosexual acts and having a homosexual inclination. While the former is always objectively sinful, the latter is not. To the extent that a homosexual tendency or inclination is not subject to one's free will, one is not morally culpable for that tendency. Although one would be morally culpable if one were voluntarily to entertain homosexual temptations or to choose to act on them, simply having the tendency is not sin. Consequently, the Church does not teach that the experience of homosexual attraction is in itself sinful. The homosexual inclination is objectively disordered, i.e., . . . the disorder is in that particular inclination, which is not ordered toward the fulfillment of the natural ends of human sexuality. Because of this, acting in accord with such an inclination simply cannot contribute to the true good of the human person. Nevertheless, while the particular inclination to homosexual acts is disordered, the person retains his or her intrinsic human dignity and value.

A considerable number of people who experience same-sex attraction experience it as an inclination they did not choose. Many of these speak of their homosexual attractions as an unwanted burden. This raises the question of whether or not a homosexual inclination can be changed with the help of some kind of therapeutic intervention. There is currently no scientific consensus on the cause of the homosexual inclination. There is no consensus on therapy. Some have found therapy helpful. Catholics who experience homosexual tendencies and who wish to explore therapy should seek out the counsel and assistance of a qualified professional who has preparation and competence in psychological counseling and who understands and supports the Church's teaching on homosexuality. They should also seek out the guidance of a confessor and spiritual director who will support their quest to live a chaste life.

There is another kind of "therapy" or healing of which we all stand in need, regardless of whether one is attracted to the same or the opposite sex: Every person needs training in the virtues. . . . In our society, chastity is a particular virtue that requires special effort. All people, whether married or single, are called to chaste living. Chaste living overcomes disordered human desires such as lust and results in the expression of one's sexual desires in harmony with God's will. "Chastity means the successful integration of sexuality within the person and thus the inner unity of man in his bodily and spiritual being." It is sad to note that in our society violation of chastity and the pervasive human suffering and unhappiness that follow in its wake are not uncommon. . . . The acquisition of virtues requires a sustained effort and repeated actions. . . . In this effort to train our desires to be in accord with God's will, as Christians we do not have to rely solely upon our own powers; we have the Holy Spirit at work in our hearts.

One way in which the Church can aid persons with a homosexual inclination is by nurturing the bonds of friendship among people. . . . There can be little hope of living a healthy, chaste life without nurturing human bonds. Living in isolation can ultimately exacerbate one's disordered tendencies and undermine the practice of chastity. It would not be wise for persons with homosexual inclination to seek friendship exclusively among persons with the same inclinations. They should seek to form stable friendships among both homosexuals and heterosexuals. . . . A homosexual person can have an abiding relationship with another homosexual without genital sexual expression. Indeed the deeper need of any human is for friendship rather than genital expression. . . . While the bonds of friendship should be carefully fostered at all levels, loving friendships among members of a family are particularly important. Those ministering in the name of the Church should encourage healthy relationships between persons with a homosexual inclination and other members of their families. The family can provide invaluable support to people who are striving to grow in the virtue of chastity. The local Church community is also a place where the person with a homosexual inclination should experience friendship. This community can be a rich source of human relationships and friendships, so vital to living a healthy life. In fact, within the Church human friendship is raised to a new order of love, that of brothers and sisters in Christ.

The Church's teaching on homosexuality is attentive to the natural law imprinted in human nature and faithful to the Sacred Scriptures. This teaching offers a beacon of light and hope in the midst of considerable confusion, intense emotion, and much conflict. . . . there are features specific to contemporary Western culture that inhibit the reception of Church teaching on sexual issues in general and on homosexuality in particular. For example, there is a strong tendency toward moral relativism in our society. Many do not admit an objective basis for moral judgments. . . . Because Church teaching insists that there are objective moral norms, there are those in our culture who portray this teaching as unjust, that is, as opposed to basic human rights. Such claims usually follow from a form of moral relativism that is joined, not with inconsistency, to a belief in the absolute rights of individuals. In this view, the Church is perceived as promoting a particular prejudice and as interfering with individual freedom. In fact, the Church actively asserts and promotes the intrinsic dignity of every person. As human persons, persons with a homosexual inclination have the same basic rights as all people, including the right to be treated with dignity. . . . Another common characteristic of Western societies that poses an obstacle to the reception of Church teaching is the widespread tendency toward hedonism, an obsession with the pursuit of pleasure. . . . Moreover, there are many in our society, particularly in the advertising and entertainment industries, who make enormous profits by taking advantage of this tendency and who work to promote it by their actions. Given such strong influences in our culture, it is not surprising that there are a number of groups active in our society that not only deny the existence of objective moral norms but also aggressively seek public approval for homosexual behavior. The message of such groups misleads many people and causes considerable harm. In the face of this challenge the Church must continue her efforts to persuade people through rational argument, the witness of her life, and the proclamation of the Gospel of Jesus Christ.[7]

Catholic psychologist Benedict J. Groeschel, who has counseled persons struggling with same-sex attraction for many years, has written about the call to chastity for such individuals. He states:

Those who argue that homosexual behavior can be an acceptable part of Christian life have had a lot of notoriety in recent years. The best representatives of this group have tried to present their position with all sincerity as part of the gentle love of Christ. They have tried to bind up wounds caused by prejudice, homophobia, and ignorance of psycho-dynamics. In a cultural situation where the mass media consistently campaign for complete sexual freedom and license, and where overtly homosexual behavior has been made to appear more and more socially acceptable, they have tried to move the moral teaching of various religious groups toward complete acceptance of a respectable and dignified homosexual lifestyle. After years of experience as a spiritual director and psychologist, I must admit that I find their efforts, however sincere, really a form of soft love that is neither spiritually nor psychologically productive in the long run. Over and over again I have seen soft love lead to bitter personal frustration at the failure to find a lasting loving relationship with God. . . . On the other hand, *I have seen the tough love taught by the Church lead many to a vibrant spiritual life and to the true dignity of an adult who is not enslaved by sexual need. It should be said that*

---

[7] Roman Catholic Church, U.S. Conference of Catholic Bishops, November 14, 2006, "Ministry to Persons with a Homosexual Inclination: Guidelines for Pastoral Care," accessed September 27, 2014, http://www.usccb.org/issues-and-action/human-life-and-dignity/homosexuality/upload/minstry-persons-homosexual-inclination-2006.pdf. Footnotes for this section list as supporting Scriptures Gen 1:27; 2:24; 19:1–19; Lev 18:22; 20:13; Matt 19:4–6; Mark 10:6–8; Rom 1:26–27; 1 Cor 6:9; Eph 5:31; 1 Tim 1:10.

large numbers of Christians in many denominations have found healing and spiritual growth in the acceptance of the tough love of the Gospel.[8]

John F. Harvey is the founder of Courage, a ministry of fellowship and support for persons with same-sex attraction. Based on his decades of counseling experience, Harvey has written numerous books on homosexuality. He comments on Catholic teaching:

> One could go on referencing other passages of Holy Scripture to demonstrate its teaching that sexual activity ought to be heterosexual and marital, but this has already been done by scholars throughout the centuries, as I have indicated [citing prominent Roman Catholic theologians]. Indeed the Second Vatican Council's document, *The Church in the Modern World*, 47–52 and *Humanae Vitae*, 11–14 sum up the teaching of Holy Scripture, of the Fathers of the Church, and of previous magisterial statements of popes and councils that the moral norm of sexual activity is a permanent union of husband and wife for the essentially inseparable purposes of love and union. This is the perennial teaching of the Church. Taken as a whole, it is at least authoritative; but the divine origin of marriage is a teaching of Faith. . . . From all this one may logically conclude that homosexual activity is objectively always seriously immoral, inasmuch as it in no way fulfills the essential purposes of human sexuality. *The Catholic teaching flows necessarily from the whole scriptural vision of the meaning of sexuality and of the complementarity of man and woman.* Specific biblical texts, moreover, confirm this general thrust of Holy Scripture.[9]

ORTHODOX CHURCHES

Globally and in the United States, the Orthodox family of churches has given a uniform witness on the issue of homosexuality. Orthodox churches highly value the historic testimony of the church; thus, their public statements on homosexuality prove consistent and clear. Despite the multitude of contemporary ecclesiastical bodies that embrace the Orthodox heritage, documents from these groups demonstrate a uniformity of belief across cultures and languages. Selections from representative documents issued by these traditions are included below.

---

[8] Benedict J. Groeschel O.F.M., "Introduction" in John F. Harvey O.S.F.S., *The Homosexual Person: New Thinking in Pastoral Care* (San Francisco, CA: Ignatius, 1987), 13. See also Benedict J. Groeschel, *Courage to Be Chaste* (Mahwah, NJ: Paulist, 1988).

[9] John F. Harvey, O.S.F.S., *The Homosexual Person, New Thinking in Pastoral Care* (San Francisco, CA: Ignatius, 1987), 97–98; italics in original. See also by Harvey: *The Truth About Homosexuality: The Cry of the Faithful* (San Francisco, CA: Ignatius, 1996); *Same-Sex Attraction: A Parent's Guide* (South Bend, IN: St. Augustine's, 2003); and *Homosexuality and the Catholic Church: Clear Answers to Difficult Questions* (West Chester, PA: Ascension, 2007).

Greek Orthodox Archdiocese of North and South America (1976)

The position of the Orthodox Church toward homosexuality has been expressed by synodical canons and Patristic pronouncements beginning with the very first centuries of Orthodox ecclesiastical life.

Thus, the Orthodox Church condemns unreservedly all expressions of personal sexual experience, which prove contrary to the definite and unalterable function ascribed to sex by God's ordinance and expressed in man's experience as a law of nature. . . .

Therefore, any and all uses of the human sex organs for purposes other than those ordained by creation, runs contrary to the nature of things as decreed by God and produces the following wrongs:

   a. They violate God's ordinance regarding both the procreation of man and his emotional life generated by his instinctive attraction to the opposite sex not only for procreating but for advancing the personalities of a man and a woman to a state of completion within the association of the Sacrament of Marriage. For all this, homosexuality is an insult to God, and since it attempts to alter the laws regulating creation it is a blasphemy.

   b. Homosexuality interferes with the normal development of societal patterns and as such it proves detrimental to all. These endangered patterns include personal values regarding sex which people normally take to be a vital part of their existence and a valuable asset to their living a normal life, esteemed by others.

   c. The homosexual degrades his own sex and thus denies to himself the self-respect that is generated from the feeling that one is in line with God's creation. . . .

The Orthodox Church believes that homosexuality should be treated by society as an immoral and dangerous perversion and by religion as a sinful failure. In both cases, correction is called for.

Homosexuals should be accorded confidential medical and psychiatric facilities by which they can be helped to restore themselves to a self-respecting sexual identity that belongs to them by God's ordinance.

In full confidentiality, the Orthodox Church cares and provides pastorally for homosexuals in the belief that no sinner who has failed himself and God should be allowed to deteriorate morally and spiritually.[10]

Standing Conference of Canonical Orthodox Bishops in the Americas

The Standing Conference of Canonical Orthodox Bishops in the Americas (SCOBA) represents more than five million Orthodox Christians in the United

---

[10] This document originated at the Twenty-Third Clergy-Laity Congress of the Greek Orthodox Archdiocese of North and South America in 1976. It appeared in print in *The Word*, January 1984, 6–11. Portions of this document are cited in "The Stand of the Orthodox Church on Controversial Issues," available on the website of the Greek Orthodox Archdiocese of America, http://www.holy-trinity.org/morality/homosexuality.html.

States, Canada, and Mexico. On several occasions the archbishops and metropolitans of this body have issued public statements on homosexuality. Two representative statements will be cited (1978, 2003). Note that the SCOBA position was essentially unaltered between 1978 and 2003 despite increasing societal pressure to accept homosexuality as a valid expression of human sexuality.

> The Christian family is currently subject to serious negative pressures from secular elements in our society. Such are the extensive campaigns of self-proclaimed homosexuals, both individually and collectively, to obtain recognition of their life-styles as being of equal worth with marriage and the home. *Without wishing to penalize anyone who deserves sympathy and pastoral assistance from the Christian community because of physical or emotional personality states over which they have no control, the Standing Conference of Canonical Orthodox Bishops in the Americas reiterates the clear directives of scriptures and tradition which condemn voluntary homosexual acts as sinful and forbidden and detrimental to the existence of the Christian home. Persons who embrace homosexual life-styles are not qualified to teach children or act as spiritual leaders.*[11]

> *The Orthodox Christian teaching on marriage and sexuality, firmly grounded in Holy Scripture, 2000 years of church tradition, and canon law, holds that marriage consists in the conjugal union of a man and a woman, and that authentic marriage is blessed by God as a sacrament of the Church. Neither Scripture nor Holy Tradition blesses or sanctions such a union between persons of the same sex.*
>
> Holy Scripture attests that God creates man and woman in His own image and likeness (Genesis 1:27–31), that those called to do so might enjoy a conjugal union that ideally leads to procreation. While not every marriage is blessed with the birth of children, every such union exists to create of a man and woman a new reality of "one flesh." This can only involve a relationship based on gender complementarity. "God made them male and female. . . . So they are no longer two but one flesh" (Mark 10:6–8).
>
> *The union between a man and a woman in the Sacrament of Marriage reflects the union between Christ and His Church (Ephesians 5:21–33). As such, a marriage is necessarily monogamous and heterosexual. Within this union, sexual relations between a husband and wife are to be cherished and protected as a sacred expression of their love that has been blessed by God. Such was God's plan for His human creatures from the very beginning. Today, however, this divine purpose is increasingly questioned, challenged or denied, even within some faith communities, as social and political pressure work to normalize, legalize and even sanctify same-sex unions.*

---

[11] Standing Committee of the Orthodox Bishops of the Americas SCOBA statement 1978, accessed September 27, 2014, http://www.frpeterpreble.com/2010/10/orthodoxy-and-homosexuality.html.

The Orthodox Church cannot and will not bless same-sex unions. Whereas marriage between a man and woman is a sacred institution ordained by God, homosexual union is not. Like adultery and fornication, homosexual acts are condemned by Scripture (Rom 1:24–27; 1 Cor 6:10; 1 Tim 1:10). This being said, however, we must stress that persons with a homosexual orientation are to be cared for with the same mercy and love that is bestowed by our Lord Jesus Christ upon all humanity. All persons are called by God to grow spiritually and morally toward holiness.

As heads of the Orthodox Churches in America and members of SCOBA, we speak with one voice in expressing our deep concern over recent developments. And we pray fervently that the traditional form of marriage, as an enduring and committed union only between a man and a woman, will be honored.[12]

Assembly of Canonical Orthodox Bishops of the United States of America (2013)[13]

1. We, the Assembly of Canonical Orthodox Bishops of North and Central America, representing millions of Orthodox Christians in the United States of America, Canada and Central America, express our deep concern over recent actions on the part of our respective governments and certain societal trends concerning the status of marriage in our countries, in particular the legalization of same-sex unions. 2. *The Orthodox Christian teaching on marriage and sexuality, firmly grounded in Holy Scripture, two millennia of Church Tradition, and Canon Law, holds that the sacrament of marriage consists in the union of a man and a woman, and that authentic marriage reflects the sacred unity that exists between Christ and His Bride, the Church.* 3. Persons with homosexual orientation are to be cared for with the same mercy and love that is bestowed on all of humanity by our Lord Jesus Christ. Moreover,

---

[12] Standing Committee of the Orthodox Bishops of the Americas, "SCOBA Statement, 1978 on the Moral Crisis of Our Nation," August 27, 2003, accessed September 27, 2014, http://www. byzcath.org/forums/ubbthreads.php/topics/28504/Re:%20SCOBA%20STATEMENT%20 ON%20MORAL%20C. This statement was signed by an archbishop or metropolitan representing the following Orthodox churches: Greek Orthodox Diocese of America, Orthodox Church in America, Antiochian Orthodox Christian Archdiocese, Romanian Orthodox Archdiocese of North America and Canada, Serbian Orthodox Church in the USA and Canada, Bulgarian Eastern Orthodox Church, Carpatho-Russian Orthodox Dioceses in the USA, Ukrainian Orthodox Church in the USA, and the Albanian Orthodox Diocese of America. This group represents more than five million Orthodox members.

[13] The Assembly of Canonical Orthodox Bishops of the United States of America is the successor of SCOBA. In 2014 the Canadian and US bishops formed separate Assemblies, and the Central American bishops joined the Assembly of Canonical Orthodox Bishops of Latin America. The purpose of the reorganization was in order to address pastoral needs and cultural diversity.

the Church is a spiritual hospital, where we all are called to find the healing of our fallen humanity through Jesus Christ, who assumed human nature in order to restore it. *All of us struggle with various passions, and it is only within the Church that we find the means of overcoming these passions with the assistance of God's grace. Acting upon any sexual attraction outside of sacramental marriage, whether the attraction is heterosexual or homosexual, alienates us from God.* 4. We exhort the clergy and faithful of the Orthodox Church to bear witness to the timeless teachings of Christ by striving for purity and holiness in their own lives, by instructing their families and communities in the precepts of the Holy Gospel, and by placing their trust in our Lord, who "has overcome the world." (John 16:33) 5. Finally, we encourage our faithful to approach their parish priest or spiritual father with any questions or concerns about this statement and its practical repercussions in their daily lives.[14]

Responding to the legalization of gay unions, the Russian Orthodox Church Outside Russia (ROCOR) issued a statement from San Francisco in 2004. The document, "Epistle of the Pastoral Conference of the Western American Diocese of the Russian Orthodox Church Outside Russia Regarding 'Same-Gender' Unions,'" made clear its opposition to this innovation.

The Russian Orthodox Church Outside Russia (2004)

We are compelled to address our flocks concerning the nature of Holy Matrimony, otherwise known as marriage. "We must obey God rather than men." (Acts 5:29). Holy Matrimony consists of the union of two persons into one, through the union of their souls and bodies, through mutual submission and obedience, and, most importantly, through the action of God's grace. It is a holy mystery, a sacrament, an avenue of the Grace of God given to us not for the indulgence of our passions, but for the working out of our salvation. . . . In addition to the salvation of the souls of husband and wife and of their children, the sacrament of marriage also serves as a guardian and standard of moral behavior. Any lustful activity outside of the bounds of sacramental marriage is damaging to the soul and creates a barrier between man and God. The sacrament defines the limits of physical and emotional intimacy between two persons. *These limits include (but are not limited to) the fact that marital relations are only possible between a man and woman, that the conception, bearing and raising of children is the natural and desired product of marital relations, and that such relations are only permitted within the sanctified bounds of marriage.*

In the modern culture, much emphasis has been placed on the "culture of the flesh" and the eternal and spiritual nature of man has been minimized. Self-indulgence has become the primary value and is protected by our

---

[14] "2013 Assembly Statement on Marriage and Sexuality," accessed March 19, 2015, http://assemblyofbishops.org/about/documents/2013-assembly-statement-on-marriage-and-sexuality.

*modern society under the pretext of individual "civil rights." Personal grati-
fication and fulfillment in this world has supplanted the spiritual striving for
purity and holiness, which is the true source of joy. The love of God has been
replaced by love of self. The desire for eternal bliss has been replaced by the
desire for worldly bliss. The fear of eternal punishment has been replaced by
the fear of worldly discomfort and condemnation. Man has supplanted God
as the measure of all things.*

Within the Church, the mystery of Matrimony is not a right; it is a calling, intended by God for a specific purpose, and not merely the fulfilling of
earthly lusts, or the comfort of a life shared together. The argument that same-
sex unions [are] "natural," while apparently a powerful argument, ignores the
truth that our human nature is fallen and corrupted by death, and driven to the
satisfaction of the desires of the flesh. The expression of sexual desires without the blessing of the Grace of God is not directed to a life that is natural, but
is an extension of a *death-directed existence.* Only by striving to live the life
of Jesus Christ, risen from the dead, can we begin to understand and achieve
a life which is truly "natural."[15]

Coptic Orthodox Church (2003)

During its annual clergy convention in 2003, leaders of the Coptic Orthodox
Church discussed the legalization of same-sex marriage and the recent decisions to ordain homosexuals in the Episcopal Church and the Uniting Church
in Australia. Pope Shenouda III, Pope of Alexandria and the Patriarch of the
See of Saint Mark, presided over the convention. Joining him were bishops
and priests from North America, Egypt, Australia, and Europe. That same year
the Coptic convention issued a press release addressing the issues facing the
church:

> Based on the teachings of the Lord Jesus Christ, and teachings of the Old
> and New Testaments, the clergy strongly condemns such activities.
> 1. *Our Lord Jesus Christ spoke against homosexuality when He made
>   reference to the abomination of Sodom and Gomorrah (Lk. 10:12;
>   Gen. 19:24; Jude 7). Similarly Saint Paul warns, "Do not be deceived.
>   Neither fornicators nor idolaters, nor adulterers, nor homosexuals,
>   nor sodomites, nor thieves . . . will inherit the Kingdom of God"*
>   (1 Cor. 6:9, 10. See also Lev. 18:22; Rom. 1:26–32).
> 2. Same-sex marriage is against the Divine Plan for marriage and its pur-
>   pose of procreation. "But from the beginning of creation, God made
>   them male and female. For this reason a man shall leave his father and
>   mother and be joined to his wife." (Mk. 10:6, 7. See also Eph. 5:31;
>   Gen. 1:27; Gen. 2:24; Matt. 19:4–6).

---

[15] Russian Orthodox Church Outside Russia, "On Same-Sex Unions," ROCOR W. Diocese
Clergy, February 28/March 28, 2004, accessed September 27, 2014, http://orthodoxinfo.com/
praxis/samesexunions.aspx.

3. Therefore, those who are ordained for church ministry must uphold the teachings of the Holy Bible. They should be ". . . blameless . . . of good behavior . . . able to teach . . ." (1 Tim. 3:2). Consequently, we disapprove of and condemn the ordination of homosexual clergy, active or not.

These movements not only contradict biblical teachings, but also pose a serious threat to the stability of the family unit, the morals of society, the purity of the Church and the future of ecumenical unity. *While we condemn homosexuality, we invite those who are under this sin to repent out of concern for their eternal life. We applaud the courageous voices of those who oppose such activities both in and outside those churches, and call on all churches to obey the Biblical teachings without compromise or change.*[16]

George Morelli, in a 2006 paper titled "Understanding Homosexuality: An Orthodox Christian Perspective," offers thoughts from his vantage point as a clinical psychologist and marriage and family therapist within the Orthodox tradition. The essay articulates the rich theological heritage of Orthodoxy and applies that heritage to the contemporary challenges of homosexuality. He writes:

For Orthodox Christians, no discussion of sex whether it is autoerotic, heterosexual, homosexual, bisexual, or the current polyamorous sex, can be divorced from an Orthodox theology of sexuality. All sexuality and sexual behavior is based on divine love; a love that is beyond any human feeling, empathy, or ethical standard, and even approaches the essence of God Himself. . . . We get a glimpse of God's love in the writings of the Church Fathers when they spoke of the interrelationships of the Persons of the Holy Trinity. . . . God's love is reflected in the anthropological ordering of creation. Genesis reveals that with the creation of Adam and Eve, man was created with two modes of being: male and female. "So God created man in His own image: in the image of God He created him; male and female He created them" (Genesis 1:27. Male and female were created for communion with each other, thereby reflecting the intercommunion within the Persons of the Holy Trinity). . . . *Christian anthropology sees the male as the appropriate complement of the female, and the female for the male which includes moral boundaries of the sexual dimension of male and female intercommunion: ". . . a man leaves his father and his mother and cleaves to his wife, and they become one flesh" (Genesis 2:24). Here we have the first reference to biblically ordered sexuality. These limitations are further elaborated later on and include prohibitions against adultery and homosexuality.* . . .

---

[16] Coptic Orthodox Church, "Coptic Orthodox Church Formally Condemns Homosexuality, Ordination of Homosexuals and Same-Sex Marriage" Coptic Orthodox Church Press Release, August 26, 2003, accessed September 27, 2014, http://copticchurch.net/news/press_release_homosexuality.html.

How is the Christian to understand the appeal for homosexual marriage? Persons with a homosexual orientation are invited to use their struggle as a means of sanctification. In scripture homosexual behavior is not blessed by God and specifically prohibited. . . . This is not the same thing as saying that a person who struggles with same-sex desire has lower value in the eyes of God. The focus is on the behavior, not the person. Rather, same-sex desire is likened to a handicap, a condition that necessarily closed off some choices that might otherwise be available, such as a paralytic who can't walk, or the deaf man who cannot hear. This is a hard saying and may strike the ear as fundamentally unfair, even harsh. But we are called to live according to God's commandments, and the struggle the homosexual might have in conforming himself to God's commands can become a pathway to holiness. . . .

Christian standards of conduct exist irrespective of sexual orientation. A heterosexual male for example, despite inclinations and predisposition to multiple females, is called by God to be bonded with one woman in marriage. . . . A homosexual has the inclination, the passion, toward same sex activity but his vocation is to overcome such a passion. It is a difficult struggle, but with God's grace all things are possible.[17]

Orthodox theologian Thomas Hopko notes the confusion about homosexuality that pervades Western society, a confusion symptomatic of dark times:

The tragic truth, however, is that countless people, especially in contemporary secularized societies, have become convinced that their sinful thoughts and feelings, including, and even especially, those having to do with sex, are perfectly normal and natural and, as such, define who they are in their essential being and life. They therefore see no purpose or need in resisting, disciplining, and ultimately destroying them. They are convinced, on the contrary, that to do so would be dishonest, would be to deny and destroy themselves as persons, and, as such, would result in their personal death, which, according to Christian Orthodoxy, is the exact opposite of the truth.[18]

Many gay men and lesbians claim that the Christian faith is the guiding rule of their lives. Some of them hold that their sexual orientation is given by God, that it is good, and that there is nothing wrong or sinful with their homosexual activities. These persons say that the Bible and Church Tradition do not condemn homosexual behavior, but have been misinterpreted and misused, sometimes unknowingly and other times quite willingly, by prejudiced and hostile people who hate homosexuals. . . . *Given the traditional Orthodox understanding of the Old and New Testament scriptures as expressed in the*

---

[17] This essay is accessible at www.orthodoxytoday.org/articles6/MorelliHomosexuality. This is a website of the Antiochian Orthodox Christian Archdiocese of North America. An early draft of this paper was presented at the Orthodox Christian Association of Medicine, Psychology, and Religion in November 2006.

[18] Thomas Hopko, *The Christian Faith and Same-Sex Attraction: Eastern Orthodox Reflections* (Chesterton, IN: Conciliar, 2006), 35.

Church's liturgical worship, sacramental rites, canonical regulations and lives and teachings of the saints, it is clear the Orthodox Church identifies solidly with those Christians, homosexual or heterosexual, who consider homosexual orientation as a disorder and disease, and who therefore consider homosexual actions as sinful and destructive. . . . The homosexual Christian is called to a particularly rigorous battle. His or her struggle is an especially ferocious one. It is not made easier by the mindless, truly demonic hatred of those who despise and ridicule those who carry this painful and burdensome cross; nor by the mindless, equally demonic affirmation of homosexual activity by its misguided advocates and enablers.[19]

CONCLUSION

Roman Catholic and Orthodox statements on sexuality and marriage mirror the testimony of Christian history. One notes from these an unbroken strand of commitment to both Scripture as historically understood for two millennia and sensitive pastoral care for Christians struggling with homosexual temptation. There is no tension in Roman Catholic and Orthodox thinking, between faithfulness to the historic teachings of the church and compassion for hurting people—the church must maintain both.

A key concept in these traditions' approach to homosexuality is the distinction between same-sex attraction, which may be beyond a person's ability to control, and acting on same-sex attraction in homoerotic behavior. The Roman Catholic and Orthodox positions take seriously the insights of modern psychology and human experience that indicate deep-seated same-sex attraction among some individuals. While acknowledging that research has produced no agreement on either the source of same-sex attraction or the effectiveness of therapy to change it, these churches nonetheless call Christians to faithful sexual obedience as defined by Scripture and two thousand years of the church's testimony. The notion that moral struggle can be positive is expressed in their teaching that one should not indulge the flesh but work toward the reordering of ungodly desires—such as same-sex attraction. Such a struggle is said to advance sanctification.

The role of spiritual disciplines and community support in sanctification is sometimes inadequately articulated by Protestants but is explained well in the Catholic and Orthodox traditions. The Orthodox Church in particular cherishes the doctrine of *theosis*,[20] that is, becoming participants in the divine nature. This teaching is based on 2 Peter 1:4–7:

---

[19] Thomas Hopko, "The Homosexual Christian," accessed August 17, 2015, http://oca.org/reflections/misc-authors/the-homosexual-christian. This is a website for the Orthodox Church in America.

[20] For a Protestant appraisal of Orthodox understandings of *theosis*, see Donald Fairbairn, *Eastern Orthodoxy Through Western Eyes* (Louisville, KY: Westminster/John Knox, 2002).

Thus he has given us, through these things, his precious and very great promises, so that through them you may escape from the corruption that is in the world because of lust, and may become participants of the divine nature. For this very reason, you must make every effort to support your faith with goodness, and goodness with knowledge, and knowledge with self-control, and self-control with endurance, and endurance with godliness, and godliness with mutual affection, and mutual affection with love.

Among modern Christians, the field of "Christian counseling" is sometimes overdependent on the social sciences and practiced by persons undertrained in Scripture and theology. Traditional "soul care" can be—although it should not be—reduced to coping mechanisms, cognitive or behavioral therapy, and other psychological remedies devoid of spiritual counsel, disciplines, and transformation. The practices of spiritual disciplines and "spiritual direction," in which a mature Christian mentors another believer struggling with sin, are ancient Christian practices and still valuable resources for the contemporary church.[21]

Roman Catholicism and the Orthodox faith regard marriage as a sacrament of the church and thus place great emphasis on the creation narrative and God's sacred design of men and women as sexual partners made for one another to propagate the human race. The sacramental marital bond may only be blessed by the church within the parameters established by God. The notion of natural law is used by both traditions to characterize homosexual practice as "unnatural," that is, a violation of the divine design.

Both of these historic faiths have spoken of celibacy having a place among God's people. According to Scripture and the Christian tradition, those unable to overcome their same-sex attraction are called to a life of celibacy—a lifestyle modeled for the church by Christ, Paul, and many other saints. Celibacy can be a significant challenge and a wonderful calling, but Christian obedience demands that sexual activity be limited to heterosexual marriage. These historic Christian traditions offer wisdom for the contemporary church to consider. Methodist scholar Richard B. Hays summarizes this point well:

It is no more appropriate for homosexual Christians to persist in a homosexual lifestyle than it would be for heterosexual Christians to maintain a lifestyle of fornication or adultery. . . . Unless they are able to change their orientation and enter a heterosexual marriage relationship, homosexual Christians should seek to live lives of disciplined sexual abstinence. Despite the illusion perpetrated by American mass culture, sexual gratification is not

---

[21] Two helpful resources which can assist Protestants with understanding and practicing the ancient disciplines include Diogenes Allen, *Spiritual Theology: The Theology of Yesterday for Spiritual Help Today* (Boston, MA: Cowley, 1997); and Bruce Demarest, *Satisfy Your Soul: Restoring the Heart of Christian Spirituality* (Colorado Springs, CO: NavPress, 1999).

a sacred right, and celibacy is not a fate worse than death. Here the Catholic tradition has something to teach those of us raised in Protestant communities. While mandatory priestly celibacy is unbiblical, a life of sexual abstinence can promote "good order and unhindered devotion to the Lord" (1 Cor. 7:35). It is worth noting that 1 Cor. 7:8–9, 25–40 commends celibacy as an option for everyone, not just for a special caste of ordained leaders. Within the church, we should work diligently to recover the dignity and value of the single life. . . . *The Church should continue to teach—as it always has— that there are two possible ways for God's human sexual creatures to live well-ordered lives of faithful discipleship: heterosexual marriage and sexual abstinence.*[22]

---

[22] Richard B. Hays, "Awaiting the Redemption of our Bodies," in *Homosexuality in the Church: Both Sides of the Debate*, ed. Jeffrey S. Siker (Louisville, KY: Westminster/John Knox, 1994), 14–15.

CHAPTER 6

EVANGELICALS ON SCRIPTURE AND CONVERSION

The term *evangelical* has received numerous definitions in contemporary times, and some wonder if it is useful anymore, given the diversity of the movement. The term has a historical trajectory beginning with its sixteenth-century usage to describe Lutheranism and its connection with the gospel. Later, seventeenth-century English Puritans and the Great Awakenings of the eighteenth century in Britain and America were identified as evangelical. Many historians of American Christianity use the term to describe the emphases that emerged as a result of the Great Awakening in that country.

British historian David Bebbington's widely acclaimed work on evangelicalism has identified four distinctives of the movement: (1) *Conversionism*—the belief that lives need to be transformed through a born-again experience and a lifelong process of following Jesus. (2) *Activism*—the expression and demonstration of the gospel in missionary and social reform efforts. (3) *Biblicism*—a high regard for and obedience to the Bible as the ultimate authority. (4) *Crucicentrism*—a stress on the sacrifice of Jesus Christ on the cross as making possible the redemption of humanity.[1]

For the purposes of this chapter, denominations will be regarded as "evangelical" based on two of Bebbingtons's distinctives—"conversionism" and "biblicism." When considering the topic of homosexuality, evangelicals typically make what Scripture says the deciding factor. In addition, evangelicals believe in a genuine conversion experience, which includes not only a personal encounter with Christ as Savior from sin but also a changed life of obedience to Christ and his commands. A genuinely converted person will exhibit a transformed life, seeking to overcome his or her old sinful lifestyle in the power of

---

[1] David W. Bebbington, *Evangelicalism in Modern Britain: A History from the 1730s to the 1980s* (London, England: Unwin Hyman, 1989), 2–3. See also *The Advent of Evangelicalism: Exploring Historical Continuities*, ed. Michael A. G. Haykin and Kenneth J. Stewart (Nashville, TN: B&H Academic, 2008).

the Holy Spirit, who progressively transforms believers into new creatures in Christ.

Undergirding the distinctives of evangelicalism is a foundational commitment to historic Christian faith and practice, that is, the "catholic" (universal) faith that makes up the indispensable substance of Christian teaching. As the nineteenth-century Princeton theologian Charles Hodge stated, "We may affirm that Christianity is a doctrine, and in another sense we may with equal truth affirm that Christianity is a life."[2] Evangelicals must be, and historically have been, committed to consensus *orthodoxy* (doctrine) and *orthopraxis* (life) as the essence of Christianity since apostolic times. And orthopraxis has always included sexual standards of conduct.

LUTHERANS

Lutheran Church—Missouri Synod (LCMS)

The LCMS, a Lutheran body with roots in the nineteenth century, has been steadfast in both its confessional and ethical standards. In a LCMS pamphlet entitled "What About Homosexuality?" the church makes plain its commitment to traditional Lutheran theology and practice. The following are excerpts from this document:

> The Lord teaches through His Word that homosexuality is a sinful distortion of His desire that one man and one woman live together in marriage as husband and wife. God categorically prohibits homosexuality. Our church, the Lutheran Church—Missouri Synod, has declared that homosexual behavior is "intrinsically sinful." . . . Through His Word, God teaches us very clearly that homosexuality is a sin. A person who persists in homosexual behavior stands under the condemnation of God's Word. This is true for anyone who persists in sin without repentance. While this may be an unpopular message, it is the truth taught to us by God in His Word. . . . *The church's most important message to homosexuals is the promise of forgiveness and eternal life through the person and the work of Jesus Christ. God sent His Son into this world to live a perfect life on our behalf, and to die a perfect death as the payment for all our sins.*[3]

The LCMS statement also speaks to the question of why some denominations have changed their positions on homosexuality. The LCMS observes:

---

[2] Charles Hodge, "What Is Christianity?," *Biblical Repertory and Princeton Review* (January 1860): 119.

[3] Lutheran Church Missouri Synod, A. L. Barry, "What About Homosexuality?," accessed October 3, 2014, http://www.lcms.org/belief-and-practice. See also Gilbert Meilaender, 1999, "Homosexuality in Christian Perspective," pdf, accessed June 23, 2014, http://www.lcms.org. Key Ministry is a Lutheran group that ministers to individuals struggling with homosexuality and also provides support for their families.

We have noticed changes particularly in many Protestant churches in our country when it comes to the issue of homosexuality. . . . What accounts for these changes in some churches? First, homosexual groups within these churches often engage in "lobbying" efforts and gain considerable influence. Second and more important, attitudes toward homosexuality have changed as a result of changing attitudes toward the authority and reliability of the Holy Scriptures. An academic philosophy about the Bible, called "higher criticism," puts man in the position of determining what is true and what is not in the Bible. With this attitude, we can understand why some churches have attempted to explain away the Bible's teaching about homosexuality.[4]

North American Lutheran Church (NALC)

The NALC was established in 2010 as a response to the Evangelical Lutheran Church of America's, or ELCA's, departure from confessional Lutheranism. One of the vision statements instrumental in the formation of the new denomination included a commitment to be "traditionally grounded," which was defined in this way: "We affirm the ecumenical creeds and *the faithful witness of the Church across time and space. We endorse the form and practices of the universal Church that are consistent with Scripture,* particularly the office of the ministry and the tradition of worship under Word and Sacrament. We seek dialogue and fellowship with other Lutheran churches and with faithful Christians of other confessions."[5] The NALC's "Standards for Pastoral Ministry" addresses the issue of sexual ethics:

The Biblical Understanding which the North American Lutheran Church affirms is that the normative setting for sexual intercourse is marriage between one man and one woman. In keeping with this understanding, chastity before marriage and fidelity within marriage are the norm. Ordained ministers of the North American Lutheran church are expected to preach, teach, and live in accordance with this Biblical standard. Adultery, promiscuity, the sexual abuse of another or the misuse of counseling relationships for sexual favors constitutes conduct that is incompatible with the character of the ministerial

---

[4] Ibid.

[5] NALC, "Core Values," accessed September 27, 2014, http://thenalc.org/core-values-2. Bishop John Bradosky of the NALC signed the January 12, 2012, statement "Marriage and Religious Freedom: Fundamental Goods That Stand Together—an Open Letter from Religious Leaders in the United States to All Americans," signed by Roman Catholics, Anglicans, Baptists, Pentecostals, and others. The document defended traditional marriage. In a press release, Bishop Bradosky stated, "Being bold in our confession of Christ to a hostile culture is never easy. There are times when making a stand for what we believe brings us into relationship with those of diverse theological perspectives. This is certainly the case among those who have joined together to sign the statement released today regarding the preservation of religious freedom, the sanctity of marriage, *and the definition of marriage preserved in the Scripture and the faithful interpretation of the Scriptures over thousands of years.*" Accessed September 27, 2014, http://thenalc.org/ecumenical-statements.

office. Persons who engage in sexual activity outside the marriage covenant of one man and one woman, whether homosexual or heterosexual, are precluded from the ordained ministry of the North American Lutheran Church.[6]

REFORMED CHURCHES

Christian Reformed Church in North America (CRC)

The CRC grew out of Dutch immigration to America in the nineteenth century and included some who left the Reformed Church in America to affiliate with the new Dutch church. In 1970 the CRC appointed a committee to study homosexuality. A thorough report was issued in 1973, which concluded with a section on pastoral advice. In this final portion of the report, the committee stated:

> *Homosexuality (male and female) is a condition of disordered sexuality which reflects the brokenness of our sinful world and for which the homosexual may himself bear only a minimal responsibility. . . . Homosexualism—as explicit homosexual practice—must be condemned as incompatible with obedience to the will of God as revealed in Holy Scripture. . . . In order to live a life of chastity in obedience to God's will, the homosexual needs the loving support and encouragement of the church. . . . Homosexuals, especially in their earlier years, should be encouraged to seek such help as may effect their sexual reorientation and the church should do everything in its power to help the homosexual overcome this disorder. . . . It is the duty of pastors to be informed about the condition of homosexuality and the particular problems of the homosexual in order that the pastor may minister to his need and to the needs of others, such as parents, who may be intimately involved in the problems of homosexuality.[7]*

In 1996 a committee was appointed by the CRC synod to give direction regarding pastoral care of persons with same-sex attraction "consistent with the decisions of Synod 1973." An extensive committee report was presented and discussed throughout the CRC. The report reaffirmed the CRC position of 1973, included lengthy advice on pastoral care, provided criteria for evaluating ministries to homosexual persons, and listed bibliographic resources. A significant section of the report dealt with questions of homosexual identity, temptation, sin, and celibacy. The report included these observations:

---

[6] "Standards for Pastoral Ministry," NALC, 2011, accessed September 27, 2014, http://thenalc.org/standards-for-pastoral-ministry.

[7] CRC, *Acts of Synod,* 1973, 51–53 and *Supplement—Report 42,* "Committee to Study Homosexuality (Art. 53)," 609–33, accessed September 27, 2014, http://www.calvin.edu/library/database/crcnasynod/1973agendaacts.pdf.

The ministry of the church to persons with same-sex attractions begins with enfolding these persons into community while at the same time sounding the message of the gospel that one's sexual identity is not one's deepest and true identity. One's core identity must not be hostage to one's sexual identity or sexual orientation. . . . Acknowledging the struggles and temptations and moving toward this new identity in Christ allow one to be honest, to receive the love of the Christian community, and, above all, to have hope. . . . We must be clear that temptation becomes sin only when we give some form of assent to it, some kind of yes. . . . In the seventh chapter of Corinthians (vv. 1, 8–9, and 32–35) the apostle Paul recommends singleness as a preferable state for Christians. These passages clearly teach that one need not be married in order to have meaning in life or to fulfil one's purpose or role in this world. . . . What about those who are sexually attracted to persons of the same sex? If marriage is not possible and they do not have the gift, or charisma, necessary to control their sexuality, what are they to do? . . . Galatians 5:22–23 speaks of self-control as one of the fruits of the Spirit. . . . The Holy Spirit promises to give Christians whatever they need in order to obey and serve God. Christians who lack self-control of their anger or their sexuality must seek it and ask God for it. Married people as well as singles need self-control, including self-control of their sexuality, for a well-disciplined life. . . . The argument that one is excused from the obligation to be sexually chaste if one does not have the gift of celibacy (or self-control) rests on questionable grounds.[8]

The CRC report concluded with a section on brokenness and healing:

The power of God is shown in changed lives, changed in all sorts of ways. . . . Some brokenness and some disease will not be healed until we come into his presence at the end of time. Some live with the pain of unhealed brokenness throughout their lives. The church must communicate all that God promises but also no more than he promises. . . . Persons with same-sex attractions testify that this healing comes in many forms and to varying degrees: (1) diminished inclinations, (2) a greater measure of self-control, (3) a supportive Christian community that brings peace and wholeness into their lives, (4) strength and support in a continuing struggle throughout their lives, (5) a greater attraction to the opposite sex, (6) and in some cases the ability to marry and have a family. All persons should be encouraged to seek whatever healing God may provide for them. They should seek it both through the common ministry of their congregations and through the specialized ministries for persons who are homosexual.[9]

---

[8] CRC, "Committee to Give Direction about and for Pastoral Care for Homosexual Members," 319–23, Agenda for Synod 2002, accessed September 27, 2014, http://www.crcna.org/sites/default/files/2002_agenda.pdf.

[9] Ibid., 324.

PRESBYTERIAN DENOMINATIONS

Presbyterian Church in America (PCA)

Established in 1973 as an alternative to the increasingly liberal Presbyterian Church in the United States (PCUS), the PCA has addressed homosexuality in a variety of public statements and publications. In 1977 the General Assembly of the PCA issued the following statement on homosexual practice:

> *1. The act of homosexuality is a sin according to God's Word; 2. Churches should actively seek to lead the homosexual person to confession and repentance that he might find justification and sanctification in Jesus Christ, according to I Corinthians 6:11; and 3. In light of the biblical view of its sinfulness, a practicing homosexual continuing in this sin would not be a fit candidate for ordination or membership in the Presbyterian Church in America.*[10]

The 1999 General Assembly declared that homosexual activity is sin and not an acceptable lifestyle. Moreover, PCA churches were warned about the aggressive homosexual agenda. The following is found in a PCA publication titled *Twenty Questions and Answers about the Presbyterian Church in America*: "Position on Homosexuality? It is sin. But just as with any other sin, the PCA deals with these people in a pastoral way, seeking to transform their lifestyle through the power of the gospel as applied by the Holy Spirit."[11]

Evangelical Presbyterian Church (EPC)

In 1981 a group of evangelically minded Presbyterians established the Evangelical Presbyterian Church, consisting primarily of churches that left the mainline Presbyterian body. As the Presbyterian Church in the United States of America, or the PCUSA, moved increasingly toward embracing gay ordination, there was a fresh exodus of clergy and congregations from the PCUSA to the EPC in recent years. The EPC has taken a definitive stance against homosexual ordination, adopting a homosexuality position paper in 1986 and amending it in 1994." The EPC paper states:

> As important as the debate regarding homosexuality is, it is but a single battlefield upon which a much larger question is being contested: How are we to determine what is right and wrong? While we affirm scientific study,

---

[10] PCA.News.com, "PCA Statements on Homosexuality," accessed September 27, 2014, http://sites.silaspartners.com/partner/Article_Display_Page/0,,PTID23682_CHID125044_CIID1620134,00.html. See also PCA Historical Center for a list of PCA statements on homosexuality: http://pcahistory.org/pca.

[11] "Twenty Questions and Answers About the Presbyterian Church in America," accessed September 27, 2014, http://sites.silaspartners.com/partner/Article_Display_Page/0,,PTID23682_CHID125044_CIID1620134,00.html.

we assert that it is an illegitimate form of moral reasoning to suggest that one can reason from what "is" to what "ought to be." History has proved science makes for poor ethics. Human frailty being what it is, it is all too easy to reinterpret scientific findings in such a way as to justify our moral (or immoral) desires. . . .

The witness of God's Word in both the Old and New Testaments is clear, declaring that the practice of homosexual behavior, including lust, is a grievous sin, and that any who continue to engage in such activity face the consequences of God's condemning judgment. However, God's grace offers love, forgiveness, hope and a new life. The necessary response to this offer is a true repentance, including turning from homosexual behavior, and commitment to a faithful obedience to the Lord according to His Word. . . . Unrepentant homosexual behavior is incompatible with the confession of Jesus as Lord, which is required of members of the EPC. Unrepentant homosexual behavior is incompatible with the ordination vows for the offices of Deacon, Ruling Elder and Teaching Elder.[12]

ANGLICANS

Anglican Church in North America (ACNA)

Departures from historic Christian practice in the Episcopal Church USA have caused numerous Episcopalians to disaffiliate from the American province and seek episcopal oversight from Anglican provinces in other parts of the world. A number of Anglican jurisdictions have aligned themselves in a new ecclesiastical structure, such as the Anglican Church in North America, with twenty-eight dioceses. The ACNA emerged from the 2008 Global Anglican Future Conference (GAFCON) in Jerusalem, which was attended by 281 bishops as well as other clergy and laity. The conference issued a "Statement on the Global Anglican Future," including a theological statement known as the "Jerusalem Declaration." It is endorsed by the ACNA. The following are citations from this document:

> The future of the Anglican Communion is but a piece of the wider scenario of opportunities and challenges for the gospel in the 21st century global culture. We rejoice in the way God has opened doors for gospel mission among many peoples, but grieve for the spiritual decline in the most economically

---

[12] EPC, "Position Paper on Homosexuality," *Minutes of the Sixth General Assembly of the Evangelical Presbyterian Church* (Evangelical Presbyterian Church, Office of the General Assembly, 1986), 35–39. This document was revised in 1994 with an appendix, "Guidelines for Christian Ministry to Homosexuals"; see *Minutes of the General Assembly*, 1994, 175–79. The EPC *Book of Discipline* defines "immorality" as "conduct inconsistent with the biblical standards for conduct, including but not limited to . . . sexual immorality such as adultery, fornication, homosexual practice, and bestiality." *EPC Governing Documents, Constitution*, vol. 1: *The Book of Order* (Evangelical Presbyterian Church, Office of the General Assembly, 2012), 78.

developed nations where the forces of militant secularism and pluralism are eating away the fabric of society and churches are compromised and enfeebled in their witness. The vacuum left by them is readily filled by other faiths and deceptive cults. To meet these challenges will require Christians to work together to understand and oppose these forces and to liberate those under their sway. It will entail the planting of new churches among unreached peoples and also committed action to restore authentic Christianity to compromised churches.

The Anglican communion, present in six continents, is well positioned to address this challenge, but currently it is divided and distracted. The Global Anglican Future Conference emerged in response to a crisis in the Anglican Communion, a crisis involving three undeniable facts concerning world Anglicanism.

The first fact is the acceptance and promotion within the provinces of the Anglican Communion of *a different "gospel" (cf. Galatians 1:6–8), which is contrary to the apostolic gospel. This false gospel undermines the authority of God's Word written and the uniqueness of Jesus Christ as the author of salvation from sin, death and judgment.* Many of its proponents claim that all religions offer equal access to God and that Jesus is only a way, not the way, the truth and the life. *It promotes a variety of sexual preferences and immoral behaviour as a universal human right. It claims God's blessing for same-sex unions over against the biblical teaching on holy matrimony. In 2003 this false gospel led to the consecration of a bishop living in a homosexual relationship.* The second fact is the declaration by provincial bodies in the Global South that they are out of communion with bishops and churches that promote this false gospel. . . . The third fact is the manifest failure of the Communion Instruments to exercise discipline in the face of overt heterodoxy. The Episcopal Church USA and the Anglican Church of Canada, in proclaiming this false gospel, have consistently defied the 1998 Lambeth statement of biblical moral principle.[13]

The "Jerusalem Declaration" also includes these affirmations:

We believe the Holy Scriptures of the Old and New Testaments to be the Word of God written and to contain all things necessary for salvation. *The Bible is to be translated, read, preached, taught and obeyed in its plain and canonical sense, respectful of the church's historic and consensual reading.* . . . We acknowledge God's creation of humankind as male and female and the unchangeable standard of Christian marriage between one man and one woman as the proper place for sexual intimacy and the basis of the family. We repent of our failures to maintain this standard and call for a renewed commitment to lifelong fidelity in marriage and abstinence for those who are not married. . . . *We reject the authority of those churches and leaders who have*

---

[13] Fellowship of Confessing Anglicans Resolution 1.10, "The Complete Jerusalem Statement," Statement on the Global Anglican Future, accessed September 27, 2014, http://fca.net/resources/the-complete-jerusalem-statement.

denied the orthodox faith in word or deed. We pray for them and call on them to repent and return to the Lord. . . . The meeting in Jerusalem this week was called in a sense of urgency that a *false gospel* has so paralyzed the Anglican Communion that the crisis must be addressed. The chief threat of this dispute involves the compromising of the integrity of the church's worldwide mission. The primary reason we have come to Jerusalem and issued this declaration is to free our churches to give clear and certain witness to Jesus Christ.[14]

Convocation of Anglicans in North America (CANA)

The Convocation of Anglicans in North America is sponsored by the Anglican Church of Nigeria and its bishops, thus connecting it to the worldwide Anglican Communion. The CANA provides orthodox clergy and congregations in North America an ecclesiastical structure with representative leadership. The long-term goal of the CANA is to assist in the establishment of the Anglican Church in North America (ACNA) as the provincial structure for orthodox Anglicanism. The CANA endorses the "Jerusalem Declaration" as well as the 2005 "Dromantine Communiqué," which states, "We continue unreservedly to be committed to the pastoral support and care of homosexual people. The victimization or diminishment of human beings whose affections happen to be ordered towards people of the same sex is anathema to us."[15]

Evangelical Anglicans in the United States (ACNA, CANA) maintain ecclesiastical connections to the Global Fellowship of Confessing Anglicans (GFCA) formed out of GAFCON. At the second GAFCON assembly in Nairobi, Kenya, in 2013, 331 bishops from thirty-eight countries reaffirmed their denunciation of the false gospel being spread among Anglicans and reasserted their separation from false churches until they repent. At the 2013 Nairobi meeting, GAFCON, recognizing the interconnectedness of doctrine and ecclesiastical structure, declared:

> The character and boundaries of our fellowship are not determined by institutions but by the Word of God. The Church is a place where the truth matters, where it is guarded and promoted and where alternatives are exposed for what they are—an exchange of the truth of God for a lie (Romans 1:25). Our willingness to submit to the written Word of God and our unwillingness to be in Christian fellowship with those who will not, is clearly expressed in The Jerusalem Statement and Declaration. This means that the divisions in

---

[14] Ibid.

[15] Anglican Communion News Service, "The Anglican Communion Primates' Meeting Communiqué, February 2005," accessed September 27, 2014, http://www.anglicannews.org/news/2005/02/the-anglican-communion-primates-meeting-communique,-february-2005.aspx. Thirty-five primates met at the Dromatine Retreat and Conference Centre in Northern Ireland in 2005. There the primates asked the Episcopal Church, USA and the Anglican Church of Canada to withdraw from the Anglican Consultative Council, a key body within the Anglican Communion.

the Anglican Communion will not be healed without a change of heart from those promoting the false gospel, and to that end we pray. . . . We urge those who have promoted the false gospel to repent of their unfaithfulness and have renewed confidence in the gospel. . . . We grieve that several national governments, aided by some church leaders, have claimed to redefine marriage and have turned same-sex marriage into a human rights issue. . . . We want to make clear that any civil partnership of a sexual nature does not receive the blessing of God. *We continue to pray for and offer pastoral support to Christians struggling with same-sex temptation who remain celibate in obedience to Christ and affirm them in their faithfulness. The gospel alone has the power to transform lives. As the gospel is heard, the Holy Spirit challenges and convicts of sin, and points to the love of God expressed in his Son, Jesus Christ. The sheer grace of God in setting us free from sin through the cross of Christ leads us into the enjoyment of our forgiveness and the desire to lead a holy life.*[16]

FREE CHURCH TRADITION

Mennonite Church USA (MCUSA)

Numerous denominations in the US have connections to the sixteenth-century Anabaptist movement. The largest such denomination is the Mennonite Church USA, the merger of the Mennonite Church (MC) and the General Conference Mennonite Church (GC) in 2001. The two former bodies began discussing the issue of homosexuality in the 1980s, producing a joint study document on human sexuality. In 1986 and 1987, the two groups each adopted a "Resolution on Human Sexuality"; it declared homosexual activity is sin. The MC's 1987 Purdue Statement incorporated this covenant:

> We covenant with each other to study the Bible together and expand our insight into the biblical teachings relating to sexuality. *We understand the Bible to teach that genital intercourse is reserved for a man and a woman united in a marriage covenant and that violation even within the relationship, i.e., wife battering, is a sin. It is our understanding that this teaching also precludes premarital, extramarital, and homosexual genital activity. We further understand the Bible to teach the sanctity of the marriage covenant and that any violation of this covenant is sin.*[17]

In the late 1980s and the 1990s, several disciplinary cases resulted in the expulsion of clergy and congregations for tolerating homosexual practice. In 1995, the MC and GC denominations adopted a new joint *Confession of Faith*

---

[16] GAFCON, "Nairobi Communiqué and Commitment," accessed September 27, 2014, http://gafcon.org/news/nairobi-communique-and-commitment.

[17] Mennonite Church, "Purdue Statement" (1987), accessed September 27, 2014, http://www-personal.umich.edu/~bpl/purdue.html.

in a Mennonite Perspective, which included an article on marriage and single-ness. The confession states:

> We recognize that God has created human beings for relationship. God intends human life to be blessed through families, especially through the family of faith. All Christians are to take their place within the household of God, where members treat each other as brothers and sisters. We hold that within the church family, the goodness of being either single or married is honored. We honor the single state and encourage the church to respect and to include single persons in the life and activities of the church family. Families of faith are called to be a blessing to all families of the earth. *We believe that God intends marriage to be a covenant between one man and one woman for life.* Christian marriage is a mutual relationship in Christ, a covenant made in the context of the church. *According to Scripture, right sexual union takes place only within the marriage relationship.* Marriage is meant for sexual intimacy, companionship, and the birth and nurture of children.[18]

In spite of continued calls for dialogue on homosexuality, the MC issued a statement declaring that the 1987 Purdue Statement was the official position of the Mennonite Church. As merger discussions continued, the General Boards of the MC and GC decided they must develop a set of "membership guidelines" before the merger could take place. The guidelines included a section called "Clarification on Some Issues Related to Homosexuality and Membership." It declares:

> We hold the Confession of Faith in a Mennonite Perspective (1995) to be the teaching position of the Mennonite Church USA. *"We believe that God intends marriage to be a covenant between one man and one woman for life"* (Article 19). We hold the Saskatoon (1986) and Purdue (1987) statements describing homosexual, extramarital and premarital sexual activity as sin to be the teaching position of the Mennonite Church USA. . . . *Pastors holding credentials in a conference of Mennonite Church USA may not perform a same-sex covenant ceremony. Such action would be grounds for review of their credentials by their area conference's ministerial credentialing body.*[19]

Evangelical Free Church of America (EFCA)
The result of a 1950 union between the Evangelical Free Church of America (Swedish) and the Evangelical Free Church Association (Norwegian-Danish), the EFCA produced a 2011 policy paper on ordination credentials as they

---

[18] *Confession of Faith in a Mennonite Perspective* (1995), Article 19: "Family, Singles, Marriage," accessed September 27, 2014, http://www.mennolink.org/doc/cof/art.19.html.

[19] Membership Guidelines for the Formation of Mennonite Church USA (Mennonite Church USA, 2001); "Clarification of Some Issues Related to Homosexuality and Membership," accessed September 27, 2014, http://www.mennoniteusa.org/wp-content/uploads/2014/07/MembershipGuidelines_2013_July.pdf.

relate to homosexual belief and conduct. The paper includes the following comments:

> Those seeking a credential within the EFCA are expected to uphold a high standard of holiness and wholeness, which includes beliefs and conduct (1 Timothy 3:1–13, Titus 1:5–9, and James 3:1). Therefore the following will be applied:

> 1. *Any person who (a) practices homosexual conduct in any form, (b) believes that homosexual behavior is a Biblically acceptable life-style for themselves or others, (c) willfully and habitually engages in conduct grounded in homosexual lust such as masturbation associated with homosexual fantasies or involvement with pornography, or (d) identifies himself or herself as homosexual, is not eligible for any level of credential for ministry within the EFCA. Furthermore, such persons who already have an EFCA credential will have their credential revoked.*

> Clarification of item 1 (d) above: *While tragically, as a result of the fall, believers might experience sexual attraction to those of the same sex, Christ's followers will not affirm this as part of God's plan for their lives nor build their identities around such attractions. Therefore, persons will not view themselves, or refer to themselves as homosexuals, but rather define their identity as new creatures in Christ.* One may (and indeed, honesty may demand that they must) acknowledge the reality of same-sex attraction, but must ground their identity in Christ, not in their sexual attractions. Thus, any person who embraces a homosexual identity, even if celibate, acts in rebellion against God's created order of male and female, demonstrating that they have not fully repented from homosexual lust and behavior.[20]

CONGREGATIONALISTS

Conservative Congregational Christian Conference (CCCC)

The "Four Cs" was organized in 1948 by a group of congregations and clergy who did not want to be a part of the emerging union of the General Council of Congregational and Christian Churches and the Evangelical Reformed Church, which formed the United Church of Christ in 1957. Over the years the CCCC has adopted numerous position papers. "Homosexuals and the Christian Fellowship" asserts:

---

[20] Evangelical Free Church, "Homosexual Belief and Conduct (Both Male and Female) as It Pertains to Credentialing in the Evangelical Free Church," accessed September 27, 2014, http://go.efca.org/sites/default/files/resources/docs/2013/02/efca_credentialing_homosexual_belief_and_conduct.pdf.

Our aim in the following statement is to combine theological thinking and Biblical commitment with contemporary understanding and compassionate pastoral care. 1. God in His Holy Word plainly condemns the practice of homosexuality as an abomination in His sight (Leviticus 18:22), as a degrading and unnatural passion (Romans 1:26, 27), as one that brings grave consequences in this life, and as a sin that, if persisted in, will exclude one from the Kingdom of God (1 Corinthians 6:9, 10). *Therefore neither individual Christians, nor ministers of the Word of God, nor congregations of the Lord Jesus Christ may take away from or lessen God's prohibition of and warning against the practice of homosexuality. . . . We specifically renounce any unbiblical prejudice against persons who are homosexual simply because of their orientation, which is just one particular form of the same sinful orientation we all have. But we do believe that every expression of that orientation is sinful, just as every expression of adulterous desire is sinful, and we believe that all practicing adulterers and homosexuals should be called to repentance* . . . individual Christians, ministers and congregations, will compassionately and in love, proclaim the Good News of forgiveness and the admonition to go and sin no more (John 8:11) to those once involved in homosexual practices, admitting such into fellowship after confession of faith and evidence of repentance, as with all those who have sinned grievously in other ways (1 Corinthians 6:11). We counsel those homosexuals who do not experience full healing and reorientation to remain celibate, trusting the Holy Spirit to give a joyous and fruitful existence as is promised to believers who cannot experience marriage (Isaiah 56:3-2). Jesus repeats the promise (Matthew 19:12).[21]

BAPTISTS

Southern Baptist Convention (SBC)

With about sixteen million members, the largest Protestant denomination in the US is the Southern Baptist Convention. Southern Baptists historically have held a high view of Scripture; thus, their public statements addressing homosexuality have affirmed historic Christian views on sexual ethics. With a congregational polity, churches that cooperate with the SBC are autonomous. However, Baptist associations, state Baptist conventions, and the SBC have withdrawn fellowship from congregations with pro-gay views. Since the 1970s the Southern Baptist Convention has issued numerous statements on homosexuality. Excerpts from a sampling of those statements are included below.

Whereas, Homosexuality has become an open lifestyle for increasing numbers of persons, and *Whereas,* Attention has been focused on the

---

[21] Conservative Congregational Christian Conference, "Homosexuals and the Christian Fellowship," accessed September 27, 2014, http://ccccusa.com/wp-content/uploads/2011/07/PPLH_Homosexuals_and_the_Fellowship.pdf.

religious and moral dimension of homosexuality, and *Whereas*, It is the task of the Christian community to bring all moral questions and issues into the light of biblical truth. Now therefore, *be it Resolved*, that the messengers to the Southern Baptist Convention meeting in Norfolk, Virginia, affirm our commitment to the biblical truth regarding the practice of homosexuality and sin. *Be it further Resolved, that this convention, while acknowledging the autonomy of the local church to ordain ministers, urges churches and agencies not to afford the practice of homosexuality any degree of approval through ordination, employment, or other designations of normal lifestyle. Be it further Resolved, that we reaffirm our Christian concern that all persons be saved from the penalty and power of sin through our Lord Jesus Christ, whatever their present lifestyle.*[22]

WHEREAS, The erosion of moral sanity continues to be a major problem in modern society; and WHEREAS, Homosexuality has become the chosen lifestyle of many in this moral decline; and Whereas, The Bible is very clear in its teaching that homosexuality is a manifestation of a depraved nature; and WHEREAS, This deviant behavior has wrought havoc in the lives of millions; and WHEREAS, Homosexuals are justified and even glorified in our secular media; and WHEREAS, Homosexual activity is the primary cause of the introduction and spread of AIDS in the United States which has not only affected those of the homosexual community, but also many innocent victims. Therefore be it RESOLVED, That we, the messengers to the Southern Baptist Convention, meeting in San Antonio, Texas, June 14–16, 1988, *deplore homosexuality as a perversion of divine standards and as a violation of nature and natural affections; and Be it further RESOLVED, That we affirm the biblical injunction which declares homosexuals, like all sinners, can receive forgiveness and victory thorough personal faith in Jesus Christ* (1 Corinthians 6:9-11); and Be it finally RESOLVED, *That we maintain that while God loves the homosexual and offers salvation, homosexuality is not a normal lifestyle and is an abomination in the eyes of God* (Leviticus 18:22; Romans 1:24–28; 1 Timothy 1:8–10).[23]

WHEREAS, A vast segment of the entertainment industry has pursued an agenda of legitimizing homosexual relationships; and WHEREAS, Public school textbooks and curricula are beginning to portray families with two homosexual "parents" as equivalent to families with a mother and a father; and WHEREAS, *Jesus states that marriage is a sacred, lifelong bond between one man and one woman (Matthew 19:4–6); and WHEREAS, Legalizing same-sex "marriage" would convey a societal approval of a homosexual lifestyle, which the Bible calls sinful and dangerous both to the individuals involved and to society at large (Romans 1:24–27; 1 Corinthians 6:9–10;*

---

[22] Southern Baptist Convention, "Resolution on Homosexuality," 1976, accessed September 27, 2014, http://www.sbc.net/resolutions/606/resolution-on-homosexuality.

[23] Southern Baptist Convention, "Resolution on Homosexuality," 1988, accessed September 27, 2014, http://www.sbc.net/resolutions/610.

Leviticus 18:22); now, therefore, be it RESOLVED, That the messengers to the Southern Baptist Convention meeting in Phoenix, Arizona, June 17–18, 2003, affirm that legal and biblical marriage can only occur between one man and one woman; and be it further RESOLVED, That we continue to oppose steadfastly all efforts by any court or state legislature to validate or legalize same-sex marriage or other equivalent unions; and be it further RESOLVED, That we call upon all judges and public officials to resist and oppose the legalization of same-sex unions; and be it further RESOLVED, That we oppose all efforts by media and entertainment outlets and public schools to mainstream homosexual unions in the eyes of our children; and be it further RESOLVED, That we call on Southern Baptist churches to commit to guard our religious liberty to recognize and perform marriages as defined by Scripture; and be it finally RESOLVED, *That we call on Southern Baptists not only to stand against same-sex unions, but to demonstrate our love for those practicing homosexuality by sharing with them the forgiving and transforming power of the gospel of Jesus Christ (1 Corinthians 6:9–11).*[24]

WHEREAS, From the beginning, the Bible establishes the basis for sexuality by declaring that human beings are created in God's image as "male and female" (Genesis 1:26–27) and that "a man leaves his father and mother and bonds with his wife, and they become one flesh" (Genesis 2:24); and WHEREAS, Jesus answered questions about marriage by reaffirming this male/female and "one flesh" creation pattern for sexuality (Matthew 19:4–6); and WHEREAS, The Apostle Paul based his teaching about marriage upon God's creation order of this one man/one woman relationship and the analogy of Christ and His bride, the Church (Ephesians 5:29–31); and WHEREAS, Any sexual behavior outside of this husband/wife marriage relationship is sinful, including premarital sex, adultery, bestiality, and pornography (Hebrews 13:4; Galatians 5:19; 1 Corinthians 6:9–11; Leviticus 18:23); and WHEREAS, *Homosexual behavior is specifically prohibited and condemned in both the Old and New Testaments (Genesis 19:1–27;* Leviticus 18:22; *Romans 1:18–25;* 1 Corinthians 6:9-11)*; and WHEREAS, Any public policy action normalizing unbiblical sexual behavior or giving homosexual unions the legal status of marriage is diametrically opposed to God's Word*; . . . now, therefore, be it RESOLVED, That the messengers to the Southern Baptist Convention meeting in Louisville, Kentucky, June 23–24, 2009, reaffirm our historic and consistent support of the biblical definition of marriage as the exclusive union of a man and a woman; and be it further RESOLVED, That we encourage all Christians to be "salt and light" on these issues by exemplifying sexual purity in our lifestyle, speaking prophetically to the culture, and acting redemptively toward individuals; . . . and be it finally RESOLVED, *That we proclaim that those who practice any unbiblical sexual behavior can be forgiven and changed, as the Apostle Paul wrote, ". . . some of you were*

---

[24] Southern Baptist Convention, "Resolution on Same-Sex Marriage," 2003, accessed September 27, 2014, http://www.sbc.net/resolutions/1128/on-samesex-marriage.

like this, but you were washed, you were sanctified, you were justified in the name of the Lord Jesus Christ and by the Spirit of our God" (1 Corinthians 6:9-11).[25]

WHEREAS, Marriage is a covenant relationship and an institution established by God rather than simply a human social construct (Genesis 2:24; Matthew 19:4–6; Ephesians 5:22–33); and WHEREAS, Southern Baptists have consistently affirmed our support of the biblical definition of marriage as the exclusive union of one man and one woman; and WHEREAS, The Scriptures indicate that all sexual behavior outside of marriage is sinful; and WHEREAS, All people, regardless of race or sexual orientation, are created in the image of God and thus are due respect and love (Genesis 1:26–27); . . . and WHEREAS, While homosexuality does not present the distinguishing features of classes entitled to special protections, like the classes of race and gender, we acknowledge the unique struggles experienced by homosexuals in some parts of society; and WHEREAS, It is regrettable that homosexual rights activists and those who are promoting the recognition of "same-sex marriage" have misappropriated the rhetoric of the Civil Rights Movement; now, therefore, be it RESOLVED, That the messengers to the Southern Baptist Convention meeting in New Orleans, Louisiana, June 19–20, 2012, oppose any attempt to frame "same-sex marriage" as a civil rights issue; and be it further RESOLVED, That we deny that the effort to legalize "same-sex marriage" qualifies as a civil rights issue since homosexuality does not qualify as a class meriting special protections, like race and gender; and be it further RESOLVED, *That we encourage Southern Baptists everywhere to fight for the civil rights of all people where such rights are consistent with the righteousness of God; and be it further RESOLVED, That we express our love to those who struggle with same-sex attraction and who are engaged in the homosexual lifestyle; and be it further RESOLVED, That we stand against any form of gay-bashing, whether disrespectful attitudes, hateful rhetoric, or hate-incited actions toward persons who engage in acts of homosexuality; and be it further RESOLVED, That we affirm that pastors should preach the truth of God's Word on human sexuality, marriage, purity, and love with all boldness and without fear of reprisal; and be it further RESOLVED, That we encourage our fellow Southern Baptists to consider how they and their churches might engage in compassionate, redemptive ministry to those who struggle with homosexuality; and be it finally RESOLVED, That we proclaim that Christ offers forgiveness of sin for those who turn from their sins and believe on Christ for the forgiveness of sin.*[26]

---

[25] Southern Baptist Convention, "On Biblical Sexuality and Public Policy," 2009, accessed October 3, 2014, http://www.sbc.net/resolutions/1196/on-biblical-sexuality-and-public-policy.

[26] Southern Baptist Convention, *"On 'Same-Sex Marriage' and Civil Rights Rhetoric,"* 2012, accessed October 3, 2014, http://www.sbc.net/resolutions/1224/on-samesex-marriage-and-civil-rights-rhetoric.

National Baptist Convention, USA Inc.

The largest African-American denomination is the National Baptist Convention, USA Inc., which has more than five million members. National Baptists have not produced position papers on homosexuality; however, black Baptists historically have regarded homosexuality as sinful, and most black Baptist churches do not allow clergy to perform same-sex commitment ceremonies. In the summer of 2012, the president of the National Baptist Convention, Julius R. Scruggs, issued a statement condemning gay marriage: "The National Baptist Convention, USA, Incorporated does not dictate to its constituent churches what position to take on issues because we believe in autonomy of the local church. However, *the National Baptist Convention, USA, Inc. affirms that marriage is a sacred biblical covenant between a man and a woman.*"[27]

METHODIST AND WESLEYAN DENOMINATIONS

African Methodist Episcopal Church (AME)

The AME Church is the largest historically black Methodist denomination in the United States. It began holding separate meetings for African-Americans in the late eighteenth century, organizing as the AME Church in 1801. Leaders of the AME Church have been clear about rejecting homosexual practice. In 2003, Bishop Richard Franklin Norris issued a public statement on gay ordination and directed all AME pastors to read it to their congregations. The statement noted, "The official position of the African Methodist Episcopal Church is not in favor of the ordination of openly gay persons to the ranks of clergy in our church. This position reaffirms our published position papers, public statements and prior rulings, all of which indicate that we do not support the ordination of openly gay persons." At the 2004 National Convention, AME delegates voted unanimously to bar clergy from officiating at marriages or civil union ceremonies for same-sex couples.[28]

---

[27] National Baptist Convention, USA, Inc., "A Statement on the Same-Sex Marriage Issue, Voting, and Christian Responsibility," accessed September 30, 2014, http://www.nationalbaptist.com/about-us/news--press-releases/the-same-sex-marriage-issue,-voting-and-christian-responsibility.html. For an overview of African-American Christian perspectives on homosexual practice, see "African American Church Traditions" in *Homosexuality and Religion: An Encyclopedia*, ed. Jeffrey S. Siker (Westport, CT: Greenwood, 2007), 48–50. This essay cites several surveys indicating almost universal condemnation of homosexuality in the Christian African-American community.

[28] Human Rights Campaign, "Stances of Faiths on LGBT Issues: African Methodist Episcopal Church," accessed September 30, 2014, http://www.hrc.org/resources/entry/stances-of-faiths-on-lgbt-issues-african-methodist-episcopal-church. The AME position on marriage has remained constant since its founding. The 1817 edition of the AME's *Doctrines and Discipline*, under "The Form of the Solemnization of Matrimony" states that the purpose of a wedding ceremony is "to join together this man and this woman in holy Matrimony: which is an honourable estate, instituted by God in the time of man's innocence, signifying the mystical union that is

Wesleyan Church

The Wesleyan Church was established in 1846 in protest of the Methodist Episcopal Church's refusal to address slavery. In 2011 the Board of General Superintendents issued a "Pastoral Letter on Homosexuality." Below are selections from this letter.

It is only a recent aberration that a few denominations—infiltrated by leaders and influencers who question or reject the authority of Christian Scriptures—have arrogantly challenged twenty centuries of orthodoxy and orthopraxy by condoning homosexual relationships as behavior compatible with a Christian profession of faith. . . . [W]e find no positive example or justification anywhere in God's Word to sanction sexual relations between same-sex partners. Instead, we find multiple, unmistakably clear passages indicating that homosexual practices are the immoral consequence of fallen human nature. . . . While science may have unresolved questions, Scripture is unequivocal about the divine design for the sexes and the sinfulness of indulging sexual lust, fantasies, and relations—gay or straight—outside a faithful marriage covenant between a man and a woman. . . . A Wesleyan outlook takes sin and human depravity seriously. To do less repudiates the holiness of God and depreciates human freewill. We believe all people are born broken, with an inherited disposition toward wrongdoing and evil. We believe people become more broken by their own choices, by habitually giving in to their sinful nature, and by willing participation in personal and corporate acts of sin. . . . The Scriptures promise more than forgiveness of sins—they promise deliverance from sin's domination over our lives. . . . We trust the testimony of Scripture that people can change. We are also confident of this because of firsthand evidence. . . . Our churches are full of persons who have experienced God's power in their lives. They have been forgiven and become forgivers. They have instantaneously or through disciplined effort and divine enablement been delivered from addiction, resentments, compulsion, and temptations. Sins and perversions they once delighted in indulging have become repulsive to them. . . . The question remains open whether genetic, hormonal, environmental, or volition factors—or some combination of factors—cause people to feel same-sex attractions. Yet, none of these potential causes changes the moral responsibility and accountability of every person to live according to God's revealed will. The heterosexually inclined are under the same rule of abstinence until marriage and self-control when married as the homosexually inclined. . . . *Speaking the truth in love, the Church must never quit calling "sin" by its proper name solely for the sake of political correctness or popularity. . . . The good news is that through dependence on Christ, true deliverance from evil is possible (the kind of deliverance asked for in the Lord's Prayer). For some this deliverance is experienced as*

betwixt Christ and his Church." *The Doctrines and Discipline of the African Methodist Episcopal Church*: Electronic Edition (Philadelphia, PA: Richard Allen and Jacob Tapisco, 1817), 137–38, accessed March 28, 2015, http://docsouth.unc.edu/church/ame/ame.html.

miraculous or instantaneous release from sinful desires, urges, compulsions, habits and addictions. For others, deliverance comes in the form of daily strength to remain faithfully obedient to God, even when it means enduring thorns in the flesh that He does not choose to remove. The Christian who continues to feel same-sex temptations, yet maintains a sexually chaste life, is experiencing the delivering power of God's grace. . . . The twenty-first century opened with a generation that faces seduction by the values of an increasingly secular, materialistic, hedonistic culture in which lesbian, gay, bisexual, and transgender lifestyles are touted as acceptable alternatives to heterosexuality. The Wesleyan Church, along with biblical Christians from many other denominations and local gatherings, is boldly responding by pointing to the glorious in-breaking of the Kingdom of God upon this world and the powers of darkness that have deluded it. The Church continues to be God's sole plan for incarnating the love and character of Jesus Christ for the sake of saving this generation. . . . It is full of inspiring examples of formerly wicked men and women who are now tangible proof of the power of the gospel to change lives.[29]

HOLINESS AND PENTECOSTAL DENOMINATIONS

Church of the Nazarene

The Church of the Nazarene's position on homosexuality is articulated in the "Human Sexuality" statement in the denomination's *Manual*. It declares:

> *Homosexuality is one means by which human sexuality is perverted. We recognize the depth of the perversion that leads to homosexual acts but affirm the biblical position that such acts are sinful and subject to the wrath of God. We believe the grace of God sufficient to overcome the practice of homosexuality (1 Corinthians 6:9–11). We deplore any action or statement that would seem to imply compatibility between Christian morality and the practice of homosexuality. We urge clear preaching and teaching concerning Bible standards of sexual morality.*[30]

An official statement by the Board of Superintendents, updated in 2011, expands on the brief statement in the *Manual*. The longer document includes the following excerpt:

> *Church tradition has for more than nineteen hundred years served to strengthen the prohibition of homosexual behavior; this behavior has always been considered contrary to the will of God. Major voices throughout the*

---

[29] The Wesleyan Church, "Pastoral Letter on Homosexuality," 2011, Board of General Superintendents, accessed September 30, 2014, http://www.wesleyan.org/234/pastoral-letter-on-homosexuality.

[30] Church of the Nazarene, *Manual*, 2009–2013, "Human Sexuality," accessed September 30, 2014, http://nazarene.org/files/docs/Perspectives_Homosexuality.pdf.

history of the Church have condemned homosexual behavior as sinful/ immoral. . . . A Wesleyan response is defined by a clear conviction that homosexual behavior is immoral. The Scriptures, along with the received tradition of the Christian Church, speak to the issue with sufficient clarity to make it plain to all that homosexual behavior is part of the fallen nature. . . . The logic that condones homosexual behavior is innately selfish. This logic claims that homosexual desires are natural and that a person has the right to act on their natural desires. "I want what I want regardless of others, regardless of what it does to society, regardless of what it does to me or to my family." As Christians we are ultimately called to discipline our desires, to lay down our lives for others, and to bear the fruit of the Spirit, which is self-control. The pit of selfish sexual pursuit is easy to fall into and hard to crawl out of. Its patterns dig tracks in our soul[s]. Homosexual behavior damages a person, a relationship, a family, a world. Choosing to practice a lifestyle regardless of its consequences is ultimately selfish. We wish to be absolutely clear. *A person who claims to be a Christian and a practicing homosexual is making two contradictory statements: 1) I am a practicing homosexual, and 2) I am a follower of Jesus Christ. Which one supersedes the other? Which one is most basic to his or her identity? If someone says "Christian," then as a disciple of Jesus this person's sexuality must bow in obedience to Christ and what Scripture says about the sin of homosexual behavior. If a person says "practicing homosexual," then God and Scripture must bow to the person's sexual orientation, and this makes homosexuality an idolatrous identity. For the practicing homosexual, his or her sexual identity supersedes identity in Christ. Anything above God is idolatry. . . . We must not shy away from telling the truth about homosexuality, its roots, and its consequences. The Church may well be the only place left in the world where homosexuals can be loved and hear the truth of God. From Scripture, Christian tradition, and the doctrines of our church, we compassionately and persistently affirm that homosexual practice is contrary to God's will and cannot be acceptable behavior for followers of Christ.* At the same time we must always point to hope in the Christ who came to redeem all of us from the power of sin. Wesleyan theology offers resources of hopeful grace for the homosexual. By grace God is able to either deliver them from homosexual desires or enable them to live celibate lives.[31]

Church of God in Christ (COGIC)

With more than five million members, the largest Pentecostal denomination in the United States is the Church of God in Christ. The COGIC was established in 1907 by African-American clergy; they believed in the ongoing gift of speaking in tongues. The following is a selection from the COGIC's official statement regarding same-sex marriage and civil unions:

---

[31] Ibid.

This divinely inspired family framework, pronounced in Old and New Testament Scripture, is without compromise. To tamper with the foundation is to disrupt the order God intended. This order is the intended structure by which all humanity is expected to govern their lives. The human body is designed by God as male and female to anatomically accommodate individuals of the opposite sex in the conception, bearing and nurture of children; the human body is unquestionably designed to accommodate individuals of the opposite sex, not of the same sex. *The Holy Bible, which is the authoritative Word of God, clearly prohibits sexual relations between members of the same sex. Though it does not isolate intercourse between individuals of the same sex as the only sin, it designates this and a series of other activities as sinful behavior from which the Christian is to abstain. 1 Cor. 6:9–11 (NKJV) says, "Do you not know that the unrighteous will not inherit the kingdom of God? Do not be deceived. Neither fornicators, nor idolaters, nor adulterers, nor homosexuals, nor sodomites, nor thieves, nor covetous, nor drunkards, nor revilers, nor extortioners will inherit the kingdom of God. And such were some of you. But you were washed, but you were sanctified, but you were justified in the name of the Lord Jesus and by the Spirit of our God." (See also: Leviticus 18:22; Romans 1:26–27; and 1 Timothy 1:8). The Bible indicates that there is nothing that can excuse or eliminate the sinfulness of sexual involvement between individuals of the same sex.* Neither so called "marriage vows," civil unions, nor homosexual drives or passions are recognized by the Bible as justifications or acceptable excuses or rationale for sexual acts between individuals of the same sex. Sinful desires and inclinations must be resisted and overcome by the power of God in Christ Jesus, and by power of the Holy Spirit who strengthens our minds and our wills. . . . The Bible defines marriage as a relationship between one man and one woman (Genesis 2:24; 1 Corinthians 7:2; 1 Timothy 3:2, 12; Titus 1:6). To define marriage otherwise is to dilute and destroy its usefulness as a word which denotes what is highest and best about human society. While we are committed to proclaim and support the tenants of the Bible, and also to persuade others to do so, we recognize that in a free and democratic society morality cannot be legislated. We oppose violence and discrimination against individuals or groups because of sexual orientation. We do not feel that it is necessary to legalize same-sex marriage to provide the civil benefits and civil rights to all regardless of sexual orientation. We proclaim the value and worth of every human being regardless of sexual orientation. But, we passionately and unapologetically defend the right of faith communities to maintain the integrity of their message, mission and identity. We welcome to the church all people who seek to serve and know God and His Word.[32]

---

[32] Charisma News, "COGIC Takes Stand Against Same-Sex Marriage," posted May 23, 2012, accessed September 30, 2014, http://www.charismanews.com/us/33464-cogic-takes-stand-against-same-sex-marriage.

Assemblies of God (AG)

The Assemblies of God was formed in 1914 from a gathering of delegates representing a number of Pentecostal ministries who organized themselves as the General Council of the Assemblies of God. Today the AG is the largest Pentecostal denomination in the world, with more than 65 million members; in the US, membership is more than 3 million. In 2001 a study committee on homosexuality reported:

> *This reaffirmation of truth has become all the more urgent because writers sympathetic to the homosexual community have advanced revisionist interpretations of relevant biblical texts that are based upon biased exegesis and mistranslation. In effect, they seek to set aside almost 2,000 years of Christian biblical interpretation and ethical teachings. We believe these efforts are reflective of the conditions described in 2 Timothy 4:3, "For the time will come when men will not put up with sound doctrine. Instead, to suit their own desire, they will gather around them a great number of teachers to say what their itching ears want to hear." (See also v. 4.) It should be noted at the outset that there is absolutely no affirmation of homosexual activity found anywhere in Scripture. Rather, the consistent sexual ideal in the Bible is chastity for those outside a monogamous heterosexual marriage and fidelity for those inside such a marriage. There is abundant evidence that homosexual behavior, along with illicit heterosexual behavior, is immoral and comes under the judgment of God. We believe, in the light of biblical revelation, that the growing cultural acceptance of homosexual identity and behavior, male and female, is symptomatic of a broader spiritual disorder that threatens the family, the government, and the church. . . . The Christian church has historically understood that although the ceremonial provisions of the Old Testament law were no longer in effect after the atoning death of Christ, the New Testament interpretation and restatement of its moral law was. On the subject of homosexuality both the Old and New Testaments speak with one voice. The moral prohibitions against homosexual behavior in the Old Testament are pointedly repeated in the New Testament. . . .* Of fundamental importance for every individual, including those who struggle with homosexual temptation or behavior, is the need for reconciliation with God through His Son Jesus Christ. Believers who struggle with homosexual temptations must be encouraged and strengthened by fellow Christians (Galatians 6:1, 2). Likewise, they should be taught that temptation is universal, that temptation itself is not sin, and that temptation can be resisted and overcome (1 Corinthians 10:13; Hebrew 12:1-6). The moral imperatives of Scripture are incumbent upon all persons. However, believers should not be surprised that unbelievers do not honor God and do not recognize the Bible has a rightful claim on their lives and conduct (1 Corinthians 1:1–18). . . . *As Christians we must both exhort believers to live in moral purity and express in word and deed Christ's love for the lost. Aware of the claims of God on every aspect of our lives, we must emphasize that we are called to holiness. To unbelievers*

we must reach out with compassion and humility. We must hold no malice toward, or fear of, homosexuals—such attitudes are not of Christ. At the same time we must not condone sexual behavior that God has defined as sinful.[33]

INDEPENDENT CONGREGATIONS

As noted in the introduction to this chapter, the evangelical movement often is traced back to the First Great Awakening (evangelical revival), which dramatically shaped the religious landscape of the United States and Britain in the eighteenth century. The evangelical movement proliferated in the nineteenth century as a result of numerous revivals on college campuses and the American frontier. In the mid-twentieth century a resurgence of this movement was spurred by the ministry of Billy Graham. Today many mainline denominations have congregations that identify with evangelicalism. Multitudes of new evangelical denominations emerged from the American revivals, and millions of church members fill independent evangelical congregations throughout the United States. Evangelicals vastly outnumber the members of mainline denominations.

The thousands of American congregations independent of any formal denominational affiliation range from ten-thousand-member megachurches to small urban and rural congregations. In the American context almost all of these congregations are classified as evangelical. Altogether there may be as many as 100 million evangelicals in America, about one-third of the population.[34] The evangelical emphases of obedience to Scripture and a transformed life as a result of Christian conversion lead evangelicals to unite in support of the traditional biblical understanding of homosexuality.

---

[33] Assemblies of God, "Homosexuality," August 6, 2001, accessed September 30, 2014, http://ag.org/top/Beliefs/Position_Papers/pp_downloads/pp_4181_homosexuality.pdf. Cf. the new official statement, "Homosexuality, Marriage, and Sexual Identity" (2014), at the same site.

[34] For a brief overview of the evangelical movement in America, see Douglas Sweeney's *The American Evangelical Story* (Grand Rapids, MI: Baker Academic, 2005). Sweeney indicates that worldwide there are more than 2 billion Christians. Of that number more than 800 million are evangelicals—if one includes Pentecostals and Charismatics as evangelicals (p. 9). According to the Institute for the Study of American Evangelicals, evangelicals make up 30–35% of the American population, some 90–100 million people. See "How Many Evangelicals Are There?," accessible at http://www.wheaton.edu/ISAE/Defining-Evangelicalism/How-Many-Are-There. These figures are similar to the results of the 2007 Religious Landscape Survey conducted by the Pew Forum on Religion and Public Life. According to the Pew statistics, if one combines the membership of evangelical Protestant churches (26.3% of the US population) with that of historically black churches (6.9% of the US population), the total would be 33.2% of the American population.

COLLABORATIVE EVANGELICAL ORGANIZATIONS

A few sample texts illustrate the virtual unanimity within the evangelical movement regarding homosexuality. Below are citations from the Lausanne Movement, the National Association of Evangelicals, the Council for Christian Colleges and Universities, and the Manhattan Declaration.

The Lausanne Movement

This movement has its roots in the 1966 World Congress on Evangelism in Berlin, an event sponsored by the Billy Graham Evangelistic Association and *Christianity Today*. Attended by 1,200 Christian leaders from 100 countries, the purpose of the meeting was to "unite all evangelicals in the common task of the total evangelization of the world." This vision for global evangelical partnership continued with the first meeting of the Lausanne Movement in Lausanne, Switzerland, in 1974. A document, "The Lausanne Covenant," was produced (drafted chiefly by John Stott), which helped define evangelical theology and practice. A second Lausanne Congress was held in Manila, Philippines, and a third in Cape Town, South Africa, in 2010. The Cape Town meeting, attended by 4,000 evangelical leaders from 198 countries, adopted "The Cape Town Commitment," which addressed human sexuality:

> 2. Walk in love, rejecting the idolatry of disordered sexuality.
>
> *God's design in creation is that marriage is constituted by the committed, faithful relationship between one man and one woman, in which they become one flesh in a new social unity that is distinct from their birth families, and that sexual intercourse as the expression of that "one flesh" is to be enjoyed exclusively within the bond of marriage.* This loving sexual union within marriage, in which "two become one," reflects both Christ's relationship with the Church and also the unity of Jew and Gentile in the new humanity.
>
> Paul contrasts the purity of God's love with the ugliness of counterfeit love that masquerades in disordered sexuality and all that goes along with it. *Disordered sexuality of all kinds, in any practice of sexual intimacy before or outside marriage as biblically defined, is out of line with God's will and blessing in creation and redemption. The abuse and idolatry that surrounds disordered sexuality contributes to wider social decline, including the breakdown of marriages and families and produces incalculable suffering of loneliness and exploitation.* It is a serious issue within the Church itself, and it is a tragically common cause of leadership failure. We recognize our need for deep humility and consciousness of failure in this area. We long to see Christians challenging our surrounding cultures by living according to the standards to which the Bible calls us.[35]

---

[35] The Lausanne Movement, "The Cape Town Commitment," 2011, accessed September 30, 2014, http://www.lausanne.org/en/documents/ctcommitment.html.

National Association of Evangelicals (NAE)

The National Association of Evangelicals began in 1942 and today has more than forty member denominations as well as thousands of individual member congregations. The NAE's public policy statements over the decades have supported historic Christian views of marriage and homosexuality. The NAE supported the Defense of Marriage Act (DOMA) in 1996 and has consistently spoken out against same-sex marriage. In its 2004 document "For the Health of the Nation: An Evangelical Call to Civic Responsibility," the NAE stated, "We commit ourselves to work for laws that protect and foster family life, and against government attempts to interfere with the integrity of the family. We also oppose innovations such as same-sex 'marriage.'" In 2004 the NAE drafted a resolution on homosexuality. A 2012 NAE publication, *Theology of Sex*, addresses homosexuality as well.

> The Scriptures declare that God created us male and female. Furthermore, the biblical record shows that sexual union was established exclusively within the context of a male-female relationship (Genesis 2:24), and was formalized in the institution of marriage. . . . Homosexual activity, like adulterous relationships, is clearly condemned in the Scriptures. . . . In the name of Christ we proclaim forgiveness, cleansing, restoration and power for godly living for all who repent and believe the gospel. . . . We believe that homosexuality is not an inherited condition in the same category as race, gender, or national origin, all of which are free from moral implication. *We believe homosexuality is a deviation from the Creator's plan for human sexuality. . . . Individual Christians, ministers, and congregations should compassionately proclaim the Good News of forgiveness and encourage those involved [in] homosexual practices to cease those practices, accept forgiveness, and pray for deliverance, as nothing is impossible with God. Further, we should accept them into fellowship upon confession of faith and repentance, as we would any other forgiven sinner (1 Corinthians 6:11).* We further call upon pastors and theologians, along with medical and sociological specialists with the Christian community to expand research on the factors which give rise to homosexuality and to develop therapy, pastoral care and congregational support leading to complete restoration.[36]

A noteworthy challenge for Christians striving to honor God in their sexuality today is how to make sense of homosexual behaviour. Consensus among Christians about the immorality of homosexual behavior has been shaken through difficult debates in many churches related to monogamous homosexual relationships, the approval of gay marriages, and complex and

---

[36] National Association of Evangelicals, "Homosexuality 2004," accessed October 3, 2014, http://www.nae.net/fullresolutionlist/180-homosexuality-2004. At the writing of this book, the 2004 resolution on homosexuality was being reviewed at the direction of the board. The NAE refers people to their publication, *Theology of Sex*.

painful questions surrounding what it means to offer acceptance, love and justice to professed homosexual individuals. . . . Although some homosexual individuals may exhibit some positive characteristics, homosexual activity does not fall in line with the fundamental purposes for sex. In fact, Romans 1, 1 Corinthians 6, and other passages throughout the Bible specifically identify homosexual behaviour as sinful. . . . The biblical emphasis on moral purity is not a devious plan to eliminate enjoyment from a Christian's life; rather, it is God's infinitely wise foundation for our collective and individual well-being and happiness, as well as long-lasting family relationships. In this area of our lives as in all others, God call[s] us to be obedient to his revealed moral rules, in no small part because these moral laws are given for our own good (see John 14:21; Deuteronomy 10:13). Righteousness is life-giving; sin has the opposite effect.[37]

Council for Christian Colleges and Universities (CCCU)

With a membership including 118 institutions in North America and 58 affiliate institutions in nineteen countries, the CCCU established a Task Force on Homosexuality; it issued a report in 2001. The report's purpose was to provide assistance to member schools engaging a host of issues related to homosexuality within academic institutions. The report put the issue in the larger context of the sexual revolution and the erosion of marital stability in North America. The report acknowledged "shared institutional commitments to the historic Christian faith . . . and fidelity to the historic understandings of the Church universal unless overwhelming contrary evidence forces a new understanding."[38] After reviewing biblical teaching, the 2001 report stated:

Historically, the Christian Church has affirmed marriage between one person of each sex as the creational norm for intimate sexual expression. . . . In light of these realities and purposes of our sexuality, the core of the traditional sexual ethic of the Christian Church for two millennia and of the Hebrew people before and since has been that God commends and commands chastity both for married people though maintaining the exclusivity of sexual intimacy with one's spouse and for unmarried people through refraining from intimate sexual relations. . . . Celibacy, voluntary restraint from intimate sexual expression, while not the creational norm for adults, is nevertheless approved in words by the Apostle Paul and by the example in the life of our Lord Jesus Christ himself. This reality ought to caution Christians about

---

[37] National Association of Evangelicals, *Theology of Sex* (2012), accessed October 3, 2014, http://nae.net/images/content/Theology_of_Sex.pdf.

[38] Council for Christian Colleges and Universities, "Report of Ad Hoc Committee on Human Sexuality," August 16, 2001, accessed September 30, 2014, http://www.cccu.org/~/media/file-folder/Taskforce-HumanSexuality. Evangelical Christian colleges face increasing pressure to capitulate on LGBT issues. A number of evangelical schools have student and alumni groups such as OneGordon.com, OneWestmont.com, and OneBiola.com that advocate the gay agenda.

accepting any view that elevates sexual intimacy to a basic necessity of full humanness or denies the possibility of a meaningful celibate existence, especially where the latter is formed and carried out in the context of a Christian community that equally and fully values the gifts of all its members.[39]

The report rehearses the scholarly challenges to traditional interpretations of Scripture yet argues for maintaining adherence to historic views:

Historically, the Church has had consensus that these biblical injunctions, which appear across a variety of genres of biblical literature, apply across chronological and cultural boundaries. . . . While there can be no question that we face challenges in applying the scriptural view in contemporary and pluralistic Western culture, there is a fair consensus that the historic stance of the Church, grounded in the unambiguous teaching of Scripture, cannot be explained away. Arguments that there are other ways to read the scriptural witness on this matter or on the broader vision for sexuality and sexual ethics have not rendered the traditional judgment irrelevant.[40]

Manhattan Declaration: A Call to Christian Conscience (2009)

The Manhattan Declaration is a manifesto issued by evangelical, Roman Catholic, and Orthodox leaders to affirm their support of "the sanctity of life, traditional marriage, and religious liberty." Signed by more than 150 American religious leaders, the statement decries the erosion of traditional marriage in American culture, also addressing the issue of homosexuality. The document states:

We acknowledge that there are those who are disposed towards homosexual and polyamorous conduct and relationships, just as there are those who are disposed towards other forms of immoral conduct. We have compassion for those so disposed; we respect them as human beings possessing profound, inherent, and equal dignity; and we pay tribute to the men and women who strive, often with little assistance, to resist the temptation to yield to desires that they, no less than we, regard as wayward. We stand with them, even when they falter. We, no less than they, are sinners who have fallen short of God's intention for our lives. We, no less than they, are in constant need of God's patience, love and forgiveness. *We call on the entire Christian community to resist sexual immorality, and at the same time refrain from disdainful condemnation of those who yield to it. Our rejection of sin, though resolute, must never become the rejection of sinners.* For every sinner, regardless of the sin, is loved by God, who seeks not our destruction but rather the conversion of our hearts. Jesus calls all who wander from the path of virtue to "a more excellent way." As his disciples we will reach out in love to assist all who hear the call and wish to answer it.

---

[39] Ibid.
[40] Ibid.

We further acknowledge that there are sincere people who disagree with us, and with the teaching of the Bible and Christian tradition, on questions of sexual morality and the nature of marriage. Some who enter into same-sex and polyamorous relationships no doubt regard their unions as truly marital. They fail to understand, however, that marriage is made possible by the sexual complementarity of man and woman, and that the comprehensive, multi-level sharing of life that marriage is includes bodily unity of the sort that unites husband and wife biologically as a reproductive unit. This is because the body is no mere extrinsic instrument of the human person, but truly part of the personal reality of the human being. Human beings are not merely centers of consciousness or emotion, or minds, or spirits, inhabiting non-personal bodies. The human person is a dynamic unity of body, mind, and spirit. *Marriage is what one man and one woman establish when, forsaking all others and pledging lifelong commitment, they found a sharing of life at every level of being—the biological, the emotional, the dispositional, the rational, the spiritual—on a commitment that is sealed, completed and actualized by loving sexual intercourse in which the spouses become one flesh, not in some merely metaphorical sense, but by fulfilling together the behavioral conditions of procreation.* That is why in the Christian tradition, and historically in Western law, consummated marriages are not dissoluble or annullable on the ground of infertility, even though the nature of the marital relationship is shaped and structured by its intrinsic orientation to the great good of procreation.[41]

CONCLUSION

Most striking in evangelical statements concerning homosexual practice is the unequivocal commitment to Scripture as the final word on the subject. Specific biblical texts are cited in most of the statements. An underlying assertion of evangelicals is that the Old and New Testaments comprehensively and consistently condemn homosexual practice as sinful before God. A common understanding of marriage as defined by the creation narrative and confirmed by Christ is evident in many of the evangelical statements.

Many evangelical position papers emphasize the transformative grace of God. This grace empowers persons for a life of self-denial, sustaining them in the midst of sexual temptation. The power of the gospel of Christ to remake men and women into godly persons who honor God in their sexual behavior is a common theme. The reality of intense struggle in the midst of sexual temptation is acknowledged along with the importance of the Christian community providing support and encouragement to persons struggling with same-sex attraction. Pastoral care and professional counseling are recommended for

---

[41] "Manhattan Declaration: A Call to Christian Conscience," November 20, 2009, accessed September 30, 2014, http://manhattandeclaration.org/man_dec_resources/Manhattan_Declaration_full_text.pdf.

ministry to believers who experience homosexual attraction. By God's grace converted homosexuals may experience varying degrees of freedom from same-sex attraction. Nonetheless, all believers are called to chastity outside of heterosexual marriage.[42]

Statements on homosexuality among evangelicals, in agreement with statements by Roman Catholics and Orthodox believers, frequently distinguish homosexual orientation from practice. Often only the practice is said to be sinful; orientation is something one should work to alter. In our view sexual ethics involves more than orientation and action. Desires of the heart can form orientation and lead to actions. Jesus recognizes this when he says, "You have heard that it was said, 'You shall not commit adultery.' But I say to you that everyone who looks at a woman with lust has already committed adultery with her in his heart" (Matt 5:27–28). Indeed, Jesus's ethical challenge to Pharisaic Judaism is largely a challenge to see righteousness not just in terms of actions but also in terms of the heart. Jesus says, "For out of the heart come evil intentions, murder, adultery, fornication, theft, false witness, slander" (Matt 15:19). Further work needs to be done on applying this teaching of Christ to the issue of homosexuality.

That a number of evangelical statements appeal to church history's steady testimony on homosexuality is significant. The congruence of evangelical Protestant perspectives on homosexual practice with those of the Roman Catholic and Orthodox churches is equally noteworthy. These traditions articulate a common set of themes and approaches to pastoral care for homosexual persons. Each of the traditions affirms the historic understanding held by Christians for two millennia that homosexual practice is incompatible with Christian discipleship, and church discipline may be necessary if the practice is habitual. This amazing unanimity over centuries of Christian ministry confirms that Christ is leading his church with clarity to uphold and practice the truths revealed in Scripture.

---

[42] A host of evangelical ministry resources point to the transforming power of the gospel for homosexuals. Several we have found useful include, Chad W. Thompson's *Loving Homosexuals as Jesus Would* (Grand Rapids, MI: Brazos, 2004). Thompson offers a balanced appraisal on the issue of change and an encouraging blueprint for loving our homosexual neighbors. Stanton L. Jones and Mark A. Yarhouse, in their book *Ex-Gays?: A Longitudinal Study of Religiously Mediated Change in Sexual Orientation* (Downer's Grove, IL: InterVarsity, 2007), report the results of a study with homosexual clients. Their clinical research has confirmed the possibility of substantive change for believers who seek it. Jones and Yarhouse state, "Every secular study of change has shown some success rate and persons who testify to substantial healings by God are legion" (p. 109).

CHAPTER 7

MAINLINE DENOMINATIONS AND REVISIONIST CHRISTIANITY

Only in the last few decades have mainline Protestants—particularly those in the West—openly tolerated homosexual behavior and allowed those practicing it to serve in church office. While it is not shocking that Western culture has turned its back on Christian sexual ethics, traditional believers are dismayed to hear of professing "Christians" doing the same. Catholics, Orthodox, and evangelical Protestants shake their heads in disbelief each time they learn of another denomination capitulating on the homosexual issue. Just as disconcerting is a recent proliferation of books by Protestant authors arguing that homosexual practice can be consistent with Christianity.

It has become popular in some Christian circles to downplay biblical authority and grant social science or the culture at large equally authoritative voices in the church. This is tragic. Such a departure from historic Christian practice has been obvious in the field of sexual ethics. In the last few decades, discussions of homosexuality have frequently focused on homosexual experience and the pronouncements of psychological associations rather than the explicit instruction of Scripture. If the Bible were silent on homosexuality, some of this might be understandable. But the wholesale abandonment of clear biblical teaching on homosexuality is inexcusable for those claiming to follow Christ.

Since the 1970s, gay and lesbian activists in mainline denominations have launched a full-scale assault on traditional, biblically defined sexual standards. As a result, a number of mainline denominations have capitulated by endorsing gay ordination. Some denominations have been willing to bless same-sex unions. In all such instances, although mainline denominations possess a rich theological heritage in the Protestant Reformation, that connection has become irrelevant. They claim biblical fidelity and seek to ground their revisionist practices in tradition, but their actions reveal a disingenuous spirit. Mainline gay advocates often claim that one cannot take the Christian tradition seriously, for the church—they insist—has misread the Bible; instead, one must locate authority in the contemporary community's reasoning and experience.

UNITED CHURCH OF CHRIST (UCC)

The United Church of Christ was established in a 1957 merger of the Congregational-Christian Churches and the Evangelical and Reformed Churches. In 1972, the Golden Gate Association (CA) of the UCC ordained openly gay William R. Johnson as a minister. Five years later in Virginia, Anne Holmes became the first ordained lesbian minister in the UCC. The 1985 General Synod of the UCC adopted an "Open and Affirming" resolution, calling congregations to commit themselves to a nondiscrimination policy and to embrace a "Covenant of Openness and Affirmation." In 2003, a resolution on "Transgender People" was adopted, and in 2005, the UCC General Synod passed an Equal Marriage Rights resolution, calling for "equal marriage rights for couples regardless of gender."

> We know, with Paul, that as Christians, we are many members, but are one body in Christ—members one of another, and that we all have different gifts. With Jesus, we affirm that we are called to love our neighbors as ourselves, that we are called to act as agents of reconciliation and wholeness within the world and within the church itself. We know that lesbian, gay, and bisexual people are often scorned by the church, and devalued and discriminated against both in the church and society. *We commit ourselves to caring and concern for lesbian, gay and bisexual sisters and brothers by affirming that: we believe that lesbian, gay and bisexual people share with all others the worth that comes from being unique individuals; we welcome gay, lesbian and bisexual people to join our congregation in the same spirit and manner used in the acceptance of any new members*; we recognize the presence of ignorance, fear and hatred in the church and in our culture, and covenant to not discriminate on the basis of sexual orientation, nor any other irrelevant factor, and we seek to include and support those who, because of this fear and prejudice, find themselves in exile from a spiritual community; we seek to address the needs and advocate the concerns of lesbian, gay and bisexual people in our church and in society by actively encouraging church instrumentalities and secular governmental bodies to adopt and implement policies of non-discrimination; and we join together as a covenantal community, to celebrate and share our common communion and the reassurance that we are indeed created by God, reconciled by Christ and empowered by the grace of the Holy Spirit.[1]

---

[1] United Church of Christ, "United Church of Christ General Synod Resolution 1985, Calling on United Church of Christ Congregations to Declare Themselves Open and Affirming," accessed March 28, 2015, http://www.ucc.org/men_open-and-affirming.

WHEREAS, God has brought forth human beings as creatures who are male, female, and sometimes dramatically or subtly a complex mix of male and female in their bodies; and WHEREAS, human cultures have created a broad diversity of roles for men and women, and have sometimes created roles for people named as neither man nor woman often revered and respected roles; and WHEREAS, rules of appearance in the Bible, such as in Deuteronomy 22:5, are certainly among the rules criticized by Jesus as focused on outward conformity rather than inward integrity grounded in the acceptance of God's love; and WHEREAS, there are numerous biblical affirmations of the goodness of creation and the love of God for all people, including Genesis 1, Psalm 139, John 1:1–5, and Acts 10:34–43; and WHEREAS, Galatians 3:26–29 calls on those who are baptized to put on Christ like a garment and to look past human divisions to become one person in Christ; and WHEREAS, transgender and intersexual people are currently offering valuable ministry within the United Church of Christ, both as lay people and as clergy; and WHEREAS, transgender people are recognized within the constitution of the United Church of Christ as appropriately sharing in the guidance of the national expression of the United Church of Christ (as part of the United Church of Christ Coalition for Lesbian, Gay, Bisexual, and Transgender Concerns); and WHEREAS, the United Church of Christ in numerous program activities in all expressions of the church has affirmed the positive virtues carried by men within traditional cultures, by women within traditional cultures, while also calling for the transformation of gender roles that are oppressive of men or women, or otherwise not fully reflective of Christian values; and WHEREAS, Christian transgender people have sometimes experienced rejection and non-acceptance within some expressions of the United Church of Christ and in other expressions of Christ's Church, and are in need of a welcoming Christian community where they are valued as Christian people, and WHEREAS, many settings of the United Church of Christ have little understanding of transgender people; of how to meet their needs and make them feel welcome, of how to integrate their gifts and capacities for ministry into the life of the church and of how to integrate them into liturgy and expressions of worship. THEREFORE BE IT RESOLVED THAT *all congregations of the United Church of Christ are encouraged to welcome transgender people into membership, ministry, and full participation; and BE IT FURTHER RESOLVED THAT all settings of the United Church of Christ are encouraged to learn about the realities of transgender experience and expression, including the gifts and callings and needs of transgender people, and are encouraged to engage in appropriate dialogue with transgender people; and BE IT FURTHER RESOLVED THAT Wider Church Ministries and Local Church Ministries are encouraged to develop appropriate resources, in consultation with a representative group of transgender people within the United Church of Christ, to encourage the participation and ministry of transgender people in the life of the church and to prepare individuals and churches to receive such participation and ministry*; and BE IT FURTHER RESOLVED THAT Justice and Witness Ministries is encouraged to develop a program of education and advocacy, in consultation with a representative group of transgender people within the United Church of Christ, and then to provide leadership in advocating for the human and civil rights of transgender people; and BE IT FURTHER RESOLVED THAT a representative group of transgender people within the United Church of Christ shall be invited to report on progress made in regard to participation within the United Church of Christ and the development of education and advocacy concerning civil and human rights by the United Church of Christ, and to make additional suggestions, to the Twenty-fifth General Synod.[2]

WHEREAS the Bible affirms and celebrates human expressions of love and partnership, calling us to live out fully that gift of God in responsible, faithful, committed relationships that recognize and respect the image of God in all people; and WHEREAS the life and example of Jesus of Nazareth provides a model of radically inclusive love and abundant welcome for all; and WHEREAS we proclaim ourselves to be listening to the voice of a Still Speaking God [and] that at all times in human history there is always yet more light and truth to break forth from God's holy word; and WHEREAS *many UCC pastors and congregations have held commitment services for gay and lesbian couples for some time, consistent with the call to loving, long-term committed relationships and to nurture family life*; and WHEREAS recognition of marriage carries with it significant access to institutional support, rights and benefits; and WHEREAS children of families headed by same-gender couples should receive all legal rights and protections; and WHEREAS legislation to ban recognition of same-gender marriages further undermines the civil liberties of gay and lesbian couples and contributes to a climate of misunderstanding and polarization, increasing hostility against gays and lesbians; and WHEREAS a Constitutional Amendment has been introduced to this Congress to limit marriage to "only the union of a man and a woman"; and WHEREAS equal marriage rights for couples regardless of gender is an issue deserving of serious, faithful discussion by people of faith, taking into consideration the long, complex history of marriage and family life, layered as it is with cultural practices, economic realities, political dynamics, religious history and biblical interpretation; and WHEREAS The Tenth General Synod pronounced that all person[s] are entitled to full civil liberties and equal protection under the law without discrimination related to sexual preference; and WHEREAS the Eleventh General Synod urged that States should legislatively recognize that traditional marriage is not the only stable living unit entitled to legal protection; and WHEREAS the Nineteenth General Synod called on the church for greater leadership to end discrimination against gays

---

[2] United Church of Christ, "Affirming the Participation and Ministry of Transgender People Within the United Church of Christ and Supporting Their Civil and Human Rights," Twenty-fourth General Synod, July 15, 2003, accessed March 28, 2015, http://uccfiles.com/synod/resolutions/ AFFIRMING-THE-PARTICIPATION-AND-MINISTRY-OF-TRANSGENDER-PEOPLE-WITHIN-THE-UNITED-CHURCH-OF-CHRIST-AND-SUPPORTING-THEIR-CIVIL-AND-HUMAN-RIGHTS.

and lesbians; and WHEREAS the Executive Council of the United Church of Christ in April, 2004 called the church to action and dialogue on marriage; THEREFORE LET IT BE RESOLVED, that the Twenty-fifth General Synod of the United Church of Christ affirms equal marriage rights for couples regardless of gender and declares that the government should not interfere with couples regardless of gender who choose to marry and share fully and equally in the rights, responsibilities and commitment of legally recognized marriage; and LET IT BE FURTHER RESOLVED, that the Twenty-fifth General Synod of the United Church of Christ affirms equal access to the basic rights, institutional protections and quality of life conferred by the recognition of marriage; and LET IT BE FURTHER RESOLVED, that the Twenty-fifth General Synod calls for an end to rhetoric that fuels hostility, misunderstanding, fear and hatred expressed toward gay, lesbian, bisexual and transgender persons; and LET IT BE FURTHER RESOLVED, that the Officers of the United Church of Christ are called upon to communicate this resolution to local, state and national legislators, urging them to support equal marriage rights for couples regardless of gender. In recognition that these resolutions may not reflect the views or current understanding of all bodies, and acknowledging the pain and struggle their passage will engender within the gathered church, the General Synod encourages the following: LET IT BE FURTHER RESOLVED, that the Twenty-fifth General Synod calls upon all settings of the United Church of Christ to engage in serious, respectful, and prayerful discussion of the covenantal relationship of marriage and equal marriage rights for couples regardless of gender, using the "God is still speaking, about Marriage" study and discussion guide produced by Wider Church Ministries of the United Church of Christ (available online at UCC.org); and LET IT BE FURTHER RESOLVED, that *the Twenty-fifth General Synod calls upon congregations, after prayerful biblical, theological, and historical study, to consider adopting Wedding Policies that do not discriminate against couples based on gender; and LET IT BE FINALLY RESOLVED, that the Twenty-fifth General Synod urges the congregations and individuals of the United Church of Christ to prayerfully consider and support local, state and national legislation to grant equal marriage rights to couples regardless of gender, and to work against legislation, including constitutional amendments, which denies civil marriage rights to couples based on gender.*[3]

While the UCC has been at the frontline of liberal Protestantism on homosexual issues, not all of its ministers and congregations are pleased with the denomination's pro-gay agenda. Congregations have left the UCC due to its affirmation of homosexuality, and resistance has risen from congregations that intend to remain a part of the denomination. Due to the congregational

---

[3] United Church of Christ, "In Support of Equal Marriage Rights for All," Twenty-Fifth General Synod of the United Church of Christ," July 4, 2005, accessed March 28, 2015, http://uccfiles.com/synod/resolutions/RESOLUTION-IN-SUPPORT-OF-EQUAL-MARRIAGE-RIGHTS-FOR-ALL-FOR-GENERAL-SYNOD-25.pdf.

polity of the UCC, traditional congregations are free to differ with the Synod's resolutions. One dissenting organization, "Faithful and Welcoming Churches of the United Church of Christ" (FWC), is a fellowship of laity, clergy, and churches that believe the UCC has departed from historic Christian faith.

The FWC identifies itself as an organization that seeks to be *"Faithful to God, our Father and Creator, to Jesus Christ, our Lord and only Savior, and to the Holy Spirit; Faithful to the Bible as our ultimate authority for faith and practice; Faithful to apostolic faith declared by the church across the years and around the world and reaffirmed in our historic traditions; Faithful to the preservation of the family, and to the practice and proclamation of human sexuality as God's gift for marriage between a man and a woman."* The FWC has opposed the UCC's recognition of gay marriage: "We in the FWC believe that the Equal Rights resolution of General Synod 25 [2005] stands in stark contrast to the teachings of Jesus, the witness of Holy Scripture, and the testimony of the historic Christian faith."[4]

THE EPISCOPAL CHURCH IN THE UNITED STATES OF AMERICA (ECUSA/TEC)

The Episcopal Church in the United States of America is part of the worldwide Anglican Communion, consisting of about 80 million Anglicans. The General Convention of the ECUSA passed a resolution on Human Sexuality in 1979, affirming orthodox Christian practice. The resolution stated:

> *Whereas*, we are conscious of the mystery of human sexuality and how deeply personal matters related to human sexuality are, making it most difficult to arrive at comprehensive and agreed-upon statements in these matters; and *Whereas*, we are aware that under the guidance of the Holy Spirit the Church must continue to study these matters in relationship to *Holy Scripture, Christian faith and tradition*, and growing insights; . . . 1. There are many human conditions, some of them in the area of sexuality, which bear upon a person's suitability for ordination; 2. Every ordinand is expected to lead a life which is "a wholesome example to all people" (*Book of Common Prayer*, pp. 517, 532, 544). There should be no barrier to the ordination of qualified persons of either heterosexual or homosexual orientation whose behavior the Church considers wholesome; 3. We reaffirm the *traditional teaching* of the Church on marriage, marital fidelity and sexual chastity as the standard of Christian sexual morality. Candidates for ordination are expected to conform to this standard. Therefore, we believe it is not appropriate for this Church to

---

[4] Faithful and Welcoming Churches, accessed September 30, 2014, http://www.faithfulandwelcoming.org/about.htm.

ordain a practicing homosexual, or any person who is engaged in hetero-sexual relations outside of marriage.[5]

Ten years later Bishop John S. Spong ordained an openly gay man living with a partner, sparking outrage in the church. At the 1991 General Convention there was long and heated debate on homosexuality, but the Episcopal Church reaffirmed its historic position on gay ordination. Meanwhile, leaders in the church continued to speak in favor or ordaining noncelibate homosexuals to the priesthood. Bishops in the global south rebuked these innovations and issued a statement in 1997 known as the "Kuala Lumpur statement on Human Sexuality." It included these declarations:

> *4. The Scripture bears witness to God's will regarding human sexuality, which is to be expressed only within the life-long union of a man and woman in (holy) matrimony. 5. The Holy Scriptures are clear in teaching that all sexual promiscuity is sin. We are convinced that this includes homosexual practices between men or women as well as heterosexual relationships outside marriage. 6. We believe that the clear and unambiguous teaching of the Holy Scriptures about human sexuality is of great help to Christians as it provides clear boundaries. 7. We find no conflict between clear biblical teaching and sensitive pastoral care. Repentance precedes forgiveness and is part of the healing process. To heal spiritual wounds in God's name we need his wisdom and truth. We see this in the ministry of Jesus, for example his response to the adulterous woman, ". . . neither do I condemn you. Go and sin no more." (John 8:11) . . . 9. We are deeply concerned that the setting aside of biblical teaching in such actions as the ordination of practicing homosexuals and the blessing of same-sex unions calls into question the authority of the Holy Scriptures. This is totally unacceptable to us.[6]*

At the 1998 Lambeth Conference (a worldwide Anglican gathering), a report on human sexuality was received and a resolution on "Human Sexuality," I.10, stated that "in view of the teaching of Scripture," the conference affirmed traditional marriage between a man and woman and believed that abstinence "is right for those who are not called to marriage." The resolution also encouraged pastoral care of gay persons. "While rejecting homosexual practice as incompatible with Scripture," the resolution called "on all our people to

---

[5] ECUSA Human Sexuality resolution, "Appendix: Selected Denominational Statements on Homosexuality" in Jeffrey S. Siker, ed., *Homosexuality in the Church: Both Sides of the Debate* (Louisville, KY: Westminster/John Knox, 1994), 196. See also Siker's *Homosexuality and Religion: An Encyclopedia* (Westport, CT: Greenwood, 2007), 107–12 for a history of evolving Episcopal views on homosexuality. This is a useful source for the history of discussions of homosexuality in mainline Protestant denominations.

[6] Global South Anglican, "The Kuala Lumpur Statement on Human Sexuality—2nd Encounter in the South, 10–14 February 1997," accessed September 30, 2014, http://www.globalsouthanglican.org/gse4/docs/GSA_docs_GSE4.pdf.

minister pastorally and sensitively to all irrespective of sexual orientation."[7] Also noteworthy in the resolution was acknowledgement of the Kuala Lumpur Statement issued by the global south bishops the previous year.

A 1998 Lambeth resolution from the Central and East Africa Region, V.1, rebuked bishops in the West who disobeyed Scripture: "All our ordained Ministers must set a wholesome and credible example. Those persons who practice homosexuality and live in promiscuity, as well as those Bishops who knowingly ordain them or encourage these practices, act contrary to the Scriptures and the teaching of the Church. We call upon them to repent."[8] A resolution from the West Africa Region, V.35, also chastised Anglicans in the West:

> This conference: (a) noting that—(i) the Word of God has established the fact that God created man and woman and blessed their marriage; (ii) many parts of the Bible condemn homosexuality as a sin; (iii) homosexuality is one of the many sins that Scripture has condemned; (iv) some Africans in Uganda were martyred in the 19th century for refusing to have homosexual relations with the king because of their faith in the Lord Jesus and their commitment to stand by the Word of God as expressed in the Bible on the subject;[9] (b) *stands on the Biblical authority and accepts that homosexuality is a sin which could only be adopted by the church if it wanted to commit evangelical suicide.*[10]

Both African resolutions were put to the Lambeth Conference in the form of amendments to Resolution I.10 but were defeated. The 1998 conference candidly acknowledged the tension within Anglicanism over homosexuality. The conference declared:

> *We must confess that we are not of one mind about homosexuality.* Our variety of understanding encompasses: those who believe that homosexuality is a disorder, but that through the grace of Christ people can be changed, although not without pain and struggle; those who believe that relationships between people of the same gender should not include genital expression, that this is the clear teaching of the Bible and the Church universal, and that such activity (if unrepented of) is a barrier to the Kingdom of God; those who believe that committed homosexual relationships fall short of the biblical norm, but are to be preferred to relationships that are anonymous and transient; those who believe the Church should accept and support or bless

---

[7] The Lambeth Conference, "Resolution I.10 Human Sexuality," 1998, accessed September 30, 2014, http://www.lambethconference.org/resolutions/1998/1998-1-10.cfm.

[8] The Lambeth Conference, "Resolution V.1 from Central and East Africa Region," accessed September 30, 2014, http://www.lambethconference.org/resolutions/1998/1998-1-10.cfm.

[9] See http://www.buganda.com/martyrs.htm.

[10] The Lambeth Conference, "Resolution V.35 from the West Africa Region," accessed September 30, 2014, http://www.lambethconference.org/resolutions/1998/1998-1-10.cfm.

monogamous covenant relationships between homosexual people and that they may be ordained.[11]

Finally, in 2003 ECUSA priest Gene Robinson, who left his wife and children to live with a homosexual lover, was elected as a bishop in New Hampshire.[12] In response, thirty-five primates, meeting at the Dromatine Retreat and Conference Centre in Northern Ireland in 2005, asked the ECUSA and the Anglican Church of Canada to withdraw from the Anglican Consultative Council, a key body within the Anglican Communion. The primates asked for the two provinces to be summoned to explain their views. A communiqué was issued which said, in part:

> We as a body continue to address the situations which have arisen in North America with the utmost seriousness. Whilst there remains a very real question about whether the North American churches are willing to accept the same teaching on matters of sexual morality as is generally accepted else-where in the Communion, the underlying reality of our communion in God the Holy Trinity is obscured, and the effectiveness of our common mission severely hindered.[13]

Henry Luke Orombi, archbishop of Uganda, stated, "In our Ireland meeting the Primates suspended the Episcopal Church of America and the Canadian Church until they repent. We are committed to other members of the Episcopal Church who are orthodox in their interpretation of the scriptures and adore Jesus Christ as their savior and Lord. We continue to provide support for them because they share with us in the same mission."[14] Despite cries for repentance from the worldwide Anglican Communion, and hundreds of congregations leaving the ECUSA, the denomination continued to affirm full inclusion of sexually active homosexuals in all ministries of the church. The following 2009 ECUSA statement summarized the denomination's position:

> *Resolved*, That the 76th General Convention affirm the value of "listening to the experience of homosexual persons," as called for by the Lambeth Conferences of 1978, 1988 and 1998, and acknowledge that through our own listening the General Convention has come to *recognize that the baptized*

---

[11] The Lambeth Conference, "Resolution I.10 Human Sexuality," 1998, accessed September 30, 2014, http://www.lambethconference.org/resolutions/1998/1998-1-10.cfm.

[12] Bishop Robinson, after divorcing his wife, "married" his homosexual partner in 2003 but subsequently "divorced" him in 2014.

[13] Anglican Communion News Service, "The Anglican Communion Primates' Meeting Communique, February 2005," accessed September 27, 2014, http://www.anglicannews.org/news/2005/02/the-anglican-communion-primates-meeting-communique,-february-2005.aspx.

[14] Episcopal News Service, "From Uganda's Primate Henri Luke Orombi," March 3, 2003, accessed September 30, 2014, http://archive.episcopalchurch.org/3577_59435_ENG_HTM.htm.

membership of The Episcopal Church includes same-sex couples living in lifelong committed relationships "characterized by fidelity, monogamy, mutual affection and respect, careful, honest communication and the holy love which enables those in such relationships to see in each other the image of God" (2000–D039); and be it further

Resolved, That the 76th General Convention recognize that gay and lesbian persons who are part of such relationships have responded to God's call and have exercised various ministries in and on behalf of God's One, Holy, Catholic and Apostolic Church and are currently doing so in our midst; and be it further

Resolved, That the 76th General Convention affirm that God has called and may call such individuals to any ordained ministry in The Episcopal Church, and that God's call to the ordained ministry in The Episcopal Church is a mystery which the Church attempts to discern for all people through our discernment processes acting in accordance with the Constitution and Canons of The Episcopal Church; and be it further

Resolved, That the 76th General Convention acknowledge that members of The Episcopal Church as of the Anglican Communion, based on careful study of the Holy Scriptures, and in light of tradition and reason, are not of one mind, and Christians of good conscience disagree about some of these matters.[15]

The 2012 ECUSA General Convention approved the blessing of same-sex unions with a liturgical rite, including the exchange of vows and rings, called "The Witnessing and Blessing of a Lifelong Covenant." Bishops may decide whether to allow the rite within the local diocese.

The ordination of Gene Robinson and other pro-gay stances provoked some Anglican provinces in Africa and Asia to break official ties with the ECUSA. The denomination's pro-gay stances were also a catalyst for the formation of several new North American groups, producing an "Anglican realignment" of churches in North America with bishops in Africa.

The Anglican Church in North America (ACNA) was initiated at the request of the Global Anglican Future Conference (GAFCON) in June 2008 and formally recognized by the GAFCON Primates—leaders of Anglican churches representing 70 percent of the active Anglicans globally—on April 16, 2009. The ACNA endorses the *Jerusalem Declaration*, which affirms the historic Christian condemnation of homosexual practice. As of October 2015, the ACNA is a partner province of the Global South, comprised of orthodox provinces representing the majority of Anglicans worldwide. The goal is for

---

[15] The Archives of the Episcopal Church, Resolution 2009–D025, "Reaffirm Participation in the Anglican Communion While Acknowledging Differences 2009–D025," General Convention, *Journal of the General Convention of . . . the Episcopal Church, Anaheim, 2009* (New York, NY: General Convention, 2009), 627–28, accessed September 30, 2014, http://www.episcopal-archives.org/cgi-bin/acts/acts_resolution.pl?resolution=2009-D025.

the ACNA to become the provincial structure for orthodox Anglicanism in North America.[16]

EVANGELICAL LUTHERAN CHURCH IN AMERICA (ELCA)

The largest body of Lutherans in America, the Evangelical Lutheran Church in America (ELCA), was established by the 1988 merger of two predecessor denominations: the Lutheran Church in America and the American Lutheran Church. Below are excerpts from official statements on homosexuality from the older Lutheran denominations before their union. These statements remained in force after the ELCA was established:

Lutheran Church in America (1970)

> Scientific research has not been able to provide conclusive evidence regarding the causes of homosexuality. Nevertheless, homosexuality is viewed biblically as a departure from the heterosexual structure of God's creation. Persons who engage in homosexual behavior are sinners only as are all other persons—alienated from God and neighbor.[17]

American Lutheran Church (1980)

Human Sexuality and Sexual Behavior

1. We note the current consensus in the scientific community that one's preferred sexual behavior exists on a continuum from exclusively heterosexual to exclusively homosexual and that homosexual behavior takes a variety of forms. We believe it appropriate to distinguish between homosexual orientation and homosexual behavior. Persons who do not practice their homosexual erotic preference do not violate our understanding of Christian sexual behavior.
2. *The church regards homosexual erotic behavior as contrary to God's intent for his children. It rejects the contention that homosexual behavior is simply another form of sexual behavior equally valid with the dominant male/female pattern.*
3. *We have reviewed the challenges to the traditional interpretation of those scripture passages that appear to proscribe homosexual behavior. We are not convinced by the evidence presented.* Among passages cited as requiring interpretations different from the traditional interpretation are Genesis 18:16–19:29; Leviticus 18:22 and 20:13; Romans 1:24–32; 1 Corinthians 6:9–10; 1 Timothy 1:10. While we

---

[16] For information on ACNA and the *Jerusalem Declaration*, see chapter 6.

[17] Lutheran Church in America, "Sex, Marriage, and Family" (Fifth Biennial Convention, 1970), "Appendix: Selected Denominational Statements on Homosexuality," in Jeffrey S. Siker, ed., *Homosexuality in the Church: Both Sides of the Debate* (Louisville, KY: Westminster/John Knox, 1994), 197.

see no scriptural rationale for revising the church's traditional teaching that homosexual erotic behavior violates God's intent, we nonetheless remain open to the possibility of new biblical and theological insights.[18]

Five years after the formation of the ELCA, some of its leaders proposed a new social statement on human sexuality, but no such statement was submitted to the Churchwide Assembly (CWA). That same year the Conference of Bishops of the ELCA issued a pastoral letter stating that they found no biblical basis to establish rites for the blessing of same-gender unions. The ECLA adopted several resolutions in the 1990s, welcoming gay and lesbian people to participate in the life of the church; still, no official policy blessed same-sex unions or allowed the ordination of practicing homosexuals. In 2001 the CWA decided to initiate a study on homosexuality. In 2003 a task force produced a study guide, *Journey Together Faithfully: The Church and Homosexuality*, which presented both sides of the debate with broad input from across the ELCA. The task force's final report, issued in 2005, acknowledged division within the ELCA regarding homosexuality and called churches to work together despite differences.[19]

At the 2007 ELCA Churchwide Assembly, a number of proposals to approve gay ordination and unions were defeated, but a motion by Bishop Landahl of Chicago passed 538 to 431; it "encourage[d] synods, synodical bishops, and the presiding bishop to refrain from or demonstrate restraint in disciplining those congregations and persons who call into the rostered ministry otherwise-qualified candidates who are in a mutual, chaste, and faithful committed same-gender relationship." In 2009 the Churchwide Assembly adopted the social statement "Human Sexuality: Gift and Trust" by a margin of 636 to 338. The statement opened the door for ordination of practicing homosexuals. Accompanying this document was Resolution 2, a "Report and Recommendation on Ministry Policies," which allowed those in "publicly accountable life-long, monogamous, same-gender relationships to serve as rostered leaders of this church." "Human Sexuality: Gift and Trust" acknowledged, "Disagreements exist in this church and in the larger Christian community about whether marriage is also the appropriate term to use to describe similar benefits, protection, and support for same-gender couples entering into lifelong, monogamous relationships."

---

[18] American Lutheran Church, "Human Sexuality and Sexual Behavior" (Tenth General Convention, 1980), "Appendix: Selected Denominational Statements on Homosexuality," in Siker, *Homosexuality in the Church,* 198.

[19] James M. Childs Jr., "Evangelical Lutheran Church in America," in *Homosexuality and Religion: An Encyclopedia,* 117–19.

Report and Recommendation on Ministry Policies

Resolution 1: *"RESOLVED, that the ELCA commits itself to finding ways to allow congregations that choose to do so to recognize, support and hold publicly accountable life-long, monogamous, same-gender relationships."* [Adopted 619-402]

Resolution 2: *"RESOLVED, that the ELCA commits itself to finding a way for people in such publicly accountable, lifelong, monogamous, same-gender relationships to serve as rostered leaders of this church."* [Adopted 559-451]

Resolution 3: "RESOLVED, that in the implementation of any resolutions on ministry policies, the ELCA commits itself to bear one another's burdens, love the neighbor, and respect the bound consciences of all." [Adopted 771-230 as amended]

Resolution 4: This resolution called upon members to respect the bound consciences of those with whom they disagree; declared intent to allow structured flexibility in decision-making about candidacy and the call process; eliminated the prohibition of rostered service by members in publicly accountable, lifelong, monogamous same-gender relationships; recognized and committed to respect the conviction of members who believe that the ELCA should not call or roster people in committed same-gender relationships; called for development of accountability guidelines; directed that amendments to ministry policy documents be drafted and approved; and stated that this church continue to trust congregations, bishops, synods and others responsible for determining who should be called into public ministry. [Adopted 667-307 as amended][20]

"Human Sexuality: Gift and Trust" incongruously cited historic Lutheran faith and practice as undergirding its revisionist interpretation:

The trust and mutuality affirmed by marriage offers one of the most beautiful, abiding, and transformative forms of human relationship. This church understands marriage as a covenant of mutual promises, commitment, and hope authorized legally by the state and blessed by God. *The historic Christian tradition and the Lutheran Confessions have recognized marriage as a covenant between a man and a woman. . . . This statement responds to this church's call for a foundational framework that will help it discern what it means to follow faithfully God's law of love in the increasingly complex sphere of human sexuality. It does not offer once-and-for-all answers to contemporary questions. Rather it seeks to tap the deep roots of Scripture and the Lutheran theological tradition for specific Christian convictions, themes,*

---

[20] Evangelical Lutheran Church in America, *2009 Worldwide Assembly, Reports and Records: Minutes*, "Report and Recommendation on Ministry Policies," accessed September 30, 2014, http://download.elca.org/ELCA%20Resource%20Repository/CWA2009.pdf. The "Human Sexuality" paper and implementing resolutions were fiercely debated. Multiple amendments were proposed by those objecting to this innovation in Lutheran practice.

and wisdom that will assist people of faith to discern what is responsible and faithful action in the midst of the complexity of daily life.[21]

Because the ELCA had departed from its Lutheran heritage, the North American Lutheran Church (NALC) was established in 2010. The new Lutheran body committed itself to the practices of the universal church consistent with Scripture. In its statement about pastoral ministry, the NALC declared, "Persons who engage in sexual activity outside the marriage covenant of one man and one woman, whether homosexual or heterosexual, are precluded from the ordained ministry of the North American Lutheran Church."[22]

PRESBYTERIAN CHURCH IN THE UNITED STATES OF AMERICA (PCUSA)

In 1978 the United Presbyterian Church in the USA (UPCUSA) adopted a "Statement on the Ordination of Homosexuals: Policy Statement and Recommendations" that welcomed gays and lesbians into church membership. However, "self-affirming, practicing homosexuals" were not eligible for ordination to church office. The Presbyterian Church in the US (PCUS) adopted a similar policy a year later. The two major branches of Presbyterianism united in 1983 to form the Presbyterian Church in the United States of America, and the 1978 statement remained in force. The statement came to this conclusion:

> The biblical revelation to Israel, reaffirmed in the teaching of Jesus and Paul, portrayed in the *theology and human creation*, specifically reflected in the ethical teaching in both the Old and New Testaments, and confirmed in nature, clearly indicates that genital sexual expression is meant to occur within the covenant of heterosexual marriage. Behavior that is pleasing to God cannot simply be defined as that which pleases others or expresses our own strong needs and identity; it must flow out of faithful and loving obedience to God. Many unselfish deeds ignore God's expressed intentions for our lives. Homosexual Christians who fail to recognize God's revealed intent for sexual behavior and who move outside God's will in this area of their lives may show many gifts and graces. They may evidence more grace than heterosexual believers who so readily stand in judgment over them. This does not

---

[21] Evangelical Lutheran Church in America, "Human Sexuality: Gift and Trust," 2009, accessed September 30, 2014, http://download.elca.org/ELCA%20Resource%20Repository/ SexualitySS.pdf. Some Lutherans apparently have convinced themselves they have not forsaken their heritage, although an objective observer would be hard-pressed not to disagree. Lutheran confessions and catechisms, along with the writings of Luther, make it abundantly clear that the ELCA is no longer historically Lutheran in the area of Christian ethics. See chap. 4.

[22] "Standards for Pastoral Ministry" NALC, 2011, accessed September 27, 2014, http:// thenalc.org/standards-for-pastoral-ministry. See chap. 6 for more information on the NALC.

mean that God approves their behavior in the area in which they are failing to be obedient.[23]

After ongoing debates through the 1980s, in 1993 the weary Presbyterians instituted a three-year voting moratorium on issues related to the ordination of gay and lesbian members to church office. In 1997, conservatives passed an amendment to the PCUSA constitution, requiring candidates for ordination "to live either in fidelity within the covenant of marriage between a man and woman, or chastity in singleness." Liberals presented a substitute amendment requiring "fidelity and integrity in marriage or singleness," which deleted references to celibacy and did not define marriage as the union of a man and woman. The substitute was defeated in 1998. Again the next year there was a move to delete the "fidelity and chastity" clause in the constitution, but it was defeated. Another attempt to remove the "fidelity and chastity" provision was defeated in 2001. Traditional views prevailed, but the votes grew closer.

A 2006 "Peace, Unity and Purity" task force recommended allowing exceptions to the "fidelity and chastity" standard. The denomination endorsed the recommendation and opened the door to homosexual ordination. Again in 2009 Presbyterians declined to modify the constitutional "fidelity and chastity" requirement for ordination, though by the smallest margin yet. Finally, the "fidelity and chastity" constitutional language was jettisoned in 2011 by a majority vote of the regional presbyteries. This paved the way for ordaining openly gay persons to the Presbyterian ministry, which began with the October 2011 ordination of Scott Anderson to serve a congregation in Wisconsin.

The PCUSA continued to discuss blessing same-sex unions, and some churches performed same-sex commitment ceremonies in violation of denominational policy. The Presbyterian General Assembly had thus far declined to approve gay marriage, but the pro-gay lobby within the denomination was unrelenting. Several Presbyterian denominations outside the US either publically chastised or officially severed ecclesiastical relationships with the PCUSA over its departures from historic Christianity. In 2012 a group of churches began departing from the PCUSA to form a new denomination, ECO—a Covenant Order of Evangelical Presbyterians. Between 2007 and 2015, the Evangelical Presbyterian Church has received more than 350 churches departing from the PCUSA.

In 2014, the Presbyterian General Assembly approved a policy allowing pastors to perform same-sex ceremonies in states where the practice is legal. The vote of 371 to 238 represented a 61percent majority for pro-gay Presbyterians. An additional vote to change the definition of marriage to "two

---

[23] United Presbyterian Church in the USA. "Statement on the Ordination of Homosexuals: Policy Statement and Recommendations" (New York, NY: Office of the General Assembly, 1978), 263.

people" rather than "a woman and a man" passed by a 71 percent majority. By March 2015 most of the regional presbyteries had voted in favor of this change, and same-sex marriage became officially part of the Presbyterian constitution in June.

REFORMED CHURCH IN AMERICA (RCA)

Organized in 1792 after the American Revolution, the RCA has written numerous papers and reports on the homosexual issue since the late 1970s. A 1978 paper on homosexuality, written by the Commission on Theology, was distributed by the General Synod to RCA churches. The paper stated:

> *When Paul rejects homosexual acts on the grounds that they are "against nature" he expresses and reaffirms the clear sense of Scripture. Human sexuality was created for heterosexual expression. . . . Heterosexuality is not only normal; it is normative. Homosexual acts are contrary to the will of God for human sexuality.* The homosexual invert [one who does not decide to become homosexual, but for whom genetic, hormonal, or psychosocial factors have influenced his or her sexual orientation] is no more to be blamed for his/her condition than a retarded child. It follows, then, that the church's ministry to the invert may best begin with the attempt to lift a burden of guilt that need not be carried. Inverts may not idealize their orientation as a legitimate alternative, but neither should they blame themselves for their sexual orientation. While we cannot affirm homosexual behavior, at the same time we are convinced that the denial of human and civil rights to homosexuals is inconsistent with the biblical witness and Reformed theology.[24]

In 1980 the General Synod adopted a resolution "to bring awareness of RCA members, congregations, classes and synods, competent programs and persons which can successfully help the practicing homosexual and lesbian, minister or layperson, overcome his or her homosexual behavior."[25] A decade later the RCA adopted an official position on homosexuality, declaring "the practicing homosexual lifestyle is contrary to scripture."[26] In 2012 the RCA General Synod voted to reaffirm its position on homosexuality:

> *While compassion, patience, and loving support should be shown to all those who struggle with same-sex desires, the General Synod reaffirms our official position that homosexual behavior is a sin according to the Holy Scriptures, therefore any person, congregation, or assembly which advocates*

---

[24] Reformed Church in America, "Summaries of General Synod Discussions and Actions on Homosexuality and Rights of Homosexuals," *Minutes of the General Synod* (1978), 233–39, accessed October 3, 2014, https://www.rca.org/homosexuality.

[25] Ibid., *Minutes of the General Synod* (1980),97.

[26] Ibid., *Minutes of the General Synod* (1990),461.

homosexual behavior or provides leadership for a service of same-sex mar-
riage or a similar celebration has committed a disciplinable offense.[27]

AMERICAN BAPTIST CHURCHES USA

The American Baptist Churches USA (ABC/USA) was formally organized in 1907 as the Northern Baptist Convention, taking its current name in 1972. In 1984 the General Board of the ABC/USA published a statement affirming marriage as the union of one man and one woman. In 1992 the General Board affirmed a one-sentence "American Baptist Resolution on Homosexuality," which asserted, "We affirm that the practice of homosexuality is incompatible with Christian teaching."[28] Despite these declarations, some congregations in the ABC/USA have accepted practicing homosexuals as church members; they formed the Association of Welcoming and Affirming Baptists. Conservatives formed their own group, American Baptist Evangelicals. A statement on human sexuality was included in the American Baptist Evangelicals' statement of faith: "God's design is that man and woman either be joined together in a perpetual monogamous relationship or live in a single state. The practice of extra-marital sex, adultery or homosexuality is inconsistent with biblical teaching."[29]

The identity statement "We Are American Baptists," adopted by the General Board in 2005, included a stance on homosexuality: "We affirm that God through Jesus Christ calls us to be . . . [a biblical people] who submit to the teaching of Scripture that God's design for sexual intimacy places it within the context of marriage between one man and one woman, and acknowledge that *the practice of homosexuality is incompatible with Biblical teaching.*[30]

Some regional fellowships of the ABC/USA have withdrawn fellowship from pro-homosexual churches, but other regions have received them, thus allowing "welcoming and affirming" churches to maintain membership in the parent denomination. The General Board's unwillingness to discipline pro-gay

---

[27] Ibid., *Minutes of General Synod* (2012), 149–50. A growing number of RCA congregations are supporting homosexual practice. A recent example is the City Church of San Francisco, which issued a letter to the congregation on March 19, 2015, stating that requiring celibacy of gays "is simply not working and people are being hurt." The letter declares, "We will no longer discriminate based on sexual orientation and demand lifelong celibacy as a precondition of joining." City Church of San Francisco, "A Letter from the Elder Board," accessed March 28, 2015, http://citychurchsf.org/A-Letter-From-The-Elder-Board.

[28] American Baptist Churches USA, "American Baptist Churches USA: Responses/Actions Pertaining to Homosexuality," accessed October 3, 2014, http://www.abc-usa.org/wp-content/uploads/2012/06/homosexuality.pdf.

[29] American Baptist Evangelicals is no longer in existence, but some ABC/USA congregations use the old statement of the American Baptist Evangelicals as their statement of faith.

[30] American Baptist Churches USA, "Identity Statement (2005)," accessed October 3, 2014, http://www.abc-usa.org/about-us/identity-statement-2005.

regional groups led to the Pacific Southwest region's vote to withdraw its membership from the ABC/USA in 2006.

UNITED METHODIST CHURCH (UMC)

Since the 1970s the second largest Protestant denomination in the United States, the United Methodist Church, has experienced internal debate on homosexuality at meetings of the General Conference, an international gathering that meets every four years and includes lay and clergy delegates from Europe, Africa, and the United States. Decisions of the General Conference are binding on Methodists in the United States. When the General Conference approves a statement, it is published in the *Book of Discipline* and/or the *Book of Resolutions*.

At the 1972 meeting of the General Conference, a "Statement on Social Principles" stirred discussion regarding homosexuality. As a result, the General Conference added a clause to the statement: "*We do not condone the practice of homosexuality and consider this practice incompatible with Christian teaching.*" Opponents tried repeatedly to change this "incompatibility clause" but to no avail. In 1984 the General Conference added a statement to the *Book of Discipline,* forbidding gay ordination: "*Since the practice of homosexuality is incompatible with Christian teaching, self-avowed practicing homosexuals are not to be accepted as candidates, ordained as ministers, or appointed to serve in the United Methodist Church.*" In 1996 the General Conference added the following to the Statement on Social Principles: "*Ceremonies that celebrate homosexual unions shall not be conducted by our ministers and shall not be conducted in our churches.*"[31]

Several UMC ministers have been convicted in high profile judicial cases and suspended from the ministry for affirming homosexual behavior.[32] These suspensions have targeted practicing homosexual clergy and ministers who celebrated same-sex unions. Despite increasing pressure from some in the denomination, the historic position of the UMC remains intact. The sections of the *Book of Discipline* cited below address the issue of ordination and "Chargeable Offenses" against church policy:

> *While persons set apart by the Church for ordained ministry are subject to all the frailties of the human condition and the pressures of society, they are required to maintain the highest standards of holy living in the world. The practice of homosexuality is incompatible with Christian teaching.* Therefore self-avowed practicing homosexuals are not to be certified as candidates,

---

[31] See citations below from the Methodist *Book of Discipline*.

[32] A recent example is the Rev. Frank Schafer, who was defrocked by the UMC in December 2013 for performing a marriage ceremony for his gay son in 2007. On appeal he was reinstated in June 2014.

ordained as ministers, or appointed to serve in The United Methodist Church. 1. *"Self-avowed practicing homosexual"* is understood to mean that a person openly acknowledges to a bishop, district superintendent, district committee of ordained ministry, board of ordained ministry, or clergy session that the person is a practicing homosexual. See Judicial Council Decisions 702, 708, 722, 725, 764, 844, 984, 1020 2. See Judicial Council Decisions 984, 985, 1027, 1028. (304.3)[33]

Ceremonies that celebrate homosexual unions shall not be conducted by our ministers and shall not be conducted in our churches. (341.6)[34]

1. A bishop, clergy member of an annual conference (370), local pastor, clergy on honorable or administrative location, or diaconal minister may be tried when charged (subject to the statute of limitations in 2702.4) with one or more of the following offenses: (a) immorality including but not limited to, not being celibate in singleness or not faithful in a heterosexual marriage; (b) practices declared by The United Methodist Church to be incompatible with Christian teachings, including but not limited to: being a self-avowed practicing homosexual; or conducting ceremonies which celebrate homosexual unions; or performing same-sex wedding ceremonies. (2702)[35]

According to the UMC *Book of Discipline*, "Wesley believed that the living core of the Christian faith was revealed in Scripture, illumined by tradition, vivified in personal experience, and confirmed by reason."[36] Despite repeated assaults on biblical faith from within the denomination, Methodists have held fast to the Wesleyan tradition's emphasis on the centrality of holiness to authentic expressions of Christianity.

CONCLUSION

A common mainline perspective on homosexuality is found in Jack Rogers's book, *Jesus, the Bible, and Homosexuality*:

We are witnessing a profound transformation in attitudes toward people who are LGBT throughout many American denominations. In the 1950's very few people knew any "out" LGBT people. Today, most Americans do. They are friends and co-workers; parents, children, and siblings; neighbors, elected

---

[33] United Methodist Church, "Homosexuality: Full Book of Discipline Statements," accessed October 3, 2014, http://www.umc.org/what-we-believe/homosexuality-full-book-of-discipline-statements.

[34] United Methodist Church, "What Is the Denomination's Position on Homosexuality?," accessed October 3, 2014, http://www.umc.org/what-we-believe/what-is-the-denominations-position-on-homosexuality.

[35] United Methodist Church, "2702 Chargeable Offenses and Statute of Limitations." accessed October 3, 2014, http://www.umc.org/what-we-believe/para-2702-chargeable-offenses-and-the-statute-of-limitations.

[36] "Theological Guideline: Sources and Criteria," in *The Book of Discipline of the United Methodist Church 2008* (Nashville, TN: The United Methodist Publishing Company, 2008), 77.

officials, and fellow church members. For many people, as ignorance has been replaced with real-world knowledge of people who are LGBT, myths and preconceptions have vanished. This remarkable transformation has given us the opportunity to read the biblical texts anew, through the lens of Jesus' redemptive life and ministry, free from some of the mistaken assumptions that had previously obscured our understanding of God's revelation for our lives. Like growing numbers of Christians across the United States and around the world, I believe that support for LGBT equality is consistent with and indeed mandated by my faith.[37]

One observes in this assessment a number of propositions that underlie the aggressive pro-gay theology within mainline denominations. The words *ignorance* and *myth* are used to belittle persons who take traditional Christian sexual ethics seriously. This condescension exhibits a shallow arrogance that denigrates the entirety of Christian tradition. It is a vain attempt to shame the orthodox into embracing the illusion that God endorses homoeroticism.

According to the new script, since contemporary Christians know coworkers, friends, and family members who are gay, they must realign their reading of the Bible to corroborate their experiences. Personal experience, then, becomes a filter to help discern the meaning of biblical revelation. Appeal is made to a fictitious Jesus, the welcoming and affirming prophet who would never turn away anyone or call people to repentance and self-denial.

Part of the myth prevalent in mainline denominations is exaggeration of the extent to which the church is "seeing the light" about homosexuality. In reality, many congregations and ministers within mainline denominations remain opposed to homosexual practice and offer counseling to persons who struggle with same-sex attraction and seek the transforming grace of God. Hosts of mainline Christians reject the gay propaganda that has been parading through their denominations since the 1970s. Many mainline believers see this for what it is—deception of the worst order, misleading the people of God into condoning sin.

At its foundation the revisionist program in mainline denominations seeks to destroy historic Christianity and replace it with a substitute that fits modern sensibilities. Revisionists denounce the universal Christian testimony, which has always declared homosexual practice sinful and subject to church discipline. The so-called "remarkable transformation" regarding homosexuality in some denominations has led mainline Protestantism into profound theological confusion. Renowned German theologian Wolfhart Pannenburg observed:

> If a church were to let itself be pushed to the point where it ceased to treat homosexual activity as a departure from the biblical norm, and recognized

---

[37] Jack Rogers, *Jesus, the Bible, and Homosexuality: Explode the Myths, Heal the Church*, 2nd ed. (Louisville, KY: Westminster/John Knox, 2009), 144–45.

homosexual unions as a personal partnership of love equivalent to marriage, such a church would stand no longer on biblical grounds but against the unequivocal witness of Scripture. A church that took this step would cease to be the one, holy, catholic and apostolic church.[38]

Those who claim to be practicing homosexuals and "Christians" delude themselves. In reality they have left historic Christianity and created a new religion. One cannot legitimately claim Christian faith and simultaneously deny essential teachings of that faith. For a Christian, it is intellectually dishonest to teach "gay is OK" when Christianity has always taught that homosexual practice is sinful.

In part II, the discussion will shift to specific biblical texts and their interpretation, observing how the gay Christian movement has attempted to distort the meaning of texts with an array of innovative interpretations. A brief excursus after part II will discuss the mistaken parallel between issues of ethnicity, gender, and sexual orientation in the Bible.

---

[38] "What Wolfhart Pannenberg Says About This Debate in the Church," *Christianity Today*, November 11, 1996, 37.

PART II

THE BIBLE AND HOMOSEXUALITY

Introduction to Part II

CHAPTER 8

SEXUAL ETHICS IN SCRIPTURE AND THE EARLY CHURCH

INTRODUCTION: WHY THINGS HAVE GONE ALL WOBBLY

The idea has recently been posited that the only sexual ethic in Scripture is an "ethic of love." This is asserted (rather than carefully argued) in order to open the door for declaring homosexual practice acceptable. If interpreters can distance themselves from the concrete commands of Scripture, if they can suggest that only the most general and abstract principle is left as a guide for believers, if they can wrestle authority from Scripture and the church's teaching throughout the centuries and deliver it to communities and individuals, then they need not worry about a scriptural teaching that this or that is a sin. As we begin to address such challenges, readers may well ask, How could people in certain Christian traditions come to entertain such radical proposals? How could they state this with so little argument, with such slight exegetical discussion, and/or with such little regard for what the church has taught? How can congregations refuse to engage Scripture and the church's teaching in the formation of their convictions—except to find ways to discount these? Indeed, what is the condition of churches that cannot distinguish orthodoxy from heresy?

Why have things gone all wobbly? No doubt a myriad of answers rather than a single answer to such questions should be considered. First, Western culture and many church congregations as a whole are biblically illiterate.

Another point may be that theology is often conducted as a discipline separate from biblical studies in seminaries. Thus, theological arguments are all too often decided on nonbiblical grounds. Also, some theological colleges and seminaries barely teach the Bible, let alone offer robust programs in careful biblical interpretation. In the 1980s one well-known seminary only required two introductory Bible courses, with the focus in each on questions such as authorship and dating rather than content, in its three-year master of divinity curriculum. Several seminaries require neither Hebrew nor Greek, the languages in which the biblical text was first penned. The sad fact is that certain well-known seminaries have put out biblically illiterate or uninformed graduates for decades.

Further, Protestant ministers, and Christians in general, are often painfully oblivious to church history and entertain novel interpretations of texts with no guidance from Christians in ages past and little understanding of how Scripture functions as a whole. Into this vacuum step biblical scholars capable of exercising their exegetical skills, though at times supporting questionable exegesis. Other scholars then cite these biblical scholars as authorities on what the Bible states—as though they have actually presented cogent arguments. This point takes us to another suggestion for the cause of confusion on homosexuality: political correctness.

Some accept that Scripture does, indeed, state that homosexual practice is sinful. Yet they deny the relevance of Scripture or church history. This dangerous position simply changes the rules of the game. Luke Timothy Johnson articulates this view:

> I think it important to state clearly that we do, in fact, reject the straightforward commands of Scripture, and appeal instead to another authority when we declare that same-sex unions can be holy and good. And what exactly is that authority? We appeal explicitly to the weight of our own experience and the experience thousands of others have witnessed to, which tells us that to claim our own sexual orientation is in fact to accept the way in which God has created us. By so doing, we explicitly reject as well the premises of the scriptural statements condemning homosexuality—namely, that it is a vice freely chosen, a symptom of human corruption, and disobedience to God's created order.[1]

Such a radical disregard of Scripture and church tradition is the true alternative to orthodox Christian faith. When this view arises, Christians must realize the issue facing the church is really one of authority, not exegesis. Are

---

[1] Luke Timothy Johnson, "Homosexuality and the Church," *Commonweal,* June 11, 2007, accessed 12 November, 2013, https://www.commonwealmagazine.org/homosexuality-church-1?utm_source=PANTHEON_STRIPPED&utm_medium=PANTHEON_STRIPPED&utm_campaign=PANTHEON_STRIPPED.

Christian convictions founded on what the Bible says or not? Does what the church has taught matter?

What this section of the book offers is a focus on reading biblical texts about homosexuality in their context. The further debate on biblical authority will need to be waged by others (as it already has been). Also, practical theological matters of how Christians might live out their convictions in Christian communities in the West must be addressed elsewhere. Readers of this book need to be aware, however, that such issues stand in the foreground of the exegetical arguments presented here.

Our opening argument is that Jews and Christians around the time of the New Testament believed in a biblical sexual ethic, and they were universally agreed that homosexuality in any form was sinful. The idea that there was no Christian or Jewish sexual ethic in the first century can only be asserted by someone who fails to work with the primary sources.

ETHICS AS GENERAL PRINCIPLES (LOVE)
OR CONCRETE COMMANDS?

The assertion that Scripture has no sexual ethic has been made, for example, by Walter Wink[2] and followed by Jack Rogers.[3] Such a claim entails arguing that Scripture is diverse and inconsistent in what it says, such that there is a lack of unity on many topics, and that a general principle, such as love, summarizes the thrust of biblical teaching. According to Wink:

> The crux of the matter . . . is simply that the Bible has no sexual ethic. Instead, it exhibits a variety of sexual mores, some of which changed over the thousand-year span of biblical history. Mores are unreflective customs accepted by a given community. Many of the practices that the Bible prohibits, we allow, and many that it allows, we prohibit. The Bible knows only a love ethic, which is constantly being brought to bear on whatever sexual mores are dominant in any given country, or culture, or period.[4]

Wink is not the first to argue that Christian ethics is nothing more and nothing less than a love ethic. Indeed, situation ethics—popularized by Joseph Fletcher in the 1960s[5]—made love the only ethical principle such that there was no content to ethics. The general principle of love was said to need no

---

[2] Walter Wink, "Homosexuality and the Bible," in *Homosexuality and Christian Faith: Questions of Conscience for the Churches*, ed. Walter Wink (Minneapolis, MN: Fortress, 1999), 44.

[3] Jack Rogers, *Jesus, the Bible, and Homosexuality: Explode the Myths, Heal the Church* (Louisville, KY: Westminster/John Knox, 2006), 61.

[4] Walter Wink, "Homosexuality and the Bible," 44. This passage is quoted and affirmed without discussion by Jack Rogers, *Jesus, the Bible and Homosexuality*, 63.

[5] Joseph F. Fletcher, *Situation Ethics: The New Morality* (Louisville, KY: Westminster/John Knox, 1966).

concrete definition through specific ethical commands because one would naturally know the loving thing to do in a given situation. The impossibility of this approach to ethics is easily demonstrated by the fact that people differ over what the loving thing to do is in many situations. For instance, one person points out that it is not loving to kill unborn children while another person argues that telling a woman what to do with her own body is not loving.[6]

For our purposes the more significant point to consider is that Scripture does not reduce Christian ethics to a general principle, such as love or freedom. But of course, love is an essential principle, value, and virtue in Christian ethics. Jesus corrects the legal ethic of the Pharisees by stating that the chief laws are love of God (Deut 6:5) and love of neighbor (Lev 19:18, 34). They undergird all other teaching in the laws of Moses and in the Prophets:

> "You shall *love the Lord your God* with all your heart, and with all your soul, and with all your mind." This is the greatest and first commandment. And a second is like it: "You shall *love your neighbor as yourself.*" On these two commandments hang all the law and the prophets. (Matt 22:37–40)

Notice, however, that these commands of love do not replace the Law and the Prophets. Rather, the other commandments hang on the love commands. A common error is to understand Jesus as affirming a love ethic and speaking against the moral commands of the Old Testament. Matthew 5:20–48 is, on such a view, read as Jesus's grand overthrow of any norm, rule, law, or concrete ethic: "You have heard it said . . . , *but* I say to you . . ."[7] Yet, in this section of Matthew, Jesus is addressing what keeps people from obeying God's law. Jesus does not say, "Forget about that old command not to murder"; rather, he affirms the ongoing validity of the law. Ulrich Luz, recognizing this point in Matthew, thinks this means that "Matthew obviously does not know Paul and

---

[6] James E. Gustafson, for example, sought to present a new method of moral enquiry that rejected the primacy of scriptural authority and church teaching in ethics in favor of input from science and historical data. The result is supposed to be more pastoral and realistic, allowing people to make their own decisions and acknowledging that the moral life is complicated and contradictory. Someone might, for example, choose to end the life of a fetus but do so with regret. See Gustafson's *Ethics from a Theocentric Perspective, Volume 1: Theology and Ethics* (Chicago, IL: University of Chicago Press, 1981). While Gustafson hopes to find a mediating position between a so-called Catholic rule and natural-law ethic and an intuitive Protestant ethic, his rejection of traditional Christian moral reasoning from Scripture and the teaching of the historical Christian church lands him in the circle of situation ethics. In the abortion example, Gustafson leaves the woman struggling with the question to her own decision with no Christian guidance.

[7] At times the "*de*" in Greek in these verses may be better translated as "*and*" rather than as "*but*": "you have heard it said . . . *and* I say to you . . ." Jesus states, after all, that he has not come to dismantle the Law but to fulfill it (Matt 5:17). This suggestion was made to Rollin Grams in the 1980s by John R. Levison. At least we might say that the stronger *alla* is not used in Matt 5:20–48.

his theology."[8] Luz suggests there is a fundamental disagreement between a rule ethic and a theology of grace. As Glen Stassen has shown, however, Jesus is confronting his audience with their compromising hearts that pull them into a vicious cycle of sin and then offering them practical advice about transforming initiatives that can help them escape this cycle.[9]

Jesus did not affirm an ethic lacking concrete practices and rules. He did not accept the ongoing sin of the tax collectors and prostitutes; he showed mercy and forgave the repentant tax collectors and prostitutes (Matt 21:28–32). He sat with sinners not because he had discovered some ethic of toleration but because he, the Physician, was willing to sit with the sick (Matt 9:12)—and he did so to make them well again. He had not come to tell them that the Ebola of their lives was perfectly OK and he would still fellowship with them; he came to them to save them from their deadly illness. His ministry, like that of John the Baptist, was a call to repentance that the tax collectors received but the Pharisees, by and large, rejected (Luke 7:29–30). John's baptism of repentance for the forgiveness of sins went along with a warning of coming judgment (Matt 3:5–12; Luke 3:1–9) and an admonition not to continue in sin (Luke 3:10–14). Jesus' healing of a paralytic began with, "Your sins are forgiven you" (Luke 5:20, 23), as did his reception of the sinful woman at a Pharisee's home (Luke 7:36–50).

Jesus' ministry to sinners led to the accusation that he was a friend of tax collectors and sinners (Matt 11:19–20). The Pharisees and scribes (and Essenes) approached ethics essentially in terms of God's holiness, and so separation from sinners was the righteous thing to do. Jesus, on the other hand, approached ethics in terms of God's mercy (Matt 9:13; 12:7; based on Hos 6:6). God was like the joyful woman whose coin had been found, the joyful shepherd whose lost sheep had been restored to the fold, and the joyful father whose prodigal son returned (Luke 15). Such mercy presupposes an ethic of right and wrong, of righteousness and sin. It also involves the belief in a final judgment. Only if there is real sin, real "lostness," and real judgment can there be real mercy—and real joy over repentance and redemption.

---

[8] Ulrich Luz, *Matthew 1–7: A Commentary*, trans. Wilhelm C. Linss (Edinburgh, Scotland: T&T Clark, 1989), 87. Willi Marxsen was even more extreme in his assessment of Matthew's Gospel: "Matthew's ethic, of course, emerged from the Christian tradition, but we cannot call it genuinely Christian. It represents rather a relapse into the Pharisaic ethic. Likewise, the other verdict is that the ethic of the Sermon on the Mount is not a truly Christian ethic, either" (*New Testament Foundations for Christian Ethics*, trans. O. C. Dean Jr. [Minneapolis, MN: Fortress, 1993], 246).

[9] Glen Stassen and David Gushee, *Kingdom Ethics: Following Jesus in Contemporary Context* (Downers Grove, IL: InterVarsity, 2003), 142.

As Wolfgang Schrage says, the law of love is a standard of interpretation. Jesus does not abrogate the law but radicalizes how it is interpreted.[10] Schrage also notes the significance of Jesus himself for his ethic. Jesus calls for and fulfills a better righteousness in word and deed; he is Emmanuel, "God with us," the one who humbly and willingly dies for others; he heals people; he is the Lord, present with his own after resurrection; he is the authoritative teacher showing his disciples a better righteousness; Jesus's disciples turn his mission into a universal mission; and Jesus (like John the Baptist) calls for obedience—to do good works, produce the fruit of righteousness, and be about God's mission.[11] We might say Jesus reveals what the law always was: not righteous requirements over against love but righteous requirements for love.[12] In Schrage's view, Jesus downgraded the law and replaced it with himself: his demands are grounded in his own authority.[13] On this understanding the law is still not understood to be abrogated by Jesus, and Jesus's teaching is not antinomian.

The narrative setting of Jesus's ministry is crucial for understanding his ethic. That setting, as N. T. Wright and others have pointed out over the past two decades, is the narrative of Israel's return from exile: "*Jesus was offering the return from exile, the renewed covenant, the eschatological "forgiveness of sins"*—in other words, the kingdom of God. And he was offering this final eschatological blessing outside the official structures, to all the wrong people, and on his own authority. That was his real offence."[14]

In the Old Testament the return from exile meant the end of punishment for sin (Lam 4:22; Jer 31:31–34; 33:4–11; Ezek 36:24–26, 33; 37:21–23; Isa 40:1–2; 43:25–44:3; 52–55; Dan 9:16–19). Jesus is offering kingdom forgiveness alongside a call to kingdom righteousness. He is doing so because he, as Messiah, is fulfilling the messianic task of saving Israel from her sins (Matt 1:21) by purifying Israel's righteousness, cleansing the temple, dying for her sins (as understood through Isaiah 53:10 [LXX]), and fighting her battles.[15] The demands of the Sermon on the Mount are predicated on Jesus' offer of the kingdom. The sermon begins with the welcoming beatitudes spoken to an

---

[10] Wolfgang Schrage, *The Ethics of the New Testament*, trans. David E. Green (Philadelphia, PA: Fortress, 1988), 149–50.

[11] Ibid., 145.

[12] Such an understanding also highlights the significance of community ethics. As Frank Matera states, Jesus' Sermon on the Mount is Jesus's interpretation of the Law in light of the kingdom of heaven and "is how disciples live." He continues, "It only becomes an impossible ideal when Christians forget the ethical horizon of the kingdom of heaven, or when they no longer live in a community of like-minded disciples" (*New Testament Ethics: The Legacies of Jesus and Paul* [Louisville, KY: Westminster/John Knox, 1996], 50).

[13] W. Schrage, *Ethics of the New Testament*, 55–68.

[14] N. T. Wright, *Jesus and the Victory of God* (London, England: S.P.C.K., 1996).

[15] Ibid., 604–5.

audience being comforted and invited to follow Jesus out of exile in sin and into the reign of God. Jesus's ministry of restoring Israel from exile in her sins is the grace on which the demands of kingdom righteousness are predicated.[16] To miss this point is to miss everything.

Jesus could be misunderstood as opposing the law because of his opposition to those quintessential lawmakers and lawkeepers, the scribes and Pharisees. Yet Jesus saw them as quintessential lawbreakers, for their intricate interpretations provided them with wiggle room to disobey the law (Matt 5:20). Jesus opposed the Pharisees where they accommodated sin, as in their abuse of the Mosaic permission to divorce (Matt 19:1–9) or the Pharisaic practice of devoting something to God to keep it from otherwise being used for good (Matt 15:1–9). Jesus particularly opposed them on their view of the Sabbath, which gave the appearance of holiness but entailed avoiding doing the right thing (e.g., Matt 12:1–14). Moreover, they, sitting in Moses's seat, failed to practice what they preached. Jesus did not say, "Do not obey them because they are teachers of Moses's law." Rather, he said,

> The scribes and the Pharisees sit on Moses' seat; therefore, *do whatever they teach you and follow it*; but do not do as they do, for they do not practice what they teach. (Matt 23:2–3)

Thus, Jesus' "love ethic" rests on the Mosaic law and the Prophets rather than replacing them. In fact, it was already part of the Mosaic law (Deut 6:5; Lev 19:18, 34) since to love God *is* to keep his commandments (Deut 11:1). Jesus, in fact, applies this to himself: "If you love me, you will keep my commandments" (John 14:15; cf. 14:21–24). In adopting the language of the Old Testament that identifies loving God with keeping his commandments, Jesus is both identifying himself with God and affirming the place of biblical commandments in any ethic of love. A general antagonism in our day—by scholars as much as by laypersons—makes it possible to misinterpret Jesus's teaching on the law and his ethic of love.[17] The reality, however, is that Jesus's ethic of love went hand-in-glove with the righteous requirements of God revealed in the Old Testament. Jesus did not come to oppose the law, but to fulfill it:

> Do not think that I have come to abolish the law or the prophets; I have come not to abolish but to fulfill. For truly I tell you, until heaven and earth pass away, not one letter, not one stroke of a letter, will pass from the law

---

[16] On the role of grace in Jesus's teaching, see Roger Mohrlang, *Matthew and Paul: A Comparison of Ethical Perspectives,* Society for New Testament Studies Monograph Series (New York, NY: Cambridge University Press, 1984). Mohrlang also understands Jesus to affirm the Law (see pp. 8–17).

[17] The following article explores this antagonism toward concrete norms and rules in Christian ethics: Rollin G. Grams, "The Use of Biblical Norms in Christian Ethics," *Journal of European Baptist Studies* 4, no. 1 (September 2003): 4–19.

until all is accomplished. Therefore, whoever breaks one of the least of these commandments, and teaches others to do the same, will be called least in the kingdom of heaven; but whoever does them and teaches them will be called great in the kingdom of heaven. (Matt 5:17–19)

Neither can Paul's ethics be reduced to a principle of love. He clearly states that certain behaviors are sinful, and he adamantly believes God will one day judge humanity for their sins (e.g., Rom 2:5–16; 2 Cor 5:10). His sin lists do not reflect mere customs to which he adheres willy-nilly but sins that will keep people from inheriting the kingdom of God (1 Cor 6:9–10). The work of Christ and the Holy Spirit washes, sanctifies, and makes righteous[18] people who acted sinfully before coming to faith (1 Cor 6:11). Believers are, therefore, to shun sexual immorality and realize that their bodies are temples of the Holy Spirit (1 Cor 6:19–20). Paul states that believers were bought with a price—Christ's death on a cross—and therefore they are to glorify God in their bodies (1 Cor 6:21). Does this in any way sound as though Paul's concrete ethic can be understood merely as a collection of "unreflective customs"?

Several other problems with Wink's approach to Scripture through a "love ethic" should be noted. First, love is, to be sure, an important part of a Christian ethic, but it lacks content. As in our example from Matthew's Gospel, so too in Paul: the "law of love" is used to interpret, not to replace, concrete content in Christian ethics (e.g., Rom 13:8–14). Indeed, in Romans 13, where Paul states that love sums up the Ten Commandments, he does not eliminate those commandments for Christians, and he concludes with the following imperative: "Instead, put on the Lord Jesus Christ, and make no provision for the flesh, to gratify its desires" (Rom 13:14). We are back to recognizing that there is a concrete ethic—indeed, a concrete sexual ethic—alongside the "law of love." The challenge Paul gives is to see how the righteous commandments of God are loving commandments and to be sure to practice them as such.

Second, those who wish to identify Christian ethics with some broad principle instead of concrete practices show themselves beholden to a Western, Enlightenment way of thinking. For several hundred years the West has tried to reduce ethics to some key principle or a few key values. John Locke's values of "life, liberty, and property" became Thomas Jefferson's values of "life, liberty, and the pursuit of happiness." The French encapsulated their values

---

[18] "Made righteous" ought to be the translation in 1 Cor 6:11, as the entire section (5:1–6:20) is ethical and the other two words in this verse, "washed" and "sanctified," are not juridical terms but speak of moral cleansing and purity. The Greek word *dikaioō* can be translated into English either as "justify" (a law-court term) or "make righteous" (a moral term). Despite significant translations opting for "justified" in 1 Cor 6:11, the translation ought to be "made righteous." Compare Titus 3:7, which should be understood ethically: the Spirit's work is not "justification" but the making righteous of God's people (see the context, vv. 5–7; cf. Ezek 36:25–33; Isa 59:20–21).

in "liberty, fraternity, and equality." Immanuel Kant suggested ethics can be derived from the principle that one should do what everyone ought to do, no matter the situation (the "categorical imperative"). Jeremy Bentham and John Stuart Mill emphasized the utilitarian principle of seeking the greatest good for the greatest number of people. This long history of reducing ethics to one or a few principles finally led to the suggestion by Joseph Fletcher that people should just do the "loving thing." They will know what that is when they are in the situation, and so no concrete ethic is needed.

This deeply rooted perspective in Western society cannot fathom concrete ethics—norms, laws, rules, the threat of divine punishment—even the concept of sin. Nor can ethics, it is claimed, be thought of in terms of acts or practices. Rather, the spokesmen for our culture aver, one must consider motivations, intentions, and, of course, orientation.[19] Acts are considered neutral; their moral worth is, allegedly, derived from these added values.[20] To say that such and such an act is itself wrong seems, from such a perspective, to be irrational. The culture can, on these grounds, criticize casual sex but has no reason to object to couples living together or homosexuals marrying each other. Yet this abstracted understanding of ethics runs contrary to biblical ethics in general. As Wolfgang Schrage has argued with respect to Paul's ethics, virtue and vice are not distinguished from concrete specifications.[21]

Third, biblical ethics works from a perspective of moral actions, and God is believed to have revealed to sinful humanity which actions are right and

---

[19] For example, James Brownson claims, "In the New Testament, purity moves from being a matter of externals to a matter of the heart and the will" and "The kind of same-sex eroticism that Paul had in mind in Romans 1 was indeed 'impure' in the sense in which that word is understood in the New Testament, that is, marked by lust and licentiousness" (*Bible, Gender, Sexuality: Reframing the Church's Debate on Same-Sex Relationships* [Grand Rapids, MI: Eerdmans, 2013], 202). This sort of statement is remarkable first for its lack of serious engagement with Paul's letters, second for its failure to engage opponents when arguing a controversial point, and third for its logical weaknesses. Are we really to believe Paul's sin lists are about motivations, attitudes, and intentions rather than the actions listed?

[20] Charles Pinches, *Theology and Actions: After Theory in Christian Ethics* (Grand Rapids, MI: Eerdmans, 2002), offers a detailed discussion of this separation of actions from morality in Western thought.

[21] Wolfgang Schrage, *Ethics of the New Testament*, trans. David E. Green (Philadelphia, PA: Fortress, 1988; German, 1982), 188. Schrage says, "The difference between Paul's ethics and casuistry lies not in a lack of concreteness but in the absence of any elaborate system embodying every possible injunction and reducing them all to a lowest common denominator of triviality" (p. 189). Schrage opposes certain scholars who have seen Paul's ethics as situational for their emphasis on the role of the Spirit and being in Christ. Rather, law remains relevant for Christian ethics (cf. Rom 8:4; 1 Cor 6:9) (p. 192). Still, Schrage fails to see the extent to which Paul advocates a concrete ethic with norms and rules, including his use of the Old Testament. What he demonstrates, as a spokesperson for concrete ethics in German biblical scholarship in the twentieth century, so dominated by existential and liberal theology, is that the Pauline ethic is a concrete ethic.

which are wrong. If the Old Testament has specific laws regulating specific acts and practices, the New Testament has specific sins in a variety of sin lists, as well as affirmations of many Old Testament laws, including an affirmation of Old Testament sexual ethics. This is the Jewish and Christian understanding of the law. Paul finds the law lacking not because there is something wrong with concrete commands, norms, rules, or laws, or because he is addressing only laws that separate Jews and Gentiles but because of human sin (Rom 2:17–3:20).[22] The problem with the law was that it was powerless to make people righteous (Rom 7:22–23; Gal 3:21). It could only enlighten people about what was right and wrong (Rom 2:20; 7:7). It actually turned "sin" into "trespass," since fallen people will inevitably sin, and fallen people with God's law will inevitably trespass that law when they do. Jews and Christians—including Paul the apostle—regularly invoked the Old Testament law to admonish one another. Wink's principle of love is what fails to qualify as an ethic, not the ethics of the early church. The early church had much more than a collection of social practices upon which they did not reflect carefully. The early church's ethics were formed in the context of a Judaism that had thought long and hard about its ethic based on Mosaic law, over against the practices of surrounding cultures. The early church's ethics were a further reflection on how that long history of Jewish ethics had to be rethought in light of Jesus Christ. Rethinking the faith involved an interpretation of authoritative Scripture and a continued use of the Law in ethical matters.

Fourth, note Richard Hays's reasons for rejecting "love" as an adequate criterion to bring scriptural ethics into focus. "'Love' is not discussed in all New Testament writings (e.g., the term is not even found in Acts). It is, furthermore, far too broad a notion and can be summoned to support "all manner of vapid self-indulgence."[23] As already noted, what happens with the criterion of "love" in a culture that highly values "freedom" is that "love" is defined in terms of "freedom." The "loving thing to do" becomes letting people do what they want to do, as long as the rights of others are not infringed. Like cake batter, love takes the shape of the mold into which it is poured. In the West this mold consists of liberation and equality. No society will stand with so meager a basis for thinking through its great moral challenges. Citizens of Western culture lack a robust enough moral vocabulary and ethic to explain why they object to things their consciences feel are wrong. In the public square they are restricted to the language of freedom and equality in all moral matters. Such

---

[22] On this point, that the problem with the law was that it could not make sinful people righteous, we agree with Stephen Westerholm, *Israel's Law and the Church's Faith* (Grand Rapids, MI: Eerdmans, 1988) and Frank Thielman, *From Plight to Solution,* Supplements to Novum Testamentum 61 (Leiden, Netherlands: E. J. Brill, 1989).

[23] Richard B. Hays, *The Moral Vision of the New Testament* (San Francisco, CA: HarperCollins, 1996), 202.

a "vapid" ethic fails to provide sensible answers for a number of great moral questions: abortion, euthanasia, gun laws, freedom of speech, sexual ethics, and so forth.

DOES A CONSISTENT OLD TESTAMENT SEXUAL ETHIC EXIST?

One of our primary points in this book is that homosexual acts are *consistently* condemned as sin in Scripture. The early church's appeal to Old Testament sexual ethics leads us to explore a little more fully whether there is a consistent Old Testament sexual ethic. The answer will help us determine whether the traditional condemnation of homosexual acts aligns with the Old Testament view of sexuality.

The traditional view has been challenged. We have already noted one of the detractors, Walter Wink, and will here look into his argument regarding the Old Testament.[24] By engaging Wink's arguments, we can see how cleverly crafted words without serious research have led some people—including some theologians—down the garden path.

As it turns out, in his article "Homosexuality and the Bible," Wink is himself actually opposed to a variety of sexual practices: rape, incest, and pederasty (pedophilia)—practices that involve domination by one person of another (although this is not always the case with incest). Moreover, Wink grants that the Bible speaks against homosexuality. So saying that the Bible has no sexual ethic and then acknowledging that it forbids a sexual act suggests a rhetorical rather than a logical approach to the subject.

What, then, is his reasoning? Wink believes there are inconsistencies in the Bible's statements about sexuality, and that leads him to the conclusion that the Bible has no sexual ethic. However, that argument falls apart easily. His approach is to list various sexual acts in groups, make some unsubstantiated claims, and create enough confusion to introduce his own view as a legitimate option. Below are Wink's groups of sexual sins:[25]

1. Acts rejected by the Bible and most of us today: "incest, rape, adultery, and intercourse with animals."
2. Acts rejected by the Bible but accepted today: "intercourse during menstruation, celibacy (some texts), exogamy (marriage with non-Israelites), naming sexual organs, nudity (under certain conditions), masturbation (some Christians still condemn this), birth control (some Christians still forbid this)."
3. Acts permitted by the Bible but rejected today: "prostitution, polygamy, levirate marriage, sex with slaves, concubinage, treatment of women as property, very early marriage (for the girl, age 11–13)."

---

[24] Walter Wink, "Homosexuality and the Bible," 33–49. See esp. p. 44.
[25] Ibid., 43.

Scripture's condemnation of homosexual acts does not mean such acts are forbidden today, Wink declares, because the Bible condemns other sexual practices that are viewed as acceptable today. Conversely, Wink says, the Bible permits some acts that are regarded by Christians today as forbidden. This is, first of all, false logic. It is like saying Scripture has no ethic and no authority in what it says about incest, rape, adultery, and bestiality because some sexual practices mentioned in the Old Testament are not forbidden now, thousands of years past its origination. Even if Scripture does have changing views on some practices, this does not render questionable the views it teaches consistently.

Yet Wink's argument has other problems. For example, in contrast to Wink's claim, Scripture nowhere affirms prostitution. A narrative about prostitution—Judah's encounter with his daughter-in-law dressed as a prostitute (Genesis 38)—is an account about Judah's descendants from whom came the Davidic kings; the chapter is not a narrative told for ethical instruction. It does not affirm prostitution. Further, Paul condemns prostitution based on Genesis 2:24 and the believer's union with Christ (1 Cor 6:15–16). Also untrue is Wink's assertion that in Scripture women were treated simply as property; even if property law could be applied to marriage—the issues covered in the Bible are far more complex than what Wink leaves the reader to believe. Sex with a slave girl who was not ransomed, for instance, was not a mere violation of property rights but was treated as a sin: the sin needed to be atoned for with a guilt offering (Lev 19:20–22). A captive slave, moreover, could become a wife. If the man was not satisfied with her, she could be released but not sold as a slave (Deut 21:10–14). Thus, she was not treated merely as property, and the separation was essentially a divorce. That the laws governing property could be applied to women does not mean women were "treated" as property or that only property law applied to them. On the contrary, other laws protected women: Deuteronomy 24 required a certificate of divorce to protect the woman from her former husband, and Deuteronomy 22:28–29 set up a law to protect girls from premarital sex. Importantly, premarital sex reduced a girl to being a sex object—a piece of property:

> If a man meets a virgin who is not engaged, and seizes her and lies with her, and they [implied: both acting willingly] are caught in the act, the man who lay with her *shall give fifty shekels of silver to the young woman's father, and she shall become his wife. Because he violated her he shall not be permitted to divorce her as long as he lives.* (Deut 22:28–29)

Also, certain conditions may indeed be cultural, such as early marriage for girls, but that does not mean there is no scriptural ethic on sexuality. Early marriage may have made sense in a culture where the average life span was half of what it is today, for example. It was also more workable when marriages were held together in larger family and community structures. This is a cultural issue.

Furthermore, Wink's lists of sexual acts are noticeably incomplete; for example, he does not mention homosexuality, sex apart from marriage, or sex by couples living together. He does not appreciate that understanding can be reached as to why something might be prohibited under the old covenant, such as sex during menstruation or "exogamy" (marriage outside a social group). In other words, he notes views without attempting to interpret why such views were held. Nor does Wink show any awareness that Scripture differentiates between various types of laws in the Old Testament. The breaking of some laws required the death penalty; others were merely civil laws and required payment of a fine when broken; others required purification and/or a sacrifice for sin because they were understood to be moral laws, and so forth. Again texts must be interpreted. Yet the larger issue is that even though some sexual practices, such as polygamy or marrying at a young age, are cultural, Scripture may still have a consistent sexual ethic. For example, the notion of fidelity in marriage is not undermined just because Scripture tells stories about girls being married at an early age; there are no laws on the subject. Indeed, practices may be cultural—not binding—while also pointing to something that is transculturally normative: cultural practices such as polygamy, levirate marriage, concubinage, and girls marrying young all demonstrate the transculturally normative conviction that marriage is binding and heterosexual.

Moreover, Wink seems to interpret narratives as though they always imply endorsement of the behavior described. For example, he cites polygamy, concubinage, and prostitution as permitted in Scripture. Proper analysis of such practices requires considerable comment, particularly regarding the relationship between narratives and ethics,[26] not facile citation as though they are scripturally endorsed simply because they are mentioned.

The point, then, is that Wink's argument against Scripture having a sexual ethic is logically flawed at numerous levels and entails an abandonment of biblical scholarship. Having such a bold argument in print by a scholar, however, allows others in a Western cultural context that devalues tradition to present the same claim and get away with it by merely referencing the supposed expert's work. The example we have in mind is Jack Rogers, a former moderator of the Presbyterian Church, USA. Rogers's popular work on homosexuality favorably quotes Wink's statement that the Bible has no sexual ethic. He treats the

---

[26] John Barton, *Understanding Old Testament Ethics: Approaches and Explorations* (Louisville, KY: Westminster/John Knox, 2003), has some helpful analysis of ethics in narrative texts, but see especially Gordon Wenham, *Story as Torah: Reading the Old Testament Ethically* (Edinburgh, Scotland: T&T Clark, 2000).

claim as though it has, thanks to Wink, already been proven.[27] Are we really ready to jettison the church's reading of Scripture on sexual ethics so quickly and with so little argument? Is this acceptable for Christian theologians in our day? Indeed, this example says more about the Western church and the state of theological enquiry than about biblical sexual ethics. Only Christians' ignorance of the Bible and the church's history allows scholars to get away with such poor argumentation. But as this ignorance often extends to pastors trying to make sense of a complex debate, two or more supposed scholarly works like those of Wink and Rogers can gain steam behind the pulpit, leaving many to assume their argument is legitimate. And though the argument is hopelessly flawed and stands in opposition to truth, it seems to have authority. After all, scholars are thought to be the experts.

To return to Wink's arguments, he claims that the Reformers' view of scriptural authority needs to be reformed in our day. Apparently, what we now need is a liberation reading of Scripture that might require us to be liberated *from Scripture.* Wink argued first that, because Scripture says different things about sexuality, it therefore offers no authoritative teaching on the subject of sexuality. Then he argued that we need to stop treating Scripture as authoritative even where it is consistent—as with the issue of homosexuality. This is the theological equivalent of a usurper slaying the allegedly erratic king and dismissing Parliament in the name of liberation, only to rule by his own autocratic whims even when good laws exist in the land.

The Old Testament does, in fact, have a sexual ethic,[28] and it excludes homosexual acts. The ethic is based on the creation narrative found in Genesis 1–3 and is grounded in the view that marriage is a *union between a man and a woman.* This rules out bestiality, homosexuality, casual sex, premarital sex, prostitution, adultery, and gender-confused sexual behavior, such as cross-dressing. Marriage is more than a covenant; it is related to a natural or creational ethic.[29] This point is the thrust of Jesus's rejection of divorce on

---

[27] See Jack Rogers, *Jesus, the Bible and Homosexuality,* 63. This is an example of someone latching onto an argument that supports his own thesis without examining the merits of the argument.

[28] For a helpful overview of Old Testament sexual ethics, see J. M. Sprinkle, "Sexuality, Sexual Ethics," in *Dictionary of the Old Testament Pentateuch,* ed. T. Desmond Alexander and David W. Baker (Downers Grove, IL: InterVarsity, 2003), 741–53.

[29] See Gordon Hugenberger, *Marriage as a Covenant: Biblical Law and Ethics as Developed from Malachi* (Grand Rapids, MI: Baker Academic, 1994). Hugenberger argues that marriage in the Old Testament is understood to be a covenant. His argument is based on understanding Mal 2:14's "the wife of your covenant" as a reference to a marital covenant. Proverbs 2:17; Ezekiel 16; Hos 2:18–22 (English translations, 2:16–20); and 1 Samuel 18–20 also support the view that marriage is a covenant. Yet he also notes that Mal 2:15a is dependent on Gen 2:23–24 and therefore references more than a covenant (p. 342). The oath-taking aspect of covenant, in the case of marriage, involves the sexual act itself. "To know" one's spouse, both sexually and covenantally, is referenced in Hos 2:22 (English, Hos 2:20). Thus, the covenant oath of marriage and

the basis of Genesis 2:24; the man and woman become *one flesh*. Since this is the basis of Jesus's interpretation of marriage, it is not difficult to extend Genesis 2:24 to homosexuality as well—even though the issue would not have been raised in a first-century Jewish context, where there was no argument in favor of homosexuality to counter. "Homosexual marriage" is impossible if marriage is understood in light of the creation story. There are nuances of sexual ethics in the Old Testament, such as laws about kinship relationships or practices such as polygamy and levirate marriage. Yet this is the starting point for an Old Testament sexual ethic and serves as the basis for consistency to Old Testament teaching on sexual ethics.[30]

Genesis 2:24 explains how male and female come together as one flesh and so fulfill the mandate to be fruitful and multiply (Gen 1:28). Sex within the context of a "one flesh" union between a male and a female is the biblical sexual ethic. The anatomical complementarity of male and female, their sexual union, and their ability to fulfill the mandate to multiply on the earth represent a complete, relational union that is more than a contract but is a matter of two people becoming inseparably one. This is an ontological (creational, natural) union possible only for complementary beings made for each other—male and female.

DID FIRST-CENTURY JEWS BELIEVE THEY HAD A SEXUAL ETHIC?

It is one thing for Wink to assert that the Bible has no sexual ethic; it is quite another to ask whether first-century Jews and Christians believed they had a sexual ethic. The evidence is clear.

Josephus, a first-century Jewish writer, explained to his non-Jewish readers that there was a Jewish ethic on sexuality stated in the laws of the Bible. That incontrovertible law included, among other things, regulations about homosexual acts—whether forced or voluntary—adultery, and premarital sex. He writes:

> But then, what are our laws about marriage? That law owns no other mixture of sexes but that which nature has appointed, of a man with his wife, and that this be used only for the procreation of children. But it abhors the mixture of a male with a male; and if anyone does that, death is its punishment. It commands us also, when we marry, not to have regard to portion, nor to

---

sexual union between a male and a female (Gen 2:24) are one and the same. As Hugenberger concludes, "Sexual union, as a marriage covenant-ratifying act, is the decisive means by which an individual 'acknowledges' his or her spouse as covenant partner" (p. 343; argued in detail in chap. 7).

[30] For a more detailed exploration of a biblical sexual ethic, see Andreas J. Köstenberger and David W. Jones, *God, Marriage, and Family: Rebuilding the Biblical Foundation,* 2nd ed. (Wheaton, IL: Crossway, 2010).

take a woman by violence, nor to persuade her deceitfully and knavishly; but to demand her in marriage of him who has power to dispose of her, and is fit to give her away by the nearness of his kindred. . . . A husband, therefore, is to lie only with his wife whom he has married; but to have to do with another man's wife is a wicked thing; which, if anyone ventures upon, death is inevitably his punishment: no more can he avoid the same who forces a virgin betrothed to another man, or entices another man's wife. . . . Moreover, the law enjoins, that after the man and wife have lain together in a regular way, they shall bathe themselves. . . . Now the greatest part of offences with us are capital; as if anyone be guilty of adultery; if anyone force a virgin; if anyone be so impudent as to attempt sodomy with a male; or if, upon another's making an attempt upon him, he submits to be so used. There is also a law for slaves of the like nature that can never be avoided. (*Against Apion* 2:199–201, 203, 215)[31]

Elsewhere, in *Antiquities of the Jews* 4:245–47, Josephus interpreted the Old Testament—showing the source for Jewish sexual ethics—to say that nobody should marry a prostitute and that women should marry as virgins. (Together these commands ruled out males having sex with women before marriage.) According to 4:252 of the same document, rape carried the death sentence. If sex occurred before marriage, the two participants were required to marry; or if the father of the girl allowed, a fine could be paid. For a marriage to end, Josephus records in 4:253, a divorce certificate had to be obtained. In 19:204 Josephus mentioned incest as wrong not only in his view but also among the Romans. He further pointed out that Jews would rather die than violate their laws, including those on sex and marriage:

Nor ought men to wonder at us, if we are more courageous in dying for our laws than all other men are; . . . *being under inviolable rules in lying with our wives*. (*Ag. Ap.* 2:234)

In all this Josephus demonstrated not only that he believed Jews to have a sexual ethic but also that their sexual ethic derived from laws in Scripture.

The perspective in Judaism appears to be that expressed in the book of *Jubilees*, which spoke of the need for Moses to write down laws for Israel in order to preserve it as a holy nation. Among those were laws about fornication; for there was, the author wrote, no greater sin on earth (*Jubilees* 33:18–20).

Details about the Jewish sexual ethic are seldom given as straightforwardly in extrabiblical literature as in the passage cited above from Josephus. The reason for this is, in large part, that Jews believed Moses's laws explained the ethic well, and Moses's teaching was considered divinely inspired and authoritative. It was constantly before the Jewish people in the synagogues and in the

---

[31] Josephus's works are quoted from the translation by William J. Whiston (1828) in public domain, available on *BibleWorks*.

teachings of the scribes and Pharisees in particular. Indeed, Jesus did not relax laws regarding sexual ethics, although he did criticize laxity toward the commandment not to commit adultery in the practice of divorce and remarriage (Matt 19:3). One reason he did not address homosexuality was that it was not practiced in Israel as it was in the Gentile world.

SEXUAL ETHICS FOR GENTILE BELIEVERS

The Old Testament's teaching on sexual ethics and Josephus's comments about sexual ethics in the first century should lead scholars to expect that the early church also held to a particular sexual ethic. This was, indeed, the case. Five points support this.

1. The early church could have developed a new sexual ethic; it did not. The early Christians did not differ from the Old Testament or first-century Judaism in their sexual ethics. This is remarkable since the Christian message engaged the cultures of the Greco-Roman world by the AD 40s at the latest and spread among Gentiles as time passed. To be sure, enculturation of sexual views posed a major problem for the church. New Testament writers took a stand against the sinful sexual practices of the Greco-Roman world creeping into the churches. However, this is hardly an instance of promoting sexual mores unreflectively, as Wink asserts.

2. New believers were instructed in sexual ethics—the topic was not ignored. Sexual ethics was part and parcel of Paul's initial instruction to new converts: an up-front course in Christian ethics was needed for persons coming from a non-Jewish background into the Christian faith. Paul's first letter to the church in Thessalonica gives us a view into his initial teaching of new converts, since he wrote it shortly after establishing the church and only had three weeks in Thessalonica to establish the church before he had to leave (Acts 17:2). In 1 Thessalonians 4, Paul *reminded* this young body of believers about what he had already (see vv. 1–2) taught them.[32] The chapter reminded this church of Paul's ethical teaching, which was, in Paul's view, critical for salvation, since "whoever rejects this [that God called us not to impurity but to holiness in sexual matters] rejects not human authority but God, who also gives his Holy Spirit to you" (1 Thess 4:8). Paul's teaching covered two areas: sexual ethics (1 Thess 4:3–8) and community ethics (1 Thess 4:9–12). The passage is tantalizing for its brevity: we are overhearing Paul's reminder to a church that already knew the details without hearing the full teaching he gave. Yet Paul reminded the Thessalonians to "abstain from fornication (*porneia*)"

---

[32] Victor Paul Furnish acknowledges (see below regarding his view on Rom 6:17) that Paul offered counsel (a softer notion than "orders") for new converts, perhaps as part of their baptismal catechesis: *1 Thessalonians, 2 Thessalonians,* Abingdon New Testament Commentaries (Nashville, TN: Abingdon, 2007), 91.

(v. 3). He warned the new converts not to "wrong or exploit a brother or sister in this matter" (v. 6). By "this matter" Paul was referring to the sexual passions of "the Gentiles," who did not know God (v. 5).[33] God called the Thessalonians to be holy, and that meant dealing with sexual passions ("abstaining" v. 3) by controlling their "vessels" in "holiness and honor" (v. 4).[34] This is consistent with Paul's view of sexuality in 1 Cor 7:1–7: the place for sex is marriage, and marriage is, among other things, a place for sexual expression. The Gentiles' view of sexual expression, on the other hand, did not confine them to sex within marriage or only to heterosexual sex. Paul, to the contrary, called Gentile converts to acknowledge a sexual ethic for the body:

> *Shun fornication!* Every sin that a person commits is outside the body; but the fornicator sins against the body itself. . . . Do you not know that *your body is a temple of the Holy Spirit*, who is in you, whom you have received from God? You are not your own; For you were bought with a price; therefore *glorify God in your body.* (1 Cor 6:18–20)

That Paul presented his churches with a "standard of ethical teaching" is also clear from yet another of his letters:

> But thanks be to God that you, having once been slaves of sin, have become *obedient from the heart to the form of teaching to which you were entrusted.* (Rom 6:17)

Some scholars deny there was a concrete ethical teaching in the early church. For example, Victor Paul Furnish (following Rudolf Bultmann) claimed that Romans 6:17 was an interpolation—Paul would surely never have spoken of obedience to a "form of teaching" that the church had given believers.[35] Such conjectures are motivated from preconceptions rather than evidence; no manuscript evidence raises doubts about the authenticity of Romans 6:17. In fact, as we have seen, there is good evidence that Paul followed his proclamation of the gospel with moral teaching for new converts (1 Thessalonians 4).

3. Pauline ethics included teaching on sexuality. At a later point in this book, we shall have opportunity to say more on Paul's ethics. Here we merely wish to note that Paul's teaching on sexuality fits into his overall understanding of Christian ethics. Much of Paul's focus in Romans is on the passions of the flesh and how they lead people into sin. The passions go beyond sexual

---

[33] An alternative proposal, but one we think without merit, is that "this matter" refers to conduct in business. If Paul had meant that, he would have said so. See the discussion of authors advocating this in Earl J. Richard, *First and Second Thessalonians* (Collegeville, MN: Liturgical, 1995), 200–202.

[34] This could have to do with acquiring a wife, understood as a "vessel" (cf. 1 Pet 3:7), instead of learning to control one's sexual "vessel" (organ) or body. See our discussion in chap. 13.

[35] Victor Paul Furnish, *Theology and Ethics in Paul* (Philadelphia, PA: Fortress, 1968), 239.

matters, but they include sexuality. Paul was no ascetic—there was a place for sex within marriage (1 Cor 7:1). Yet the passions in a fallen, sinful world caused people to be enslaved to sin. Only in Christ could individuals be freed from such passions and become obedient to righteousness. Romans 6–8 is an explanation of how such freedom is attained, not by human effort or by the law but by the work of Jesus Christ and the Holy Spirit. Indeed, Paul's sexual ethic looks not only to the acts but also to the passion that accounts for twisted sexuality and other sins. While we cannot reduce Romans to a treatise on sexual ethics, Paul's arguments do address the matter—including the particular matter of homosexuality—at a profound level: the passions.[36]

4. The Old Testament teachings were an important source for early Christian ethics, including sexual ethics. As James Thompson has demonstrated, ancient Jewish and Christian teaching on sexuality was based on the Old Testament, particularly chapters 18 and 20 of Leviticus, which are part of the so-called Holiness Code of chapters 17 through 26.[37] The importance of the Holiness Code for sexual ethics needs to be recognized in the discussion of homosexuality and the Bible since some attempt to undermine its relevance.

As Thompson argues regarding Hellenistic Judaism:

> The emphasis on sexual vices and care for the poor and disadvantaged is based primarily on a "canon-within-the canon" from the Pentateuch. Of special importance is the Holiness Code (Lev 17–26), especially Leviticus 18–20, which contains both the sexual laws and the regulations for the care of disadvantaged people within the community. This list of laws repeats and elaborates on the rules of the Decalogue. Because the Holiness Code covered the spheres of family life, work, and relationships with others, it was useful for catechetical instruction in a variety of contexts.[38]

Later, regarding Paul's catechesis and vice lists, Thompson states:

> The list of sexual offenses suggests that Paul derives the specific vices from the Holiness Code in Leviticus 17–26. He envisions the church as a holy community separated from the society around them, as does Leviticus. Paul's instructions on sexuality reflect his Jewish heritage, according to which the Holiness Code defines obedience to the law in a pagan environment. Paraeneses [moral exhortations] in Jewish literature focused on separating the sexual practices of the communities to abstain from *porneia* and homosexual relationships. Just as the Holiness Code was important in Hellenistic Jewish paraenesis [moral exhortation], it shaped Paul's sexual paraenesis, for

---

[36] See James Thompson, *Moral Formation According to Paul: The Context and Coherence of Pauline Ethics* (Grand Rapids, MI: Baker Academic, 2011).

[37] Ibid., 72–79. The Holiness Code contains explicit instructions on what constitutes sexual immorality (in Leviticus 18 and 20, homosexuality is addressed).

[38] Ibid., 40.

Paul placed the paraenetic [moral] instructions on sexuality under the rubric of holiness in 1 Corinthians.[39]

The Holiness Code was not the only part of the Old Testament used by the early church to define sexual immorality. Yet it appeared to be significant once again in the Jerusalem Council's decision about what Gentiles ought to do as believers in Jesus Christ (Acts 15:20, 29; 21:25). The decision included a warning to avoid sexual immorality (*porneia*, which is sometimes translated as "fornication"). There was no need to explain this further: the early Christians knew what this meant. In fact, as in 1 Thessalonians 4:3, the Leviticus Holiness Code is probably alluded to in this council's decision regarding idolatry, sexual immorality, and regulations about blood.[40]

5. The early church countered false teaching on sexual ethics. Paul accuses the non-Christian Gentiles of intentionally propagating false teaching on a host of ethical issues, including homosexuality (see Rom 1:24–28). He concludes, *"They* [the Gentiles] *know God's decree*, that those who practice such things deserve to die—yet they not only do them but even applaud others who practice them. (Rom 1:32)."

In Ephesians 4:1–5:20, Paul covers a number of subjects that have to do with *unity* in the church. In the process he notes where it is appropriate to maintain *disunity*. Believers are *not* to be like unbelievers in a variety of ways, including sexual practices.

As in Romans 1:28, Paul insists in Ephesians 4 that those outside of Christ have a fatal flaw: they lack understanding such that they fail to discern right from wrong (Eph 4:17–18). This works itself out in an abandonment to sexual sin (v. 19). Paul counters this by speaking of "learning Christ" and being "taught in him" (vv. 20–21). This teaching involves putting away the former life, corrupt and deluded by its lusts (v. 22). What believers learn instead is to be renewed in the spirit of their minds, clothed with a new self, and created anew in the image of God "in true righteousness and holiness" (vv. 23–24).[41]

A few verses later Paul returns to the subject of sexual immorality, stating that it must not characterize God's "saints"—people set apart to him and called to be holy. Paul says, "But fornication and impurity of any kind, or

---

[39] Ibid., 99.

[40] See I. Howard Marshall, *Acts,* Tyndale New Testament Commentaries (Grand Rapids, MI: Eerdmans, 1980), 246.

[41] Ephesians 4:18–24 says: ". . . because of their ignorance and hardness of heart. They have lost all sensitivity and have abandoned themselves to licentiousness, greedy to practice every kind of impurity. That is not the way you learned Christ! For surely you have heard about him and were taught in him, as truth is in Jesus. You were taught to put away your former way of life, your old self, corrupt and deluded by its lusts, and to be renewed in the spirit of your minds, and to clothe yourselves with the new self, created according to the likeness of God in true righteousness and holiness."

greed, must not even be mentioned among you, as is proper among saints" (Eph 5:3). Those who will inherit the kingdom of Christ are distinguished from those who will not by sexual purity—a point Paul had already mentioned in 1 Corinthians 6:9–11. There he included general and specific terms referring to sexual sin. Those terms referenced fornication, adultery, and engaging in homosexual conduct. Here he uses broader terms so as to include all forms of sexual immorality:

> Be sure of this, that no *fornicator* or *impure* person, or one who is greedy (that is, an idolater), has any inheritance in the kingdom of Christ and of God. Let no one deceive you with empty words, for because of these things the wrath of God comes on those who are disobedient. Therefore do not be associated with them. For once you were darkness, but now in the Lord you are light. Live as children of light. (Eph 5:5–8)

Thus Paul calls believers to put on the breastplate of righteousness (6:14) in every way, including in their sexuality. He also defines the dividing line between those who are "in" and those who are "out," between those who are obedient—children of light—over against those who are disobedient—in the darkness—and not in the Lord. Moreover, in his day as in ours, there were those who deceived believers "with empty words," saying that fornicators and impure persons *would* inherit the kingdom of Christ and of God.

Other New Testament authors kept their warnings about sexual immorality general so as to cover all possible sexual sins, assuming their audiences knew precisely what constituted sexual immorality. The author of Hebrews, for example, has a few general words to say about sexual immorality, but he says just enough that we know he finds sex between a married male and female to be the only appropriate sexual expression:

> Let marriage be held in honor by all, and let the marriage bed be kept undefiled; for God will judge fornicators and adulterers. (Heb 13:4)

If, indeed, marriage is the only legitimate place for sexual intimacy, then one did not have to spell out that particular acts were sinful, such as homosexuality or bestiality. If the proper place for sex was the marriage bed, then all the particular aberrations of this did not need to be provided. Similarly, Jesus did not need to address homosexuality or bestiality in Israel.

Yet there were in the Hellenistic context, as the church spread beyond Israel, false teachings about sexuality Christians had to address. Jude spoke of false teachers who had disseminated a teaching about sex that perverted the grace of God:

> For certain intruders have stolen in among you, people who long ago were designated for this condemnation as ungodly, who pervert the grace of our

God into *licentiousness* and deny our only Master and Lord, Jesus Christ (Jude 4; cf. vv. 16, 18).

As Jude also mentioned Sodom's "sexual immorality and unnatural [homosexual] lusts," these false teachers may have been teaching that homosexual acts were not sinful. Whether or not this was part of the false teaching, Jude let his readers know in no uncertain terms that such sexual sins would result in a "punishment of eternal fire" (v. 7).

Second Peter 2, possibly rewording the text of Jude, speaks in general terms of false teachers who promote sexual immorality: "Even so, many will follow their *licentious* ways, and because of these teachers the way of truth will be maligned" (v. 2). The chapter continues (following Jude) with two examples of how God delivered his people from sexually immoral cultures: God delivered Noah and his family after the angels had illicit sex with the daughters of men (2:4–5; cf. Genesis 6), and Lot was delivered from Sodom (2:6–8; cf. Genesis 19). Still using general terms, 2 Peter refers to "those who indulge their flesh in depraved lust" (2:10). Included in this is adultery, but also those who are "insatiable for sin" (v. 14). This powerful chapter concludes with a strong word against sexual immorality and those who advocate it in the church:

> For they speak bombastic nonsense, and with *licentious desires of the flesh* they entice people who have just escaped from those who live in error. They promise them freedom, but they themselves are slaves of corruption; for people are slaves to whatever masters them. For if, after they have escaped the defilements of the world through the knowledge of our Lord and Savior Jesus Christ, they are again entangled in them and overpowered, the last state has become worse for them than the first. For it would have been better for them never to have known the way of righteousness than, after knowing it, to turn back from the holy commandment that was passed on to them. It has happened to them according to the true proverb, "The dog turns back to its own vomit," and, "The sow is washed only to wallow in the mud." (2 Pet 2:18–22)

While adultery and homosexuality are in view in Jude and 2 Peter, the authors intentionally keep the discussion at a general level. True, the sexual sin of Sodom—homosexuality—is mentioned. But the authors are only using this as one example of sexual immorality. The problem they address is not a particular type of sexual immorality so much as any sexual immorality.

Revelation also condemns sexual immorality without specifying what is entailed (Rev 2:14, 20–21; 9:21). Where general references to sexual immorality are found, we can be certain the audience understood what was sexually immoral. Authors using general terminology did so in order not to restrict their comments to some sins and so leave out others. In so doing, they demonstrated that the church knew full well what "sexual immorality" was—this did not need a detailed explanation. Sexual immorality was defined by an ethic clearly laid out in the Old Testament. Indeed, the early church in the Gentile world confidently addressed that world's sexual practices with the sexual ethic of Old Testament Scripture.

CONCLUSION

We conclude, then, that the Old Testament—the Scriptures of the early church—contained a consistent sexual ethic, including teaching on homosexuality. The place for sex was understood to be within a marriage between a man and a woman. A first-century Jewish author, Josephus, assumed there was an identifiable Jewish teaching on sexuality, and the New Testament bears this out in its use of the Old Testament for teaching on sexuality (a point that will be developed later). While some specific Old Testament commandments did not apply within the early church, no Christian author argued against Old Testament sexual ethics. The fact that there was an Old Testament sexual ethic served as the basis for the early church's consistent sexual ethic, and a critical section of the Old Testament for the early church was the Holiness Code in Leviticus, where teaching on homosexuality is found. This early Christian teaching on sexuality, we have seen, was fundamental to initial instruction for new believers. Not only did the early church need to reform the thinking and behavior of Gentile converts on sexuality, but New Testament authors also had to combat attempts by some new converts to introduce Gentile practices into the churches.

Thus, readers should keep in mind that a look at texts on homosexual practice fits within a larger discussion of sexual ethics. Proponents of new teaching on homosexuality need to engage the larger matter of biblical sexual ethics as well. To accept homosexual practice as somehow acceptable for Christians entails a rethinking of Christian sexual ethics—indeed, Christian ethics!—over against what Scripture says.

**Creation and Law: Old Testament
Texts and Homosexuality**

CHAPTER 9

THE OLD TESTAMENT TEXTS
ADDRESSING HOMOSEXUALITY

Just what does the Old Testament say about homosexuality? This question will be addressed in this chapter through an overview of relevant Old Testament passages. The next two chapters address Sodom's sins and homosexuality in the ancient Near East respectively. The evidence is straightforward, although various attempts to read the texts differently in recent times will be addressed. Since we will also examine Jewish texts up to the fifth or sixth century AD, we might as well add here that Jews saw the issue straightforwardly. Jews and Christians consistently taught that homosexual acts were sinful, and they supported their views with the Scriptures. Both the Old and New Testaments, Judaism and the early church, taught a consistent view on sexuality in general and on homosexuality in particular, clearly differing from the surrounding cultures. Debate over this matter in recent times is not due to fresh illumination of biblical texts that our predecessors misread; rather, it stems from our culture's unwillingness to accept what the text says clearly.

When questions arise regarding the Christian use of the Old Testament to formulate ethics in the church, we have the New Testament authors as our guide. Paul, for example, nowhere overrides Old Testament views on sexual sin and, moreover, affirms Old Testament teaching on ethics—particularly on this matter of homosexuality. Thus, while some Old Testament practices such as circumcision, food laws, sacrifices, and following the Jewish calendar, were dropped in the early church, sexual ethics were not revised. Instead, there is a consistent understanding of sexuality in the Old and New Testaments. This consistency has extended all the way to our time in orthodox churches of the Christian faith.

THE OVERALL CONTEXT: A BIBLICAL UNDERSTANDING OF SEX IN MARRIAGE BETWEEN A MALE AND A FEMALE

We begin with a survey of Old Testament passages explaining God's intention to create humans as male and female so that they might unite to become one flesh and populate creation.

> God created humankind in his image, in the image of God he created them; *male and female he created them*. God blessed them, and God said to them, "Be *fruitful and multiply*, and fill the earth and subdue it; and have dominion over the fish of the sea and over the birds of the air and over every living thing that moves upon the earth." (Gen 1:27–28)

> Then the LORD God said, "*It is not good that the man should be alone; I will make him a helper as his partner*.". . . So the LORD God caused a deep sleep to fall upon the man, and he slept; then he took one of his ribs and closed up its place with flesh. And the rib that the LORD God had taken from the man he made into *a woman* and brought her to the man. Then the man said, "This at last is bone of my bones and flesh of my flesh; this one shall be called Woman, for out of Man this one was taken." *Therefore a man leaves his father and his mother and clings to his wife, and they become one flesh*. And the man and his wife were both naked, and were not ashamed. (Gen 2:18–25)

> This is the list of the descendants of Adam. When God created humankind, he made them in the likeness of God. *Male and female he created them*, and he blessed them and named them "Humankind" when they were created. (Gen 5:1–2)

THE LEGAL CONTEXT: NO HOMOSEXUAL UNIONS

Second, some texts explicitly forbid homosexual unions. The plain reading of these passages has been challenged in recent years, and so some discussion is needed.

> You shall not lie with a male (Septuagint: *arsenos*) as with a woman; it is an abomination. (Lev 18:22)

> If a man lies with a male (Septuagint: *arsenos koitēn*) as with a woman, both of them have committed an abomination; they shall be put to death; their blood is upon them. (Lev 20:13)

Some interpreters have suggested a contextual limitation to Leviticus 18:22 and 20:13.[1] For example, Letha Scanzoni and Virginia Mollenkott suggest three possible contextual readings of these laws:

> The reasons given for these proscriptions [in the Leviticus Holiness Code] involve several factors: (1) separation from other nations and their customs (Lev 18:1–5); (2) avoidance of idolatry and any practices associated with it (Lev 20:1–7); (3) ceremonial uncleanness. The prohibition of male homosexual acts in these passages may be partially understood in the light of the first two reasons, the context of the proscriptions in both chapters suggesting the association of such practices with the idolatrous neighboring nations. But the third reason—ceremonial uncleanness—may also be relevant.[2]

The flaw in this argument lies not in noting that laws come to be written in certain contexts but in assuming the laws are limited to those contexts. Situations arise that lead people to write certain laws, but those writing laws write them to apply in various contexts. If a law needs to be limited and not applied to every situation, those forming the law clarify what the limitations are. The sexual laws of Leviticus 18 are written, contextually, because Israel is to be distinct from Canaan and Egypt. No one has ever entertained the view that should Canaanites and Egyptians start obeying these laws themselves, the Israelites should then start to practice what had previously been forbidden in order to be different from Canaan and Egypt. Indeed, the peoples in the region of Canaan were not to be exterminated by Israel because they were foreign but because they were sinful, idolatrous, and would lead Israel into sin (Gen 15:16; Deut 20:16–18; Judg 2:2–3). The formation of Israel is the occasion for writing the laws, but the laws forbidding homosexual behavior in Leviticus 18 and 20 are not limited to this context. They are, on the contrary, related to God's character. God is holy, and Israel is to be holy too. In the Holiness Code, we read,

> Speak to all the congregation of the people of Israel and say to them: You shall be holy, for I the LORD your God am holy. (Lev 19:2)

Moreover, when Paul mentions male homosexual unions in sin lists (1 Cor 6:9–11 and 1 Tim 1:8–10), he demonstrates that prohibitions of these unions were not limited to the original context in which they were written.

One reason for attempting to limit Leviticus 18:22 and 20:13 to some particular context focuses on the word "abomination" (*tō'ēbāh*), which is used

---

[1] See discussion of such interpretations in Andreas Köstenberger, with David Jones, *God, Marriage, and Family: Rebuilding the Biblical Foundation*, 2nd ed. (Wheaton, IL: Crossway, 2010), 205–6.

[2] Letha Dawson Scanzoni and Virginia Ramey Mollenkott, *Is the Homosexual My Neighbor? A Positive Christian Response*, rev. ed. (New York, NY: HarperCollins, 1994), 64.

in religious contexts (cf. 2 Kgs 16:3; Isa 44:19; Jer 16:18; Ezek 7:20). Yet, as Andreas Köstenberger points out, the term is also found in nonreligious contexts (Gen 43:32; Ps 88:8; Prov 6:16–19; 28:9).[3] Thus, the term does not provide a limiting context (such as homosexual unions at Canaanite shrines of the fertility god Baal) for a text in which it is found. Moreover, Köstenberger states, the term is used elsewhere in the immediate context of Leviticus 18 and 20 to reference incest (Lev 18:6–18), adultery (Lev 18:20), bestiality (Lev 18:23), and a summary of all the sins discussed (Lev 18:26)—acts not limited to rites associated with the fertility god. Köstenberger adds the caution that, of course, a sin can be a sin in its own right even if practiced, on occasion, in a specific context—such as homosexual acts in temple prostitution or child sacrifice associated with the god Molech.

As noted in chapter 11, temple prostitution is addressed in the Old Testament, and particular language was available in Hebrew to reference it. It could, therefore, have been clearly mentioned here had the author wanted to limit the laws to that context. We shall also consider other prohibitions of certain homosexual acts in the ancient Near East. These laws do not oppose homosexuality in general; they refer to specific types of homosexual acts. If, then, these laws specified what was prohibited, why did Lev 18:22 and 20:13 not specify particular kinds of homosexual acts? The answer to this question seems clear: *any* type of homosexual act was being prohibited.

Another scholar attempting to apply contextual limitations to Leviticus 18:22 and 20:13 is Jacob Milgrom. First, Milgrom argues that lesbianism, a sexual practice where there is no spilling of seed, is not forbidden. He assumes the problem for males was that the spilling of seed was thought to be a wasting of life—a conjecture without any base. Moreover, not many would view the patriarchal society of Israel, with its understanding of sex being restricted to marriage, as allowing lesbianism but restricting males from homosexual acts. The forbidden unions in Leviticus 18 are described from a male's perspective, which was the way laws were written even though they also applied to women. The Ten Commandments, for example, apply to women just as they do to men—even though the verbs are all in the second person masculine singular.[4] Moreover, how much must our credulity be stretched to suppose that a patriarchal society would allow women to indulge in lesbian acts while men were restricted from homosexual acts?

Milgrom further argues that given the context of laws forbidding other types of unions in these chapters of Leviticus, only homosexual unions *of the*

---

[3] Andreas Köstenberger, with David Jones, *God, Marriage, and Family: Rebuilding the Biblical Foundation*, 205–6.

[4] For this example, we are grateful to a colleague, Catherine McDowell.

same sort as the forbidden heterosexual unions are in view.[5] So, for example, Milgrom avers that only male homosexual unions between persons *within the same family* would be forbidden. However, if, as is the case, later Jewish and early Christian texts appealed to Leviticus in forbidding homosexual unions, this should give an Old Testament commentator pause about his unique reading. Milgrom apparently feels no sense of obligation to deal with later interpretations—and none of them would support his suggestions. He steps out of the history of interpretation in order to venture his new theory, which turns out to support the peculiarities of Western culture at the beginning of the twenty-first century. What makes Milgrom's argument all the more improbable is the fact that a prohibition of bestiality follows the prohibition of homosexuality. Shall we, following his logic, argue that only bestiality with, say, a dog in the family is prohibited? Both male homosexual unions and bestiality are said to be "abominations" (Lev 18:22–23). Even Erhard Gerstenberger, who believes the Bible wrongly promotes persecution of homosexuals, states that Leviticus 18:22's condemnation of homosexuality (by declaring it an "abomination") goes beyond "the parameters of the clan"—that is, prohibitions of having sex with someone in the clan (i.e., incest).[6]

Dan O. Via contends that these Leviticus laws against homosexuality are about what makes one ceremonially "unclean."[7] This thesis was mentioned above by Scanzoni and Mollenkott. While it proves rather difficult to imagine that incest and child sacrifice, also mentioned in Leviticus 18, are condemned merely for violating Israelite purity laws, the "purity limitation" argument should be addressed further as it has, surprisingly, garnered support from various quarters. Via sees this violation of purity as having to do with occupying two different classes or roles at the same time. This clever interpretation would then understand Leviticus 18:22 and 20:13 to be about heterosexuals engaging in homosexual relations (occupying two different roles at the same time). Via further contends that the violation of a purity law is not the same as committing a sin.

But it is unreasonable to view the prohibitions against homosexuality in Leviticus as mere purity laws. Some acts that caused a person to be ceremonially unclean were also obvious sins, and often the consequences prescribed for forbidden actions indicate whether they are merely violations of ritual cleanliness or whether they are also sinful. While a wrongdoing such as pollution of the temple can be dealt with through a ritual, there is no ritual to

---

[5] Jacob Milgrom, *Leviticus: A Book of Ritual and Ethics,* A Continental Commentary (Minneapolis, MN: Augsburg Fortress, 2004), 196–97.

[6] Erhard Gerstenberger, *Leviticus: A Commentary*, trans. Douglas W. Stott (Louisville, KY: Westminster/John Knox, 1996), 254.

[7] Dan O. Via and Robert Gagnon, *Homosexuality and the Bible: Two Views* (Minneapolis, MN: Fortress, 2003), 6–7.

cleanse apostasy (Lev 20:1–5, 27; Deut 13:7–12; 17:2–7), sexual immorality (Leviticus 18), or murder (Deut 19:13; 21:8).[8] To collapse distinctions between purity laws, thus eliminating the notion of sin from the sexual laws of Leviticus 18, is Via's error. Indeed, are we really to believe the death penalty is meted out for a homosexual act merely because it is an impure and not a sinful act?[9] This is illogical when compared with how mere impurities were addressed: someone touching a corpse, having an emission, or touching something unclean that swarms needs only to bathe and will be unclean until evening (Lev 22:4-5; cf. Num 9; 19; and 31:19). Moreover, treating homosexual acts as a matter of impurity that is not also sin renders nonsensical Paul's linking of impurity with sexual sin in Romans 1:24: "Therefore God gave them up in the lusts of their hearts to *impurity* [*akatharsia*], to the degrading of their bodies among themselves."[10]

A final comment must be made about the laws against homosexual acts in Leviticus 18:22 and 20:13: these are acts of *consensual* sex, and still Leviticus 20:13 calls for the death penalty for both males involved in a homosexual act. Deuteronomy 22:22–29 discusses cases of both illicit sex and that of consent, showing that, in cases of forced heterosexual sex, the aggressor is punished but not the victim. Therefore, in Leviticus 20:13, where both persons are guilty and to be punished, the assumption is that this same-sex act is consensual.

Note these attempts to restrict the meaning of the text are recent in the history of interpretation. We live in a peculiar world where novel interpretations are applauded rather than questioned. Any alternative reading of a biblical text that affirms pro-homosexual, Western culture is celebrated. It is rushed to print like a soldier, not yet through basic training, to the front lines of battle, and, if it falls, it has nevertheless served its purpose for the day, holding the line just long enough for some fresh recruit to take its place.

---

[8] See the helpful overview of interpretations of purity in the Old Testament by Susan Hamer, *They Shall Purify Themselves: Essays on Purity in Early Judaism* (Atlanta, GA: Society of Biblical Literature, 2008). Also see Jay Sklar, *Sin, Impurity, Sacrifice, Atonement: The Priestly Conceptions* (Sheffield, England: Sheffield Phoenix, 2005). Sklar demonstrates that *kipper* in Hebrew references both atoning for sin and removing impurity. Both sin and impurity require ransoming and purification, and blood sacrifice accomplishes both. The relevance of this for our study is that the concepts of sin and impurity cannot be so easily separated as Dan Via hoped.

[9] We will examine holiness and purity in the Old Testament again in this book when 1 Corinthians is discussed.

[10] One simply cannot neatly distinguish impurity from sin. Whereas the Greek translation of Leviticus uses "*akatharsia*" (unclean/impure) to describe things such as a woman's monthly period or food that is considered unclean (Lev 18:19; 20:21), Paul can use the same term of sexual sin—homosexuality in particular (Rom 1:24–28). Even within Leviticus, there is a close relationship between what is holy and what is clean, what is profane and what is unclean: "You are to distinguish between the holy and the common [profane], and between the unclean and the clean" (Lev 10:10). The sacrifice of atonement is for uncleanness, transgression, and sin (Lev 16:16)—overlapping concepts rather than three separate things.

NO GENDER DEVIATION FROM ONE'S BIOLOGICAL MAKEUP

Third, there are texts forbidding gender deviation, that is, a woman acting as a man or a man acting as a woman. From a biblical perspective, gender is not something one feels about oneself but is what one is: one is male because one is a man; one is female because one is a woman. Thus,

> A woman shall not wear a man's apparel, nor shall a man put on a woman's garment; for whoever does such things is abhorrent to the LORD your God. (Deut 22:5)

Clearly, this passage is not talking about matters of style or a costume party. The verse is warning against crossing gender boundaries.

NO MALE OR FEMALE TEMPLE PROSTITUTION

Fourth, male and female temple prostitution is forbidden in the Old Testament. This will be discussed in more detail later, but here several passages summarize the general structure of the argument.

> None of the daughters of Israel shall be a temple prostitute; none of the sons of Israel shall be a temple prostitute. You shall not bring the fee of a prostitute or the wages of a male prostitute [in Hebrew, literally, "dog"] into the house of the LORD your God in payment for any vow, for both of these are abhorrent to the LORD your God. (Deut 23:17–18)

> There were also male temple prostitutes in the land. They committed all the abominations of the nations that the LORD drove out before the people of Israel. (1 Kgs 14:24)

In 1 Kings 14:24, not simply prostitution but "the abominations of the nations" are mentioned. The passage also refers specifically to idolatry (v. 23). This passage reminds one of a great "clearing" of two cities for the sins they committed: Sodom and Gomorrah. Sodom's wickedness was not one particular sin, but the extent of their sin was illustrated in the homosexual acts mentioned in Genesis 19 (more on Sodom later).

> Asa did what was right in the sight of the LORD, as his father David had done. He put away the male temple prostitutes out of the land, and removed all the idols that his ancestors had made. (1 Kgs 15:11–12)

> He broke down the houses of the male temple prostitutes that were in the house of the LORD, where the women did weaving for Asherah. (2 Kgs 23:7)

> They die in their youth, among male prostitutes of the shrines. (Job 36:14 NIV)

THE NARRATIVES OF HOMOSEXUAL SINFULNESS: SODOM (GENESIS 19) AND GIBEAH (JUDGES 19)

Fifth, two separate narratives depict cultures abhorrent to God that combined a variety of sins, among which was homosexual union. The first is the story of Sodom in Genesis 19, which will be discussed in the next chapter as so much has been said about it. The second is a similar story:

> While they were enjoying themselves, the men of the city, *a perverse lot*, surrounded the house, and started pounding on the door. They said to the old man, the master of the house, "*Bring out the man who came into your house, so that we may have intercourse with him.*" And the man, the master of the house, went out to them and said to them, "No, my brothers, *do not act so wickedly*. Since this man is my guest, do not do this vile thing. Here are my virgin daughter and his concubine; let me bring them out now. Ravish them and do whatever you want to them; but against this man do not do such a vile thing." (Judg 19:22–24)

These passages show that homosexual acts were condemned in Israel. They were, as Leviticus 18 and 20 clearly state, sin. Such acts even required the death penalty. Both Genesis 19 and Judges 19 identify the Canaanites (and Israelites succumbing to their example) with a customary practice of homosexual rape of strangers and see it as more heinous than heterosexual rape of family. (The biblical texts are not, of course, endorsing the latter.) Homosexual acts might be associated with other sins, such as violence, prostitution, and idolatry. Yet these associations, when present, did not negate the fact that homosexual acts were sinful in themselves—just as violence, prostitution, and idolatry were.

GENERAL REFERENCES TO SEXUAL SIN IN THE OLD TESTAMENT INCLUDE HOMOSEXUAL ACTS

Sixth, any general references to sexual sin in the Old Testament imply that specific sexual sins, such as homosexuality, are illicit. As an example, consider the following passage from Proverbs:

> [Wisdom] will save you from the way of evil, from those who speak perversely, who forsake the paths of uprightness to walk in the ways of darkness, who rejoice in doing evil and delight in the perverseness of evil; those whose paths are crooked, and who are devious in their ways. (Prov 2:12–15)

This passage speaks generally of evil, perversity, darkness, crooked paths, and devious ways. In the context we see that Wisdom's pupil is being warned to follow a wise path over against practicing sexual sins. Proverbs 2:16–19 identifies a particular sexual sin: adultery. This application of the general warning, of course, does not rule out other sexual sins.

This point is a response to some who have highlighted the small number of texts explicitly addressing homosexual behavior in the Old Testament (and New Testament). While counting texts in order to derive biblical ethics is ludicrous (where would we be if we did so with bestiality or pederasty, for instance?), the fact of the matter is that the number is not small in the case of homosexuality. Once one understands that there is a biblical sexual ethic—sex is for a man and a woman in marriage—then one grasps that all general statements forbidding sexual sin cover every act between two people other than that which is allowed.

EZEKIEL 16

The sixteenth chapter of Ezekiel includes a noteworthy passage meriting consideration. Ezekiel 16:50 refers to Sodom's sins and uses the term "abomination," found in the prohibitions of homosexual acts in Leviticus 18:22 and 20:13. In particular, consider Ezekiel 16:48–50:

> As I live, says the LORD GOD, your sister *Sodom* and her daughters have not done as you and your daughters have done. This was the guilt of your sister Sodom: she and her daughters had pride, excess of food, and prosperous ease, but did not aid the poor and needy. They were haughty, and did *abominable things (tō'ēbāh)* before me; therefore I removed them when I saw it.

In this text, Sodom is said to have been guilty of a variety of sins. Yet, as Andrew Marin notes, some interpreters cite this text in support of the view that Sodom's sin was not homosexual practice. He writes,

> None of the themes in Ezekiel 16 are even remotely close to resembling the committed monogamous same-sex relationships we know of today. Because of that, pro-gay theologians assert that the overarching theme to Genesis 19 is not homosexuality.[11]

John McNeill, for example, avers that "the sin of Sodom was never interpreted in Old Testament times as being primarily sexual, to say nothing of involving homosexual practices; rather, it is portrayed as a sin of pride and inhospitality."[12] This is simply untrue, not only because Genesis 19 itself needs to be read as, among other things, a story of sexual immorality, but also because Ezekiel 16 has many sins of Sodom in view and does not rule out homosexual acts. The matter turns on the meaning of the phrase "abominable

---

[11] Andrew Marin, *Love Is an Orientation: Elevating the Conversation with the Gay Community* (Downers Grove, IL: InterVarsity, 2009), 118.

[12] John McNeill, *The Church and the Homosexual* (Boston, MA: Beacon, 1993), 68.

things" in Ezekiel 16:50. (The term *tō'ēbāh* also appears in Ezek 18:12; 22:11; and 33:26.)

A number of points are worth noting about Ezekiel 16's use of *tō'ēbāh* and the relation between idolatry and sexual perversions, including homosexual acts. First, the Hebrew word *tō'ēbāh* (in Greek: *anomia* [or "lawlessness"] or *bdelygma* ["detestable thing"—at which someone turns up his or her nose]), is as general as the English "abominable thing." It is found thirty-one times in Ezekiel and is a general term for anything of which God disapproves. In Ezekiel 8:6, 13, and 15 it refers primarily to idolatry. In Ezekiel 16:50 it functions well to capture the various sins of Sodom and Israel, including but not limited to idolatry, that led God to purge them from the land. Second, note that nothing is said here about the sin of inhospitality. Third, Sodom's sin is not singular: the very point of Ezekiel 16 is to say that Sodom's sins were many and varied. Fourth, Ezekiel elsewhere uses *"tō'ēbāh"* to refer to sexual sin:

> If he has a son who is violent, a shedder of blood, who does any of these things (though his father does none of them), who eats upon the mountains, defiles his neighbor's wife, oppresses the poor and needy, commits robbery, does not restore the pledge, lifts up his eyes to the idols, commits *abomination* [*tō'ēbāh*], takes advance or accrued interest; shall he then live? He shall not. (Ezek 18:10–13)

> One commits *abomination* [*tō'ēbāh*] with his neighbor's wife; another lewdly defiles his daughter-in-law; another in you defiles his sister, his father's daughter. (Ezek 22:11)

> You rely on the sword, you commit *abominations* [*tō'ēbāh*], and each of you defiles his neighbor's wife; shall you then possess the land? (Ezek 33:26)

In Ezekiel 18:12, the term follows a reference to idolatry and likely has in view the sexual sins, including homosexual acts, committed at shrines with prostitutes of both genders. In Ezekiel 22:11, the term is used in reference to adultery. In Ezekiel 33:26, the term is distinguished from adultery and precedes a reference to adultery. Thus, it is not unreasonable to assume it is here also a reference to a sexual sin, although the term in this chapter likely includes a variety of Israel's sins, not only—but definitely including—her sexual practices. Fifth, the connection between idolatry and sexual perversions is that the latter were performed as a part of fertility cults, such as those Israel failed to eradicate in its midst. The logical connection between idolatry and homosexuality is that both entail paying unnatural attention to the wrong object, contrary to creation. Quite understandably, therefore, Ezekiel 16 mentions Sodom in its rebuke of Israel's idolatry. Finally, and sixth, both the reference to Sodom and the use of the phrase "abominable thing"—*tō'ēbāh*—in Ezekiel 16:50, directly relate Ezekiel 16 to the specific use of the term in reference to homosexual practice in Leviticus 18:22 and 20:13. This connection between Ezekiel 16's reference to Sodom and the Leviticus Holiness Code—through the word "abominable"—also demonstrates that things declared to be abominable are by no means limited to ceremonial uncleanness.[13]

Yet Marin attempts to narrow the referent of "abominable things" so that homosexuality is excluded. He says "monogamous same-sex relationships" are not in view. If he were able to support the idea that homosexual relationships were valued or at least tolerated in Israel at any point in its biblical history, he may have a point worth considering: some homosexual relationships might be acceptable and others sinful. But this is not at all the case, and the contrary is in fact true and obvious. As the passages cited demonstrate, homosexuality was one of the sins of Sodom, and differentiations between types of homosexuality were not in view because homosexual acts *per se* were viewed as an abomination. Primary sources illustrate further the weakness of Marin's overall approach to interpreting biblical texts: they must be interpreted in the context of other literature, not in isolation. What the primary texts demonstrate is that Sodom was not only associated with "sin" but in particular the sin of homosexuality (as well as pride and overindulgence).

CONCLUSION

The Old Testament is not a collection of unrelated laws against sexual sin. It articulates an overall understanding of the place for sex: in marriage between one male and one female. Understanding this situates discussion about specific sexual sins within a general understanding of sexual unions. It also helps one see that general references to sexual sin would include any sexual practice outside of marriage between a male and a female. Thus, one cannot say, for instance, that the Old Testament has only a few references to homosexual sin. Counting how many times a sin is mentioned in the Bible has nothing to do with whether it is sinful.

Indeed, several factors make the case against homosexuality strong in the Old Testament. First, every text addressing the issue portrays homosexual unions as sinful. Second, homosexual unions are forbidden through different genres of biblical writing: in both legal and narrative literature. Third, homosexual unions are inconsistent with the Old Testament view that the place for sex is within marriage between a male and a female—there is rationale for the opposition to this sin, and it is grounded in an understanding of God's

---

[13] We have discussed the relationship between impurity and sin already. The overlap of the concepts is clear when we place Ezek 16:50 alongside Lev 18:22 and 20:13. Moreover, what is abominable because it is *sin* needs to be cleansed because it is *impure*. That is why Genesis 19 tells of Sodom's destruction and why Lev 20:13 advocates the death penalty for both partners in a consensual homosexual act. Indeed, the abominable acts of Israel (Ezekiel 16) ultimately led to her exile.

purpose in creation. Fourth, as we shall see, interpretation of the relevant Old Testament texts on this issue in later Judaism and the early church consistently concluded that homosexual acts of any sort were sinful.

CHAPTER 10

SODOM'S SINS

We now turn to how to interpret the story of Sodom, found in Genesis 19 but referenced several times in both the Old and New Testaments.[1] In the Old Testament, Judaism, the New Testament, and the early church, the city of Sodom was viewed as receiving divine judgment for homosexual practices, a prideful spirit, and/or other sins. As Sodom became the extreme example of a sinful city, so homosexuality and pride came to be viewed as extreme examples of sin.

THE VARIETY OF SODOM'S SINS

Scripture's first characterization of Sodom states, "Now the people of Sodom were wicked, great sinners against the LORD" (Gen 13:3). We find a similar statement in Genesis 18:20. Thus, before we get to the story in Genesis 19, we are aware Sodom was a wildly wicked city; we can hardly expect it to be guilty merely of a single sin. Yet some try to reduce Sodom's sin to a single transgression, such as gang rape[2] or inhospitality.[3] Such suggestions beg credibility

---

[1] Readers should be aware of an entire book on this subject: J. A. Loader, *A Tale of Two Cities: Sodom and Gomorrah in the Old Testament, Early Jewish and Early Christian Traditions,* Contributions to Biblical Exegesis and Theology 1 (Kampen, Netherlands: Kok, 1990). Our arguments are our own.

[2] Walter Barnett, *Homosexuality and the Bible: An Interpretation* (Wallingford, PA: Pendle Hill, 1979).

[3] D. Sherwin Bailey, *Homosexuality and the Western Christian Tradition* (London, England: Longmans, Green and Co., 1955), 3–5. Others following this particular reductive and/or nonsexual reading of Genesis 19 include John Boswell, *Christianity, Social Tolerance, and Homosexuality: Gay People in Western Europe from the Beginning of the Christian Era to the Fourteenth Century* (Chicago, IL: University of Chicago Press, 2005), 92; John J. McNeill, who first included pride with inhospitality as Sodom's sins, *The Church and the Homosexual,* 4th ed. (Boston, MA: Beacon, 1993), 68, and then suggested the city's sins were inhospitality and idolatry (*Sex as God Intended* [Maple Shade, NJ: Lethe, 2008], 31–36); James B. Nelson,

in vain. If gang rape is the focus of the story, why does Lot offer his daughters to the mob? If inhospitality is the issue, why is Gomorrah also destroyed? If pairing with angels is the issue (though the men of the city were unaware their visitors were angelic), why is Sodom accused of being extremely sinful before the angels appear? Certainly other sins contributed to Sodom's sinfulness, but the sin of homosexual practice should not be ignored. Indeed, the men's homosexual behavior illustrated just how depraved Sodom was.

This leads to another point. Genesis often characterizes human sinfulness in sexual terms and identifies tribes with particular sexual unions. The narrative following the story of Sodom's destruction, that of Lot's incestuous relations with his daughters, connects their sons Moab and Ben-Ammi to the Moabites (meaning, "from the father") and the Ammonites (meaning "son of my people"), linking those groups with sexual sin (Gen 19:37–38). Also, the Ishmaelites' origin was associated with Abraham's ill-advised childbearing with his concubine, Hagar (Genesis 16). The wickedness of the people of Noah's generation, furthermore, was epitomized in the illicit sexual union between the "sons of God" and the "daughters of men" (Genesis 6). Noah's son, Ham, who some have suggested had a homosexual encounter[4] with his father, was the father of the Canaanites (Gen 10:19–20). The Egyptians, on the other hand, were absolved of sexual guilt when Pharaoh returned Sarai

---

Embodiment: An Approach to Sexuality and Christian Theology (Minneapolis, MN: Augsburg, 1978), 183.

[4] The story appears to be about incestuous homosexual rape. Robert Gagnon (*The Bible and Homosexual Practice: Texts and Hermeneutics* [Nashville, TN: Abingdon, 2001], 64ff.), following Donald J. Wold (*Out of Order: Homosexuality in the Bible and the Ancient Near East* [Grand Rapids, MI: Baker, 1998], 69–76) and Martti Nissinan (*Homoeroticism in the Biblical World* [Minneapolis: Fortress, 1998], 52–53), presents the case for this interpretation. Why was Noah uncovered? Why was his garment outside the tent? How did Noah discover what had been "done" to him by his son? To "uncover the nakedness of" is a euphemism for "have sex with" (Lev 18:6–19; 20:11, 17–21). Leviticus 20:17 refers to sibling incest in terms of "sees his/her nakedness." The Mediterranean context saw homosexual rape as a way of domineering over someone. This was a contextual attempt to overcome his father's authority and replace him. Noah's curse on Ham's son, Canaan, fits with why the Canaanites were replaced by Israel—due to their abominable practices of incest and same-sex intercourse (Lev 18:24–30; 20:22–26). Genesis 10:19 mentions that Canaanite territory included Sodom and Gomorrah. That Canaan is the focus of the story explains why Noah cursed Canaan, not Ham, who did the evil thing. Finally, just as Ham committed a terrible deed with his "seed," so too was his "seed" cursed (p. 67). A text in the Babylonian Talmud (late fifth or early sixth century AD), *Sanh.* 70a, says that Rab and Samuel disagreed over whether Gen 9:24 meant "castrate" or "have homosexual relations with" Noah. Three Greek translations use "shamefulness" (*tēn aschēmosunēn*) instead of "nakedness," suggesting a sexual act. "Shamefulness" is used in Lev 18:6–19; 20:11, 17–21 of incest, as well as by Paul in Rom 1:27. The story, then, is about homosexual intercourse, rape, incest, and dishonoring one's father (p. 69). The later indictment of the Canaanites suggests that sexual immorality was among the sins committed by Ham against Noah (69). The *sexual* act of which Ham was guilty was a homosexual act, even though Ham's sinful act included other horrific dimensions as well.

to Abram (Genesis 12). Similarly, Abimelech returned Sarah to Abraham under comparable circumstances, and the consequence was that the house of Abimelech was healed of infertility (Genesis 20). Esau, although forbidden by his father to marry Canaanite wives (Gen 28:6), married a woman from the Hittites and another from the Hivites (Gen 26:34; Gen 36:2–3)—groups considered "Canaanite"—as well as a woman descended from Ishmael (Gen 28:9). Through these marriages Esau gave rise to the Edomites (cf. Gen 36:1, 8, 43). The Shechemites were associated with rape (Genesis 34); thus, Genesis 19 is one of several passages connecting certain tribes with some sort of sexual sin. We cannot, on such a reading of Genesis, limit the story of Sodom to a nonsexual sin, such as inhospitality.

As Robert Gagnon notes, "Three elements (attempted penetration of males, attempted rape, inhospitality), and perhaps a fourth (unwitting, attempted sex with angels), combine to make this [story in Genesis 19] a particularly egregious example of human depravity that justifies God's act of total destruction."[5]

Later Old Testament references to Sodom also show that the city was remembered for a diversity of sins. William Loader states that early interpretation of the Sodom story of Genesis 19 had to do with violent inhospitality rather than sexuality (Isa 1:10; 3:9; Jer 23:14; Ezek 16:48–50). This claim is groundless, as anyone reading the cited passages can see: nothing is said about violent inhospitality.[6] Rather, Sodom was remembered as the quintessential example of open sinfulness, with a variety of sins attributed to it in the literature. Ezekiel in particular lists several of Sodom's sins, including "abominable things."

---

[5] Robert Gagnon, *The Bible and Homosexual Practice Texts and Hermeneutics*, 75.

[6] See William Loader, *The New Testament on Sexuality* (Grand Rapids, MI: Eerdmans, 2012), 30. Compare Isaiah 1:9–10: "If the LORD of hosts had not left us a few survivors, we would have been like Sodom, and become like Gomorrah. Hear the word of the LORD, you rulers of Sodom! Listen to the teaching of our God, you people of Gomorrah!" [The context suggests the comparison has to do with the people being "laden with iniquity," v. 4; destined for punishment and destruction, v. 7; characterized by open, hypocritical sinfulness, vv. 12–16; unjust toward the oppressed, orphan, and widow, v. 17; and given the chance to repent, vv. 19–20.] Isaiah 3:9: "The look on their faces bears witness against them; they proclaim their sin like Sodom, they do not hide it. Woe to them! For they have brought evil on themselves." Jeremiah 23:14: "But in the prophets of Jerusalem I have seen a more shocking thing: they commit adultery and walk in lies; they strengthen the hands of evildoers, so that no one turns from wickedness; all of them have become like Sodom to me, and its inhabitants like Gomorrah." Ezekiel 16:48–50: "As I live, says the Lord GOD, your sister Sodom and her daughters have not done as you and your daughters have done. This was the guilt of your sister Sodom: she and her daughters had pride, excess of food, and prosperous ease, but did not aid the poor and needy. They were haughty, and did abominable things before me; therefore I removed them when I saw it."

CANAAN AND HOMOSEXUAL PRACTICE

One sin of the Canaanite city of Sodom was homosexual practice. Indeed, Canaan appears to have been associated with homosexual practice far beyond Sodom's borders. Several passages show this association. First, and though some may find the theory shocking since the passage is often read to refer to parental dishonor only, Genesis 9 likely tells of some homosexually aberrant treatment of Noah by his son Ham, father of the Canaanites (v. 22). Judges 19 tells the story of the gang rape of a concubine in Gibeah, a city of the Benjaminites. The offenders first intended to have intercourse with the concubine's male partner (Judg 19:22). This led, much like Sodom's behavior did, to the destruction of both the town and the people involved in the sin, Gibeah and the tribe of Benjamin. The entire story illustrates Israel's slipping into the practices of Canaan. As Judges 3:4 states, the Canaanites and some other non-Israelite people remained in the land in order to test Israel, to see if they would obey the Lord's commandments. By ending the book of Judges with the horrendous story of Gibeah, the author concludes with the emphatic point that some (in this case, the Benjaminites) surrendered their obedience to God for the practices of the Canaanites. Moreover, the Holiness Code of Leviticus warns Israel not to engage in the abhorrent practices of the Canaanites and Egyptians (Lev 18:3)—including homosexual acts. Finally, the Canaanites practiced prostitution with both women and men under sacred trees, influencing Israel in her conduct as well (see the discussion of homosexual prostitutes in the following chapter).

THE INTENSITY OF SODOM'S SINS AND A NARRATIVE READING OF THE TEXT

In light of the fact that some recent interpreters have tried to locate the sin of Sodom entirely in its inhospitable reception of the strangers—the angels— who visited Lot, we should note several reasons such a narrow interpretation is impossible:

1. Genesis, as we have just noted, tells us that Sodom's citizens were "great sinners" *before* the incident with the strangers ever took place (Gen 13:3; 18:20). Their sins cannot be focused narrowly on a single act.
2. The visit of the strangers (angels) to Sodom was in order to see if there were even ten righteous persons in a city known for its *sinfulness in general* (Gen 18:32).
3. The issue of ancient Near Eastern *hospitality* is a feature of the story *as it pertains to Lot*: *because* he takes the strangers in as guests, he is willing to protect them even to the point of sacrificing his own daughters (Gen 19:8). Since Sodom's citizens have *not* received the strangers as

guests, they do not understand themselves to be under an obligation to treat them hospitably. They even view Lot, who has lived for some time among them, to be a stranger in their midst, and they plan to treat him the same way (Gen 19:9). The similar story in Judges 19 demonstrates the same logic: strangers can be violated as the practice of hospitality does not apply to them. *The law of hospitality applies to members of a people group and to those who have been received as guests, not to just anybody.*[7] Thus, while hospitality is a piece of the story, it is not the focus.

4. Even if one of the sins of Sodom against the strangers was inhospitality (as a few later texts interpreting the incident suggest), one would still have to say that *homosexual acts and gang rape* were sinful in themselves. That is, one must accept that these were sins in order to accept them as examples of inhospitality.

5. The fact that the Sodomites reprimand Lot for judging their customs (Gen 19:9) shows they in no way thought they were breaking a Near Eastern hospitality code. Rather, they were practicing the custom of homosexual rape of foreigners that would later resurface in the Benjaminite city of Gibeah (Judges 19), which had evidently adopted Canaanite practices.

6. The Pentateuch identifies several ethnic groups with sexual sins, so it is no surprise that the Sodomites are identified with sexual sin in this story meant to illustrate how sinful they had become. The Canaanites and Egyptians are identified with various sexual sins in Leviticus 18, and the story of Ham gazing on his father's nakedness (Gen 9:22–25) illustrates the homosexual and incestuous sin of the Canaanites who descended from him. Moabite women, who came from the incestuous relationship between Lot and his elder daughter (Gen 19:37), later enticed the Israelite men to sin sexually and engage in idolatry (Num 25:1–3).

7. *Later interpretations* of the story of Sodom show the narrative was read as a tale about the *intensity of the city's sinfulness*, not normally as a story about the sin of inhospitality.

8. *Later interpretations* of the account of Sodom show that homosexuality was among a variety of sins explicitly associated with the city, though some interpretations locate the root of its sinfulness in luxury or pride.

Attempts to interpret Genesis 19 as a story that does not illustrate homosexual sin fail. Even if there were a strong tradition in Judaism identifying

---

[7] This point applied in Jesus's day as well. Hospitality customarily was denied to people from a different group, which can be seen in the Samaritan woman's response to Jesus's request for a drink of water (John 4:9). Jesus's parable of the good Samaritan (Luke 10:30–36) is so powerful because it turns this thinking on its head. One should love one's neighbor, but, he argues, one's "neighbor" is to be defined not as a member of one's own group but as the one in need—even a stranger from a hated ethnic group.

Sodom's sin as inhospitality alone—which there is not—Christians would have to note that Jude 7 sees Sodom's sin as sexual and unnatural. Diverse interpretations of texts may arise from ambiguities in those texts or from a lack of training in the interpretation of ancient texts written in other languages in cultures not entirely understood. But this need not be the case here. Indeed, ancient references to the story of Sodom *never* attributed the city's sin to inhospitality alone (or to any other singular sin). While there is some basis for saying Sodom was inhospitable, this was not its primary sin.[8] Such an interpretation in our day comes from those wishing to defend their own agenda of affirming homosexuality. Those trying to argue their position *against* Scripture, not *from* it, need to dismiss the relevance of the story in Genesis 19 and the subsequent understanding of the text in Judaism and the New Testament.

We now consider the story more directly. In Genesis 19 we learn about the depths of Sodom's sinfulness: its citizens attempted to commit gang, homosexual rape of guests (who turned out to be angels) in someone else's home. The narrative of Sodom includes multiple emphases. It would be an error to read something into the narrative that is not there or to limit an interpretation to only one dimension of the story. The narrative of Sodom is intended to show just how sinful this city was, so the narrative allows the reader to be horrified by many sinful acts. Whatever else the story suggests of Sodom's sins, the sexual dimension is present:

> Before they lay down, the men of the city, the men of Sodom, both young and old, all the people to the last man, surrounded the house; and they called to Lot, "Where are the men who came to you tonight? Bring them out to us, so that we may know [i.e., have sex with] them." (Gen 19:4–5)

---

[8] One may read this argument in some detail in Michael Cardin, *Sodomy: A History of a Christian Biblical Myth* (London, England: Equinox, 2004), 86–103. He begins the section, "*The Men of Sodom Have No Portion in the World to Come,*" by saying, "The cities are constantly associated with oppression, injustice, greed and hostility towards strangers. These crimes are often augmented with the practice of idolatry and sexual sins, especially adultery, but these evils remain secondary to Sodom's greed and oppression of the poor and outsiders." In concluding this section, he says, "In other words, sexual misdeeds alone, such as the Sodomites threatened upon Lot's guests, do not constitute an evil warranting divine intervention in Sodom. It is Sodom's sanctioned use of violence including sexual violence in order to maintain a cruel, oppressive and selfish social system that incurs divine wrath" (103). Cardin's discussion involves several targumim (Aramaic paraphrases of the Old Testament) and rabbinic texts, but the important point to note is that he tries to sweep Sodom's sexual sins under the rug not by denying that they are in the texts but by demoting them to a secondary significance. His attempt to link a story about Lot's wife being inhospitable—a narrative not in the biblical text or key Jewish texts—to the men of Sodom being inhospitable simply does not convince us. Yet the issue is decided not by the texts Cardin considers but by those noted here, as well as the fact that sexual sin is, as he admits, a part of the matter. We would simply say it is the primary matter, particularly for those taking the biblical texts as authoritative.

The way the story is told in Genesis 18–19 highlights similarities and differences between Abraham and Lot. Abraham's rural, nomadic setting contrasts with Lot's urban, settled situation. The behavior of both men dignifies the strangers as honored guests in their homes. Abraham runs (an undignified thing to do!) out from his tent to meet them, bows before them, and arranges for their feet to be washed and for them to rest from the heat of the midday sun. He offers them the best of his food, refers to himself as their "servant," and stands by while they eat rather than eating with them as an equal or even a host. The "gift" the guests offer childless Abraham and his wife, Sarah, is the promise of a son—yet another reaffirmation of God's covenant with Abraham (Gen 12:1–3; 15:3–4; 17:4–8). Abraham also travels with the men to set them on their way. He pleads with them not to destroy Sodom and Gomorrah, further demonstrating his righteous character: Abraham is merciful. Thus, in Genesis 18, Abraham is doing much more than showing hospitality to strangers. Speaking to one of the visitors, Abraham asks if he will destroy the righteous in Sodom along with all the others (v. 23). By this time he is aware that he is entertaining either the Lord in the flesh or an angel of God.

Like Abraham, Lot invites the now two messengers from God to his house, entreating them not to spend the night in the city square. The mob gathering at Lot's house nevertheless insists that Lot bring the men out to them, and Lot replies, "Do nothing to these men, for they have come under the shelter of my roof" (Gen 19:8). The response of the mob clarifies that they do not see themselves as breaking the custom of hospitality: they have neither received the strangers nor Lot as guests but consider them to be aliens outside their laws (v. 9). This point takes the story of Lot beyond being a story about hospitality.

Indeed, the account illustrates the intensity of Sodom's sins, for its residents go well beyond inhospitality. That grievance worsens into a desire to mistreat the strangers. Over against righteous Abraham's quick recognition that the visitors were righteous men, the males of Sodom only see them as sex objects. They not only want to mistreat the strangers, but they also want to have sexual relations with them. They not only want to have sex; but, as is illustrated by their passing up the offer of women instead, their desire is specifically for homosexual sex. Genesis 19:5 focuses the sin of Sodom on sexuality: "to know" is an Old Testament euphemism for "to have sexual relations with."[9] The narrative as a whole, however, presents the Sodomites as committing a multitude of reprehensible practices.

---

[9] Some writers on this subject mishandle primary texts. Not understanding the Hebrew, D. Sherwin Bailey suggested that "to know" here means "to get acquainted with" (*Homosexuality and the Western Christian Tradition*, 3–5). For the use of "to know" in terms of "to have sex with," see Gen 4:1, 17, 25; 1 Kgs 1:4; Judg 11:39; 19:25 (a parallel story to Genesis 19); 21:12; 1 Sam 1:9. This language for sexual relations is also found in Matt 1:25.

The entire story in Genesis 18–19 involves three themes: righteousness/sin, sex, and the survival/destruction of a people. The righteousness of Abraham is coupled with the promise that he and Sarah will miraculously produce a son, Isaac. This heir becomes the father of the Israelites. The unrighteousness of Lot's wife results in her death, and so Lot is left with only his daughters and no wife with whom to produce sons and heirs. Thus, his daughters get him inebriated and mate with him. The offspring of these incestuous relationships produce two nations, the Moabites and the Ammonites. Between these two stories lies the account of the Sodomites, whose repugnant custom of committing homosexual acts (indeed, *every* male of the city comes out to have forced intercourse with the strangers, Gen 19:4) is described. Their practice resulted in the destruction of their city by God, even as homosexual practice leads to the destruction of a people because no children can be produced.

SUBSEQUENT INTERPRETATION OF SODOM'S SIN

Jewish texts from the first century AD and earlier continued to speak of the sinful city of Sodom, as did Jesus. Christ's references to Sodom focus not on the city's sinful practices but on its failure to receive God's warning through heavenly visitors (Matt 10:15; 11:23–24; Luke 10:12; 17:29).[10] Sodom's sinfulness is not reduced to a single transgression.

At times authors may focus on a single sin, but this does not mean they fail to recognize that Sodom practiced various sins. For example, *3 Maccabees* and Sirach identify Sodom's sin as arrogance:

> You consumed with fire and sulfur the people of Sodom who acted arrogantly, who were notorious for their vices; and you made them an example to those who should come afterward. (*3 Macc* 2:5)[11]

> He did not spare the neighbors of Lot, whom he loathed on account of their arrogance. (Sir 16:8)

A number of Jewish texts focus on the homosexual nature of the sin in Genesis 19. Two texts from the *Testament of the Twelve Patriarchs* from the second century BC should be noted. The *Testament of Naphtali* refers to homosexual practice as changing "the order of its nature":

---

[10] Paul, quoting Isa 1:9, also references Sodom and Gomorrah but only in terms of their being destroyed: "And as Isaiah predicted, 'If the Lord of hosts had not left survivors to us, we would have fared like Sodom and been made like Gomorrah'" (Rom 9:29).

[11] This reference to Sodom follows a reference to the evil generation of Noah's day. The examples of sin in Noah's day and in Sodom also occur in Jude and 2 Peter 2. Third Maccabees is difficult to date, but speculations tend to locate it in the first century AD.

> But you will not be so, my children: you have recognized in the vault of heaven, in the earth, and in the sea, and in all created things, the Lord who made them all, so that you should not become like *Sodom which changed the order of its nature*. (*T. Naph.* 3:4)[12]

Note the relationship between not knowing God as Creator and changing the order of nature (homosexuality). This is Paul's argument in Rom 1:18–28.

The *Testament of Levi* also points to the sexual sin of Sodom and Gomorrah, and it appears to speak of homosexual acts as well:

> You take gentile women for your wives and your sexual relations will become like Sodom and Gommorah. (*T. Levi* 14:6)[13]

Another Jewish text written before AD 70 (*Jubilees*) focuses on Sodom's sexual sin and exceeding wickedness (cf. Wis 13:18; 20:5):

> And in this month the Lord executed his judgments on Sodom, and Gomorrah, and Zeboim, and all the region of the Jordan, and He burned them with fire and brimstone, and destroyed them until this day, even as [lo] I have declared unto thee all their works, that they are wicked and sinners exceedingly, and that they *defile themselves and commit fornication in their flesh, and work uncleanness on the earth*. And, in like manner, God will execute judgment on the places where they have done according to *the uncleanness of the Sodomites*, like unto the judgment of Sodom. (Jub. 16:5–6)[14]

Later the text speaks of Sodom's "fornication and impurity" and "corruption of sin" (20:5–6). Homosexual acts, such as pederasty, are wrong, according to 2 Enoch, because the acts are sins against nature. In present times such acts might firstly be condemned for their involvement of a child, whether or not the child consents. Our focus in the moral discussion might be on freedom of choice in sexual acts, and our assumption is that a child is not at the age of consent. Whatever we make of the strength of moral arguments that highlight freedom, 2 Enoch places the focus elsewhere—on "nature." Indeed, to practice a sin against nature with a child will possibly lead to a corruption of the child so that when he (or she) is able to make moral choices, his (or her) choices will

---

[12] Translated by M. DeJonge, *The Apocryphal Old Testament*, ed. H. Sparks (New York, NY: Clarendon, 1984), 569. The date of the testaments is uncertain, and, though Jewish, there are Christian interpolations. In the case of the Testament of Naphtali, a Qumran text, 4Q215, supports its existence prior to AD 70. Another text in the *Testament of the Twelve Patriarchs*, the Testament of Levi 17.11, mentions those who corrupt boys (*paidophthoroi*).

[13] "Testament of Levi," trans. Howard C. Kee in *The Old Testament Pseudepigrapha*, vol. 1: *Apocalyptic Literature and Testaments*, ed. James H. Charlesworth (Peabody, MA: Hendrickson, 1983), 793.

[14] R. H. Charles, *The Apocrypha and Pseudepigrapha of the Old Testament* (New York, NY: Clarendon, 1913).

be against nature as well. The focus is not on the child's lack of freedom or consent but on the corruption of the child's nature:

> "Woe, woe, how very terrible is this place," and those men said to me: This place, O Enoch, is prepared for those who dishonour God, *who on earth practice sin against nature*, which is *child-corruption after the sodomitic fashion*, magic-making, enchantments and devilish witch-crafts, and who boast of their wicked deeds, lies, calumnies, envy, rancour, fornication, murder. (*2 En.* 10:4)[15]

The first-century Alexandrian, Jewish philosopher, Philo, had much to say about Sodom's sin against nature, although he attributed other sins to the city as well:

> [Regarding Sodom] And the cause of its excessive and immoderate intemperance was the unlimited abundance of supplies of all kinds which its inhabitants enjoyed. . . . And he was a wise man and spoke truly who said—"The greatest cause of all iniquity is found in overmuch prosperity." As men, being unable to bear discreetly a satiety of these things, get restive like cattle, and become stiff-necked, and *discard the laws of nature*, pursuing a great and intemperate indulgence of gluttony, and drinking, and *unlawful connections*; for not only did they go mad after women, and defile the marriage bed of others, but also those who were *men lusted after one another, doing unseemly things, and not regarding or respecting their common nature*, and though eager for children, they were convicted by having only an abortive offspring; but the conviction produced no advantage, since they were overcome by violent desire; and so, *by degrees, the men became accustomed to be treated like women, and in this way engendered among themselves the disease of females, an intolerable evil; for they not only, as to effeminacy and delicacy, became like women in their persons, but they made also their souls most ignoble, corrupting in this way the whole race of man, as far as depended on them.* At all events, if the Greeks and barbarians were to have agreed together, and to have adopted the commerce of the citizens of this city, their cities one after another would have become desolate, as if they had been emptied by a pestilence. (*Abraham* 1:134–36)[16]

> But God, having taken pity on mankind, as being a Savior and full of love for mankind, increased, as far as possible, the natural desire of men and women for a connection together, for the sake of producing children, and *detesting the unnatural and unlawful commerce of the people of Sodom*, he

---

[15] "2 Enoch, or the Book of the Secrets of Enoch," trans. Nevill Forbes and R. H. Charles, in *Apocrypha and Pseudepigrapha of the Old Testament*, vol. 2, ed. R. H. Charles (New York, NY: Clarendon, 1913).

[16] All translations of Philo are taken from *The Works of Philo Judaeus, the Contemporary of Josephus*, trans. C. D. Yonge, 4 vols. (London, England: Henry G. Bohn, 1854–55).

extinguished it, and destroyed those who were inclined to these things, and that not by any ordinary chastisement, but he inflicted on them an astonishing novelty, and unheard of rarity of vengeance. (*Abraham* 1:137 XXVII)

Nor did the inhabitants of Sodom, blind in their minds, who were insanely eager to defile the holy and unpolluted reasonings, "find the road which led to this" [Genesis 29.11] object; but, as the sacred scriptures tell us, they were wearied with their exertions to find the door, although they ran in a circle all round the house, and left no stone unturned for the accomplishment of their *unnatural and impious desires* [*tēs ekphylou kai asebous epithymias*]. (*Flight* 1:144)

Moreover, Philo speaks of pleasure "contrary to nature" when commenting on Leviticus 20:13, and he applies this text to the practices of pederasty and effeminacy—speaking of "male-female" men (*androgynoi*)—and states that both active and passive partners in homosexual acts deserve death (*Special Laws* 1:325; 2:50; 3:37–42).[17] This is the punishment stated in Leviticus 20:13.

Philo also says Lot was spared judgment because he declined to be involved with the Sodomites in a life of luxury and effeminacy:

[Lot] was spared only because he did not join the multitude who were inclined to luxury and *effeminacy* [*habrodiaitos*], and who pursued every kind of pleasure and indulged every kind of appetite, gratifying them abundantly, and inflaming them as one might inflame fire by heaping upon it plenty of rough fuel. (*Moses* 2.58)[18]

The first-century Jewish historian Josephus also commented on Sodom's various sins: pride, injustice toward men, impiety toward God, and hatred of strangers. In the following quotation Whiston's translation, "abused themselves with sodomy" (1.194), might be rendered something like, "turned to their own advantage associations with other men." Just what this means is clarified because Josephus mentions the "lust" of the Sodomites for the strangers: homosexual desire and intercourse for the Sodomites' own gratification. Josephus read the account of Sodom as a story about the sinfulness of homosexual acts and not about a lust for angels. He likely did not mean to limit Sodom's homosexual sin to rape or self-gratification without the other's consent since he elsewhere stated outright that for Jews, men lying with other men was a capital offense (*Against Apion* 2:199, 215).

About this time the Sodomites grew proud, on account of their riches and great wealth: they became unjust toward men, and impious toward God,

---

[17] Philo also opposed the arguments for same-sex intercourse put forth in Plato's *Symposium* (Philo, *On the Contemplative Life*, 59–62).

[18] Note that "*habrodiaitos*" would be a synonym for *malakos*, Paul's term for "soft men" in 1 Cor 6:9.

insomuch that they did not call to mind the advantages they received from him: they hated strangers, and *abused themselves with sodomy [or: "and turned to their own advantage associations with other men"]*. . . . Now, when the Sodomites saw the young men to be of beautiful countenances, and this to an extraordinary degree, and that they took up their lodgings with Lot, they *resolved themselves to enjoy these beautiful boys* by force and violence; and when Lot exhorted them to sobriety, and not to offer anything immodest to the strangers, but to have regard to their lodging in his house; and promised, that if their inclinations could not be governed, he would expose his daughters to their lust instead of these strangers—neither thus were they made ashamed. (*Antiquities* 1.194, 200–201)[19]

An Aramaic paraphrase of Genesis, perhaps from the second century AD, expanded the text by listing several sins of Sodom, including sexual sins:

And the men of Sodom were depraved in their wealth one with another, and they *sinned in their bodies*; they sinned with *open nakedness*, and the shedding of innocent blood, and practised strange worship, and rebelled greatly against the name of the Lord. (*Tg. Onq.* Gen. 13:13)[20]

Such texts from Judaism not only help us understand how Genesis 19 was interpreted but also give us a context for reading New Testament references to the sins of Sodom.

THE NEW TESTAMENT AND REFERENCES TO SODOM

The New Testament interprets the story of Sodom in various ways for a variety of purposes. Jesus refers to Sodom in statements about God's judgment (Matt 10:15; 11:23–24; Luke 10:12; 17:29–33). For example:

On that day, anyone on the housetop who has belongings in the house must not come down to take them away; and likewise anyone in the field must not turn back. Remember Lot's wife. Those who try to make their life secure will lose it, but those who lose their life will keep it. (Luke 17:31–33)

There is no mention of homosexuality here.[21] Paul, too, refers to the story with reference to God's judgment (Rom 9:29, quoting Isa 1:9). Yet such a use of

---

[19] All translations of Josephus's works are taken from the translation by William J. Whiston (1828) in the public domain, available on *BibleWorks*.

[20] *Targum Onqelos, Genesis*, trans. J. W. Etheridge (1862). See http//www.targum.info/pj/psjon.htm.

[21] James De Young believes that since the sin of homosexuality is generally associated with Sodom, it should be associated with it here. But my point is that Sodom could be used to symbolize a variety of sins, or the intensity of sin, and need not always refer to homosexuality. Even so, homosexuality is a significant manifestation of Sodom's sin, beginning in Genesis 19 and continuing in subsequent references. Luke 17:31–33, though, is not one of them. Cf. James B.

Genesis 19 by Jesus does not mean he regarded Sodom's homosexual behavior as morally acceptable. Indeed, Christ's understanding of sexual practice is based on Genesis 2:24 in particular: the place for sex is between a married man and woman (Mark 10:6–9; Matt 19:4–6). Anything else is sin.

Two references to Sodom in the New Testament do have its sexual sins in view. Jude specifically has homosexual sin—unnatural lust—in view:

> Likewise, Sodom and Gomorrah and the surrounding cities, which, in the same manner as they, indulged in *sexual immorality* [*ekporneusasai*] and *pursued unnatural lust* [*apelthousai opisō sarkos heteras*; literally, "going after a different flesh"], serve as an example by undergoing a punishment of eternal fire. (Jude 7)

Jude 6, the previous verse, mentions the sin of the angels, likely a reference to the story in Genesis 6:1–7 of the "sons of God" leaving their position and having sex with the "daughters of men." Thus, Jude 7 seems to have in view a comparison between the unnatural lust of Genesis 6 and the unnatural lust of Sodom and Gomorrah in Genesis 19. For Jude, the sin in view in verse 7 is sexual and unnatural.

Second Peter 2 and Jude are related literarily, and it appears the former is an edited version of Jude. Peter, too, understands Sodom's sin as sexual ("licentious"):

> If he [God] rescued Lot, a righteous man greatly distressed by the *licentiousness of the lawless* (for that righteous man, living among them day after day, was tormented in his righteous soul by their lawless deeds that he saw and heard). (2 Pet 2:7–8)

Thus, those who have tried to argue that Genesis 19 has nothing to do with sexual sin but is merely about inhospitality must reckon with Jude and 2 Peter saying that the sin of Sodom was sexual. Whatever other sexual sins one might wish to attribute to Sodom, foremost among them must be same-sex acts. Also, that Jude and 2 Peter interpret Sodom's sin as sexual means *Scripture* claims Sodom's sin must be understood this way—even if other aspects of it could be discussed as well. For believers who accept canonical authority, Jude and 2 Peter are not just historical witnesses to how a text was read; they are also authoritative texts clarifying how to read Genesis 19.

More should be said about Jude 7 as commentaries differ over its interpretation. In light of the various Jewish interpretations of the sins of Sodom we have surveyed, we need to challenge Richard Bauckham's interpretation in a number of ways. He says:

> In Jewish tradition the sin of Sodom was rarely specified as homosexual practice (though Philo, *Abr.* 135–136 is a notable account of Sodomitic

homosexuality, and cf. *Mos.* 2.58). The incident with the angels is usually
treated as a violation of hospitality, and the Sodomites are condemned especially for their hatred of strangers (Wis 19:14–15; Josephus, *Ant.* 1.194;
Pirqe R. El. 25), their pride and selfish affluence (Ezek 16.49–50; *3 Macc*
2:5; Josephus *Ant.* 1.194; Philo, *Abr.* 134; *Tg. Ps.-J.* Gen 13:13; 18:20), or
their sexual immorality in general (*Jub.* 16:5–6; 20:5; *T. Levi* 14:6; *T. Benj.*
9:1). So it is not very likely that Jude means to accuse the false teachers of
homosexual practice (Kelly), and we can hardly speculate that they desired
sexual relations with angels—even in their "dreams" (v 8). . . . In rejecting the
commandments of God, the false teachers were rebelling against the divinely
established order of things as flagrantly as the Watchers [the angels who had
sex with women, Gen 6.1–7] and the Sodomites had done. Moreover, they
were motivated, like the Watchers and the Sodomites, by sexual lust, and, like
the Sodomites, insulted angels.[22]

First, as we have seen, Genesis 19 was not typically interpreted as only a
violation of hospitality. Second, Bauckham misses some of the evidence that
we have presented which shows that a sexual interpretation is more common
than he is aware. Third, some texts he references need to be more carefully
read. As we have seen, Josephus, *Antiquities* 1:194 is not presented fully here.
There are clear references to sexual sin, including males turning their associations with other men to their own (sexual) advantage, amid other sins. Ezekiel
16:50 has in view not only the haughtiness that Bauckham rightly notes but
also other "abominable things," which we take to include homosexual sin.
Wisdom 19 is a peculiar chapter. While it does refer to receiving strangers with
hostility (v. 15), verse 18 speaks of a disorder in nature in various ways. Also,
we have suggested that *T. Levi* 14:6 actually refers to homosexual acts. Fourth,
more texts than those cited need to be considered. Philo has more than one
reference to Sodom's sins and homosexual practices as sinful, and Bauckham
does not mention all the Jewish texts that speak of Sodom's sin as including
homosexuality (e.g., *T. Naph.* 3:4, though he notes it in the next paragraph, and
2 En. 10:4). Targum Onkelos is also significant. Thus, Bauckham's handling of
the primary texts is uncharacteristically inadequate here.

Bauckham takes the phrase "indulged in sexual immorality and pursued
other flesh" in Jude 7 as a hendiadys (two words or phrases expressing a single
thought). For him that single thought is that the sexual immorality of Sodom
and Gomorrah was the pursuit of sex with angels, as in the case with the watchers in Genesis 6:1–7. Peter H. Davids takes "departing after flesh of a different
type" (his translation) as a reference to humans pursuing sex with angels, but
he does not consider all the evidence from Jewish interpretations. However, he

---

[22] Richard Bauckham, *Jude, 2 Peter*, Word Biblical Commentary 50 (Waco, TX: Word, 1983),
54. In this quotation Bauckham refers to J. N. D. Kelly, *A Commentary on the Epistles of Peter
and Jude* (London: A. & C. Black, 1969).

does note Philo (*Abraham* 135–36), which supports his reading.[23] One should note, on the other hand, that 2 Peter 2's use of Jude omits the ambiguous language such that there is no longer a possibility of interpreting the sexual sin in Sodom as a desire to pair with angels. Moreover, the problem Jude addresses is a false teaching about the grace of God such that licentiousness is allowed or even advocated (Jude 4). This is similar to the false teaching mentioned in 2 Peter 2, as well as that of the Nicolaitans (Rev 2:6; 14–15) and followers of Jezebel (Rev 2:20–21) in Revelation. Relating the story of Sodom to homosexuality, therefore, fits the context better than relating it to intercourse with angels.

Robert Gundry offers a second interpretation. He, like Bauckham, takes the phrase as a hendiadys, but the single thought for him is that the sexual immorality in question was the pursuit of homosexual unions. He says:

> The men of Sodom, Gomorrah, and surrounding cities engaged in sexual intercourse with "another kind of flesh," that is, flesh other than that of the females God created for them to copulate with. Jude has correctly deduced from the Sodomites demanding Lot deliver to them his guests, who they thought were human males, that the Sodomites and their neighbors practiced homosexuality (and bestiality?).[24]

A third view is that the phrase conveys two ideas and is not a hendiadys. Robert Gagnon says that "indulged in sexual immorality" led to the further sin of desiring to have sex with beings of another "flesh." Thus, he also takes the language to refer to sex with angels. However, this was not something of which the Sodomites were aware, and so the focus of their sin is on sexual indulgence with the "strangers"—and therefore on homosexual indulgence (among other sins).[25] (Note, however, that Jude says nothing of violent, nonconsensual sex.) Jude 7's "indulged in sexual immorality" has the specific sin of homosexual acts in view while using more general language so that it could be applied to various sexual sins in Jude's context.

Gagnon's view is attractive, but Gundry's view is equally viable. Jude 7's "other flesh" may be a way of using general language to describe both the sin of the angels of Genesis 6:1–7 and the sin of the Sodomites in pursuing intercourse with persons different from those God intended—not with women but men. As Douglas Moo notes, the word "flesh" is an unlikely word to be applied

---

[23] Peter H. Davids, *A Theology of James, Peter, and Jude: Biblical Theology of the New Testament* (Grand Rapids, MI: Zondervan, 2014), 272.

[24] Robert H. Gundry, *Commentary on First and Second Peter, Jude* (Grand Rapids, MI: Baker Academic, 2010).

[25] Robert Gagnon, *The Bible and Homosexual Practice*, 87.

to angelic beings.[26] Bauckham's view seems too narrowly focused on relations between humans and angels when Jude wants to apply the example of sexual immorality to his own context and therefore more broadly. Similarly, when a text such as 2 Peter 2:6–7 interprets Jude 7 as a reference to lawless deeds and licentiousness, and when it does so as a warning about contemporary teaching, then the specific sin of sex with angels—if it ever was in view—fades into the background. The Greek and Roman culture engaged in homosexual practice, not sex with angels. Sodom was relevant for Jude and 2 Peter because there was a false teaching about sexuality seeping into the church from the culture via the teachers. As Romans 1:26–27 demonstrates, Jews saw the Gentile culture as particularly wayward in its practice of homosexual acts. While many sexual perversions may be in view, they would certainly include such acts in the culture when a passage such as Genesis 19 is cited to illustrate how God deals with sexual immorality.

EARLY CHURCH REFERENCES TO SODOM

Since it has already been demonstrated that the early church understood homosexuality as sinful, we might briefly note in this chapter that it identified Sodom's sin in various ways, including as homosexual acts.

First Clement (written at the end of the first century AD), notes a variety of sins in Sodom in the context of mentioning Lot's hospitality and godliness:

> On account of his hospitality and godliness, Lot was saved out of Sodom when all the country round was punished by means of fire and brimstone, the Lord thus making it manifest that He does not forsake those that hope in Him, but gives up such as depart from Him to punishment and torture. For Lot's wife, who went forth with him, being of a different mind from himself and not continuing in agreement with him *as to the command which had been given them*, was made an example of, so as to be a pillar of salt unto this day. This was done that all might know that those who are of a double mind, and who distrust the power of God, bring down judgment on themselves, and become a sign to all succeeding generations. (11:1–2)[27]

This quotation rather nicely illustrates the point that the narrative genre allows interpreters to focus on different aspects of the story. Both the themes of hospitality and godliness are mentioned, and Lot's wife becomes an illustration of double-mindedness. About a century later a different Clement (Clement

---

[26] Douglas Moo, *2 Peter and Jude*, NIV Application Commentary (Grand Rapids, MI: Zondervan, 1996), 242.

[27] *The First Epistle of Clement to the Corinthians*, trans. by Alexander Roberts and James Donaldson in vol. 1: *The Apostolic Fathers with Justin Martyr and Irenaeus* (Christian Literature Publishing Company, 1885; repr., Peabody, MA: Hendrickson, 1994).

of Alexandria) listed various sins of Sodom, including sexual acts specified as uncleanness, adultery, paedophilia, and licentiousness:

> The Sodomites having, through much luxury, fallen into uncleanness, practising adultery shamelessly, and *burning with insane love for boys*; the All-seeing Word, whose notice those who commit impieties cannot escape, cast His eye on them. Nor did the sleepless guard of humanity observe their *licentiousness* in silence; but dissuading us from the imitation of them, and training us up to His own temperance, and falling on some sinners, lest *lust* being unavenged, should break loose from all the restraints of fear, ordered Sodom to be burned, pouring forth a little of the sagacious fire on *licentiousness*; lest lust, through want of punishment, should throw wide the gates to those that were rushing into *voluptuousness*. (*The Instructor*, III.8)[28]

Two other texts from the early church speak of Sodom's sin as "unnatural," that is, homosexual. The second quotation distinguishes laws against nature from violations of the Mosaic code. As sins against nature, homosexual acts and bestiality are acts of impiety toward the Creator himself.

> The inhabitants of Sodom, gathering their vintage from these vines, were provoked to an *unnatural and fruitless passion of men*.[29]

> But we do not say so of that mixture that is *contrary to nature*, or of any unlawful practice; for such are enmity to God. For *the sin of Sodom is contrary to nature*, as is also that with brute beasts. But adultery and fornication are against the law; the one whereof is impiety and the other injustice and in a word, no other than a great sin. But neither sort of them is without its punishment in its own proper nature.[30]

CONCLUSION

The focus on hospitality in the Genesis account of Sodom's destruction is almost completely lacking in later reflections on what Sodom's sin was really all about.[31] Instead, pride, with its related sin of overindulgence, and homosexuality are seen as the primary sins of this most sinful city. Homosexual rape, mob violence, casual sex, sex outside marriage on any definition of that

---

[28] *The Instructor,* III. 8, trans. William Wilson, in *Ante-Nicene Fathers*, vol. 2, ed. Alexander Roberts, James Donaldson, and A. Cleveland Coxe (Buffalo, NY: Christian Literature Publishing Co., 1885), revised and edited for New Advent by Kevin Knight, accessed July 30, 2009, http://www.newadvent.org/fathers/0209.htm.

[29] *St. Methodius: A Treatise on Chastity*, *Ancient Christian Writers*, vol. 27, trans. Herbert Musurillo (New York, NY: Paulist, 1958).

[30] *Constitution of the Holy Apostles*, VI.XXVIII (*ANF* 7:462), trans. W. Whiston, in *Ante-Nicene Fathers*, vol. 7: *Constitutions of the Holy Apostles* (Peabody, MA: Hendrickson, 1994), 462.

[31] Incidentally, Jesus's references to Sodom are not about hospitality.

phrase, and so forth are not in view even though they occurred. Rather, as several texts demonstrate, sex between persons of the same gender is what later readers saw to be the primary problem with the behavior in Sodom. This should not surprise anyone, since that is indeed one of the points of the original story in Genesis 19.

Sodom's story may be used to illustrate several principles, but there are some things that it is not about. It is not about homosexuality associated with male prostitutes in temple worship—the problem was not one of idolatry or pagan worship. The problem in Sodom was not nonconsensual sex, whether heterosexual or homosexual. The problem was not sex outside marriage or in groups or sex involving men and boys.

The problem in Sodom was that its citizens were *so sinful they turned to unnatural sexual practices*. This is not to say that this particular sin cannot also be related to other sins. Indeed, Genesis 13:3 and 18:20 make the point that Sodom's citizens were great sinners, and this no doubt means they were sinful in a variety of ways and in the extreme. Homosexuality was just one of their sins, but it was the sin that illustrated the extreme degree of their sinfulness, for in their sinning they even turned against nature itself.

Robin Scroggs, whose *The New Testament and Homosexuality* has significantly influenced the arguments of many since the 1980s even though it has been discounted at a number of essential points, famously stated that "Sodom is mentioned a few times [in the New Testament], but never in connection with homosexuality."[32] As we have seen, he was, quite simply, wrong (cf. Jude 7 and 2 Pet 2:7). Yet one still finds people proclaiming his theory as fact these decades later.[33]

This is, frankly, one of the major problems with the entire debate: people latch onto the arguments they wish to tout without concern for their merit and without actually checking the primary sources. One author just quotes some previous author who is favorable to his or her case, leaving unsuspecting readers to assume the argument is well established because of the footnote references

---

[32] Robin Scroggs, *The New Testament and Homosexuality* (Minneapolis, MN: Fortress, 1983), 100. Also David K. Switzer, *Coming Out as Parents: You and Your Homosexual Child* (Louisville, KY: Westminster/John Knox, 1996), 77.

[33] Jude 7 is significant for believers, as it is not just another ancient text but a text within the biblical canon. Thus, when an author suggests Genesis 19 is not about sexual immorality or homosexuality in particular, he needs to explain why he rejects the reading of Genesis 19 in the canonical book of Jude. For example, Steve Chalke has recently supported homosexuality on the grounds that Genesis 19 is about "indulgence, indifference to others and social injustice" rather than homosexuality ("The Bible and Homosexuality," *Christianity* [Feb. 2013], accessed November 2, 2013, http://www.christianitymagazine.co.uk/sexuality/stevechalke.aspx). This kind of statement shows not only an ignorance of the history of interpretation of Genesis 19 but also of Jude 7, which states that Sodom "indulged in sexual immorality and pursued unnatural lust" (as the NRSV translation has it).

to earlier books when in fact no assessment has been made. Moreover, the fields of theology and practical theology are not typically associated with study in primary sources in our day, with the result that scholars in these areas rely on the work of others if they are even interested in primary sources. This practice is open to abuse, and one will find a tendency in such scholarship to "arrange" arguments in favor of a case rather than argue points from texts.

Some biblical scholars, trained in the use of primary sources, offer inadequate work. At times, as in the case of Scroggs, their real intention appears to be to pull together primary sources that can support their presupposition rather than survey all the evidence in order to discover what conclusion emerges. Some scholars offer radically new interpretations of the primary texts, ones never before entertained, leaving those without an understanding of those primary texts or any knowledge of the history of interpretation stymied. Precisely for this reason those who are interested in this topic need to read the primary sources for themselves. As we continue to present the primary sources in this book, readers should be able to draw their own conclusions about the evidence, which is, far more often than not, clear and compelling.

CHAPTER 11

HOMOSEXUALITY IN THE ANCIENT NEAR EAST

I n this chapter we will discuss homosexual practice in the ancient Near East.[1] Research on this topic serves at least two purposes. First, it demonstrates that there were different types of homosexual practices in the ancient Near East, defined by intent and context. Second, it reveals the significance of homosexual acts committed as part of cultic activity (i.e., activity associated with a religion). At junctures in the discussion where the relevant primary and secondary sources include graphic depictions of sexual acts, we will provide references for further reading rather than reproducing material some readers may find distasteful.

If the ancient Near East differentiated between various types of homosexual acts, then unspecified laws against homosexuality, as we have in Leviticus 18:22 and 20:13, should be understood to forbid any sort of homosexual practice—otherwise authors would have been expected to specify which acts were intended. Homosexual acts in the ancient Near East were, at times, forms of rape and attempts to dominate another person. They could, at other times, relate to social status or cultic practices. Thus we need to look carefully at what is promoted or opposed in regard to homosexual acts in the ancient Near Eastern context. Apart from the Old Testament, ancient Near Eastern texts specify only certain types of homosexual acts as forbidden or punishable. This has led some authors to suppose that the Old Testament prohibitions of homosexual acts are not absolute either. We shall, however, argue that the Old Testament's prohibition of any homosexual act is one of the factors that made Israel distinct among ancient Near Eastern nations.

As for homosexual acts related to cultic practices, we will argue that there was idolatrous, cultic prostitution in Israel's territories and that this included male prostitutes used by other males. The context for this activity is relevant, yet the practice is not abominable merely because it is within the context of

---

[1] On this topic, readers should, in particular, note Donald J. Wold, *Out of Order: Homosexuality in the Bible and the Ancient Near East* (Grand Rapids, MI: Baker, 1998).

idolatry and/or because it is prostitution. Indeed, the biblical sexual ethic is primarily an "action" ethic, not having to do with how someone feels about another person. In Scripture sexual acts are justified as acts of union in a marriage between a man and a woman and, relatedly, as acts of procreation.

THE PRACTICES OF EGYPT AND CANAAN

Part of the Holiness Law Code (Lev 17–26) is introduced with the following words:

> The LORD spoke to Moses, saying: Speak to the people of Israel and say to them: I am the LORD your God. You shall not do as they do in the land of Egypt, where you lived, and you shall not do as they do in the land of Canaan, to which I am bringing you. You shall not follow their statutes. My ordinances you shall observe and my statutes you shall keep, following them: I am the LORD your God. You shall keep my statutes and my ordinances; by doing so one shall live: I am the LORD. (Lev 18:1–5)

From this introduction we anticipate that the list of sins to follow will include practices of Egypt and Canaan. Among the laws that follow is the law against homosexual conduct in Leviticus 18:22: "You shall not lie with a male as with a woman; it is an abomination." The prohibition is repeated in Leviticus 20:13, where both persons involved in the act—both consenting to the act—are condemned to death.

What is it about mutually consenting homosexual acts that was wrong in the Old Testament? On the face of the matter, several possibilities might be considered. (1) Is homosexual conduct said to be wrong because it involved dominance in some unacceptable way of one person over another? (2) Is homosexual conduct said to be wrong because it was associated with idolatry? (3) Is homosexual conduct said to be wrong because it was a sinful sexual practice in itself? (4) Is homosexual conduct said to be wrong simply because it was foreign—Egyptian or Canaanite—and not because there was anything wrong about it in itself? Note that we are not asking, (5) Is homosexual conduct prohibited because it involved sex with a minor? The literature does not give any reason to consider this option (contrary to evidence from the Greek context).

These questions lead us to both an examination of Leviticus and of the ancient Near Eastern context. The latter concerns us here. Just what did ancient Near Eastern societies think about homosexual acts?[2]

---

[2] For further discussion, see Donald J. Wold.

HOMOSEXUAL CONDUCT AND DOMINANCE

Some of the evidence we have from the ancient Near East relates homosexual conduct to dominance of a certain kind.[3] The possible kinds of dominance to consider as the sources are read include: (1) someone in a higher social position dominating someone in a lower social position;[4] (2) someone trying to dominate a person in the same social position;[5] (3) someone in a lower social position trying to dominate someone in a higher social position.[6]

The practice of homosexual acts can and did include dominance and submission.[7] Sex is used this way in our day as well, although the ancient Near East appears to have accepted the practice and to have accepted particularly violent expressions of dominance (the practice of slavery offers another example). In these texts, when a wrong is alleged to have been committed, it is because the sexual act is done to a person of higher status.

Yet the Old Testament does not condemn homosexual acts because they are acts of dominance except perhaps, and only partly, in the story of Noah and Ham. The laws against homosexual acts in the Leviticus Holiness Code are *not* qualified but absolute. They do not differentiate homosexual acts in terms of personal or social dominance and are intended to distinguish Israel from its sinful cultural context. Same-sex unions are an abomination to God.

As Robert Gagnon says, in Middle Assyrian law, accusing a person wrongly of homosexually dominating others could lead to punishment (the *lex talionis* of meting out to false witnesses the penalty due homosexual offenders). Yet the act of homosexual sex in itself generally was not viewed negatively by the nations surrounding Israel. Gagnon concludes:

---

[3] This is depicted on several Egyptian coffin texts (Raymond O. Faulkner, *The Ancient Egyptian Coffin Texts* [Warminster: Aris & Phillips, 1973]). See 2.162, 264; Adriaan de Buck, *The Egyptian Coffin Texts VI* (Chicago, IL: University of Chicago Press, 1956), 258f-g.

[4] See Tablet A, a Middle Assyrian text (trans. Martha Roth, *The Context of Scripture: Monumental Inscriptions from the Biblical World,* vol. II, ed. William Halo [Leiden: Brill, 2000], 355).

[5] See *Šumma alu* 51, a Mesopotamian text (trans. Ann K. Guinan in *The Context of Scripture: Canonical Compositions from the Biblical World,* vol. I, ed. William Hallo [Leiden: Brill, 1997], 425); and A20, a Middle Assyrian text (trans. Martha Roth, *The Context of Scripture,* 355).

[6] The Egyptian story of Seth and Horus, an older and younger brother among the gods, respectively, gives us insight into the recurrent theme of brotherly rivalry for dominance, as in the Genesis stories of Cain and Abel, Esau and Jacob, and Joseph and his brothers. However, in the Egyptian story, dominance is established sexually (*The Contest of Horus and Seth for the Rule,* Section XI, Section XI, in David F. Greenberg, *The Construction of Homosexual Identity* (Chicago, IL: University of Chicago Press, 1988), 130; Albert K. Grayson and Donald B. Redford, *Papyrus and Tablet* (New York, NY: Prentice-Hall, 1973), 76; see further, Robert Gagnon, *The Bible and Homosexual Practice* (Nashville, TN: Abingdon, 2001), 52).

[7] This may in part help us understand what Ham attempted to do to his father, Noah (Gen 9:20–25). However, it seems more likely that the story is meant to be read at the national level: what Ham, the father of the Canaanites, did was the sort of thing the Canaanites were known for, as illustrated in the story of Sodom (Gen 19). If so, the story in Genesis 9 is about more than any attempt by a person of lesser status of a person of higher status.

In the Levitical laws, the penalty for homosexual intercourse was death for both the passive partner (presumably consenting) and the active partner (whether acting with the consent of the passive partner or not). The level at which the Levitical laws stigmatize and criminalize all homosexual intercourse, while not discontinuous with some trends elsewhere, goes far beyond anything else currently known in the ancient Near East.[8]

The penalty for same-sex unions in Leviticus 20:13 is death. The penalty is to be applied to both persons involved. If there were a concern for social status and dominance, the penalty would apply to only one person. The focus in Leviticus is rather on consenting adults engaging in homosexual practices. In this matter Israel truly did stand out from its neighbors. It not only considered these acts sinful but also applied the death penalty to those practicing them.

HOMOSEXUAL CONDUCT AND TEMPLE PROSTITUTION

In a helpful essay on the Old Testament and homosexuality, Gordon Wenham addresses the issue of male cult prostitution. He says:

> Deut 23:17 prohibits male and female cult prostitution in Israel. The following verse describes a male homosexual prostitute as a "dog," a description also found in Mesopotamian texts and in the book of Revelation (22:15). The books of Kings state that when Canaanite religious practices were introduced into Israel, so was cult prostitution and three reforming kings attempted to abolish the male prostitutes (1 Kgs 15:12; 22:46; 2 Kgs 23:7). . . .

> Since male prostitutes were sometimes castrated and often took part in ceremonies flaunting their effeminacy, it may well be that aversion to homosexuality partially explains the ban on castrated men participating in the public assembly, or on wearing women's clothes. The latter is described as "an abomination to the LORD" (Deut 23:1; 22:5). It could well be that the law is banning anything suggestive of homosexual practice.[9]

There is a debate over whether any of these texts actually do refer to male cult prostitution. The debate turns on (1) the meaning of the word *qādēš* in the Hebrew and (2) whether we have any historical evidence for male cult prostitutes in Israel and the ancient Near East generally.[10] Several Hebrew words share the three consonants *qdš*, which is all a reader of the Old Testament saw until vowels were added much later (Hebrew was originally written without vowels). The most common meaning of the consonants *qdš* is "a holy thing"

---

[8] Robert Gagnon, *The Bible and Homosexual Practice*, 56.

[9] Gordon Wenham, "The Old Testament Attitude to Homosexuality," *Expository Times* 102 (1991): 259–363, accessed December 24, 2012, http://www.biblicalstudies.org.uk/article_attitude_wenham.html#10.

[10] On this second matter, see Phyllis Bird, "The End of the Male Cult Prostitute: A Literary-Historical and Sociological Analysis of Hebrew *QĀDĒŠ-QĔDĒŠÎM*," in *Congress Volume Cambridge 1995*, ed. J. A. Emerton (Leiden: Brill, 1995), 37–80.

(*qōdesh*), which makes it likely that a person designated as *qādēš* is connected to a shrine or temple—the cult (and here "cult" is not used pejoratively but simply in reference to the practices of a religion). The debate over the meaning of *qādēš* concerns whether a *qādēš* is simply someone involved in the cult at a shrine or temple or more specifically involved *as a prostitute* functioning at a shrine. This is the question before us as we proceed in the next few paragraphs. For this discussion one should note the following about the Hebrew terms:

1. A *qādēš* is a male person involved in the cult (and possibly as a prostitute).
2. *qĕdēši'm* is the plural of *qādēš* (both masculine terms).
3. A *qĕdēšah* is a female person involved in the cult (and possibly as a prostitute).
4. *qĕdēšôth* is the plural of *qĕdēšah* (both feminine terms).
5. The general Hebrew word for a female "prostitute" is *zōnāh* (plural, *zōnôth*).
6. Apparently, *keleb* (literally, "dog") is a term that could be used for a male prostitute.

Note the use of such terms in Deuteronomy 23:17–18:

> None of the daughters of Israel shall be a temple prostitute [*qĕdēšah*]; none of the sons of Israel shall be a temple prostitute [*qādēš*]. You shall not bring the fee of a prostitute [*zōnāh*] or the wages of a male prostitute [*keleb*] into the house of the LORD your God in payment for any vow, for both of these are abhorrent to the LORD your God.

The terms *qĕdēšah* and *qādēš* appear in this passage to be associated with temple prostitution. This supposition is corroborated by the fact that the terms *qĕdēšah* and *zōnāh* are used interchangeably in Deuteronomy 23:17–19 (Hebrew and LXX Deut 23:18–19) as well as in Genesis 38:15, 21–22, 24 (the story of Judah and his daughter-in-law Tamar), and Hosea 4:14. If the female *qĕdēšah* is a temple prostitute, the male *qādēš* must be a male prostitute. This also explains the use of "dog"—the assumption being that the sexual behavior of male dogs is associated with these male temple prostitutes.

Following this linguistic argument, the interpreter next needs to ask whether there were male cult prostitutes in the ancient Near East. Two Mesopotamian texts might be cited:

> If a man copulates with a male cult prostitute (*assinnu*), a hard destiny (or: care, trouble) will leave. (*Šumma alu*)[11]
>
> He will hand over seven priests and seven priestesses to Adad, who dwells in Kurbail, and will give seven male prostitutes and seven female prostitutes to Ishtar, who dwells in Arbail. (*Nimrud*, pl. XVI)[12]

---

[11] As quoted by Martti Nissinen, *Homoeroticism in the Biblical World: A Historical Perspective* (Minneapolis, MN: Augsburg Fortress, 1998), 27.
[12] As quoted John Day, "Does the Old Testament Refer to Sacred Prostitution and Did It Actually Exist in Ancient Israel?" in *Biblical and Near Eastern Essays: Studies in Honour of*

Because cults typically were associated with fertility in this region, it makes sense that the *qĕdēšah* and *qādēš* would engage in sexual activity with devotees. However, Phyllis Bird argues that fertility cults did not involve homosexual prostitution because same-sex acts have nothing to do with fertility. Previously, Robin Scroggs had similarly reasoned that men must have had sex at cultic sites for *fertility* gods with *female* prostitutes.[13] We do not find such arguments compelling. The Mesopotamian text quoted above relates homosexual intercourse with a cult prostitute with removing some trouble. Moreover, sex with female prostitutes could, conceivably, celebrate fertility without anyone intending the act to result in procreation. Thus the sexual act seems to be the main focus, and it could, therefore, be an act with a female, a male, or even an orgy. Indeed, some evidence points to the act as having to do with fulfilling sexual desire.[14] There is really no reason to believe that cultic sex even in fertility cults was meant for procreation.

Bird's argument is detailed and involves some beliefs she has about sources underlying Deuteronomy 23:17–18. She distinguishes the source allegedly behind Deuteronomy 23:17, with its reference to female and male groups serving at a temple in some capacity (not sexual), from the source behind Deuteronomy 23:18, with its references to prostitution (*zōnāh* for a female prostitute and *keleb* for a male prostitute).[15] If the verses derive from different sources, then there is, she avers, no reason to suggest that the prostitution mentioned in verse 18 has anything to do with the "*qĕdēšah*" or "*qādēš*" in verse 17.

This seems to us a rather weak argument. Which is more significant, the *supposed* meaning in *alleged* source documents or the use to which an author or editor put his sources (assuming there really are sources)? If the author of Deuteronomy had two sources in Deuteronomy 23:17–18, his placing them together demonstrates an understanding that the verses speak to the same thing, and the Hebrew terms under discussion are related. Moreover, theories about underlying sources where there are no existing source texts have proven highly speculative and debatable.[16] Bird actually appreciates this counterargument, despite her argument about sources. She suggests that, while the underlying literary sources of Deuteronomy 23:17–18 may have distinguished prostitution from whatever it meant to be a *qādēš*, the editor of Deuteronomy

---

Kevin C. Cathcart, ed. Carmel McCarthy and John F. Healey (London: T&T Clark, 2004), 15.

[13] Robin Scroggs, *The New Testament and Homosexuality* (Philadelphia, PAA: Fortress, 1983), 71.

[14] One text in the *Šumma alu* refers to having sexual desire like a Mesopotamian, homosexual, cult prostitute, an *assinnu*. Another text refers to sexual arousal of a *kalu*, a lamentation priest. For quotations, see Robert Gagnon, *The Bible and Homosexual Practice*, 49; David Nissinen, *Construction*, 97–98. We recommend that persons wanting to pursue these Ancient Near Eastern quotes further should begin with Gagnon in particular.

[15] Phyllis Bird, "The End of the Male Cult Prostitute," 48f.

[16] See C. Clifton Black III, *The Disciples According to Mark: Markan Redaction in Current Debate*, 2nd ed. (Grand Rapids, MI: Eerdmans, 2012). Black demonstrated (as in his 1989 first edition) the wildly different conclusions three scholars offer depending on their assumptions about sources and their redaction in Mark's Gospel.

and subsequent readers of the text naturally understand the two as related.[17] We find it interesting that a scholar in our day would claim to know more than an ancient redactor about the practices of pagan cults, and we find it interesting that someone would use redaction criticism (the study of how an author edited sources) to demonstrate that the author did not know how to use his sources wisely—sources we do not have. Frankly, we find it troubling that someone would interpret Scripture in this highly speculative way that also entails reading against the meaning of the text as we have it. Still, even following Bird, we are back to reading the edited text, verses 17–18 taken together, as a text with its own meaning. Consequently, whatever her views about sources and the meaning of words, the end of the matter for someone interested in what the text of Scripture actually says would be the same: homosexual cultic prostitutes are condemned, and the basis for this is not only their association with a cult but also that homosexual practices were condemned in any context in Israel.

Bird's other major argument is that there is no historical evidence for cultic prostitution in ancient Israel. This, too, is unconvincing. Some evidence for an association of idolatry with prostitution in Israel can be presented. While "prostitution" can be a metaphor for idolatry and not necessarily something sexual done in relation to idolatry,[18] the evidence suggests that at least some Old Testament references to idolatry as prostitution were more than metaphors. (Even as metaphors, they entail disapproval of both idolatry and prostitution.) Evidence is fairly strong for the practice of cultic prostitution in ancient Israel and also for homosexual prostitution. The Old Testament disapproves of prostitution, idolatry, and homosexual acts in and of themselves, let alone in some combination. The following texts should be considered.

Note that Canaanite (in this case, Moabite) worship involved idolatry, food, and sex, whether or not this was specifically prostitution.

> While Israel was staying at Shittim, the people *began to have sexual relations with the women* of Moab. These invited the people to the *sacrifices of their gods*, and the people ate and bowed down to their gods. Thus Israel yoked itself to the Baal of Peor, and the LORD's anger was kindled against Israel. (Num 25:1–3, emphasis added)

In Ezekiel 16, Israel is pictured as a woman whom God married but who prostituted herself at idolatrous shrines:

> You took some of your garments, and made for yourself colorful shrines, and on them *played the whore*; nothing like this has ever been or ever shall be. You also took your beautiful jewels of my gold and my silver that I had given you, and made for yourself male images, and with them played the whore. (Ezek 16:16–17, emphasis added)

---

[17] Phyllis Bird, "The End of the Male Cult Prostitute," 72.

[18] For example, "You [Israel] played the whore with the nations, and polluted yourself with their idols" (Ezek 23:30).

A connection between idolatrous shrines and sexual practices is also found in Isaiah 57. The text is addressed to "children of a sorceress" engaged in idolatry and "offspring of an adulterer and whore," suggesting fornication (adultery is a metaphor for idolatry but likely implies that sexual practices were involved in the associated religious practices—as Wisdom 14, at a later date, explicitly states). Those seeking places for idol worship among the rocks and trees engage in sacrifice and sexual acts:

> You that *burn with lust among the oaks, under every green tree*; you that slaughter your children in the valleys, under the clefts of the rocks. . . . Upon a high and lofty mountain you have *set your bed*, and there you went up to offer sacrifice. Behind the door and the doorpost you have set up your symbol; for, in deserting me, you have *uncovered your bed*, you have gone up to it, you have made it wide; and you have made a bargain for yourself with them, *you have loved their bed, you have gazed on their nakedness* [literally, "hand," i.e., the male sexual organ]. (Isa 57:5, 7–8, emphasis added)

Verse 8 suggests rather strongly that homoerotic acts at pagan shrines are in view. English translations seem inadequate here. We know from Egyptian and possibly Ugaritic texts that "hand" was used in the ancient world as a euphemism for the male genitals,[19] and that seems to be the intent here. But by translating the word *yad* as "nakedness," the NRSV, ESV, and NIV leave unclear that the gazing is on male genitals (the practice is also noted in Hab 2:15 and Gen 9:21–22). The Holman Christian Standard Bible has "genitals" but does not specify male genitals, as it should. The Complete Jewish Bible (1998) misses the point with its translation: "whose bed you loved when you saw their hand beckoning." No one will catch the homoerotic reference in the text with such translations.

Something similar is said in Hosea, where idolatry that includes prostitution and sexual acts appears to be in view:

> They sacrifice on the tops of the mountains, and make offerings upon the hills, under oak, poplar, and terebinth, because their shade is good. Therefore *your daughters play the whore, and your daughters-in-law commit adultery.* I will not punish your daughters when they play the whore, nor your daughters-in-law when they commit adultery; for *the men themselves go aside with whores (hazōnôth), and sacrifice with temple prostitutes (haqᵉdēshôth)*; thus a people without understanding comes to ruin. (Hos 4:13–14, emphasis added)

A similar passage connecting what is done under trees in idolatry and what is done sexually can be found in Jeremiah:

---

[19] See John N. Oswalt, *The Book of Isaiah, Chapters 40–66,* The New International Commentary on the Old Testament (Grand Rapids, MI: Eerdmans, 1998), 480.

> Only acknowledge your guilt, that you have rebelled against the LORD your God, and *scattered your favors among strangers under every green tree,* and have not obeyed my voice, says the LORD. (Jer 3:13, emphasis added)

With an ironic twist, God speaks of Israelites lying amid the idols in a different sense in Ezekiel 6:13. They will indeed lie amid the idols: he will slay these worshippers! This passage gives us a picture of what took place at the shrines. The idols were laid out around the altars at sacred places, and sexual encounters took place amid incense sacrifices.

> And you shall know that I am the LORD, when *their slain lie among their idols* around their altars, on every high hill, on all the mountain tops, under every green tree, and under every leafy oak, wherever they offered pleasing odor to all their idols. (Ezek 6:13, emphasis added)

Given the connection in such passages between idolatry and sexual immorality at shrines, and given the connection between idolatry and prostitution in Deuteronomy 23:17–18, the conventional argument that *qĕdēsôth* and *qĕdēšîm* refer to female and male cult prostitutes seems likely, contrary to Bird's arguments.

One might note that the above texts in Isaiah, Jeremiah, Ezekiel, and Hosea depict Israel's sin as idolatry and prostitution, which are intermingled in the sense that idolatry was Israel's prostitution with foreign gods and in the sense that prostitution took place at the shrines. The language of *qedēsôth* (female, plural) and *qĕdēšîm* (male, plural) brings in the additional thought of both female and male prostitutes at these shrines of fertility gods. Prostitution is not wrong because it is in the context of idolatry; both are wrong. Homosexual encounters are not wrong because they are outside of committed relationships or because they are in the context of worshipping idols; homosexual acts, prostitution, and idolatry are all wrong.

The relationship between idolatry and other accompanying sinful practices—and the fact that they are all sinful—is outlined in detail in the book of Wisdom, chapters 13–14:

> For *the idea of making idols was the beginning of fornication,* and the invention of them was the corruption of life (Wis 14:12, emphasis added).

The author elaborates the connection between idolatry and other sinful behaviors, explaining that places of idolatrous worship became places for all sorts of sinful practices. Some of those practices, as the following quotation shows, were sexual in nature, including homosexual acts:

> Then it was not enough for them to err about the knowledge of God, but though living in great strife due to ignorance, they call such great evils peace. For whether they kill children in their initiations, or celebrate secret mysteries, or hold frenzied revels with strange customs, they no longer keep

either their lives or their marriages pure, but they either treacherously kill one another, or grieve one another by adultery, and all is a raging riot of blood and murder, theft and deceit, corruption, faithlessness, tumult, perjury, confusion over what is good, forgetfulness of favors, defiling of souls, sexual perversion, *disorder [or "inversion"] in marriages*, adultery, and debauchery. *For the worship of idols not to be named is the beginning and cause and end of every evil.* (Wis 14:22–27, emphasis added)

The point here, of course, is not that these sins are wrong because they are practiced in the context of idol worship. The point is rather that idolatry (turning away from what is right in the worship of God) is the beginning of turning away from everything else that is right. People learn sinful practices that have been incorporated into idol worship. While several hundred years elapsed between Isaiah and Hosea (eighth century BC), Jeremiah and Ezekiel (sixth century BC), and the book of Wisdom (perhaps second century BC), Wisdom represents a Jewish way of thinking about the origin of sin and the connection between idolatry and sin. Two centuries later Paul presents the same logical connection between idolatry, homosexual acts, and other sins (Rom 1:18–32).

So, did the periodic reforms in preexilic Israel (1 Kgs 14:24; 15:12; 22:46; 2 Kgs 23:7) involve merely tearing down shrines and removing female and male persons associated with the cults, or were the reforms more particularly a matter of removing idolatry and the attendant practice of cultic prostitution (female and male)?[20] The book of Wisdom suggests the latter, as do Isaiah, Jeremiah, Ezekiel, and Hosea.

We support the view, summarized by Brian Rosner, that Israel faced a challenge because it did not eradicate but incorporated the cult prostitution of the Canaanites. As Rosner says:

Religious prostitution was commonly practiced by the cults of the ancient Near Eastern fertility religions. Israelite participation was thus condemned as tantamount to apostasy. It was a problem for Israel from the moment they entered the promised land (Num 25:1; cf. Judg 2:17), becoming especially prevalent in Judah and Israel during the divided monarchy (from Rehoboam, 1 Kings 14:24, to Josiah, 2 Kings 23:7). According to Exodus 34:11-16 the extermination of the inhabitants of the land was commanded so that the Israelites would avoid the practice. Deut. 23:17(18) forbids cult prostitution for Israel (cf. Amos 2:7).[21]

---

[20] Phyllis Bird ("The End of the Male Cult Prostitute," 73) suggests that *qĕdēši̇m* in 1 Kgs 23:7 does not refer to people but storehouses—treasuries—at the temple. In 1 Kgs 15:12-15, we hear of Asa's reform, which involved a removal of alien votaries (*qĕdēšîm*) and a bringing into the temple votive offerings (*qodāšîm*) (cf. 1 Kgs 7:51, where Solomon also brings votive offerings into the temple). Thus 1 Kgs 23:7 is about removing the votive storehouses related to the goddess Asherah.

[21] Brian S. Rosner, "Temple Prostitution in 1 Corinthians 6:12–20," *Novum Testamentum* 40, no. 4 (October 1998): 343.

Having made the association between some forms of pagan worship or idolatry and sexual immorality, including homosexual acts, the question might arise in the minds of some whether this is the practice condemned in Leviticus 18 and 20. Are we to assume homosexual cultic prostitution, not homosexuality in general, is the point of the prohibitions in Leviticus 18:22 and 20:13?

While homosexual cultic acts seem to have been a part of at least some cultic practices, there is no reason whatsoever to claim that the problem with such practices was only their idolatrous context.[22] The evidence we have considered suggests that a term in Hebrew was available, *qĕdēšîm,* for male temple prostitutes (as also in the Babylonian tongue, *assinnu*). Therefore the laws in the Leviticus Holiness Code (Lev 18:22; 20:13) should not be taken, to refer only or even primarily to this cultic practice. If the author had wanted to limit his laws in this way, he would have said so. Instead, he words the laws as broadly as possible in order to prohibit any lying of two men together. This observation comports with the fact that most other sins in Leviticus 18 relate to sexuality, not idolatry, and the sins in Leviticus 20 are grouped according to the penalty, not according to cultic contexts. Furthermore, later texts interpreting Leviticus 18:22 and 20:13 do not limit the meaning to cultic contexts and prostitution. Rather, the texts are interpreted as they ought to be—as references to a sexual act between males.

HOMOSEXUAL CONDUCT AND SEXUAL PRACTICE

In addition to homosexual relations being related to dominance and worship in the ancient Near East, homosexual acts were, of course, also related to sexuality itself. Various types of homosexual acts occurred. A Hittite text has a father denying incestuous relations with his son and daughter (Hittite Law 189).[23] An Egyptian text from about 1400 BC involves someone denying having sex with another male.[24] Some tomb depictions in Egypt also suggest the possibility

---

[22] Robert Gagnon gives a list of persons who have maintained the view that the problem with homosexual acts in Leviticus is not the acts themselves but idolatry. See Gagnon, *The Bible and Homosexual Practice,* 129n202. Gagnon states that "few today give this argument much credence" (129).

[23] Quoted in Gordon Wenham, "The Old Testament Attitude to Homosexuality," *Expository Times* 102 (1991): 259–363, here 361. Wenham agrees with the conclusion of the Hittitologist H. A. Hoffner that "it would appear that homosexuality was not outlawed among the Hittites" ("Incest, Sodomy, and Bestiality in the Ancient Near East" in *Orient and Occident: Essay in Honor of C. H. Gordon* [Neukirchen: Neukirchener Verlag, 1973], 85). Given the mention of both the daughter and the son, what makes the same-sex act a capital crime is incest. No other Hittite texts mention same-sex acts, although bestiality, adultery, rape, and incest are mentioned in other texts. This might suggest that homosexual acts were permitted among the Hittites as long as they were not incestuous, adulterous, or instances of rape.

[24] *The Book of the Dead,* chap. 125. James B. Pritchard (*ANET,* 35) translated the passage such that it refers to pederasty. However, according to David F. Greenberg (*The Construction of Homosexuality* [Chicago, IL: University of Chicago, 1988], 132f), the age of the partner in this text is indeterminate.

of consensual, adult, homosexual relations:[25] The tomb of Pharaoh Niuserre (ca. 2600 BC) pictures his two manicurists and hairdressers as holding hands, embracing, and touching noses.[26] Pharaoh Ikhnaton (ca. 1370 BC) is shown with his son-in-law and probable coregent, Smenkhare. Ikhnaton has a feminine shape, and the two are nude and stroking each other's chins. Smenkhare is described with terms of endearment that typically apply to Ikhnaton's queen and concubines.[27] Finally, men who changed their masculinity into femininity in their cultic roles for the fertility goddess Eanna are mentioned in another Mesopotamian text, and the text also suggests a sexual indulgence associated with cultic activity:[28]

> They rouse Eanna, the party boys and festival people who changed their masculinity into femininity to make the people of Ishtar revere her. (*Erra and Ishum* IV)

CONCLUSION

We see from surviving ancient Near Eastern texts that people surrounding Israel practiced homosexuality. Some homosexual practices were condemned. Others were accepted.

Male (and female) cult prostitutes were condemned in the Old Testament, and we have argued that this included condemnation of idolatry, prostitution, and homosexual practice in themselves as well as in some combination. Effeminacy (as in the wearing of women's clothing) was also condemned in Israel. Most importantly, no qualifications regarding context or intent can be found for prohibitions of male homosexuality in the Old Testament, whereas we do find qualifications of what is condemned or accepted in other ancient Near Eastern literature. The absolute or unqualified condemnation of homosexual acts in Leviticus 18:23 and Leviticus 20:13 or Israel shows that any homosexual act was out of bounds. Indeed, it carried the death penalty (Lev 20:13).

This conclusion concurs with later understandings of Israel's view on homosexual practice. Indeed, Josephus, Paul, Jude, 2 Peter, and Philo demonstrate that first-century Jews and Christians condemned homosexual practice without qualification. Jews and Christians never deemed some forms of homosexual behavior acceptable.

---

[25] See Greg Reeder, "Same-Sex Desire, Conjugal Constructs, and the Tomb of Niankhkhnum and Khnumhotep," *World Archaeology* 32, no. 2 (October 2000): 193–208.

[26] Ibid. See also David Greenberg, *The Construction of Homosexuality*, 130; David Greenberg, *The Construction of Homosexuality*, 130.

[27] David Greenberg notes the debate about how to interpret this material. We cannot be certain that we know these are instances of homosexual activity (*The Construction of Homosexuality*, 130).

[28] *Erra and Ishum* IV, as quoted in Stephanie Dale, *Myths from Mesopotamia: Creation, the Flood, Gilgamesh, and Others* (Oxford, UK: Oxford University Press, 1989), 305.

CHAPTER 12

JEWISH VIEWS ON HOMOSEXUALITY
AFTER OLD TESTAMENT TIMES

What did Jews writing after the Old Testament period, from the fifth century BC through the sixth century AD think about homosexual practice? By considering this question, we will (1) see how Jews in this period interpreted Old Testament teaching on homosexuality and (2) set the Jewish context of the early church's treatment of this issue. The early church was, after all, largely a Jewish movement in much of the first century AD.

If we discover Jewish statements about homosexuality in this post-Old Testament period are at odds with our findings to this point, we might have a reason to rethink the argument given so far. We will find, however, that there is no debate at all: Jews consistently condemned homosexual practice of any sort after the return from exile and right through the early church period. Jews understood the Old Testament to speak against homosexual behavior, and they accepted biblical authority in matters of sexual ethics. On this point Jews and Christians were in total agreement.

Our procedure in this chapter will be to present the various Jewish texts on homosexual practice after the Old Testament up until the writing of the Babylonian Talmud in the fifth or sixth century AD.[1] Some of this material

---

[1] Readers should note a series of recent publications by William R. G. Loader. In addition to his studies on the Scriptures (*Sexuality in the New Testament: Understanding the Key Texts* [London: SPCK; Louisville, KY: Westminster/John Knox, 2010]; *Sexuality and the Jesus Tradition* [Grand Rapids, MI: Eerdmans, 2005]), Loader has undertaken a major study of primary sources from the Jewish context. See *The Septuagint, Sexuality, and the New Testament: Case Studies on the Impact of the LXX in Philo and the New Testament* (Grand Rapids, MI: Eerdmans, 2004); *Enoch, Levi, and Jubilees on Sexuality: Attitudes towards Sexuality in the Early Enoch Literature, the Aramaic Levi Document, and the Book of Jubilees* (Grand Rapids, MI: Eerdmans, 2007); *The Dead Sea Scrolls on Sexuality: Attitudes towards Sexuality in Sectarian and Related Literature in Qumran* (Grand Rapids, MI: Eerdmans, 2009); *The Pseudepigrapha on Sexuality: Attitudes towards Sexuality in Apocalypses, Testaments, Legends, Wisdom, and*

has already been presented (particularly that on Sodom), and it will only be repeated in a few instances.

WISDOM OF SOLOMON

In this book we read:

> For the idea of making idols was the beginning of fornication, and the invention of them was the corruption of life; for they did not exist from the beginning, nor will they last forever. For through human vanity they entered the world, and therefore their speedy end has been planned. . . . For whether they kill children in their initiations, or celebrate secret mysteries, or hold frenzied revels with strange customs, they no longer keep either their lives or their marriages pure, but they either treacherously kill one another, or grieve one another by adultery, and all is a raging riot of blood and murder, theft and deceit, corruption, faithlessness, tumult, perjury, *confusion over what is good*, forgetfulness of favors, *defiling of souls, sexual perversion (miasmos geneseōs), disorder in marriages (enallagē gamōn)*, adultery, and debauchery. For the worship of idols not to be named is the beginning and cause and end of every evil. (14:12–14, 23–27)

Wisdom makes a connection between idolatry and all sorts of evils, including sexual sins. The connection is of two sorts. First, idolatrous worship involves other sinful practices, not just worship of an idol. One might, for example, think of cult prostitution, as discussed in the previous chapter, or child sacrifice. Second, because idolatrous worship involves these other sins, people begin to practice such sins in other contexts as well. In this way idolatry is "the beginning and cause and end of every evil."

One sin in the list of verse 26 is "sexual perversion," according to the NRSV. Yet the Greek more literally reads "corruption of origin" (*miasmos geneseōs*). This appears to be a reference to altering one's nature, whether in homoerotic practices or by castration. The preceding item in the list, "defiling of souls," should probably also be taken as a sexual term; compare 2 Peter 2:10's "who indulge their flesh in depraved [*miasmou*] lust." The subsequent sin, "disorder in marriages" (*enallagē gamōn*), as the NRSV puts it, is also a reference to sexual sin. It includes a Greek word (*enallagē*) that means "exchange."[2] Paul uses a word with the same root (*metēllaxan* from the root word *allagē*) in Romans 1:26 for lesbians, who "exchange" the natural use of their bodies for what is against nature. The *Testament of Naphtali* 3.4 also

---

Related Literature (Grand Rapids, MI: Eerdmans, 2011); *Philo, Josephus, and the Testaments on Sexuality: Attitudes Towards Sexuality in the Writings of Philo, Josephus, and the Testaments of the Twelve Patriarchs* (Grand Rapids, MI: Eerdmans, 2011).

[2] Henry George Liddell and Robert Scott, *An Intermediate Greek-English Lexicon* (New York, NY: Oxford University Press, 1945).

uses the term (*enallagē*) in reference to homosexual practice: Sodom is said to have "changed" the order of its nature. In place of the NRSV's "disorder in marriages" in Wisdom 14:26, David Winston suggests the translation "interchange of sex roles."[3] Winston also notes a parallel passage in Philo, where "exchange" (*enellagē*) again occurs:

> In every festival then and assembly among men, the following are the most remarkable and celebrated points, security, relaxation, truce, drunkenness, deep drinking, reveling, luxury, amusement, music at the doors, banquets lasting through the night, unseemly pleasures, wedding feasts during the day, violent acts of insolence, practices of intemperance, indulgence of folly, pursuits of shameful things, an utter destruction and renunciation of what is good, wakefulness during the night for the indulgence of immoderate appetites, sleep by day when it is the proper time to be awake, a turning upside down of the laws of nature [*physeōs ergōn enallagē*].[4]

Thus, the reference in Wisdom 14:26 likely indicates an exchange of the natural relations of men and women in marriages for homosexual relations, but it could also refer to sexual exchanges outside marriage—or both. The two terms following "disorder in marriages" are also sexual sins: "adultery, and debauchery." All this strongly suggests these sins are sexual sins. Since "adultery" is listed separately, "disorder in marriages" should probably be translated "exchange of marriages" and read along with "corruption of origin" (and perhaps also "defiling of souls") to refer to same-sex practices (with other sexual sins that fit such a description possibly in view as well). What seems certain is that sexual deviations from nature and from marriage between a man and a woman are intended in the list.

The Wisdom of Solomon makes two references to Sodom, without mentioning the city by name. The "exceeding wickedness" of the city with regard to its hatred of guests is highlighted in 19:13–17. Emphasizing the great wickedness and folly of Sodom in general terms is 10:1–14—Sodom's sins were many and extreme and not limited to the hatred shown toward guests.

TESTAMENT OF THE TWELVE PATRIARCHS

This document condemns various sins, including sexual sins between persons of the same gender such as pederasty and homosexual acts among men.

---

[3] David Winston, *The Wisdom of Solomon: A New Translation with Introduction and Commentary,* The Anchor Bible 43 (New York, NY: Doubleday, 1979), 280. James B. DeYoung agrees and offers further discussion: *Homosexuality: Contemporary Claims Examined in Light of the Bible and Other Ancient Literature and Law* (Grand Rapids, MI: Kregel, 2000), 81–82.

[4] *On the Cherubim* 92, in *The Works of Philo Judaeus, the Contemporary of Josephus*, trans. C. D. Yonge, 4 vols. (London, England: Henry G. Bohn, 1854–55).

Homosexuality, as in Romans 1:26–28, is seen as a violation of God's created order.

> In the seventh week [of the seventy weeks of Daniel] there will come priests: idolaters, adulterers, money lovers, arrogant, lawless, voluptuaries, pederasts, those who practice bestiality. (*T. Levi* 17:11)[5]

> For the unjust will not inherit the kingdom of God, nor will the adulterers, nor the accursed, nor those who commit outrages and have sexual intercourse with males. (*T. Jac* 7:20)[6]

> The gentiles, because they wandered astray and forsook the Lord, have changed the order, and have devoted themselves to stones and sticks, patterning themselves after wandering spirits. But you, my children, shall not be like that: In the firmament, in the earth, and in the sea, in all the products of his workmanship discern the Lord who made all things, so that you do not become like Sodom, which departed from the order of nature. (*T. Naph.* 3:3–4)[7]

> Sometimes I strangle men, sometimes I pervert them from their true natures. (*T. Sol* 4:5, manuscript D [first through third centuries AD])[8]

OTHER INTERTESTAMENTAL JEWISH LITERATURE

The *Letter of Aristeas* concurs with the views expressed in the *Testament of the Twelve Patriarchs*:

> Therefore he compels us to recognize that we must perform all our actions with discrimination according to the standard of righteousness—more especially because we have been distinctly separated from the rest of mankind. For most other men defile themselves by promiscuous intercourse, thereby working great iniquity, and whole countries and cities pride themselves upon such vices. For they not only have intercourse with men but they defile their own mothers and even their daughters. But we have been kept separate from such sins. *Letter of Aristeas* 151–153 [early second century BC or earlier])[9]

---

[5] "Testament of Levi," in *The Old Testament Pseudepigrapha*, vol. 1, ed. James H. Charlesworth, trans. H. C. Kee (Garden City, NY: Doubleday, 1983), 794.

[6] "The Testament of Jacob," in *The Old Testament Pseudepigrapha*, vol. 1, ed. James H. Charlesworth, trans. W. F. Stinespring (Garden City, NY: Doubleday, 1983), 917.

[7] "Testaments of the Twelve Patriarchs," in *The Old Testament Pseudepigrapha*, vol. 1, ed. James H. Charlesworth, trans. H. C. Kee (Garden City, NY: Doubleday, 1983), 812.

[8] "Testament of Solomon," in *The Old Testament Pseudepigrapha*, vol. 1, ed. James H. Charlesworth, trans. D. C. Duling (Garden City, NY: Doubleday, 1983), 965.

[9] *The Letter of Aristeas*, trans. H. T. Andrews, in *The Apocrypha and Pseudepigrapha of the Old Testament*, ed. R. H. Charles (New York, NY: Clarendon, 1913), 83–122.

The author is contrasting Jewish laws to the practices of other nations. He attributes Jewish ethics to Moses and so must have Leviticus 18:22 and 20:13 in mind. He places males who have sex with other males—without any qualification related to certain contexts or practices—in the same category of non-Jewish unrighteousness as those who pair with their mothers or daughters.

Pseudo-Phocylides appears to have been written by a Jew just before or after the earthly lifetime of Christ. The work professes to state Jewish standards of morality in order to attract unbelievers.[10] It captures the Jewish view on homosexuality over against the Greco-Roman culture.

> Neither commit adultery nor rouse homosexual passion. (*Sentences*, 3)[11]

> Do not transgress with unlawful sex the limits set by nature. For even animals are not pleased by intercourse of male with male. And let women not imitate the sexual role of men. (*Sentences*, 190–92)

> Guard the youthful prime of life of a comely boy, because many rage for intercourse with a man. (*Sentences*, 213–14)

Second Enoch, originally written in the early first century AD in Egypt and later expanded, is like Romans 1:18–28 in that it sees the connection between confusion, idolatry, and "abominable fornications," including homosexuality:

> And all the world will be reduced to confusion by iniquities of wickednesses and abominable fornications, that is, friend with friend in the anus, and every other kind of wicked uncleanness which it is disgusting to report, and the worship of [the] evil [one]. (*2 Enoch* 34:2)[12]

According to Qumranic literature (pre-AD 70),[13] exposure of oneself before other males was punishable in the Qumran community:

> And whoever walks about naked in front of his fellow, without needing to, shall be punished for six months. And whoever takes out his "hand" from under his clothes, or if these are rags which allow his nakedness to be seen, he will be punished thirty days. (*Community Rule* [1QS] 7:14)[14]

---

[10] See James Charlesworth, *The Pseudepigrapha and Modern Research* (Atlanta, GA: Scholars, 1976), 173–74.

[11] All translations of Pseudo-Phocylides' *Sentences* are by P. W. van der Horst, *The Old Testament Pseudepigrapha*, vol. 2, ed. R. H. Charlesworth (New York, NY: Doubleday, 1985).

[12] "2 Enoch," in *The Old Testament Pseudepigrapha*, vol. 1, ed. James H. Charlesworth, trans. F. I. Andersen (Garden City, NY: Doubleday, 1983), 158.

[13] Also see the discussion in William Loader, *The Dead Sea Scrolls on Sexuality* (Grand Rapids, MI: Eerdmans, 2009), 361.

[14] *The Dead Sea Scrolls Translated: The Qumran Texts in English*, 2nd ed., ed. Florentino Garcia Martinez, trans. Wilfred Watson (Grand Rapids, MI: Eerdmans, 1996).

As with Isaiah 57:8, "hand" is a euphemism for the male sex organ. The possibility of a homosexual indication in this quotation is supported by the fact that the Qumran community was a male community. The text attempts to eradicate any homosexuality.

Confusion of genders was also condemned at Qumran in 4Q159, frs. 2–4: "Let no man's garment be worn by a woman all [the days of her life]. Let him [not] be covered with a woman's mantle, nor wear a woman's tunic, for this is an abomination."

In about the first century AD, the Jewish *Apocalypse of Abraham* speaks of the place of eternal punishment for men who have homosexual passion for one another: "I saw also naked men, the foreheads against each other, and their disgrace, and their passion which (they had) against each other, and their retribution" (24.8).[15]

PHILO

A prolific first-century Jew from Alexandria, Philo mentions the sin of homosexuality at various points in his writings. He was eager to relate Greek philosophy to Judaism, but he rejected Greek attitudes toward sexuality— including the acceptance of homosexual unions. In the following quote, Philo is responding to Plato's *Symposium*. Note that for Philo the root issue is homosexual acts of any sort, not merely the *Symposium's* discussion of pederasty. Homosexual acts, he insists, are rejected as sins against nature by all Jews (cf. Rom 1:26–27).

> But the entertainment recorded by Plato is almost entirely connected with love; not that of men madly desirous or fond of women, or of women furiously in love with men, for these desires are accomplished *in accordance with a law of nature*, but with that *love which is felt by men for one another*; differing only in respect of age; for if there is anything in the account of that banquet elegantly said in praise of genuine love and heavenly Venus [goddess of love], it is introduced merely for the sake of making a neat speech; for the greater part of the book is occupied *by common, vulgar, promiscuous love, which takes away from the soul courage*, that which is the most serviceable of all virtues both in war and in peace, and which engenders in it instead the *female disease, and renders men men-women*, though they ought rather to be carefully trained in all the practices likely to give men valor. And having *corrupted the age of boys, and having metamorphosed them and removed them into the classification and character of women*, it has *injured their lovers also in the most important particulars, their bodies, their souls, and their properties*; for it follows of necessity that the mind of a *lover of boys* must be kept on the stretch towards the objects of his affection, and must have no acuteness

---

[15] *The Apocalypse of Abraham Together with the Testament of Abraham*, trans. G. H. Box and Moses Gaster (Charleston, SC: CreateSpace Independent Publishing, 2011).

of vision for any other object, but must be blinded by its desire as to all other objects private or common, and must so be *wasted away*, more especially if it fails in its objects. Moreover, the man's property must be diminished on two accounts, both from the owner's neglect and from his expenses for the beloved object. There is also another greater evil which affects the whole people, and which grows up alongside of the other, for *men who give into such passions produce solitude in cities, and a scarcity of the best kind of men, and barrenness, and unproductiveness. . . .* All these things are very attractive, being able by novelty of their imagination to allure the ears, but they are despised by the disciples of Moses, who in the abundance of their wisdom have learnt from their earliest infancy to love truth, and also continue to the end of their lives impossible to be deceived. (*On the Contemplative Life* 1:59–63)[16]

Philo describes human life allegorically by saying that each of us, as it were, cohabits with two argumentative wives: Pleasure and Virtue (*Sacrifices of Cain and Abel,* 1:20). His lengthy description of the vices associated with the life of pleasure calls to mind the "softness" characterizing the lifestyles of certain persons in Greek and Roman society that included homosexuality. This was rejected as sinful by Jews and Christians. The life of pleasure was considered "effeminate" or "womanly" (the term in italics includes the word for "female," *thēlu*):

> Know, then, my good friend, that if you become a votary of pleasure you will be all these things: . . . a demagogue, a bad steward, stiffnecked, *effeminate* [*thēludrias*], outcast, confused, discarded, mocking. (*Sacrifices of Cain and Abel* 1:32)

About this life of pleasure, Philo has much to say. It is an "effeminate" (*thrypsis*) luxury which stems from indulgence of the "irrational passion of pleasure" (*On the Cherubim* 1:12). Philo regards the "daughters of men" to whom the sons of God were attracted in Genesis 6 as symbolic of "dissolute and effeminate passions" (*On the Unchangeableness of God* 1:3). He says there are three kinds of persons: those who enjoy basic foods, those who enjoy healthy foods, and those who enjoy delicacies (*On Drunkenness* 1.214). The last of these three is skilled in making life luxurious and effeminate (1.219). Philo says he is aware of fathers who have taken to the countryside in shame so they can pursue a life of extreme delicacy (effeminacy and/or luxury; "*habrodiaitos*," *On Flight and Finding* 1.3). In *On Moses*, he also reflects on the possibility of an effeminate social trend:

---

[16] Translations of Philo are taken from *The Works of Philo Judaeus, the Contemporary of Josephus*, trans. C. D. Yonge, 4 vols. (London, England: Henry G. Bohn, 1854–55).

> When the chief of a nation begins to indulge in luxury and to turn aside to
> a delicate and effeminate life, then the whole of his subjects, or very nearly
> the whole, carry their desire for indulging the appetites of the belly and the
> parts below the belly beyond all reasonable bounds. (1:160)

The soft, luxurious life involves, *necessarily* for Philo, sexual excess and
deviancy. Indeed, an unbridled tongue, intemperate appetite, and sexual indulgence—including unnatural, homosexual acts—characterize the orientation of
some men:

> A man who is in every respect unfortunate and miserable, in his tongue,
> and his belly, and all his other members, since he uses the first for the utter-
> ance of things which ought to be secret and buried in silence, and the sec-
> ond he fills full of abundance of strong wine and immoderate quantities of
> food out of gluttony, and the rest of his members he uses for *the indulgence
> of unlawful desires and illicit connections, not only seeking to violate the
> marriage bed of others, but lusting unnaturally, and seeking to deface the
> manly character of the nature of man, and to change it into a womanlike
> appearance, for the sake of the gratification of his own polluted and accursed
> passions.* (*Special Laws* 2:49–50)

Philo describes such men as "delicate and effeminate of soul" (*habrodi-
aitois kai tēn psychēn ektethēlummenois*), indicating an orientation derived,
rather than innate, that is a corruption of male nature (*On Moses* 2.184). He
offers a vivid description of what this involved:

> Moreover, another evil, much greater than that which we have already
> mentioned, has made its way among and been let loose upon cities, namely,
> *the love of boys*, which formerly was accounted a great infamy even to be
> spoken of, but which sin is a subject of boasting not only to those who prac-
> tice it, but even to those who suffer it, and who, being accustomed to bearing
> the *affliction of being treated like women, waste away as to both their souls
> and bodies*, not bearing about them a single spark of a manly character to
> be kindled into a flame, but having even the hair of their heads conspicu-
> ously curled and adorned, and having their faces smeared with vermilion,
> and paint, and things of that kind, and having their eyes penciled beneath,
> and having their skins anointed with fragrant perfumes (for in such persons
> as these a sweet smell is a most seductive quality), and being well appointed
> in everything that tends to beauty or elegance, are not ashamed to devote their
> constant study and endeavors to the task of *changing their manly character
> [physin, nature] into an effeminate one [eis thēleian].* (*Special Laws* 3:37)

Note the following in this last quotation from Philo: he opposes pederasty,
gives a description of what is meant by "effeminate," and sees cross-dressing as
an example of changing one's nature. Moreover, pederasty is not condemned
as a form of child abuse, as in the present day when society opposes pedophilia,

but as a form of effeminacy. In other words, it is not merely sexual abuse of boys but "soul" abuse, corrupting them toward a soft, effeminate, homosexual lifestyle. Thus,

> He who is about to go through the operations of matrimony ought by all means first of all to cut away *concupiscence, reproving all lascivious and effeminate persons* as those who bring together superfluous mixtures which were not for the sake of the generation of children but *to gratify incontinent desires.*" (*Questions and Answers on Genesis* 3:61)

FLAVIUS JOSEPHUS

A number of relevant quotations come from the first-century Jewish historian Flavius Josephus. As with two other significant first-century Jewish authors in this study, Philo and Paul, Josephus sees homosexual acts as against nature. Those who argue that Paul does not understand homosexual acts as sins against nature in Romans 1:26–27 must explain why Philo and Josephus present similar arguments—to say nothing of similar arguments among non-Jewish, non-Christian authors such as Epictetus. Note the following quotations from Josephus. The final one references a time in the first century (after Jesus and Paul—during the war with Rome) when gangs of effeminate men terrorized Jerusalem.

> But then, what are our laws about marriage? That law owns no other mixture of sexes but that which nature has appointed, of a man with his wife, and that this be used only for the procreation of children. But it abhors the mixture of a male with a male; and if anyone does that, death is its punishment. (*Against Apion* 2:199)[17]

> Now the greatest part of offences with us are capital; as if anyone be guilty of adultery; if anyone force a virgin; if anyone be so impudent as to attempt sodomy with a male; or if, upon another's making an attempt upon him, he submits to be so used. There is also a law for slaves of the like nature, that can never be avoided. (*Against Apion* 2:215)

> And why do not the Eleans and Thebans abolish that *unnatural and impudent lust, which makes them lie with males*? For they will not show a sufficient sign of their repentance of what they of old thought to be very excellent, and very advantageous in their practices, unless they entirely avoid all such actions for the time to come: nay, such things are inserted into the body of their laws, and had once such a power among the Greeks, that they ascribed these *sodomitical practices* to the gods themselves, as a part of their good character; and, indeed, it was according to the same manner that the gods

---

[17] All translations of Josephus's works are taken from the translation by William J. Whiston (1828) in public domain, available on *BibleWorks*.

married their own sisters. This the Greeks contrived as an apology for their own *absurd and unnatural pleasures*. (*Against Apion* 2:273–75)

When this letter was brought to Herod, he did not think it safe for him to send one so handsome as was Aristobulus, in the prime of his life, for he was sixteen years of age, and of so noble a family, and particularly not to Antony, the principal man among the Romans, and one that *would abuse him in his amours*, and besides, one that *openly indulged himself in such pleasures as his power allowed him, without control*. (*Antiquities of the Jews* 15:29)

And during this time did the mischievous contrivances and courage [of John] corrupt the body of the Galileans; for these Galileans had advanced this John and made him very powerful, who made them suitable requital from the authority he had obtained by their means; for he permitted them to do all things that any of them desired to do, while their inclination to plunder was insatiable, as was their zeal in searching the houses of the rich; and for the murdering of the men, and abusing of the women, it was sport to them. They also devoured what spoils they had taken, together with their blood, and *indulged themselves in feminine wantonness*, without any disturbance, till they were satiated therewith; while *they decked their hair, and put on women's garments, and were besmeared all over with ointments; and that they might appear very comely, they had paints under their eyes, and imitated, not only the ornaments, but also the lusts of women, and were guilty of such intolerable uncleanness, that they invented unlawful pleasures of that sort.* And thus did they rove up and down the city, as in a brothel house, and defiled it entirely with their impure actions; nay, while their faces looked like the faces of women, they killed with their right hands: and when their walk was *effeminate*, they presently attacked men, and became warriors, and drew their swords from under their finely dyed cloaks, and ran everyone through whom they came to. (*The Jewish War* 4:558–63)

THE SIBYLLINE ORACLES[18]

Several quotations from the Sibylline Oracles also attest to an abhorrence of homosexual acts.

Immediately compulsion to impiety will come upon these men. Male will have intercourse with male and they will set up boys in houses of ill-fame and in those days there will be a great affliction among men and it will throw everything into confusion. (3.184–87)[19]

---

[18] The second oracle is likely a Christian addition to the collection of oracles, as the use of *arsenokoitein* suggests: "Do not practice homosexuality [*arsenokoitein*], do not betray information, do not murder" (Sibylline Oracles 2:73 in *Old Testament Pseudepigrapha*, vol. 1, ed. James H. Charlesworth, trans. J. J. Collins [New York, NY: Doubleday, 1983], 347). This word for homosexuality is not found outside Christian literature.

[19] *Old Testament Pseudepigrapha*, vol. 1, ed. James H. Charlesworth, trans. J. J. Collins (New York, NY: Doubleday, 1983), 366–67.

But quicken your thoughts in your breasts; evade unlawful cults; worship the Living One. Beware of adultery and homosexual intercourse with men. Raise your offspring and do not kill it. For the Immortal will be furious at anyone who commits these sins. (3.2.6.762–66)[20]

With you are found adulteries and illicit intercourse with boys. Effeminate and unjust, evil city, ill-fated above all. Alas, city of the Latin land, unclean in all things, maenad, rejoicing in vipers, as a widow you will sit by the banks, and the river Tiber will weep for you its consort. (5.162–70)[21]

Jewish writings during the era of the early church continued to prohibit homosexuality—there was no change in perspective, and there was no diversity of views.

THE MISHNAH AND TOSEFTA

Two Jewish collections of law from the second century AD, the Mishnah and the Tosefta, forbid practices that could lead to homosexual acts.

R. Juday says: An unmarried man may not herd cattle, nor may two unmarried men sleep under the same cloak. But the Sages permit it. (*Kiddushin* 4.14 [Mishnah])[22]

And two unmarried men should not sleep in a single cloak. (*Qiddushin* 5.10 E [Tosefta])[23]

These are the felons who are put to death by stoning. He who has sexual relations with (1) his mother, (2) with the wife of his father, (3) with his daughter-in-law, (4) with a male, and (5) with a cow. (*Sanhedrin* 7.4 [Mishnah])[24]

A significant Jewish text from the second or third century AD that interprets Leviticus is called *Sifra,* and it is frequently cited in the Babylonian Talmud. In this passage, *Sifra* is clear about the meaning of Leviticus 18:22 and 20:13:

"You shall not do as they do in the land of Egypt . . . and you shall not do as they do in the land of Canaan" (Lev 18:3). . . . And what did they do?

---

[20] *Book III of the Sibylline Oracles and Its Social Setting*, trans. Rieuwerd Buitenwerf (Boston, MA: Brill, 2003).

[21] *Old Testament Pseudepigrapha*, trans. J. J. Collins, 397.

[22] *The Mishnah*, trans. H. Danby (New York, NY: Clarendon, 1933).

[23] *The Tosefta*, trans. Jacob Neusner (New York, NY: Ktav, 1979).

[24] Jacob Neusner, *The Mishnah: A New Translation* (New Haven, CT: Yale University Press, 1988), 596.

A man married a man and a woman, and a man married a woman and her daughter, and a woman was married to two men.[25]

Regulations from the Babylonian Talmud—a document compiled at the end of the fifth century or beginning of the sixth—continue to condemn homosexual practice. The Babylonian Talmud quotes the second-century AD Jewish Mishnah first, and then adds commentary on it from rabbinic teaching over the centuries.

THE BABYLONIAN TALMUD[26] AND MIDRASH *RABBAH*

The following teaching relates to thirty commandments the "sons of Noah" (that is, all humans, particularly the Gentiles) allegedly accepted. The author asserts that the "sons of Noah" only abide by three of those commandments. The idea of the first law mentioned is that while Gentiles may be suspected of homosexual behavior, they at least do not go so far as to draw up marriage contracts (*kethubah*) between two men.

(i) they [Gentiles] do not draw up a kethubah document for males, (ii) they do not weigh flesh of the dead in the market, and (iii) they respect the Torah. (*Chittin* 92b)

Lesbianism is also mentioned in the Talmud:

Women who practice lewdness with one another are disqualified from marrying a priest. (*Yebamoth* 76a [fifth or sixth century AD])

Sanhedrin 54a, also fifth or sixth century AD, discusses the punishments for different sins mentioned in Leviticus 18, including homosexuality. Under discussion is the meaning of "the nakedness of your father" (Lev 18:8), which is said to reference sexual union either with one's father's wife, or one's father, or both. The conclusion is that, in the case of sex with one's father or uncle, a twofold penalty is incurred because both the commandment not to uncover one's father's nakedness and the commandment against same-sex unions in Leviticus 18:22 and 20:13 are broken.

[The] Mishnah [says:] He who commits sodomy with a male or a beast, and a woman that commits bestiality are stoned. . . . [The interpretation of the Mishnah] Gemara [is as follows:] Whence do I know that pederasty is punished by stoning?—Our Rabbis taught: [*If a man lieth also with mankind, as the lyings of a woman, both of them have committed an abomination:*

---

[25] Translated by Bernadette J. Brooten, *Love Between Women* (Chicago, IL: University of Chicago Press, 1996), 65.

[26] All translations of the Babylonian Talmud are taken from I. Epstein, ed., *The Babylonian Talmud* (London, England: The Soncino Press, 1948).

they shall surely be put to death; their blood shall be upon them.] A man—
excludes a minor; *that lieth also with mankind*—denotes whether an adult
or a minor; *as the lyings of a woman*—this teaches that there are two modes
of intimacy, both of which are punished when committed incestuously. . . .
[54b] This teaches the punishment: when do we derive the formal prohibition? From the verse, *Thou shalt not lie with mankind, as with womankind:
it is an abomination.* From this we learn the formal prohibition for him who
lies [with a male]: when do we know a formal prohibition for the person who
permits himself thus to be abused?—Scripture saith: There shall be no sodomite of the sons of Israel.

The same tractate, and others, have more to say on the issue of homosexual
unions. Also in these texts from the same period, note the concern to produce
biblical and rabbinic teaching on the issue—Scripture and tradition.

For it has been taught: *Therefore shall a man leave his father and his
mother* [Gen 2.24]. R. Eliezer said: His *father* means "his father's sister"; his
mother, "his mother's sister." . . . *And he shall cleave,* but not to a male; to his
wife, but not to his neighbor's wife. (*Sanhedrin* 58a)

[The discussion here regards Ham's sin against his father, Noah.] Rab and
Samuel [differ,] one maintaining that he castrated him, *whilst the other says
that he sexually abused him.* (*Sanhedrin* 70a)

Our Rabbis taught: Six things are unbecoming for a scholar. He should
not go abroad scented. . . . R. Abba the son of R. Hiyya b. Abba said in the
name of R. Johanan: This applies only to a place where people are suspected
of *pederasty.* (*Berakoth* 43b)

Samuel's father did not permit his daughters to go out with threads, nor
to sleep together; and he made *mikwa'oth* for them in the days of Nisan, and
had mats placed in the days of Tishri. (*Shabbath* 65a)

*How art thou fallen from heaven, O day star, son of the morning! How art
thou cut down to the ground, thou holesh [who didst cast lots] over the nations,*
etc. Rabbah son of R. Huna said: This teaches that he [Nebuchadnezzar]
cast lots over the royal chiefs to ascertain whose turn it was for pederasty.
(*Shabbath* 149b)

[It was stated in] the text: "Things which are permitted, yet others that
[are] forbidden, you many not permit it in their presence." Said R. Hisda: This
refers to Cutheans. Yet not [to] all people? Surely it was taught: Two brothers may bathe together, yet two brothers do not bathe [together] in Cabul.
(*Pesahim* 51a)

Our Rabbis taught, when the sun is in eclipse it is a bad omen for idolaters. . . . Our Rabbis taught, On account of four things is the sun in eclipse:

On account of an *Ab Beth din* who died and was not mourned fittingly; on account of a betrothed maiden who cried out aloud in the city and there was not [time] to save her; on account of *sodomy*, and on account of two brothers whose blood was shed at the same time. (*Sukkah* 29a)

Finally, *Leviticus Rabbah* may date from the fifth century AD, although it could be later. This text, like the Talmud, is consistent with what we have found in the earliest Jewish teaching of the Old Testament.

R. Huna says in the name of R. Jose: The generation of the Flood were only blotted out of the world on account of their having written hymenean songs for *sodomy*. (*Midrash Rabbah Leviticus* 23.9)[27]

CONCLUSION

For a period of about 2,000 years, all Jews everywhere taught that homosexual unions of any sort were sinful and against nature. On this point Christians fully agreed, even as they increasingly became a Gentile church in a culture that permitted homosexual acts of various sorts. Arguments were based on Scripture, for that was the authoritative basis for sexual ethics among both Jews and Christians.

---

[27] *Midrash Rabbah, Leviticus*, vol. 4, ed. H. Freedman and Maurice Simon, trans. Judah J. Slotki (London, England: The Soncino Press, 1961).

Creation, the Law, and the Gospel: New Testament Texts and Homosexuality

CHAPTER 13

THE NEW TESTAMENT TEXTS ADDRESSING HOMOSEXUALITY

INTRODUCTION

The following New Testament texts should be considered when discussing homosexuality. They offer no critique of the Old Testament texts that oppose homosexual acts. Rather, they affirm the same ethic. A more detailed consideration of several of these texts will follow, but here we lay out which texts from the New Testament deserve consideration.

MARRIAGE, ONE FLESH, AND THE IMPORTANCE OF GENESIS 2:24

Jesus's teaching on marriage, consistent with the Old Testament and Judaism, affirms heterosexual unions based on Genesis 2:24:

> But from the beginning of creation, "God made them male and female." "For this reason a man shall leave his father and mother and be joined to his wife, and the two shall become one flesh." So they are no longer two, but one flesh. Therefore what God has joined together, let no one separate. (Mark 10:6–9)

This passage and its parallel in Matthew 19:4–6 reference divorce and remarriage. They show that the creation story defined sexual relationships and limited marriage to a man and a woman. The obvious implication is that marriage is not between men and animals or people of the same gender. If homosexual practice were common in first-century Israel, Jesus might have developed his argument from Genesis 2:24 in that direction as well. As it was, though, the issue for Jews was not homosexual practice, which all abhorred, but divorce and remarriage, which was both common and addressed in various ways by rabbis.

Paul also references Genesis 2:24 to explain marriage in terms of becoming "one flesh." The Genesis passage is used to exclude extramarital sexual relations, such as with a prostitute:

> Do you not know that whoever is united to a prostitute becomes one body with her? For it is said, "The two shall be one flesh." (1 Cor 6:16)

Genesis 2:24 is used to describe marriage in Ephesians as well. Because the husband is one flesh with his wife, he should love, nourish, and tenderly care for her just as he does his own body:

> In the same way, husbands should love their wives as they do their own bodies. He who loves his wife loves himself. For no one ever hates his own body, but he nourishes and tenderly cares for it. . . . "For this reason a man will leave his father and mother and be joined to his wife, and the two will become one flesh." This is a great mystery. (Eph 5:28–29, 31–32)

The doctrine of spouses as "one flesh" undoubtedly stands behind Paul's view that the body of each spouse belongs to the other, and therefore neither should withhold sexual relations from the other:

> The husband should give to his wife her conjugal rights, and likewise the wife to her husband. For the wife does not have authority over her own body, but the husband does; likewise the husband does not have authority over his own body, but the wife does. (1 Cor 7:3–4)

Our point is that for Jesus—and for Mark and Matthew in their recording of Jesus's teaching—and for Paul, Genesis 2:24 is an important passage regarding sexual ethics and marriage. It can be used to address various issues, including homosexuality. Indeed, the creation narrative stands behind Paul's comments about idolatry and homosexuality in Romans 1:18–28. Homosexual relations are said to be "against nature," contrary to the natural coming together of male and female as one flesh in marriage.

WHAT DID THE JERUSALEM COUNCIL SAY
ABOUT GENTILE CHRISTIAN PRACTICES?

The decision of the Jerusalem Council regarding Gentile converts is recorded in Acts 15. The speaker in verses 19–21 is James, the half brother of Jesus and a leader in the church at Jerusalem:

> "Therefore I have reached the decision that we should not trouble those Gentiles who are turning to God, but we should write to them to abstain only from things polluted by idols and *from fornication* and from whatever has been strangled and from blood. For in every city, for generations past, Moses has had those who proclaim him, for he has been read aloud every sabbath in the synagogues." Then the apostles and the elders, with the consent of the whole church, decided to choose men from among their members and to send them to Antioch with Paul and Barnabas. They sent Judas called Barsabbas, and Silas, leaders among the brothers, with the following letter: "The brothers, both the apostles and the elders, to the believers of Gentile origin in Antioch and Syria and Cilicia, greetings. Since we have heard that certain persons who have gone out from us, though with no instructions from us, have said things to disturb you and have unsettled your minds, we have decided unanimously to choose representatives and send them to you, along with our beloved Barnabas and Paul, who have risked their lives for the sake of our Lord Jesus Christ. We have therefore sent Judas and Silas, who themselves will tell you the same things by word of mouth. For it has seemed good to the Holy Spirit and to us to impose on you no further burden than these essentials: that you abstain from what has been sacrificed to idols and from blood and from what is strangled and *from fornication*. If you keep yourselves from these, you will do well. Farewell." (Acts 15:19–29)

As various scholars have suggested over the past eighty years, the Jerusalem Council's discussion regarding Gentiles appears to involve reasoning based on the Holiness Code in Leviticus (Leviticus 17–26, particularly chapters 17–18). Ernst Haenchen, following an earlier argument by H. Waitz, notes that the decree in Acts 15:20 and 29 was based on the teaching in "Moses" (Acts 15:21), and, second, that the order of the stipulations in Acts 15:29 follows the order of those in Leviticus 17–18.[1]

1. Idolatry: Lev 17:8–9 forbids sacrifices that are idolatrous.
2. Blood: Lev 17:10, 12 states that no alien among the Israelites shall eat blood.

---

[1] Ernst Haenchen, *The Acts of the Apostles: A Commentary* (Philadelphia, PA: Westminster, 1971), 468–72, citing the argument laid out earlier by H. Waitz, "Das Problem des sogenannten Aposteldekrets," *Zeitschrift für Kirschengeschichte* 55 (1936): 227. See also Richard Bauckham, "Chapter 15: James and the Jerusalem Church," in *The Book of Acts in Its Palestinian Setting*, vol. IV, ed. R. Bauckham (Grand Rapids, MI: Eerdmans, 1995), 459–60.

3. Pouring out of the blood: Lev 17:13 stipulates that any animal killed for food must have its blood poured out so that the blood might not be consumed—hence nothing strangled should be eaten.

4. Sexual Immorality: Finally, Lev 18:26 forbids committing any of "these abominations." The abominations listed in vv. 3–23 include various sexual sins, for which the Canaanites had been removed from the land.

A third argument for the relation of Acts 15 to Leviticus 17–18 is that the stipulations in Acts 15 include prohibitions in the Holiness Code for the aliens living among the Israelites (cf. Lev 17:8, 10, 12–13; 18:26).[2] A fourth argument has been mentioned in a previous chapter: Jewish authors regularly turned to the Leviticus Holiness Code for their sexual teaching.[3] A fifth reason for relating Leviticus 17–18 to the Jerusalem Council's decision is that the post-apostolic church continued to engage these passages in their discussions of Christian ethics.[4] A sixth reason is that the Holiness Code does not require of aliens living among God's people obedience to circumcision laws, food laws, or the observance of special days.[5] It should, finally, be noted that included in the list of sexual sins in Leviticus 18 is the prohibition against homosexuality (Lev 18:22).

---

[2] See also Lev 16:29; 19:10, 33–40. In addition to the passages already listed, a number of others in the Mosaic law apply to foreigners (Exod 12:19; 12:48; 20:10; Lev 24:22; Num 15:14–16, 29; 19:10; 35:15; Deut 1:16; 5:14; 23:7; 24:17–22; 27:19). See Richard Bauckham, "James and the Jerusalem Church," 459. The issue is not settled. Ben Witherington III argues it is problematic to draw a parallel between Acts 15 and the Holiness Code's laws regarding aliens since Leviticus has to do with aliens living in Israel and not with Gentiles in the Gentile world (*The Acts of the Apostles: A Socio-Rhetorical Commentary* [Grand Rapids, MI: Eerdmans, 1998], 464–65). Yet this seems to miss the point: both Leviticus and Acts are addressing the situation of non-Jews living amid God's people—whether in Israel or the church. Witherington shifts the focus of interpretation from the sources to the setting of the commands: Gentile feasts associated with idolatry. Craig Keener, on the other hand, favors a common suggestion in rabbinic literature that is possibly also present before the first century AD: there were certain laws attributed to God's covenant with Noah (and therefore all humans). See Craig Keener, *Acts: An Exegetical Commentary,* vol. 3 (Grand Rapids, MI: Baker, 2014), especially 2,265–66.

[3] See James Thompson, *Moral Formation According to Paul* (Grand Rapids, MI: Baker Academic, 2011), chap. 6.

[4] See the discussion in Richard Bauckham, "James and the Jerusalem Church," 464–68.

[5] See also Eckhard Schnabel, *Paul the Missionary: Realities, Strategies, and Methods* (Downers Grove, IL: InterVarsity, 2008), 54–56. A possible seventh argument involves linking texts to one another based on a common word or phrase (in typical first-century Jewish fashion). The two phrases "in your midst" and "raise up" in Leviticus 17–18; Jer 12:16; and Zech 2:11 may explain James's scriptural application to the question in Acts 15. For this argument, see Richard Bauckham, "James and the Jerusalem Church," 461–62.

PAUL'S TEACHING ON HOMOSEXUALITY

The lengthiest discussion of homosexuality in the New Testament occurs in the following passage.

> Therefore God gave them up in the lusts of their hearts to impurity, to the degrading of their bodies among themselves, because they exchanged the truth about God for a lie and worshiped and served the creature rather than the Creator, who is blessed forever! Amen. For this reason God gave them up to degrading passions. Their women exchanged natural intercourse for unnatural, and in the same way also the men, giving up natural intercourse with women, were *consumed* [*exekauthēsan*, from *ekkaiō*] with *passion* [*en tē orexei*] for one another. Men committed *shameless acts* [*aschēmosunēn*] with men and received in their own persons the due penalty for their error. And since they did not see fit to acknowledge God, God gave them up to a debased mind and to things that should not be done. They were filled with every kind of wickedness, evil, covetousness, malice. Full of envy, murder, strife, deceit, craftiness, they are gossips, slanderers, God-haters, insolent, haughty, boastful, inventors of evil, rebellious toward parents, foolish, faithless, heartless, ruthless. They know God's decree, that those who practice such things deserve to die—yet they not only do them but even applaud others who practice them. (Rom 1:24–32)

Romans 1:27 has several words of interest, noted in italics and with the Greek terms bracketed. The first two words suggest uncontrolled sexual desire and passion, and the third suggests an act considered shameful. The "due penalty for their error" has been variously understood as a painful condition due to anal intercourse or to some sexually transmitted disease. It may, however, simply be a way of saying sexual sin is a sin against one's own body (cf. 1 Cor 6:18), and homosexual sin is a changing of one's order of nature (*T. Naph.* 3:3–4). Epictetus speaks of homosexuals "losing the man" (*Disc.* 2:10); Philo understands the homosexual to have defaced his manly character (*Spec. Laws* 2:50) and to be wasting away in soul and body (*Spec. Laws* 3:37); and Aeschines speaks of the homosexual who has "sinned against his own body" (*Against Timarchus* 1:185; also 194). Jewish thought involves the notion that the penalty of sin pursues the sinner (cf. Wis 14:30; John 9:1).

Another important passage addressing homosexuality appears in Paul's letter to the Corinthians. The NRSV translation will be quoted first, but the Greek must be considered in order to understand what Paul has in mind.

> Do you not know that wrongdoers will not inherit the kingdom of God? Do not be deceived! *Fornicators, idolaters, adulterers, male prostitutes, sodomites* [*malakoi oute arsenokoitai*, literally, "neither soft (effeminate) men nor homosexuals"], thieves, the greedy, drunkards, revilers, robbers—none of these will inherit the kingdom of God. And this is what some of you used to

be. But you were washed, you were sanctified, you were justified in the name
of the Lord Jesus Christ and in the Spirit of our God. (1 Cor 6:9–11)

The last two Greek terms of verse 9, *malakoi* and *arsenokoitai*, "soft men"
and "men having sex with one another" (to offer a literal translation), have
been variously translated. (A whole chapter will be devoted to examining
1 Cor 6:9–11 in greater detail.) The ESV of 2002 has translated this phrase
as "nor men who practice homosexuality." That is, the two terms are taken
together. The NIV has "nor male prostitutes nor homosexual offenders," and
Today's New International Version has "male prostitutes nor practicing homosexuals." The term *malakos* means "soft," and it carries clear connotations of
effeminate behavior, orientation, and identity and homosexual activity. "Male
prostitute," therefore, is too limiting.

The term translated "sodomites" in the NRSV is *arsenokoitai*, which cor-
responds to the phrase *arsenos koitēn* in Leviticus 20:13 (LXX). Paul seems to
have coined the single term from this Septuagint reference, so he is possibly
affirming this Old Testament law for Christians—not just deriving his vocabulary from the Old Testament.

We find another interesting passage later in the same epistle:

> Does not *nature* [*physis*] itself teach you that if a man wears long hair, it
> is degrading to him, but if a woman has long hair, it is her glory? For her hair
> is given to her for a covering. (1 Cor 11:14–15)

First Corinthians 11:2–16 is speaking against the confusion of genders
in appearance and in worship. Some interpret the word "nature" in verse 14
to mean "convention." After all, men *can* grow long hair. There were people
groups, such as the Parthians or Germans, so the argument goes, whose men
wore long hair in the first century. Writing at the end of the second century,
Clement of Alexandria discusses ethnic groups in which the men had long
hair (*The Instructor*).[6] Still, an alternative interpretation needs to be considered: Paul does indeed mean "natural," not "conventional." He does not intend
to suggest men cannot grow long hair or that the convention of long-haired
men was unknown in the first century. Rather, he is associating long hair with
effeminacy, and it is what long hair symbolizes that he considers "against
nature." As we have seen elsewhere, ancient Jews, Christians, and even some
pagans deemed unnatural any behavior or attire that seemed inconsistent with
one's biological gender. Jewish, Greco-Roman, and early Christian texts can
be cited in support of this view.[7]

---

[6] The long-haired locusts of Rev 9:7–8 likely symbolize Parthian warriors.

[7] See, e.g., Sirach 9:2; Susanna 31–32; *Sentences of Pseudo-Phocylides*, 110–14; Philo, *Special Laws*, 3.7; Josephus, *The Wars of the Jews*, 4.9.10; *mBava Kamma*, 8.6; Clement of Alexandria, *Paedagogus*, 3.11; Gaius Musonius Rufus, Lecture XXI; Plutarch, *Old Men in Public*

First Thessalonians gives us a window into the teaching Paul gave to new Gentile converts, since he writes a "reminder" of what he had said to a congregation he recently established.[8] His teaching to new converts included instruction regarding sexual ethics:

> For this is the will of God, your sanctification: that you *abstain from sexual immorality*; that each one of you know how to *control his own body* in holiness and honor, not in the *passion of lust* (*pathei epithymias*) like the Gentiles who do not know God; that no one transgress and wrong his brother in this matter, because the Lord is an avenger in all these things, as we told you beforehand and solemnly warned you. For God has not called us for impurity, but in holiness. Therefore whoever disregards this, disregards not man but God, who gives his Holy Spirit to you. (1 Thess 4:3–8)

On the one hand, one might understand this passage primarily as a teaching about marriage as the only appropriate venue for sexual expression—which would fit our argument well. This view is based on understanding "control his own body" as a reference to marriage. Yet behind this translation of the NRSV is a more ambiguous statement in the Greek: literally, "acquire/control his vessel." If "vessel" refers to a wife, as in 1 Peter 3:7, then the meaning in 1 Thessalonians 4:4 is actually that one should acquire a wife in holiness and honor.

However, "vessel" may also denote the male sexual organ, as perhaps in 1 Samuel 21:5 ("the vessels of the young men are holy"). If one follows this interpretation, 1 Thessalonians 4:4 may more generally reference controlling sexual passion. Thus, while one might understand "wrong his brother" in verse 6 as a reference to adultery, the text might equally be a reference to homosexuality. Strengthening such a reading is the fact that Romans 1:24–28 and Ephesians 4:18–19 also associate the Gentiles' not knowing God with homosexual acts. In addition, Romans 1:27 speaks of being on fire with desire and engaging in same-sex intercourse. Such arguments are not conclusive, but understanding verse 4 in terms of controlling sexual desire rather than acquiring a wife was an interpretation known in the patristic era. John Chrysostom, for instance, understood 1 Thessalonians 4:4 to refer to gaining control over sexual passion (*Homilies on 1 Thessalonians* V).[9]

Affairs; Epictetus, *Discourses*, 3:1; Dio Chrysostom, *Discourses* 33, 52; Juvenal, *Satire* II, 90–100; Cicero, *In Catilinam*, II, x. 22–23; Dionysius of Halicarnassus, 7.9; Pseudo-Lucian, *Affairs of the Heart* 3; Seneca, *Epistles*, 95.24; Horace, *Epode* 11; Lucius Apuleius, *The Golden Ass*, II.

[8] To his credit (given what he says about Rom 6:17), Victor Paul Furnish says of 1 Thess 4:1–8 that we have here Paul's "counsels" for new converts, perhaps for baptismal catechesis (*1 Thessalonians, 2 Thessalonians,* ANTC [Nashville, TN: Abingdon, 2007], 88).

[9] John Chrysostom, "Homilies on Thessalonians" in *Nicene and Post-Nicene Fathers*, vol. 13, trans. John A. Broadus, ed. Philip Schaff (Peabody, MA: Hendrickson, 1994), 344–45

The last pertinent passage from Paul's letters contains a direct reference to homosexuality.

> Now we know that the law is good, if one uses it legitimately. This means understanding that the law is laid down not for the innocent but for the lawless and disobedient, for the godless and sinful, for the unholy and profane, for those who kill their father or mother, for murderers, fornicators, *sodomites* [*arsenokoitais*], slave traders, liars, perjurers, and whatever else is contrary to the sound teaching that conforms to the glorious gospel of the blessed God, which he entrusted to me. (1 Tim 1:8–11)

The term translated in the NRSV as "sodomites" in verse 10 is the same term employed in 1 Corinthians 6:9–11 (discussed above). Its appearance here is most appropriate, for Paul has the law in view (v. 8), and it is in Leviticus 18 and 20 that the two words Paul combines into one appear beside each other.

TWO FURTHER TEXTS: JUDE 7 AND 2 PETER 2:7–9

Remarkably, Jude 7 is omitted in significant presentations of the issue of homosexuality and the Bible.[10] Recall that these passages were discussed in detail in chapter 10. In these last two New Testament passages to consider, the reference to Sodom clarifies that homosexuality is in view when sexual immorality is mentioned.

> Likewise, Sodom and Gomorrah and the surrounding cities, which, in the same manner as they, indulged in *sexual immorality [ekporneusasai] and pursued unnatural lust [apelthousai opisō sarkos heteras]*, serve as an example by undergoing a punishment of eternal fire. (Jude 7)

> If he rescued Lot, a righteous man greatly distressed by *the licentiousness of the lawless* (for that righteous man, living among them day after day, was tormented in his righteous soul by their lawless deeds that he saw and heard), then the Lord knows how to rescue the godly from trial, and to keep the unrighteous under punishment until the day of judgment. (2 Pet 2:7–9)

Second Peter 2 appears to be an edited version of Jude. While "unnatural lust" is not repeated in 2 Peter, Sodom's sexual sin is still in view, as evidenced by the term "licentiousness" (*aselgeia*). This terminology still includes homosexual acts but also encompasses sexual sin in general. In chapter 10, we noted that some scholars see Jude 7 as having to do with unnatural lust of men for

---

[10] For example, Jeffrey Siker somehow omits this verse in his article on homosexuality in *Dictionary of Scripture and Ethics,* ed. J. Green, J. Lapsley, R. Miles, and A. Verhey (Grand Rapids, MI: Baker, 2011), 371–74. (He also omits any discussion of 2 Pet 2:7–9.) The article raises questions about how to understand and apply biblical texts dealing with homosexuality. Siker leans toward a dismissive reading of Scripture on this issue.

angels and not homosexual lust. Here we repeat that 2 Peter 2:7–9 omits any reference to angels and keeps the focus on sexual immorality. We might also add that the men of Sodom, even if they knew the angels were angels, wanted to engage with angels who had assumed the form of human *males*. The attempt to limit these texts to nonsexual sins and nonhomosexual acts seems strained.

Conclusion

These texts present a uniform position on the issue of homosexuality that is consistent with the Old Testament. Homosexual acts are considered sins characteristic of the life believers have left behind. To continue in such a practice means exclusion from the kingdom of God and the punishment of eternal fire. It is a most heinous sin, twisting God's intent in creation for sex between a husband and wife. There is simply no deviation from this perspective in all of Scripture. This point is worth expanding in the next section: when homosexual acts are considered sinful, then general references to sexual sin should be understood to include homosexual acts.

GENERAL TEACHING ON SEXUAL ETHICS IN THE NEW TESTAMENT

We might add to our list of texts on homosexuality from the previous section a large number of passages that pertain to homosexuality but do not explicitly mention it. These texts use general terms for sexual desire, excess, and sin. The reason for studying such passages is simple: if homosexual practices were considered sinful, then general terms for sexual sin would include homosexual practices, whatever else was also in view. One peculiar argument found in popular discussions about the Bible and homosexuality is that same-gender sexual acts are permissible because only a few biblical texts address the issue. While this constitutes frightfully poor hermeneutics (if we were to count texts to establish doctrine, we would deny the virgin birth and possibly begin to advocate bestiality), it is also simply wrong. Numerous texts are added to the explicit texts addressing homosexual practices once we include the general references to sexual sins and understand that the basis for sexual ethics in Scripture lies in the husband and wife becoming one flesh. On such a reading, there are remarkably many texts to note.

Porneia

The word *porneia* and its cognates (*porneuō, pornos*) are used for various types of sexual immorality. As Roy Ciampa notes:

> The term *pornos* may be taken as a catch-all term for people who engage in any of those sexual relationships explicitly or implicitly prohibited in the OT. The term does not refer to a concrete list of particular sexual activities,

but serves as a general term for illicit sexual activity, especially any sexual activity that takes place outside the marital context. It would also include rape, adultery, incest, same-sex relations, bestiality and marital relations during the menstrual period among other things. In [1 Cor.] 5:1 Paul uses the related term *porneia* (sexual immorality) in referring to the incestuous relationship between a man and (presumably) his stepmother (Lev 18:8; 20:11; cf. Ezek. 22:10).[11]

Context sometimes clarifies which type of sexual immorality is in view, and the form *pornē* refers specifically to female prostitutes. In the New Testament the term *pornos* is used fifty-two times in forty-nine verses. A number of these occurrences include a prohibition against homosexuality since it was considered a prime example of sexual immorality or "fornication" for Jews and Christians. Each use of this term needs to be considered with reference to the possibility that homosexuality is a part of the prohibition in view. For brevity's sake, only three occurrences are noted here: Matthew 15:19; Acts 15:20; and Ephesians 5:3.

> For out of the heart come evil intentions, murder, *adultery (moicheia)*, *fornication (porneia)*, theft, false witness, slander. (Matt 15:19)

Here we know that *porneia* does not mean "adultery" because the term preceding it specifically means "adultery." It is therefore used as a general term for sexual immorality in Matthew 15:19.

> We should write to them to abstain only from things polluted by idols and *from fornication (tēs porneias)* and from whatever has been strangled and from blood. (Acts 15:20)

As we discussed in the previous section, the list of things forbidden for Gentile Christians by the Jerusalem Council in Acts 15 appears to be taken from the Leviticus Holiness Code (Leviticus 17–26). In Leviticus 18 and 20, various sexual sins are forbidden, including homosexuality (Lev 18:22; 20:13). The letter to the Gentile believers in Acts 15:20, therefore, includes a warning against sexual sin in general, including incest, homosexual practices, and bestiality in particular.

The term probably has a general sense in Ephesians 5:3 as well:

> But *fornication (porneia)* and *impurity of any kind*, or greed, must not even be mentioned among you, as is proper among saints.

---

[11] Roy Ciampa, "'Flee Sexual Immorality': Sex and the City of Corinth," in *The Wisdom of the Cross: Exploring 1 Corinthians*, ed. Brian Rosner (Downers Grove, IL: InterVarsity, 2011), 110.

Darkened Understanding and Its Effects

Consider Ephesians 4:18–29:

> They are darkened in their understanding, alienated from the life of God because of their ignorance and hardness of heart. They have lost all sensitivity and have *abandoned themselves to licentiousness, greedy to practice every kind of impurity.*

Note that the idea of progressive faltering in this text is reminiscent of the argument in Romans 1:18–28. A darkened understanding leads to an insensitivity to what is right, and this leads to various sins, including sexual immorality. A similar argument can be found in the apocryphal book of Wisdom, chapters 13 and 14.

Three terms are used in Ephesians 4:19 that refer to or include sexual immorality, further supporting the idea that in a biblical text using general terms for sexual sin, particular sins (like homosexuality) may be included without being specified:

- *aselgeia*: debauchery, licentiousness, sensuality. See also Mark 7:22; Rom 13:13; 2 Cor 12:21; Gal 5:19; 1 Pet 4:3; 2 Pet 2:2, 7, 18; Jude 4.
- *akatharsia*: uncleanness, impurity, immorality. See also Matt 23:27; Rom 1:24; 6:19; 2 Cor 12:21; Gal 5:19; Eph 4:19; 5:3; Col 3:5; 1 Thess 2:3; 4:7.
- *pleonexia*: greediness, insatiableness, covetousness. See also Mark 7:22; Luke 12:15; Rom 1:29; 2 Cor 9:5; Eph 5:3; Col 3:5; 1 Thess 2:5; 2 Pet 2:3, 14.

Passions out of Control

In Romans 13:13, we find three terms referring to passions out of control.

> Let us live honorably as in the day, not in *reveling* (*kōmos*) and drunkenness, not in *debauchery* (*koitē*) and *licentiousness* (*aselgeia*), not in quarreling and jealousy.

The three Greek terms *kōmos, koitē*, and *aselgeia* suggest sexual immorality. The first term could also refer to excessive feasting, thus capturing the idea of one's passions being out of control in various ways. The term appears again in Galatians 5:21, where the ESV and NIV translate it as "orgies" and the NRSV translates it as "reveling." The term appears in 1 Peter 4:3 in a list of sins that begins with licentiousness (*aselgeia*) and passions, continues with three terms (including *kōmos*, reveling) that suggest excessive partying, and concludes with lawless idolatry. In Romans 1, Paul's reason for choosing homosexuality as the sin to highlight is that it illustrates an extreme, a turning away from God's created order. In Jewish references to Sodom, homosexuality represents an extreme sin—as we have seen. Thus, while *kōmos* is a general term, it could well be used in reference to homosexual acts and practices.

The second term simply means "bed," so, as in English, it can refer to sexual acts done in bed. In the Greek Old Testament, one finds the phrase "to know the bed of" as a way of referencing sexual intercourse (Num 31:17). The third term, *aselgeia*, means licentiousness, sensuousness, lewdness, or debauchery. It appears in sin lists of Mark 7:22; 2 Corinthians 12:21; Galatians 5:19; Ephesians 4:19; 1 Peter 4:3; 2 Peter 2:2, 7, 18; and Jude 4. In 2 Peter 2:7 the term is used to describe the sin of Sodom. Here a general term describing excessive "lawlessness" in sexual matters includes homosexuality.

Asōtia

Another term translated "debauchery" is *asōtia*:

> Do not get drunk with wine, for that is *debauchery* (*asōtia*); but be filled with the Spirit. (Eph 5:18)

This passage illustrates the close connection between drunkenness, excessive feasting, and sexual immorality. Several of the Greek terms we have been considering capture the scene of a wild party, where excesses of all sorts are pursued. Sexual excesses come in a variety of forms, though homosexuality is considered one of the chief among them (with Sodom as the great example for Jews and Christians). There is no Jewish or ancient Christian text that regards homosexual acts or homosexual marriage as morally permissible and no text that permits homosexual acts within a stable, loving relationship or marriage. Homosexual acts committed in any and every context are considered to be like any other sexual sin; they represent sexual passion gone wrong.

Desire, Flesh

The word group referencing "desire" (*epithymein* and cognates) occurs fifty times in the New Testament, though not always as sinful desire and not always as sexual desire. Often it functions in relation to "flesh" (*sarx*) and its cognates, which occur 160 times (not always as a moral term, of course). "Flesh" is the locus of the senses (taste, touch, smell, hearing, and sight), the seat of desire and passion. The Christian life involves addressing desires that have gone awry outside of life in Christ:

> And those who belong to Christ Jesus have crucified the flesh with its passions and desires. (Gal 5:24)

> Put to death, therefore, whatever in you is earthly: fornication (*porneia*), impurity (*akatharsia*), passion (*pathos*), evil desire (*epithymian kakēn*), and greed (*pleonexia*) (which is idolatry). (Col 3:5)

. . . treacherous, reckless, swollen with conceit, lovers of pleasure (*philēdonos*) rather than lovers of God . . . (2 Tim 3:4)

. . . someone who is blameless, married only once, whose children are believers, not accused of debauchery (*asōtia*) and not rebellious. (Titus 1:6)

For we ourselves were once foolish, disobedient, led astray, slaves to various passions (*epithymia*) and pleasures (*ēdonē*), passing our days in malice and envy, despicable, hating one another. (Titus 3:3)

But one is tempted by one's own desire (*epithymia*), being lured and enticed by it; then, when that desire has conceived, it gives birth to sin, and that sin, when it is fully grown, gives birth to death. (Jas 1:14–15)

. . . especially those who indulge their flesh in depraved lust (*epithymia miasmou*), and who despise authority. Bold and willful, they are not afraid to slander the glorious ones. (2 Pet 2:10)

CONCLUSION

Passages such as these demonstrate that the biblical authors used general terms to reference sexual sin, portraying it as the result of unchecked desire. Desire can find expression in ways that are simply wrong, and both its excess and misdirection were—and are—major ways in which worldly society differs from that of God's people. Homosexuality, like adultery or bestiality, is one sin among others in which desire has gone unchecked and is misplaced. Such sins are never permitted among those who have been washed, sanctified, and made righteous in the Lord Jesus Christ and by the work of the Holy Spirit (1 Cor 6:11).

In this chapter we have surveyed the particular texts and the general terms for sexual immorality in the New Testament. We have suggested there is a uniform position taken in the New Testament on the issue of homosexuality, that it is consistent with the Old Testament, and that the early church's understanding of sexual immorality was well enough known that general terms for immorality could be used without explanation. The church, as also the Jews, was clearly distinct from the larger society in its sexual ethic. Moreover, sexual practices were a result of forces at work in the human heart, whether the sinful flesh or the empowering presence of the Holy Spirit. In the following chapters, several key New Testament texts will be examined further in light of the cultural context of the Greco-Roman world.

CHAPTER 14

LAW, HOLINESS, AND PURITY FOR GOD'S PEOPLE: 1 CORINTHIANS 5–7

INTRODUCTION

We have, so far, concluded that Jewish literature before and after the beginnings of the church uniformly opposed homosexual acts. Any argument that the church permitted homosexual practices is an argument that the church opposed its Jewish context in favor of Greco-Roman morality. This may apply to the Nicolaitans of Pergamum or the followers of "Jezebel" in Thyatira (Rev 2:6,15), but as a thesis regarding the church and the New Testament writers, this contention borders on preposterous. All the evidence strongly supports that the early church affirmed Jewish views on sexuality.

Both Judaism and the early church derived their ethical convictions from the authoritative Old Testament—the Scriptures. That is, neither Jews nor Christians held their views on sexual ethics merely as cultural mores; both based their stances on their interpretation of Scripture. Christians, moreover, had to determine just how this canon of authority should apply to Gentile converts. This was true as much for Paul as any other early Christian writer.

The church reevaluated certain Jewish practices in light of Christ and its mission. From its earliest times the church revised Jewish practices in regard to circumcision, food laws, purity laws, sacrifices, and observance of the Jewish calendar—as is recorded in Acts 15; Galatians 4:10; 5:6, 11; 6:15; 1 Corinthians 7:18–19; Philippians 3:2–3; Romans 2:25–29; 14–15; and Colossians 2:11, 16–17. Jesus and his followers revised Jewish practices regarding divorce and remarriage, and some practiced celibacy for the sake of mission in the context of persecution and suffering (Matt 19:10–12; 1 Corinthians 7). Yet they did not revise their basic sexual ethic, including what they believed about homosexual practices.

Greek and Roman sexual practices posed a challenge to the early church, so Christians had to articulate their counterviews according to the authorities that guided them. At times sexual immorality occurred in the churches as Gentiles were "taught in Christ,"[1] but these errors were corrected and condemned as inconsistent with the Christian faith.

Almost hopelessly confusing this issue for some Christians today is the erroneous notion that Paul's statements about the Mosaic law involved a complete rejection of the Old Testament law for Christians. Our question in this chapter, then, is, Did Paul see the Old Testament Law as an authoritative guide for Christian ethics? The answer is, without question, yes.

PAUL, THE LAW, AND THE CHURCH OF CHRIST JESUS

Paul used the Old Testament law as a guide for Christians. To establish this, one might examine how Paul uses it in a passage such as 1 Corinthians 5–7, where he addresses several matters related to sexual ethics. This has been the subject of a book by Brian Rosner, who demonstrates against the tide of much scholarship that Paul's ethical arguments were an articulation and application of the Old Testament as an authority for believers.[2] More recently,

---

[1] See Eph 4:20–24: "That is not the way you learned Christ! For surely you have heard about him and were taught in him, as truth is in Jesus. You were taught to put away your former way of life, your old self, corrupt and deluded by its lusts, and to be renewed in the spirit of your minds, and to clothe yourselves with the new self, created according to the likeness of God in true righteousness and holiness." One could, of course, say that the churches debated such issues. That there were different views on sexual ethics in some of the churches is clear from the fact that New Testament writings had to correct certain people. We know what Paul's teaching on sexual ethics was precisely because, for example, certain Corinthians in the church were practicing incest, going to prostitutes, and refraining from sex within their marriages (1 Corinthians 5–7). Our point is not that there was a unanimous view on sexual ethics in the churches but that the New Testament authors—and early church authors in general—were unanimous in their view that practices such as adultery, prostitution, fornication, and homosexual acts were sinful. Indeed, the issue in the church today is similar. Those with a high view of biblical authority—the authority of the Old Testament Scriptures and the apostolic witness in the New Testament— accept that homosexual practice is a sin, whereas those promoting homosexual practice either discount the biblical witness in one way or another or deny the Bible's authority, even though they accept that the ethic to which the Bible testifies condemns homosexual practice.

[2] Brian S. Rosner, *Paul, Scripture and Ethics: A Study of 1 Corinthians 5–7* (Leiden, Netherlands: Brill, 1994). The history of scholarship on this issue, including anti-Semitic scholarship, is also part of Rosner's work. Rosner has more recently explored how to determine which parts of the law still applied to Christians for Paul and which did not. *Paul and the Law: Keeping the Commandments of God*, New Studies in Biblical Theology (Downers Grove, IL: Apollos, 2013). A common answer to this question (which Rosner dates back at least to Origen—see 36) has been that the civil (or social) and ceremonial (or cultic) law applied only to Israel and did not continue as an authority for Christians, whereas the moral law did. Rosner, however, argues that the question is not which parts of the law remained authoritative for Christians according to Paul but what kind of "law"—law as commandments, prophecy, or wisdom—remained authoritative (29–30). He concludes that Paul repudiated the law as Jewish commandments for Christians but

James Thompson's excellent *Moral Formation According to Paul* has corroborated this thesis and expanded the argument.[3] Such careful studies are needed because some scholarship since the early twentieth century has perpetuated a notion that Paul's qualifications of the law were actually repudiations of the law as a guide for believers. Nothing could be further from the truth as far as Jesus and the early church were concerned.

In 1 Corinthians 5, Paul opposes the "sexual immorality" of a man living with his father's wife. This may be the man's stepmother or his real mother. The language "father's wife" seems to have been chosen by Paul because it involves an allusion—an appeal—to texts in Leviticus and Deuteronomy, as will be demonstrated shortly. Thus, it is irrelevant whether the woman is the man's real mother or not: the law covers both situations. And such behavior was not even tolerated among the Gentiles, as Paul puts it (1 Cor 5:1).

Among various primary sources indicating Greek disapproval of sex with one's mother[4] is a play by Sophocles, *Oedipus Rex* (fifth century BC). The main character of the play, Oedipus, was a man who survived to adulthood despite his parents' trying to kill him because of a prophecy that, should he live, he would kill his parents. As a man Oedipus was traveling from Corinth (note the city) to Thebes when he met and killed another man who, unbeknown to Oedipus, was his father. In Thebes he married Jocosta, whom he discovered

---

reappropriated the law as prophecy and wisdom. This hermeneutical solution to the question of Paul's use of the law is not, in our view, successful. For Paul the issue is not whether to read the Law as commandments, prophecy, or wisdom; after all, Paul frequently utters commandments, gives lists of sins, and calls for judgment within the churches. Rather, Paul's negative comments on the law concern its impotence. Sin is a power; the law is not. Through the law comes knowledge of sin but no deliverance (Rom 3:19–20). The law continues to function as moral commandment for Christians (Rom 13:9–10), but once Christ is "put on," he empowers believers to cease making provision for the flesh (Rom 13:14). Freedom from the law is not freedom from its righteous commandments but freedom from the reign of sin in the flesh through the law that led to death and freedom to live through Christ in the Spirit that leads to righteousness. (This is Paul's point in Romans 6–8.)

[3] James W. Thompson, *Moral Formation According to Paul*. Also see Eckart Reinmuth, *Geist und Gesetz: Studien zur Voraussetzung und Inhalt der paulinschen Paränese* (Berlin, Germany: Evangelische Verlagsanstalt, 1985); Peter J. Tomson, *Paul and the Jewish Law: Halakah in the Letters of the Apostle to the Gentiles*, Jewish Christians in Christian Literature, Section 3, vol. 1 (Assen, Netherlands: Van Gorcum & Co., 1990) (noted also by James Thompson). Tomson concludes, "Halakah [Jewish Law] was pervasive in Paul's thought" (264).

[4] According to Sextus Empiricus, ca. AD 200, "With us it is forbidden to have intercourse with one's mother, whereas with the Persians this sort of marriage is very much the custom" (*Outlines of Pyrrhonism* 1.151–52; *Sextus Empiricus: Outlines of Pyrrhonism*, translated by Benson Mates [New York, NY: Oxford University Press, 1996]). Also, as Brian Rosner ("Temple Prostitution in 1 Corinthians 6:12–20," *Novum Testamentum* 40, [Oct. 1998]: 340) notes, Dio Cassius (*Roman History* 58:22) refers to sexual relations between a man and his stepmother as "criminal," and Martial (*Epigrammata* 4.16) says there is no acquittal for such an offense.

was his mother after inquiring into the reason for the gods' visiting a plague on the city. As a result Oedipus was ostracized from Thebes.

This popular play, written centuries before Paul's birth, built on the common association of pre-first-century Corinth with sexual sin, and it tells the story of a person committing sins that not even the Gentiles or the immoral gods of Greece permitted: patricide and incest with one's mother. The Old Testament guides Paul's view on this issue, and he echoes the laws of Leviticus 18:8; 20:11 and Deuteronomy 22:30; 27:20. While Gentiles would have understood Paul's verdict that one guilty of incest with his mother should be ostracized, Paul's reasoning entails a direct quote of a repeated phrase from Deuteronomy: "purge the evil from your midst" (cf. 1 Cor 5:13; Deut 13:5; 17:7, 12; 19:13, 19; 21:21; 22:21, 24; 24:7).

Deuteronomy 17:8–12 shows the link between Paul's conclusion in 1 Corinthians 5 and his comments about judging in the congregation in 1 Corinthians 6:1. Deuteronomy 17 describes how difficult judgments regarding bloodshed are to be made in the community by Levitical priests and the judge so that evil might be purged from Israel's midst (vv. 8–13). Similarly, 1 Corinthians 6:1–6 addresses the authority of Christians to render judgment within the community. Roy Ciampa and Brian Rosner suggest that Old Testament passages calling for unity between brothers also underlie Paul's comments (Gen 13:8; Exodus 18; Deuteronomy 1; Ps 133:1).[5]

In 1 Corinthians 7, Paul says, "Circumcision is nothing, and uncircumcision is nothing; but obeying the commandments of God is everything" (v. 19). Paul's distinction between laws regarding circumcision and the "commandments of God" would be surprising to a Jew. It shows that he saw circumcision not as a matter of spiritual life but only as a matter of Jewish ethnic identity. Yet the "commandments" of the Old Testament continue to apply to the church. Peter Tomson argues that these commandments (1 Cor 7:17–20), Paul's "rule for all the churches," entail the three commandments for Gentiles (Acts 15:29) of "no idolatry, unchastity, and bloodshed."[6] Wherever and however the line is to be drawn between Jewish practices such as circumcision and still relevant laws for believers, laws regarding sex unquestionably continue to apply to the church. Old Testament laws repeatedly underlie what Paul says to the Corinthian church about sexuality and marriage, including his teaching on incest (1 Corinthians 5; Lev 18:8; 20:11; Deut 22:30; 27:20), adulterers (1 Cor 6:9; Exod 20:14; Lev 20:10; Deut 5:18), homosexuals (1 Cor 6:9; Lev 18:22; 20:13), and persons going to prostitutes (1 Cor 6:15–16; Lev 19:29; Prov 7:24–27). While more might be said about Paul's use of the Old Testament in

---

[5] Roy E. Ciampa and Brian S. Rosner, *The First Letter to the Corinthians*, The Pillar New Testament Commentary (Grand Rapids, MI: Eerdmans, 2010), 224.

[6] Peter Tomson, *Paul and the Jewish Law*, 274.

1 Corinthians 5–7, this may suffice to demonstrate that his statements about ethics, particularly sexual ethics, are based on Old Testament law.

Second, while the New Testament does abrogate laws that apply merely to Jewish culture and practices, no New Testament author foregoes Old Testament laws having to do with ethics, unless it is to "tighten" a law where a supposed loophole for sin has been discovered or to extend the law in new directions.[7] Laws regarding clean and unclean foods, celebration of special religious days, sacrifices, and the practice of circumcision are not imposed on Gentile Christians. The law permitting divorce is tightened to disallow divorce except in the case of sexual immorality (Matt 5:31–32) or when an unbeliever abandons his or her Christian spouse (1 Cor 7:15). But no New Testament author suggests relaxing the code of righteousness found in Old Testament law. Indeed, as 1 Timothy 1:8 says, "Now we know that the law is good, if one uses it legitimately" (and two verses later Paul stipulates that the law's prohibition of homosexuality still applies—v. 10).

When Paul says the believer is no longer under law but is under grace (Rom 6:14), his point is that the one under law is a slave to sin. The believer who has been freed from slavery to sin is now a slave to righteousness, and such a slave has no need for the corrective authority of law for its warnings and punishments. The law corrects those who are disobedient, but the believer is obedient from the heart "to the form of teaching to which [he or she was] entrusted" (Rom 6:17). Now it is possible to stand without condemnation from the law in Christ, who fulfilled the righteous requirements of the law (Rom 8:2–3). Thus, the law's righteous requirements are not erased for believers. Rather, the need to live under the law's correction is done away with when people are released from their imprisonment in sin. The need to establish one's own righteousness has been brought to an end for those who stand in Christ's righteousness (Rom 9:30–10:4; 2 Cor 5:21; Phil 3:6, 9).

New Testament authors continued to use the law as a moral guide: it was not obsolete for Gentile believers. Paul, who said that "Christ [was] the end of the law" (Rom 10:4), explicitly stated that the law was holy, just, and good (Rom 7:12). Indeed, he used the law in his writings on Christian ethics, including sexual ethics.

PURITY AND HOLINESS FOR THE CHURCH

We will now examine Paul's use of the Old Testament notions of "holiness" and "purity" in 1 Corinthians 5–7. Roy Ciampa and Brian Rosner

---

[7] For example, as Richard Bauckham points out, Jesus used Leviticus 19 to extend the law to love one's neighbor (Lev 19:18) to include anyone, not just Israelites (Matt 5:44–47; 22:39–40; Luke 10:29–37). See Richard Bauckham's chapter on "Holiness for the People" in his *The Bible in Politics*, 20–40.

confirm our reading of 1 Corinthians that "Paul's attempt to sort out the serious problems within the largely Gentile church in Corinth consists primarily of a confrontation with the church over purity concerns in general and two vices in particular [sexual immorality and idolatry]."[8] We have already discussed purity in our examination of the mistaken claim that Leviticus 18:22 and 20:13 merely reference ritual impurity, not sinful practices. This matter now needs to be considered for New Testament ethics and applied to 1 Corinthians and the issue of homosexuality.

To see the need for this discussion, note that Bernadette Brooten has argued Paul's use of Leviticus 20's purity laws in 1 Corinthians 5 is outmoded and not applicable to contemporary ethical arguments. Modern ethicists should, she suggests, evaluate the permissibility of a sexual act by considering other factors, such as the intentions of the person committing the act.[9] Yet the particular concern she raises is off the mark, and a fine critique of her objections to Paul has elsewhere been given by Robert Gagnon.[10] We would simply say that Leviticus 20 does not merely provide purity laws: none of the capital offenses—which comprise most of the chapter—is merely a matter of purity. This is not to say Paul never *associates* impurity with sin (e.g., sexual sin in Rom 1:24). Indeed, he thinks about the effect of one person's sin on the purity of the church, the "saints" or "holy ones" of God, in 1 Corinthians 5. Paul uses the Old Testament notions of "holiness" and "purity" when discussing various issues, including sin, in 1 Corinthians 5–7. These notions are not outmoded but helpful in contemporary ethics. The commentary here will begin by distinguishing "holiness" from "purity" in Old Testament law. It will then note how this distinction is employed by Paul in 1 Corinthians 5–7.

1. Holiness and Purity in the Old Testament

In the Old Testament, God calls Israel, his people, to be both holy and pure. "Holiness" has to do with God's being, who he is. Anything or anyone who is "holy" has been separated to God. Something separated to him is said to be "consecrated," and once it is consecrated, it is said to be "made holy" (sanctified). For example, Aaron and his sons are "consecrated" to God so they

---

[8] Roy Ciampa and Brian Rosner, *The First Letter to the Corinthians*, 21. They state their overall view of 1 Corinthians this way: Paul attempts in this letter "*to tell the church of God in Corinth that they are part of the fulfillment of the Old Testament expectation of worldwide worship of the God of Israel, and as God's eschatological temple they must act in a manner appropriate to their pure and holy status by becoming unified, shunning pagan vices, and glorifying God in obedience to the lordship of Jesus Christ*" (52). Part of their convincing demonstration of this argument entails tracking Paul's use of the Old Testament, especially Deuteronomy.

[9] Bernadette Brooten, *Love Between Women: Early Christian Responses to Female Homoeroticism* (Chicago, IL: University of Chicago Press, 1996), 281–94.

[10] Robert Gagnon, *The Bible and Homosexual Practice: Texts and Hermeneutics* (Nashville, TN: Abingdon, 2001), 122.

might serve him as priests (Exod 30:32). In the same way, some specific oil used for anointing priests through the generations was to be considered holy and not used for any common purpose (Exod 30:31–32).

This understanding of holiness is also applied to God's people. The Holiness Code in Leviticus 17–26 is of particular significance in this regard. God says to Moses, "Speak to all the congregation of the people of Israel and say to them: You shall be holy, for I the LORD your God am holy" (Lev 19:2). Again in the Holiness Code, God says, "Consecrate yourselves therefore, and be holy; for I am the LORD your God" (Lev 20:7). This verse begins a section in the Holiness Code that lists various infractions serious enough to warrant the death penalty, including the sin of a man taking his father's wife (Lev 20:11), applied by Paul in 1 Corinthians 5:1, and the sin of homosexuality (Lev 20:13), mentioned in 1 Corinthians 6:9. (Of course, the death penalty does not apply any longer for Paul since the church is not a theocratic state as Israel was.)

"Holiness" is different from "purity." Purity in the Old Testament is better understood with reference to our word "cleanliness" in its literal and figurative senses. People encountered "impurity" regularly and needed to be cleansed: from death (Lev 5:2), from eating "unclean" foods (Leviticus 11), from giving birth (Lev 12:2), from certain skin diseases (Leviticus 13), and from having bodily emissions (Lev 15:2). There were, then, things that could make an Israelite impure; thus, there were ways, such as bathing, to become pure again. Purity has to do with being untainted or clean.

Israelites, then, as God's holy people, were to avoid becoming impure or, if they could not avoid this, they were to cleanse themselves to become pure again. This is the basis of Old Testament laws concerning holiness and purity. God's people were to deal with all sorts of impurities, constantly attending to the purity required of those set apart as holy to God.[11]

While not all impure things are sinful,[12] all sinful things make one impure (cf. 1 Tim 5:22; Eph 5:5). Certain impurities may easily be cleansed, but sin requires sacrifice and repentance in the Mosaic law. As Robin Routledge says, "Offering sacrifices for sin was significant in preserving the holiness of God's people, and to fulfil this role, the priest too needed to be in a state of consecration to God (e.g., Exod 28:41; 1 Chr 15:14; 2 Chr 5:11; 29:34)."[13]

---

[11] For distinctions between holy and profane, clean and unclean, see Philip Peter Jenson, *Graded Holiness: A Key to the Priestly Conception of the World* (Sheffield, England: Sheffield Academic, 1992).

[12] Examples of things that make someone impure (unclean) include touching a carcass or some swarming thing or a person that can make one unclean, menstruation, leprosy, bodily discharges, eating something that dies by itself (discussion occurs in Leviticus 11–15, 17, and 22; and Numbers 19).

[13] Robin Routledge, *Old Testament Theology: A Thematic Approach* (Downers Grove, IL: InterVarsity, 2008), 185.

Separation of what is sinful and therefore impure from God's holy people is necessary. A close association in the Old Testament exists between holiness and moral purity. Routledge states:

> In the [ancient Near East], holiness had little to do with moral purity; so, for example, cult prostitutes were regarded as holy. In the [Old Testament], though, because holiness is bound up with the character of God, it is closely related to purity (e.g., Josh 24:19; Pss 15; 24:3–4; Isa. 5:16; 6:5; Hab. 1:13). An important aspect of this is that people who belong to God are called to be holy too: *be holy because I am holy* (Lev 11:44–45; cf. 1 Pet. 1:16; Lev 20:26).[14]

Thus "cleansing" involves cutting off the sinful person from God's holy people in order for God's people to be pure again and so remain a people separated to God, as we read repeatedly in the Holiness Code of Leviticus 17–26. Otherwise, the sinful person would make the rest of the people impure.

Leviticus 20 mentions sins requiring a person to be cut off from God's people: sacrificing children to the god Molech, witchcraft, cursing one's parents, adultery, sex with one's father's wife or with a daughter-in-law, homosexuality (a man lying with another man as with a woman), sexual relations with a mother and her daughter, bestiality, incest, sex with a menstruating woman, and sex with an aunt or a sister-in-law. If the individuals who commit such acts are not cut off by God's people, God himself will cut them off. Using the imagery of ingesting and vomiting out impurities, Leviticus 18:25, 28; 20:22 state that if God's commands and ordinances are not kept, the land will "vomit" the people out.

In other words, just as a person must "wash" to become clean, so a people must wash themselves of those practicing sin in their midst. Attempting to deny the ethical character of these laws in the Holiness Code because they include language of ritual purity and separation involves a false disjunction.[15] Sometime later John the Baptist's baptism, as an example, was an act of ritual purification *and* of repentance for the forgiveness of sins (Mark 1:4; Luke 3:3). He was calling all Israelites to wash themselves of their impurities—their sinful practices—in preparation for their consecration to God as he came in all of his holy splendor to establish his kingdom. Failure to repent would eventually

---

[14] Ibid., 106.

[15] The argument may be met in a variety of articles and books attempting to get around the obvious prohibition of homosexual acts in the Holiness Code. See, e.g., Phyllis A. Bird, "The Bible in Christian Ethical Deliberation Concerning Homosexuality: Old Testament Contributions," in *Homosexuality, Science, and the Plain Sense of Scripture*, ed. David Balch (Grand Rapids, MI: Eerdmans, 2000), 142–76. The source for these considerations distinguishing morality from purity begins with Mary Douglas, *Purity and Danger: An Analysis of the Concepts of Pollution and Taboo* (London, England: Routledge and Kegan Paul, 1966), 43, 49.

result in a separation of the wheat and the chaff, which will be burned up with unquenchable fire (Luke 3:17).

2. Holiness and Purity in 1 Corinthians

The New Testament uses the same concepts, but there are crucial differences. The first difference lies in the fact that the church is not a geopolitical nation. Quite the contrary: the church is God's holy people dispersed throughout a sinful world. Thus, the church can cut off a person from the congregation of God's holy people, but it cannot cut off sinful people from a land or a nation. Second, the church does not hold civil power. Thus, it can cut someone off from fellowship, but it cannot administer broader judicial punishment. Third, the church's punishment of ostracism (the "ban") is equally a process offering the sinful person hope through repentance.

All this can be seen in 1 Corinthians 5. Paul applies Leviticus 20 to a situation in the Corinthian church, saying a man having sexual relations "with his father's wife" (cf. Lev 20:11; 1 Cor 5:1) must be handed over by the congregation to Satan for the destruction of the flesh. As just noted, the difference between Paul and Leviticus is that, whereas the people of God in the Old Testament were a nation, the church is not a nation and has no land. Thus, the church is not an agent that exercises governmental authority within a state. The death penalty is not applied in the local church but is reinterpreted ethically and communally: instead, the goal is to destroy the "flesh" in a moral sense. As in Leviticus, Paul says the church should put the sinful person out of God's people. For Christians this means putting a sinner into the impure sphere of Satan—excommunicated from the sanctified people of God, the holy church— and hoping the experience will drive that person to repentance.[16]

The logic is that as long as the person remains part of the church, he or she will think his or her sin is not all that bad—or perhaps not sin at all. Only by cutting the person off from the church (dealing with impurity in the midst of what is holy) and by handing the person over to Satan is there any hope of the church remaining pure and holy and of the person realizing his or her sinfulness and turning from it—thereby destroying the "flesh." Yet whether or not the person repents of the sin, the primary concern in Leviticus and in 1 Corinthians 5 is for the holy people of God. They must remove the sin from their midst because, as God's holy people, they must not tolerate impurity. Thus, Stanley Grenz's suggestion that the church can welcome but not affirm homosexuals (or any other open, unrepentant sinners) fails to account for the

---

[16] So, e.g., Gordon D. Fee, *The First Epistle to the Corinthians*, New International Commentary on the New Testament (Grand Rapids, MI: Eerdmans, 1987).

fact that Paul appropriates Old Testament teaching on purity even as he affirms Christ's welcoming of sinners—repentant sinners.[17]

Paul says:

> Do you not know that a little yeast leavens the whole batch of dough? Clean out the old yeast so that you may be a new batch, as you really are unleavened. For our paschal lamb, Christ, has been sacrificed. Therefore, let us celebrate the festival, not with the old yeast, the yeast of malice and evil, but with the unleavened bread of sincerity and truth. (1 Cor 5:6–8)

The local church at Corinth is depicted as God's holy people: they must remove the "yeast" of sin from their midst so they can celebrate the Feast of Unleavened Bread, at which the Passover lamb is eaten. Christ is identified as this lamb. God's people must be pure in order to partake of Christ. The incestuous man's sin means he is no longer "holy" or separated unto God, and so the holy people of God are to separate him into Satan's realm. This is not only in hope of the man's eventual repentance but because the people of God are impure as long as they tolerate such sin in their midst. They must send the unholy person out from among them, like leaven removed from a Jewish home before Passover, in order not to be impure. Only then can they partake of the paschal lamb, Christ.

This application of Leviticus in 1 Corinthians is an important aspect of the church's stance toward sin. As a holy people living in the context of a sinful world, the church must keep itself pure for the sake of its own relationship to Christ. The church, of course, cannot enforce God's ethical standards among non-Christians. Thus Paul says,

> I wrote to you in my letter not to associate with sexually immoral persons—not at all meaning the immoral of this world, or the greedy and robbers, or idolaters, since you would then need to go out of the world. (1 Cor 5:9–10)

Only those *within* the church can and should be held by the congregation to God's standards of purity:

> I am writing to you not to associate with anyone who bears the name of brother or sister who is sexually immoral or greedy, or is an idolater, reviler, drunkard, or robber. Do not even eat with such a one. For what have I to do with judging those outside? Is it not those who are inside that you are

---

[17] Stanley Grenz, *Welcoming but Not Affirming: An Evangelical Response to Homosexuality* (Louisville, KY: Westminster/John Knox, 1998). Of course, Christians do sin, and they can repent without being put out of the church. Other "spiritual believers" can help restore them (Gal 6:1). Cf. Jas 5:16. What is intolerable in 1 Corinthians 5 is the person's willful continuance in sin and the congregation's tolerance of it—their "welcoming" the sinner not as repentant but without repentance.

to judge? God will judge those outside. ^aDrive out the wicked person from among you." (1 Cor 5:11–13)

The local church, then, is seen to be a "holy" people, a people set apart by God for God. The church needs to separate a willfully sinful person from its fellowship for several reasons:

1. *For the church (ecclesiology).* The local church cannot continue to function as a holy people with impurity in its midst. Believers may associate with sinful people outside the church (1 Cor 5:9–10), but they must drive out wicked people from their fellowship (1 Cor 5:11–13).

2. *For the individual (soteriology).* The sinful person has no hope of repenting as long as he or she thinks such practices do not separate him or her from the people of God (1 Cor 5:5). Inclusion of a willfully sinful person in a local church involves a level of acceptance that will nevertheless lead to eternal exclusion on the day of judgment.

3. *For God (theology).* God is holy. To permit ongoing sin in the church is to associate God with unholiness. Paul also argues this point in 1 Thessalonians 4:7–8 (quoted below).

4. *For Christ (Christology).* Thinking of the Christian life as a Passover celebration, Paul makes the point that Christ is our sacrifice for the feast. The church, therefore, needs to prepare itself for this celebration by cleansing the house of yeast, that is, removing sin from its midst (1 Cor 5:7–8).

5. *For the Holy Spirit (pneumatology).* First Thessalonians 4:7–8 brings together a concern for the church as a holy people (number one above) and a concern for understanding the dynamics of Christian life. Christian life involves the transforming, empowering work of the Holy Spirit, a point Paul also makes in 1 Corinthians 6:11. Christianity is not merely a belief, a certain way of thinking about God and sin without a real change in one's life. The Christian life entails the work of the Holy Spirit:

   For God did not call us to impurity but in holiness. Therefore whoever rejects this rejects not human authority but God, who also gives his Holy Spirit to you (1 Thess 4:7–8).

Churches that regard sexual sin as something to be contained rather than overcome fail to understand Paul's point that the Spirit, God's empowering presence, is at work in believers.[18] Paul continues to explain the concept of separation to God in 1 Corinthians 6 and 7. In 1 Corinthians 6:11, he states clearly that members of the church in Corinth are now holy:

---

[18] See Gordon D. Fee, *God's Empowering Presence: The Holy Spirit in the Letters of Paul* (Peabody, MA: Hendrickson, 1994).

> And this is what some of you used to be. But you were washed, you were
> sanctified, you were [made righteous] in the name of the Lord Jesus Christ
> and in the Spirit of our God. (1 Cor 6:11)

They had been cleansed (washed, purified) from various sins so they could be
made holy (sanctified) and righteous, including with respect to homosexual
practices (v. 9).

In 1 Corinthians 6:12, Paul addresses those Corinthians who, having been
set apart to God, returned to what is impure (idolatry, visiting prostitutes). He
reminds them they are holy—consecrated to God—and therefore must not join
themselves to what is impure:

> Do you not know that your body is a temple of the Holy Spirit within
> you, which you have from God, and that you are not your own? For you were
> bought with a price; therefore glorify God in your body. (1 Cor 6:19–20)

Again, in 1 Corinthians 7, Paul argues that what is holy can make holy that
which is unholy:

> For the unbelieving husband is made holy through his [believing] wife,
> and the unbelieving wife is made holy through her [believing] husband.
> Otherwise, your children would be unclean, but as it is, they are holy. (1 Cor
> 7:14)

The failure in some denominations and churches to condemn certain
sinful practices, and the failure to deal with willfully sinful persons in the
church, then, entails a failure not only on that specific ethical issue (e.g.,
homosexuality) but also a failure in ecclesiology, soteriology, theology,
Christology, and pneumatology.

While Paul's specific concern in 1 Corinthians 5 is about a man living with his father's wife, the same arguments would apply to the sin of
homosexuality. In such cases the church must realize it is God's holy people
who must keep themselves pure, honor the holiness of God, and expect God's
empowering presence to transform sinners. Tolerating sin in the church is like
keeping unleavened bread in the house during Passover. Christ, our Passover
lamb, has been sacrificed for us. In order to keep the feast, therefore, we must
remove sin from our midst. If we do not, the leaven of sin will affect the whole
church. One man's sin will make the community impure and therefore no longer holy, unqualified to partake of Christ.

CONCLUSION

The mention of "soft men" and "homosexuals" in 1 Corinthians 6:9
involves more than saying these, along with other sinners, will not inherit
the kingdom of God. The larger context of the verse involves the hope that

transformation can occur in such people's lives through the divine work of Jesus Christ and the Holy Spirit (1 Cor 6:11). In the still larger context (1 Cor 5:1–6:20), the perspective is that a certain ecclesiology of holiness is inextricably related to the personal purity of the church's members. Moreover, how the church includes and excludes persons is a matter of soul care, which is also a matter of eternal significance for individuals. Indeed, how a church handles willful sin in its midst involves the outworking of the gospel in the midst of a community.

CHAPTER 15

"SOFT MEN" AND "HOMOSEXUALS" IN 1 CORINTHIANS 6:9

INTRODUCTION

In 1 Corinthians 6:9–11, Paul says homosexual men will not inherit the kingdom of God and that while some Corinthian Christians had practiced homosexuality, they had experienced a life-transforming, cleansing work of our Lord Jesus Christ and the Spirit of our God.

This statement makes three claims. First, sinful behaviors were expected of those outside of Christ; one such behavior was homosexuality. Second, both those with a particular orientation and life style as "soft men" (*malakoi*) and those engaging in homosexual practice or acts (*arsenokoitai*) are mentioned in the sin list. Third, those in Christ had been transformed by him and the Holy Spirit. When we examine Romans 1:24–28 in a later chapter, we will consider the third claim in reference to the transition between depravity of the mind (Rom 1:28) and renewal of the mind (Rom 12:2).

An argument has surfaced regarding the translation of *malakoi* and *arsenokoitai* in 1 Corinthians 6:9. There has, indeed, been considerable confusion regarding these two words (unnecessarily, as we shall see), as a look at several English translations demonstrates:

> King James Version: "nor effeminate, nor abusers of themselves with mankind"
> New American Standard Bible: "nor effeminate [*malakoi*], nor homosexuals [*arsenokoitai*]"
> New Revised Standard Version: "male prostitutes, sodomites"
> English Standard Version: "men who practice homosexuality"

Robert Gagnon proposes translating *malakoi* with the phrase "effeminate males who play the sexual role of females."[1] He later says, "In my own reading, the meaning of *malakoi* in 1 Cor 6:9 probably lies somewhere in between 'only prostituting passive homosexuals' and 'effeminate heterosexual and homosexual males.'"[2] This is, in our view, partly correct. While agreeing that the term involves certain homosexual practices, we believe *malakoi and its synonyms* reference both practices *and orientation.* Also, we would not limit the meaning as Gagnon does later and as many others do to "passive partners in homosexual intercourse."[3] One might say this is currently the standard view. Whether it or our slightly different view is correct, the text is insisting at the very least that homosexual practices are sins to be overcome by the work of Jesus Christ and the Spirit in the believer's life. While the more general "immoral sexual intercourse" is "an identifying mark" of *malakoi*,[4] and while homosexual acts also seem to be among the practices of "soft males," these men are, we shall see, persons with a particular orientation—not just those engaged in certain acts.

All four translations above understand the second term to be speaking of homosexuals as well, although they render it with different expressions. The second Greek word, *arsenokoitai*, appears to be Paul's own term, one he made up by combining the Greek words for "male" (*arsenos*) and "bed" (*koitē*, implying sex). The ESV collapses *malakoi* and *arsenokoitai* into the one idea of "men who practice homosexuality." The NRSV interprets "soft men" to be male prostitutes—an impossibly limiting translation, as we shall see. The designation "effeminate" in the NASB and KJV is partly correct, but also imprecise and could be misleading if understood merely as a cultural interpretation of maleness. If it did not carry so negative and pejorative a connotation, the slang word *queers* would capture the meaning of *malakoi* and related words[5] better in English since it conveys much of the same range of meaning. *Malakoi* also seems to be somewhat pejorative but not to the same extent. Thus, we suggest translating the term simply as "soft men"—a direct translation of the Greek.

This chapter has in view three questions:

1. Who are the *malakoi* ("soft men") of 1 Corinthians 6:9?
2. How does the answer relate to homosexual sin?

---

[1] Robert Gagnon, *The Bible and Homosexual Practice* (Nashville, TN: Abingdon, 2001), 303.

[2] Ibid., 307–8.

[3] Ibid., 312. See, e.g., Gordon D. Fee, *The First Epistle to the Corinthians*, The New International Commentary on the New Testament (Grand Rapids, MI: Eerdmans, 1987).

[4] Robert Gagnon, *The Bible and Homosexual Practice*, 308.

[5] See chap. 17. Related words to "soft men" include *habrodiaitos* (effeminate), *kinaidoi* (men who play the role of women, transvestites), *euthryptos* (easily broken, crumbling, soft), *thēlydrios* and *tethēlusmenos* (effeminacy), *pathētikōs* (males playing the female, passive role with other males), and *androgynos*" (man-woman).

3. What does Paul mean by *arsenokoitai* in 1 Corinthians 6:9 and 1 Timothy 1:10?

The major focus of this chapter will be on the first question.

JOHN BOSWELL'S ARGUMENTS AGAINST UNDERSTANDING *MALAKOI* IN 1 CORINTHIANS 6:9 AS HOMOSEXUALS

First, consider an argument against using 1 Corinthians 6:9 to condemn homosexual practice. John Boswell's argument should be considered because of its importance to those addressing the question of homosexuality—his work, though fatally flawed in many ways, has been highly influential. His overall view is that the terms should not be translated in reference to homosexuality. Our argument will be that Boswell misrepresented some evidence, failed to consider enough of the evidence (whether intentionally or not), and reasoned poorly from the evidence he did accept.

Regarding *malakoi*, Boswell argues that the term was not used in Paul's day in reference to homosexuals but had to do with other practices. He gives six reasons:

1. The term can be used in a nonsexual way: e.g., "unruffled by others' anger" (Dionysius of Halicarnassus VII.2.4).
2. If it means "effeminate" in a writing, this is a cultural assessment of behavior.
3. It was used in reference to masturbation and moral laxity (no references given).
4. Greek words for "effeminacy" were *thēludrios* (Tatian, *Adversus Graecos* 29; Clement, *The Instructor* 3.3.76); *androgynos* (Justin Martyr, *1 Apology* 27; Tatian, *Adversus Graecos* 29; Clement, *The Instructor* 3.2.41); and the phrase *tōn andrōn hoi gynaikōdeis* (Clement, *The Instructor* 2.10)—not *malakos*.
5. If the term was used of homosexuals, it was not used to designate them as such but just as a general derogatory term that was also used of others.
6. It is not a term for passive partners in male homosexual relationships—other terms are used: *drōntes* (active) and *paschontes* (passive) or *paiderastai* (active) and *paidika* (passive).[6]

Boswell's first point misrepresents the matter by suppressing information. The actual quotation from Dionysius of Halicarnassus shows an awareness that *malakoi* could refer to someone who could control his anger *and* to someone who was engaged in a homosexual relationship as a boy, allowing himself to be treated as a woman:

---

[6] John Boswell, *Christianity, Social Tolerance, and Homosexuality* (Chicago, IL: University of Chicago Press, 1980), 335.

> The tyrant of Cumae at that time was Aristodemus, the son of Aristocrates, a man of no obscure birth, who was called by the citizens *Malacus or "Effeminate"*—a nickname which in time came to be better known than his own name—either because when a boy he *was effeminate and allowed himself to be treated as a woman*, as some relate, *or because he was of a mild nature and slow to anger*, as others state. (VII.2.4)[7]

This passage could, therefore, be used against the claim Boswell makes in his sixth point. Strangely enough, Boswell gives no support for his third claim. His fourth and sixth points concern words used for "effeminacy" and passive partners in male homosexual relationships. He is, first, wrong in saying that the term *malakos* is not used for effeminacy—we shall note more evidence than just the quote from Dionysius. He is, second, correct that the evidence suggests *malakos* is not so much a limited term for passive homosexual males as a term with a wide range of meaning, not always sexual and not only passive. Indeed, Boswell should not have focused his comments only on passages where the word occurs but where the notion of "soft" or "smooth" men appears in the literature, whatever terms are used. We will see in the texts to be quoted that men could be designated "soft" for being effeminate in the sense of playing the role of women. We will also see that these "men-women" could involve themselves in heterosexual as well as homosexual relationships—at least in Egypt. In addition, not only their sexual acts but also their whole effeminate way of life could be in view. In more modern times Joris-Karl Huysmans's 1884 *Against Nature* (*À Rebours*) and Oscar Wilde's *The Picture of Dorian Gray* seem to capture the essence of *malakoi*: effeminate, hedonistic, aesthetic, profligate, decadent, sexually loose, and homosexual, sometimes bisexual, "soft men." Yet sources from antiquity are needed to establish this definition.

HOW SHOULD WE UNDERSTAND *MALAKOI* IN 1 CORINTHIANS 6:9 IN LIGHT OF SOURCES FROM ANTIQUITY?

Perhaps we should begin by noting that Polycarp, early second-century bishop of Smyrna, understood Paul to be using the word *malakos* in reference to sexual lusts (*epithymiōn/epthymia*) in the following quotation:

> In like manner, let the young men also be blameless in all things, being especially careful to preserve purity, and keeping themselves in, as with a bridle, from every kind of evil. For it is well that *they should be cut off from the lusts* [*epithymiōn*] *that are in the world*, since "every lust [*epithymia*] warreth against the spirit;" [Gal 5:16–17] and "neither fornicators, nor effeminate, nor abusers of themselves with mankind, shall inherit the kingdom of God," [quoting from 1 Cor 6:9] nor those who do things inconsistent and

---

[7] *Dionysus of Halicarnassus: Roman Antiquities,* vol. 6, trans. Earnest Cary (Cambridge, MA: Harvard University Press, 1947).

unbecoming. Wherefore, it is needful to abstain from all these things, being subject to the presbyters and deacons, as unto God and Christ. The virgins also must walk in a blameless and pure conscience. (Philippians 5)[8]

Polycarp understands Paul to say that sinful actions stem from passions of the flesh (Paul's term) or world (Polycarp's term) that war against the Spirit. It will not do to discuss sexual orientation without understanding how passions derive from the sinful "world." What Christianity offers people living in a sinful world is release through the work of the Holy Spirit from the "lusts [or sinful passions] that are in the world." Polycarp notes three resources that help believers deal with sin: guidance in moral matters from the presbyters and deacons, a focus on abstaining from sinful actions, and the empowering presence of the Holy Spirit to redirect the desires of sinful persons. He understands Paul's sin list that includes *malakoi* to be about sexual desires, or lusts, that find their expression in sinful actions. He does not suggest merely that people should control their actions but that the Holy Spirit will also transform their desires.

The Greek term *malakos*, however, had a range of meaning that extended beyond sexuality. Its basic meaning was simply "soft," but it had other extended meanings, too. Aristotle used *malakos* in a passage where the related words are "timid" and "cowardly" (*Eudemian Ethics* 3.1229b). In *Nichomachean Ethics* (7.7), he discusses the "soft" male as a pushover or intemperate person— someone who could not endure.

A few paragraphs earlier, Aristotle discusses two main reasons people may be intemperate: nature and habit. In the course of the discussion, he suggests that some people sexually desire children either because of nature (*physis*) or because they somehow formed a habit (*Nichomachian Ethics* 7.5). When Aristotle turns to discuss "soft men," he applies the same options.

> [5] One who is deficient in resistance to pains that most men withstand with success, is *soft [malakos]* or luxurious (*for Luxury is a kind of Softness*): such a man lets his cloak trail on the ground to escape the fatigue and trouble of lifting it, or feigns sickness, not seeing that to counterfeit misery is to be miserable. . . . But we are surprised when a man is overcome by pleasures and pains which most men are able to withstand, except when his failure to resist is *due to some innate tendency [dia physin tou genous]*, or to disease: instances of the former being the *hereditary effeminacy* [malakia] of the royal family of Scythia, and the inferior endurance of the female sex as compared with the male. (*Nichomachian Ethics* 7.7)[9]

---

[8] Polycarp, "Epistle to the Philippians," in *Ante-Nicene Fathers* (*ANF* 1:34), vol. 1, ed. Alexander Roberts and James Donaldson (Peabody, MA: Hendrickson), 1999.

[9] *Aristotle in 23 Volumes*, vol. 19, trans. H. Rackham (Cambridge, MA: Harvard University Press; London, William Heinemann Ltd, 1934).

Aristotle's discussion demonstrates the connection between "soft" and "effeminate"—the words are used alongside each other. The sexual understanding of *malakos* is certainly in view in 1 Corinthians 6:9, but other primary sources help us understand this better.

Philo, for example, uses the term *malakos* of the men of Sodom. Their softness related to being unable to withstand their sexual urges and being given to a feminine orientation:

> They were overcome by *violent desire*; and so, by degrees, the men became *accustomed to be treated like women*, and in this way engendered among themselves the disease of females, an intolerable evil; for they not only, as to *effeminacy and delicacy* [*malakotēti kai thrupsei*], *became like women in their persons*. (*Abraham* 1.135–36)[10]

Manetho Ptolemy (first to second century AD) argues that astrology can explain the various sexual orientations of men and women, including a sexual orientation contrary to nature. In the course of his argument, Ptolemy uses the term *malakoi* to reference male homosexuals with feminine dispositions:

> The men, on the contrary, become effeminate [*malakoi*] and *unsound with respect to natural [kata physin] congresses* and the *functions of women* [*gynaikōn erga*], and are dealt with as *pathics* [*pathētikōs*], though privately and secretly. (*Tetrabiblos* III.14.172)[11]

This quotation demonstrates that contrary to Boswell's contentions, *malakoi* can refer to effeminate men in the sense of homosexuals exhibiting feminine dispositions. Ptolemy has in view *malakoi* who are both homosexual and males playing the role of women; in other words their behavior is a matter of orientation and identity. Ptolemy also shows that *malakos* is one of several ways to speak of effeminate men: he uses the terms *euthryptos* (easily broken or soft)[12] and *tethēlysmenos* (effeminate) as well (III.14.172). Other texts employ terms such as *androgynoi* (male-female men) and *thēlydrios* (effeminate). So, even where the term *malakos* is not found, the notion of a soft male can be conveyed using other terms. This is key to our own presentation, for the meaning of *malakoi* can be discerned not only from passages where the word appears but also from other passages where the idea of "soft men" is found in ancient

---

[10] All translations of Philo are taken from *The Works of Philo Judaeus, the Contemporary of Josephus*, trans. C. D. Yonge, 4 vols. (London, England: Henry G. Bohn, 1854–55).

[11] Ptolemy, *Tetrabiblos*, trans. W. G. Waddell and F. E. Robbins (Cambridge, MA: Harvard University Press, 1940), 371.

[12] The Loeb Classical Library edition of Ptolemy cited above translates *euthryptos* as "soft," whereas the classical Greek dictionary suggests the translation "easily broken" or "crumbling." See Henry George Liddell and Robert Scott, *A Greek-English Lexicon* (Oxford, UK: Clarendon, 1940), 715.

literature. Had the word actually been a technical term for such persons, it no doubt would have occurred more often. Instead, a variety of words are used for the common notion of softness in men. We are here in search of an idea, not simply the meaning of a particular word.

We will next examine references to soft men from the centuries surrounding the New Testament era. Often the notion of male softness references homosexual or bisexual debauchery. We have already noted an astrological understanding of personality and orientation. Medical teaching also discussed personality types and orientation.

The second-century AD physician Galen, following Hippocrates and others, presented a system for describing body humors and personality types. Such an approach to psychophysiological characteristics may reach back to Aristotle (*Problema* XXX.1), who suggested that black bile produces different dispositions depending on whether it is hot (euphoria) or cold (apoplexy, torpor, depression, and various phobias). It may also produce melancholy, and, in various mixtures of temperature and amount, it will produce still other characteristics. When it is cold and plentiful, a person may be lazy and stupid; when warm and plentiful, a person may be crazed, brilliant, and oversexed, easily angered and passionate, and so forth. Galen's view may be presented briefly this way:[13]

Humors	Condition	Element	Features	Temperament
Yellow bile	hot + dry	fire	yellow	keenness of intellect
Black bile	cold + dry	earth	thin, dark	constancy and stability
Phlegm	cold + wet	water	pale, fat	soft
Blood	hot + wet	air	red skinned	simplicity or stupidity of mind

Thus, a relationship is established between the body and the temperament. As Kyle Harper says, "Folk belief had long held that women were underheated and incompletely formed men: moist, clammy, the female body had been contrived by nature to play its role in the continuous regeneration of the species, "born to be penetrated." For men, too, manliness was a matter of degree, and

---

[13] Expanded from the table in Maria Michela Sassi, *The Science of Man in Ancient Greece*, trans. Paul Tucker (Chicago, IL: University of Chicago Press, 2001), 155.

the insufficiently masculinized male became damp, soft, in extreme cases an "androgyne" [man-woman]."[14]

For our purposes we note first that antiquity could and did discuss orientations from a medical point of view—as well as philosophically and astrologically. Second, we see that this discussion could and did include ideas about sexual inclinations. Third, we see that the idea of "softness" related to a person's physical and temperamental characteristics. Ancient medical considerations, then, allow "wetness" and "softness" to apply to a particular range of persons. This may be one reason the concept of "softness" could be applied to women, men acting as women or overly attached to domestic comforts and luxury, children (including boys engaged in pederasty), and eunuchs.

Even before Hippocrates and Aristotle, the playwright, Aristophanes of the fifth to fourth century BC, describes a person with a "man-woman" orientation in the following excerpt from his play, *Women at the Thesmophoria* (*Thesmophoriazusae* 1.35). This person, Agathon, has an effeminate orientation—including a sexual orientation—that, Aristophanes suggests, is found typically among poets:

> [Euripedes says to Mnesilochus]: And yet *you have made love to him* [Agathon, the poet]. Well, it must have been without knowing who he was. . . . [Agathon is depicted in the play as effeminate. This is said to be a result of certain poets needing to take on a more effeminate demeanor in order to write sweet poetry.]
>
> [Mnesilochus] [130] Oh! ye venerable Genetyllides, what tender and voluptuous songs! They surpass the most lascivious kisses in sweetness; I feel a thrill of delight pass up me as I listen to them. [To Euripides] Young man, if you are one, [135] answer my questions, which I am borrowing from Aeschylus' "Lycurgeia." Whence comes this androgyne [man-woman]? What is his country? his dress? What contradictions his life shows! A lyre and a hair-net! A wrestling school oil flask and a girdle! What could be more contradictory? [140] What relation has a mirror to a sword? [To Agathon] And you yourself, who are you? *Do you pretend to be a man?* Where is your tool, pray? Where is the cloak, the footgear that belong to that sex? Are you a woman? Then where are your breasts? Answer me. But you keep silent. Oh! [145] just as you choose; your songs display your character quite sufficiently.
>
> [Agathon:] If the heroes are men, [155] everything in him will be manly. What we don't *possess by nature*, we must acquire by imitation. . . . Besides, it is bad taste for a poet [160] to be coarse and hairy. Look at the famous Ibycus, at Anacreon of Teos, and at Alcaeus, who handled music so well; they wore head-bands and found pleasure in the lascivious and dances of Ionia. And have you not heard [165] what a dandy Phrynichus was and how careful

---

[14] Kyle Harper, *From Shame to Sin: The Christian Transformation of Sexual Morality in Late Antiquity* (Cambridge, MA: Harvard University Press, 2013), 33.

in his dress? For this reason his pieces were also beautiful, for the works of a poet are copied from himself.

[Mnesilochus:] Ah! so it is for this reason that Philocles, who is so hideous, writes hideous pieces; Xenocles, who is malicious, malicious ones, [170] and Theognis, who is cold, such cold ones?

[Agathon:] Yes, necessarily and unavoidably; and it is because I knew this that I have so well cared for my person.[15]

Also, in the fourth century BC, Aeschines delivered a speech against a certain man, Timarchus, who was being considered for an official post. Aeschines claimed Timarchus had endeared himself to the luxurious life and was "a slave to shameful lusts," including a sexual relationship with an older man, Misgolas. Misgolas, too, enjoyed a soft life (though the word "soft" is not used). Here we see that the lifestyle of soft men included luxury, weak morals, and homosexual relationships:

[41] Fellow citizens, there is one Misgolas, son of Naucrates, of the deme Collytus, a man otherwise honorable, and beyond reproach save in this, that he is bent on that sort of thing like one possessed, and is accustomed always to have about him singers or cithara-players. I say this, not from any liking for indecent talk, but that you may know what sort of man Misgolas is. Now this Misgolas, perceiving Timarchus' motive in staying at the house of the physician, paid him a sum of money in advance and *caused him to change his lodgings, and got him into his own home*; for Timarchus was well developed, young, and lewd, just the person for the thing that Misgolas wanted to do, and Timarchus wanted to have done.

[42] Timarchus did not hesitate, but *submitted to it all*, though he had income to satisfy all reasonable desires. For his father had left him a very large property, which he has squandered, as I will show in the course of my speech. But he behaved as he did because he was *a slave to the most shameful lusts*, to gluttony and extravagance at table, to flute-girls and harlots, to dice, and to *all those other things no one of which ought to have the mastery over a man who is well-born and free*. And this wretch was not ashamed to abandon his father's house and live with Misgolas, a man who was not a friend of his father's, nor a person of his own age, but a stranger, and older than himself, a man who knew no restraint in such matters, while Timarchus himself was in the bloom of youth.[16]

Aeschines also refers negatively to male prostitution. Male prostitutes, he says, are excluded from a number of offices and places (*Speeches,* "Against

---

[15] Translated by Eugene O'Neill Jr., in Aristophanes, *Women at the Thesmophoria: The Complete Greek Drama,* vol. 2 (New York, NY: Random House, 1938), accessed September 11, 2008, http://www.perseus.tufts.edu/cgi-bin/ptext?doc=Perseus:text:1999.01.0042:line=1.

[16] Aeschines, "Against Timarchus" 1.41, 42 in *Speeches*, trans. Charles Darwin Adams (Cambridge, MA: Harvard University Press, 1919), 37, 39.

Timarchus" 1.21). But Aeschines makes a distinction between male prostitution and having a male lover, which goes beyond pederasty (1.136–7). Sexual indulgence, a penchant for the luxurious, aesthetic life, and being a slave to shameful lusts like homosexuality describe the "soft" male.

The first-century AD Roman philosopher Musonius Rufus, like Aeschines centuries before in Greece, tied the "life of luxury and self-indulgence" to sexual excess, including the craving of sex with both women and men (*Fragment* 12). "Softness" can cover a number of excesses since it has to do with yielding to urges of all sorts, including sexual desires and particularly homoerotic ones. Such behaviors characterize a person ruled by unchecked desire.

The first-century AD Spanish poet Martial mentions adult homosexuality in his writings (*Epigrams* 1.24; 2.47). He specifically mentions adult males who want to receive anal intercourse (*Epigrams* 2.51; 6.56; 9.47; 11.88). Thus, one should not limit "softness" to boys or youths involved in pederastic relationships with older men.

In *Special Laws* 1.325 Philo, a first-century AD Jewish philosopher from Egypt, says:

> He previously excludes all who are unworthy from the sacred assembly, beginning in the first instance with those who are afflicted with the *disease of effeminacy [thēleian noson], men-women [androgynōn], who, having adulterated the coinage of nature [physeōs]*, are willingly driven into the appearance and treatment of licentious women. He also banishes all those who have suffered any injury or mutilation in their most important members, and those who, seeking to preserve the flower of their beauty so that it may not speedily wither away, have *altered the impression of their natural manly appearance into the resemblance of a woman [thēlumorphon]*.

Philo says some men sought a life of pleasure rather than virtue. Such a life was characterized by luxury, uncontrolled passions, sexual excesses, and deviancy that included homosexual acts. Evidence from Philo is extremely valuable in a consideration of how first-century writers defined "soft man." Without using the word *malakos*, Philo demonstrates precisely what is involved in this concept. It is a man who has abandoned his masculine nature to pursue womanly ways, including sex with other men and boys.

The first- and second-century AD Roman satirist Juvenal was aware of two kinds of homosexuals: the manly homosexual who fulfills his desires in secret, and the effeminate homosexual who lives openly as a woman. In this passage, both are said to play the passive part (receiving anal intercourse), but Juvenal sees the former as choosing his orientation and the latter as genetically predisposed to his.

And do you rebuke foul practices, when you are yourself the most notorious delving-ground among Socratic reprobates [Latin: "*cinaedos*"; i.e., persons engaging in same-sex intercourse]? A hairy body, and arms stiff with bristles, give promise of a manly soul: but sleek are your buttocks when the grinning doctor cuts into the swollen piles [from anal intercourse]. Men of your kidney talk little; they glory in taciturnity and cut their hair shorter than their eyebrows. Peribomius himself is more open and more honest; his face, his walk, betray his distemper, and I charge Destiny with his failings. Such men excite your pity by their frankness; the very fury of their passions wins them pardon. Far worse are those who denounce evil ways in the language of a Hercules; and after discoursing upon virtue, prepare to practice vice. (*Satire* II, lines 10–21)[17]

Juvenal also speaks of a tightly knit homosexual community: "Great is the concord among soft men" (*Satire* II.47).[18] He uses the Latin word *molles*, which would be the direct translation of the Greek *malakoi*, as both words mean "soft men." A tightly knit group of individuals who are sexually active with persons of the same gender seems what is today termed the LGBT (lesbian, gay, bisexual, transgender) community.

A passage from another of Juvenal's satires mentions bisexual adult males, male prostitutes naturally oriented to same-sex attraction and receiving payment for their services, and effeminate catamites who appear to be adults rather than youths:

Not long ago, as I remember, you used to frequent the Temple of Isis and that of Peace with its Ganymede, and the secret courts of the Foreign Mother and Ceres—for in what temple are there not frail fair ones to be found?—you, a more notable adulterer than Aufidius, and what you say nothing of, you would corrupt the husbands themselves.

Many men have found profit in my mode of life; but I have made nothing substantial out of my labours. I sometimes have a greasy cloak given me that will save my toga—a coarse and crudely dyed garment that has been ill-combed by the Gallic weaver—or some trifle in silver of an inferior quality. Many is ruled by destiny; even those parts of him that lie beneath his clothes. . . . What greater monster is there in the world than a miserly debauchee [*mollis*]? "Gave you this," says he, "and then that; and later you got ever so much more." Thus he makes a reckoning with his lusts. . . .

---

[17] All quotes to Juvenal, *Satires* are from *Juvenal and Persius*, trans. G. G. Ramsay, Loeb Classical Library (Cambridge, MA: Harvard University Press, 1957).

[18] Our translation. As other quotations offered here from *Satire* II demonstrate, the topic is the homosexual male. *Molles* is not a term that can be reduced in meaning simply to men with some feminine characteristics. In assessing the meaning of the Greek word *malakoi*, we should include evidence from the Latin equivalent. *Satire* II gives us a good understanding of "soft males."

> Be not afraid; so long as these seven hills of ours stand fast, pathic [Latin: "*pathicus*," an adjective describing a person who submits to homosexual use] friends will never fail you: from every quarter, in carriages and in ships, those gentry who scratch their heads with one finger will flock in. (*Satire* IX.20–40, 130–33)

Juvenal also mentions the Great Mother Cult of Cybele, which predated Christianity in Rome but originated farther east. In the first century AD, the cult was popular in Asia Minor. The city of Sardis paid special homage to Cybele, and the remains of an altar to this goddess may still be seen there.[19] Male priests in this cult were initiated through a ceremony involving self-castration. As Everett Ferguson explains, a myth related to this cult explains the practice:

> Zeus begat Agdistis, a wild creature half male and half female. Dionysus made it drunk and tied its male member to a tree so that on awakening suddenly from sleep it mutilated itself. From the severed male member an almond tree sprang up. Nana, the daughter of Sangarius, took fruit of the tree into her bosom and conceived Attis. The youth grew up and was about to be married to the daughter of the king of Pessinus, but Agdistis had fallen in love with him and to prevent the marriage caused Attis to castrate himself.[20]

Juvenal also describes men cross-dressing and joining in orgies associated with various religions: the normally female-only religion of Bona Dea, devotees of Cotytto, and the eunuch priests of Cybele (*galli*). He also depicts the emperor Ortho in this way.

> Some day you will venture on something more shameful than this dress; no one reaches the depths of turpitude all at once. By degrees you will be welcomed by those who in their homes put long fillets round their brows, swathe themselves with necklaces, and propitiate the Bona Dea with the stomach of a porker and a huge bowl of wine, though by an evil usage the Goddess warns off all women from entering the door; none but males may approach her altar. "Away with you! Profane women" is the cry; "no booming horn, no she-minstrels here!" Such were the secret torchlight orgies with which the Baptae [those who worshiped Cotytto, the Thracian deity] wearied the Cecropian [Cecrops was the first king of Athens: hence, "an Athenian"] Cotytto. One prolongs his eyebrows with some damp soot staining the edge of a needle, and lifts up his blinking eyes to be painted; another drinks out of an obscenely shaped glass, and ties up his long locks in a gilded net; he is clothed in blue

---

[19] See photo, accessed April 24, 2014, http://via.lib.harvard.edu/ via/deliver/chunkDisplay?_collection=via&inoID=339395&recordNumber=1&chunkNumber=4 &method=view&image=full&startChunkNum= 0&endChunkNum=0 &totalChunkCount=0.

[20] Everett Ferguson, *Backgrounds of Early Christianity* (Grand Rapids, MI: Eerdmans, 2003), 283.

checks, or smooth-faced green; the attendant swears by Juno like his master. Another holds in his hand a mirror like that carried by the effeminate [*pathicus*] Otho. . . . You will hear all the foul talk and squeaking tones of Cybele; a grey-haired frenzied old man presides over the rites; he is a rare and notable master of mighty gluttony, and should be hired to teach it. But why wait any longer when it were time in Phrygian fashion to lop off the superfluous flesh [a reference to initiates of the goddess Cybele, associated especially with Phrygia, emasculating themselves]? (*Satire* II, lines 82–99, 110–16)

Thus, Juvenal is aware of various types of males who engage in homosexual acts, whether in devotion to a particular deity or because of orientation or choice. He even envisions homosexuals marrying.

Gracchus has presented to a cornet player—or perhaps it was a player on the straight horn—a dowry of four hundred thousand sesterces. *The contract has been signed; the benedictions have been pronounced; a crowd of banqueters seated, the new made bride is reclining on the bosom of her husband.* O ye nobles of Rome! Is it a soothsayer that we need, or a Censor? Would you be more aghast, would you deem it a greater portent, if a woman gave birth to a calf, or a cow to a lamb? The man who is now arraying himself in the flounces and train and veil of a bride once carried the nodding shields of Mars by the sacred thongs and sweated under the sacred burden!

O Father of our city, whence came such wickedness among thy Latin shepherds? How did such a lust possess thy grandchildren, O Gradivus? Behold! *Here you have a man of high birth and wealth being handed over in marriage to a man*, and yet neither shakest thy helmet, nor smites the earth with thy spear, nor yet protestest to thy Father? Away with thee, then; begone from the broad acres of that Martial Plain which thou has forgotten!

"I have a ceremony to attend," quoth one, "at dawn to-morrow, in the Quirinal valley." "What is the occasion?" "No need to ask: a friend is taking to himself a husband; quite a small affair." Yes, and if we only live long enough, we shall see these things done openly: people will wish to see them reported among the news of the day. *Meanwhile these would-be brides have one great trouble: they can bear no children wherewith to keep the affection of their husbands; well has nature done in granting to their desires no power over their bodies.* (*Satire* II, lines 117–40)[21]

The second-century AD Stoic philosopher Epictetus gives us yet another understanding of "soft men." In the following quotation Epictetus is addressing the topic of adornment and what makes a person beautiful. He argues that beauty has first to do with the virtues and not outward appearance, and that

---

[21] Let the reader recall that Manetho Pompey (*Tetrabiblos* III.172), quoted above, spoke of women who lived with other women as their wives. Whether cohabitation by homosexual males or by lesbians was sealed in a marriage ceremony, as Juvenal here suggests, is uncertain. That this is satire may mean Juvenal is using hyperbole.

beauty in regard to outward appearance is defined by remaining as one was made. He says, "Know, first, who you are; and then adorn yourself accordingly." This sort of argument from nature/creation speaks against a certain young man's appearance, for he had ornamented his hair and dressed himself in fine clothing, as a woman might do. In *Discourses* 3.1 Epictetus says:

> You are a human being; that is, a mortal animal, capable of a rational use of things as they appear. And what is this rational use? A perfect conformity to Nature. What have you, then, particularly excellent? Is it the animal part? No. The mortal? No. That which is capable of the mere use of these things? No. The excellence lies in the rational part. Adorn and beautify this; but leave your hair to him who formed it as he thought good.
>
> Well, what other appellations have you? *Are you a man or a woman? A man. Then adorn yourself as a man, not as a woman. A woman is naturally smooth and delicate*, and if hairy, is a monster, and shown among the monsters at Rome. It is the same thing in a man *not* to be hairy; and if he is *by nature* not so, he is a monster. But if he depilates himself, what shall we do with him? Where shall we show him, and how shall we advertise him? "A man to be seen, who would rather be a woman." What a scandalous show! Who would not wonder at such an advertisement? I believe, indeed, that these very persons themselves would; not apprehending that it is the very thing of which they are guilty.
>
> Of what have you to accuse your *nature*, sir, that it has made you a man? Why, were all to be born women, then? In that case what would have been the use of your finery? For whom would you have made yourself fine, if all were women? But the whole affair displeases you. Go to work upon the whole, then. *Remove your manhood itself and make yourself a woman entirely*, that we may be no longer deceived, *nor you be half man, half woman*. To whom would you be agreeable, to the women? Be agreeable to them as a man. [22]

In his work *Paedegogos* (*The Instructor*), the second-century Alexandrian Christian author Clement has much to say about the culture of effeminacy in his urban, Egyptian context:

> To such an extent, then, has *luxury* advanced, that not only are the female sex deranged about this frivolous pursuit, but *men also are infected with the disease*. For not being free of the love of finery, they are not in health; but inclining to voluptuousness, they become *effeminate* [*gynaikizontai*], cutting their hair in an ungentleman like and meretricious way, clothed in fine and transparent garments, chewing mastic, smelling of perfume. What can one say on seeing them? Like one who judges people by their foreheads, he will divine them to be adulterers and *effeminate* [*androgynous*; literally,

---

[22] *The Works of Epictetus: His Discourses, in Four Books, the Enchiridion, and Fragments*, trans. Thomas Wentworth Higginson (New York, NY: Thomas Nelson and Sons, 1890). Higginson's translation will be used throughout for Epictetus.

"male women"], addicted to both kinds of venery, haters of hair, destitute of hair, detesting the bloom of manliness, and adorning their locks *like women.* (3.3.21)[23]

It appears the emphasis on hair is tied, in part, to a tendency among these men to have their bodily hair pulled out in shops where passersby could observe. Thus, says Clement:

> For those who are *men to shave and smooth themselves*, how ignoble! As for dyeing of hair, and anointing of grey locks, and dyeing them yellow, these are practices of *abandoned effeminates* [*androgynōn*]; and their *feminine* [*thēludriōdeis*] combing of themselves is a thing to be let alone. (3.3.16)

The passage clearly indicates that these are grown men; indeed, some have grey hair. Thus, we are not to identify this group with boys, young catamites in pederastic relationships. They also wear jewelry and "are dragged to the women's apartments, amphibious and lecherous beasts" (*The Instructor* 3.3.17). This line shows that the effeminate men being described are bisexual. Later Clement says, "If [removing hair, smoothing] is to attract men, [it] is the act of an effeminate person,—if to attract women, [it] is the act of an adulterer; and both must be driven as far as possible from our society" (*The Instructor* 3.3.19). To some extent, then, we agree with Roy Ciampa, who says of the term *malakos*: "While the whole set of associations cannot be expressed in one or two words, and the tie with feminine weaknesses in particular would be lost, I would suggest that "promiscuous men" or "sexual profligates" (or, for a longer expression, "those who engage in sexual license") may get to a key part of what effeminacy (as well as womanly behaviour) suggested to the ancient reader."[24]

Some support exists for emphasizing promiscuity in the definition of "soft male," as we have seen. Plutarch, moreover, speaks of a soft life in terms of the pursuit of pleasure or indulgence:

> But that other lax and housebound love, that spends its time in the bosoms and beds of women, ever pursuing a *soft life*, enervated amid *pleasure devoid of manliness* and friendship and inspiration. (*Dialogue on Love* 751 D–E)[25]

---

[23] All quotes from Clement are translated by William Wilson, in *Ante-Nicene Fathers*, vol. 2, ed. Alexander Roberts, James Donaldson, and A. Cleveland Coxe (Buffalo, NY: Christian Literature Publishing Co., 1885.) Revised and edited for New Advent by Kevin Knight, accessed September 26, 2013, http://www.newadvent.org/fathers/02093.htm.

[24] Roy Ciampa, "'Flee Sexual Immorality': Sex and the City of Corinth," in *The Wisdom of the Cross: Exploring 1 Corinthians*, ed. Brian S. Rosner (Nottingham, England: Apollos, 2011), 118.

[25] Translated by E. L. Minar, F. H. Sandbach, W. C. Helmbold, *Plutarch: Moralia*, vol. IX, ed. G. P. Goold (Cambridge, MA: Harvard University Press, 1961), 317–25.

The difficulty we find in defining softness as promiscuity in general, though, is that it fails to account for the emphases in primary sources on femininity as well as male homosexual orientation and conduct. This is a primary feature of the term that must not be lost in any translation. Plutarch elsewhere makes the connection between softness and male homosexual practices:

> Rather is it bestial, we reply, and irrational and pitiable that a man who knows the better should be led astray by the worse as a result of a weak will and soft living. And again: "Tis character persuades, and not the speech."
>
> No, rather it is both character and speech, or character by means of speech, just as a horseman uses a bridle, or a helmsman uses a rudder, since virtue has no instrument so humane or so akin to itself as speech. And: "To women more than men is he inclined? Where there is beauty, either suits him best."
>
> But it were better to say "Where there is virtue, either suits him best," of a truth, and there is no difference in his inclination; but the man who is influenced by pleasure or outward beauty to shift his course hither and thither is incompetent and inconstant. (*Quomodo adolescens poetas audire debeat* 12)[26]

Clement of Alexandria supports his view on homosexuality by relating softness to the creation story. Thus, he sees such a lifestyle as unnatural—as we also saw in Epictetus. In *The Instructor* 3 Clement says, "Whatever *smoothness and softness* was in him [Adam] He [God] abstracted from his side when He formed the woman Eve, physically receptive, his partner in parentage, his help in household management, while he (for he had parted with all smoothness) remained a man, and shows himself man."

It would be wrong to limit Clement's condemnation to, say, oversexed men, men presenting themselves naked in public places, heterosexual men who engage in occasional homosexual acts, or bisexual men who have casual sex rather than settle into monogamous relationships. Among Clement's various concerns about these soft and smooth men in his culture is that they are defying God's created order. As with all Christian writers, this conviction rules out any same-sex practices. One key aspect of "soft men" is that they are behaving contrary to God's design for males.

These primary sources lead us to agree in part with Kyle Harper's claim that "soft men" was a concept that covered a variety of males:

> The essence of malakia was softness, an interior disposition formed of luxuriance, effeminacy, and weakness. Sexual deviance was not the sole mark of softness, but it was a practically inevitable consequence of the inability to impose one's hard will on the enervating poison of desire. Excessive fondness for bathing, fine food, and soft clothing were characteristic of the malakos,

---

[26] Plutarch, *Moralia*, trans. Frank Cole Babbitt (Cambridge, MA: Harvard University Press, 1927).

but "above all and with the least self-control" he was possessed by "a sharp and scalding madness for sex, for coition with both women and with men, and even for inexpressible and unknown acts of shame." The malakos was as likely to surrender to the love of women as to the love of men. The desire underlying the sexual behavior of the malakos was not so much deviant as excessive, a surplus of lust dissolving the steely power over the self that was the surest guarantee of manliness in the ancient Mediterranean. [27]

Yet we think Harper, too, should stress more than he does that "soft men" committed homosexual acts even though the term includes other nuances. The primary source evidence indicates that participation in homosexual acts was central to the definition of "soft men," even though the term was not a mere synonym for "homosexuals." Also, softness referenced not only inability to control oneself. It characterizes a man who is unnaturally nonmale, and therefore also oriented to the feminine side of life. It entails being soft, womanly, boyish, a eunuch, and interested in feminine things. As we read in Pseudo-Lucian (ca. fourth century AD), luxury, feminine males, hedonism, and homosexual unions among men are related interests for soft males:

> [Aphrodite, the goddess of love] linked them [males and females] to each other, ordaining as a sacred law of necessity that each should retain its own nature and that neither should the female grow unnaturally masculine nor the male be unbecomingly soft. . . . (19) But gradually the passing years degenerated from such nobility to the lowest depths of hedonism and cut out strange and extraordinary paths to enjoyment. *Then luxury, daring all, transgressed the laws of nature herself.* And who ever *was the first to look at the male as though at a female* after using violence like a tyrant or else shameless persuasion? *The same sex entered the same bed.* Though they saw themselves embracing each other, they were ashamed neither at what they did nor at what they had done to them, and, sowing their seed, to quote the proverb, on barren rocks they bought a little pleasure at the cost of great disgrace. (*Amores* 20)[28]

In light of these primary sources, we can rule out the imaginations of some prominent scholars who have swayed many in their false understandings of what Paul meant by "soft men" in 1 Corinthians 6:9. Boswell's attempt to understand *malakoi* as something nonsexual is fatally flawed once the evidence is accumulated and properly presented. Another argument ventured by revisionist scholars is that 1 Corinthians 6:9's *malakoi* and *arsenokoitai* referred to passive and active participants, respectively, in pederastic relationships. This suggestion received prominence in the 1980s, but it too stemmed from a failure to attend to the primary sources, which—as we have seen—point to the term

---

[27] Kyle Harper, *From Shame to Sin,* 97–98.

[28] Lucian, vol. 8, *Amores,* trans. A. M. Harmon, Loeb Classical Library (Cambridge, MA: Harvard University Press, 1967).

malakoi as describing adult males behaving as women. While the term *mala-koi* has various nuances of meaning that could be emphasized in different texts, part of its essential overall meaning is the notion of men involved in same-sex acts.

Finally, the primary sources presented here suggest a broader meaning for *malakoi* than simply the passive partner in a homosexual act. This is a common suggestion regarding 1 Corinthians 6:9, with *arsenokoitai* taken as referring to the active partner. The evidence, however, suggests a distinction between those men fully immersed in a feminine way of life—including unrestrained, sexually loose behaviors that could be passive, homosexual, or bisexual—and men engaged in homosexual acts, possibly in secret. The distinction, then, might be between those possessing an open, effeminate *orientation* and those who merely commit homosexual *acts*, whether open or secretive. The next section of this chapter examines the second term, *arsenokoitai*, in more detail.

ARSENOKOITAI IN 1 CORINTHIANS 6:9 AND 1 TIMOTHY 1:10

According to Arland Hultgren, *arsenokoitai* should be taken with *malakoi* (which he wrongly understood as boys receiving sex) to mean pederasts, adult males having sex with boys.[29] Thus, he conjectured, the two terms refer to the practice of pederasty, not homosexuality in general. This had, notes Hultgren, been the argument of Robin Scroggs,[30] as well as Wolfgang Schrage,[31] and Eduard Lohse.[32] Victor Paul Furnish had suggested that prostitution was in view: the *arsenokoitai* were customers of call-boys.[33] All these biblical scholars failed to do adequate work in the primary sources.

Arsenokoitai is a word not found in Greek literature outside Christian circles. It is a rare compound word that may well have been coined by Paul. The word is a blend of "male" and "bed." Boswell suggests it simply means oversexed males, and he posits that it refers to male prostitutes. How could it, he argues, mean "homosexuals" if, in all the literature we have from the Greeks on the subject, the term is not used (other than in Paul's writings and those quoting them)?[34]

On this reasoning the word could not mean anything at all, let alone "homosexual." Boswell also misses the fact that in 1 Corinthians 5–7 Paul is

---

[29] Arland Hultgren, "Being Faithful to the Scriptures: Rom 1:26–27 as a Case in Point," *Word and World* 14 (1994).

[30] Robin Scroggs, *The New Testament and Homosexuality* (Minneapolis, MN: Fortress, 1983).

[31] Wolfgang Schrage, *Der Erste Brief an die Korinther* (Zürich: Benzinger, 1991), 431.

[32] Eduard Lohse, *Theological Ethics of the New Testament* (Philadelphia, PA: Fortress, 1991), 119–20.

[33] Victor Paul Furnish, *The Moral Teaching of Paul: Selected Issues*, rev. ed. (Nashville, TN: Abingdon, 1985), 72.

[34] John Boswell, *Christianity, Social Tolerance, and Homosexuality*, 345.

making reference to the Holiness Code (Leviticus 17–26)—something pointed out clearly by Brian Rosner.[35] Key correlations between 1 Corinthians 5–6 and the Holiness Code include:

> Incest: Lev 18:6–18; 20:11; and 1 Cor 5:1–13,
> Homosexuality: Lev 18:22; 20:13; and 1 Cor 6:9,
> Idolatry: Lev 18:21 and 1 Cor 10:7,[36]
> Imitating God: Lev 19:2 and 1 Cor 11:1,
> Not causing someone to stumble: Lev 19:14 and 1 Cor 8:9, and
> Warning against spiritual prostitution: Lev 20:5 and 1 Cor 6:12–20.

Thus, we might expect that the background for *arsenokoitai* in 1 Corinthians 6:9 will be found in Leviticus 17–26. Significantly, the Greek translation of Leviticus 20:13 offers the words needed to understand how the word *arsenokoitai* came into existence:

> *Kai hos an koimēthē meta arsenos koitēn gynaikos . . .*
> And whoever lies with a man sexually as with a woman . . .

Not only are the words found together, but a Greek manuscript in Paul's day would not have separated them with spaces. While Paul would have known the two words were distinct, he would have seen them together in Leviticus 20:13 and apparently chose to keep them that way. Another compound constructed to convey the same notion is more widely used: the "man woman" compound of *androgynos*. Since the word *arsenokoitai* is not found elsewhere in Greek literature—except where Christian authors use it and usually in reference to 1 Corinthians 6:9—it apparently is a word Paul coined from Leviticus 20:13.[37]

Robert Gagnon's discussion of *arsenokoitai* in 1 Corinthians 6:9 and 1 Timothy 1:10 says all that needs to be stated, including his definitive responses to those offering other interpretations.[38] In order to emphasize that early Christians understood the word to refer to a sexual sin, and in particular as homosexual practice, he notes numerous texts where the term is found

---

[35] Brian Rosner, *Paul, Scripture and Ethics: A Study of 1 Corinthians* 5–7 (Leiden: Brill, 1994), 50. Rosner further points out Paul's use of Leviticus 17–26 in Romans: Rom 13:9 uses Lev 19:18 ("love your neighbor"); the sin list in Rom 1:29–31 overlaps considerably with Leviticus 20; and the sin list ends (Rom 1:32) with "those who do such things deserve death," as in Leviticus 20 (51). Rosner's work demonstrates definitively that Paul is using the Old Testament in 1 Cor 5–7: Paul has not abandoned the law's relevance for Christian ethics.

[36] We would suggest for idolatry this correlation of texts: Lev 19:4; 1 Cor 6:9.

[37] The word does appear in *Sybylline Oracle* 2.73, but this is an addition by a Christian writer from around the year 150. See Robert Gagnon, *The Bible and Homosexual Practice*, 317–18. Otherwise, the word appears in Christian literature only after the time of Paul and often in reference to 1 Cor 6:9.

[38] Ibid., 312–36.

in Christian literature penned after Paul's writings. These texts, including the Christian addition to the *Sibylline Oracles* (first quote), state:

1. "Do not *arsenokoitein* [verbal form of the word] . . . , do not betray information, do not murder" (*Sib. Or.* 2.73).

2. There will be a double measure of judgment on "the poisoner, sorcerer, robber, swindler, and *arsenokoitēs* [singular form of the word], the thief and all his band" (*Acts of John* 36).

3. The term is twice found in sin lists from Theophilus of Antioch's *To Autolychus*: in 1.2 it appears after "adultery, *porneia* [sexual immorality], thief, plunderer, defrauder/robber," and before, "savagery, abusive behavior, wrath, jealousy, etc."; in 1.14 it appears after "adultery and *porneia*," and before "greed and idolatry."

4. Hippolytus uses the term in his description of the "Naasene" Gnostic myth (*Haer.* 5.26.22–23). In the myth the evil "Naas (a Greek transliteration of the Hebrew word for serpent) approached Eve and after deceiving her committed adultery with her, which is contrary to the law; and he also approached Adam and possessed him like a boy (an allusion to pederasty), which is also itself contrary to the law. From that time on, adultery and *arsenokoitia* have come into being."

5. "From the Euphrates River (eastward) . . . a man who is derided as a murderer or thief will not be the least bit angry; but if he is derided as an *arsenokoitēs*, he will defend himself to the point of murder. [By contrast, the Greeks take male lovers.]" (Eusebius, *Preparation for the Gospel* (6.10.25), quoting a third-century Christian, Bardesanes (the comment about the Greeks may come from Eusebius, early fourth century).

6. Aristides, *Apology* (c. 125–145): stories about the gods say they practice "mutual slaughter and poisoning/witchcraft and adultery and theft and *arsenokoitias* (13.7)." [Previously, in chap. 9, Aristides mentions Zeus's carrying off Ganymedes, a shepherd boy, as his beloved.]

7. Gagnon says "the abstract noun *arsenokoitia* is grouped together with *porneia* (sexual immorality, fornication, prostitution, incest) and *moicheia* (adultery) in Origen, Theodoret of Cyrrhus (ca. 450), a homily dubiously ascribed to Cyril of Alexandria (where *malakia* also appears), Nilus of Ancyra (ca. 410; where *aselgeia*, "licentiousness," also appears), and the *Sacra Parallela* attributed to John of Damascus (where *arsenokoitia* is linked explicitly to Lev 20:13). This grouping of *arsenokoitia, porneia*, and *moicheia* parallels the grouping of *porneia, moicheia*, and *paidophthoria* (corruption of boys) in *Barnabas* 19.4; *Did.* 2:2; Clement of Alexandria, Origen, and *The Apostolic Constitutions*."

8. "In his *Demonstration of the Gospel* Eusebius (ca. 340) at one point states: 'Moses issued commands to adulterers and to the unbridled (*akolastois*) not to commit adultery, nor (*mēde*) to *arsenokoitein*, nor to pursue pleasures contrary to nature . . . , but I do not want my disciples to even look at a woman with unbridled desire' (1.6.67)."

9. "In a collection of homilies attributed probably falsely to Macarius of Egypt (ca. 425) the men of Sodom are charged with 'wanting to commit [*arsenokoitia*] with the angelic visitors' (*Homo. Spir.* 50.4.354; *Serm.* 64.49.5.6)."

10. "The translations of *arsenokoitai* in the early translations of Scripture confirm a general reference to 'men who have sex with males': in Latin, *masculorum concubitores* ('men lying together with males'); in Syriac, 'those who lie with men'; and in Coptic, 'lying with males.'"[39]

We could add to these points of Gagnon two later uses of the term by early Christians in reference to Sodom—John IV (*Oratio de Monasteriis* 16.632) and Damascenus Studites (*Thesaurus* 11.560).

Many Christian writers quote Paul's usage in 1 Corinthians 6:9, but the term is not found outside Christian writings.[40] Thus, it is a term probably coined by Paul or at least biblical language that must be understood in light of Scripture. But as noted, we can explain how the term arose in Leviticus 20:13 (LXX). Greek, furthermore, is a language in which words can be combined to form new words that can be understood because of their context and components—as in the German language, for instance. Finally, the importance of the Holiness Code to the early church (e.g., Acts 15) further increases the likelihood that Leviticus 20:13 explains the meaning of *arsenokoitai*.[41]

Therefore, the only possible meaning of this word is men lying with other men as with women. This would apply to *any* male homosexual relationship. It would not merely reference the male playing a dominant role in a homosexual act, but either male involved in a homosexual act, since Leviticus 20:13 speaks of both males equally (they are both to be put to death for their abominable act).[42] Had Paul wanted to distinguish passive and active partners in a

---

[39] Ibid., 317–22. For points 1–5, Gagnon references Dale Martin (*Arsenokoitēs* and *Malakos*: Meanings and Consequences," in *Biblical Ethics and Homosexuality: Listening to Scripture*, ed. Robert L. Brawley [Louisville, KY: Westminster/John Knox, 1996], 117–36). For points 6–9, he references David F. Wright, "Homosexuals or Prostitutes: the Meaning of ARSENOKOITAI (1 Cor 6:9; 1 Tim 1:10)," *Vigilae Christianae* 38 (1984), 125–53.

[40] Based on a search of *Thesaurus Linguae Graeci*, the following writers quote 1 Cor 6:9: Ignatius, Clement of Alexandria, Polycarp, Flavius Claudius Julianus, Epiphanius, Athanasius, Basilius, Origen, John Chrysostom, Theodorus Studites, Barsanuphius, Joannes, Anastasius, John of Damascus, Neophytus Inclusus, Pseudo-Mthodius, Symeon Neotheologus, Gregorius Palamas, Theodoretus, Severianus, Basil of Caesarea, Paulus Helladicus, John of Damascus, and Theodoret. Also, the works *Vitae Andreae Sali* and *Typica Monastica* mention the term.

[41] As Robert Gagnon points out, when the word *arsenokoitai* is used in *Sybylline Oracle* 2.73, it is added into a section taken from another work, *The Sentences of Pseudo-Phocylides* 2.56–148, which is heavily dependent on Leviticus. See Robert Gagnon, *The Bible and Homosexual Practice*, 317–18. Thus, *arsenokoitai* is associated with Lev 20:13 here as in 1 Cor 6:9, and perhaps because of 1 Cor 6:9.

[42] Roy E. Ciampa has suggested that *malakos* refers to the passive partner and *arsenōkoitē* refers to the active partner in a homosexual act ("'Flee Sexual Immorality': Sex and the City of Corinth," in *The Wisdom of the Cross: Exploring 1 Corinthians*, ed. Brian S. Rosner [Nottingham, UK: Apollos/InterVarsity, 2011], 116). Yet he also sees *malakos* as having a broader

homosexual act, he might have done so with the vocabulary available to him in Greek: *erastēs* was used of a male who penetrated another male, and *erōmenos* was used of a male who was penetrated. By using different terms, Paul showed he did not have this distinction in mind. By extension Paul's point would, of course, also apply to lesbian acts (a suggestion confirmed by what Paul says in Rom 1:26 about lesbians).[43]

Since *malakoi* refers to an *orientation* that includes homosexuality as well as other dimensions of "softness," the addition of *arsenokoitai* in 1 Corinthians 6:9 makes sense in order to focus on the *act* of same-sex intercourse and to cover homosexuals other than "soft men" in the list.

ORIENTATION AND "SOFT MEN"

Two different positions appear in popular discussions about homosexual orientation. One has been that the ancient world knew nothing of orientation and only in modern times have we developed this concept. Given this supposed fact—one we have already shown to be false—the argument proceeds to insist that any biblical passages appearing to oppose homosexuality are in reality only opposing heterosexual persons engaging in homosexual acts as a part of idol worship, sexual debauchery, or pederasty. Such interpretations relocate the problem being addressed to anything other than same-sex intercourse *per se*.

The evidence is actually rather strong that some in antiquity believed homosexuals were oriented to same-sex practices. Given this fact, one must conclude that Paul's unqualified statements against same-sex practices are just that—unqualified. Had Paul wanted to oppose pederasty, he would have said so—Greek had a complete vocabulary for this. If sex associated with idols was the issue rather than the same-sex act itself, Paul would have said so. Were the issue simply adultery or debauchery as opposed to committed, long-term, covenantal marriages between same-sex couples, Paul could have made those distinctions too; after all, such relationships are attested in antiquity. If antiquity entertained the notion of sexual orientation—and it did—then Paul's opposition to same-sex practices is not due to an ignorance of sexual orientations.

In 1 Corinthians 6:9–11, when he uses the word *malakoi*, Paul has in view men whose entire lives—actions, desires, and inclinations—are lived in a feminine manner. He is condemning their orientation, not just their behavior. He is not just condemning the passive role in a homosexual act, with *arsenokoitai*

---

meaning than just the passive partner. A man could "also be called effeminate for being overly active in sexual pursuits of women—that is, for being what we might call a 'ladies' man'" (115). See also Roy Ciampa, "Ideological Challenges for Bible Translators: The Terms of Translation," *International Journal of Frontier Missiology* 28, no. 3 (Fall, 2011): 139–48; see n19 and n21.

[43] Another term identified the more dominant lesbian: *gynaikerastria*.

then referring to the active partner in that act. The word *malakoi* and its synonyms overwhelmingly point toward men *oriented* to live as women, and it can also refer to *sexually wanton* persons, not just to those playing a passive role in sexual acts. Yet—and this is the good news—Paul concludes,

> And this is what some of you used to be. But you were washed, you were sanctified, you were justified [*or* made righteous] in the name of the Lord Jesus Christ and in the Spirit of our God. (1 Cor 6:11)

Paul does not merely say, "And this is what some of you used to *do*"; he says, "And this is what some of you used to *be*." The sin list in 1 Corinthians 6:9–10 includes both acts and lifestyles or orientations. The gospel, however, offers the new creation (2 Cor 5:17) a reality of real transformation. This is something Paul articulated in one of his earliest letters.

In 1 Thessalonians 4:8, as Volker Rabens notes, "The gift of the Spirit is placed by Paul in opposition to fornication, lustful passion and impurity (1 Thess 4:3–7). This contrast clearly foreshadows what Paul would later formulate *expressis verbis* as the Spirit-flesh opposition (e.g., Gal 5:17; 1 Cor 3:1)."[44] The eschatological Spirit, the Spirit of the restoration of God's people (Jer 31:31–34; Ezek 36:24–29),[45] is the Spirit of moral transformation now present, sent into the lives of those in Christ Jesus who are no longer oriented to the sinful life of the flesh.

Orientation, then, must be understood in light of both the grip of sin on human life outside of Christ, and, on the other hand, in light of what it means to be a new creation in Christ and to enjoy the empowering presence of the

---

[44] Volker Rabens, "1 Thessalonians," in *A Biblical Theology of the Holy Spirit*, ed. Trevor J. Burke and Keith Warrington (Eugene, OR: Wipf and Stock, 2014) 203. Rabens ably argues against E. D. Schmidt, *Heilig ins Eschaton. Heiligung und Heiligkeit als eschatologische Konzeption in 1 Thessalonicherbrief* (Berlin, Germany: DeGruyter, 2010), 316–18. Schmidt attempts to limit the Spirit to being the theological guarantor of a new status. This is rather like limiting the work of Christ to justification without any transformation to live a righteous life—a mere change of status—or the even more limiting notion that justification is not even a term of salvation but only of covenant fidelity. If Romans 6 and 8 say anything, it is that the work of Christ (chap. 6) and of the Spirit (chap. 8) empowers believers to live the righteous life. Overcoming the power of sin, flesh, and death, and the impotent law (Rom 7:7–25), Christ and the Spirit offer righteousness and new life. In the same book, Trevor J. Burke discusses Paul's theology of the Spirit in terms of, among other things, the Spirit of empowerment for the moral life. For example, referencing Rom 8:13–14, Burke says, "The Spirit is therefore the divine energy and dynamic power to enable the Roman Christians to honour God in the way that they live, which includes the daily responsibility to kill and to conduct themselves in a manner befitting of members of God's new household" ("Romans," in *A Biblical Theology of the Holy Spirit,* 137).

[45] Regarding Ezekiel 36, Volker Rabens, "1 Thessalonians," 207, quotes J. E. Robson's conclusion in his *Word and Spirit in Ezekiel* (London, England: T&T Clark, 2006): "The book of Ezekiel, then, highlights the effecting power of *ruach* [Spirit]. . . . Yahweh, by his *ruach,* brings about moral and ethical transformation and renewal, creating a new community obedient to his word" (276).

Spirit to bring about moral transformation. Many are the sins that imprison the human heart. The law, in Paul's view, is a powerless vessel when it comes to fighting the relentless passions of the flesh. Only in Christ can they who once presented their "members to sin as instruments of wickedness" (Rom 6:13), who were under sin's dominion (Rom 6:14), and who were once "slaves of sin" (Rom 6:17) be set free to become "slaves of righteousness" (Rom 6:18), "obedient from the heart" (Rom 6:17), and able to present their "members to God as instruments of righteousness" (Rom 6:13). Paul's theology is all about the transformation of orientation: "Therefore, do not let sin exercise dominion in your mortal bodies, to make you obey their passions" (Rom 6:12). Instead, "live according to the Spirit" (Rom 8:5).

CONCLUSION

In this chapter we have examined the meanings of two words Paul uses to reference homosexuality. One, *malakoi*, means "soft men." It was used, along with other words conveying the same idea, as a broad notion. "Soft men" were aesthetes, persons with loose morals, sexually promiscuous persons, and, in particular, men with an unnatural female orientation who engaged in homosexual practices. They were "men-women," males who presented a feminine appearance in public. Most importantly, they were oriented to this sort of life. A variety of words, not just *malakoi,* was used to describe this group. In antiquity "soft men" included devotees of the Great Mother Cult, sexually loose and effeminate males in Egypt, and male couples living the "soft life" together.

The other term discussed in this chapter, *arsenokoitēs*, pertains to homosexual acts more than orientation. It appears to be a compound word that Paul formed in 1 Corinthians 6:9 and 1 Timothy 1:10 from two words appearing together in Leviticus 20:13, "men" and "bed." The term has to do with males engaging in sex with one another, whether in active or passive roles.

While we believe the evidence is strong for this conclusion about the two words, our interpretation differs from that of scholars who see *malakos* as depicting the passive homosexual partner and *arsenokoitēs* as depicting the active male partner. Our definition of the terms would certainly include both partners in a homosexual act, but we believe more is behind these words. Even so, one can be certain the desperate attempts by some to understand the words as pertaining to something other than homosexuality, such as pederasty, are in error. The primary sources leave no alternative but to understand that Paul is addressing primarily adult homosexuality with these two terms. This is true even if *malakos* suggests additional dimensions of lifestyle and sexual looseness. Our suggestion, then, is to translate the terms in 1 Corinthians 6:9 as "soft men and homosexuals," thus making the primary distinction in meaning not passive and active homosexuals but those men living as women (emphasizing orientation) and those performing same-sex acts (emphasizing behavior).

CHAPTER 16

HOMOSEXUAL ORIENTATION IN ANTIQUITY AND IN PAUL'S WRITINGS

INTRODUCTION

In 1985 Victor Paul Furnish stated that the Bible cannot be used to argue against homosexuality because the biblical authors had no concept of "sexual orientation." He claimed:

> There was no word for homosexuality in any ancient language, including the biblical languages (Hebrew, Aramaic, Greek); nor were there any words for heterosexuality or bisexuality. . . .
>
> Not only the terms, but the concepts "homosexual" and "homosexuality" were unknown in Paul's day. These terms like "heterosexual," "heterosexuality," "bisexual," and "bisexuality" presuppose an understanding of human sexuality that was possible only with the advent of modern psychology and sociological analysis. The ancient writers were operating without the vaguest idea of what we have learned to call "sexual orientation."[1]

Furnish raises an important question: With regard to homosexuality, are we talking about the same thing as the biblical authors? Many in our day are inclined to accept a comment such as Furnish's since we tend to believe that we are today a more informed society than lived in Paul's time, thanks to the sciences—even the soft sciences. Of course, our understanding is more advanced than that of the ancients when it comes to treating cancer or rocketing to the moon. But is our understanding of sexuality and ethics also more advanced?

Here we will answer this question specifically with regard to sexual orientation. In the previous chapter we explored the primary source evidence

---

[1] Victor Paul Furnish, *The Moral Teachings of Paul: Selected Issues,* 2nd ed. (Nashville, TN: Abingdon, 1985), 85.

303

for homosexual orientation related to the concept of soft men. In this chapter broader evidence for a notion of sexual orientation in antiquity will be discussed, contrasting Furnish and others. In chapter 18 still further evidence will be cited in the discussion of "nature versus nurture" in ancient writings. In our view, people in antiquity had many of the same ideas about sexual practices as we hold today, including the notion of sexual orientation. The difference between ancient and modern views lies in the explanation of what shapes sexual orientation, not in the notion of sexual orientation itself. Scholars who contended several decades ago that only in modern times did people discover the concept of orientation have been proven wrong, as the evidence has been accumulated over time. Our discussion of sexual orientation in general will be followed by a brief look at Paul's specific contribution to the discussion.

TERMS FOR HOMOSEXUALITY IN GREEK AND LATIN

Over against Furnish's claim that ancient languages had no terms for "heterosexual" or "homosexual," we would note the existence of a rich vocabulary in Greek and Latin that referenced both homosexuals and homosexual practices. Some key terms (mostly from Greek) are listed below.

Terms for Homosexuals
- *para physin*, "against nature"—a way of speaking of homosexual acts and orientations
- *kata physin,* "according to nature"—a way of speaking of heterosexual acts and orientations

Terms for Male Homosexuals
- *erastēs*—a male who penetrates another male
- *erōmenos*—a male who is penetrated by another male

Terms for Lesbians
- *gynaikerastria*—a woman who loves other women; a woman-lover[2]
- *hetairistria*—"women who, like men, are oriented (*tetrammenai*) toward women companions for sex"[3]

---

[2] The second-century AD Egyptian text, P. Oxy. XV 1800, says that Sappho was a "woman-lover" (*gynaikerastria*). She is also said to be an "*erastēs* of women." As noted in Dominic Montserrat, *Sex and Society in Graeco-Roman Egypt* (1963, repr.; London, England: Routledge, 2011), 160.

[3] As noted by Bernadette J. Brooten, *Love Between Women: Early Christian Responses to Homoeroticism* (Chicago, IL: University of Chicago, 1996), 5, in reference to Kurt Latte, ed., *Hesychii Alexandrini Lexicon* (Berlin, Germany: Munksgaard, 1953), 1:451. Bernadette Brooten also lists the Greek word *dihetaristria,* found in Hesychius (a fourth-century AD Greek lexicographer).

- *tribas* (pl. *tribades*)—having the basic meaning of "to rub," the word was used of homosexual women;[4] Latin: *frictrix/ fricatrix*
- *lesbia*—from the word Lesbos, a Greek island, associated with the homosexual or bisexual poetess Sappho and certain other women, the term is used of women who love other women and engage in sexual acts with them; Latin: *lesbis, lesbiacus, lesbius, lesbous*

Terms for Pederasty
- *paiderastia*—pederasty
- *paiderastai*—adult male in a pederastic relationship
- *paidika*—youth in a pederastic relationship
- *philoneos*—lover of young boys

Terms for Effeminate, Soft Men Acting Out This Orientation Sexually
- *habrodiaitos*—effeminate
- *kinaidoi*—men who play the role of women, transvestites; Latin: *virago*—a man-like woman, heroic maiden, female warrior, heroine
- *malakos*—soft, used of effeminate, homosexual males; Latin: *mollis*
- *euthryptos*—easily broken, crumbling, soft
- *thēlydrios*—effeminacy (also the participial form, *tethēlysmenos*)
- *pathētikōs*—males playing the female, passive role with other males
- *androgynos*—man-woman (effeminacy)

Some of these terms could primarily reference actions, but most have to do with deeper tendencies, regular practices, and orientations.

SEXUAL ORIENTATION IN ANTIQUITY

The impossibility of Furnish's declaration that antiquity knew no such thing as sexual orientation is further highlighted by various texts that address the subject. Many texts from antiquity that reference sexual orientation do so in discussing the larger question of whether nature or nurture causes human behavior. We shall explore the matter of sexual orientation first in terms of romantic love, then in terms of arguments from nurture, and finally in terms of arguments from nature. Readers should understand that ancients offered a variety of opinions on these matters, as analysts do today. We shall conclude this discussion by noting how Paul's biblical argument eclipses the nature/nurture discussion of sexual orientation.

---

[4] While Liddell-Scott says *tribas* referenced "a woman who practises unnatural vice with herself or with other women," Bernadette Brooten, *Love Between Women*, questions whether the term ever meant females who masturbate (4).

1. Romantic Love, Desire, and Sexual Orientation

Ancient literature, as much as literature today, spoke about sex in terms of passion that drove people to pursue love. That is, sex could not be reduced to rational choice. In addition to ancient novels, such as Xenophon's *Ephesian Tale of Anthia and Habrocomes*, there was also love poetry. Tibullus, of the first century BC, writes of a man possessed and taunted by love of boys and gives advice on how to enter a relationship with a boy (*The Love of Boys*). This is romantic pederasty, not mere sexual indulgence. Virgil (37 BC) says in *Eclogue* II,

> Cruel Alexis, heed you naught my songs?
> Have you no pity? You'll drive me to my death . . .
> . . . beauteous boy.[5]

Pseudo-Lucian, of the fourth century AD, offers a more philosophical discussion of pederasty in *Amores* 46, yet it, too, describes pederasty in terms of romantic love:

> *Who would not fall in love with such a youth?* Whose eyesight could be so blind, whose mental processes so stunted? How could one fail to love him who is a Hermes in the wrestling-school, an Apollo with the lyre, a horseman to rival Castor, and one who strives after the virtues of the gods with a mortal body? For my part, ye gods of heaven, I pray that it may for ever be my lot in life to sit opposite my dear one and hear close to me his sweet voice, to go out when he goes out and share every activity with him.[6]

Suffice it to say that where our society considers pedophilia to be a deviant, sexual perversion, the Greeks understood pederasty in terms of romance. Platonic philosophers even portrayed it as superior to the love of a woman because they understood the love of boys as the pursuit of ideals or universals, such as beauty (as in *Amores* or Plato's *Phaedrus*). Yet most significantly, the power of love, what we would call romantic love, played an important role in the literature of antiquity and could explain unreasoned desire of one person for another—whether heterosexual or homosexual involvement was in view.

2. Nurture and Sexual Orientation

The historical, anthropological, and sociological arguments in antiquity, as might be expected, pointed toward nurture as the reason different people pursued different types of sexual relationships. Yet nurture could be understood as

---

[5] The Internet Classics Archive by Daniel C. Stevenson, Web Atomics 1994–2000, accessed May 4, 2011, http://classics.mit.edu/Virgil/eclogue.mb.txt.

[6] Lucian, *Amores,* Loeb Classical Library, trans. A. M. Harmon (Cambridge, MA: Harvard University Press, 1967).

leading to a reshaping of what a person or culture experiences as "natural." So, for example, Herodotus says in *The Histories* 1.135.1,

> The Persians more than all men welcome foreign customs. They wear the Median dress, thinking it more beautiful than their own, and the Egyptian cuirass in war. Their *luxurious practices are of all kinds*, and all borrowed: *the Greeks taught them pederasty*. Every Persian marries many lawful wives, and keeps still more concubines.[7]

A *Sibylline Oracle* (3.595–600) further states that the Persians, Greeks, Phoenicians, Egyptians, Romans, Galatians, and the people of Asia Minor practiced pederasty. Plato, too, suggests that same-sex eroticism, particularly pederasty, arose among the Cretans (*Laws* 1.636b–c). Plutarch speaks of the practice as particularly notable among the Spartans (*Lycurgus* 17.1; 18.4).[8] Interestingly, Philo argued that the love of boys was a social development (*Special Laws* 3.37–42). And Sextus Empiricus (ca. AD 200) says in *Outlines of Pyrrhonism* 3:198–200,

> Amongst us *sodomy* is regarded as [199] shameful or rather illegal, but by the Germanic they say, it is not looked on as shameful but as a customary thing. It is said, too, that in Thebes long ago this practice was not held to be shameful, and they say that Meriones the Cretan was so called by way of indicating the Cretans' custom, and some refer to . . . the burning love of Achilles for Patroclus. And [200] what wonder, when both the adherents of the Cynic philosophy and the followers of Zeno of Citium, Cleanthes and Chrysippus, declare that this practice is indifferent (*adiaphoron*)?[9]

Xenophon, of the fourth century BC, also addresses social differences regarding pederasty in *The Constitution of the Lacedaemonians* 2.12:

> I think I ought to say something also about *intimacy with boys*, since this matter also has a bearing on education. In other Greek states, for instance among the Boeotians, man and boy live together, like married people; elsewhere, among the Eleians, for example, consent is won by means of favours. Some, on the other hand, entirely forbid suitors to talk with boys.[10]

---

[7] *Herodotus, with an English translation by A. D. Godley* (Cambridge, MA: Harvard University Press, 1920).

[8] Plutarch, *Lives,* vol 1: *Theseus and Romulus, Lycurgus and Numa, Solon and Publicola*, Loeb Classical Library 46, trans. Bernadotte Perrin (Cambridge, MA: Harvard University Press, 1914), accessed September 26, 2013, http://penelope.uchicago.edu/Thayer/E/Roman/Texts/Plutarch/Lives/Lycurgus*.html.

[9] *Sextus Empiricus: Outlines of Pyrrhonism*, Loeb Classical Library 273, trans. R. G. Bury (Cambridge, MA: Harvard University Press, 1933).

[10] *Xenophon in Seven Volumes*, vol. 7, Loeb Classical Library, trans. E. C. Marchant and G. W. Bowersock (Cambridge, MA: Harvard University Press, rev. ed. 1925; London: William Heinemann, Ltd., 1984).

Juvenal, who lived in the first and second centuries AD, speaks of the spread of pederasty, noting that it was practiced by Romans in his day and could catch on in Armenia:

> And yet they say that one Zalaces, an Armenian more effeminate than any of our youth, has yielded to the ardour of a Tribune! Just see what evil communications do! He came as a hostage: but here boys are turned into men. Give them a long sojourn in our city, and lovers will never fail them. They will throw away their trousers and their knives, their bridles and their whips, and thus carry back to Artaxata the manners of our Roman youth. (*Satire* II.27)[11]

3. Nature and Sexual Orientation

Other ancient writings present the view that same-sex eroticism is more a matter of nature than nurture. We have already noted some astrological and medical discussion of orientation while exploring the meaning of "soft males" (*malakoi*) and will examine more here. Also, physiognomy (i.e., the discipline of judging character based on physical characteristics) and philosophy addressed the question of sexual orientation. Without extensive duplication of what has been said, we turn to consider further evidence for the concept of sexual orientation in antiquity.

a. Medical Theory, Physiognomy, and Sexual Orientation

The famous medical author Galen represents a line of writers that attempted to explain personality and temperament from a biological perspective. This included a "soft" temperament associated with sexual orientation.

Aristotle wrote a work on physiognomy in which he associated soft characteristics in humans or animals with femaleness. For example, the feet, buttocks, belly, back, and shoulders can be described physically and then associated with maleness or femaleness (*Physiognomonica* 5–6). Moreover, in 2–3 he states:

> Signs of low spirits are lean and wrinkled brows; enfeebled eyes (but you should notice that weak eyes may signify softness and effeminacy as well as dejection and low spirits); a weak bearing and weary gait. The pathic [passive partner in male, homosexual relationships] is weak-eyed and knock-kneed; his head hangs on his right shoulder; his hands are carried upturned and flabbily; and as he walks he either wags his loins or else holds them rigid by an effort; and he casts a furtive gaze around.[12]

---

[11] Juvenal, *Satires* are from *Juvenal and Persius*, Loeb Classical Library, trans. G. G. Ramsay (Cambridge, MA: Harvard University Press, 1957).

[12] *The Works of Aristotle,* vol. 6, trans. T. Loveday and E. S. Forster, ed. W. D. Ross (Oxford, England: Clarendon, 1913).

The effeminate demeanor of soft men is discussed by Aristotle in terms of the pathic, that is, the passive partner in male homosexual relationships. Such a person has adopted an entire way of life that anyone can identify at a glance. Aristotle further describes the pathic:

> Shrill, soft, broken tones mark the speech of the pathic, for such a voice is found in women and is congruous with the pathic's nature.[13]

b. Astrology and Sexual Orientation

Claudius Ptolemy penned *Tetrabiblos*,[14] a work that was cited earlier. The work is a second-century AD text exploring the effects of astral phenomena on human behavior. That is, the author is searching for an explanation of certain orientations in light of astrology. While we might reject the "science" of the second century (along with some psychological theories today), we see in this work the concept of a sexual orientation beyond one's control, like any other disease. Thus, Ptolemy writes in *Tetrabiblos* III.14.171–72,

> But if likewise Mars [planet/god of war] or Venus [planet/god of love] as well, either one of them or both, is made masculine, the males become addicted to *natural* [*kata physin*] sexual intercourse, and are adulterous, insatiate, and ready on every occasion for base and lawless acts of sexual passion, while the females are lustful for *unnatural congresses* [*para physin*], cast inviting glances of the eye, and are what we call *tribades*; for *they deal with females and perform the functions of males* [*andrōn erga*]. If Venus alone is constituted in a masculine manner, they do these things secretly and not openly. But if Mars likewise is so constituted, without reserve, so that sometimes they even designate *the women with whom they are on such terms as their lawful "wives."*
>
> But on the other hand, when the luminaries in the aforesaid configuration are unattended in feminine signs, the *females exceed in the natural* [*kata physin*], and the *males in unnatural practice* [*para physin*], with the result that their souls become *soft* [*euthrypton*] and *effeminate* [*tethēlysmenos*]. If Venus too is made effeminate, the women become depraved, adulterous and lustful, with the result that they may be dealt with in the *natural* manner [*kata physin*] on any occasion and by any one soever, and so that they refuse absolutely no sexual act, though it be base or unlawful. The men, on the contrary, become *effeminate* [*malakoi*] and unsound with respect to *natural* [*kata physin*] congresses and the functions of women [*gynaikōn erga*], and are dealt with as *pathics* [*pathētikōs*], though privately and secretly. But if Mars also is constituted in a feminine manner, their shamelessness is outright and frank and they perform the aforesaid acts of either kind, assuming the

---

[13] Ibid.

[14] Ptolemy, *Tetrabiblos*, Loeb Classical Library, trans. by W. G. Waddell and F. E. Robbins (Cambridge, MA: Harvard University Press, 1940).

guise of common bawds who submit to general abuse and to very baseness until they are stamped with the reproach and insult that attend such usages.

Here, in a work written within a century after the New Testament, we have an astrological theory to explain sexual orientation. Note that the terminology of *kata physin* (according to nature), *para physin* (against nature), and *malakoi* (soft males) was standard during multiple centuries. Also, the terms as well as the concepts employed (since various terms are used) suggest homosexual orientation for women and men. Indeed, language about gender (male, female) and function (according to one's sexuality) is used—as in Romans 1:26–27. Females assuming the "functions of males" or males assuming the "functions of females" are considered deviant from a "natural" standard, and this deviation is due to an orientation one may have from birth. In other words, in this astrological text, people are said to be born with a particular sexual orientation distinct from their biological makeup or their nurturing.

c. Philosophy, Mythology, and Sexual Orientation

Pre-Socratic philosophers known as the Sophists focused their discourses on the question of whether people developed particular traits because of nature or nurture. This philosophical question was in the background as Aristotle discussed nurturing virtue through the development of habits and friendship in his treatise on ethics (*Nichomachean Ethics*).[15] The philosophical schools of Cynicism and Stoicism emphasized nature in ethics. The Cynics opposed nurture, social mores, customs, and laws and attempted to live purely according to "nature." They demonstrated their contempt for supposedly human-generated customs by remaining unkempt, defecating or having sex in public, and having no regard for social authorities. The Stoic philosophical movement grew out of Cynicism and emphasized finding contentment in the way things are. For example, if one was a slave, one should accept this and learn contentment as a slave. Thus, in a general sense, Greek philosophy had been discussing for centuries whether people possess certain traits and commit certain acts because of their nature or because of their social nurturing. One finds the matter of homosexual identity being discussed in light of this larger philosophical question.

One theory about sexual orientation is presented through a myth told by the character Aristophanes in Plato's *Symposium*, written in the fifth century BC. Aristophanes retells an old fable that humans were originally created in pairs: male-male, male-female, or female-female. After the gods sliced them

---

[15] While Aristotle linked actions to habits that became part of one's character, his virtue ethics failed to do what biblical ethics does: distinguish good or righteous acts from bad or unrighteous acts. The focus on virtue (*aretē*) came at the expense of a clear understanding of moral acts. His virtue ethics did ask what helps a person accomplish his purpose well, but Aristotle understood purpose in terms of functioning in society rather than in terms of how God made a person. A virtue ethic, like a value ethic, turns out to be too abstract and open to various interpretations.

in half, they sought their other half. Thus, heterosexuality as well as male and female homosexuality are seen as natural dispositions. In Plato's *Symposium* 191 Aristophanes says:

> Each of us, then, is but a tally of a man, since every one shows like a flat-fish the traces of having been sliced in two; and each is ever searching for the tally that will fit him. All the men who are sections of that composite sex that at first was called *man-woman* are woman-courters; our adulterers are mostly descended from that sex, [191e] whence likewise are derived our man-courting women and adulteresses. *All the women who are sections of the woman have no great fancy for men: they are inclined rather to women*, and of this stock are the she-minions. Men who are sections of the male pursue the masculine, and *so long as their boyhood lasts they show themselves to be slices of the male by making friends with men and delighting [192a] to lie with them and to be clasped in men's embraces; these are the finest boys and striplings, for they have the most manly nature.*[16]

Despite such strong evidence from antiquity, some contemporary scholars have claimed that sexual orientation was an unknown concept until the modern age. Gillian Clark, for example, says that "a Lesbian identity was not an option in late antiquity."[17] Like Furnish and others, David Halperin, following Michel Foucault,[18] believes homosexual orientation was something discovered in the latter part of the nineteenth century. The basic problem with such arguments—which have been important in attempts to distance opposition to homosexual practice in Scripture from homosexuality today—is that their proponents ignore considerable evidence to the contrary.

Halperin is aware of Plato's *Symposium.* Thus, he attempts to offer an explanation of the *Symposium* that does not involve sexual orientation. He argues that since Aristophanes describes the love of some boys for men and the love these boys have for other boys once they are grown (see *Symposium* 191e–92b), the passage is about pederastic relationships and not sexual orientation.[19]

---

[16] *Plato in Twelve Volumes*, Loeb Classical Library 9, trans. Harold N. Fowler (Cambridge, MA: Harvard University Press; London, William Heinemann Ltd. 1925).

[17] Gillian Clark, *Women in Late Antiquity: Pagan and Christian Lifestyles* (New York, NY: Clarendon, 1993), 90.

[18] Michel Foucault, *The History of Sexuality,* vol. 1: *An Introduction*, trans. Robert Hurley (New York, NY: Vintage, 1978). Foucault writes, "Homosexuality appeared as one of the forms of sexuality when it was transposed from the practice of sodomy into a kind of interior androgyny, a hermaphrodism of the soul. The sodomite had been a temporary aberration; the homosexual was now a species" (43) (as quoted by John Thorp, "Review Article/Discussion: The Social Construction of Homosexuality," *Phoenix* 46, no. 1 [1992]: 54–65, accessed April 19, 2012, http://www.fordham.edu/halsall/med/thorp.asp). David Halperin, *One Hundred Years of Homosexuality: And Other Essays on Greek Love* (New York, NY: Routledge, 1990).

[19] David Halperin, *One Hundred Years of Homosexuality and Other Essays on Greek Love*, 19–21.

This argument fails for three reasons. First, Aristophanes's speech in the *Symposium* is crafted in order to *explain orientation*. The argument is that people are wired to pursue certain sexual partners because of how they were originally made. Pederasty is only an illustration, whereas same-sex orientation is the issue. Second, Aristophanes refers to adult women pursuing love with one another, not just adult male to boy sexual attraction. Third, Aristophanes's example envisages the boys who are attracted to men then growing up to be attracted to boys, not girls or women. As adults, they continue in same-sex attractions and relationships.

As John Thorp says, Aristophanes "doesn't seem to want to explain just an anatomical or mechanical sexual preference, but a whole way or tenor of life. The males who desire males do not just want to copulate with them, but to spend their lives with them (192c)." Also:

> Aristophanes explicitly says that the sexual pleasure cannot explain the desire of these males to be together; their souls are longing for something else which they cannot name (192d). Far from being a superficial point of taste, the homosexual desire and activity is an expression of something which lies deep in the soul—so deep that its nature is altogether unclear. . . . With this genealogical explanation, Aristophanes is effectively assigning the three groups to something like different races or species; he is undertaking to tell the story of the origins of three different races.[20]

A further problem with the idea that people in antiquity did not know of homosexual orientation should be noted here. There are clear examples of adult males and females involved in homosexual relationships in antiquity. These people did not just perform homosexual acts. Their passionate love of one another, their long-term same-sex desire, and even, on occasion, their marriage or cohabitation with one another are discussed in the sources we have. There is, in short, nothing distinct about contemporary conversations concerning homosexual orientation.

THE ACTIVE FEMALE AND PASSIVE MALE

Part of Halperin's argument is his claim that Greek political thinking did not accept a male citizen playing a passive role, which the citizen would do if he permitted himself to be penetrated sexually. This raises the question, Is the problem with homosexuality in antiquity merely that it involves a man playing a passive role in sex and a woman playing an active role in sex? Various scholars present this kind of argument, saying negative views of homosexuality in

---

[20] John Thorp, "Review Article/Discussion: The Social Construction of Homosexuality." Footnote 7 states, "In 1869 *'homosexuelle'* was coined by Karl Maria Kertbeny; in the same year Carl Westphal introduced the phrase *'die conträre Sexualempfindung.'*" The terminological history is told by Halperin, *One Hundred Years of Homosexuality,* 155.

antiquity referenced only passive males and active females. So, for example, Furnish states, in regard to Romans 1:26–27, that a negative view of "same-sex intercourse compromises what patriarchal societies regard as the properly dominant role of males over females."[21] Such a conjecture falters when applied to Paul because Greek had precise language to reference the male who penetrates (*erastēs*) and the male who is penetrated (*erōmenos*). That Paul does not use this terminology when he could have in order to limit his meaning suggests Furnish's theory is incorrect. In fact, Paul rather clearly states that same-sex relationships are the issue, not females playing male roles or males playing female roles in sex.

Furthermore, "against nature" never means merely a female playing an active role or a male playing a passive role; it means women or men involved in same-sex acts. While Ptolemy distinguishes between women and men who play the active and passive roles (*Tetrabiblos* III. 14.172), a theory of dominance is not only absent from his writing but could not make sense of what he says. Ptolemy works from the notion that what is according to nature is heterosexual sex. The language of "against nature" and "according to nature" refers to homosexual and heterosexual sex, respectively.

Epictetus also understands "according to nature" by the use of body parts for the purposes for which they were created. What is natural is for the male and female parts to be connected (*Disc.* 1.6). Also, he says that both the active and the passive partner in a male homosexual relationship "lose the man" (*Disc.* 2.10). There is nothing here of Halperin's or Furnish's notion that only passive males and active females were considered moral failures in antiquity. This is not the issue in Romans 1:26–27.

PAUL'S UNDERSTANDING OF SEXUAL ORIENTATION IN ROMANS 1:24–28

For Paul, as we saw in the previous chapter, orientation can be understood either in terms of what God intended in creation or in terms of passions that drive a person to desire and do certain things. It can refer either to the intentions of God or to the intentions of the human heart, either in its fallen or restored state. This can be seen in Romans and in Paul's notion of desires of the flesh. But how did his view relate to those of his contemporaries?

As did a Stoic philosopher like Epictetus, Paul understood the world as God made it to be natural. God's law is written into the design of his creation. On the matter of sex, God designed creation so that males come together with females. The ancients often commented on how animals do not pair off in

---

[21] Victor Paul Furnish, "The Bible and Homosexuality: Reading the Texts in Context," in *Homosexuality in the Church: Both Sides of the Debate,* ed. Jeffrey Siker (Louisville, KY: Westminster/John Knox, 1994), 20.

homosexual relationships like some people do. Animals show humans what
is natural, but humans sometimes live against nature, as Pseudo-Phocylides,
Pseudo-Lucian, Plutarch, and Pliny the Elder state.

> Transgress not for unlawful sex the natural [*physeōs*] limits of sexuality.
> For even animals are not pleased by intercourse of male with male. And let
> not women imitate the sexual role of men. (Pseudo-Phocylides, *Sentences*
> 190–92)[22]

> If each man abided by the ordinances prescribed for us by Providence,
> we should be satisfied with intercourse with women and life would be uncor-
> rupted by anything shameful. Certainly, among animals incapable of debas-
> ing anything through depravity of disposition the laws of nature are preserved
> undefiled. Lions have no passion for lions but love in due season evokes in
> them desire for the females of their kind. The bull, monarch of the herd,
> mounts cows, and the ram fills the whole flock with seed from the male.
> Furthermore do not boars seek to lie with sows? Do not wolves mate with
> she-wolves? And, to speak in general terms, neither the birds whose wings
> whir on high, nor the creatures whose lot is a wet one beneath the water
> nor yet any creatures upon land strive for intercourse with fellow males, but
> the decisions of Providence remain unchanged. But you who are wrongly
> praised for wisdom, you beasts truly contemptible, you humans, by what
> strange infection have you been brought to lawlessness and incited to outrage
> each other? With what blind insensibility have you engulfed your souls that
> you have missed the mark in both directions, avoiding what you ought to
> pursue, and pursuing what you ought to avoid? If each and every man should
> choose to emulate such conduct, the human race will come to a complete end.
> (Pseudo-Lucian, *Amores* 22)[23]

> Whence it comes about that to this very day the desires of beasts have
> encompassed no homosexual mating. But you have a fair amount of such traf-
> ficking among your high and mighty nobility, to say nothing of the baser sort.
> Agamemnon came to Boeotia hunting for Argynnus, who tried to elude him,
> and slandering the sea and winds . . . then he gave his noble self a noble
> bath in Lake Copaïs to drown his passion there and get rid of his desire. Just
> so Heracles, pursuing a beardless lad, lagged behind the other heroes and
> deserted the expedition. On the Rotunda of Ptoian Apollo one of your men
> secretly inscribed FAIR IS ACHILLES—when Achilles already had a son.
> And I hear that the inscription is still in place. But a cock that mounts another
> for the lack of a female is burned alive because some prophet or seer declares
> that such an event is an important and terrible omen. On this basis even men
> themselves acknowledge that beasts have a better claim to temperance and

---

[22] P. W. van der Horst, *The Sentences of Pseudo-Phocylides* (Leiden, Netherlands: E. J. Brill, 1978), 101.

[23] Pseudo-Lucian, *Affairs of the Heart*, Loeb Classical Library, trans. A. M. Harmon (Cambridge, MA: Harvard University Press, 1925).

the non-violation of nature in their pleasures. Not even Nature [*physis*], with Law [*nomos*] for her ally, can keep within bounds the unchastened vice of your hearts; but as though swept by the current of their lusts beyond the barrier at many points, men do such deeds as wantonly outrage Nature, upset her order, and confuse her distinctions. For men have, in fact, attempted to consort with goats and sows and mares, and women have gone mad with lust for male beasts. From such unions your Minotaurs and Aegipans, and, I suppose, your Sphinxes and Centaurs have arisen. Yet it is through hunger that dogs have occasionally eaten a man; and birds have tasted of human flesh through necessity; but no beast has ever attempted a human body for lustful reasons. But the beasts I have mentioned and many others have been victims of the violent and lawless lusts of man. (Plutarch, *Whether Beasts Are Rational* 7)[24]

In the human race also, the men have devised various substitutes for the more legitimate exercise of passion, all of which outrage Nature; while the females have recourse to abortion. How much more guilty than the brute beasts are we in this respect! (Pliny the Elder, *Nat. Hist.* x.83 [63])[25]

What Paul is saying in Romans 1:24 is that just as God the Creator has faded from the understanding of sinful humanity, so too God's intention in creation has faded from the understanding of sinful humanity. Just as people turned to make and worship idols, so too they have turned from God's purpose for men and women sexually to use the sexual instruments God gave them for other purposes—same-sex unions. This is why we find the words "natural use" in Romans 1:26—a fact obscured by some English translations:

For this reason God gave them up to degrading passions. Their women exchanged natural intercourse [so the NRSV; ESV, NIV: natural relations; Greek: *physikēn chrēsin,* natural use, function] for unnatural.

Romans 1:27 speaks of men who give up the "natural use of women" (*physikēn chrēsin tēs thēleias*)—again obscured in English translations. The focus on "use" (*chrēsis*) means that Paul is thinking in terms of the function of body parts as God intended them to be used. This notion reappears in Romans 6:

No longer present your members to sin as instruments of wickedness, but present yourselves to God as those who have been brought from death to life, and present your members to God as instruments of righteousness. (v. 13)

The notion of the proper use of one's body appears again in the paragraph concluding Paul's theological argument and beginning his ethical argument

[24] Plutarch, *Moralia*, trans. Harold Cherniss and William C. Hembold (Cambridge, MA: Harvard University Press, 1957).

[25] Pliny the Elder, *The Natural History*, trans. John Bostock and H. T. Riley (London, England: Taylor and Francis, 1855).

in Romans: "Present your bodies as a living sacrifice, holy and acceptable to God, which is your spiritual worship" (Rom 12:1). Paul not only develops this ethic of "the use of body parts as God intended" in Romans; he also develops his ethic in terms of "the transformation of sinful desires." The terms Paul uses for the notion of desires in Romans 1:26–27 are "sinful passions" (*pathē atimias*), verse 26, "enflamed" (*ekkaiō*), and "desire" or "passion" (*orexis*), verse 27. Such things result in a depraved mind, where one thinks the sinful desires are natural and should be followed and accepted (Rom 1:28, 32). As noted in the previous chapter, Paul later argues that such slavery to sin can be changed into a slavery to righteousness (Rom 6:16–18). The transformation of sinful desire, like the appropriate use of body parts, is possible. Paul argues that in light of God's mercies, humans can be transformed by the renewing of their minds such that they will no longer be conformed to this world and can again know God's will (Rom 12:2). Thus, Paul's overall argument in Romans involves a solution to the problem of sinful sexual orientation. Whether this is articulated in terms of the misuse of body parts contrary to nature or in terms of the depraved mind of fallen humanity passionately desiring what is unnatural, the solution is the same. The gospel provides the answer to the problem of misusing body parts in the acting out of sinful desires.

One scholar, Mark Smith, has suggested that antiquity thought more in terms of humans being first bisexual and then expressing their sexuality in one direction or another. He suggests thinking of a continuum, with heterosexual on one end and homosexual on the other; the idea is that people fit onto the scale somewhere in between. The variety of sexual orientations is fairly diverse on this sort of scale, and people can lean in one direction or the other for various reasons.[26]

This does not explain Paul's view in Romans 1:26–27, but where Smith is helpful is in his observation that, for Paul, sexual passion stands prior to orientation, and orientation can take a variety of forms (not just heterosexual or homosexual). Indeed, Paul does not seem to think merely in terms of homosexual and heterosexual orientations. He is aware of a great variety of sexual orientations, and he considers a number of heterosexual orientations to be sinful: fornication, adultery, and lust. Paul's basic understanding of orientation is that human passions have become sinful because of the fall. Homosexual passion is one of many distortions of what God intended for human desire. While God made males and females to desire one another and fit together naturally, humans have turned away from God's good design in creation and refocused their desires so that some have even—against nature—desired same-sex unions.

---

[26] Mark Smith, "Ancient Bisexuality and the Interpretation of Romans 1:26–27," *Journal of the American Academy of Religion* 64, no. 2 (Summer 1996): 223–56.

In Paul's writings God has a design for sex: its place is in marriage between a man and a woman. This has been the standard view in Judaism and Christianity (until the past few decades in some quarters of the Western church). Among the forms of sexual sin listed in the New Testament are immorality (*akatharsia,* Rom 1:24; 6:19; 2 Cor 12:21), sexual immorality (*porneia,* Matt 15:19; Gal 5:19; 2 Cor 12:21; Eph 5:3; Col 3:5), adultery (*moicheia,* sometimes *porneia,* Mark 7:22; Matt 15:19), gender confusion (*malakos,* 1 Cor 6:9; cf. 11:2–16), orgies (*kōmoi,* Rom 13:13; Gal 5:21; 1 Pet 4:3), sexual encounters (*mē koitais,* Rom 13:13), sexual impurity (*akatharsia,* Gal 5:19; 1 Thess 4:7; Rom 6:19; 2 Cor 12:21; Eph 4:19; 5:3; Col 3:5), debauchery or licentiousness (*aselgeia,* Mark 7:22; Gal 5:19; Rom 13:13; 2 Cor 12:21; Eph 4:19; 1 Pet 4:3; 2 Pet 2:2, 7, 18; Jude 4), disgusting things associated with idolatry (*athemitois eidōlolatriais,* 1 Pet 4:3), sexual passion (*pathos,* Rom 1:26; 1 Thess 4:5; Col 3:5), bad desires (*epithymia kakē,* Col 3:5), and lawlessness (*anomia,* what is against the law, Rom 6:19).

One word in this list, *epithymia,* occurs throughout Paul's writings and gets to the heart of his "psychology of sin." Paul's understanding of "orientation" involves passions and sin. Twice, in Romans 7:7–8 and 13:9, Paul quotes only part of the tenth commandment (Deut 5:21), "You shall not covet" (in Greek, the word for "covet" is related to the noun *epithymia*). By quoting this part alone and not the rest of the commandment, he emphasizes not the object of desire but the passions or desires themselves that lead people into sin. *Epithymia* means "passion" or "desire," and Paul has in mind *sinful passions* in these verses. He often uses this word in reference to sexual passion and almost always in a negative way: Romans 1:24 (associated specifically with homosexual passion); 6:12; 7:7–8; and 13:9 (used in quoting the tenth commandment from Deut 5:21); 13:14; 1 Corinthians 10:6 (very broadly, desire of evil things); and Galatians 5:16–17, 24; Ephesians 2:3; 4:22; Colossians 3:5; 1 Thessalonians 4:5; 1 Timothy 6:9; 2 Timothy 2:22; 3:6; 4:3; Titus 2:12; 3:3. In these passages Paul understands humans to be driven by sinful passions, particularly sinful sexual passions. Of course, there is a place for sexual desire, but he regards marriage between a man and a woman as the only acceptable place to express it (1 Cor 7:5, 36). If married people do not practice sex in marriage, their passions will lead them into sin (1 Cor 7:5). Conversion does not do away with passions, but believers are taught to put away their sinful passions. Paul says:

> They [those outside of Christ] have lost all sensitivity and have abandoned themselves to licentiousness, greedy to practice every kind of impurity. That is not the way you learned Christ! For surely you have heard about him and were taught in him, as truth is in Jesus. You were taught to put away your former way of life, your old self, corrupt and deluded by its lusts [*epithymia*],

and to be renewed in the spirit of your minds, and to clothe yourselves with the new self, created according to the likeness of God in true righteousness and holiness. (Eph 4:19–24)

The church today encounters suggestions that one's sexual passions are only natural and should be indulged as long as one has a willing partner. Thus, couples living together before marriage and homosexual relationships are being endorsed by some in a clear contradiction of Paul's teaching.

A conceptually related term to *epithymia* ("desire") is *sarx* ("flesh"). This relationship comes out where the two words are used together, as in Galatians 5:16–17: "Do not bring *desires of the flesh* to their goal, for the *flesh desires* against the Spirit" (our translation). Also note Ephesians 2:1, 3: "And you, being dead in your trespasses and sins, . . . in which we all once conducted ourselves in the *desires of our flesh*, acting according to the wishes of the *flesh* and of our thoughts" (our translation). "Flesh" is a common term in Paul's ethics, capturing, like "desire," the notion that behind sinful acts is the fundamental problem of sin: it has control over human passions or desires. (In fact, Paul's use of the term *flesh* for sinful desire related to our bodies might stem from reflection on the creation story, as Herman Ridderbos has maintained.)[27] Thus, Paul aims his ethical teaching at the root of the problem, sinful desires of the flesh, even though he takes note at times of the specific sins that result from humanity's sinful condition.

This bears some similarity to Plato's view in the *Phaedrus* (246a–254e). In this work Plato describes the human soul as comprised of a charioteer (reason) who tries to drive two winged horses. One horse is noble, the other ignoble. The noble horse rises up on wings fed by noble things: truth, modesty, and temperance. These virtues exist in the realm of the ideals. The other horse has not been fed with such ideals or universals, and it desires to plunge to the earth, or it has such feeble wings that it cannot rise to the heavens. It is drawn to the world of the particulars. The result is a turbulent ride for the human soul that, at times, soars to the heavens and at other times plummets to the earth.

In this myth the horses represent desire that needs to be guided by the charioteer, reason, and "fed" with ideals. Desire is both good and bad. It is good when reason and an attraction to the heavenly realm of ideal virtues guide the soul. It is bad when reason is absent and an attraction to the earthly realm of lesser things guides. Each person experiences the pull of both kinds of desire.

---

[27] Herman Ridderbos, *Paul: An Outline of His Theology* (Grand Rapids, MI: Eerdmans, 1975), 104. As Ridderbos argues, the "theological" understanding of humanity is prior to the anthropological understanding. This stands in contrast to R. Bultmann, who says it is not a weak creation which could not stand against temptation that accounts for sin in the world but a sinful choice (Adam's) which accounts for the sinful state of the world.

While this offers some parallel to Galatians 5:16–17, Paul's ethics are different in two ways. First, Paul's ethic is not based on Platonic ideals but on God's intention for his creation. Thus, Plato says in the *Phaedrus* that a pedophile appreciates the ideal of beauty in the boy that he finds attractive, whereas Paul would say that this same-sex attraction is a perversion of God's good intention in creation. Second, Paul teaches that conflict in the soul between good and evil is overcome in the life of believers because they are led by the Spirit (Gal 5:16–18; Rom 7:7–25; 8:1–17; Rom 12:1–2).

Thus, Paul has a theology of sexual orientation. While desire and anatomical design are part of God's intention for males and females, passions and practices have become corrupted due to sin. Humanity's fallen orientation produces various sinful sexual desires, whether desire for a neighbor's wife, prostitutes, orgies, homosexual unions, or something else outside biblical marital union. In Christ, however, the mind of the Spirit replaces a mind-set set on the flesh (Rom 8:5; Gal 5:16–18).[28] The Spirit directs and empowers the believer to live according to God's design once again. By putting on the Lord Jesus Christ, believers make no provision for the flesh, to gratify its desires (Rom 13:14). Belonging to Christ means crucifying the flesh with its passions and desires (Gal 5:24). Those outside Christ live according to the passions of their flesh and follow its desires (Eph 2:3), but, even though we are dead in our trespasses, God has made believers alive together with Christ (Eph 2:5). Thus, the good news Paul proclaims is not only forgiving grace but transforming grace: not only have we been saved through faith (Eph 2:8), we have also been created in Christ Jesus for good works (Eph 2:10). The indicative of God's grace includes transformation that makes the imperative possible: "For once you were darkness, but now in the Lord you are light. Live as children of light" (Eph 5:8). This is not just an eschatological hope—that one day we will be righteous; it is also a present reality "in the Lord": righteousness is an already and not-yet reality into which believers have been initiated. Believers are no longer *non posse non peccare*—unable not to sin—but, because of Christ and the Spirit, are *posse non peccare*—able not to sin.

Paul is not alone in his theology. For example, Jesus also taught on the relationship between actions and inward, driving forces. Where Paul speaks of the "passions," Jesus speaks of the sinful "heart." His critique of the Pharisees and scribes is that they focus only on actions but not on the root cause—orientation, if you will (Matt 5:20–48). As sinful people we are oriented toward any number of sins, including sexual sins, and what we need is a transformation. As Jesus says,

---

[28] The phrase "desires of the flesh" also appears in 1 Pet 2:11 (where they war against the soul and where believers, who are aliens and exiles, are to abstain from them) and 2 Pet 2:18 (where false teachers are said to entice believers with licentious desires of the flesh).

> For it is from within, from the human heart, that evil intentions come: fornication, theft, murder, adultery, avarice, wickedness, deceit, licentiousness, envy, slander, pride, folly. All these evil things come from within, and they defile a person. (Mark 7:21–23)

This same understanding is found in the Old Testament. David, after his adulterous liaison with Bathsheba and murder of her husband Uriah, recognizes his sinful orientation from the earliest stages of life: "Indeed, I was born guilty, a sinner when my mother conceived me" (Ps 51:5). Yet he knows that God can have mercy on him and cleanse him from his sin (Ps 51:1–2). Then he asks God to change him: "Create in me a clean heart, O God, and put a new and right spirit within me" (Ps 51:10).

Thus, a biblical understanding of orientation—including sexual orientation—regards desire as reflecting a measure of what God intended in creation but also as having been altered by sin. Paul says in Romans 1:24–28 that "God gave them up in the lusts of their hearts to impurity" and "to a debased mind." He let sinful humanity go its sinful way. Yet the redemptive mercies of God in Christ Jesus have made it possible to present our bodies as spiritual sacrifices to God, no longer conforming to this world: our minds can be renewed (Rom 12:1–2). Apart from this redemption, humanity became so debased by its sinful passions that people not only practiced sin and did so thinking that it was natural but also sinned by supporting others in their sinful practices. Paul says that knowing "God's decree, that those who practice such things deserve to die . . . they not only do them but even applaud others who practice them" (Rom 1:32). Now, transformed by the renewing of their minds, those in Christ are once again able to "discern what is the will of God—what is good and acceptable and perfect" (Rom 12:2).

CONCLUSION

Our focus in this chapter has been on the notion of sexual orientation in antiquity. We have seen there was a rich discussion in antiquity about why people not only performed certain acts but also why they were disposed to do so. Underlying the various views was the philosophical question of whether nature or nurture was responsible for what people were and did. The surviving literature, to be sure, offers us a limited insight to the discussion as it pertains to sexuality. Yet we have seen that, indeed, there were arguments in antiquity about sexual orientation being a result of natural inclinations.

We shall see in the next chapter that Paul applies this discussion of nature and nurture to his argument in Romans. For Paul, nature is understood in terms of God's creation and eternal law; nurture is essentially understood in terms of the Mosaic law, given by God to direct Israel. Yet the guidance of both nature and nurture is obstructed by sin, which results in desires that run counter to both. In Romans 1:24–28, Paul states that nature can no longer serve as a guide because people have been given over to a depraved mind as a result of sin. The examples he uses to illustrate this point are, indeed, lesbianism and male homosexuality. In 1 Corinthians 6:9 and 1 Timothy 1:10, Paul's reflection on moral guidance turns to the Mosaic law, with both passages alluding to the nurturing righteousness referenced in Leviticus 18:22 and 20:13. Yet this law, as much as nature or God's intention in creation, was inadequate to address the human condition caused by sin. Thus, a righteousness apart from the law was necessary, a righteousness to which the Law and the Prophets bore witness but which came from God himself (Rom 3:21–26).

CHAPTER 17

PAUL'S NATURE/CREATION AND NURTURE/ LAW ARGUMENT IN ROMANS

INTRODUCTION

I n this chapter we will examine Paul's argument in Romans regarding homosexual practices, Romans 1:24–28. The text states:

> Therefore God gave them up in the lusts of their hearts to impurity, to the degrading of their bodies among themselves, because they exchanged the truth about God for a lie and worshiped and served the creature rather than the Creator, who is blessed forever! Amen. For this reason God gave them up to degrading passions. Their women exchanged *natural* intercourse for *unnatural*, and in the same way also the men, giving up *natural* intercourse with women, were consumed with passion for one another. Men committed shameless acts with men and received in their own persons the due penalty for their error. And since they did not see fit to acknowledge God, God gave them up to a debased mind and to things that should not be done. (Rom 1:24–28)

We will argue that this text has in view the desires and practices of lesbians and male homosexuals. We will first establish what Paul meant by "natural" and "unnatural" in verses 26–27 in light of primary sources from his time period. A study of primary sources leaves no doubt as to what he meant, since the terminology had been well established in philosophical circles for centuries by Paul's time. This is important to note because erroneous conjectures by certain scholars have affected the recent debate on homosexuality. This part of the chapter will involve several arguments. An important one here is that Paul employs a common philosophical distinction of "nature" (*physis*) versus "convention/law" (*nomos*) in Romans 1:18–3:31. We also argue that Paul's comments about homosexuality in Romans 1:26–27 appear within a passage addressing creation (Rom 1:18–28). We have seen that Paul had *nomos* (the law of Moses) in view in 1 Corinthians 5–7, including a term for homosexuals in 1 Corinthians 6:9; now we see that in Romans 1:26–27 he had creation and nature (*physis*) in view. However, his point in Romans is that righteousness comes neither through *physis* nor *nomos* but from God.

I. WHAT DOES PAUL MEAN BY "NATURAL" (*PHYSIKOS, KATA PHYSIN*) AND "UNNATURAL" (*PARA PHYSIN*) IN ROMANS 1:26–27?

When Paul speaks of what is "natural," *kata physin*, he means what is according to the way God made the world. God made humans as either male or female (Gen 1:27), and they come together as one in marriage (Gen 2:24). This may seem obvious, but, in fact, it is questioned by some revisionist readings of Romans 1:26–27.

We will consider the views of two revisionist scholars in this section before examining Paul's view of "natural" in light of Greek philosophy. Both of the revisionist scholars contend that Paul meant "conventional" when he said "natural" in Romans 1:26–27. From what we have examined of Paul's overall argument in Romans and his perspective as seen in a variety of his letters, it should be clear to the reader that these will not be successful arguments. Neither of these scholars considers the primary source evidence for the meaning of "according to nature/natural," *kata physin*, and "against nature/unnatural," *para physin*. Further, neither considers the use of these Greek phrases in relation to homosexuality. Such research is precisely what is required. The two scholars considered here are a theologian, Jack Rogers, and a biblical scholar, Dan Via. Rogers tries to make "natural" mean "conventional" by appealing to Romans 11:24; Via attempts to do the same by appealing to 1 Corinthians 11:14–15.

The Suggestions of Jack Rogers and Dan Via

Jack Rogers argues that Romans 11:24 unlocks the meaning of "according to nature" in Romans 1:26–27.[1] In Romans 11:24, Paul describes the "unnatural" growth of a tree when a foreign branch is grafted into an established stump:

> For if you have been cut from what is by nature [*kata physin*] a wild olive tree and grafted, contrary to nature [*para physin*], into a cultivated olive tree, how much more will these natural [*kata physin*] branches be grafted back into their own olive tree.

---

[1] Jack Rogers, *Jesus, the Bible, and Homosexuality: Explode the Myths, Heal the Church* (Louisville, KY: Westminster/John Knox, 2006), 76–78.

Rogers wishes to understand "contrary to nature" here as referencing an event or practice outside the ordinary. He then wants to apply this meaning to Romans 1:26–27. "Against nature," then, would mean "what is out of the ordinary," that is, a heterosexual person engaging in and out of the ordinary act for him or her. Paul is therefore interpreted as saying that heterosexual persons should not engage in homosexual acts. One could extend this further and say that people who are homosexual should not engage in heterosexual acts. Thus, Rogers takes Paul's word against homosexual acts in Romans 1:26–27 and turns it into an affirmation of heterosexual practice for heterosexuals and homosexual practice by homosexuals.

Yet such fanciful and speculative interpretation is impossible. Romans 11:24's "contrary to nature" means just that: foreign branches are not natural branches. Nor is this any way to do a word study. Rogers takes a phrase he finds in one passage and applies the meaning in that context (about which he is incorrect) to another passage without considering either the general meaning of the phrase in Greek or its specific meaning in the new context. Rogers also fails to examine the use of the phrases *kata physin* ("according to nature," "natural") and *para physin* ("contrary to nature," "unnatural") in Greek literature. The following passage, loosely translating *para physin*, captures the typical meaning of the phrase:

> The women also boldly took part with them in the fight, hurling tiles from the houses and enduring with a courage *beyond their sex (para physin)*.[2]

Had Rogers examined uses of the phrase, he would have discovered that it was, when used of sex, a typical way to reference homosexual practice. He also neglects to note the use of the term *physis* as an antonym to various terms for convention.

Dan Via also argues that Romans 1:26–27 condemns homosexual acts performed by people who are heterosexual.[3] In Via's case the meaning of "natural" is derived from what Paul says in 1 Corinthians 11:14–15:

> Does not nature [*physis*] itself teach you that if a man wears long hair, it is degrading to him, but if a woman has long hair, it is her glory? For her hair is given to her for a covering.

On first glance, *physis* as "conventional" here appears to have merit. Paul could not be arguing that men are unable to grow long hair naturally. In fact, in some cultures of his day—such as the German and Parthian cultures—men did grow

---

[2] Thucydides, *History of the Peloponnesian War* 3.74, Loeb Classical Library 108 (Cambridge, MA: Harvard University Press, 1919), 131.

[3] Dan O. Via and Robert A. J. Gagnon, *Homosexuality and the Bible: Two Views* (Minneapolis, MN: Fortress, 2003), 15.

their hair long, and Cynic philosophers were known for letting their hair grow out. Yet the Greeks and Romans did not typically wear their hair long in Paul's time. So Paul must be saying, the argument proceeds, that men had short hair as a matter of style or convention in Roman times. The line of interpretation suggested by Via, however, is not consistent with the primary source evidence. As the next section makes clear, the Greco-Roman world generally and Paul in particular were perfectly capable of differentiating "nature" and "convention," and Paul really does mean "nature" in 1 Corinthians 11:14–15.

The Meaning of *Physis* and *Nomos*

We cannot make words mean what they do not, and *physis* does not mean "conventional." The Greek word for "law" is *nomos,* and it can carry the connotation of conventional. Synonyms of *nomos* include *ethos* (custom, usage), *themis* (established order, usage), *hrētra* (ordinance, injunction),[4] and *epitēdeuma* (institution, national custom). William Guthrie, following earlier scholars of Greek philosophy, has an extended discussion of the *physis–nomos* antithesis in Greek philosophy of the fifth and fourth centuries BC.[5] Guthrie begins by noting that *physis* means "nature" but can also be translated "reality" when found in contrast to *nomos.*[6] Students of the Greek New Testament are accustomed to translate *nomos* as "law," yet in contrast to *physis* the term can mean "convention." Guthrie explains this point with reference to etymology:

> *Nomos* for the men of classical times is something that *nomizetai,* is believed in, practiced or held to be right; originally, something that *nemetai,* is apportioned, distributed, or dispensed. That is to say, it presupposes an acting subject—believer, practitioner or apportioner—a mind from which the *nomos* emanates. Naturally therefore different people had different *nomoi,* but . . . the devising mind could be the god's, and so there could be *nomoi* that were applicable to all mankind.[7]

The *laws* that societies draw up are the codification of the *conventions* of those societies. Guthrie notes both these meanings of *nomos*:

> [*Nomos'*] more important uses are two: (i) usage or custom based on traditional or conventional beliefs as to what is right or true; (ii) laws formally

---

[4] The terms to this point are among those suggested as synonyms for *nomos* by Alexandre Pillon, *Handbook of Greek Synonyms,* ed. with notes by T. K. Arnold (London, England: Francis and John Rivington, 1850), 312. One other synonym Pillon suggests points to universal law rather than convention: *thesmos* (established order, natural law).

[5] W. K. C. Guthrie, *A History of Greek Philosophy* (Cambridge, MA: Cambridge University Press, 1969), 56.

[6] Ibid., 55.

[7] Ibid.

drawn up and passed, which codify "right usage" and elevate it into an oblig-
atory norm backed by the authority of the state.[8]

Guthrie further notes that in English, "law" has the second meaning, but in
Greek both meanings existed. In light of this discussion, we can see that had
Paul wanted to speak of convention in 1 Corinthians 11:14, he would not have
used the term *physis* but perhaps *nomos* in the first sense of the term—or some
other term such as *epitēdeuma*. Paul was not unaware of the fact that men
could grow long hair; he was opposing this very thing. Nor would he have been
unaware that, in some cultures of his day, men did wear their hair long.

Paul's point in 1 Corinthians 11:14–15 is certainly different from Via's
interpretation of the passage. Paul is saying there is a natural distinction
between men and women; if a man crosses this barrier and dons the appearance of a woman by growing his hair long, he is degrading himself. Texts
noted in previous chapters about "soft men" with long hair help us understand
this perspective. As we have already noted, priests (known as *galli*) of the
goddess of the Great Mother cult, Cybele, would emasculate themselves, dress
as women, and grow their hair long.[9] As Anna Clark says, "These men wore
yellow or multi-colored robes with a tiara" and "adorned [themselves] with
ornaments, rings, and earrings; they wore white make-up and curled their long
hair."[10] The feminine appearance of the male *galli* was a most unnatural thing,
and they were not the only effeminate men with long hair known to Roman
culture. As Epictetus says in *Discourses* 3.1, a young man's ornamented hair
is not "natural" for a male; the writer is not discussing conventions of his day
but what it means for men to live according to or against their nature *as males*.

Paul uses *physis* in accordance with its traditional meaning: "the way
things are because they were created by God to be so." Thus, Paul's point
is not that long hair is impossible for a man to grow but that an effeminate
appearance for a man is unnatural. In 1 Corinthians 11:2–16, Paul is saying
that men should be men and women should be women, according to nature.
While hairstyles are a matter of custom, in Paul's day long hair on men suggested effeminacy in Greek and Roman culture. For a man to have long hair,
then, was like cross-dressing—purposefully appearing contrary to his nature.

How, then, might Paul be using "natural" and "unnatural" in Romans
1:26–27?

---

[8] Ibid., 56–57. Guthrie quotes Aristotle on this point: "The law has no power to compel obedience beside the force of custom" (*Politics* 1269a20).

[9] The cult was widespread in Paul's day, including in Rome. While it had eastern origins, it
was associated with Phrygia by the Greeks—that is, an area of Paul's ministry. Paul would have
been well aware of it in his missionary travels.

[10] Anna Clark, *Desire: A History of European Sexuality* (New York, NY: Routledge, 2008), 28.

> For this reason God gave them up to degrading passions. Their women exchanged natural intercourse for unnatural, and in the same way also the men, giving up natural intercourse with women, were consumed with passion for one another. Men committed shameless acts with men and received in their own persons the due penalty for their error.

The contrast of "natural" and "unnatural" here relates to the contrast between the "truth" and a "lie": people had given up the truth about God for a lie in turning away from worshipping the Creator to pursue idolatry. "Natural," too, is defined in terms of the created order.

Moreover, Romans 1:26–27 is phrased in terms of the typical contrast between what is "against nature" (*para physis*) and what is "according to nature" (*physikēn,* also *kata physin*). The "Athenian" in Plato's *Laws* 1.636b-c, for example, discussing different city states' laws and homosexual acts, says that

> . . . this institution [the gymnasium, with its naked males], when of old standing, is thought to have *corrupted the pleasures of love which are natural not to men only but also natural to beasts.* For this your States [Lacedaemon and Crete] are held primarily responsible, and along with them all others [636c] that especially encourage the use of gymnasia. And whether one makes the observation in earnest or in jest, one certainly should not fail to observe that *when male unites with female for procreation the pleasure experienced is held to be due to nature* [kata physin], *but contrary to nature* [para physin] *when male mates with male or female with female*, and that those first guilty of such enormities were impelled by their slavery to pleasure.[11]

In Paul's day the same language, *para physin*, still applied to homosexuality. Texts (by Musonius Rufus XII, Plutarch, Josephus, and Philo) will be quoted later in which this phrase references homosexual acts and orientation. In contrast, *kata physin* is used of heterosexual sex and orientation in other works such as Josephus's *Against Apion* 2.199.

The Philosophical Context of Paul's Nature/Nurture Argument in Romans 1:18–3:20

Paul's use of *physis* and *nomos* in Romans 1:18–3:20 seems to relate to the age-old philosophical debate about nature and nurture. By speaking of nature and nurture as the two ways in which people might be kept in line, and by doing so in part in relation to homosexual practices, Paul is saying something also found in Plutarch's work. Writing a few decades after Paul, Plutarch argues that animals do not pursue same-gender relations or cross-species sex

---

[11] *Plato in Twelve Volumes*, vol. 10, trans. R. G. Bury (Cambridge, MA, Harvard University Press; London, England: William Heinemann Ltd. 1967 & 1968).

as humans pursue homosexual and bestial unions. Like Paul he uses the language of *physis* and *nomos* in the course of his argument:

> Not even *Nature* [*physis*], with *Law* [*nomos*] for her ally, can keep within bounds the unchastened vice of your hearts; but as though swept by the current of their lusts beyond the barrier at many points, men do such deeds as wantonly outrage Nature, upset her order, and confuse her distinctions. (*Whether Beasts Are Rational* 7)[12]

Aristotle (384–322 BC) employed the nature versus nurture distinction in a way similar to Paul's use of the terms in Romans 2:1–3:20:

> Let us now classify *just (dikaiōmata)* and unjust actions generally, starting from what follows. *Justice (dikaia)* and injustice have been defined in reference to *laws (nomous)* and persons in two ways. Now there are *two kinds of laws*, particular and general. By particular laws I mean those established by each people in reference to themselves, which again are divided into written and unwritten; by general laws I mean those *based upon nature (kata physin)*. In fact, there is a general idea of *just (dikaion)* and *unjust (adikon)* in accordance with *nature (physei)*, as all men in a manner *divine*, even if there is neither communication nor agreement between them. (*Rhetoric* I.13.1–2)[13]

This quote from Aristotle illustrates the distinction between the particular laws of a certain community and the general laws that all should agree upon because they are in accordance with nature. Note that Aristotle's discussion also relates to what is just (*dikaiōmata, dikaion*). In Romans, Paul approaches the subject of justification/righteousness (*dikaiosunē*) through consideration of the two types of law as well: one that is according to nature (Rom 2:14–16) and one that is particular to a certain people, the Jews (Rom 2:12–14, 17–3:20). Note the two understandings of "law" (the written Mosaic law and the divine law that accords with creation/nature) in Romans 2:12–16:

> All who have sinned apart from the law will also perish apart from the law, and all who have sinned under the law will be judged by the law. For it is not the hearers of the law who are righteous in God's sight, but the doers of the law who will be justified. When Gentiles, who do not possess the law, do instinctively what the law requires, these, though not having the law, are a law to themselves. They show that what the law requires is written on their hearts, to which their own conscience also bears witness; and their conflicting thoughts will accuse or perhaps excuse them on the day when, according to my gospel, God, through Jesus Christ, will judge the secret thoughts of all.

---

[12] This text was quoted at greater length in the previous chapter.

[13] Aristotle, *The Art of Rhetoric,* trans. J. H. Freese (Cambridge, MA: Harvard University Press, 1926), 193.

Such distinctions between nature and law are also found in the work of Greek orator and statesman Demosthenes (384–322 BC). In the following quote, Demosthenes, like Paul centuries later in Romans 1:18–32, sees nature as corrupted by its base desires. Not unlike Paul in Romans 7:10, where the (Mosaic) law is said to be holy, just, and good, Demosthenes characterizes human laws as aiming toward what is just, good, and beneficial.

> The whole life of men, Athenians, whether they dwell in a large state or a small one, is governed by *nature* [*physis*] and by the *laws* [*nomoi*]. Of these, *nature* is something irregular and incalculable, and peculiar to each individual; but the *laws* are something universal, definite, and the same for all. Now *nature*, if it be evil, often chooses wrong, and that is why you will find men of an evil *nature* committing errors. But the *laws* desire what is *just* and honourable and salutary; they seek for it, and when they find it, they set it forth as a general commandment, equal and identical for all. The *law* is that which all men ought to obey for many reasons, but above all because every *law* is an invention and gift of the gods, a tenet of wise men, a corrective of errors voluntary and involuntary, and a general covenant of the whole State, in accordance with which all men in that State ought to regulate their lives. . . . If once they [the laws] were done away with and every man were given license to do as he liked, not only does the constitution vanish, but our life would not differ from that of the beasts of the field. (*Orations* 25.15–16, 20)[14]

The notion of divine law, seen in the above quote, is also found among other authors. Heraclitus taught that human laws depended on the one divine law (fr. 114). Hesiod and Plato spoke of Zeus laying down a law for all people (Hesiod, *Erga* 276; Plato, *Protagoras* 322d). Plato also stated that Zeus gave laws to Crete but Apollo gave the laws to Sparta (*Laws* 624a). Thucydides complained that politicians in his day did not obey divine law (*History of the Peloponnesian War,* 3.82.6). Sophocles wrote of divine laws that were unwritten, eternal; they could not be defied by mortals. He also said that laws of religious purity had been given directly by the gods of Olympus (*Oedipus Tyrannus* 863). Isocrates spoke of the ancient custom (*ethos*) and ancestral law (*nomos*) of burying the dead, which was ordained by divine power (*Panathenaicus* 169).[15] In similar fashion we suggest that Paul, having discussed the external religious and moral guidance of nature in Romans 1:18–32, next considers the internal divine law in Romans 2:1–16—written down for the Jews but placed in the hearts and consciences of all (Romans 2:12–16)—and then turns to consider the particular divine law Moses wrote down for the Jews in Romans 2:17–3:20. The

---

[14] Demosthenes, "Oration 25, Against Aristogeiton 1," in *Demosthenes Orations 21–26,* vol. 3, trans. J. H. Vince, Loeb Classical Library 299 (Cambridge, MA: Harvard University Press, 1935).

[15] For these references, see W. K. C. Guthrie, *A History of Greek Philosophy*, 55–56.

philosophical context for Paul's argument in Rom 1:18–3:20 can best be seen in a comparison between Epictetus and Paul.

EPICTETUS AND PAUL: DIVINE LAW, NATURE, AND SEXUALITY

Writing not much later than Paul, the Stoic philosopher Epictetus, spoke about divine law and nature at length in his *Discourses*. In that work he addressed sexuality as it related to this distinction. Epictetus offers a contemporary, non-Jewish, non-Christian parallel to Paul's argument. For him there are two senses in which *nomos* or "law" can be used: as divine law, in which case it is equivalent to nature, or as human law, in which case it is equivalent to nurture or convention. Divine law is the same for all, whereas human laws differ from one state to the next. Thus, law can either be God's universal law that accords with nature, or it can be human convention.

In *Discourses* Epictetus speaks of the "divine and mighty and inescapable law," and he warns against disobeying it (3.24.42). God "administers the universe" (1.12.7), and so there is a "law of nature" (1.29.19; 3.17.6). According to Stoic philosophy, people should conform to this divine law rather than work against it, and they should act according to nature (*kata physin*), not contrary to it (*para physin*). Diogenes Laertius described living according to nature as an essential tenet of Stoicism:

> This is why Zeno [the originator of Stoicism] was the first (in his treatise *On the Nature of Man*) to designate as the end [i.e., the moral goal] "life in agreement with *nature*" [or living agreeably to *nature*], which is the same as a virtuous life, virtue being the goal towards which *nature guides us*. So too Cleanthes in his treatise *On Pleasure*, as also Posidonius, and Hecato in his work *On Ends*. Again, living virtuously is equivalent to *living in accordance with experience of the actual course of nature*, as Chrysippus says in the first book of his *De finibus*; for our individual *natures* are parts of the *nature* of the whole universe. (*Lives of Eminent Philosophers* 7.87)[16]

According to *Discourses* 1.6.12–18 there is, however, a distinction between animals and humans in this regard. Irrational animals only concern themselves with the "use" (*chrēsis*) for which their parts were created. Paul, we should note, uses *chrēsis* in the same way in Romans 1:26–27 with respect to God's purpose in creating the body parts of males and females for heterosexual union. Rational humans, Epictetus continues, not only need to attend to the natural "use" of their bodies but additionally must act according to their understanding (*parakolouthētikē*). Herein lies the complication, for humans must employ their understanding to reason what their true end is. Should their

---

[16] Diogenes Laertius, *Lives of Eminent Philosophers*, trans. R. D. Hicks (Cambridge, MA: Harvard University Press, 1972).

reasoning not accord with the natural use of things, they will not reach the end for which they were created by God:

> ... while for us, to whom He has made the additional gift of the faculty of understanding, these things are no longer sufficient, but unless we act appropriately, and methodically, and in conformity each with his own nature [*kaia-kolouthōs tē hekastou physei*] and constitution, we shall no longer achieve our own ends. (Epictetus, *Discourses* 1.6)[17]

Divine law conforms to nature, and one should not only instinctively put the body to the right use but also be able, as a rational being, to understand the purpose in creation:

> Another tenet of theirs [the Stoics] is the perpetual exercise of virtue, as held by Cleanthes and his followers. For virtue can never be lost, and *the good man is always exercising his mind, which is perfect.* Again, they say that justice, as well as law and right reason, *exists by nature and not by convention*: so Chrysippus in his work *On the Morally Beautiful.* (Laertius, *Lives of Eminent Philosophers* 7.128)

Paul, in contrast, says the improper use of sexual organs in homosexual acts results in a debased mind such that people not only do things that should not be done (Rom 1:28) but also applaud others who practice them (Rom 1:32). Those who misuse their sexual organs have lost the ability to reason from the observation of nature to moral laws.

On one occasion, Epictetus challenges a man who claimed to have acted "naturally" (*physikōs*, an adjective Paul uses in Rom 1:26–27):

> But really, you must first convince me of this, that you *were* acting *naturally*, said he [Epictetus], and then I will convince you that whatever is done *in accordance with nature* is rightly done. (*Discourses* 1.11.5–6)

A human is "a rational and mortal being" (*Disc.* 2.9). Epictetus argues that humans have an innate idea of moral principles given by nature:

> But, on the other hand, who has come into being without an *innate concept* of what is good and evil, honourable and base, appropriate and inappropriate, and happiness, and of what is proper and falls to our lot, and what we ought to do and what we ought not to do? ... The reason is that we come into the world with a certain amount of instruction upon this matter already given us, as it were, *by nature,* and that starting with this we have added thereto our opinion.—Yes, by Zeus, for do I in my own case not have by gift of *nature*

---

[17] Epictetus, *Discourses*, volumes 1 (discourses 1 and 2) and 2 (discourses 3 and 4), trans. W. A. Oldfather, Loeb Classical Library 218 (Cambridge, MA: Harvard University Press, 1925). The following quotations are from this translation.

knowledge of what is noble and base; do I not have a concept of the matter? (*Discourses* 2.11.3–4, 7)

The problem arises, Epictetus continues, with trying to apply these innate principles. Similarly, Paul argues that there is an inward witness of God's law and a conscience that also bears witness (Rom 2:14–16). This is different from the mind's reasoning from observations of nature—an outward or objective moral reasoning. Divine law that is *within* a person's *heart* (Rom 2:15) is instinctive ("by nature," v. 14). As the Cynics taught, the conscience is an inward power that can reprove a person (Epictetus, *Disc.* 3.22). Paul sees the conscience positively but also as a subjective, adjudicatory faculty (Rom 2:15; 1 Cor 8:7, 10, 12), and adds that God will ultimately judge the secret thoughts of all (Rom 2:14–15). People are designed, says Epictetus, so that they want to live according to nature, the way God made them:

> Yet if you tell a man, "Your desires are feverish, your attempts to avoid things are humiliating, your purposes are inconsistent, your choices are out of *harmony with your nature* (*asymphōnai tēi physei*), your conceptions are hit-or-miss and false," why, immediately he walks out and says, "He insulted me." (*Disc.* 2.14.23–24)

This understanding of "natural law" or living according to the way God made the world is further explained by Epictetus in terms of sexuality—in the same logic Paul uses in Romans 1:26–27:

> And the male and the female, and the passion of each for intercourse with the other, and *the faculty which makes use of the organs which have been constructed for this purpose*, do these things not reveal their artificer either? (*Disc.* 1.6.9–10)

For a man to practice homosexual acts, on the other hand, is to lose his manhood. Epictetus does not understand the homosexual act as unnatural only for the passive partner in male homosexuality: both participants lose their male nature:

> What is lost by the victim of unnatural lust [*cinaedus, the passive homosexual*]? His manhood. And by the agent? Beside a good many other things he also loses his manhood no less than the other. (*Disc.* 2.10.17–18)

The translation "victim," which is not in the Greek, is here unfortunate as Epictetus intends to describe the passive and active men in this example as complicit in a homosexual relationship. Both act against their nature; therefore, both lose their manhood. Men are male, women are female. The Creator intends each for the other and not for same-sex attraction or unions. In a later discourse, Epictetus encounters a young man whose hair is too elaborately dressed, whose clothes are highly embellished, and who plucks out his body hair (one who, we might say, is tending toward the identity of a "soft male"). He advises the young man not to find fault with his male nature, for women, not men, are naturally smooth and delicate, having little hair on their bodies, whereas men are naturally hairy. A man who chooses to be a woman is, indeed, a terrible sight says Epictetus in *Discourses* 3.1. For Epictetus, one struggling with a shameful lifestyle first needs to come to the conviction that the behavior is wrong and then must exercise will power repeatedly until he has mastered himself (*Disc.* 3.9). This is where Paul differs so radically from the Stoic. For Paul, moral correction requires much more than an exercise of the will. In Romans chapters 6 and 8 he argues that humans are enslaved to sin and can be released only by God's transforming grace in Jesus Christ and the empowering presence of the Holy Spirit.

Natural Law and Sexuality in Other Greek and Roman Authors

Epictetus's teacher, Musonius Rufus, who lived in Rome in the first century AD, held a similar view of living according to nature and what this meant sexually. He condemned sex outside marriage, such as adultery, nonprocreative sex, and homosexual sex, which he called "contrary to nature" (*para physin*; compare Rom 1:26):

> Not the least significant part of the life of luxury and self-indulgence lies also in sexual excess; for example those who lead such a life crave a variety of loves, not only lawful but unlawful ones as well, not women alone but also men; sometimes they pursue one love and sometimes another, and not being satisfied with those which are available, pursue those which are rare and inaccessible, and invent shameful intimacies, all of which constitute a grave indictment of manhood. Men who are not wantons or immoral are bound to consider sexual intercourse justified only when it occurs in marriage and is indulged in for the purpose of begetting children, since that is lawful, but unjust and unlawful when it is mere pleasure-seeking. . . . But of all sexual relations those involving adultery are most unlawful, and no more tolerable are those of men with men, because it is a monstrous thing and contrary to nature. (Fragment 12.1–2)[18]

Other Greek authors from well before and during the time of the early church expressed similar views, as we can see in the works of Aeschines (389–314 BC) and Plutarch (ca. AD 46–120):

> Or what man will not be regarded as lacking intelligence who is angry with her who errs by an impulse of nature [adultery], while he treats as

---

[18] *Musonius Rufus: Lectures and Fragments*, trans. Cora Lutz, Yale Classical Studies (New Haven, CT: Yale University, 1947).

adviser the man who *in despite of nature has sinned against his own body* [homosexually]? (Aeschines, *Speeches,* "Against Timarchus" 1.185)[19]

> If union *contrary to nature* [*para physin*] with males does not destroy or curtail a lover's tenderness, it stands to reason that the love between men and women, being natural will be conducive to friendship developing in due course from favor. . . . But the union with males, either unwillingly with force and plunder, or willingly with *weakness* [or softness, *malakia*] and *effeminacy* [*thēlytēs*], surrendering themselves, as Plato says, "to be mounted in the custom of four-footed animals and to be sowed with seed *contrary to nature*"—this is an entirely ill-favored favor, shameful and contrary to Aphrodite [goddess of love]. (Plutarch, "Dialogue on Love" 751C–E)[20]

Plutarch further states that humans have so departed from nature and become confused in their thinking that they need to learn right and wrong from animals (whose instincts are not clouded by opinions, adventitious judgments, cleverness, love of freedom, irrational impulses, and desires) and plants (which lack imagination and impulse). By studying Plutarch, we understand more clearly Paul's notion of the debased mind (Rom 1:28), although he sees it to be the result not only of suppressing the truth (Rom 1:18–19) but also of God's judgment. In *De Amore Prolis* ["On Affection for Offspring"] 493 B-E Plutarch says:

> Is it thus, then, that philosophers also, because of their disagreements with each other, refer some of their questions to the nature of irrational animals, as though to a foreign city, and submit the decision to the emotions and character and habits of these creatures as to a court that cannot be influenced or bribed? Or is this also a common charge against human depravity—that, being in doubt about the most necessary and important things, we seek among horses and dogs and birds how we ourselves should marry and beget and bring up children (as though we had no plain indication of Nature in ourselves) and that we term the traits which brute beasts have "characters" and "emotions," and accuse our life of a great deviation and *departure from Nature* [*kata physin*], confused and disordered as we are at the very beginning concerning even the first principles? For in dumb animals *Nature* preserves their special characteristics pure and unmixed and simple, but in men, through reason and habit, they have been modified by many opinions and adventitious judgements so that they have lost their proper form and have acquired a pleasing variety comparable to the variety of perfumes made by the pharmacist on the basis of a single oil. And let us not wonder if irrational animals follow *Nature* more

---

[19] Aeschines, *Against Timarchus*, trans. Charles Darwin Adams, Loeb Classical Library 106 (Cambridge, MA: Harvard University Press, 1919).

[20] Plutarch, "Dialogue on Love," in *Moralia*, vol. 9, trans. W. C. Helmbold, Loeb Classical Library 425 (Cambridge, MA: Harvard University Press, 1939).

closely than rational ones; for animals are, in fact, outdone in this by plants, to which *Nature* has given neither imagination nor impulse, nor desire for something different, which causes men to shake themselves free from what *Nature* desires; but plants, as though they were fastened in chains, remain in the power of *Nature*, always traversing the one path along which *Nature* leads them. Yet in wild beasts versatility of reasoning and uncommon cleverness and excessive love of freedom are not too highly developed; and though they have irrational impulses and desires and often wander about on circuitous paths, they do not go far afield, but ride, as it were, at the anchor provided by *Nature*, who points out to them the straight way, as to an ass which proceeds under bit and bridle. But in man ungoverned reason is absolute master, and, discovering now one way of deviation and innovation and now another, has left no clear or certain vestige of *Nature* visible.[21]

Plutarch applies his point to marriage and childbearing, noting that humans discover "now one way of deviation and innovation and now another" through their clever reasoning against nature. He also shows that during New Testament times, residents of the Roman Empire held varying views of homosexuality. People did what they wanted to do, and there were no laws against homosexuality in general (even if there were laws against using free born male youths for sex). In short, there were competing philosophical views on sexuality. Thus, people did not hold views because of convention but by choice. What Paul says in Romans 1:26–27 agrees with what Jews and Christians taught based on the law, but it also agrees with what some Greek philosophers, particularly the Stoics like Musonius Rufus and Epictetus, taught based on their understanding of divine law or nature. Moreover, "according to nature" and "against nature" were *the* way to discuss these points. Paul was following conventional language in Romans 1:26–27 and 2:14–15. However, when it came to arguing his point from a Judeo-Christian mind-set, he did so by focusing on the Genesis 1–3 account of creation.

Jewish Texts on "Against Nature"

Jewish texts also spoke of homosexuality as "against nature." Thus, the entire Greco-Roman world, including Judaism, could speak of homosexuality using the phrase "against nature" (*para physin*). Consider these texts:

> Having gone astray and forsaken the Lord, the Gentiles changed their order. . . . But you shall not be so, my children . . . so that you will not become as Sodom, which *changed the order of its nature.* (*T. Naph* 3.3–4)

---

[21] Plutarch, "On Affection for Offspring," in *Moralia*, vol. 6, trans. W. C. Helmbold, Loeb Classical Library 337 (Cambridge, MA: Harvard University Press, 1939).

Do not transgress with unlawful sex *the limits set by nature.* For even animals are not pleased by intercourse of male with male. And let women not imitate the sexual role of men. (Pseudo-Phocylides, *Sentences* 190–92)

What are our marriage laws? The law recognizes only sexual intercourse that is *in accordance with nature,* [that] with a woman, and that only for the procreation of children. (Josephus, *Against Apion* 2.199)[22]

Sexual intercourse with males which is *contrary to nature* and without restraint. (Josephus, *Against Apion* 273–75)

Philo speaks of "pleasure *contrary to nature*" in commenting on Lev 20:13. (Philo, *Special Laws* 3.39)

In the same vein, then, Paul says:

For this reason God gave them up to degrading passions. Their women exchanged natural intercourse [*physikēn chrēsin*] for unnatural [*tēn para physin*]. (Rom 1:26)

II. PAUL'S USE OF THE CREATION NARRATIVE IN ROMANS 1:18–28 AND ITS SIGNIFICANCE FOR THE HOMOSEXUAL DEBATE

Some, such as Dale Martin and Martti Nissinen, have argued that Romans 1:24–28 does not have the creation account of Genesis in view. Thus, they say, Paul is not arguing that same-sex intercourse is rebellion against the pattern for sexuality established in Genesis 1–2.[23] Others, such as Jack Rogers and Dan Via, as we noted already, have attempted to make "against nature" mean something other than against God's creative purposes seen in nature. Given what we have just demonstrated, such arguments should be viewed as unsound. Additionally, there are indications in Romans that Paul does have creation—and therefore nature—in view.

Paul's Use of Creation Language in Romans 1:18–28

First, as Robert Gagnon has ably demonstrated, Paul employs language pertaining to creation in Romans 1:18–28.[24] The significance of this, for our purposes, is that Paul's opposition to homosexual acts is based on a view of marriage that is grounded in God's creation of the world. Marriage is not based

---

[22] All translations of Josephus's works are taken from the translation by William J. Whiston (1828) in public domain, available on *BibleWorks*.

[23] Dale Martin, "Heterosexism and the Interpretation of Romans 1.18–32," *Biblical Interpretation* 3 (1995): 332–55, and Martti Nissinen, *Homoeroticism in the Biblical World* (Minneapolis, MN: Fortress, 1998) 107.

[24] Robert Gagnon, *The Bible and Homosexual Practice: Texts and Hermeneutics* (Nashville, TN: Abingdon, 2001), 289.

on mere attraction between two people, nor is it merely contractual. *Marriage is, rather, a creational union*: the coming together of a male and a female in accordance with how God created them. Such a coming together entails a permanent union: the two become "one flesh":

> Then the man said, "This at last is bone of my bones and flesh of my flesh; this one shall be called Woman, for out of Man this one was taken." Therefore a man leaves his father and his mother and clings to his wife, and they become one flesh. (Gen 2:23–24)

Paul's argument in Romans 1:18–28 first affirms that God is the Creator. Further, his language reflects wording from Genesis (the Greek in Old Testament quotations below reflects the Septuagint):[25]

> They exchanged the glory of the immortal God for images [*eikonos*] resembling a mortal human [*anthrōpou*] being or birds [*peteinōn*] or four-footed animals [*tetrapodōn*] or reptiles [*herpetōn*]. (Rom 1:23)

> And God said, "Let the earth bring forth living creatures of every kind: cattle [*tetrapoda*] and creeping things [*herpeta*] and wild animals [*thēria*] of the earth of every kind." And it was so. (Gen 1:24)

> Then God said, "Let us make humankind [*anthrōpon*] in our image [*eikona*], according to our likeness; and let them have dominion over the fish of the sea, and over the birds *[peteinōn]* of the air, and over the cattle, and over all the wild animals of the earth, and over every creeping thing [*herpetōn*] that creeps upon the earth." (Gen 1:26)

> God blessed them, and God said to them, "Be fruitful and multiply, and fill the earth and subdue it; and have dominion over the fish of the sea and over the birds [*peteinōn*] of the air and over every living thing that moves upon the earth [Septuagint adds: and all the reptiles [*herpetōn*] creeping over the earth]." (Gen 1:28)

> "And to every beast of the earth, and to every bird [*peteinois*] of the air, and to everything that creeps [*herpetōi*] on the earth, everything that has the breath of life, I have given every green plant for food." And it was so. (Gen 1:30)

The language of creation is also found in the Mosaic prohibition of making images for worship:

> Since you saw no form when the LORD spoke to you at Horeb out of the fire, take care and watch yourselves closely, so that you do not act corruptly by making an idol for yourselves, in the form of any figure—the likeness of

---

[25] Similarly, the vision of Acts 10:12 and 11:6, in which God told Peter to eat any food, describes animals with words from Genesis.

male [*arsenikou*] or female [*thēlykou*], the likeness of any animal that is on
the earth, the likeness of any winged bird [*pterōtou*] that flies in the air, the
likeness of anything that creeps [*herpetou*] on the ground, the likeness of any
fish that is in the water under the earth. (Deut 4:15–18)

Also, Paul uses *arsen*, "male," and *thēlys*, "female," to reference the genders in Romans 1:26–27. This language can be found in the Septuagint of
Genesis 1:27:

> God made man (*anthrōpos*—the generic sense). According to the image
> of God he made him. Male (*arsen*) and female (*thēlys*) he made them. (LXX,
> our translation)

This language is repeated in Genesis 5:2 (regarding creation); 6:9 (taking male
and female creatures into the ark); and Deuteronomy 4:16 (as seen above).
The only other place where Paul uses "female" (*thēlys*) and "male" (*arsen*)
is in Galatians 3:28; there he states that there is no longer any female or male
in Christ Jesus. The word *arsen* is only otherwise found in Paul as part of a
compound word for "homosexual" (1 Cor 6:9; 1 Tim 1:10). Thus, the language
points to Genesis as the source of Paul's thought in Romans 1:26–27. His point
in Romans 1 is that people abandoned creation by turning from the Creator to
idols and by turning from their God-given gender orientation to homosexual
perversions.

The Logical Relationship Between Idolatry and Homosexuality in Romans 1:18–28

If Paul has the Genesis creation story in mind and sees idolatry as the worship of what was created rather than who created it, then his understanding of
"natural" will relate to God's created order.

Idolatry is a confusion of creation, an unnatural worshipping of the crea-
ture instead of the Creator. Not only does it involve turning away from God to
what he created; it also involves humans, whom God placed in charge of creation, worshipping images of the lower creatures. Idolaters turn their devotion
away from the glory of the immortal God, in whose image they were created,
to things that have lesser glory than they themselves enjoy.

Homosexuality involves a similar choosing of the unnatural over the natural in God's creation. God created humankind in his image, both male and
female (Gen 1:27). This was so that together they might be fruitful and multiply and so fill the earth and have dominion over it. To be created in God's
image was to have dominion over creation. As part of their mandate to exercise
authority over creation, men and women were to come together to multiply
(Gen 1:28). Union between the sexes is an expression of being created in the
divine image. Homosexuality is a perversion of God's design for men and

women to express his glory. Rather than declaring God's glory by creating and subduing the earth through offspring, those who practice homosexuality participate in a "degrading of their bodies among themselves" (Rom 1:24).

Paul's Interest in Creation Elsewhere in Romans

Note, further, that Paul's appeal to creation in Romans 1:18–28 is not isolated. He returns to the theme of creation elsewhere in Romans. In Romans 5:12–21, Paul contrasts the sin of Adam to the justifying/making righteous work of Christ. In Romans 8:18–39, Paul discusses creation's future freedom from bondage and the universal triumph of God in Jesus Christ. The mind, depraved due to sin (Rom 1:28), is already renewed in those who have presented their bodies as a living sacrifice, holy and acceptable to God, and chosen not to conform to this world but to be transformed (Rom 12:1–2). Creation, then, is a theme running throughout Romans.

Unnatural "Use" in Romans 1:26–27

In light of the Greek and Jewish texts discussed above, we are in a better position to understand Paul's argument in Romans 1:26–27. Paul's comments about homosexuality are one component of the proof that nature's witness cannot produce righteousness. Paul is concerned to lay the blame for this at the feet of sinful humanity, not God, for they "suppress the truth" that "God has shown to them" (Rom 1:18–19). What is revealed by nature ought to be clear to people, but they have, instead, turned away from the Creator to idolatry. This theological error is mirrored in its moral consequence: people have turned away from the way they were created to pursue homosexual relations. A look around creation ought to be enough for people to realize that it was produced by God, not an idol. Nevertheless, people have turned to idolatry, and so God turned them over to their own misguided ways. They who turn away from the Creator no longer behave as they were created to behave but do things that are contrary to nature. A prime example of this is same-sex attraction and unions, since God created the world in such a way that male and female—not female and female or male and male—should desire one another and unite sexually to become one flesh (Gen 2:24). To emphasize the point that homosexual unions are against nature, Paul says the women exchanged "natural use" for what is "against nature" (Rom 1:26) and the men gave up "the natural use of females" (Rom 1:27).

The focus on "use" (*chrēsis*) in Romans 1:26–27, discussed above, continues Paul's thought from verse 18: the misuse of the sexual organs in homosexual unions is as unnatural as failing to honor the Creator by making idols. Paul draws several parallels between idolatry and homosexual unions—a point that renders impossible any attempt to limit his teaching to a specific kind of homosexuality. Note the verbal parallels: "not honoring God" in idolatry (Rom 1:21) is equivalent to the "dishonoring" (*atimazesthai*—which the NRSV translates "degrading") of their bodies committed by those who participate in same-sex acts and to the "dishonorable (*atimias*) passions" of homosexual union (Rom 1:26). The "exchange" (*ēllaxan*) of the glory of the immortal God for idols (Rom 1:23) is equivalent to the "exchange" (*metēllaxan*) of the natural use of body parts for uses against nature (Rom 1:26). Idolaters, claiming to be wise, have become fools (Rom 1:22), just as homosexuals have been given over to debased minds (Rom 1:28). The parallels are not only verbal but also consequential: for dishonoring the Creator, the idolaters were handed over to "against nature" practices. All this points to the fact that Paul is speaking of homosexual unions *per se*. He is addressing the failure to live in conformity to nature and not narrowing his comments to particular forms of homosexuality, such as pederasty or homosexual acts associated with idol worship or homosexual acts committed by heterosexual persons or homosexual acts committed due to out-of-control passions or unclean homosexual acts in which the penis comes into contact with fecal matter or bisexual abuse of slaves or homosexual sex outside of committed, loving relationships—or any other nuanced variety of homosexual practice. Paul's focus is rather on how males and females were created: God made them for each other, and the male and female sexual organs were created to be joined together.

The Penalty for Living Against Nature and God's Transformation

Paul's argument from nature also explains the statement that men committing shameless homosexual acts "received in their own persons the due penalty for their error" (Rom 1:27). Paul's understanding is that going against nature has consequences. He makes a similar argument with regard to sexual sin in 1 Corinthians 6:18: since God made sex to be the union between a husband and a wife (Gen 2:24), any sexual act that defies this creation paradigm is a sin against one's own body. As suggested previously, some ancient authors understood homosexual acts to involve changing the order of nature, losing one's maleness, and wasting away one's soul and body (*T. Naph.* 3:3–4; Epictetus, *Discourses* 2:10; Philo, *Special Laws* 2:50; 3:37, respectively). In *Against Timarchus* (1:185, 194), Aeschines, like Paul, speaks of the homosexual as one who has "sinned against his own body." Similarly, in Romans 1:27, Paul asserts that homosexual acts, being attempts to defy nature, carry consequences—just as much as jumping off a cliff would, for instance.

The situation we confront in the sinful world, Paul argues, is that people's minds have become debased or depraved (*adokimon noun*, Rom 1:28). They now think that what is contrary to God's created order is actually right. Paul will argue later in Romans that this situation has been reversed for those made righteous in Christ, such that the debased minds of sinful humans are renewed; thus, people can once again know God's good, acceptable, and perfect will.

This development from Romans 1:28 to 12:1–2 is not noted often enough as a key to the structure of Paul's argument:

> Since they did not see fit to acknowledge God, God gave them up to a *debased mind* and to things that should not be done. (Rom 1:28)

> I appeal to you therefore, brothers and sisters, by the mercies of God, to present your bodies as a living sacrifice, holy and acceptable to God, which is your spiritual worship. *Do not be conformed to this world, but be transformed by the renewing of your minds*, so that you may discern what is the will of God—what is good and acceptable and perfect. (Rom 12:1–2)

Those who have returned to right worship (v. 1, cf. Rom 1:18–24) no longer conform to the way of this world. Their minds that had become debased (Rom 1:28) are renewed, and they once again know God's design—His good, acceptable, and perfect will (v. 2).

The only other place where the Greek word for "conform" (*syschēmatizein*) appears in the New Testament is in a similar passage in 1 Peter that also speaks of "desires":

> Like obedient children, do not be *conformed* to the desires (*epithymiais*) that you formerly had in ignorance. Instead, as he who called you is holy, be holy yourselves in all your conduct; for it is written, "You shall be holy, for I am holy." (1 Pet 1:14–16)

First Peter 4:1–3, seen below, parallels the thought of Romans 12:1–2:

> Since therefore Christ suffered in the flesh, arm yourselves also with the same intention (for whoever has suffered in the flesh has finished with sin), so as to live for the rest of your earthly life no longer by human desires but by the will of God. You have already spent enough time in doing what the Gentiles like to do, living in licentiousness, passions, drunkenness, revels, carousing, and lawless idolatry.

How this transformation happens is the subject of Romans: through the righteousness of God that comes in Jesus Christ (e.g., Rom 3:21–26; 5:12–21; 8:1–4). This divine solution to the human plight can apply to those trying to follow nature (creation) as a guide as much as those trying to follow nurture (the law). In both cases human sin has blocked the possibility of obtaining righteousness. A third option is needed: a righteousness that comes from God himself. God's solution is his own righteousness in Christ Jesus; therefore, faith in Christ is the only path to our righteousness and justification (Rom 1:16–17; 3:21–5:21).

III. PAUL'S WIDER ARGUMENT IN ROMANS 1:18–3:31 AND 4:1–8:39 AND HIS THEOLOGY OF TRANSFORMING GRACE

What remains to consider in this chapter is how Paul's particular argument in Romans 1:26–27 fits into the larger argument in Romans. Paul addresses both the larger problem of sin and the solution of God for humanity. Paul is not only concerned to discuss sin as acts but also as a power and God's righteousness not only as forgiveness but also as transforming power. This is important to see because Romans offers much more than a condemnation of homosexuality. Homosexuality demonstrates the depth of human departure from nature and God's law. While law has no power to make people righteous, God's righteousness brings transformation. Paul's larger argument in Romans offers hope to the person overwhelmed by the power of sin, not only homosexuality but also many other sins. Here we see that Christian counsel for those struggling with such sins, if it is to be biblical, offers more than justification or atonement for sins; it offers life in the power of God's transforming righteousness, the resurrection power of Jesus Christ, and the empowering presence of the Holy Spirit. This is a major theme in Romans, but it can also be found in Isaiah, which Paul uses significantly in his theological interpretation. To these points we now turn.

Romans 1:18–3:31

Romans 1:24–28 is part of Paul's first argument in Romans, Romans 1:18–8:39: on the one hand, both Gentiles and Jews have sinned and fallen short of the glory of God (Rom 1:18–3:20, 23), and on the other hand, God has provided righteousness to both Jews and Gentiles in Christ despite the disobedience of Adam and later of Israel (Rom 3:21–8:39). Romans 3:21–31 is a transitional passage declaring God's solution to the problem of sin. This first argument highlights not only the Gentile/Jew distinction but also the *physis/ nomos* distinction in Romans 1:18–3:31:

A   *Creation/Nature*
       Romans 1:18–32: Creation/nature's revelation has failed
       to produce righteousness due to a suppression of the truth
       (particularly an argument regarding Gentiles).

      B   *Divine Law and Judgment*
           Romans 2:1–16: Divine law/nature has failed to produce
           righteousness but leads to judgment by God due to sin
           (an argument regarding Jews and Gentiles).

           C   *Written (Mosaic) Law*
               Romans 2:17–3:20: Mosaic law/nurture has
               failed to produce righteousness for Jews.

> D   *God's Righteousness*
>   Romans 3:21–31: God has produced
>   righteousness apart from the law for
>   both Jews and Gentiles through Jesus
>   Christ.

In what follows in Romans, Paul possibly continues to reason chiastically to explain the contrast of how God's righteousness comes:

> C   *Faith* (not works of law)
>   Romans 4:1–4:25: Righteousness comes by faith
>   not law.

> B   *Peace and Reconciliation* (not divine judgment)
>   Romans 5:1–11: Justification through the blood of Jesus
>   Christ produces peace/reconciliation with God.

> A   *First Adam/Second Adam* (fall and new creation)
>   Romans 5:12–21: Justification/righteousness through Jesus has
>   undone the condemnation/trespass of Adam (the dominion of sin
>   coming after creation).

While Romans 1:18–3:31 certainly has a Gentile and Jew distinction within it, the nature and nurture distinction of Greek philosophy is also evident and needs to be understood. In Romans 1:18–32, with the Gentile primarily in view, Paul argues that sin prevents humans from receiving the ethical guidance of nature. Also regarding nature, with both Jew and Gentile in view, Paul argues in Romans 2:1–16 that sin prevents humans from receiving the ethical guidance of divine law. [26] Regarding nurture, in Romans 2:17–3:20 Paul argues that sin prevents humans from receiving the external guidance of Israel's Mosaic law. Sin is the problem in all three approaches to moral guidance, and therefore a solution needs to come apart from external and internal moral guidance and from human actions proposed by Gentiles or Jews.

Paul then concludes this part of his argument in Romans: if neither nature (*physis*; Romans 1:18–2:16) nor nurture (*nomos*, law; Romans 2:17–3:20) leads people to righteous acts, then only the righteousness of God can deliver people from their sin (Rom 3:21–26). The solution to the problem of sin is not some other guidance but God's own righteousness, which brings atonement for sin and empowers believers to understand what is right and to live righteously.

---

[26] The NRSV translates *physei* (by nature) as "instinctively" in Rom 2:14: "When Gentiles, who do not possess the law, do instinctively what the law requires, these, though not having the law, are a law to themselves." This translation captures Paul's point but causes the English reader to miss that he is addressing an argument about "nature" throughout 1:18–2:16. *Physis*, "nature," is mentioned in this first section of Romans in 1:26 (twice), 27; 2:14, and 27. Otherwise, Paul uses the term in Gal 2:15; 4:8; Rom 11:21, 24 (three times); 1 Cor 11:14; and Eph 2:3.

PAUL'S POSSIBLE USE OF ISAIAH 59 REGARDING
SIN AND THE RIGHTEOUSNESS OF GOD

In Romans 3:10–26, Paul is not presenting an entirely new understanding of sin and righteousness. While we have seen similarities between Paul and a Stoic such as Epictetus, his thinking is fundamentally scriptural. Paul may well be interpreting Isaiah 59 in Romans 3:10–26 regarding the problem of human sin, the inadequacy of the law to deal with it, and the solution of God's righteousness in the form of Christ's redemption.

First, in the chain of scriptural texts cited by Paul in Romans 3:10–18, he relies heavily on Isaiah 59. Robert Jewett, for example, suggests the following quotations and allusions in Romans 3:10–18:[27]

1. Romans 3:10b   Ecclesiastes 7:20
2. Romans 3:11–12   Psalm 14:1–3
3. Romans 3:13a   Psalm 5:9
4. Romans 3:13b   Psalm 139:4
5. Romans 3:14   Psalm 10:7
6. Romans 3:15–17   Isaiah 59:7–8[28]
7. Romans 3:18   Psalm 35:2

In the above list, note that a major quotation appears in Romans 3:15–17 and is believed to come from Isaiah 59:7–8. Indeed, the importance of Isaiah 59 needs to be noted in Romans generally. Another use of Isaiah 59 occurs in Romans 11:25–27, where Paul uses Isaiah 59:20–21 to explain the hope he has for Israel's future redemption. Our suggestion is that this text from Isaiah is part of Paul's argument in Romans 3:21–26. First note what Paul says:

> But now, apart from law, the righteousness of God has been disclosed, and is attested by the law and the prophets, the righteousness of God through faith in Jesus Christ for all who believe. For there is no distinction, since all have sinned and fall short of the glory of God; they are now justified by his grace as a gift, through the redemption that is in Christ Jesus, whom God put forward as a sacrifice of atonement by his blood, effective through faith. He did this to show his righteousness, because in his divine forbearance he had passed over the sins previously committed; it was to prove at the present time

---

[27] Robert Jewett, *Romans: A Commentary,* Hermeneia (Minneapolis, MN: Fortress, 2007), 35.

[28] Jewett sees Rom 3:15–17 as a "citation and abbreviation of Isa 59:7–8" (p. 255). Yet he states on p. 262 that these verses are adapted from Isa 59:7–8 and Prov 1:16. He also demonstrates the relationship between Rom 3:16 and LXX Ps 13:3b and Isa 59:7c (stating that the "psalmist exactly quotes Isaiah") and between Rom 3:17 and LXX Ps 13:3 and Isa 59:8a (noting that only different words for knowing are used, otherwise the passages are the same) (262). (Psalm 13 in the Septuagint is Psalm 14 in English. Compare it to Isa 59:7–8. Also note that Psalm 53 is parallel to Psalm 14.)

that he himself is righteous and that he justifies the one who has faith in Jesus. (Rom 3:21–26)

This sounds much like Isaiah's argument from the chapter Paul quoted in Romans 3:15–17. Both Isaiah and Paul move from declaring the utter sinfulness of Israel (despite its having the law—Isaiah 58:1–59:15) to speaking of God's righteousness as the solution. Isaiah declares God will don *righteousness* (cf. Rom 3:21–22), and the *redeemer* (Hebrew: *gō'ēl*) will come to Zion (cf. Rom 3:24):

> He saw that there was no one, and was appalled that there was no one to intervene; so his own arm brought him victory, and his righteousness upheld him. He put on righteousness like a breastplate, and a helmet of salvation on his head; he put on garments of vengeance for clothing, and wrapped himself in fury as in a mantle. According to their deeds, so will he repay; wrath to his adversaries, requital to his enemies; to the coastlands he will render requital. So those in the west shall fear the name of the LORD, and those in the east, his glory; for he will come like a pent-up stream that the wind of the LORD drives on. And he will come to Zion as Redeemer, to those in Jacob who turn from transgression, says the LORD. And as for me, this is my covenant with them, says the LORD: my spirit that is upon you, and my words that I have put in your mouth, shall not depart out of your mouth, or out of the mouths of your children, or out of the mouths of your children's children, says the LORD, from now on and forever. (Isa 59:16–21)

The coming of God's own righteousness establishes righteousness for a sinful people. If Paul is still interpreting Isaiah 59 in Romans 3:21–26, as we suggest, then God's righteousness in Christ is understood by Paul to be the fulfillment of the salvation and redemption the Redeemer brings to Zion in Isaiah 59:20. The righteousness of God is far more than his covenant faithfulness.[29] Also, the "righteousness of God" in Romans 3:21—so much discussed by commentators—is, with Isaiah 59:16–21 in view, a possessive genitive (God's own righteousness), a genitive of source (a righteousness that comes from God), and a subjective genitive (a righteousness that God works for sinful Israel). This righteousness comes after a protracted period of God's forbearance (cf. Rom 3:25–26).[30] It is the only solution to Israel's sin (Isa 58:1–59:15) despite their

---

[29] Note that the term for "redeemer" (Isa 59:20) occurs in its verbal form in Isa 52:9, where God is similarly said to redeem exiled Jerusalem. The passages are linked through the same word and thought. In near proximity to Isa 52:9, the prophet speaks of one who announces the "good news" (cf. "Gospel") of salvation (Isa 52:7) and, a little later, that the Suffering Servant will provide a guilt offering (Isa 53:10). Often Jews interpreted one text in light of another if the texts shared a term in common. Using this technique, Isa 59:20 and 52:9 and its surrounding texts can be interpreted together.

[30] Thus, John Ziesler wrongly suggested that God's forbearance was his way of being righteous (John A. Ziesler, *Paul's Letter to the Romans*, New Testament Commentaries

claiming to have "done righteousness" and belief that they had not forsaken the ordinances of God (Isa 58:2; cf. "works of law" in Paul). It is an apocalyptic righteousness, related to God's bringing his judgment and wrath. The Redeemer comes to Zion (Isa 59:20), which Paul interprets as Christ's sacrifice of atonement by his blood (in Jerusalem, Rom 3:25). The righteousness of God is also an ethical righteousness, in that it provides transformation by God's Spirit. Indeed, the coming of God's righteousness means redemption for those who turn from transgression (Isa 59:20), *and* it means the empowering presence of the Holy Spirit, who makes new covenant obedience possible (Isa 59:21)—Paul's point in Romans 8:1–17.

Transforming Grace in Romans and in Other Pauline Texts

God's transforming grace—not simply forgiving grace—is fundamental to Pauline theology. Paul expresses this theology of participation in Christ in various ways in Romans. For example, the transforming grace of God in Christ Jesus can be spoken of in terms of baptism into Christ's death, living according to the Spirit, Christ in us, dying and rising with Christ, and putting on Christ:

> How can we who died to sin go on living in it? Do you not know that all of us who have been baptized into Christ Jesus were baptized into his death? Therefore we have been buried with him by baptism into death, so that, just as Christ was raised from the dead by the glory of the Father, so we too might walk in newness of life. (Rom 6:2–4)

> For those who live according to the flesh set their minds on the things of the flesh, but those who live according to the Spirit set their minds on the things of the Spirit. (Rom 8:5)

> But if Christ is in you, though the body is dead because of sin, the Spirit is life because of righteousness. If the Spirit of him who raised Jesus from the dead dwells in you, he who raised Christ from the dead will give life to your mortal bodies also through his Spirit that dwells in you. (Rom 8:10–11)

> Put on the Lord Jesus Christ, and make no provision for the flesh, to gratify its desires. (Rom 13:14)

A similar understanding of transforming grace is presented in Ephesians. Paul describes people who have not come to Christ as "dead through the trespasses and sins in which you once lived" (Eph 2:1–2a). He continues:

> All of us once lived among them in the passions of our flesh, following the desires of flesh and senses, and we were by nature children of wrath, like everyone else. But God, who is rich in mercy, out of the great love with which he loved us even when we were dead through our trespasses, made us

[Harrisburg, PA: Trinity, 1989], 115).

alive together with Christ—by grace you have been saved—and raised us up with him and seated us with him in the heavenly places in Christ Jesus. (Eph 2:3–6)

Paul writes in a similar way to Titus about the dramatic contrast between life before and after salvation:

For we ourselves were once foolish, disobedient, led astray, slaves to various passions and pleasures, passing our days in malice and envy, despicable, hating one another. But when the goodness and loving kindness of God our Savior appeared, he saved us, not because of any works of righteousness that we had done, but according to his mercy, through the water of rebirth and renewal by the Holy Spirit. (Titus 3:3–5)

The argument advanced by some that homosexual practice should be accepted by Christians because some people cannot change their orientation to this sin runs contrary to biblical texts such as these. Christians are told that God's grace only forgives and is really in essence more like a divine tolerance; it does not change sinners; it has no such power. On such a view, culture sets moral norms for the church, and Christians holding to biblical teaching are seen as out of step with the advance of our culture. Calling something sinful is, in such thinking, nothing more than being phobic, unkind, and intolerant toward those who have an "alternative lifestyle."

The scriptural answer to this is to see that a non-Christian culture, whatever goods it may have by God's grace, represents the collective perspective of people with debased minds. The church needs to call people to repentance from their sinful passions rather than bless their depravity. Moreover, God's people need to pray for his transforming power to be at work among them that they may know his will and, by his strength, live holy lives.

The passages of Scripture noted above emphasize the transforming work of God among believers. Salvation cannot be reduced only to being forgiven. To be saved from captivity in Babylon meant not only that God would bring Israel out of captivity but also that he would transform his people from the sinners they were into his righteous children (Isa 59:21; Jer 31:31–33; Ezek 36:25–27). Similarly, salvation from sin through the cross of Christ meant not only forgiveness but also the transforming power of God whereby one could then die to sin and be raised to new life in Christ Jesus, walking in step with the Holy Spirit (Romans 6–8). In Ephesians salvation is expressed as undressing from a former way of life and being clothed with a new way of life:

Put off the old person with its former way of life—the corruptible person with its deceitful desires, to be renewed in the spirit of your mind, and to be

clothed with the new person, created in conformance to God in the righteousness and holiness that derives from the truth. (Eph 4:22–24)[31]

One of the earliest Pauline epistles, 1 Thessalonians, gives us a window
into the sort of teaching given to Gentile converts. Paul would "teach Christ"
to these converts. First on his list was teaching that becoming a Christian
involved a change of lifestyle:

> Finally, brothers and sisters, we ask and urge you in the Lord Jesus that, as
> you learned from us how you ought to live and to please God (as, in fact, you
> are doing), you should do so more and more. For you know what instructions
> we gave you through the Lord Jesus. For this is the will of God, your sanc-
> tification: that you abstain from fornication; that each one of you know how
> to control your own body in holiness and honor, not with lustful passion, like
> the Gentiles who do not know God; that no one wrong or exploit a brother
> or sister [Greek: his brother] in this matter, because the Lord is an avenger
> in all these things, just as we have already told you beforehand and solemnly
> warned you. For God did not call us to impurity but in holiness. Therefore
> whoever rejects this rejects not human authority but God, who also gives his
> Holy Spirit to you. (1 Thess 4:1–8)

Parallels between Paul's warnings to new Gentile converts in
1 Thessalonians 4 and Ephesians 4:17–20 are noteworthy:

> Now this I affirm and insist on in the Lord: you must no longer live as
> the Gentiles live, in the futility of their minds. They are darkened in their
> understanding, alienated from the life of God because of their ignorance and
> hardness of heart. They have lost all sensitivity and have abandoned them-
> selves to licentiousness, greedy to practice every kind of impurity. That is not
> the way you learned Christ!

We might list the parallels between 1 Thessalonians 4:1–8 and Ephesians
4:17–20: (1) an old way of life versus a new way of life; (2) living as the
Gentiles do; (3) the need for a change of mind regarding sexual ethics that
God makes possible; (4) being taught the new way of life not merely by human
teachers but in accordance with God's authority and will—being taught Christ.
These same points can be found in Romans 1:24–28 and 12:1–2.

---

[31] This is our translation of the passage. Translations such as the NRSV, the NEV, and the NIV
undertranslate "the truth" in the last verse by making "the truth" function as an adjective: "true
righteousness and holiness." This is certainly wrong since this passage—before and after this
verse—has in view "speaking the truth" (4:15, 25) and being "taught Christ" (4:20), in whom
truth is found (4:21). Thus, 4:24 is saying the new person has been created in conformity with
God, that is, in conformity with the righteousness and holiness that derives from the truth that
Christ is, that the believers have been taught, and that the believers speak to one another.

Thus, Paul does not expect Gentiles outside of Christ to understand that their sexual passions are corrupt and that their thinking about sexuality is corrupt. In truly coming to Christ, their thinking will change as their minds are renewed. They will no longer applaud sinful acts (Rom 1:32). They will be able to know how to live righteous and holy lives (Rom 12:2). And they, who were "unable not to sin" (*non posse non peccare*), will now be "able not to sin" (*posse non peccare*)[32] as God's power works within them and as they present their bodies as living sacrifices, holy and well-pleasing to God (Rom 12:1).

CONCLUSION

In light of other ancient sources, readers of Romans 1:26–27, then, can appreciate how Paul's original audience would have understood what he says about "against nature" and "according to nature." Gentile believers, perhaps some of which had actually heard Musonius Rufus teach on the subject in Rome along with his student Epictetus, and Jewish believers in the Roman church would have known what Paul meant by "according to nature" and "against nature." They would also have known how to understand such language in regard to the issue of homosexuality. "Against nature" did not mean someone behaving against his or her sexual orientation but against the nature of God's created order. A "man-woman" or "soft man" was a man who was living "against nature." Lesbians, too, were using their parts against nature. Such people not only committed homosexual acts but were given over to an orientation against nature. Paul's use of this language in Romans 1:26–27, then, is standard fare. Yet Paul understands that all people have sinned and fallen short of the glory of God and are beholden to the power of sin at work in their members. Only in Christ can a person find freedom from sin, a renewed mind, and the empowering presence of the Holy Spirit to live the righteous life. Paul not only says to believers, "Do not do these things"; he explains how the righteousness of God in Christ Jesus and the empowering presence of the Spirit free them from the predicament of sin and reconcile them to God.

The evidence cited in this chapter from Greek and Jewish sources demonstrates that Paul's language comes from the literature of his day. Attempts to say he is speaking about homosexual acts only in certain circumstances are undermined precisely because Paul is using standard terminology of "according to nature" and "against nature" for heterosexual and homosexual unions, respectively.[33] Moreover, Paul's wording reflects thinking based on the Genesis

---

[32] Cf. Augustine, *De Correptione et Gratia* 12.33.

[33] Cf., e.g., James E. Miller, "The Practices of Rom 1:26," *Novum Testamentum* 37, no. 1 (1995): 1–11; James E. Miller, "Response: Pederasty and Romans 1:27: A Response to Mark Smith," *Journal of the American Academy of Religion* 65, no. 4 (1997): 861–66. Miller's arguments fall apart at a number of levels: misconstruing ancient awareness of lesbianism, misrepresenting the continuing practice of pederasty, and offering illogical arguments.

creation story. "Natural," then, means the way God ordered creation, including the pairing of male and female. In the creation story the separation of the rib from Adam (the man) means that when he marries Eve (the woman), he reconforms to the way God made him: the man and the woman become "one flesh." Being created in the image of God, Adam and Eve are to be fruitful and multiply in order to have dominion over the earth. This is sex "according to nature."

In our study of Romans 1:24–27, we see that the time-honored interpretation of the church through the ages is correct: Paul was speaking about homosexuality. We also agree with the conclusion reached by Robert Jewett in his commentary on Romans, which gives particular attention to primary sources. Jewett writes with respect to Romans 1:26–27:

> Paul's language served to remove any vestige of decency, honor, or friendship from same-sex relations. Neither distinguishing pederasty from relationships between adult, consenting males, nor distinguishing between active and passive partners as Roman culture was inclined to do, Paul simply follows the line of his Jewish cultural tradition by construing the entire realm of homosexual relations as evidence that divine wrath was active therein.[34]

We would add to Jewett's conclusion that Paul also likely follows the Stoic tradition, as seen in Epictetus. Paul's argument, however, is neither derived simply from his "Jewish cultural tradition" nor Stoicism: it is an interpretation of Scripture. What he says in this passage is what the church has understood all along. As Jewett notes:

> There is no mistaking the direction of Paul's argument or its consistency with all other known branches of ancient Judaism and early Christianity. Convinced that heterosexuality was part of the divinely created order for humankind and that sexual identity is essential to humans as *soma* [physical beings], he presents deviations from traditionally Judaic role definitions as indicative of an arrogant assault on the Creator and as a sign of current and forthcoming wrath. The evidence [in Rom 1:26, which speaks against lesbianism] is particularly damaging to the [qualifying] hypothesis by [Robin] Scroggs[35] that the critique of homosexuality in this [passage] aims solely to attack pederasty and thus has no bearing on homoerotic relationships between consenting adults.[36]

Jewett is not pleased with Paul's perspective, but he makes the case well enough that there really is no other way to read Romans 1 than as a condemnation of same-sex practices. By citing various primary texts in Greek, Roman, and Jewish literature and by attending to Paul's logic, he too eliminates the various

---

[34] Robert Jewett, *Romans*, Hermeneia (Minneapolis, MN: Fortress, 2007), 179.

[35] Robin Scroggs, *The New Testament and Homosexuality* (Minneapolis, MN: Fortress, 1983).

[36] Jewett, *Romans*, 177.

suggestions put forward to make Paul say something other than what he actually says. Reading a commentary such as Jewett's, one gets the impression that all the fanciful exegetical arguments of the past thirty years will eventually fade from the discussion. This will take time though, since some authors will perpetuate inadequate arguments without engaging more serious scholarship and without checking the ancient literature.

CHAPTER 18

REVISIONIST READINGS OF ROMANS 1:24–28

INTRODUCTION

I n this chapter we examine how revisionist interpretations of Romans 1:24–28 have played a role in the growing Western abandonment of the church's understanding that homosexual practice is a sin. We will note several proposals, yet our primary interest is in how these proposals conflict with one another and how their failure nonetheless has not hindered pro-homosexual interpretation of this passage. This fact—a disagreement over reasons and yet an agreement over the conclusion—points to the true issue facing denominations that have affirmed homosexual practice. They have begun with their conclusion rather than a commitment to scriptural authority. The real issue is not exegesis but authority.

NARROWING THE ARGUMENT TO SOME TYPE OF HOMOSEXUAL ACT

Nowhere in Scripture is pederasty specifically condemned. Rather, by condemning same-sex unions, the Bible makes plain that pederasty is also wrong. Yet, when Robin Scroggs argued in 1983 that Paul's condemnation of homosexuality in Romans 1:27 was limited to pederasty, a number of scholars, such as Victor Paul Furnish, thought they at last had a way to affirm biblical authority yet still allow adult, mutually loving, monogamous homosexual relationships.[1] Remarkably, Scroggs believed "pederasty was the only *model* [for homosexuality] in existence in the world of [Paul's] time."[2] Such a belief could

---

[1] Robin Scroggs, *The New Testament and Homosexuality* (Minneapolis, MN: Fortress, 1983); Victor Paul Furnish, *The Moral Teachings of Paul: Selected Issues*, 2nd ed. (Nashville, TN: Abingdon, 1985), 52–83.
[2] Ibid., 139.

not stand for long, since it was the result of seriously inadequate scholarship. It also involved a farfetched claim: that in Paul's day people were only practicing pederasty, but at the same time a segment of the population was naturally disposed to same-sex attraction. As Kyle Harper states in his 2013 work, after a survey of evidence for adult, same-sex relationships or marriages, "It is time to lay to rest the bizarre notion, which is still sometimes expressed, that same-sex eros was, materially and ideologically, on the wane by the second century [AD]."[3] Once the sources were examined, the argument dissolved. Yet one wonders how many were misled in their ecclesiastical proceedings by such erroneous scholarship from the 1980s.[4]

After Scroggs published his argument, pro-homosexual, revisionist interpreters of Scripture had something of an open season on Romans 1:24–28. Various reasons were offered not to take Paul's words at face value. Eleven years later Arland Hultgren of the Evangelical Lutheran Church of America still touted the view that Paul had pederasty in mind in Romans 1. This was a view on the way out in scholarship even as his denomination was solidifying its argument that Scripture posed no barrier to same-sex marriage. Hultgren and others also added reasons for departing from the church's traditional reading of Romans 1:24–28. The following are some of the arguments revisionist interpreters have attempted.

Could Paul Be Speaking of Pederasty and Promiscuity in Romans 1:26–27?

Hultgren says: "In Romans 1 Paul attacks homosexual activity known in his world—massive pederasty and promiscuity among gentiles. He had no idea that there could be persons who actually have a homosexual orientation; he could not have done so."[5]

---

[3] Kyle Harper, *From Shame to Sin: The Christian Transformation of Sexual Morality in Late Antiquity* (Cambridge, MA: Harvard University Press, 2013), 36.

[4] We also wonder how many Presbyterians were persuaded by Jack Rogers in 2006 when he argued the impossible thesis that Paul was condemning temple prostitution in Rom 1:26–27. For counterarguments to Rogers's unique claim, see Robert Gagnon's "Bad Reasons for Changing One's Mind: Jack Rogers' Temple Prostitution Argument and Other False Starts," March 1, 2004, accessed October 7, 2013, http://www.robgagnon.net/responsetorogers2.htm. See Jack Rogers, *Jesus, the Bible, and Homosexuality: Explode the Myths, Heal the Church* (Louisville, KY: Westminster/John Knox, 2006).

[5] Arland Hultgren, "Being Faithful to the Scriptures: Rom 1:26–27 as a Case in Point," *Word and World* 14 (1994): 322. Regarding promiscuity, Hultgren says that in Rom 1:27, Paul uses a word for sexual passion that means "utterly consumed by fire" (319). He contrasts this with what he says is Paul's normal word for sexual passion, *pyrein* (1 Cor 7:9). Thus Rom 1:27 refers to "something beyond normal sexual desire; it is a lust that destroys the self and ends in abusive behavior" (320). Of course, the natural reading of the passage is that homosexual union is precisely that: "something beyond normal sexual desire" which "destroys the self" (whether or not

Could Anyone, Including Paul, Be Thinking of Sexual Orientation at All in the First Century?

A previous chapter has demonstrated that people offered various explanations for sexual orientation in the time of the early church—even centuries before then. Yet this is one of the most common arguments from revisionist interpreters. Hultgren states outright that people in the first century could not have entertained the notion of sexual orientation: "The concept of sexual orientation, including homosexual orientation, had to wait another nineteen centuries to be formulated."[6] This argument proceeds by conjecture without adequate examination of primary sources. We have seen that mythological, medical, physiognomical, philosophical, astrological, and contextual arguments about sexual orientation were entertained, in addition to the scriptural argument that people are sinful.

In the course of his argument that Romans 1:27 is about pederasty, Hultgren

1. *supposed* that Paul is speaking about pederasty in Rom 1:27 without proving it.
2. *ignored* the fact that Rom 1:26, the previous verse, condemned lesbianism (and therefore more than pederasty is involved in his argument).
3. *did not investigate* the meaning of "against nature" and "according to nature" in the primary sources.
4. *missed the fact* that Paul's argument in Rom 1:18–28 is based on understanding nature in terms of creation: God's creation of male and female for sexual union is "natural" orientation; any other orientation is unnatural, no matter how "natural" it seems to the sinner.
5. *claimed* that Paul would not have known about homosexual orientation without investigating the literature in antiquity that indicates society was well aware of it.
6. *misunderstood* 1 Cor 6:9 as being about pederasty and, consequently, erroneously applied this wrong conclusion to his reading of Rom 1:26–27. In his interpretation of 1 Cor 6:9, he . . .
    a. failed to investigate the use of *malakoi* in Greek writings and assumed it applied to boys in pederastic relationships;
    b. failed to see the likely connection between Paul's term *arsenokoitoi* and Lev 18:22 and 20:13.
7. *failed* to explain how idolatry is related to homosexuality in Rom 1:18–28.
8. *did not mention* that his restricted interpretation of Paul is not found in the church fathers.

That so many errors were made in interpretation is partly due to Hultgren's dependence on previous scholarship, such as that of Scroggs. One reason this kind of scholarship received a "pass" is that its audience wanted to believe the

---

it entails abusive behavior). The natural reading of the verse involves contrasting the natural use of women with men being enflamed toward one another.

[6] Arland Hultgren, "Being Faithful to the Scriptures," 319.

conclusion. Another reason is that the audience likely got lost in the academic material—original languages and primary sources. They trusted scholars to have done their homework and to have been careful, correct, and complete in what they presented.

In the 1990s still other suggestions for revising the church's reading of Romans 1:24–28 were advanced.

Could "Natural" in Romans 1:26–27 Actually Mean "Conventional"?

As we noted in the previous chapter, Dale Martin and Martti Nissinen argued that Paul meant by "nature" not what is natural but what is convention-al.[7] We have already disproven this suggestion with overwhelming evidence to the contrary in ancient texts, let alone the fairly obvious meaning of Romans 1:26–27.[8]

Could "Natural" in Romans 1:26–27 Mean a Female Stepping Out of Her Subordinate Role or a Male Taking on a Subordinate Role?

Following Bernadette Brooten, Robert Jewett has suggested Paul's concern is that females play the subordinate role and males the dominant role in their relations, including sexual intercourse. As Jewett says, "'Natural' intercourse means penetration of a subordinate person by a dominant one."[9] Over against this suggestion the previous chapter has demonstrated that in other ancient texts, "according to nature" references heterosexual unions. Also, we might recall that Epictetus says *both* the one who penetrates *and* the one penetrated in a male homosexual relationship "lose the man" (*Disc.* 2.10). One cannot limit the understanding of "natural" to men who penetrate and women who are penetrated sexually. While there may have been disdain in some circles for men who were penetrated and women who penetrated, the fact remains that "natural" in antiquity had to do with the union of male and female; "unnatural" had to do with same-sex unions of any sort. For Paul, unnatural use has to do with putting one's sexual organs to use in a way God did not intend, as when women join together sexually with women and men with men. There is no suggestion of social stigmatization in Romans 1:26–27 for a woman who penetrates another woman or for a man who is penetrated. Had Paul wished

---

[7] Dale Martin, "Heterosexism and the Interpretation of Romans 1:18–32," *Biblical Interpretation* 3 (1995): 332–55; Martti Nissinen, *Homoeroticism in the Biblical World* (Minneapolis, MN: Augsburg Fortress, 1998), 107.

[8] See the helpful discussion of "natural" and "unnatural" in James B. De Young, *Homosexuality: Contemporary Claims Examined in Light of the Bible and Other Ancient Literature and Law* (Grand Rapids, MI: Kregel, 2000), 147.

[9] So Robert Jewett, "The Social Context and Implications of Homoerotic References in Romans 1:24–27," 232, quoting Bernadette Brooten, *Love Between Women: Early Christian Responses to Homoeroticism* (Chicago, IL: University of Chicago Press, 1996), 232.

to say this, as some authors did, he could have done so. The Greek language was perfectly capable of expressing this thought, but this was not Paul's point.

Is Paul Opposing Heterosexual Oral or Anal Intercourse in Romans 1:26–27?

A particularly unpopular attempt to reinterpret Paul is that proposed by James F. Miller. Miller ventured the notion in 1995 that Paul is speaking about heterosexual anal or oral intercourse.[10] This suggestion is sheer speculation without textual basis and has garnered little support from others.

Is Paul Opposing Bestiality in Romans 1:26–27?

Possibly the most imaginative suggestion came from Klaus Haacker, who proposed that Romans 1:24–28 is actually about bestiality.[11] This suggestion, like the previous one, shows exegetical desperation by those wanting to revise the traditional interpretation of Romans 1:24–28.

Readers of the literature should note that these different suggestions are thoroughly at odds with one another: if one is right, the other is wrong. They do not support one another. This undercuts the notion that there is an increasing consensus of scholars who have argued in favor of homosexual relations with respect to biblical texts. That there is so much disagreement among those trying to find a reason to read biblical texts in novel ways should alert readers to the possibility that new interpretations are flawed.

Still, the various suggestions have a numbing effect in the overall argument about homosexuality. Some, hearing the cacophony of misguided interpretations, assume there is uncertainty about what Paul meant in Romans 1:24–28. This is not the case at all. Scholars such as those noted simply stirred up clear waters.[12]

In 1996, Mark Smith put Scroggs's theory that Paul was addressing pederasty to rest in a scholarly article that demonstrated wide study of ancient texts. First, he noted, Philo of the first century AD used both general language to condemn all homosexual practices (as Paul in Rom 1:24–28) and specific language to condemn pederasty. Thus, Smith appropriately reasoned, an author could distinguish homosexual practices from pederasty. Paul, therefore, would have identified the issue in Romans 1:27 as pederasty had he wished to limit his comments in the way Scroggs suggested. He did not, so he must have

---

[10] James F. Miller, "The Practices of Rom 1:26: Homosexual or Heterosexual?" *Novum Testamentum* 37 (1995): 1–11.

[11] Klaus Haacker, "Exegetische Gesigtspunkte zum Thema Homosexualität," *Theologische Blätter* 25 (1994): 173–80.

[12] For alternative views of Rom 1:24–28 that emerged after Scroggs, see Robert Gagnon, *The Bible and Homosexual Practice: Texts and Hermeneutics* (Nashville, TN: Abingdon, 2001), 258; William Loader, *The New Testament on Sexuality* (Grand Rapids, MI: Eerdmans, 2012), 308.

intended to oppose homosexual practices of any sort. Second, said Smith, Paul was reaffirming what he already knew from Leviticus 18:22; 20:13.[13] Paul stood in a Jewish tradition of interpretation, and on the issue of homosexuality he perpetuated that tradition. Third, and most importantly, Smith disproved Scroggs' hypothesis that Paul and others in his day only knew of pederasty: knowledge of a wide variety of homosexual practices, orientations, and relationships can be demonstrated well enough in ancient literature. Romans 1:26–27 most naturally reads as a reference to adult female and male homosexuality. The following evidence for such in antiquity mostly follows Smith (with some expansion). It is offered to establish the fact that adult homosexuality was very much a known entity in Paul's day.

FURTHER EVIDENCE OF MALE HOMOSEXUALITY FROM GREEK AND ROMAN LITERATURE AND ARTIFACTS

This work has a goal to present and discuss primary sources, and yet an attempt to present all the primary sources on homosexuality in Greece would be exhausting. Many primary texts have already been cited and discussed. Here we point interested readers to some further texts and artifacts:

- Vases showing bearded males engaging in homosexual acts (sixth century BC)
- Statue of young, hermaphrodite in Louvre Museum, Paris, France (Roman period)
- Agathon and Pausanias in Plato's *Symposium*
- Ctessipus and Cleinias in Plato's *Euthydemus*
- Charmides is a lover of other youths in Plato's *Charmides*
- Aristotle, *Nichomachian Ethics*[14]
- Philolaus and Dioclese set up house together, remained in their relationship throughout their lives, and wished to be buried side by side (Aristotle, *Politics* 2.96–97 [1247a])
- Plutarch's description of the Sacred Band of Thebes (*Pelopidas* 18–20)[15]

---

[13] Mark Smith, "Ancient Bisexuality and the Interpretation of Romans 1:26–27," *Journal of the American Academy of Religion* 64 (Summer 1996): 223–56, 245–47.

[14] Aristotle says men who are effeminate or practice pederasty can be accounted for either because of their nature or the way in which they were raised: "the habit of plucking out the hair or of gnawing the nails, or even coals or earth, and in addition to these paederasty; for these arise in some by nature and in others, as in those who have been the victims of lust from childhood, from habit" (*Nichomachian Ethics* 7.5).

[15] Male lovers were paired for fighting so they would fight better, wanting to impress each other.

- Plutarch, *Erotikos* (761d) says Epaminondas and Caphisodoros were lovers and buried together as a married couple[16]
- Achilles Tatius mentions two pairs of young male lovers (*Leucippe and Clitophon* 1.7; 2.33–34)
- Oxyrhynchus Papyrus 3070[17]

Roman primary sources also offer considerable evidence. Restrictions may be evident regarding classes, and there may be some tendency to look askance at the flourishing of homosexual activity in Greek territories, but the general picture seems fairly similar to that of the Greeks: homosexual acts of various sorts were not uncommon. Consider these examples:

---

[16] Note Plutarch's description of a pederasty that is pursued not alongside heterosexual relations but in opposition to them: "He rails against and vilifies that great conjugal Love which co-operates to win immortality for the human race by kindling afresh through new generations our being prone as it is to extinction. . . . Boy-love denies pleasure; that is because it is ashamed and afraid. It needs a fair pretext for approaching the young and beautiful, so it pretends friendship and virtue. It covers itself with the sand of the wrestling-floor, it takes cold baths, it plays the highbrow and publicly proclaims that it is a philosopher and disciplined on the outside— because of the law. But when night comes and all is quiet, sweet is the harvest when the guard's away" ("Dialogue on Love" 751D–E, trans. E. L. Minar, F. H. Sandbach, W. C. Helmbold, *Plutarch: Moralia*, vol. 9, ed. G. P. Goold [Cambridge, MA: Harvard University Press, 1961], 317–25).

[17] The text states, "Says Apion and Epimas to Epaphroditus, (1) the Dearest, that if you were to grant us the opportunity to bugger (*pugazein*) you, (2) well will it go for you when no longer will we thrash you (3) if you grant us the opportunity to bugger you. Farewell. Farewell" (as quoted in Marguerite Johnson and Terry Ryan, *Sexuality in Greek and Roman Society and Literature: A Sourcebook*).

- Emperors Tiberius,[18] Caligula,[19] Nero (with Sporos and then Doryphorus),[20] Galba,[21] and Hadrian all took male lovers.[22]
- Seneca, *Epistulae Morales* 47.7 mentions the topic.[23]
- Xenophon of Ephesus, writing in second or early third century AD, penned *Ephesian Tale of Anthia and Habrocomes*. It tells of a man in love with another man his own age, an older woman, and a younger man.
- Cicero (*Philippics*) mentions a permanent marriage between Marcus Antonius and Curio, another male.
- Martial mentions two male marriages (Martial 1.24; 12.42).
- Juvenal mentions two men getting married (*Satire* 2.117–42), a bisexual adulterer, Aufidius, and a homosexual, Virro (*Satire* 9).
- Emperor Elagabalus married Zoticus, an athlete, and insisted on his courtiers also marrying men if they wanted advancement (*Lampiridius* 10–11; third century AD).

---

[18] Suetonius, *Tiberius* 3.44: "Some of his criminal obscenity are almost too vile to discuss, much less believe. Imagine training little boys, whom he called his 'minnows,' to chase him while he went swimming and to get between his legs to lick and nibble him. . . . The story goes that once, while sacrificing, he took an erotic fancy to the acolyte who carried the incense casket, and could hardly wait for the ceremony to end before hurrying him and his brother, the sacred trumpeter, out of the temple and indecently assaulting them both" (Suetonius, *The Twelve Caesars*, trans. Robert Graves [London, England: Penguin, 1979]).

[19] Suetonius, *Caligula* 36.1: "He is said to have had unnatural relations with Marcus Lepidus, the pantomimic actor Mnester, and certain hostages. Valerius Catullus, a young man of a consular family, publicly proclaimed that he had violated the emperor and worn himself out in commerce with him" (trans. J. C. Rolfe, Loeb Classical Library 31 [Cambridge, MA: Harvard University, 1913]).

[20] Suetonius, *Nero* 28: "[Having] . . . tried to turn the boy Sporus into a girl by castration, he [Nero] went through a wedding ceremony with him—dowry, bridal veil and all—which the whole Court attended; then brought him home and treated him as a wife. He dressed Sporus in the fine clothes normally worn by an Empress and took him in his own litter not only to every Greek assize and fair, but actually through the street of Images at Rome, kissing him amorously now and then" (Suetonius, *The Twelve Caesars*, trans. Robert Graves [Baltimore, MD: Penguin, 1957]).

[21] Regarding Galba, Suetonius writes, "A homosexual invert, he showed a decided preference for sturdy men. It is said when Idelus, one of his trusty bed-fellows, brought the news of Nero's death, Galba showered him with kisses and begged him to undress without delay; whereupon intimacy took place" (Suetonius, *The Twelve Caesars*.)

[22] Hadrian had a twenty-year-old male lover, Antinous. Upon Antinous's death by drowning in the Nile, Hadrian established a city and statue in his honor and had him deified.

[23] The text states: "Another, as wine-steward, is dressed like a woman and struggling with his own growth to adulthood; he cannot escape boyhood but is dragged back and his appearance, already fit for military service, has been smoothed out, with the bristles pumiced away or completely plucked: he divides the night between his master's drunkenness and lust, as a man in the bedchamber and boy at the dinner party" (*Seneca: A New Translation*, trans. Elaine Fantham [New York, NY: Oxford University Press, 2010], 69).

- *Theodotian Code* 9.7.3: In the Christian era a law was passed against a man marrying another man as though he were a woman, suggesting such a scenario needed to be addressed (AD 342).
- An Egyptian magical text suggests the practice of adult, male homosexuality.[24]

A look at the evidence for lesbianism in Greek and Roman contexts shows that this practice was, indeed, known and present during the early Christian centuries. Its existence, of course, undercuts any attempt to limit ancient references to homosexuality to pederasty.[25]

Evidence for the practice of lesbianism is not as strong as that for male homosexuality, but it is present. The following texts mention lesbian orientation, attraction, and/or acts:

- Sappho (seventh century BC) and her poetry[26]
- Aristophanes's speech in *Symposium* (189c–193d)
- Plato, *Laws* 636C–D: unnatural pleasure (when a male unites with a male or female with female) is practiced by the Cretans, who likely concocted the myth about Zeus's same-sex love for Ganymede in order to legitimatize their desires

---

[24] This text, written after the Greco-Roman period, describes one man's attempt to secure the love of another man. Papollo was to place the following written text on the threshold of Phello son of Maurê's home so that when he walked over it he would be smitten with desire: "You will take over his heart and his mind, and you will have mastery over his whole body. When he wishes to stand, you will not allow him to stand; when he wishes to sit down, you will not allow him to sit down; but let him seek after me from village to village, from city to city, from country to country, until he comes to me and becomes subject under my feet . . . until I have fulfilled the desire of my heart and the longing of my soul, with a good will and an inextinguishable physical desire, now now, quickly quickly!" (As quoted in Dominic Montserrat, *Sex and Society in Graeco-Roman Egypt* [Abingdon, UK: Routledge, 1963], 156–57.)

[25] Mark Smith ("Ancient Bisexuality and the Interpretation of Romans 1:26–27," 243) states that Paul's mention of lesbianism in Rom 1:26 is all the more remarkable if we think there is not sufficient ancient evidence outside of Scripture to establish its widespread practice in the ancient world. Second, the evidence does not point to a connection with pederasty: these were mutually consenting women. That anyone would think to argue that Rom 1:27 should be limited to pederasty is incredible when the previous verse is about lesbianism.

[26] For example, a woman speaks to another woman: "'I simply wish to die.'/ Weeping, she left me / and said this too: / 'We've suffered terribly / Sappho I leave you against my will.' / I answered, go happily / and remember me, / You know how we cared for you, / if not, let me remind you /. . . the lovely times we shared. / Many crowns of violets, / roses and crocuses / . . . together you set before me / and many scented wreaths / made from blossoms / around your soft throat . . . / with pure, sweet oil /. . . you anointed me, / and on a soft, gentle bed . . . / you quenched my desire." Translation by Diane J. Rayor, *Sappho's Lyre: Archaic Lyric and Women Poets of Ancient Greece* (Berkeley, CA: University of California, 1993). See further Jane McIntosh Snyder, *Lesbian Desire in the Lyrics of Sappho* (New York, NY: Columbia University Press, 1997).

- Pseudo-Phocylides, *Sentences* 192[27]
- Plutarch, *Whether Beasts Are Rational* 990D–F
- Plutarch, *Life of Lycurgus* 18.4[28]
- Clement of Alexandria, second-century Christian author, wrote in *The Instructor* 3.3.21 that men play the part of women, and women of men, contrary to nature; women are both wives and husbands, and this promiscuity is a public institution.
- Pseudo-Lucian, *Erotos* 28 argues that there is no logical reason to forbid lesbian sex, which was thought to be abhorrent, if male homosexuality is permitted.
- Lucian of Samosata, in the second century, penned *Dialogues of the Courtesans*[29]: Megilla was married to a woman, could satisfy females' desires as well as any man's, and seduced Laena, "whom she love[d] as a man" (5).
- Ovid, *Metamorphoses* 9.715–48[30]
- Several vases depict women engaged either in homosexual activity or actively courting one another:

  ~ R207 one woman caressing another's genitals
  ~ R223 two women using a double *olisbos* (a facsimile of male genitalia) for sexual stimulation

---

[27] Quoted earlier. The relevant part here states, "And let women not imitate the sexual role of men."

[28] Quoted earlier. The relevant part here states, "Even the maidens found lovers in good and noble women."

[29] Lucian's fifth dialogue addresses the love of three women. Megilla, from Lesbos, sees herself as male and is able to seduce Leaena. She and another courtesan, Demonassa, want Leaena to sleep between them. When confronted with performing homosexual practices, Leaena replies, "Quite true . . . But I'm ashamed, for it's unnatural." Regarding her lover it is stated: "She's a sort of woman for the ladies. They say there are more women like that in Lesbos, with faces like men, and unwilling to consort with men, but only with women, as though they themselves were men" (*Lucian Vol. VII, Dialogues of the Courtesans*, Loeb Classical Library, ed. T. E. Page, E. Capps, W. H. D. Rouse et al., trans. M. D. Macleod [Cambridge, MA: Harvard University Press, 1961]).

[30] Ovid tells of a girl, Ianthe, who was raised by her mother as a boy, since the father had said that if the mother gave birth to a girl the baby should be put to death. This passage has to do with the girl's approaching wedding: she is to marry another girl, Iphis, whom she has loved while growing up with her. As this is deemed an impossible situation in the story, the goddess turns Iphis into a young man and the wedding continues. Ianthe says, "O what will be the awful dreaded end, with such a monstrous love compelling me? If the Gods should wish to save me, certainly they should have saved me; but, if their desire was for my ruin, still they should have given some natural suffering of humanity. The passion for a cow does not inflame a cow, no mare has ever sought another mare. The ram inflames the ewe, and every doe follows a chosen stag; so also birds are mated, and in all the animal world no female ever feels love passion for another female—why is it in me?" (trans. Brookes More, *Ovid: Metamorphoses* [Boston, MA: Cornhill, 1922]).

~ an Aegean vase from Thera (ca. 620 BC) with two women in courting position, one touching the other's chin

- Alcman of the seventh century BC, in *Partheneion* I, tells of the homoerotic love between two Spartan girls.
- Asclepiades, of the third century BC, writes *Epigrams* that mentions two women who defy the law of Aphrodite and engage in sexual activities that "are not seemly."[31]
- Seneca, *Controversiae* 1.2.23 tells of a man who catches his wife in bed with a woman and kills them both.
- Phaedrus (from the time of Seneca) explains why males and females are at times homosexual: Prometheus mistakenly put sexual organs on the wrong people, such that "lust now enjoys perverted pleasure" (*Liber Fabularum* 4.16).
- Martial mentions two lesbians: Philaenis, a "lesbian of lesbians" (*tribadum tribas*) and "an insatiable Nymphomaniac," was said to engage in sexual relations with boys and girls daily; Bassa's lust imitated that of a man (*Epigrammata* 7.67).
- Iamblicus, *Babyloniaca* is a lost novel of the second century AD. In it Berenice, queen of Egypt, marries another woman, Mesopotamia. The story is preserved in Photius, *Biblioteca* 94.
- Evidence from Egypt suggests lesbianism.[32]

---

[31] Asclepiades, *Epigram* IX: "*Bittó* and *Nánnion* are two Samian women, women who / Wish not to visit Love's domains / By rules the goddess preordains, / Deserting her prescribed delight / For other joys that are not right. Hate, Aphrodite, those who've fled / From your dominion's marriage bed!" (trans. in Gordon L. Fain, *Ancient Greek Epigrams: Major Poets in Verse Translation* [Berkeley, CA: University of California Press, 2010], 79).

[32] *Papyri Graecae Magicae* 32: "I adjure you, Eangelos [possibly a dead spirit], by Anoubis [an Egyptian god of the underworld] and Hermes [a Greek god able to enter Hades] and all the rest down below [that is, in Hades]; attract and bind Sarapias whom Helen bore, to this Herais, whom Thermoutharin bore, now, now; quickly, quickly. By her soul and heart attract Sarapias herself, whom (Helen) bore from her own womb. *maei ote elbōsatok alaoubētō ōeio* [. . .] *aēn* [magical words not translated into Greek]. Attract and [bind the soul and heart of Sarapias], whom [Helen bore, to this] Herais, [whom] Thermoutharin [bore] from her womb [now, now; quickly, quickly.]" (trans. as found in Bernadette J. Brooten, *Love Between Women*, 78–79. Our explanations are added.) *Tablet* in *Supplementum Magicum* 1.42: "Fundament of the gloomy darkness, jagged-toothed dog, covered with coiling snakes, turning three heads, traveler in the recesses of the underworld, come, spirit-driver, with the Erinyes, [savage with their stinging whips; holy serpents, maenads, frightful maidens, come to my wroth incantations. Before I persuade by force this one and you, render him immediately a fire-breathing daemon. Listen and do everything quickly, in no way opposing me in the performance of this action; for you are the governors of the earth. . . . By means of this corpse-daemon inflame the heart, the liver, the spirit of Gorgonia, whom Nilogenia bore, with love and affection for Sophia, whom Isara bore. Constrain Gorgonia, whom Nilogenia bore, to cast herself into the bath-house for the sake of Sophia, whom Isara bore; and you, become a bath-woman. Burn, set on fire, inflame her soul, heart, liver, spirit with love for Sophia, whom Isara bore. Drive Gorgonia, whom Nilogenia

- And even Jewish literature mentions lesbianism:

  ~ *Sifre*, a commentary on Leviticus 18, and
  ~ Jerusalem Talmud, which debates over whether a female who has committed homosexual acts should be said to have lost her virginity and therefore be disqualified from marrying a priest.

Thus, in light of the evidence for adult male homosexuality and lesbianism in antiquity, Scroggs and others following him misled many during the 1980s and early 1990s with their focus on pederasty. But Smith's work marks a turning point in refutation of the argument offered by Scroggs.

Remarkably, when Jack Rogers, from the same Presbyterian denomination as Scroggs, wrote in 2006 in favor of homosexual unions, he did so without one reference to Scroggs.[33] But the battle continued, even if one had to ignore "heroes" on one's own side who had carried the wrong argument into the fray. A further surprise was that Rogers, a theologian with far weaker exegetical arguments than Scroggs, introduced his own imaginative interpretation of

---

bore, drive her, torment her body night and day, force her to rush forth from every place and every house, loving Sophia, whom Isara bore, she, surrendered like a slave, giving herself and all her possessions to her, because this is the will and command of the great god. . . . Blessed lord of the immortals, holding the scepters of the Tartaros and of terrible, fearful Styx (?) and of life-robbing Lethe, the hair of Kerberos trembles in fear of you, you crack the loud whips of the Erinyes; the couch of Persephone delights you, when you go to the longed bed, whether you be the immortal Sarapis, whom the inverse fears, whether you be Osiris, star of the land of Egypt; your messenger is the all-wise boy; yours is Anoubis, the pious herald of the dead. Come hither, fulfill my wishes, because I summon you by these secret symbols [a lengthy section of Egyptian magical words follow]. Constrain Gorgonia, whom Nilogenia bore, to cast herself into the bath-house for the sake of Sophia, whom Isara bore, for her. Aye, lord, king of the chthonic gods, burn, set on fire, inflame the soul, the heart, the liver, the spirit of Gorgonia, whom Nilogenia bore, with love and affection for Sophia, whom Israra bore; drive Gorgonia herself, torment her body night and day; force her to rush forth from every place and every house, loving Sophia, whom Isara bore, she, Gorgonia surrendered like a slave, giving herself and all her possessions. Aye, lord, king of the chthonic gods, carry out what is inscribed on this tablet, for I adjure you who divided the entire universe, a single realm, [more Egyptian magical words]. So, do not disobey my request, but cause Gorgonia, whom Nilogenia bore, force her to cast herself into the bath-house for the sake of Sophia, whom Isara bore, for her. Burn, set on fire, inflame the heart, the liver, the spirit of Gorgonia, whom Nilogenia bore, with love and affection for Sophia, whom Isara bore, for a good end." [The text continues with the same requests repeated again.] (Translation is in Bernadette J. Brooten, *Love Between Women*, 82–88.)

Tablet in *Supplentum Magicum* 1.37:

Tablet A: Horion, son of Sarapous, make and force [drawing of a mummy] Nike, daughter of Apollonous, to fall in love with Paitous, whom Timesios bore.

Tablet B: Make Nike, daughter of Apollonous, fall in love with Paitous, whom Timesios bore, for five months.

[33] Jack Rogers, *Jesus, the Bible, and Homosexuality: Explode the Myths, Heal the Church* (Louisville, KY: Westminster/John Knox, 2006). The 2009 revised edition also lacks any reference to Scroggs.

Romans 1:26–27. The banner for homosexual practice and marriage would be carried by someone with an even weaker argument.

Rogers imagined that Paul was opposing temple prostitution when writing the Roman church from Corinth. We say "imagined" not only because Rogers is involved in some dubitable psychological interpretation of Paul but also because there is no evidence of temple prostitution in Corinth in Paul's day.[34] As Robert Gagnon points out, Rogers picked up some information as a tourist of ancient Corinth that he apparently did not understand correctly.[35] Corinth, in an earlier era, did have temple prostitution. But the city was destroyed and then later rebuilt. The practice of temple prostitution in Corinth, mentioned by the ancient geographer Strabo, related to the first city of Corinth in an era well before Paul's.[36] Also, there is no mention in Strabo of male prostitutes being used by other males. This confusion on Rogers's part led him to imagine that Paul was addressing temple prostitution in Romans 1:26–27, which, in turn, led Rogers to change his mind about homosexuality and argue that his denomination ought to do so as well.

While we cannot accept the validity of Rogers's view about the temple of Aphrodite in Corinth, there is some evidence of male prostitution at temples in the first century AD. We earlier noted this passage from Juvenal:

---

[34] Brian S. Rosner ("Temple Prostitution in 1 Cor 6:12–20," *Novum Testamentum* 40 [October 1998]: 336–51) has argued that 1 Cor 6:12–20 opposes neither secular nor sacred prostitution, but prostitution available on the occasion of festive events associated with a cult—what Rosner calls "temple prostitution." (This language will confuse persons reading his argument too quickly—better "festal prostitution.") Rosner says, "As Catherine Edwards notes, various ancient texts indicate that sexual pleasure was often the expected sequel to a banquet (Cicero, *Phil.* 2:104–5; *De. fin.* 2:23; Seneca, *Ep.* 47:7; 95:23) and sometimes prostitutes were explicitly mentioned as part of the after-dinner entertainment (e.g., Juv. 11:162–170; Cicero, *Pro Mur.* 13). We may add Dio Chrysostom (*Or.* 77/78.4), who writes that brothel-keepers 'drag their stock' to the 'great festive occasions'" (cf. Catherine Edwards, *The Politics of Immorality in Ancient Rome* [Cambridge: CUP, 1993], 188). While Rosner presents solid evidence that prostitution following banquets was a cultural practice in the Roman Empire, the textual argument from 1 Corinthians seems to us rather slim. We might grant some religious association with prostitution in Corinth, but we would not have any reason to limit Paul's words against sexual sin to idolatry. That is, even with such an association, Rogers's argument still fails.

[35] For Jack Rogers's description of why he argues that Paul is addressing temple prostitution, see "How I Changed My Mind on Homosexuality" (October 11, 2003), accessed October 16, 2013, http://covnetpres.org/2003/10/how-i-changed-my-mind-on-homosexuality. See Robert Gagnon's response in "Bad Reasons for Changing One's Mind."

[36] See Strabo, *Geography* 8.6.20c: "And the temple of Aphroditê was so rich that it owned more than a thousand temple slaves, courtesans, whom both men and women had dedicated to the goddess. And therefore it was also on account of these women that the city was crowded with people and grew rich; for instance, the ship captains freely squandered their money, and hence the proverb, 'Not for every man is the voyage to Corinth'" (*The Geography of Strabo*, trans. H. L. Jones, Loeb Classical Library (Cambridge, MA: Harvard Press, 1927], accessed October 16, 2013, http://penelope.uchicago.edu/Thayer/E/Roman/Texts/Strabo/8F*.html.

Not long ago, as I remember, you used to frequent the Temple of Isis and that of Peace with its Ganymede, and the secret courts of the Foreign Mother and Ceres—for in what temple are there not frail fair ones to be found?—you, a more notable adulterer than Aufidius, and what you say nothing of, you would corrupt the husbands themselves. (*Satire* IX.20–40, 130–33)[37]

That Paul is not limiting his discussion in Romans 1:26–27 to homosexual acts in temples should, however, be clear for the following reasons:

1. Given the variety of homosexual practices in antiquity, an author could be expected to clarify if he was limiting his discussion to a particular variety, such as pederasty or acts performed in temples. The vast amount of literature on homosexuality from antiquity does not suffer from confusion over which activity is in view.
2. The reference to lesbians alongside male homosexuals in Romans 1:26–27 expands rather than narrows Paul's focus.
3. Paul's overall argument is about how humans have defied God's created order in their pursuit of idolatry (worshipping what was created rather than the Creator) and homosexuality (turning from sexual relations between male and female, as God created humans, to homosexual relations).

HERMENEUTICS AND HOW TO USE ROMANS 1:26–27

These new interpretations of Romans 1:24–28 demonstrate how wild ideas, unsupported by academic research, are touted by scholars writing in favor of homosexuality. The modus operandi appears to be for people to line up behind a new interpretation of the text, push their denomination in new directions, and then line up behind an alternative, contradictory interpretation of the text when the first one fails. Onward the cause advances, no matter the discounted arguments. The carnage of inadequate interpretations does not hinder the movement. When all the arguments fail, the argument for homosexuality will have, nevertheless, won the day in some denominations. This strategy works well enough since, in fact, the exegetical arguments are not really important. The real issue, as it turns out, is neither exegesis nor what the church has taught but whether the Bible is authoritative.

Indeed, alongside clever reinterpretations of texts, two other kinds of arguments have helped carry the cause. One is hermeneutical; the other concerns Scripture's authority. Hermeneutically, the argument is advanced that while Paul clearly opposed same-sex unions of any sort, this does not really speak to the issue of homosexuality in our day. This view has already been noted in

---

[37] *Juvenal and Persius*, trans. G. G. Ramsay, Loeb Classical Library (Cambridge, MA: Harvard University Press, 1957).

considering the false claim that antiquity knew nothing of homosexual orientation—a view that, as we have demonstrated, the primary sources easily discount. It can take other forms, however. Robert Jewett, for example, argues that the social context of both the church in Rome and first-century society generally should give us pause in applying Paul's words to homosexuality in Western culture today. Jewett avers that the original audience of Romans consisted of "house and tenement churches that [were] situated mainly in the slum districts of the city [of Rome]."[38] This suggestion—which we do not accept—leads him to conclude that Paul was speaking to persons who were sexually used and abused by persons in more powerful classes. Jewett quotes Seneca: "Sexual servicing is a crime for the freeborn, a necessity for a slave, and a duty for the freeman" (*Controversiae* 4 preface 10).[39] Thus, on Jewett's interpretation, many Roman Christians were sexually exploited slaves whom Paul attracted to his cause—a mission to Spain—by speaking to their cause against their masters. Since sex in Paul's day was aggressively bisexual, and therefore involved multiple partners, Jewett says, Paul was speaking to exploitation of others in sexual relations, particularly slaves, who could not resist whatever their masters wished to do with them.[40]

Jewett offers passages from Petronius's racy novel *Satyricon* in support of his view:

> When I came from Asia I was about as tall as this candle-stick. In fact I used to measure myself by it every day, and grease my lips from the lamp to grow a moustache the quicker. *Still, I was my master's favourite for fourteen years. No disgrace in obeying your master's orders. Well, I used to amuse my mistress too.* You know what I mean; I say no more, I am not a conceited man. (75)

Jewett's unprecedented argument, however, needs to be challenged. He is correct that Paul was undoubtedly writing to an audience that would agree with his views on homosexual relationships: in Romans 1:26–27 he did not have to elaborate on his statement that lesbianism and male homosexuality are sinful. Yet this indicates that the early church followed the Scriptures and Judaism over against Greco-Roman culture in saying that homosexual relationships were sinful. Paul's Gentile converts were immediately taught Christian sexual ethics (cf. 1 Thess 4:1–8). Whether or not some in the Roman church were slaves in the homes of sexually perverted masters, Paul's point in Romans

---

[38] Robert Jewett, "The Social Context and Implications of Homoerotic References in Romans 1:24–27," in *Homosexuality, Science, and the "Plain Sense" of Scripture*, ed. D. L. Balch (Grand Rapids, MI: Eerdmans, 2000), 223.

[39] *Petronius Arbiter*, trans. Michael Hesseltine (London, England: William Heinemann, 1913).

[40] Robert Jewett, "The Social Context and Implications of Homoerotic References in Romans 1:24–27," 240.

1:24–28 remains the same: he is arguing that nature—God's law written in the created order itself—is incapable of keeping people from sin. He is not at this juncture trying to score points in support of a Spanish mission or addressing the social context of his audience. If he wanted to address the possible sexual exploitation of slaves, he would need to do so more directly and with reference to both heterosexual and homosexual forced sex.

Moreover, we have already stated that Josephus notes a firm Jewish law against a Jewish slave ever submitting to sex with a master (*Against Apion* 215), and Josephus writes this in first-century Rome. We might also note what Musonius Rufus, a pagan first-century philosopher who lived in Rome, says. In his twelfth lecture he objected to masters having heterosexual or homosexual sex with slaves. While his comments demonstrate that the practice did occur, they also show it was generally considered detestable, characteristic of those pursuing "unlawful" excesses. One is left with the impression that sex with slaves was more rare than the above quotation from Seneca suggests to Jewett. Note, too, that Musonius's discussion does not condemn homosexual acts as an abuse of power. He condemns them because homosexual acts are against nature. While Musonius acknowledges that some have sex with slaves, he also says everyone knows this is wrong. While parts of the passage in question have been quoted earlier, the whole text is presented here so that the reader can appreciate the context and argument Musonius provides:

> Not the least significant part of *the life of luxury and self-indulgence lies also in sexual excess*; for example those who lead such a life *crave a variety of loves not only lawful but unlawful ones as well, not women alone but also men*; sometimes they pursue one love and sometimes another, and not being satisfied with those which are available, pursue those which are *rare and inaccessible, and invent shameful intimacies*, all of which constitute a grave indictment of manhood. Men who are not wantons or immoral are bound to consider sexual intercourse justified only when it occurs in marriage and is indulged in for the purpose of begetting children, since that is lawful, but unjust and unlawful when it is mere pleasure-seeking, even in marriage. But of all sexual relations those involving *adultery* are most unlawful, and *no more tolerable are those of men with men, because it is a monstrous thing and contrary to nature*. But, furthermore, leaving out of consideration adultery, all intercourse with women which is without lawful character is shameful and is practiced from lack of self-restraint. So *no one with any self-control would think of having relations with a courtesan or a free woman apart from marriage, no, nor even with his own maid-servant*. The fact that those relationships are not lawful or seemly makes them a disgrace and a reproach to those seeking them; whence it is that no one dares to do any of these things openly, not even if he has all but lost the ability to blush, and *those who are not completely degenerate dare to do these things only in hiding and in secret*. And yet to attempt to cover up what one is doing is equivalent to a confession

of guilt. "That's all very well," you say, "but unlike the adulterer who wrongs the husband of the woman he corrupts, the man who has relations with a courtesan or a woman who has no husband wrongs no one for he does not destroy anyone's hope of children." I continue to maintain that everyone who sins and does wrong, even if it affects none of the people about him, yet immediately reveals himself as a worse and a less honorable person; for the wrong-doer by the very fact of doing wrong is worse and less honorable. Not to mention the injustice of the thing, there must be sheer wantonness in anyone yielding to the temptation of shameful pleasure and like swine rejoicing in his own vileness. *In this category belongs the man who has relations with his own slave-maid, a thing which some people consider quite without blame, since every master is held to have it in his power to use his slave as he wishes.* In reply to this I have just one thing to say: if it seems neither shameful nor out of place for a master to have relations with his own slave, particularly if she happens to be unmarried, *let him consider how he would like it if his wife had relations with a male slave.* Would it not seem completely intolerable not only if the woman who had a lawful husband had relations with a slave, but even if a woman without a husband should have? And yet surely one will not expect men to be less moral than women, nor less capable of disciplining their desires, thereby revealing the stronger in judgment inferior to the weaker, the rulers to the ruled. In fact, it behooves men to be much better if they expect to be superior to women, for surely if they appear to be less self-controlled they will also be baser characters. *What need is there to say that it is an act of licentiousness and nothing less for a master to have relations with a slave? Everyone knows that.* (Lecture XII)[41]

This might make one wonder whether sex with slaves really was that common in Rome. Yet even if it were, why would Paul only condemn homosexual sex with slaves if both homosexual and heterosexual acts took place? And why would Paul merely condemn homosexual sex with slaves when a pagan like Musonius Rufus condemns homosexual acts in general as unnatural and sexual excesses performed by persons who lack self-control? Finally, even if Jewett were correct that sexual exploitation of slaves by masters was common, this does not at all seem to fit Paul's context. He is, after all, addressing the problem of human sin by beginning with how humans have usurped what is according to nature.

BIBLICAL AUTHORITY AND HOW TO USE ROMANS 1:26–27

When imaginative interpretations of texts and erroneous exegetical arguments fail, a final argument is to deny the authority of Scripture. For an increasing number of scholars, it appears, exegetical arguments no longer matter.

---

[41] *Musonius Rufus: Lectures and Fragments*, trans. Cora Lutz, Yale Classical Studies (New Haven, CT: Yale University, 1947).

This takes us to the real issue. Once the exegetical games and the hermeneutical degrading of Paul's arguments are set aside, scriptural authority must be addressed. This point relates to the Presbyterian Robin Scroggs. Just twelve years after he attempted to read Romans 1:26–27 in terms of pederasty, when this argument was being shown decisively to be wrong (1995), he offered a new line of argument. He advocated simply abandoning the concept of biblical authority and speaking of the Bible as a "foundational document"—language intended to shift authority to the interpreting community.[42]

The ELCA scholar Arland Hultgren for his part in 1995 asked whether it really matters what the Bible says about homosexuality. In the space of a single article, Hultgren does what it took Scroggs ten years to do: he moves from exegetical attempts to approve of homosexual practice to issues of biblical authority. He asks, "But what if my exegetical arguments are wrong?"[43] His answer is that ELCA Lutherans do not abide today by the view they took on divorce and remarriage in 1925, even though it was biblically based. To be consistent, he concludes, they should not follow other teachings from Scripture that undermine their practices today. Hultgren ironically presented this argument in a talk entitled, "Being Faithful to the Scriptures." We might thank Hultgren for stating the point so bluntly, for he identifies the real issue underlying all the fanciful, new arguments in regard to the meaning of scriptural texts: unfaithfulness to the Scriptures.

We saw the same bluntness by Luke Timothy Johnson, a former Benedictine monk, at the beginning of the second section of the book. We also saw it in Walter Wink, a Methodist who suggested moving away from what he called the Reformers' view of Scripture and being liberated from Scripture in our ethics. Wink apparently thought the Reformers' view of Scripture was an innovation. However, Augustine, a great Christian scholar writing in the early fifth century, represents not only his own view but also that of the early church on biblical authority when he says in a letter to Jerome:

> I have learned to yield this respect and honour only to the canonical books of Scripture: of these alone do I most firmly believe that the authors were completely free from error. And if in these writings I am perplexed by anything which appears to me opposed to truth, I do not hesitate to suppose that either the manuscript is faulty, or the translator has not caught the meaning of what was said, or I myself have failed to understand it. (82.3)[44]

---

[42] Robin Scroggs, "The Bible as Foundational Document," *Interpretation* 49, no. 1 (1995): 17–30.

[43] Arland Hultgren, "Being Faithful to the Scriptures," 322.

[44] Philip Schaff, ed., *The Confessions and Letters of Augustine, with a Sketch of His Life and Work*, vol. 1, in *Nicene and Post-Nicene Fathers* (Peabody, MA: Hendrickson, 1994), 350.

Augustine speaks of the truth in Scripture being certain simply because it is found in Scripture, which he calls the "highest (even the heavenly) pinnacle of authority" (*Letter* 82.5). The trustworthiness of Scripture's statements is not to be questioned (*Letter* 82.5) for its truthfulness is "universal and unquestionable" (*Letter* 82.6). Later in the same epistle, Augustine reaffirms his position with these words: "It is to the canonical Scriptures alone that I am bound to yield such implicit subjection as to follow their teaching, without admitting the slightest suspicion that in them any mistake or any statement intended to mislead could find a place."[45] Thus, the attempt to confine the doctrine of biblical authority to a single period in church history—even the Reformation—fails because orthodox Christianity has always upheld Scripture as God's Word. Indeed, as Jesus said to the Sadducees, "You are wrong, because you know neither the scriptures nor the power of God" (Matt 22:29). And then he quoted God's words to Moses in Exodus, saying, "Have you not read what was said to you by God?" Such a view of scriptural authority goes further back than the Reformers and far exceeds their opinions or authority.

CONCLUSION

The authority of Scripture will undoubtedly be where the debate comes to rest. As the matter settles on accepting or abandoning scriptural authority itself, any number of issues will further divide the church. Denial of scriptural authority means open season on Christian orthodoxy: Jesus' bodily resurrection, his divinity, his being crucified according to the Father's will, and so forth. There are often other heretical teachings in the closets of those who defend homosexual practice. The true church, however, will continue to maintain what it has always taught about biblical authority:

> All scripture is inspired by God and is useful for teaching, for reproof, for correction, and for training in righteousness, so that everyone who belongs to God may be proficient, equipped for every good work. (2 Tim 3:16–17)

By denying God's decrees in one way or another, several entire denominations have baptized themselves not into Christ but into Western culture. Paul concludes his argument about homosexual acts and other sins in Romans 1 by saying that sinners "know God's decree, that those who practice such things deserve to die[46]—yet not only do them but even applaud others who practice them" (Rom 1:32).

---

[45] Ibid., 358.

[46] Paul will later say, "The wages of sin is death, but the free gift of God is eternal life in Christ Jesus our Lord" (Rom 6:23). By stating that people who practice sin deserve to die, he is not calling for executing immoral persons but restating what we read in the creation story: sin will result in death (Gen 2:17; 3:3).

The approval of homosexual practice in our day is now a social pressure. Believers who affirm what Scripture teaches are considered phobic at best and haters of humanity at worst, and in this we are back to being a minority group facing opposition or even persecution. What Earle Cairns says of the early church might, with slight adjustment, be said of the orthodox Christian church in the West today:

> Christians separated themselves from pagan temples, theaters, and places of recreation. This nonconformity to accepted social patterns brought down on them the dislike that the non-conformist always faces in any period of history. The purity of their lives was a silent rebuke to the scandalous lives that people of the upper class were leading. The Christians' nonconformity to existing social patterns led the pagans to believe that they were a danger to society and to characterize them as "haters of mankind" who might incite the masses to revolt.[47]

Yet it has always been the case that truly Christian society is a challenge to non-Christian society. As Stanley Hauerwas observed several decades ago:

> The church first serves the world by helping the world to know what it means to be the world. For without a "contrast model" the world has no way to know or feel the oddness of its dependence on power for survival.[48]

While his particular point was about the contrast of the way of the cross to the power of the world, Hauerwas's broader notion is that as a matter of urgent priority, *the world* needs to know that it is not *the church*. These three decades later, after intense pressure to conform culturally and an open rejection of biblical authority, parts of the church in the West now need to realize that *the church* is not *the world*.

---

[47] Earle E. Cairns, *Christianity Through the Centuries: A History of the Christian Church*, 3rd ed. (Grand Rapids, MI: Zondervan, 1996), 89.

[48] Stanley Hauerwas, "Jesus: the Story of the Kingdom," in *A Community of Character: Toward a Constructive Christian Social Ethic* (Notre Dame, IN: University of Notre Dame Press, 1981), 50.

CONCLUSION: ORTHODOX CHRISTIAN PRACTICE

> *To the angel of the church in Thyatira write: These are the words of the Son of God, who has eyes like a flame of fire, and whose feet are like burnished bronze: "I know your works—your love, faith, service, and patient endurance. I know that your last works are greater than the first. But I have this against you: you tolerate that woman Jezebel, who calls herself a prophet and is teaching and beguiling my servants to practice fornication and to eat food sacrificed to idols. I gave her time to repent, but she refuses to repent of her fornication. Beware, I am throwing her on a bed, and those who commit adultery with her I am throwing into great distress, unless they repent of her doings; and I will strike her children dead. And all the churches will know that I am the one who searches minds and hearts, and I will give to each of you as your works deserve. But to the rest of you in Thyatira, who do not hold this teaching, who have not learned what some call 'the deep things of Satan,' to you I say, I do not lay on you any other burden; only hold fast to what you have until I come. To everyone who conquers and continues to do my works to the end, I will give authority over the nations; to rule them with an iron rod, as when clay pots are shattered—even as I also received authority from my Father. To the one who conquers I will also give the morning star. Let anyone who has an ear listen to what the Spirit is saying to the churches."*
> (Rev 2:18–29)

We would like to offer some concluding thoughts based on many years of working through all the texts cited in this book. Observing the severe rifts in American Christianity in recent years, it is clear to us that the modern Western church is at a watershed moment. We humbly offer the following reflections, trusting the Head of the church will preserve his people in the truth.

THE GOSPEL AND HOMOSEXUAL PRACTICE

The present debate in certain sectors of Western Christianity over homosexuality represents but one aspect of a larger debate that is much less prominently in view. Specifically, those arguing in support of homosexuality are making claims about the human situation and the reality of the work of Christ and the Holy Spirit in the believer's life. The pro-homosexuality position looks at the human situation not in terms of God's purposes in creation and the results of sin in the world; instead, it endorses the present human condition as normative.

Christian orthodoxy has affirmed over the centuries the biblical view that the way God created the world is different from the way the world presently is. The move from Genesis 1 and 2 to Genesis 3 sets forth the radical distinction between creation and the fall. This distinction is vital in Scripture: what we now see as normative in the world is not what God intended in creation. A succinct statement of this view is found in Ephesians 2:3: "All of us once lived among them in the passions of our flesh, following the desires of flesh and senses, and we were by nature children of wrath, like everyone else." Becoming a Christian calls for a radical change of life. As Paul says:

> Let us then lay aside the works of darkness and put on the armor of light; let us live honorably as in the day, not in reveling and drunkenness, not in debauchery and licentiousness, not in quarreling and jealousy. Instead, put on the Lord Jesus Christ, and make no provision for the flesh, to gratify its desires. (Rom 13:12–14)

First John addresses a division in the church over this matter. Some denied their sinfulness and did not see a need to change their way of life. The various religions of the Greeks and Romans were distinct from Judaism and Christianity precisely on this matter. The former told stories of their gods that depicted them engaged in the same sordid behaviors as humanity, albeit magnified to superhuman levels. Rape, war, fighting, trickery, cannibalism, cruelty, and homosexual acts—whatever evil was found among humans was to be found among the gods as well. What the gods did, humans did. Moreover, the Greek and Roman religions did not address the problem of sinfulness. To be sure, the gods might get angry over bad behavior of one sort or another. Religion, however, did not address the moral human condition. It was, instead, a means to negotiate human relationships with the cantankerous deity or deities of the region. It involved extending human interactions to the metaphysical plain. No distinction was made between a holy God and sinful humanity, and there was no distinction between those outside a religion and those inside it in terms of behavior. Religion involved no change, other than change of devotion from one divine patron to another.

Thus, the situation within the church addressed in 1 John comes as no surprise. A local perspective crept into the church and challenged its teaching on sin, just as it does in our own day and context. Does Christianity really address sinfulness? Could one not simply express devotion to Jesus and thus receive all his benefits? To this, John replies:

> If we say that we have no sin, we deceive ourselves, and the truth is not in us. If we confess our sins, he who is faithful and just will forgive us our sins and cleanse us from all unrighteousness. If we say that we have not sinned, we make him a liar, and his word is not in us. (1 John 1:8–10)

This view of the human condition is tied inseparably to what is said about Jesus:

> My little children, I am writing these things to you so that you may not sin. But if anyone does sin, we have an advocate with the Father, Jesus Christ the righteous; and he is the atoning sacrifice for our sins, and not for ours only but also for the sins of the whole world. (1 John 2:1–2)

Similarly, Paul states in Galatians 2:21, "If righteousness comes through the Law, then Christ died for no reason" (our translation). Whereas John was engaging a Greco-Roman challenge to the notion of human sinfulness, Paul was engaging a Jewish Christian challenge that did not see the transforming work of Christ as sufficient to deal with the power of sin.[1] Both challenges to apostolic Christianity in the first century downplayed the need for Jesus to die for our sins and for the power of Christ to transform our lives.

In our day the challenge comes through a democratic form of religion in which the golden rule of "do to others as you would have them do to you" (Matt 7:12) is misinterpreted as tolerance of all behavior rather than as a word about how to treat others, even our enemies. The ethic of tolerance, in theory, accepts no notion that there are evil people other than those who are intolerant of others' views and behaviors. (Such a view, of course, is never consistently held.) Tolerance is surely a virtue, but not a cardinal virtue let alone *the* cardinal virtue. This democratic religion is, indeed, a religion of the people, for the people, and by the people. It cannot tolerate a doctrine of human sinfulness. While such a teaching might equalize everyone, it fails to distinguish between people in the issue that makes Jesus Christ's death meaningful. As Paul says, "For our sake he [God] made him [Jesus] to be sin who knew no sin, so that in him we might become the righteousness of God" (2 Cor 5:21). This is why Paul says of those who refuse the life-transforming work and forgiveness of Jesus Christ, "None of these will inherit the kingdom of God" (1 Cor 6:10). If we do not think that we are sinful, it is rather sad and embarrassing to have a wonderful Person—someone who inspires our devotion—die to deal with how awful we are! The modern democratic religion wants to speak of Jesus as accepting us for who we are, not his dying for us because of who we are.

---

[1] Galatians 2:15–21 is not simply about the justification Jesus offers to sinners. It is also about the work of Christ to make sinners righteous. Thus, Paul says, "For through the law I died to the law, so that I might live to God. I have been crucified with Christ; and it is no longer I who live, but it is Christ who lives in me" (Gal 2:19–20).

At the heart of Paul's letter to the Romans is his affirmation that Jesus not only provides forgiveness of sins but also introduces into our lives the transforming power of his resurrection (Rom 8:1–17). The modern religion of tolerance denies the "power of the cross" (1 Cor 1:17–18). Paul, however, argues that the depravity into which humanity has sunk—illustrated by the confusion people have about homosexual practice despite the obvious way in which males and females were created (Rom 1:24–28)—can be overcome. The work of Christ and the Holy Spirit—God's mercy toward unjust sinners—offers the possibility of transformation by the renewing of our minds (Rom 12:2). Those who were slaves of sin have become slaves of righteousness (Rom 6:16–18). Or, to return to the text noted at the beginning of this argument, those who were dead in their transgressions have been made alive together with Christ (Eph 2:5). If the gospel is not about the transforming power of God at work in our lives through Jesus Christ, it is nothing at all.

What remains to be said here is that the "power of the cross" is a "power at work within us" (Eph 3:20). It is not, as it were, a static idea, as though Christ's work effects an immediate and complete change. It is about a real power at work—not a wish or a hope for something better. Yet it calls for a relationship with God that entails his working his will in our lives. Transformation does not take place in our own strength, not even in our own strength having been given a boost by God. Transformation takes place as the Spirit of God works in us. As Paul says in Romans, "If you live according to the flesh, you will die; but if *by the Spirit* you put to death the deeds of the body, you will live. For all who are led *by the Spirit of God* are children of God" (8:13–14, italics ours).

Thus, the challenge of the pro-homosexuality advocates in parts of Western Christianity extends beyond their view of homosexuality. These advocates not only challenge the orthodox teaching of the church through the centuries; they also challenge scriptural authority, the Bible's teaching on human sinfulness, the work of Christ on the cross, and the transformative power at work in believers' lives through Christ and the Holy Spirit. In a word, these advocates challenge the essence of the gospel.

CATHOLICITY AND THE HOMOSEXUAL HERESY

As the preceding chapters have attempted to demonstrate, homosexual practice has been affirmed nowhere in the history of Christianity. Our overview of texts has revealed unequivocally that the Fathers, Reformers, Evangelicals, Pentecostals, Roman Catholics, and Orthodox churches are *unanimous* in their condemnation of homoerotic behavior among those who profess Christ as Lord. In contrast, in the West a handful of denominations in recent decades have capitulated to the gay Christian movement, and they are currently losing members *en masse*. They are losing members because the ordination of gay clergy and the blessing of gay marriages are wholesale departures from what Scripture and Christian tradition have always taught. The homosexual crisis in the church has become a dividing line between orthodox Christianity and those who no longer confess the faith of the church across the centuries.

The historic witness of the church on the topic of homosexual practice could not be more transparent. The church's constant verdict on homosexuality is completely reasonable given the unambiguous testimony of Scripture. The historic texts explored in this volume are filled with biblical references because the Bible has always been the final authority behind Christian condemnation of homosexual practice. The historical evidence for a consistently negative assessment of homosexual practice is indisputable. In fact, as evidenced in the texts cited, there are no dissenting voices at all. In light of the unanimous historic witness, it is not surprising that 90 percent of the Christian churches in America find the gay Christian arguments unconvincing.[2] In order to jettison traditional Christian teaching about homosexuality, one would need to identify overwhelming exegetical evidence in Scripture. The lack of dissenting voices in church history confirms that there is no such exegetical evidence.

Secular gay scholars have discerned the deception underlying the gay Christian movement and Boswell's thesis in particular. It is apparent to gay academics that one cannot be a practicing homosexual and claim to be a faithful Christian following the moral demands of that tradition. The duplicity in Boswell's rereading of Christian history is evident to objective historians, gay and straight. Commenting on Boswell's book, *Homosexuality, Intolerance and Christianity*, gay author John Lauritsen writes:

> It is not surprising that Professor Boswell has been *enthusiastically hailed by the gay Christians, to whom he appears as a new Savior* who will rescue them not only from queer-hating religionists, but from gay liberation secularists as well, by demonstrating historically that it's all right to be a gay Christian. . . . I cannot remember reading a more frustrating book. Undeniably, it is a formidable work of scholarship. . . . On the other hand, Boswell's arguments, his use of evidence, are fatally flawed by his doomed attempt to reconcile the irreconcilable. . . . It is regrettable that one must be harsh on a work with such considerable merit, but *willful dishonesty in a scholar must not be condoned.* . . . We should invite John Boswell to join gay liberation wholeheartedly; he has skills and knowledge that we need. To join us, Boswell must first extricate himself from *the impossible position he's in:*

---

[2] This percentage is based on denominational membership statistics from the 2008 "U.S. Religious Landscape Study" of The Pew Forum on Religion and Public Life. According to the Pew study, Catholics, evangelical Protestant churches, historically black churches, and Orthodox churches (which all affirm biblical sexual ethics) comprise 57.7% of the US population. The pro-homosexual UCC, ECUSA, ELCA, and PC (USA) are 5.6% of the population. See http://www. Pewforum/prg/files/2013/05/report-religious-landscape-study-full.pdf.

attempting to reconcile Christianity and homosexuality. It would be an act of maturity for Boswell to graduate from Christianity to secular humanism. . . . Comrade lovers of the future will have no need for religion; they will have exchanged the illusory happiness of religion for the happiness of the real world.[3]

Much of the historical record has been ignored, discounted, or obscured by Boswell's deceptive and dishonest arguments. Ignoring the reality that Boswell's thesis has been discredited by numerous scholars, gay Christians continue to refer to his work as an authoritative reference. For some, this may be naiveté. For others who know the texts, it may be willful fraudulence. Historians know what the historic texts say, and it is clear what Christians in the past believed about homoerotic behavior. The choice to overlook or explain away these historic testimonies undermines the credibility of "gay Christians." Closing one's eyes to this material is to cut oneself off from the communion of the saints and to deny the fundamental importance of catholic (universal) faith and practice.

The great trinitarian battle in the ancient church arose in the fourth century when Arius, a presbyter of Alexandria, began to articulate publicly his views that the Son of God did not share in the divinity of the Father. In 325, more than 200 bishops met in Nicaea, rejecting the views of Arius, but there was considerable debate over the appropriate language that would be incorporated into the creedal testimony to the equal deity of the Father and Son. The ongoing ecclesiastical struggle was as much political as it was theological. The church gradually became Arian or semi-Arian in numerous places, and emperors over the next fifty years usually supported the position that was politically expedient at the moment. In 381, Emperor Theodosius summoned the general Council of Constantinople, which reaffirmed Nicaea and added several statements declaring the deity of the Holy Spirit. This second ecumenical Council of Constantinople is associated with the consensus document popularly known as the Nicene Creed.

Due in large measure to the determination of bishop Athanasius of Alexandria to stay the course over several decades of controversy, the Nicene

---

[3] John Lauritsen, "*Culpa ecclesiae*: Boswell's Dilemna," in *Homosexuality, Intolerance and Christianity: A Critical Examination of John Boswell's Work*, Gai Saber Monograph No. 1 (New York, NY: The Scholarship Committee, Gay Academic Union of New York City, 1981), 16, 20. Gay professor Jonathan Goldberg writes that the attempt of Bailey and Boswell to make Sodom's crime merely inhospitality is not convincing: "Such readings have attempted to efface sexual matters entirely, and this is difficult to do, since, even if the Sodomites had not unambiguously sought sexual relations with the angels, Lot's offer of his daughters as a substitute is a far less equivocal act." Jonathan Goldberg, ed., *Reclaiming Sodom* (New York, NY: Routledge, 1994), 5–6. This is the same point made by evangelical John Stott, who states, "Bailey's case is not convincing." John Stott, *Same-Sex Partnerships: A Christian Perspective* (Grand Rapids, MI: Fleming H. Revell, 1998), 21.

Creed would set the essential standard for orthodox Christianity. While unorthodox teaching gained traction for a season, truth prevailed in the end. In a similar vein the twenty-first century Western church is facing an Arian-like moment in the ecclesiastical politics of homosexuality. This time it is a matter of *orthopraxis*—biblically defined sexual ethics affirmed by the unanimous testimony of the saints since the time of Moses. Commitment to scriptural holiness in sexual practice has always been a defining characteristic of Christianity. Heterodox forces are gathered to combat this universal practice of the church, and the battle may be long and difficult. But nothing less than orthodox Christianity is on the line.

Contemporary Christians would do well to heed the advice of Vincent of Lerins, who in 434 counseled believers to cling to the church's heritage when faced with novel teachings without precedent among God's people:

> What will a Catholic Christian do, if a small portion of the Church have cut itself off from the communion of the universal faith? What, surely, but prefer the soundness of the whole body to the unsoundness of a pestilent and corrupt member? What, if some novel contagion seek to infect not merely an insignificant portion of the Church, but the whole? Then it will be his care to cleave to antiquity, which at this day cannot possibly be seduced by any fraud or novelty. (*Commonitory* 2.7)[4]

Credimus in unam, sanctum, catholicam et apostolicam ecclesiam.[5]

---

[4] "The Commonitory of St. Vincent of Lerins, for the Antiquity and Universality of the Catholic Faith Against the Profane Novelties of All Heresies," in *Sulpitius Severus, Vincent of Lerins, John Cassian*, ed. John Schaff, trans. C. A. Heurtley *Nicene and Post-Nicene Fathers*, vol. 11 (Edinburgh, Scotland: T&T Clark; repr., William B. Eerdmans, 1991), 132.

[5] We believe in one holy catholic and apostolic church. (Nicene Creed)

EXCURSUS: SLAVERY AND WOMEN

O ne approach of gay-affirming scholarship has been to claim the church has modified its interpretations of the Bible over the centuries. Mainline gay advocates claim one should not grant too much weight to traditional Christian interpretations of Scripture, for the church has often misread the Bible. Instead, one must follow the leading of the Spirit in the present. Presbyterian theologian Jack Rogers asserts:

> Christian people for centuries assumed that their Bibles condoned slavery and the subordination of women to men. Yet, over time and often reluctantly, people came to follow the Holy Spirit's leading to accept people of African origin and women as full and equal members of the church. . . . The Holy Spirit is once again working to change our church—making us restless, challenging us to give up culturally conditioned prejudices against people of homosexual orientation.[1]

AMERICAN RACIAL SLAVERY

This supposed parallel between Christians in the past using the Bible to justify slavery and the contemporary church using Scripture to condemn homosexuality is misleading. Historically, there is no connection between Christian attitudes toward slavery and homosexuality. Yet there does appear to be a parallel between present-day attempts to reinterpret the Bible to support

---

[1] Jack Rogers, *Jesus, the Bible, and Homosexuality: Explode the Myths, Heal the Church*, 2nd ed. (Louisville, KY: Westminster/John Knox, 2009), 58. New Testament professor Richard B. Hays rejects this theory of drawing a parallel between homosexuality, subordination of women, and slavery. Hays observes: "Though only a few biblical texts speak of homoerotic activity, all of them express unqualified disapproval. In this respect, the issue of homosexuality differs significantly from matters such as slavery or the subordination of women, concerning which the Bible contains internal tensions and counterposed witnesses." Richard B. Hays, "Awaiting the Redemption of our Bodies," in *Homosexuality in the Church*, ed. Jeffrey S. Siker (Louisville, KY: Westminster/John Knox, 1994), 9–10. See also chap. 16, "Homosexuality," in Hays's book: *The Moral Vision of the New Testament: A Contemporary Introduction to New Testament Ethics* (New York, NY: Harper Collins, 1996).

homosexuality and past misuse of the Bible to prop up race-based slavery. In both cases biblical teaching has been co-opted to support a politically popular position and enable Christians to adopt the sinful cultural values of their times.

Slavery was a reality of life in the ancient Mediterranean world during the Greco-Roman period when Christianity emerged; however, it was regulated in both Old Testament Israel and within the New Testament community. In ancient cultures persons were forced into lifelong servitude as spoils of war or became slaves in order to repay debts. Ancient slavery was not based on one's ethnic identity, and it did not always involve kidnapping followed by forced servitude.

Christ's apostles attempted to regulate slavery among believers according to ethical principles consistent with Christian faith. The apostles did not direct Christians to immediately free slaves. However, Christianity taught the equality of all men and women before God. The book of Philemon bears witness to the continuing reality of slavery among converts to Christianity. Paul exhorted believing slave owner Philemon to treat his slave Onesimus, who was also a Christian, as a brother (Phlm 16). To the church at Colossae, Paul wrote, "Masters, treat your slaves justly and fairly, for you know that you also have a Master in heaven" (Col 4:1). These were radical ideas for the first-century Roman world. One observes these same themes in the writings of the church fathers, who continued to challenge the slave-holding Christian empire to live out the gospel implications of human equality.[2]

The New Testament unmistakably affirms the equal value of all men and women: "For in Christ Jesus you are all children of God by faith" (Gal 3:26). Due to this new reality, "There is no longer Jew or Greek, there is no longer slave or free, there is no longer male and female; for all of you are one in Christ Jesus" (Gal 3:28). Part of the apostolic ministry was to transform master-slave relations based on the new reality of oneness in Christ. The New Testament also reaffirmed the Old Testament prohibition of stealing and selling humans (Exod 21:16). Included in the list of those living "contrary to the sound teaching that conforms to the glorious gospel of the blessed God" were "murderers, fornicators, *sodomites, slave traders*, liars, perjurers" (1 Tim 1:10). According to Scripture, homosexuality and slave trading are both sinful.[3]

Slavery in the New World was different from most slavery in the ancient world. New World slavery was not necessarily less cruel: slavery in ancient times could be brutal. The primary difference had to do with the manner in

---

[2] For a brief survey of the church fathers on slavery, see Jennifer A. Glancy, *Slavery as a Moral Problem in the Early Church and Today* (Minneapolis, MN: Fortress, 2011). Her discussion of Basil's opposition to Christian slave holding is particularly noteworthy. See also Glancy's New Testament study, *Slavery and Early Christianity* (New York: Oxford University Press, 2002).

[3] See also Rev 18:13, which references traders in "human lives."

which slaves were obtained and the prejudicial nature of American slavery. Anyone in the ancient world could be a slave; one's ethnic identity was not the key factor. By contrast New World slavery targeted Africans based on their ethnicity. Dark-skinned men and women from Africa were sold by fellow Africans or kidnapped by slave traders and brought across the Atlantic for profit.

In the colonial era Christians spoke out against the slave trade, and it was outlawed in the United States by 1808. Making the transatlantic trade illegal was an implicit acknowledgement that American slavery was inherently wicked. The long journey to the final abolition of slavery in America is a well-known story; that many leaders of the nineteenth-century abolitionist movement were Christians is well documented too. Understanding that slavery as it was practiced in the United States violated biblical standards, Christians opposed it.

Christians' influence in America was so strong during the early nineteenth century that even in the South state legislatures and a majority of the population were moving toward abolition.[4] Beginning in the 1830s, however, things changed. Anti-Southern rhetoric escalated, and abolitionist violence along with threats to the slave-based economy pushed southern Christians to rally behind slavery. Where previously there had been significant agreement among Christians in both the North and South that American slavery was inconsistent with the principles of the gospel, some in the South began to push for maintaining the slave system by interpreting the Bible as supportive of American slavery and the racism behind it.[5] Multitudes of Christians found this reversal of views deplorable and continued their support of emancipation.

While the New Testament appears on the surface to support all forms of slavery, in fact, the apostles were only concerned with regulating Roman slavery. They were not offering an apology for perpetual slavery. Such regulation of slavery also occurred in the Old Testament. One significant New Testament passage on slavery, Ephesians 6:5–9, sought to prevent the abuse of slaves. Another passage taught that a human master was not the slave's highest authority and that masters who acted wickedly were subject to God's judgment (Col 4:22–25). Also, Paul encouraged slaves to secure their freedom if they could (1 Cor 7:21). In the church and in the Lord, slaves were regarded as possessing equal worth with masters (Gal 3:28; Col 3:11).

In a world where as much as one third of the population was enslaved, the New Testament did not affirm slavery and undermined it in various ways. This is vastly different from the Bible's treatment of sexual immorality.

---

[4] See Alice Dana Adams, *The Neglected Period of Anti-Slavery in America, 1801–1831* (Williamston, MA: Corner House, 1973).

[5] See Mark Noll's *The Civil War as a Theological Crisis* (Chapel Hill, NC: University of North Carolina Press, 2006).

The nineteenth-century American South bowed to social pressure to reinterpret the Bible in ways that supported race-based slavery. As a society the South viewed itself as suffering injustice at the hands of a self-righteous North. This cultural ethos put enormous pressure on southern Christians to justify the norms of their culture. A similar pattern can be observed in modern American churches succumbing to cultural demands to reinterpret the Bible to support homosexuality. The current revisionist approach to the Bible and homosexuality is just as odious as older attempts to support race-based slavery and prejudice with Scripture.

WOMEN'S ORDINATION

The gay Christian movement frequently pictures itself as the next stage in the struggle for human rights, following the Civil Rights Movement and the quest for women's rights. Often a comparison between women's ordination and the ordination of noncelibate homosexuals is suggested, but this distorts both Scripture and Christian history. While historically the majority of the church has advocated male pastoral leadership, there have been some exceptions, and the biblical testimony is regarded by some as unclear. By contrast, there is unequivocal biblical testimony opposing all homosexual practice; historically, the church has not placed homosexuals in leadership positions.[6]

Portions of Scripture limit women's roles as teachers or leaders within the church (1 Cor 14:34; 1 Tim 2:11–3:7; Titus 1; 5–9). Other sections of the Bible mention women prophesying (Exod 15:20; Judg 4:4; Luke 2:35; Acts 2:17; 21:9; 1 Cor 11:5), which some have argued implies a teaching or leading role in the assembly of believers. Much ink has been spilled debating these issues, and Protestants differ on these matters. The key issue in the Protestant debate, however, is what do the Scriptures teach? While there may be different hermeneutical approaches to key texts, the final arbiter for Christians is Scripture— not the shifting sands of cultural values.

Historically, some diversity of practice regarding women's roles in the church has long existed, although the church fathers and Protestant Reformers

---

[6] For a rebuttal of the pro-gay "Misogyny Argument," see Robert Gagnon's essay "The Scriptural Case for a Male-Female Prerequisite for Sexual Relations: A Critique of the Arguments of Two Adventist Scholars" in *Homosexuality, Marriage, and the Church*, ed. Roy E. Gane, Nicholas Miller, and Peter Swanson (Berrien Springs, MI: Andrews University Press, 2012), 125–29. Gagnon states, "In the Greco-Roman milieu, opposition to male homosexual practice intensified as appreciation for women grew. . . . Hence it is no surprise that as trends developed toward greater roles for women in early Christianity (compared with early Judaism generally), opposition to homosexual practice in no way diminished. . . . If we follow the misogyny theory, one can only arrive at the absurd corollary that the writers of Scripture, and Jesus, were among the biggest misogynists of the ancient Near East and the Greco-Roman world. This claim flies in the face of evidence in both Testaments, but especially in the New Testament, of significant roles for women."

tended to follow the directives of the Pastoral Epistles. The office of deaconess was prominent during some periods of church history, especially in the ancient Eastern Church. In the West numerous women were highly esteemed as prophetesses and martyrs. The Roman Catholic Church and Eastern Orthodox churches continue the long-established practice of limiting the priesthood to males. This belief is grounded in their understanding of Scripture and supported by church tradition. These enormous global traditions have also preserved the historic denunciation of homosexual practice.

The largest Protestant movement in the world, Pentecostalism, is divided on women's roles, but the Holiness-Pentecostal tradition historically has been open to female leadership. Yet alongside this openness to women in ministry, Pentecostals universally condemn homosexual practice and have been leaders in ministries to those who seek a way out of the gay lifestyle.[7] For Pentecostals, the determining factor is Holy Scripture; the New Testament speaks of women prophesying and exercising gifts in the church, but the Bible nowhere hints at practicing homosexuals being placed in any leadership or teaching positions.

The only attempts to link women's ordination and the ordination of non-celibate homosexuals have come from a few Protestant groups abandoning their Reformation heritage of *Sola Scriptura*. For these culture-accommodating churches, God's Word is no longer the final authority, and a plethora of voices have equal weight on the homosexual question. These Protestants have discarded their historic roots in the catholic tradition of worldwide Christianity and have substituted their own sectarian homosexual theologies of liberation.

---

[7] See General Council of the Assemblies of God website for position papers: "The Role of Women in Ministry as Described in Holy Scripture," accessed June 25, 2015, https://www.vulcanhammer.org/island/4191_women_ministry.pdf and "Homosexuality, Marriage, and Sexual Identity," accessed June 25, 2015, http://ag.org/top/Beliefs/Position_Papers/pp_downloads/pp_4181_homosexuality.pdf.

NAME INDEX

SUBJECT INDEX

SCRIPTURE INDEX